Richard Flood

jesus

the man,
the mission,
and
the message

Jesus

the man,
the mission,
and
the message

second edition

c. milo connick

Professor of Religion, Whittier College

Prentice-Hall, Inc., Englewood Cliffs, New Jersey

Library of Congress Cataloging in Publication Data

CONNICK, C. MILO.
   Jesus: the man, the mission, and the message.

   Bibliography: p.
   1. Jesus Christ—Biography.   I. Title.
BT301.2.C6 1974   232.9'01   74-6264
ISBN   0-13-509521-2

Printed in the United States of America

10   9   8   7   6   5   4   3

The view of Jerusalem on p. 329 was furnished through the
courtesy of the Arab Information Center, New York.

The map of Jerusalem in the time of Jesus on p. 330 is
based upon Plate XVII, B in *The Westminster Historical
Atlas to the Bible*, rev. ed., eds. George Ernest Wright
and Floyd Vivian Filson, copyright 1956 by W. L. Jenkins,
published by The Westminster Press, and is used by permission.

The Plan of the Temple Area on p. 330 is based upon the
plan in *Sacred Sites and Ways* by Gustav Dalman,
copyright 1935 by The Macmillan Company, and is used
by permission.

PRENTICE-HALL INTERNATIONAL, INC., *London*
PRENTICE-HALL OF AUSTRALIA, PTY. LTD., *Sydney*
PRENTICE-HALL OF CANADA, LTD., *Toronto*
PRENTICE-HALL OF INDIA PRIVATE LIMITED, *New Delhi*
PRENTICE-HALL OF JAPAN, INC., *Tokyo*

*To Darren and Brent,
"for to such belongs
the kingdom of God"
(Mk. 10:14)*

Contents

The Sources   2

The Formative Years   3

The Work　　4

The Message, Miracles, and Master　　5

The Work Resumed 6

The Rejection and Resurrection 7

Preface

The enthusiastic response to the first edition of *Jesus: The Man, the Mission, and the Message* was singularly encouraging. But more than a decade has now passed. Many new and insightful books and articles have been published. The infant discipline called redaction criticism has reached its teens and rushes toward adulthood. Clearly the time has come to review and revise our understandings of Jesus in the light of current knowledge.

The specialist is forced to focus his attention upon a smaller and smaller sphere of interest. This shrinking sphere, paradoxically, produces a larger and larger body of facts. Knowledge is increasing at such a rapid rate that it doubles every five years. No longer can anyone know everything about anything.

The problem of the specialist is simple compared with that of the scholar who elects to cover a wider field. Such a scholar must first familiarize himself with the findings of the experts. Then, since these findings are often at odds, he must carefully weigh the conflicting claims and attempt to bring order out of chaos. Finally, if the end product is not to be mistaken for a prescription for insomnia, he must communicate his conclusions in attractive verbal attire.

In the last fifteen years, scores of books have been written about Jesus. In most of them, the author, defending his position with vigor and learning, expresses a particular point of view. Opposing views are sometimes minimized or omitted. Such books are not to be scorned. Because they challenge accepted modes of thought and furnish valuable insights and information, they are quoted in this work, referred to in footnotes, and included among suggestions for further reading. They contribute to our understanding of Jesus in much the same way that an article of food contributes to our diet. Unfortunately, the personal and professional demands made on most readers do not permit them the luxury of acquiring a complete sampling of the tempting variety of books provided by publishers. Readers usually can purchase only a few offerings—and thus run the risk of malnutrition.

Jesus: The Man, the Mission, and the Message is the product of over thirty years of teaching and research. It does not claim to tell the reader all he needs to know about Jesus. No book can do that. Its aim is to provide a balanced account—accurate, up-to-date, and absorbing. A variety of viewpoints is presented. Although we indicate our own conclusions on occasion, we do not indulge in special pleading. Controversial questions are probed from different vantage points. Our intention is not to prove these points but to help the reader understand them. Partisans are permitted to speak for themselves. Space limitations make hearing the case of every advocate impossible, but major positions are given their due. The method is deliberate. We have full confidence that when readers are provided with the facts and with a broad spectrum of informed opinion, they are capable of deciding for themselves "what sort of man" Jesus of Nazareth was.

Jesus lived in a world radically different from our own. To help the reader avoid the pitfall of modernizing him, considerable effort is made to place him in the context of first century Palestine. Many pages are devoted to the history of his people, the land in which he lived, the government which ruled over him, and the life of the people with whom he lived. These verbal descriptions are supplemented by more than sixty photographs, maps, and woodcuts. The photographs, except where noted, were taken by the author.

Jesus: The Man, the Mission, and the Message is not a substitute for Scripture; it is a supplement. The Gospels and other Scripture are quoted extensively in the text. Topics are accompanied by Biblical references which should be read in connection with them. The suggestions for further reading, which are found at the end of the book, are not intended to be inclusive. They provide a rich and varied field for further exploration, however, and the accompanying explanatory comments should enable the reader to continue his quest at the level of his own background and interest.

A book of this kind would be impossible apart from the creative work of hundreds of scholars. Many are mentioned in the footnotes. To them and their publishers, who generously granted permission to quote from their valuable books, I am deeply indebted. Others to whom I owe special thanks are: Religion Editor Norwell F. Therien, Jr., Production Editor Brian N. Lokker, and their associates at Prentice-Hall, Inc., for expert editorial assistance; President Frederick M. Binder and the Trustees of Whittier College, for a sabbatical leave and a research grant; Miss Mary Stacy, for her fine work on the indexes; and my wife, Genevieve, for her patient proofreading and perceptive suggestions.

C. MILO CONNICK

part 1

The World

Jesus has indelibly influenced the world. His birth date marks the division of history into B.C. and A.D. His life and teachings have caused millions to model their lives after him. His death and resurrection have resulted in his being called Lord by the largest group of worshipers in the world. It may not be far from the truth to claim that "all the armies that ever marched, and all the navies that ever were built, and all the parliaments that ever sat, and all the kings that ever reigned, put together, have not affected the life of man upon this earth as powerfully as has that One Solitary Life" (source unknown).

But how did the world influence Jesus? He was not born in a vacuum, nor was he reared on another planet. He was born with a heritage, a race, and a nation. He soon acquired a language and a religion. He grew up in a large family, worked in a carpenter's shop, attended synagogue and Temple services, joined in wedding festivities, and paid taxes to Caesar.

Whatever else Jesus may have been, he was a man of his milieu. We err if we transpose him to the twentieth century and create him in our own image. He must first be understood in the context of his own world—the legacy, the land, the law, the life, and the legends.

chapter one

The Legacy

If a visitor from outer space should ask us to define an American, we would at first be hard pressed for a rational reply. We could not point to a common national origin, a common racial background, or even a common language. America is a melting pot. We have fallen not from a single family tree but from a forest. The only thing we have in common is our history.

Once we understand this basic fact, we can begin a definition. We can review the highlights of our heritage: the discovery by Columbus, the landing of the Pilgrims, the Boston Tea Party and the Revolutionary War, the Declaration of Independence, the Constitution and the Bill of Rights, the War between the States and Lincoln's Gettysburg Address, the War to End Wars, and the more recent events which have plunged us into a position of world leadership. To be an American is to remember and to share a special history.

Jesus was a Jew. His people adhered to diverse theologies, embraced differing cultures, and exhibited varying racial characteristics. One of their most distinctive features was their sense of history. It bound them together and made them a separate people. When they celebrated the Passover, when they heard the Law being read in the synagogues, when they taught their children the tradition of the elders, they nourished their feeling of uniqueness.

In Western civilization, a man's life begins at birth. For a Chinese person, it commences at conception. But for a Jew, life starts with Abraham, traditional ancestor of his people. This is why Matthew began his account of Jesus with the words, "Abraham was the father of Isaac" (Mt. 1:2).[1] We cannot gain an adequate understanding of Jesus unless we acquaint ourselves with the legacy bequeathed to him by the forebears of his faith.

Patriarchs

Abraham was not a Jew; he was a Semite. Although most Jews are Semites, most Semites are not Jews. The Semites formed that much larger division of the Caucasian race which included the Babylonians, Assyrians, Aramaeans, Phoenicians, and other peoples of southwestern Asia, and later rightfully laid claim to the Hebrews and the Arabs. The term "Jew" was not used extensively until the sixth century B.C. When the Southern Kingdom of Judah lost its independence, many Hebrews were taken to Babylonia. Far removed from the Holy Temple and the Holy Land, they were forced by necessity to develop new forms of religious expression and organization. The layman's religion of the synagogue eventually resulted. When these exiles were released from Babylonian captivity in 538 B.C., they returned to Jerusalem, where the natives quickly noted their altered religious practices. Since the released exiles had originally come from Judah, they were called "Jews." Henceforth "Jew" specified a man's religious commitment.[2]

Abraham, the Semite, came to be regarded as the Father of the Hebrews. At the prompting of the Lord, he migrated from Mesopotamia to the land of Canaan about the turn of the nineteenth century B.C. The established settlers called him "a sojourner." He was one of the Habiru, those by no means exclusively Semitic "gypsies" who lived a nomadic life on the periphery of society. He stopped first at Shechem but soon moved on to greener pastures. With his family and flocks he wandered through the thinly settled hill country until he reached the plain of Mamre, near Hebron.

Famine finally forced the Abraham clan to take refuge in Egypt. In order to save his own skin, Abraham suggested to his wife that he misrepresent her as his sister. Although Sarah was, in fact, his half-sister, this was not the relationship under which they were living. The Pharaoh's scouts soon noticed Sarah and took her to their master to be his wife. As the Pharaoh's "brother-in-law," Abraham profited handsomely. Angered by Abraham's deceit, God sent plagues to punish the Pharaoh. The Pharaoh eventually got the point and sent Abraham away with his wife and "all that he had" (Gen. 12:20).

After the clan had returned to Canaan, a dispute arose between the herdsmen of Abraham and the herdsmen of his nephew, Lot. The incident

[1]All Biblical quotations, except where noted, are reprinted by permission and are taken from the Revised Standard Version of the Holy Bible, copyright 1946, 1952 by the Division of Christian Education of the National Council of Churches.

[2]This is the *religious* definition. The *cultural* definition depicts those who, without formal religious affiliation, accept the teachings of Judaism (its literature, ethics, and folkways) as their own. The *practical* definition applies to people who consider themselves Jews or are so considered by others.

portrays a remarkable facet of Abraham's faith. He believed in a purely partisan God, one who promised the Patriarch, "I will bless those who bless you, and him who curses you I will curse" (Gen. 12:3). Since Abraham believed that the Egyptians were beyond the pale of Providence, he felt he could lie to the Pharaoh with impunity. However, when it came to dealing with his clansmen, Abraham's obligations were stringent. In a burst of generosity, he summoned Lot and said, "Let there be no strife between you and me . . . for we are kinsmen. Is not the whole land before you? Separate yourself from me. If you take the left hand, then I will go to the right; or if you take the right hand, then I will go to the left" (Gen. 13:8–9).

We should not assume that Abraham lived by the Ten Commandments and the Sermon on the Mount, since these lofty revelations of God's commands and character had not yet been made. Judged by modern standards, Abraham was a liar, a cheat, and a bigamist. He was motivated by religious and racial bigotry. His picture of Providence was so parochial that it prompted him to think he could change the mind of God (Gen. 18:16–33)! We honor him for the strength of his faith, not for its limitations (which he shared with his contemporaries). When God spoke to him, he heeded, as when he went out "not knowing where he was to go" (Heb. 11:8). By faith he sired a son in his old age, and by faith he nearly slaughtered him (Gen. 22:1–14). It is little wonder that to such a man the Lord promised, "To your descendants I give this land, from the river of Egypt to the great river, the Euphrates" (Gen. 15:18). About eighteen hundred years later, Jesus reportedly quoted Exodus 3:6 as proof that Abraham still lived in the presence of God (Mk. 12:18–27); and nearly two millenniums after that, convinced Christians continue to derive comfort from singing, "Rock-a my soul in the bosom of Abraham."[3]

Abraham was succeeded as tribal head by his son Isaac and his grandson Jacob. Jacob warred incessantly with his redheaded twin brother and craftily stole from Esau his birthright and his father's final blessing. His triumph was temporary, for Esau's hostility forced him to flee for his life. All was not lost, however, for in a dream at Bethel, Jacob received a renewal of the promise that the Lord had made to Abraham. He would inherit the land, produce a mighty people, and through them bless all the families of the earth. Fortified by these assurances, Jacob made haste to Haran, acquired a harem from among his kinsmen, begat twelve sons, prospered, and prepared to make peace with Esau. In a nocturnal dream beside the river Jabbok, he wrestled with an angel and was crowned with a new name, "Israel."[4]

Joseph

Joseph was the foremost of Israel's sons. His father dressed him in a long robe (symbol of his special status) and sent him out to spy on his

[3]See Gen. 11:27–25:11 for a more complete account of Abraham.
[4]See Gen. 21–50 for a more complete account of Isaac and Jacob.

brothers. If this did not completely demolish his relationship with his brothers, his "delusions of grandeur" did. In addition to having dreams in which the entire family genuflected in his presence, he had the unmitigated gall to publicize them. As a result, his brothers sold him into Egyptian slavery. In a vain attempt to soften Israel's sorrow, they contrived a story about Joseph, saying he had been devoured by wild beasts.

Little did Joseph's brothers realize that their secret sin would one day turn out to be their salvation. God was with Joseph in Egypt. In rapid succession he became Potiphar's household overseer, victim of his wife's seduction charges, prisoner par excellence and assistant warden, deft interpreter of dreams, and the Pharaoh's Prime Minister in charge of peace, prosperity, and progress. When famine struck the land of Canaan, the sons of Israel made repeated visits to Egypt to buy food. On one such occasion they were ushered into the Prime Minister's presence. He disclosed to them some spine-chilling news: "I am your brother Joseph, whom you sold into Egypt." Then he continued, "Do not be distressed ... for God sent me before you to preserve life" (Gen. 45:4–5). The brothers were elated and hurried home to tell Israel. The whole family then joined Joseph in Egypt, taking up residence in the land of Goshen. There they and their descendants lived for 430 years (Ex. 12:40).[5]

Moses

After Joseph's death, the family of Israel lost favor in Egypt. There arose "a new king ... who did not know Joseph" (Ex. 1:8). The Hebrews were gradually enslaved and put to work in the Nile delta. They built the store cities of Pithom and Raamses. When the oppression became intolerable, God raised up a prophet by the name of Moses, whom He commanded to "go down and tell ole Pharaoh to let my people go." Moses staged a four-fold rebuttal, but the Lord overcame his objections, and Moses set out to sell the hard-headed Hebrew elders on the notion of liberation. When they finally fell in line, he approached the Pharaoh. That wily tyrant flatly refused to submit to Moses' demands for work-free days of worship. Instead, he ordered a speed-up and withdrew the straw which he had previously provided for brickmaking. Crestfallen, Moses turned to the Lord, who then empowered him to plague the Pharaoh into submission. Moses had to count to ten before his efforts were crowned with success. Only when the angel of death *passed over* the Hebrews and struck dead the first-born of the Egyptians did the Pharaoh yield. He told Moses to take his people with him, worship the Lord, and return. The Hebrews went (shortly after 1290 B.C.), but they had no intention of returning. The Pharaoh's

---

[5]"Admittedly, the Biblical story about Jacob and Joseph contains elements of folklore. It was intended to be an interesting and edifying story, rather than a straight biographical account.... Nevertheless the Biblical account ... in its broad outline, as well as in many details ... agrees with the historical setting of the second millennium, B.C." B. W. Anderson, *Understanding the Old Testament*, 2nd ed. (Englewood Cliffs, N.J.: Prentice-Hall, Inc., © 1957, 1966), p. 30. Reprinted by permission.

melting heart soon hardened, and he followed in hot pursuit. The sea parted for Moses and his company, but it closed on the Egyptians. "Thus the Lord saved Israel that day... and the people feared the Lord and they believed... in his servant Moses" (Ex. 14:30–31).

As the Hebrews plunged into the uncharted wilderness, their fiery faith flickered. Scarcity of food and water magnified the good old days under the Pharaohs and minimized the stature of Moses. Disciplined by daily dependence on manna and disturbed by attacks from men, the beleaguered band staggered into the oasis of Sinai. There they reflected on the meaning of their deliverance. There God offered them a special relationship (covenant). Out of gratitude for what He had done for them (their escape from Egypt), they accepted His covenant and obligated themselves to live in accordance with His Ten Commandments. Then for "forty years" they wandered as a crowd in search of community.[6]

Joshua

Under the leadership of Joshua, a new generation fought its way into Canaan. The conquest was not as sudden and total as Joshua 1–12 would have us believe. Joshua did smash his way into the hill country and deal the natives a decisive blow. The broken terrain was ideal for his guerrilla-type tactics. But against the Iron-Age weapons of the lowlanders he was about as effective as a rifleman in a nuclear war. The conquest of Canaan continued for over two hundred years before victory was complete. It was not achieved by force alone, but by intermarriage, treaties, and absorption.

Judges

During the protracted probing of the promised lowlands, the Hebrews operated in a loose confederation. The twelve-fold tribal pattern stemmed from the twelve sons of Israel. The tribes held festivals at a central sanctuary (Shechem, then Shiloh), rehearsed their history, recalled their deliverance from Egypt, renewed their commitment to the Sinai covenant, and recited their mutual regulations and obligations. They called their covenant community "Israel" to signify that they had personally participated in the Exodus experience. They welcomed others to the community if they were willing to make that saving saga their own (Joshua 24). The alliance was theocratic, not democratic. Yet it encouraged considerable tribal autonomy. Crises called to the fore charismatic (spirit-filled) leaders called judges. Although they functioned from time to time as internal arbitrators, their main role was military, and their term of service tended to coincide with the

---

[6]See Exodus, Leviticus, Numbers, and Deuteronomy for a fuller account. Actually most of the wilderness sojourn was spent at Kadesh-barnea, a desert oasis about fifty miles south of Beersheba.

length of the peril. Foremost among these charismatic leaders were Deborah, Gideon, Samson, and Saul.

United Kingdom

The Tribal Confederacy proved to be too weak to cope with Israel's enemies. The monopoly on iron weapons held by the Philistines effectively thwarted Israel's expansionist aims. Moreover, it humiliated her farmers who were compelled to go to Philistia to get their tools sharpened (I Sam. 13: 19–22). The Israelites clamored to keep up with the Canaanites. They, too, wanted a king. Since Saul had saved them in the Ammonite crisis (I Sam. 11:6–7), they turned to him in the hope that he could deliver them from the Philistine menace. Samuel (last of the judges) anointed Saul and ushered in the United Kingdom (*c.* 1020–922 b.c.). This period transmuted Philistia's Iron Age into Israel's Golden Age.

Saul resembled a judge more than he did a king. He failed to centralize the government, levy taxes, or conscript an army. With a band of volunteers he fought Israel's wars. With charismatic leadership he exercised authority over the tribes. His was a transitional time between the collapse of the confederacy and the birth of the powerful monarchy. Caught between two radically different orders, his life was cast in dark shadows. The "spirit" departed from him. Samuel (who represented the old order) rejected him. David (who personified the new order) threatened him through his rising popularity with the people. During a losing battle on Mt. Gilboa, Saul took his own life.

Saul's death paved David's way to power. He was soon anointed king of Judah and for seven years reigned at Hebron. All the while he shrewdly calculated how to win the allegiance of the northern tribes, which were headed by Saul's sole surviving son, Ishbaal. Saul's male descendants were either liquidated or taken into custody. Saul's daughter became David's wife. At the age of thirty-seven David became the undisputed king of all Israel. During his total rule of forty years he captured Jerusalem, made it the political and religious center of the realm, broke the power of the Philistines, and completed the conquest of Canaan. Whatever his personal faults (and they were numerous), he reached the pinnacle of political greatness. A thousand years later his kingdom was dust and Rome dominated his descendants; yet pilgrims on their way to Jerusalem expectantly sang, "Blessed be the kingdom of our father David that is coming!" (Mk. 11:10). The die of their deliverer (king, messiah, "anointed one") had been permanently cast in David's image.

Solomon succeeded his father, David, as king. His leadership came not from charisma but from cunning. He arrived at the throne by the customary route, the ruthless removal of possible contenders. Israel had indeed caught up with the Canaanites! Aided by the weakness of his political foes, Solomon allied himself with the foremost figure on the political horizon, Hiram I, King of Tyre. This set the stage for a period of unparalleled material prosperity. Cedars were brought from the Lebanon mountains to build the Temple in Jerusalem. This great architectural achievement was dwarfed in size and splendor by Solomon's palace and his chariot cities. His enormous building programs, his extensive commercial enterprises, and his massive display of wealth provoked the wide-eyed wonder of such lovely luminaries as the Queen of Sheba.

Divided Kingdom: Israel

At Solomon's death in 922 B.C. the kingdom was split in two. His son Rehoboam ruled in the southern kingdom of Judah. The ten northern tribes (called Israel) chose Jeroboam as their king.

Civil war between the two kingdoms gave way to close collaboration when Omri became king of Israel (c. 876–869 B.C.). Omri's son, Ahab, succeeded him. Ahab had married Jezebel, a Phoenician woman. While he himself remained faithful to the Lord, he permitted his wife to worship Melkart (Baal), a Phoenician deity. As "man" of the monarchy, Jezebel promoted her alien faith with calculated zeal. Had it not been for Elijah (c. 850 B.C.). she might have converted the country.

Elijah was charismatic successor to the judges and early kings. He challenged the prophets of Melkart to a climactic contest on Mt. Carmel. Elijah won a resounding victory, and Israel was saved for the Lord (I Kings 18). Elijah's contemporaries said that he never died; instead he was whisked up to heaven by a whirlwind. Later prophets claimed he would return before the Day of Judgment and "turn the hearts of fathers to their children and the hearts of children to their fathers" (Mal. 4:6). Jesus reportedly amended the tradition when he called John the Baptist the "Elijah who is to come" (Mt. 11:14).

While these events were taking place in the Northern Kingdom, a herdsman named Amos began his career in Judah. About 850 B.C. Amos went to Israel to sell his wool. What he saw there seared his sensitive soul. The rich were getting richer at the expense of the poor. Worshipers paid lipservice to God, but their hearts were in their possessions. Seized by the charisma, Amos (first of the writing prophets) thundered the doom of the Lord. He reminded Israel of her covenant, demanded that she repent, and cried, "Let justice roll down like waters, and righteousness like an ever-flowing stream" (Amos 5:24).

Hosea, a native of the north, was a prophetic contemporary of Amos. His wife, Gomer, bore him three children, then deserted him to become a prostitute. His world tumbled in. In time, however, Hosea made an amazing discovery; he loved Gomer in spite of her infidelity. Swallowing his pride, he paid her ransom and put her under quarantine until her promiscuous passions had been purged. Then he restored her as his wife. This bittersweet experience revealed to him a new dimension of deity. His way with Gomer was God's way with Israel. The Lord had chosen Israel as His "wife." Her fidelity had been as fickle as the morning dew. No sooner had she gained a foothold in the Promised Land than she had begun to copy the Canaanites. The natives believed their gods caused the crops to grow. Israel, unwilling to risk a crop failure, rejected the Lord of history and courted the favor of Canaanite gods with adolescent abandon. But the Lord's love was steadfast; He would not let Israel go. He would use Assyria, a pagan nation, to discipline her by empowering Assyria to conquer her. Through this tragic experience Israel would be disciplined, purged of her perversions, and restored to her "husband." To Amos' storm of doom that blanketed Israel, Hosea added a rainbow of hope. "The external judge is now seen as the involved redeemer."[7]

Not long after Hosea's death, Assyria attacked Israel. After a three-year siege Israel's capital fell in 721 B.C. Thousands upon thousands of Israelites were deported to Persia. The lament of Amos (5:2) had come to pass: "Fallen, no more to rise, is the virgin Israel."

Divided Kingdom: Judah

As long as Israel lived, Judah existed in the shadow of her stronger and more prosperous sister. Not all advantages accrue to the powerful, however. While Israel dashed violently from dynasty to dynasty, the single royal line of David occupied Judah's throne. This made her transition from tribalism to town life less traumatic, and she enjoyed a relative degree of political and economic stability.

Judah reached the summit of her success under King Uzziah (783–742 B.C.). During his forty years on the throne he captured control of important trade routes, expanded commerce, and stimulated agriculture. When he died, the atmosphere of Judah hung heavy with foreboding. He had been the only king most of the people had ever known. They must have felt like modern Americans who were numbed by the sudden demise of Franklin Roosevelt. Having elected him President for four terms, they had come to regard him as untouched by time.

Who could be a worthy successor to Uzziah? Out of the awful void came the voice of Judah's priest-prophet, Isaiah (742–700 B.C.). In a glorious vision in Solomon's Temple he cried, "My eyes have seen *the* king, the Lord of hosts!"[8] What a pointed reminder that Judah's real dependence was not upon the dynasty of David but upon the King of Kings!

Isaiah (whose writings are confined to the bulk of Isaiah 1–39) was to become the prophet most frequently quoted in the New Testament. His ideas about the coming Messiah (9:2–7 and 11:1–9), later applied to Jesus, are among the most beautiful and moving passages of Scripture. His central contribution to the stream of prophecy, however, was his concept of God's holiness. "Holy, holy, holy is the Lord of hosts; the whole earth is full of

---

[7]Norman K. Gottwald, *A Light to the Nations* (New York: Harper & Row, Publishers, Inc., 1959), p. 300. Reprinted by permission.
[8]Is. 6:5, emphasis added.

his glory" (6:3). When Isaiah's insight was added to that of Amos and Hosea, there resulted the finest definition of religion in the Old Testament (Micah 6:8): "what does the Lord require of you but to do justice [Amos 5:24], and to love kindness [Hosea 6:6], and to walk humbly with your God [Isaiah]?"

During the century after Isaiah's death Assyria reached the pinnacle of her power. For forty-five years (687–642 B.C.) Manasseh sat on Judah's throne and wallowed in servility to his Assyrian superiors. With Madison Avenue efficiency he promoted paganism, including sacred prostitution and child sacrifice. No prophet's voice was heard during his entire reign.

Manasseh's malmonarchy was continued for two years by his son. Then a court coup placed the eight-year-old Josiah on the throne. During his reign (c. 640–609 B.C.) the death of Assyria's last great king made possible a modicum of independence for Judah. The voice of prophecy, muted for nearly a century, broke forth in the persons of Zephaniah and his greater contemporary Jeremiah (626–587 B.C.).

King Josiah's early efforts at religious reform were greatly advanced by a momentous discovery in 621 B.C. While the Temple in Jerusalem was undergoing repairs (designed to erase from it all alien symbols), a remarkable manuscript was uncovered. It categorically condemned Canaanism, advocated unswerving loyalty to the Lord, and demanded that his worship be centralized in Jerusalem. The manuscript (probably Deut. 5:1b–28:68) was purportedly from Moses. Josiah was impressed. He summoned his people to the Temple, read the newly discovered "book of the covenant," and renewed their commitment to the Lord. The royal reform that followed received the enthusiastic endorsement of Jeremiah. It went far beyond tidying up the Temple. Hinterland high places, hotbeds of heathen worship, were demolished and their priests deposed. The reform even penetrated the former land of Israel (now under nominal Assyrian control) and destroyed the rival temple at Bethel. This feat left the Jerusalem Temple as the only authorized place of worship.

Josiah's purification of religion (called the Deuteronomic Reform) provoked public piety, but it failed to produce ethical fruit. Jeremiah was quick to find the flaw. Book learning was no substitute for dynamic divine direction. He denounced "the book of the covenant" as "deceptive words" (Jer. 7:3) and pleaded for a "new covenant" which would be written "upon their hearts" (Jer. 31:33). His challenge went unheeded. The new covenant did not become a historical reality, according to Christian thought, until centuries later. On the day of Jesus' death Jesus reportedly said to his disciples, "This cup is the new covenant in my blood" (I Cor. 11:25).

Babylonian Exile

The Assyrian capital, Nineveh, fell to the Babylonians and their allies in 612 B.C. By 605 B.C. Babylonia had become the undisputed mistress of the world. Four years later Jehoiakim, Josiah's son and successor on Judah's throne, thought he saw a chance to win freedom for his people. In a brash bid for independence he refused to pay tribute to his overlord, Nebuchadnezzar. At this affront, the Babylonian ruler mobilized his mighty army and sent it marching. Judah capitulated in 597 B.C. The Temple and royal treasuries were confiscated. The royal family, the prophet Ezekiel, and other prominent figures were taken into captivity. Phase I of the Babylonian Exile had begun.

Nebuchadnezzar elevated Josiah's youngest son to the throne and called him Zedekiah. He was a weak king. Deprived of the skills of the "good figs" in captivity, he was unable to cope with his second-rate subjects. Under Egyptian influence they revolted. Nebuchadnezzar acted swiftly. His army soon surrounded Jerusalem. The walls were pierced in 586 B.C., and the city was seized. Phase II of the Babylonian Exile followed. Zedekiah's sons were slain before his eyes. He was blinded and then taken into captivity. What an ignominious end for the last member of the Davidic dynasty to sit on Judah's throne!

Contrary to common belief, the Exile did not result in a mass movement of people to Babylonia. Only the upper strata of Judean society were deported. The peasantry was left behind to harvest the crops. Enough people were taken, however, to paralyze the country and remove any threat of national revival. Much of the land lay in ruins. Many Judeans found the political and economic conditions intolerable. In large numbers they migrated to Egypt. Only a hardy handful remained in the battered environs of Jerusalem.

Life among the exiles was far less severe than had been expected. Nebuchadnezzar had neither the mood nor the means to imprison thousands of people. Many of his newly acquired subjects were skilled artisans. He allowed them to live in their own communities, practice local autonomy, and prosper. Following Jeremiah's advice, they built houses, planted gardens, reared families, and sought the welfare of the city (Jer. 29:4–7). At the end of the Exile, many were unwilling to return to Judah. They had never had it so good!

The most critical adjustment the exiles had to make was religious rather than economic. Circumstances raised many questions concerning the exiles' faith. Had the Lord been defeated by the Babylonian Marduk? Had He defaulted on His promises to protect His people? Could He be worshiped in a pagan city? King Josiah's Deuteronomic Reform had insisted that the Lord could be worshiped only in the Temple in Jerusalem. Now the Temple lay in ruins, and the Lord's people were separated from the Holy Land. Prophetic proclamations suggested answers to these perplexing problems. In a letter to the exiles Jeremiah declared that despite the Temple's loss, God could be reached through prayer (Jer. 29:12–14). He had not abandoned His people. They had abandoned Him. He had not been defeated by Marduk. On the contrary, He was using Marduk's devotees to punish His people. Ezekiel (593–573 B.C.) insisted that it would do no good for them to hide behind the comforting proverb: "The fathers have eaten sour

Mt. Gerizim is the site of the Samaritan temple which rivaled the Temple of the Jews in Jerusalem. According to the Samaritans, Abraham prepared to sacrifice Isaac on top of this mountain.

grapes, and the children's teeth are set on edge" (Ezek. 18:2). Collectively they had sinned, and in community they were being disciplined. However, Ezekiel proclaimed the justice of the Lord, saying, only "the soul that sins [and does not repent] shall die" (Ezek. 18:4). Ezekiel's doctrine of individual responsibility for sin liberated the exiles from the vise of social determinism and prepared the way for his startling picture of the restored community (Ezekiel 37).

The power structure of the East began to shift once again about the middle of the sixth century B.C. A Persian king, called Cyrus, conquered Media, then Lydia, and made menacing gestures toward Babylonia. Quick to read the handwriting on the wall, an anonymous prophet (for convenience called II Isaiah, author of most of Isaiah 40–55) boldly predicted a New Exodus. Cyrus, whom he called the Lord's "messiah," would soon conquer Babylonia, release the exiles, and rebuild Jerusalem and the Temple. II Isaiah further asserted that the restored community would be a "light to the nations," enabling God's salvation to "reach the end of the earth" (Is. 46:6). His concept of the servant of the Lord who would attain victory through suffering (Isaiah 53) was to have a profound effect upon the mind of Jesus and his early followers.

Restored Community

Cyrus conquered the Babylonians in 539 B.C. and inaugurated a two-hundred-year period of Persian power. He turned out to be one of the most enlightened rulers in history. Instead of slaughtering his royal rivals, he permitted them to retain their retinues. He protected the treasures of Babylon and allowed the exiles to return to their homeland.

A small band of Judeans made their way to Jerusalem in 538 B.C. Their dreams of dynasty and destiny were deflated by the sight of the desolate city. Almost at once, according to Ezra 3, they built an altar, installed the Levites, and laid the foundation of the Second Temple. The work, however, was soon interrupted when Zerubbabel, leader of the Jews, spurned the offer of the Samaritans to help in the construction. Although the

Samaritan priests display a copy of the Pentateuch. Only a few hundred Samaritans are alive today. About half of them live in the shadow of Mt. Gerizim near Nablus, ancient Shechem.

Samaritans were descendants of the Israelites who once formed the Northern Kingdom, they had mixed their blood with the foreigners whom the Assyrians had settled in the area. Zerubbabel judged them unfit to participate in a sacred task. This rebuke constituted the first brick in a wall of separation between the two peoples; open hostility eventually resulted. The Samaritans built a rival temple on Mt. Gerizim overlooking Shechem. Centuries later a Galilean prophet asked a Samaritan woman for a drink from Jacob's well at Shechem. His request was met with the question: "How is it that you, a Jew, ask a drink of me, a woman of Samaria?" (Jn. 4:9).

The prophets Haggai and Zechariah attributed the Jewish community's prevailing poverty to a lack of housing for the Lord. Prophetic prodding prompted the Jews to resume Temple construction in 520 B.C. Five years later the project was completed, but the poverty persisted.

The sordid conditions in Jerusalem eventually reached the ears of Nehemiah, cup-bearer to the Persian king. He persuaded his sovereign to send him to the Holy City as governor in 445 B.C. and again in 432 B.C. Nehemiah roused the dispirited Jews, rebuilt the city walls, instituted tithing and Sabbath observance, and banned marriage with "the people of the land."

Shortly after Nehemiah's governorships, a priest named Ezra journeyed to Jerusalem to survey the religious situation. He brought with him a copy of "the book of the law of Moses" (Neh. 8:1) and read it to the assembled people.[9] There followed a covenant-renewal ceremony similar to the ones once conducted by Josiah and Joshua. Ezra's exaltation of Moses' Law earned him the title, "Father of Judaism." Under his influence, prophecy was nearly smothered, and the Law molded the mind and manners of the Jews.

Ezra multiplied the restrictive measures of Nehemiah. He not only denounced mixed marriages but declared that foreign wives (and their children) should be cast aside. Against these parochialists two notes of subtle protest were subsequently sounded. The book of Ruth recalled that a foreigner was the ancestress of David, Israel's greatest king. The book of Jonah dramatized the Lord's abiding concern for the salvation of aliens.

Hellenism

In the latter part of the fourth century B.C. the political tide turned once again. Alexander of Macedonia (336–323 B.C.) attacked Persia. Victory followed victory until he found himself on the Indus River in modern Pakistan. There, according to legend, he wept for want of more worlds to conquer. He dreamed of one world united by Greek culture, but he died before his dream could materialize. His huge empire was divided among his many generals. Ptolemy received Egypt and Seleucus eventually secured

[9]Scholars are divided as to whether the book refers to the Pentateuch or the Priestly Code.

Syria and Mesopotamia. Once again the Promised Land became a pawn in the power structure of the Fertile Crescent.

Alexander's successors vied with each other in sponsoring things Greek. Theaters, museums, and gymnasiums sprouted like potatoes. It became fashionable to wear Greek dress and to speak *koine* Greek, the nonclassical language of commerce. The cultural penetration (called Hellenism, from Hellas, the ancient name for Greece) was markedly successful. By the time of Ptolemy II (285–246 B.C.), Hebrew had become a dead language for most Jews. Even their sacred Scriptures had to be translated into Greek, forming the Septuagint.

Palestine was controlled by the Ptolemys of Egypt throughout the third century B.C. But in 198 B.C., Ptolemy V was decisively defeated by the Syrian Seleucid, Antiochus III. His son, Antiochus IV, eventually occupied his throne (175–163 B.C.). He called himself Epiphanes ("The Manifest" of Zeus), but his subjects dubbed him Epimanes ("The Madman"). A fanatical Hellenist, he made the worship of Zeus mandatory. When the stubborn Jews refused to submit to his impossible demands, he determined to wipe out their religion. Circumcision, Sabbath observance, and possession of a copy of the Law were decreed capital offenses. Then, in 168 B.C., Antiochus brazenly desecrated the Temple. An altar to Zeus was set up in the Temple, and swine were sacrificed upon it.

Maccabean Revolt

Antiochus' desecrating act (called "the abomination that makes desolate," Dan. 11:31) stiffened the spine of Jewish resistance. When a Syrian officer forced a Jew to worship Zeus in 168 B.C., Mattathias, a village priest, slew them both. With his sons and sympathizers, Mattathias took refuge in the hills and carried on guerrilla warfare. Just prior to his death in 166 B.C. he selected his oldest son, Judas, to carry on the revolt. Judas was such a ferocious fighter that he was named Maccabeus ("The Hammerer"). The revolution which he headed came to be known as the Maccabean Revolt.

Against seemingly insuperable odds Judas and his men won a resounding victory. They captured Jerusalem, rebuilt the altar of the Temple, and restored the worship of the Lord. Each year, about the time Christians celebrate Jesus' birth, the Jews celebrate the Temple's rededication through their ceremony of Hanukkah (Dedication), the Feast of Lights.

A tract for these times—the book of Daniel—appeared shortly after the Maccabean Revolt had begun. Its author was horrified by Hellenism's infection of the Jews. He determined to rekindle his people's faith and to renew their loyalty in the face of severe persecution. In his magnificent (and often misunderstood) work he declared that history is in the hand of the Lord, that His heavenly kingdom is near, and that steadfastness is required of those who would have a place in it. His convictions were expressed in a new idiom (apocalypse) and served to fan the fires of Judah's faith once again.

The Maccabean Revolt had begun as a struggle for religious freedom.
It soon developed into a drive for political independence. After Judas'
death, leadership passed in turn to his brothers. Freedom was wrested from
the Seleucids, fresh territory was wrung from neighbors, and Judah became
the strongest military power in the Syrian empire. However, her position
of strength soon crumbled.

Roman Rule

Fierce feuding for Judah's throne broke out in 67–63 B.C. The royal
rivals scrambled for the support of Pompey, prominent Roman general. A
citizen's committee, sick of the venal rule of their native princes, urged him
to restore the high priest to power. Pompey jumped at the invitation their
civil war offered him. He marched to Jerusalem in 63 B.C. and besieged the
city for three months. A breach in the wall became a prelude to horrible
butchery. He spared the Temple treasures and permitted Temple worship;
but he appalled the inhabitants when he barged into the Holy of Holies.
That sacred spot could be entered only by the high priest; it was commonly
believed to be the dwelling place of the Lord.

Pompey shrank the size of the Jewish state to Judea, Idumea, Galilee,
and Perea. He abolished the kingship and established Hyrcanus II as high
priest and ethnarch. The real power behind Hyrcanus, however, was An-
tipater, a wealthy and powerful Idumean governor. He scrupulously carried
out Roman policies and saw to it that his sons became prefects of Galilee
and Judea. The Roman Senate later appointed one of the sons, Herod, to
be king of the Jews. It took Herod three years to capture Jerusalem and
ascend the throne.

Like his father, Herod (40–4 B.C.) was an outstanding success as a
Roman vassal. He switched sides during Rome's civil war with the alacrity
of a race-track tout. His kingdom grew to include all of Palestine. As a
promoter of Hellenism he had no peer. He supported emperor worship,
built temples to the divine Augustus, and beautified Samaria. Hippodromes,
theaters, amphitheaters, and stadiums multiplied like rabbits. He restored
old cities and named them after relatives. He built new cities like Caesarea,
which became the talk of the times. But by far the most famous of Herod's
edifices was the rebuilt Temple in Jerusalem. He graced its stones with gold
and increased its size with courts and porticoes until it became the pride of
pilgrims. One of Jesus' disciples was awed by its magnificence. As he came
out of the Temple he turned to Jesus and exclaimed, "Look, Teacher, what
wonderful stones and what wonderful buildings!" (Mk. 13:1).

Herod was capable but cruel. He maintained peace, promoted the arts,
and gave unstinting loyalty to Rome. He probably deserved his political
title, "The Great." But to the Jews he was a self-seeking, bloodthirsty
tyrant. Even though he was half Hebrew and his first wife was of Maccabean descent, the Jews could not tolerate his devotion to Hellenism,
polygamy, and fratricide. He coldly executed his beloved wife and three

sons and (according to Mt. 2:16) massacred all the male children of Bethlehem who were two years old or under. It is small wonder Josephus records that the lot of those who survived Herod's sword made them envy those who were slain (*Antiquities*, XVII, 11,2). If Jesus of Nazareth had not been born late in his reign, Herod would long since have become a minor memory in the Western world.

We have moved swiftly through the eighteen hundred years that separate Abraham from Jesus. Jesus was a Jew, not a Greek or a Roman. He remembered and shared a special history, a history that had a divine dimension. God had spoken to his people in many ways—through their perils (such as the Exodus) and through prophets. He had called his people to be a community and had disciplined them to be a servant. Apart from this special history, there could have been no Jew, no Jesus, and no new covenant.

chapter two

The Land

Someone once remarked that the British and the Americans are united by common culture and customs and divided by a common language. Although there is some truth in this statement, language is only one of the distinguishing marks of a people. Such characteristics as clothes, mannerisms, and attitudes also enable one to recognize a stranger in a foreign land. One's native land plays a crucial role in the life of any person. If we are to understand Jesus, we must familiarize ourselves with his homeland.

Goethe grasped this truth when he wrote,

> Whoever the poet will understand
> Must go into the poet's land.

Name

It is easier to define the land of Jesus than to designate it, for it is a land with many names. The most common Old Testament designation was "Canaan" (Gen. 11:31). The word literally means "lowland" and was an appropriate term when the inhabitants were confined to that territory. The time came, however, when the lowlanders mastered the hill country also; then the designation for the entire land became a misnomer.

Another name for the territory is "Promised Land." This stems from the promise the Lord made to Abraham, father of the Hebrews: "To your descendants I give this land, from the river of Egypt to the great river, the river Euphrates" (Gen. 15:18). Since claims and counterclaims of ownership have echoed down through the centuries, it is sometimes referred to as the "much promised land."

Today we often speak of the cradle of Christianity as the "Holy Land." Fearsome fratricide notwithstanding, it is the holiest spot on earth for three of the world's great religions—Judaism, Christianity, and Islam. It might properly be called the Holy, Holy, Holy Land.

Finally, the land of Jesus is known as "Palestine." Throughout the twelfth and eleventh centuries B.C. the Hebrews were sorely troubled by a people who poured out of the Aegean onto the eastern shores of the Mediterranean. They swarmed into Cannan by land and sea and established a beachhead on the coastal plain. Their characteristic aggressiveness was intensified by their near monopoly in the production of iron weapons. They soon moved inland, easily overcame Canaanite resistance, and almost succeeded in destroying the entrenched and powerful Hebrews. The irony of it —that the land promised to the Hebrews should later derive its name from their archenemies, the Philistines!

Location and Size

Early man was cradled in the two great alluvial plains of the Nile and the Tigris-Euphrates. As he multiplied, the excess population overflowed into the areas of Syria and Palestine. Soon Palestine was recognized as one of the most strategic spots on earth. It was the land link for three continents (Europe, Asia, and Africa) and two great civilizations (Egypt and Assyria-Babylonia).

Palestine's importance has not diminished with the passing parade. All of the forceful countries of the world have struggled to control it. Only recently have France and Great Britain responded to pressures and reluctantly released it from their grasp. Today it is a pawn in the power struggle between East and West. It is little wonder, since nearby are over half of the world's proven oil supplies.

In Jesus' day the boundaries of Palestine were as elastic as a rubber band. They expanded in periods of national strength and contracted in times of national weakness. A favorite Biblical phrase defined the populated limits of the country as extending "from Dan [nestled in the foothills of Mt. Hermon in the north] to Beersheba," a desert outpost in the south. The country was bordered on the north by Phoenicia (modern Lebanon) and Syria, on the east by the Arabian Desert, on the south by the Arabian Desert and the Sinai Peninsula, and on the west by the Mediterranean Sea. Its length was about 150 miles, and its width varied from 35 miles in the north to 70 miles in the south. It contained only 10,000 square miles, making it roughly equivalent to New Hampshire or Vermont, one-fifth the size of Pennsylvania or England, and one-fifteenth the size of California. A jet plane can fly across its widest part in a matter of minutes.

The Kishon river, which cuts the Valley of Esdraelon in two, is shown here to the north of Mt. Carmel as it makes its way across the Plain of Acre toward the Mediterranean Sea. This river played a prominent part in scenes from the lives of such Old Testament personalities as Deborah, Barak, Sisera, and Elijah.

Topography

As one travels from west to east, the lay of the land of Palestine can easily be distinguished. It falls naturally into four parallel areas, running from north to south.

The Coastal Plain extends along the Mediterranean Sea for the entire length of Palestine. Like all Gaul it is divided into three parts.

1. The Plain of Acre lies to the north. It is only three miles wide where it touches Phoenicia. As it moves south it gradually broadens until it is ten miles wide at the foot of Mt. Carmel where it terminates. It derives its name from Acre, its principal city and seaport (ancient Accho). Barely above sea level, the whole plain is extensively cultivated. The "tells" (ruins of ancient cities) which are scattered over the area bear mute testimony to its importance in Biblical times.

Two rivers flow across the plain into the Mediterranean Sea. The Belis, on whose banks the Phoenicians first learned to make glass, flows past the city of Acre. The larger Kishon wends its way along the southern base of the plain. During the summer, the river is no larger than a modest creek. A memorable Old Testament happening, however, underscores the fact that it may become a raging torrent after a cloudburst. According to the story, the Israelites, led by Deborah and Barak, clashed with Sisera's Canaanite army near Megiddo. (Ar-megeddon, the ultimate battle depicted in Revelation 16:16, literally means "hill of Megiddo.") Thanks to a violent rainstorm, the Kishon burst its banks. Canaanite charioteers were helplessly trapped in the miry clay. Judges 5:20 celebrates the providential victory:

> From heaven fought the stars,
> from their courses they fought against Sisera.

2. The Plain of Sharon begins at the base of Mt. Carmel where it is less than a mile wide. In its forty-four-mile journey to Jaffa (Biblical Joppa) it recedes from the shore to a maximum width of fifteen miles. Jaffa, at the plain's southern end, has one of the oldest harbors in history. To this harbor, Hiram, King of Tyre, shipped the cedars of Lebanon which Solomon used to build the first Temple in Jerusalem (II Chr. 2:15). Legend has it that all shipwrecked gold, silver, and precious stones in all the seas flow to Jaffa. The reluctant prophet, Jonah, in flight from the Lord, "went down to Joppa and found a ship going to Tarshish" (Jonah 1:3). There too lived Simon, a tanner. On the roof of his house his kosher-conscious guest, Simon Peter, had a vision that signaled the extension of Christianity into the Greco-Roman world (Acts 10:5–16).

The city of Dor, just south of Mt. Carmel, was the most important city of Sharon in ancient times. About 22 B.C. Herod the Great built a new city a few miles to the south. It quickly became the main seaport and capital of Palestine, and it remained so for nearly five hundred years. Herod

The northern end of the Plain of Sharon is perhaps the most productive part of Palestine.

named the city Caesarea in honor of Augustus Caesar. There it was that St. Paul later languished in prison for two years while awaiting trial before the sluggish courts (Acts 24:27). There also, in the fourth century, Eusebius, Bishop of Caesarea, wrote his monumental *Ecclesiastical History*.

The red, sandy soil of Sharon is perhaps the most fertile in the country. The oranges and other citrus fruit it grows are the delight of Europe. In springtime the plain becomes a veritable garden. Wild flowers (which Jesus called "the lilies of the field," Mt. 6:28) blossom profusely. The rose of Sharon was an Old Testament byword for beauty. Along the coast the active sand dunes pose permanent peril. Modern Israelis slow their advance with an army of eucalyptus trees. Attractive resort areas are built on the sand overlooking the buoyant, blue Mediterranean.

3. The Plain of Philistia starts where Sharon ends, near Jaffa. As it continues toward the south, it becomes somewhat wider until it vanishes in the desert that separates Palestine from Egypt. Wadi el-Arish ("the Brook of Egypt," Num. 34:5) marks its southern boundary.

The sand dunes along the coast are more extensive than in Sharon. At times they stretch inland for as much as two miles. In contrast with the low plains of the north, with their wide patches scarcely above sea level, Philistia gradually rises. The rolling expanse reaches a height of over three hundred feet in the south. Wheat and barley fields and olive orchards grace the landscape.

The five great towns of the Philistines were Gaza, Ashkelon, Ashdod, Ekron, and Gath. Gaza has been burned into modern minds as "the strip" that contains more than 200,000 Arab refugees. Located athwart the great

Jaffa (Biblical Joppa), at the southern end of the Plain of Sharon, is the site of Jonah's departure to Tarshish and Simon Peter's vision.

trade route from Egypt to the north, Gaza alone stood in the way of Egyptian conquest. The five fortified cities, cogent in confederation, intermittently warred with the Israelites. One such battle cost the life of Saul and his son, Jonathan.

The Western Highlands comprise the second section of Palestine. They form the backbone and watershed of the Holy Land. The Highlands are merely a southern continuation of two mountain ranges in Syria—the Lebanon and Anti-Lebanon. The Syrian mountains were a happy hunting ground for cedar-loving Solomon. In the Anti-Lebanon range, Mt. Hermon hunches its massive shoulders upward to 9,232 feet. Its huge bulk and towering height are an unforgettable landmark. The Arabs call it Sheikh Mountain because it is chief of them all. On a clear day, sharp-eyed Bedouins can see it from as far south as Bethlehem. Tourists along the Sea of Galilee are awed by its majesty. In the winter it is covered by a blanket of snow down to the 2,800-foot level. By late summer, however, only scattered patches of snow are likely to remain. For a reader of the Gospels, Mt. Hermon is pregnant with portent. A tradition points to one of its lesser summits as the place where Jesus, in the company of Peter, James, and John, experienced the Transfiguration (Mk. 9:2–8).

The Western Highlands fall naturally into six sections.

1. The Highlands of Galilee are less rugged than the Lebanon mountains. They approach 4,000 feet in the north, but the altitude drops appreciably as they move south. Their small, picturesque valleys are frequent and highly cultivated. Easy accessibility to the hills from all sides makes effective fortification impossible. Nature, it seems, issued an open invitation to all comers, making the area a melting pot. Isaiah rightly called the land "Galilee of the nations" (Is. 9:1). The hotheaded super-patriotic "Zealots," from whose midst Jesus chose a disciple, headquartered in the hills. They plotted revolution and did their best to change the melting pot into a pressure cooker.

2. The Plains of Esdraelon and Jezreel lie to the south of Galilee and interrupt the march of the Highlands to the southern desert. Esdraelon, sliced in two by the upper Kishon river, slopes toward the northwest and the Mediterranean. East of Esdraelon is the much narrower Valley of Jezreel. The two plains were famous as the breadbasket and battlefield of Palestine. Together they formed the most traveled pass across the country. From Egypt to Damascus the route followed the seacoast from Gaza to Carmel, through Esdraelon and Jezreel, and then across the Jordan Valley. To protect the trade route and to defend the interior from marauding Bedouins, a mighty fortress was constructed at Beth-shean, at the eastern end of Jezreel. The region was so renowned for its fertility that the Sages of Israel sang, "If the Garden of Eden is in the land of Israel—then its gate is at Beth-shean."

As Jesus walked along the edge of Nazareth, he could see the steady stream of merchants, soldiers, and pilgrims that passed through the Esdraelon Valley. No doubt he ventured close enough to hear the babble of many languages and observe the contrasting customs of "the world." In his imagination he could rehearse the heart of history. Across those plains

The Plain of Esdraelon is famous as the breadbasket and battlefield of Palestine. This photograph was taken from near Nazareth and indicates what a commanding view Jesus had of the valley below.

once marched the mighty Pharaohs of Egypt. There Deborah and Barak fought against Sisera. There Gideon and his three hundred braves smote the enemies of the Lord who were "like locusts for number" (Judges 6:5). There Saul and Jonathan fell in defeat. There the Assyrians, the Babylonians, the Persians, the Greeks, the Syrians, and the Romans all came to conquer. After Jesus, conquerors continued to come—the Arabs, the Crusaders under Richard the Lion-Hearted, Saladin, the Turks, Napoleon, and Allenby.

3. Mount Carmel lies to the southwest of the Plain of Esdraelon. Its northwestern end juts out into the Mediterranean Sea and is so steep and rugged as to defy trespassing. The Carmel range reaches a height of over 1,800 feet. Today its northern end boasts the exquisitely beautiful, three-tiered city of Haifa, the San Francisco of Israel. Somewhere near here, on a promontory, Elijah brought to a dramatic halt the perverse penetration of Phoenician worship sponsored by King Ahab's wife, Jezebel, and her devoted allies, the 450 prophets of Baal (I Kings 17 and 18).

4. The Samaritan Highlands start at the southern end of Carmel-Esdraelon-Jezreel and extend to the Judean Highlands in the south. They early went by the name of Ephraim but were later called after their principal city, Samaria. Omri began the construction of Samaria and made it the capital of the Northern Kingdom of Israel. His son, Ahab, completed

it. Adorned by natural beauty and protected by natural defenses, the city was a monument to Omri's political astuteness. Its masonry, fortifications, and luxurious palaces have yielded to the excavators spade in recent times. Jerusalem's rival was a rival indeed!

Mention nearly any spot in Samaria and you are swiftly immersed by a flood of holy history: Bethel, where Jacob dreamed about a ladder that reached to heaven (Gen. 28:10–19); Shiloh, home of the priest Eli and his protégé Samuel; Shechem, where Jesus spoke to a Samaritan woman at Jacob's Well about "living water" (Jn. 4:7–24).

5. The Judean Highlands have no certain northern border since the Samaritan Highlands are not separated from them by any natural break. The boundary may be fixed not far north of Jerusalem. It probably begins with the Valley of Aijalon in the west and extends to the Wadi Kelt in the east.

Judea is principally a highland country. Her chief towns are built on the fifteen-mile-wide plateau which runs south for thirty-five miles from the northern border to below Hebron. From Jerusalem, which is 2,600 feet above sea level, the general slope is upward. At Hebron, Judea reaches its

The three-tiered city of Haifa, the San Francisco of Israel, overlooks the Bay of Haifa and (in the extreme background) the Bay of Acre. Somewhere on Mt. Carmel, on which Haifa is built, Elijah challenged and defeated Jezebel's 450 prophets of Baal. This dramatic encounter reversed the tide of pagan penetration and saved Israel for the Lord. The Bahai Temple is in the left foreground.

Jacob's Well at Nablus (Biblical Shechem) was the place where Jesus conversed with the woman of Samaria about "living water." Her observation that "our fathers worshiped on this mountain" (Jn. 4:20) referred to nearby Mt. Gerizim. After a rift with the Jews, the Samaritans had built their own temple on top of this mountain. The Jewish leader John Hyrcanus destroyed their temple in 128 B.C., about 200 years after its completion.

highest point, over 3,000 feet. So abundant are the barren rocks and crags of Judea that they have fathered a legend. During creation, the story goes, an angel responsible for the proper distribution of rocks and boulders flew over Palestine. His mission came to a premature end when the bag broke over Judea!

Where the plateau falters, ridges and shallow glens are formed. The ridges are often crowned with villages and the glens covered with vines, fig trees, and olive orchards. Some of the breaks in the plateau are rich with vegetation, such as Bethany (residence of Mary, Martha, and Lazarus, and Jesus' "home away from home" when he visited Jerusalem); the Valley of Hinnom ("Gehenna," the Hebrew equivalent of hell); the Gardens of Solomon at Bethlehem (the cradle of Christ); and the Valley of Eschol near Hebron (where Moses' spies—Joshua, Caleb, and company—discovered a cluster of grapes, proof positive of the fertility of the Promised Land, Numbers 13:23).

In spite of these fertile exceptions, Judea is so bleak and barren as to make the modern pilgrim gasp. This howling wasteland east of Jerusalem (the wilderness in which Jesus was tempted) was never very productive. However, the landscape has not always been naked; many of the Judean hills as Jesus saw them were covered with trees and blanketed with three feet of superb topsoil.

Men have been poor stewards of the soil. Vindictive conquerors punished the defeated by destroying their woodlands. The Turks imposed a stiff tax on every well, vine, and tree; consequently, the farmers felled their trees rather than pay the taxes on them. Bedouin goats completed the

This rocky hillside near Jerusalem is a mute monument to man's faithless stewardship of the soil. Some leading conservation experts are convinced that in Jesus' day such hills were shaded with trees and covered with three feet of superb topsoil.

A pine tree nursery near Jerusalem furnishes saplings for the extensive
reforestation program currently under way in Israel. The small trees in
the background were planted in nearly solid rock five years before this
photograph was taken.

erosion by clipping off every green shoot as soon as it appeared. Deprived of
vegetation, the topsoil was washed into the sea.

Israelis are now hard at work restoring the land to its Biblical splendor.
They blast holes in the rock in order to plant saplings; then for two years
they carry buckets of water from tank trucks up the hillsides for the tiny
trees. Gradually nature is able to manage on her own. The growing trees
break up the rock, provide humus for the soil, prevent erosion, beautify
the countryside, and air-condition the atmosphere. Millions of trees have
been planted since 1948, and many a desolate hillside has already been
transformed into a young pine or cedar forest. When completed, the Valley
of Martyrs alone will contain six million trees—one for each Jew who lost
his life under Adolf Hitler.

6. The Negeb forms a triangle that comprises the southern end of
Palestine. The name literally means the "Dry or Parched Land." From the
elevated dome of Hebron the land slopes downward. An undulating plain
fans eastward to the Dead Sea and southward to Aqaba on the right arm
of the Red Sea. From Gaza, on the Mediterranean, it extends thirty miles
south to the Egyptian border.

As the southernmost Palestinian city in Biblical times, Beersheba separated the settlers from the nomads. It played an important role in the lives
of the Patriarchs. It was there that Abraham planted a tamarisk tree and

made a covenant with Abimelech (Gen. 21:25–36). Today the rapidly expanding city is the throbbing capital of the Negeb. Made up of newcomers from the four corners of the earth, its industrial and arid-zone research centers spearhead Negeb colonization.

The Jordan Valley, sometimes called "a fault of God," forms the third main section of Palestine. It can best be viewed in its five natural divisions.

1. The Upper Jordan, at the extreme northern end of Palestine, begins in the foothills of Mt. Hermon. In the region of Dan and Caesarea Philippi (where Peter confessed, "You are the Christ," Mk. 8:27–33), four separate streams drain snow, rain, and spring water from the mountains and vie with each other for the honor of being called the source of the Jordan river.

The river soon reaches a marshy area where papyrus plants once grew in profusion. From such bulrushes the ancients made boats (Is. 18:2), baskets (Ex. 2:3), and mats. But their chief utility was in the manufacture of "paper." The pith of the papyrus was cut into small, thin strips which were placed side by side in rows to form a single layer. Another layer was put on top of the first at right angles and the whole was welded together by pounding. The thin white product was then burnished. No adhesive was required except that found in the pith itself. Many chapters of the Bible were originally written on the papyrus pith of the Upper Jordan.

At the southern end of the marshes lies Lake Huleh (Semechonitis),

The Negeb is a dry, parched triangle comprising the southern end of Palestine. The land in the foreground has been plowed for planting for the first time in history. In the background is a lush crop of cotton, said to be second in quality only to that of Egypt.

highest, smallest, and shallowest of Palestine's three inland bodies of water. Some scholars have equated it with the Old Testament waters of Merom (Josh. 11:5). Only seven feet above sea level, it once boasted a length of two miles, a width of three miles, and a depth of twenty-six feet. Since 1957, however, its modest size has shrunk severely. Two deep channels, dug by the Israelis, have drained the stagnant waters from the marshes into the lake. At Huleh's southern end, a straightened and deepened river bed speeds the water on its way to Galilee. The once malarial marshes have become fruitful fields and plantations. Fish ponds dot the landscape. A large peat area, uncovered by the drainage, furnishes fertilizer for the fields.

From Lake Huleh the Jordan tumbles headlong down a narrow gorge in one almost continuous cascade. It drops nearly 700 feet in less than nine miles. Then, through a delta of its own deposits, it slides noiselessly into the Sea of Galilee. How appropriate that this river should be named the Jordan, "the Descender!"

2. The Sea of Galilee is 682 feet below sea level. It is thirteen miles long and eight miles wide. Its name is variable; it has been called Chinnereth (Deut. 3:17), Tiberias (Jn. 6:1), and Gennesaret (I Macc. 11:67). Modern Israelis prefer the name "Kinneret," because the Sea is shaped like a harp (*Kinnor* in Hebrew).

Pith from papyrus plants like these near Lake Huleh (Semechonitis) furnished the raw material for the "paper" (scrolls) on which the New Testament was written. Papyri once grew in profusion in Egypt. The baby Moses floated in a basket on the Nile among the papyrus plants (Ex. 2:3).

The thriving green fields and productive fish hatcheries of the Jordan Valley at the southern end of the Sea of Galilee were made possible by fresh water from the Sea, scientific agriculture, and the dedicated enterprise of Israel's kibbutzim. This area contrasts sharply with the arid, sun-scorched land in the foreground. The Eastern Highlands form the background of the picture.

The Sea is closely hemmed in by mountains on the east and the west. During the summer the sun beats down upon the basin with unmitigated fury, making it hotter than Gehenna. Without warning, cold air currents from the west pounce upon the superheated depression and provoke sudden storms (Mk. 4:35–41). The natives usually respect this danger and keep their boats tied up from noon till nine. The climate moderates in winter, and eager vacationers rush to the lakeside for respite and release.

Sizable cities girdled the Sea in Jesus' day. Nine of them are believed to have had populations of at least fifteen thousand each.[1] On the southwestern shore was Tiberias, Herod's new city, noted for its hot springs and curative baths. To the north lay Tarichaea (pickling places), center of the bustling fishing industry. So far as the Gospels are concerned, Jesus never entered either city. Beyond Tarichaea lay Magdala (home of the seven-deviled Mary whom Jesus healed), Capernaum (site of Jesus' early and fabulously successful ministry), and Chorazin (chastised by Jesus for its unresponsiveness to the Gospel, Mt. 11:21). On the northern tip of the lake was Bethsaida (to which Jesus withdrew after he had heard of the death of John the Baptist, Lk. 9:10). Down the east coast lay Gergesa, Hippos,

[1]George Adam Smith, *The Historical Geography of the Holy Land*, 14th ed. (New York: A. C. Armstrong & Sons, 1908), p. 447.

The Jordan river is shown here as it makes its way from the Sea of Galilee toward the Dead Sea. Somewhere in its sacred waters, John baptized his converts and one "whose sandals I am not worthy to stoop down and untie" (Mk. 1:7).

and, somewhat removed from the shore, Gadara (where Jesus healed the demoniacs and the swine rushed into the sea and perished, Mt. 8:28–34). The multitudes of people who lived in these and other cities that formed an almost unbroken ring around the Sea of Galilee earned their living by agriculture, fruit-growing, dyeing, tanning, boat-building, and fishing.

Nowhere in Palestine can one recover the authentic Jesus as surely as by the Sea of Galilee. From her shores he called his first disciples (Mk. 1:16–20). From her secret depths he snatched a shoal of fish (Lk. 5:1–11). On her surface he rode in boats that sometimes served as a pulpit from which he spoke his parables (Mk. 3:7–12). Other sacred sites are strewn with shrines and sanctuaries, but as yet no one has built a church over the Sea of Galilee.

3. The Lower Jordan extends sixty-five miles from the southern end of the Sea of Galilee to the Dead Sea. It is flanked on the west by the Highlands of Galilee and Samaria (interrupted only by the Valley of Jezreel) and on the opposite side by the Eastern Highlands (pierced by the Yarmuk and Jabbok rivers). Between these ranges the land is from three to fourteen miles wide and from 600 to 1,200 feet below sea level. The Ghor or Rift, as the Arabs call it, is actually a long, narrow valley which twice expands (at Beth-shean and Jericho) to the status of a plain.

Many streams from the Highlands swell the Jordan river as it wends its way toward the Dead Sea. So serpentine is the river's course that to reach its destination it travels three times the distance of a crow's flight. Devotees of Mark Twain's mighty Mississippi have their dreams drastically deflated when they first gaze on the Jordan. "The most storied river in the world" is not more than one hundred feet wide and fifteen feet deep!

The Jordan Valley has two levels. The first is a narrow, twisting depression, from two hundred yards to a mile wide. It marks the river's broadened bed at floodtide. An almost impenetrable thicket masks its surface. From the air it looks like a monstrous green serpent. When Jeremiah wanted to steel his people for tougher times ahead, he cried, "If in a safe land you fall down, how will you do in the jungle of the Jordan?" (Jer. 12:5).

The Valley's second level, perhaps 150 feet above the first, serves as a broad footing for the Highlands on either side. Where irrigation is practiced, a lush blanket of green covers the land.

What a hollow of hallowed memories is the Jordan Valley! Picture Moses atop Mt. Nebo casting a covetous eye over the land denied to him personally (Deut. 34:1–4). Imagine the surprised delight of Joshua's advance

From the ruins of ancient Jericho, oldest city of Palestine, the Jordan Valley is viewed at its widest point where it is fourteen miles across. Date palms, bananas, and other fruit grow where the land is irrigated. The descent from Jerusalem to Jericho is about 3,300 feet. Jesus spoke like an informed topographer in relating the parable of the Good Samaritan. "A man was going *down* from Jerusalem to Jericho..." (Lk. 10:30, emphasis added).

The Dead Sea, vast storehouse of mineral wealth, is the lowest place
on earth. Its surface is nearly 1,300 feet below sea level.

guard as the waters of the Jordan part for their crossing (Josh. 3:14–17).
Hark to the sound of the trumpets that seal the doom of Jericho (Joshua 6).
Witness the explosive anger of Naaman as Elisha commands him to wash
seven times in the dirty Jordan to rid himself of leprosy (II Kings 5:1–14).
Note the surge of the multitudes as John the Baptist calls them to be immersed in the river. Mark the One who stands out from all the rest. He it is
who is baptized with water *and* the Spirit (Mk. 1:9–11).

4. The Dead Sea is fifty miles long, ten miles wide, and reaches a depth
of 1,300 feet. Like its sister to the north, its names are numerous: Sea of
Salt (Gen. 14:3), Sea of the Wilderness (Deut. 3:17), Eastern Sea (Ezek.
47:18), Sea of Lot (among the Arabs), and Lake Asphaltitus (among the
Greeks). Its surface is nearly 1,300 feet below sea level. This fact provides
a photographer with an unparalleled opportunity. He may take pictures of
his friends standing on the shore and then declare that they are literally
the lowest people on earth!

An average of nearly six million tons of water pours into the Dead Sea
daily. Yet the level of the Sea remains relatively constant. The scorching
sun and dry winds lap up the incoming waters almost as rapidly as they
appear. The concentrated solution that remains is oily to the touch and
bitter to the taste; when four buckets full are allowed to evaporate, one
bucket full of salt and other minerals is left. The Dead Sea is an enormous
storehouse of valuable minerals: 22 billion tons of magnesium chloride, 11

billion tons of sodium chloride (salt), 7 billion tons of calcium chloride, 2 billion tons of potassium chloride, and 1 billion tons of magnesium bromide.[2]

Swimming in the Dead Sea is great sport. One does not swim *in* it but *on* it. Like the Great Salt Lake of Utah, the bitter water is so buoyant that a person's arms and legs lie suspended on the surface. Face-down swimming is hazardous since one's feet bob merrily topside. Divers have drowned because they could not right themselves. One can literally sit on the Sea and read a book! After a swim, three fresh-water showers are required to wash away the oily film.

A perceptive parable is told about Palestine's two seas.

One is fresh, and fish are in it. Splashes of green adorn its banks. Trees spread their branches over it, and stretch out thirsty roots to sip of its healing waters. Along its shores the children play, as children played when He was there. He loved it. He could look across its silver surface when He spoke His parables.
The river Jordan makes this sea with sparkling water from the hills. Men build their houses near to it, and birds their nests; and every kind of life is happier because it is there.
The river Jordan flows on south into another sea. Here is no splash of fish, no fluttering leaf, no song of birds, no children's laughter. Travelers choose another route unless on urgent business. The air hangs heavy above its water, and neither man nor beast nor fowl will drink.
What makes this mighty difference in these neighbor seas? Not the river Jordan. It empties the same good water into both. Not the soil in which they lie, not the country round about. The difference is this. The Sea of Galilee receives but does not keep the Jordan. For every drop that flows into it another drop flows out. The other sea is shrewder, hoarding its income jealously. It will not be tempted into any generous impulse. Every drop it gets it keeps. The Sea of Galilee gives and lives. This other sea gives nothing. It is named The Dead.
There are two seas in Palestine, and there are two kinds of people in the world.[3]

Somewhere along the shore of the Dead Sea the unsavory cities of Sodom and Gomorrah once stood. Even Abraham's plea on their behalf could not save them from annihilation (Gen. 18:16–19:24). Ever since, their destruction has served as a searing symbol of punishment for sin. Yet Jesus declared that it would be "more tolerable on the day of judgment for the land of Sodom and Gomorrah" than for the privileged towns of his own day that heard but did not heed the Gospel (Mt. 10:15).

5. The Wadi Arabah is the name for the Jordan Valley to the south of the Dead Sea. It extends to the Gulf of Aqaba, modern Israel's gateway to Africa and the Far East. The northern part of this "valley of the desert" may once have been covered by an extensive oil flow which killed the trees

---

[2]Zev Vilnay, *Israel Guide*, 3rd ed. (Jerusalem: The Central Press, 1960), p. 17.

[3]Bruce Barton, "There Are Two Seas," *McCall's*, LV, No. 7 (1928), 7. Reprinted by permission of the author.

and preserved their stumps for centuries. But by far the most fascinating survival of the Arabah is the rose-red city of Petra. This magnificent Nabatean capital, carved out of the multicolored sandstone cliffs, reminds one of Utah's Zion National Park. Its spectacular tombs, temples, altars, and monastery (rediscovered in 1812) are among the most breathtakingly beautiful sights in the world.

The Eastern Highlands form the fourth and final part of Palestine's topography. The region to the northeast of Galilee had no single name in Jesus' day. Its various parts (Gaulanitis, Auranitis, Batanea, Trachonitis, and Ituraea) made up the tetrachy of Philip. When combined with Hauran to the south, it was called Bashan in the Old Testament. It was famous for its oaks (Is. 2:13), pastures (Micah 7:14), and well-fed cattle (Amos 4:1).

South of the Yarmuk river (which joins the Jordan just below the Sea of Galilee) is the ill-defined area called the Decapolis ("ten cities"). The Old Testament refers to it as Gilead. The cities formed a league and were built up by the Greeks as a buffer to prevent the northward expansion of the Nabateans. Four of the ten actually lay to the north of the Yarmuk. The southernmost city was Philadelphia (modern Amman, capital of Jordan).

Southwest of the Decapolis lies Perea. It was linked to Galilee not by land but by politics (Herod Antipas) and population (Jewish). For Galilean pilgrims who set out for Jerusalem to attend the feasts, the shortest route was through Samaria. Many of them preferred to go through Perea in order to travel all the way on Jewish soil. When the Samaritans proved inhospitable to Jesus (Lk. 9:51–56), he may also have taken the Perean route.

South of Perea lie the mountains of Moab. Like Gilead they form a large rolling plateau. Insufficient moisture makes stretches of fine soil appear unfertile. Moab reaches a height of 4,000 feet and then merges with Mt. Seir, southeast of the Dead Sea.

Palestine's fourfold topography reveals a unique feature. No comparable area has such varied formations—plains, plateaus, deserts, snow-capped peaks, river valleys and mountain caves, fresh- and salt-water seas, and rocks of every degree of hardness from chalk to granite. Southern California would be ranked second in topographical variety, but its huge area dwarfs the Holy Land and blurs the comparison. Palestine is, in fact, a compressed continent.

Climate

Palestine and Southern California are remarkably similar not only in topography but also in climate. Both lie between 31° and 33° north latitude. Both are semitropical. Both have sharply defined dry and rainy seasons. Both boast extremes of temperature and rainfall. Both defy description. Both inspire immodest claims!

Mediterranean breezes cool Palestine during the summer, but they bring no rain. The Western Highlands are not tall enough to push the breezes to a level where they would clash with cooler air and cause precipitation.

Abundant dew is the land's salvation and thus a symbol of God's grace. It is carried by the winds at night from the sea to the higher levels of the hills and mountains. Its drenching nature is vividly illustrated by the story of Gideon and his fleece (Judges 6:37–40).

Summer temperature sometimes exceeds 90°F. to 100°F. in the Jordan Valley. But in the highlands the air cools rapidly as soon as the sun sets, and the evenings are likely to be crisp. The average annual mean temperature is 62–68°F. When winds blow from the desert, the land suffers from intense heat. The dry, dust-laden air (called the *sirocco* by the Arabs, meaning "easterner") turns green vegetation to dying brown in a day's time. "And when you see the south wind blowing," Jesus reminded his hearers, "you say, 'there will be a scorching heat'; and it happens" (Lk. 12:55).

The summer's heat lessens appreciably in September. By the end of the month the warmer winds from the sea strike the Highlands and produce the "early rains" mentioned so frequently in the Bible. They are an advance installment that softens the hard, sun-baked soil and permits farmers to plow and plant the ground before the protracted rains arrive. "When you see a cloud rising in the west," Jesus remarked, "you say at once, 'a shower is coming'; and so it happens" (Lk. 12:54). The light rains increase in quantity until December when they become heavy. Most of the precipitation falls during December, January, and February. It may rain for a week or ten days at a time. Everything becomes damp and clammy. Jesus' parable of the two houses, one built on sand and the other on rock, is an authentic description of a Palestinian rainstorm (Mt. 7:24–27). While the temperature rarely falls below freezing, it does sometimes get cold enough to snow. The rains moderate in March, and the air becomes warmer. The "'latter rains" of March and April (Amos 4:7) never bring much moisture. They are, however, extremely important for agriculture. The total rainfall averages between twenty and twenty-four inches. Over ninety percent of it falls from November through April.

The Gospels are not geographies. They do not describe Palestine by name, location, size, topography, or climate; they declare the Good News of God in Jesus Christ. Yet the Good News is not isolated from geography. The Gospels are replete with references which tie them to the land. They mention the lilies of the field, grapes, thorns and thistles, a fatted calf, laborers in the vineyard, a house built on rock and another on sand, a farmer bent on building bigger and bigger barns, and children playing in the marketplace. "The Word became flesh and dwelt among us" (Jn. 1:14), and it cannot be fully understood apart from the land that cradled it.

chapter three

The Law

A power problem faced Palestine at the death of Herod the Great in 4 B.C. Herod had been able to designate his own successor. In his last will he had divided his kingdom among his three sons: Archelaus was named king of Judea; Antipas was made tetrarch of Galilee and Perea; and Philip was designated tetrarch of the region northeast of Galilee (including Trachonitus, Batanea, Gaulinitus, and other areas). All might have gone well had Herod not included a special stipulation: Augustus had to approve the will.

The rush to Rome was on. After cruelly crushing a revolt, Archelaus hastened to the emperor. He was soon followed by Antipas and Philip. A delegation of Jews from Jerusalem also appeared. They brought with them a catalog of Herod's crimes and pleaded for self-government under Roman supervision. While Augustus deliberated, Judea rioted. The rebellion spread like wildfire; Galilee, Perea, Jericho, and Idumea were soon aflame. Only the prompt intervention of Roman legions halted the holocaust. Thousands of Jews were penalized with slavery or death. Augustus finally approved Herod's will with one exception. He demoted Archelaus to ethnarch until such time as he should prove worthy of being king. Archelaus' quest for a kingdom probably suggested the allegory recorded in Luke 19:11–27: "A nobleman went into a far country to receive kingly power and then return. . . ."

Archelaus ruled Idumea, Judea, and Samaria recklessly and despotically from 4 B.C. to 6 A.D. He quickly proved himself to be the blackest of Herod's sheep. He shocked Jewish sensibilities by marrying his brother's widow while both of them had living spouses. His extensive building projects impoverished the people, and his highhanded removal of high priests dismayed them. When Jesus' father "heard that Archelaus reigned over Judea in place of his father Herod, he was afraid to go there" (Mt. 2:22). After enduring a decade of his dastardly deeds, Archelaus' subjects charged him with misgovernment. Augustus banished him to Gaul, and his ethnarchy became an imperial province under the control of a Roman procurator. Archelaus had muffed his chance to become king.

At least fourteen procurators, directly responsible to the Roman emperor, were sent to Judea from 6 to 66 A.D. Only three of them are mentioned in the New Testament—Pilate, Felix, and Festus. They made Caesarea their capital and usually came to Jerusalem only during the great religious festivals when disorder threatened. They had at their disposal cohorts of soldiers recruited from non-Jewish cities. Although they possessed complete military, administrative, financial, and judicial authority, their primary tasks were to keep the peace and to speed the flow of tax money into the imperial treasury. Doubtless they heartily endorsed Jesus' admonition to "render therefore to Caesar the things that are Ceasar's" (Mt. 22:21).

The popular notion that for a triple decade Judea writhed beneath the boots of sadistic and predatory procurators lacks scholarly support. The financial abuses which once ravaged the provinces no longer prevailed. Procurators and tax collectors received a fixed salary, and the latter's books were subject to intense scrutiny. Internal revenue or customs, however, was still farmed out to the highest bidder. In the Gospels these people are called "publicans" and are regularly linked with prostitutes and sinners.

The procurators usually respected local customs, and they granted the Jews a maximum of local control. The Jews ruled themselves through their Sanhedrin, a court composed of seventy priests, scribes, and elders. At only one point was its authority restricted: the death penalty apparently required the procurator's approval. The Sanhedrin was presided over by a high priest who owed his appointment to the Roman administrator. By the simple expedient of releasing or witholding the sacred vestments, Rome made the office a prize to be grasped. The Law of Moses governed the Sanhedrin and regulated all phases of existence. Civil law and religious law were one. (Local Sanhedrins, composed of twenty-three members, had jurisdiction over each of Judea's eleven districts.) Although the authority of the Sanhedrin was technically confined to Judea, its influence on Jewish life and practice was far more extensive.

The first four procurators are only names to most of us, but the fifth played a prominent role in the Christian drama. Pontius Pilate (26–36 A.D.) presided at Jesus' trial, and he alone was legally responsible for the Galilean's death. These facts have blackened his image in Christian circles beyond repair. Unfortunately they do not stand out as isolated incidents of malice or stupidity. Pilate found it difficult to respect Jewish sensitivities. He smuggled military insignia bearing the emperor's image into Jerusalem by night. Such stubborn defiance of the commandment that forbade images enraged the populace. When protesting Jews were threatened with death, they boldly bared their necks, and Pilate's soldiers were forced to withdraw. On another occasion, at the cost of many lives, Pilate took money from the Temple treasury to build an aqueduct to Jerusalem. He mingled the blood of Galileans with their sacrifices (Lk. 13:1). Although he could find no crime in Jesus, in order to placate the crowd he reportedly made the illegal suggestion that Jesus be chastised. When the crowd protested such temperate treatment, he washed his hands of Jesus and justice (Mt. 27:11–26). Pilate's downfall was brought about by his ruthless attack upon a credulous crowd of Samaritans. They had come to Mt. Gerizim to inspect some sacred objects believed to have been hidden there by Moses. What they saw instead was the sword. Pilate was summoned to Rome and dismissed for his brutality, and Eusebius indicates that he was forced to become his own executioner.[1]

Pilate is often viewed through prisms of prejudice, but scholars tend to regard him with mixed emotions. They readily acknowledge his occasional heavy-handed clashes with his subjects, but they also point to his vigorous maintenance of order and his sincere desire to improve his province. He held office longer than any other procurator. For ten years Tiberius, who kept close tabs on his subordinates and tolerated no unrest or mismanagement, found no serious fault in Pilate's administration.

Herod Antipas (4 B.C.–39 A.D.) was the second son of Herod the Great to benefit from his father's will. He was made tetrarch of Galilee and Perea. It was under his rambunctious rule that Jesus reached maturity and began his ministry. Herod shared his father's cleverness and conceit. Jesus called him "that fox" (Lk. 13:32). He, too, was a builder. He rebuilt Sepphoris, the ancient capital located a short distance from Nazareth. His most ambitious and imposing project was the city of Tiberias. It was located on the shores of Galilee, constructed in part over an old cemetery. The Jews regarded the city as unclean and avoided it as they would a Samaritan. Antipas was forced to import Gentiles to provide the place with a population. What irony that of all the lakeside cities, Tiberias alone has survived to the twentieth century!

Herod's forty-three-year tenure as tetrarch testifies to his Roman worth, but the Jewish people gave him a considerably lower rating. His worst troubles were feminine plural. To protect himself from Nabatean attacks, he married the daughter of their king. The Nabateans were a vigorous Arab people whose rose-red capital at Petra is said to be the Eighth Wonder of the World. All went well with Herod until he lost his head over Herodias, who was described by Mark as "his brother Philip's wife" (Mk. 6:17–18). When Herod audaciously decided to marry her, his Nabatean wife ran home to her father, Aretas. From that moment not even Lloyd's of London would have considered Herod insurable. Antipas decapitated John the Baptist because he denounced the tetrarch's marital muddle.[2] War broke out between Antipas and Aretas in 36 A.D., and the army of Antipas was demolished. The Jews saw Herod's defeat as divine punishment for the beheading of John.

Herod's harsh treatment of John apparently troubled his conscience. As

---

[1]*Ecclesiastical History*, II, 7.

[2]Josephus attributed John's early demise to his popularity with the masses (*Antiquities*, XVIII, 5,2).

Jesus increased in favor among the populace, Herod reasoned that he was John the Baptist raised from the dead (Mt. 14:1–2). Later, according to rumor, he determined to kill Jesus (Lk. 13:31). On the night before Jesus was crucified Herod grilled him to no avail. Herod should have known that the peaceful Galilean did not threaten his position. The danger lay in the bosom of his ambitious wife, Herodias. She pestered her husband to travel to Rome to demand a royal title. Damning charges tarnished his image, his demand was denied, he was banished, and his tetrarchy was turned over to his wife's brother, Agrippa.

Philip (4 B.C.–34 A.D.) was made tetrarch of the region northeast of the Sea of Galilee. By far the best of Herod's sons, he ruled without renown or reproach. He was content with one wife, Salome, daughter of Herodias. His subjects, who were largely Gentiles, regarded him with genuine affection. Like the other Herods, he indulged his desire to build. For his capital he constructed a splendid city near the source of the Jordan river. He called it Caesarea in honor of the emperor. "Philippi" was added to the name to distinguish it from the more important city on the seacoast. It was at Caesarea Philippi that Peter later acknowledged Jesus to be the Christ (Mk. 8:27–33). Philip also rebuilt Bethsaida, a city situated on the left bank of the Jordan where it enters of Sea of Galilee. He called it Julias in honor of the daughter of Augustus. Almost certainly it was to Bethsaida Julias that Jesus retired to escape the clutches of Herod Antipas (Lk. 9:10). At Philip's death in 34 A.D. his territory was united with Syria. Then for a brief period (41–44 A.D.) Agrippa I ruled over all the kingdom of his grandfather, Herod the Great.

Throughout the lifetime of Jesus, Palestine was conquered territory. To be sure, local rule was allowed the Jews through their Sanhedrin, and Jewish religious customs were generally respected. However, taxes were excruciating, and ethnarchs, tetrarchs, and procurators were often cruel and oppressive. Their very presence galled the Jews and reminded them of their Roman yoke. There were many malcontents. Some nursed the notion of independence. Others separated themselves from politics and declared full devotion to the Law of Moses. Still others longed for divine intervention to defeat their oppressors. Some simply acquiesced, since they loved shekels and assumed that subservience was the only way to acquire them. We shall become better acquainted with these diverse groups in the chapter that follows.

chapter four

The Life

The ability to generalize separates man from the monkeys. A monkey can dream about bananas, but he cannot think about food. He can distinguish between kind people and sadists, but he cannot speculate about kindness or sadism. He can cope with particulars, but he is utterly lost when it comes to universals. Only man can generalize.

Generalization has its hazards. Under the façade of every general term lies an embarrassing diversity. The word "Protestant," for example, covers a broad spectrum of convictions. It includes over two hundred denominations. They range from ritualistic churches to unprogrammed meetings. They embrace theologies from the fundamentalist right to the modernist left. The "life" of the Jews in first-century Palestine is a general term with similar hazards. Jewish life was not monolithic. It evidenced an astonishing variety and vitality.

Priests, Levites, and Scribes

During the hectic history of the Hebrews, different types of religious leaders arose—patriarchs, judges, kings, and prophets. By the first century of our era, patriarchs, judges, and prophets were no more, and kings no longer exercised religious authority. The Jews took their cues from priests, Levites, and scribes.

The priests, according to tradition, first appeared at Sinai. Moses' brother Aaron and his sons were consecrated there, and the rest of the tribe of Levi were designated priestly assistants. Actually, the priesthood underwent several stages of development. Any Israelite could perform priestly functions in the primitive period. During the Deuteronomic stage, priestly prerogatives were restricted to members of the tribe of Levi. Then a time of transition occurred, illustrated by Ezekiel 40–48, when the Zadokite priests were favored. Finally, after the Exile and continuing into the Christian era, only supposed descendants of Aaron were allowed to function as priests.

The priests were not permitted to own property but were supported by tithes and parts of the offerings. In return, they cared for the sanctuary and its utensils, presided at the altar, consulted the oracle and rendered judgment, preserved the purity and holiness of the people, performed rites of atonement, and pronounced the blessing. They exercised great power through their professional monopoly. Although their number doubtless varied, in David's day there were twenty-three thousand of them.[1] They were arranged in twenty-four divisions. Each division performed Temple duties for a week semiannually; then another division would be called into service. When priests were off duty, they secured other types of employment.

The High Priest stood at the top of the priestly pyramid. He became a forceful figure in Jewish life during the Persian period. As the nominal head of his people he negotiated with the various nations to which they were subject. From the second century B.C., at least, he served as head of the Sanhedrin. When the Maccabean kings assumed the office, its religious character was compromised by political considerations. The Herods and the procurators reduced the power and prestige of the High Priests, but they continued to wield considerable authority and influence until the Temple's destruction in 70 A.D. Some priestly families succeeded in amassing great wealth.

The Levites were a lesser religious order. They acted as Temple assistants, guards, porters, and musicians. The priests and the Levites were so closely associated in the popular mind that they are frequently lumped together in the Bible (Jn. 1:19).

The scribes were probably initially priests. They specialized in the Torah and guarded it against corruption. When a certain lawyer asked Jesus what he should do to inherit eternal life, he was not making an idle inquiry. His whole life was devoted to the subject. Jesus quite properly responded with a counter-question: "What is written in the law? How do *you* read?"[2] The scribe was the accepted authority on such matters. Like the Psalmist (Ps. 119), he delighted in the Law day and night. He organized schools and taught without pay. As a layman in religion he earned his living by practicing a trade or a profession. When the sacred scrolls needed to be replaced, he copied them with utmost care. Hence he was called a scribe.

The scribes became a unique group during the Exile. It was then that the Law became the center of the Jewish faith, and the people studied it with unremitting zeal. Under Ezra, the "Father of Judaism," the scribes

[1]Josephus, *Antiquities*, VII, 14,7.
[2]Lk. 10:25–26, emphasis added.

(*Sopherim*) became a distinct and influential class of teachers and inter-preters of the Law. When priests became preoccupied with the activities of the Second Temple and their interests became increasingly political, the field of scholarly study was gradually appropriated by the scribes. Schools were set up in the homes of wise men or in synagogues to train them. They were not mere copyists. They interpreted and applied the command-ments of the Torah to the full spectrum of life. Their verbal commentaries, called "the tradition of the elders" (Mk. 7:3), became as binding to their devotees as the written Law itself. The Hellenization of many priests under the Seleucids and their subsequent corruption under the Romans hastened the transfer of spiritual authority from priests to scribes. A certain scribe, called a "Teacher of Righteousness," profoundly influenced the people associated with the Damascus Document and the Qumran Scrolls. Although priests were probably numbered among the scribes in Jesus' day, the majority of scribes were laymen who comfortably allied themselves with their ideological cousins, the Pharisees. Priestly influence was on the wane in the first century, and it ended altogether after the Temple's destruction in 70 A.D. The scribe rode the wave of the future, and his successor, the rabbi, continues to exercise authority in Judaism today.

Places of Worship and Religious Education

Jewish religious interest expressed itself through two well-known institu-tions, the Temple and the synagogue.

The Temple was the center of priestly activity. Ever since the Deuter-onomic Reform (621 B.C.) it had been the only legal place of worship. Facing the east, its twenty-five-acre area was marked off from the rest of Jerusalem by porticoes, gates, and chambers for the priests. Gentiles had access to an outer court. Signs warned them not to venture beyond it. If they should do so, even by accident, the penalty would be death. The white limestone sanctuary was divided into sections. Each one was thought to be holier than the last. Beyond the eastern gate was situated the Court of Women. To the west was the Court of Men. Then come the Court of Priests. Here sacrifices were offered twice daily, at dawn and at midafter-noon. Special sacrifices, accompanied by more elaborate rituals, occurred on such festival days as Passover and the Feast of Weeks (Pentecost). Private offerings were also made daily by individuals in keeping with the myriad commands of the Torah. Consequently, the Temple area resembled a department store during a January clearance sale. It was crowded with priests and penitents, with sacrificial animals and their salesmen, and at times with money changers and their tables. Beyond the Court of Priests lay the Holy of Holies, popularly believed to be the dwelling place of the Lord, separated from the Court of Priests by a curtain. Only the High Priest could go behind the curtain, and he only once a year, on the Day of Atonement. The special character of the Holy of Holies stimulated Gentile curiosity and spawned scandalous stories concerning the contents of the room and the conduct of its visitors. It is reported that on the day that Jesus was crucified "the curtain of the Temple was torn in two, from top to bottom" (Mk. 15:38; Mt. 27:51).

The synagogue was the special province of the scribes who were its natural leaders. Although its origin and early development are shrouded in mystery, the synagogue is usually supposed to have arisen spontaneously during the Babylonian Exile. Bereft of the Holy Land and the Holy Temple, the people came together to sustain their faith, study the Law, and worship. Synagogue means "assembly," and a synagogue exists whenever ten or more adult male Jews come together for religious instruction. The place of assembly bears the same name. In New Testament times there were synagogues scattered throughout Palestine and the Dispersion.

The synagogue was a democratic layman's organization. People gathered there for prayer, instruction, discussions, and legal decisions. An elder of the community served as ruler. A paid attendant acted as custodian of the building and the sacred scrolls. Sometimes he also doubled as schoolmaster. The synagogue was open daily, and meetings were held on several weekday evenings. Attendance was considered mandatory only on the Sabbath and on special holy days. In Palestine, as long as the Temple remained, the synagogue building tended to resemble a Quaker meetinghouse in its simplicity. Jews of the Dispersion, however, deprived of direct Temple contact, endowed their synagogues with features of the Temple. The ark or chest, which housed the sacred scrolls, was located on a raised platform. From a lectern, appointed selections from the law and freely chosen passages from the prophets were regularly read in Hebrew. An interpreter translated the selections into Aramaic, for most of the Jews did not understand Hebrew. Any adult male Jew was permitted to act as reader. Jesus and Paul reportedly availed themselves of this privilege (Lk. 4:16; Acts 13:13–16). So did the priests, but not in fulfillment of their priestly office since animals were not sacrificed in the synagogue. The people sat on benches facing the ark. Opposite to them sat the scribes. The seat nearest the ark was called "Moses' seat" (Mt. 23:2) and was considered the seat of honor. The Sabbath service consisted of the Shema ("*Hear*, O Israel: The Lord our God is one Lord. . . ."[3]), a kind of creed, prayers (which became known as the Eighteen Benedictions), the reading of the Scripture, and a homily or sermon which interpreted the Scripture. The sermon was delivered by different persons, although the scribes were regarded as best fitted for the task. The synagogue service, in contrast with that of the Temple, emphasized religious education rather than worship.

Parties

The party spirit was rife in Jesus' day. There were Pharisees, Sadducees, Essenes, "Zealots," Herodians, and others. They largely owed their existence

---

[3]Deut. 6:4–9, emphasis added.

to two unpleasant facts of life, Hellenism and Romanism. The manner in which people reacted to the cultural penetration that was Greek and the political domination that was Roman determined to which party they gave their support.

The Pharisees were authentic sons of their spiritual ancestors, the Hasidim. These "Pious Ones" joined the Maccabean Revolt to protest the Hellenization zealously championed by Antiochus Epiphanes. Although they regarded Ezra as their founding father, their roots reached back into the preexilic period. They were already an established religious-political entity when they first appear in the historical record. Josephus indicates that they were one of three parties existing at the time of Jonathan (*c.* 145 B.C.) and that they first broke with the Hasmonean dynasty during the reign of Hyrcanus.[4] The historian records their contempt for Alexander Janneus, his persecution of them, and his subsequent repentance. Alexandra permitted the party a large share in government, but its power swiftly shrank under the Romans. Henceforth, most Pharisees were content to concentrate on their religious vocation and leave politics to the Sadducees. They practiced a policy of passive resistance to the Romans and the Herods until the national crisis of 66 A.D.

The derivation of the name "Pharisee" is uncertain. Many scholars think that it stems from a Hebrew word meaning "one who is separate." Their punctilious practice of the Law, especially its Levitical requirements, separated them from all that was ritualistically unclean—particularly from the "people of the land" who were careless about compliance. Whether the name was a self-designation or a derisive label bestowed by their enemies cannot be determined.

The Pharisees were legalists, but they were not supporters of the status quo. They believed in progressive revelation. Since the Lord had spoken directly to Moses and to the people through the Exodus, the Pharisees honored the Pentateuch.[5] The Lord had also spoken to prophets, seers, and psalmists in later times and through different happenings. The Pharisees, therefore, labored to enlarge the canon of Scripture. To the Law they added the Prophets and (after 90 A.D.) the Writings, forming what Christians call the Old Testament. They endorsed new rites for Temple worship and sponsored new religious festivals (Hanukkah and Purim). They urged the baptism of converts and the hallowing of the Passover meal.

To their expanded Scripture they added a second authority, the oral law ("the tradition of the elders," Mk. 7:3). This far more detailed and extensive body of legislation contained the verdicts of the rabbis concerning the Pentateuch. Later codified in the Mishna and Talmud, the oral law occupied the same place in Pharisaic thought as legal decisions related to our Constitution hold in our courts. The oral law was as binding as Scripture. Its genius was that it permitted the Pharisees to adjust the written Law to new conditions. Its flaw was that it often reduced religion to a list of great and small duties. Thirty-nine kinds of work were banned on the

---

[4]*Antiquities*, XIII, 5,9; 10,5–6.
[5]The first five books of the Bible.

Sabbath. Each kind of work was defined to death. Six hundred and thirteen prohibitions baffled the layman. It took a Philadelphia lawyer (scribe) to make sense out of the minutiae.

The enlarged Scripture and the oral law enabled the Pharisees to incorporate into their thinking many apocalyptic and eschatological ideas that attained prominence after 200 B.C. Such concepts as angels and demons, the coming of the Messiah, the resurrection, judgment, and future life played an increased part in their theology.

The Pharisees fasted frequently, tithed above and beyond the call of duty, reveled in ritualistic washings, ate only kosher food, attended synagogue and Temple services, abstained even from the appearance of work on the Sabbath, and avoided contact with Gentiles. Their aim was not prudery but piety. Strict obedience to the Law, both written and oral, brought them life and joy. Their disdain for the crowd was not personal but religious. They considered the common people, in whose ranks they counted Jesus and his disciples, ignorant concerning the law and careless about its observance.

The Gospels are saturated with caustic criticism of the Pharisees. They are pictured as sanctimonious hypocrites who tithe with abandon, neglect justice, strain out gnats but swallow camels (Mt. 23:23–24), and thank God they are not like other men (Lk. 18:11). Certainly some deserved the condemnations, but to most Pharisees they were a rank injustice. "There was no finer standard of righteousness in the ancient world than the Pharisaic, with its emphasis on personal holiness and social responsibility."[6] The Pharisees probably never numbered many more than six thousand, but their influence far exceeded their number.[7] They enjoyed great prestige and were the real leaders of Jewish life. Jesus had far more in common with them than is generally believed. Modern Judaism stands as a mighty monument to their devotion.

The Sadducees bore a label of disputed parentage. Some scholars believe that it was derived from Zadok, Solomon's priest (I Kings 2:35). The Old Testament indicates that the legitimate priestly office of Aaron was given to Zadok and his descendants. Since the Sadducees claimed exclusive right to preside over sacrificial worship in the Temple, this derivation of the name has merit.

The influence of the Sadducees was disproportionate to their limited numbers. Their ranks were filled with priests drawn from the top echelon of the Temple hierarchy and from landed laymen who lived near Jerusalem. Their religious attitude has often been contrasted with that of the Pharisees. The Sadducees were friendly to Hellenism; the Pharisees abhorred it. The Sadducees were wealthy aristocrats; the Pharisees generally belonged to the middle class. The Sadducees were conservative; the Pharisees were progressive. The Sadducees recognized only the Pentateuch as Scripture; the

[6]Sherman E. Johnson, "Introduction and Exegesis, The Gospel According to St. Matthew," in George Arthur Buttrick, ed., *The Interpreter's Bible* (New York and Nashville: Abingdon Press, © 1951), VII, 293–94.

[7]Josephus, *Antiquities*, XVII, 2,4.

Pharisees also accepted the Prophets, the tradition of the elders, and later the Writings. The Sadducees denied the resurrection, judgment, future life, angels, and spirits; all these the Pharisees affirmed. The Sadducees remained aloof from the people; the Pharisees canvassed "sea and land to make a single proselyte" (Mt. 23:15).

The activities of the Sadducees were not confined to the Temple. They played a dominant role in the Sanhedrin and served as official representatives of the Jews in their relations with Rome. As astute political opportunists, they practiced coexistence with their conqueror. Their motives may have been as pure as the driven snow—the preservation of the theocratic state (headed by the High Priest) and uninterrupted Temple services. Nevertheless, their popularity plummeted because of their alliance with the oppressor and their accumulation of worldly treasures. Their interpretation of the Torah was too rigid to meet changing circumstances, and their religious practices were too narrowly focused on the Temple. When the Temple suffered destruction in 70 A.D., their reason for being was demolished. They soon disappeared from the scene, assuring the triumph of their chief rivals, the Pharisees.

The Essenes are not mentioned in the New Testament, and until rather recently our knowledge of them was dependent upon secondary sources. The most productive mines of information were found in the writings of Josephus, Philo, and Pliny the Elder.[8] In the spring of 1947, however, a startling discovery was made at Qumran. Two shepherd lads were tending a mixed flock of goats and sheep at the base of the crumbling cliffs that border the Dead Sea on the northwest. In search of a stray animal, one of the shepherds tossed a stone into a small opening in the rock. The resultant crash was heard round the world. He had broken a jar filled with ancient manuscripts, a portion of the now-famous Dead Sea Scrolls! His unwitting act triggered an avalanche of scientific investigations. Many caves (eleven of major significance) yielded hundreds of manuscripts and tens of thousands of fragments. One of the manuscripts, the Isaiah Scroll, pushed Old Testament scholarship a thousand years closer to the original writing.

Although the work of publishing and evaluating the findings at Qumran is still incomplete, sufficient progress has been made to permit specialists to reach tentative conclusions. An impressive group of Jewish and Christian scholars now believe that the people who composed and preserved the Qumran Scrolls were Essenes. These scholars readily acknowledge the claim of their critics—that omissions and differences exist between the Josephus-Philo-Pliny accounts and the Scrolls: (1) The Teacher of Righteousness, so prominent in the Scrolls, is not mentioned in the secondary sources. (2) The secondary sources betray no hint that the Essenes considered themselves to be the people of the "new covenant." (3) No equivalent of the Essene paradise is found in the Scrolls even though the Qumran community espoused an eschatological bliss for the righteous and eternal punishment for the wicked. (4) Attitudes of the secondary sources toward the Temple and its

---

[8]Josephus, *Antiquities*, XIII, 5,9; XV, 10,4–5; XVIII, 1,5; *Wars*, II, 8,2–13; Philo, in Eusebius, *Praeparatio Evangelica*, VIII, 11; Pliny, *Natural History*, V, 17.

In these caves at Qumran the famous Dead Sea Scrolls were discovered.

animal sacrifices conflict with those in the Scrolls. (5) Philo's picture of Essene pacificism is hard to harmonize with the militant spirit and organization for war revealed in the "War Scroll."

Explanations of the omissions and differences between the Qumran Scrolls and the Essene writings are not lacking. Many of the discrepancies have flowed from faulty interpretations of the secondary sources whose authors were not Essenes. They wrote for Gentiles unfamiliar with sectarian Judaism. No wonder their descriptions appear to be incomplete and incongruous. Allowances must also be made for diversity within the order at any particular period and for developments in Essene doctrine over the years. Finally, if the Covenanters at Qumran and the Essenes were different groups, is it not odd that Josephus, Philo, and Pliny should have overlooked such a significant sect?

Careful examination of the evidence suggests that the similarities between the inhabitants of Qumran and the Essenes far outweigh any differences suggested by the different sources. They lived at the same time in the same area, sponsored common beliefs and practices, and read (composed?) the same books. If the two groups were not one and the same, they were so similar as to make differentiation difficult if not impossible. The import of this conclusion, if accepted, is considerable, for it means that we now possess extensive firsthand sources for the study of Essene beliefs and practices.

The failure of the New Testament to mention the Essenes may have been the result of their lack of hostility toward the Jesus movement. The Pharisees and Sadducees appear primarily in polemic passages. The absence of the term "Essenes" from the Scrolls suggests that it was not a self-designation. The origin of the name is uncertain, and the sect's history can be outlined only with considerable caution and conjecture.

The Essenes, like the Pharisees, were apparently the spiritual kin of the Hasidim. Just when the Essenes achieved separate existence is debatable. Jewish tradition indicates that they were active in Jerusalem until 105 B.C., and archeological evidence places them at their Qumran headquarters no later than the reign of Alexander Janneus (104–78 B.C.). They were appalled by the Hellenistic tendencies of the Hasmoneans and by their ridiculous claims to the office of High Priest. The hateful occurrence that hastened the Essenes' departure to the desert was the "wicked priest's" persecution of the "Teacher of Righteousness." The persecutor was doubtless a Has-monean, and an increasing number of experts assert that he was Alexander Janneus. The identity of the Teacher of Righteousness is far more difficult to determine. Concrete references to him are infrequent and sometimes confusing. He was, of course, a formative figure in the faith of the Essenes. They regarded him, rather than the Hasmonean pretenders, as the legiti-mate representative of the Zadokite priesthood. This helps to explain the priestly nature of the Essenes and their antipathy toward the Temple hierarchy. Their Teacher was able to speak with authority because he possessed the Spirit of Truth. The community he founded was the only one that held the authentic priestly offices and preserved the proper interpreta-tion of the Torah.

The Essenes remained at Qumran until the Herodians terminated Hasmonean rule in 36 B.C. At this time, according to archeological data, they abandoned their desert headquarters. They probably returned to Jerusalem where their anti-Hasmonean bent would have been welcomed by Herod the Great. The King granted them unrestricted religious freedom, which enabled them to establish Essene communities throughout Judea. After Herod's death in 4 B.C. they returned to Qumran, as archeological evidence again testifies. Motivation for the move was probably furnished by the slaying of three thousand worshipers during the Passover or the crucifixion of two thousand Jews by Gentile soldiers from Syria. Either horror would have freshened their memories of Alexander Janneus.

The Essenes numbered about four thousand,[9] but only a few hundred regularly dwelt in the wilderness retreat. The entire group may have as-sembled at Qumran for special occasions such as the Feast of Weeks, but most of the membership were scattered throughout the small towns and villages of Judea. They usually shunned the cities since the inhabitants of the cities welcomed Gentiles and were careless about ceremonial cleanness. An Essene writing called the *Damascus Document* depicts the organization

9Josephus, *Antiquities*, XVIII, 1,5.

of the dispersed communities. They were founded with a minimum of ten people, one of whom had to be a priest. Certain accommodations in religious practice were imperative since they lacked the privacy of Qumran, but as far as possible they conformed to the monastic mold of the movement.

Membership was not easily acquired. Prospective members had to serve a rigorous three-year probation period before they were admitted to full rank. The *Rule of the Community* gives a detailed account of the initiation rites participated in by priests, Levites, and laymen. Candidates were sworn to secrecy and compelled to take "tremendous vows." At the same time, established members reviewed their own obedience and renewed their commitment. The climax came with baptism and cleansing by the Holy Spirit.

The Essenes began their day at sunrise with special prayers for the community. Then they were dismissed by their superiors to work at various crafts (the remains of a bakery, grain mills, storage silos, pottery kilns, and a smith shop have been discovered) until eleven o'clock. After a purification bath, they assembled for breakfast. The single-course meal began and ended with a priestly blessing. Then they returned to their labors until the evening repast. Only full-fledged members could participate in the common meal, and at least some of the meals had eschatological significance. They

The ruins of an Essene community at Qumran are seen here against the background of the Dead Sea and the Eastern Highlands. Archeologists have uncovered ovens, a banquet hall, domestic equipment, stores, a scriptorium, and an intricate system of cisterns.

were consumed in anticipation of the Messianic banquet that would follow God's final victory over the forces of evil.

The Essenes studied the Scriptures daily, but the Sabbath was especially devoted to this activity. The large scriptorium at Qumran and the myriads of Biblical texts found there bear witness to their zeal for reading, copying, interpreting, and preserving the sacred writings. They were driven by a compelling conviction: the promises of God proclaimed by the prophets were actually being fulfilled in the history of their own community. They saw their retreat to Qumran as a righteous response to the call of Isaiah 40:3: "In the wilderness prepare the way of the Lord; make straight in the desert a highway for our God." They scanned the Scriptures to understand the present and to discern the future. They believed that they were the people of the New Covenant, consisting of both the Old Covenant renewed and the Eternal Covenant that would be established in the Age to Come. God would soon defeat His enemies and reestablish His sovereignty. As the Righteous Remnant or the New Israel, the Covenanters would dwell in the New Eden. Meanwhile they lived as though they were on the periphery of the Promised Land preparing to penetrate it once again. They submitted to the strictest discipline under an overseer. They held all things in common, opposed oaths, slavery, and anointing with oil, usually avoided marriage and strangers, wore white garments, and ritually bathed after being exposed to any kind of pollution. They constituted a kind of Salvation Army with battle divisions and a liturgy of Armageddon. So scrupulously did they observe the Sabbath that they strove to disregard even normal bodily needs on that day.

The Essenes refused to participate in the Temple sacrifices even though they sent into the Temple what they had dedicated to God. Their behavior was grounded in their radical requirements concerning ceremonial purity and their disdain of the Jerusalem priesthood. It is unclear whether they performed sacrifices at Qumran[10] or spiritualized the concept of sacrifice.[11] They did, however, celebrate the great religious festivals of the Jews at Qumran.

Messianic hopes characterized the Essenes, as the *Testimonia Document* proves. It is a collection of Biblical prooftexts intended to support the Messiah's advent. Although Messianic fever was not new to the Jews, the Qumran version exhibited two unusual characteristics. The Covenanters were infected with a particularly virulent strain, and they expected the arrival of not one Messiah but two! The more prestigious one, the Messiah of Aaron, would come from the priestly line. He would establish the New Jerusalem and the New Temple. The Messiah of Israel, a descendent of the royal line, would lead the community to victory in its holy war.

The Essenes continued to live at Qumran until the siege of Jerusalem. Sometime during that fateful offensive, probably about 68 A.D., Roman soldiers sacked and destroyed the settlement. Many of the inhabitants, sparked by the mistaken notion that this was the Holy War for which they

---

[10]As Josephus, *Antiquities*, XVIII, 1,5 and some archeological evidence suggest.
[11]As Philo indicates in *Every Good Man Is Free*, XII.

had been preparing, were slaughtered. Those who escaped death soon suffered disillusionment. They had mistakenly interpreted the Torah. Some of them subsequently became Christians, later called Ebionites. But before death and disillusionment destroyed the community, the Essenes concealed in nearby caves a mighty monument to their zeal for Zion and their conviction that they were the *Community of the New Covenant.*

The discovery of the library at Qumran has shed new light on the Good News. The New Testament was written in *koine* Greek (the nonclassical common language of the Middle East). Although that language is remarkably supple, it sometimes obscures the Hebrew idiom it attempts to express. Prior to the Qumran collection, Hebrew and Aramaic sources from the period surrounding the birth of Christianity were nearly nonexistent. Now philologists have access to a considerable body of Semitic literature from near the turn of time. New Testament translations have already benefited from this additional source of information.

A remarkable similarity exists between the thought patterns of the Essenes and those of the New Testament. The Essenes thought the world was a battleground of two warring spirits, the Spirit of Truth and the Spirit of Wickedness. They believed that they were living in the last days, that a new age in some sense had already dawned. They regarded themselves as the people of the New Covenant and looked forward to the coming of a priestly Messiah. Their pattern of community organization was roughly akin to the democratic assembly, council of twelve, and episcopal overseer that existed in the early church. Some scholars assert that John the Baptist was "a kind of Essene." Since he baptized Jesus and Jesus later took over his work, Jesus must have been closely related to the Essenes. His single state, critical attitude toward wealth, conflict with the Pharisees and Sadducees, and silence concerning the Essenes are seen as confirming evidence. Consequently, it is believed that the Scrolls illuminate some of Jesus' sayings and that he probably counted Essenes among his disciples.[12]

Similarity of thought patterns between the Essenes and the writers of the New Testament do not necessarily imply identity of the two groups, however. John the Baptist was not an Essene just because he lived in the desert and ate locusts and wild honey. Jesus was not an Essene merely because he shared some of their central ideas. The church was not a grown-up Qumran community because the structures of the two had common features. The striking parallels can be matched with striking differences. What can be said is this: the Essenes lived in the same conceptual world as did John, Jesus, and New Testament writers. "The people of the scrolls and early Christianity drank from a common source of theological ideas, chose or rejected institutions belonging to a common environment, and responded with new solutions to common problems of faith."[13]

12See Otto Betz, "Dead Sea Scrolls," in George Arthur Buttrick, ed., *The Interpreter's Dictionary of the Bible* (New York: Abingdon Press, 1962), A–D, 801.

13Frank Moore Cross, Jr., "The Dead Sea Scrolls," in George Arthur Buttrick, ed., *The Interpreter's Bible* (New York and Nashville: Abingdon Press, © 1957), XII, 659. The entire article, pp. 645–67, presents an illuminating summary of the story of the Dead Sea Scrolls.

The Zealots were pious cutthroats whose aim was to slit every Roman throat in sight. Their slogan was "The sword and not sparingly; no king but the Lord." Strictly speaking the Zealots did not appear as a specific party until 66 A.D. Josephus identified them as the followers of the doughty John of Gischala, a leader of the disastrous revolt against Rome. (*Wars*, IV, 3). Zealot roots, however, reached back many generations. Their ideological ancestors prided themselves on their exclusive worship of the one true God of Israel. By Maccabean times, zeal for this covenantal God was shifted to His Law, and the foundation of later Zealotism was firmly established. As strict interpreters of the Law, these people defended it with their lives. Support of the Law sired nationalistic feelings. Revolutionary groups had spontaneously sprung up ever since the time of Pompey. As long as life remained reasonably tolerable, their movements were minimal. But when overt Roman oppression occurred, as it often did, simmering patriots broke out with independence fever. They were ever present, eager to detect abuses, and ready to goad their more moderate brethren into revolt.

It was difficult, however, for the superpatriots to arouse the nation. The Pharisees usually saw their mission in the religious sphere and were quite happy to continue as the religious leaders of the people. In their eyes the revolutionaries were misguided fanatics to be treated with contempt. The Essenes were of a similar mind; they believed that only the Lord could overthrow Rome. Consequently, they forsook the normal life of men. Although their way was personally beyond reproach, it was largely divorced from the problems of occupation. The Sadducees loved lucre too much to endanger their privileged position. The masses were generally indifferent. The liberty-lovers had to go it alone. When at times their enthusiasm overreached their power, they were swiftly and severely crushed. Even with popular support the Zealot-sparked uprising of 66 A.D. led to utter disaster.

People

The Pharisees, Sadducees, Essenes, and Zealots were not the only religious parties in first-century Palestine. The others were unimportant, though, except as witnesses to the rich diversity in Judaism. All the religious parties put together probably did not comprise ten percent of the total Jewish population. The great mass of people did not belong to any party. Ignorance of and indifference to the Law made them casual in its observance. Many of them doubtless lived good lives, but their failure to maintain ceremonial purity stained their reputation.

The priests and Pharisees judged the common people to be accursed (Jn. 7:49). In the Gospels they are called "sinners" and linked with the despised tax collectors (Mk. 2:15). Strict Jews were scandalized by their carelessness. Yet Jesus sought them out and ate with them. Their response was heartening. They "heard him gladly" (Mk. 12:37). Neither Jesus nor his disciples followed all the traditions about fasting, Sabbath observance, or ritual washings. The horrified purists classed Jesus and his disciples with the crowd and simultaneously professed shock that they hobnobbed with heathens.

Population

There are no official records which disclose the population of first-century Palestine. Estimates range from a few hundred thousand people to millions. While knowledgeable experts are by no means unanimous, consensus converges on the figure three million. With slight variation this number is supported by such distinguished authorities as Drs. Nelson Glueck, F. C. Grant, and Walter C. Lowdermilk.[14]

Products and Occupations

Agriculture was the primary occupation of the Palestinian, and peasants were the mainstay of the nation. They populated most of the villages and the small and medium-sized towns. Their small holdings usually provided them with an adequate but limited subsistence. They grew such grain crops as barley, wheat, rye, millet, oats, and rice. They ate grapes from the vine, dried them into raisins, or crushed them underfoot for wine. Olive trees were plentiful, as "Mount of Olives" indicates. The oil was prized domestically and as an export to Phoenicia, Syria, and Egypt. Palm dates, figs, pomegranates, apricots, plums, almonds, apples, pears, and mulberries were grown. Vegetables included lettuce, cucumbers, beans, peas, onions, cabbage, carrots, melons, and garlic.

The small landowners lived by their own labor. The entire family worked in the fields, plowing, sowing, reaping, binding sheaves, threshing, and winnowing. They consumed most of their own produce. The rest they bartered or sold for necessities. They were unable to lay aside sums for an unrainy day. One or two seasons of drought could cost them their property and reduce them to the status of hirelings or slaves. Hirelings worked for specified periods in the hope of later improving their position, but many never gained their objective. Jewish slaves could not change their work or master; however, they were set free after six years. Even during their slavery they were in a sense more enviable than the hirelings, since they never lacked for work or food.

Misfortune for many meant fortune for the few. The land of some peasants earned more for them than they needed. They lent their extra seed or money to impoverished small holders who put up their property as security. When the small holders could not manage their debts, their property and

14See Walter C. Lowdermilk, *Palestine, Land of Promise*, rev. ed. (New York and London: Harper & Row, Publishers, Inc., 1944), pp. 51–59.

often their persons passed into the possession of the lenders. The lenders enlarged their acreage and pulled down their barns to build bigger ones (Lk. 12:18).

Pastoral life was also prominent in Palestine. Herds of sheep, goats, and cattle grazed on the uncultivated hills and along the roadways. They furnished milk, cheese, and wool for the family. The Psalmist (23:1) and the Gospel-writer chose a familiar figure when they spoke respectively of the Lord as "my shepherd" and of Jesus as "the good shepherd."

Many Palestinians were practiced in handicrafts. Every father was expected to teach his son a trade. No less than forty different craftsmen are mentioned in first-century Jewish literature: carpenters (like Joseph and Jesus), masons, dyers, potters, tailors, weavers, tanners, shoemakers, smiths, glassmakers, fishermen (like Peter, Andrew, James, and John), and others. Whole cities were famous for a particular kind of work. As in modern Hong Kong, tasks were farmed out to groups of families. Smaller units operated on a free-lance basis.

Commerce also flourished. Jewish ships, manned by Jewish crews and laden with Jewish goods, sailed to Africa, Europe, and India. Some Jews became wealthy. At home, Monday and Thursday market days were crowded. Some streets became permanent markets, devoted exclusively to trade. Pilgrims stimulated activity during the festivals. Wine from Sharon, fruit from Jericho, and corn and vegetables from Galilee were sold, bought, and bartered on such occasions.

Prosperity and Poverty

A tiny but conspicuous minority of Palestinians were wealthy. They were normally members of the royal or high-priestly families, although prosperous merchants managed to push their way into the social register. All of them loved luxury. They lived in huge palaces or spacious homes, feasted sumptuously, dressed in soft clothing of purple and fine linen, and practiced a studied indifference toward the less fortunate. The management of their affairs was entrusted to a steward who supervised an army of servants (Lk. 16:1–8).

Far removed from this wealthy class was a somewhat larger, relatively prosperous group of people. They were the financial wizards of the peasantry. These money-lending, land-grabbing status seekers were the envy of the multitudes of small landholders and the proletariat (artisans, hirelings, landless peasants, tenants, servants, and slaves), who had nothing to sell but their manpower. As long as they could find work, life was good. But they were at the mercy of every adverse economic wind, and in a day's time they could be swept into the pitiable ranks of the unemployed. Then they could empathize with the eleventh-hour laborers in the parable who stood idle all day "because no one has hired us" (Mt. 20:7).

While a few Palestinians lived on islands of prosperity, most of them were surrounded by a sea of actual or potential poverty. Their plight was compounded by a double system of taxation. (1) Rome farmed out the collection of her taxes to publicans who personally pocketed what they could collect above the stipulated amount. Rome taxed both imports and exports. The boundary of every city was regarded as a frontier, and some tax was collected at nearly every stopping place. Rome imposed a tax on everything bought and sold in the marketplace. She levied a city tax, a road tax, a house tax, and a water tax. Such taxes impoverished the people and caused goods to sell "in the Roman market at a hundred times higher cost than at the place of their origin or manufacture"[15] (2) Devout Jews also paid stiff religious taxes. They tithed their crops. They presented payments for the first-born child and animal, the first fruits of fields and trees, parts of animals at slaughtering, wool at shearing, and various other payments. There were offerings for the poor, the synagogues, the rabbis, vows, thanksgiving, and sins. Every adult male was required to pay a half shekel annually for the support of the Temple.

Total taxation amounted to more than one-third of a person's income. In our day this amount would be considered excessive. For the poor Palestinian peasant it was positively staggering. It nearly wiped out the middle class, leaving only the very poor and the very rich. It severely aggravated the problems of what people should eat, what they should drink, and what they should wear. It placed them in a receptive frame of mind for one who would say, "Blessed are you poor, for yours is the kingdom of God" (Lk. 6:20).

There is no hint in the Gospels that Jesus personally experienced poverty, but many of his countrymen did. For them poverty was a continual threat or a constant companion. It would be faulty, though, to place too much emphasis on the economic aspect of their lives, for they were rich in other realms. It was religion more than any other factor which·thrust them onto the stage of history. And it was religion, not economics, that played the decisive role in the career of Jesus of Nazareth.

15Joseph Klausner, *Jesus of Nazareth*, tr. Herbert Danby (New York: The Macmillan Company, 1925), p. 188.

chapter five

The Legends

Alexander Hamilton had Hebrew blood. Lincoln fought the Civil War to free the slaves. Robert E. Lee tendered his sword to General Grant. George Herman (the Babe) Ruth pranced to the plate in a crucial Yankee inning, pointed his index finger at the right-field fence, and poked the first pitched ball out of the park. Adolf Hitler escaped death in his Berlin bunker and began a new life in South America.

All of these claims have been disproved, but unlike old soldiers they will not fade away. They persist as tabloid tributes to the people's interest in public figures. When claims about human beings cannot be supported by facts, they are called legends. Legends about Jesus are many. We shall briefly consider examples which relate to three phases of his career.

Existence

The legend that Jesus never existed is of late origin. It was advanced for the first time in the eighteenth century. Some, impressed by contradictions and obscurities in the Gospels, have claimed that Jesus was a solar deity. Others, believing that the church resulted from the merging of different thought currents (Jewish, Greek, Roman) at the turn of the second century, have argued that Jesus was created by the church and was thus the consequence rather than the cause of Christianity. Still others, attributing Jesus to the reappearance of an ancient Semitic myth, have described him as the latest manifestation of a divinity called Joshua. Marxists have denied Jesus' historicity on the dogmatic ground that Christianity is a mere social phenomenon, which arose as the result of contact between Jewish Messianic hopes and the oppressed Roman proletariat.[1]

Christian sources, since they would be considered biased, cannot be used to refute the legend that Jesus never existed. However, no such onus is attached to non-Christian witnesses. Let us consider what they have to say about Jesus.

Three Roman writers, all lacking in love for Christianity, yield valuable information. *Pliny the Younger* was governor of the province of Bithynia (North Central Turkey) from 111–115 A.D. In a letter to Emperor Trajan he asked advice regarding the methods employed at the trials of Christians. The devotees of this "absurd and extravagant superstition" had become numerous enough to create a real problem. Pliny's practice was to pardon those who renounced Christ, invoked the gods, and offered incense before Trajan's statue. He executed faithful Christians unless they were Roman citizens, in which case the death penalty was the prerogative of the Emperor.

Pliny's letter to Trajan gives a remarkable picture of the followers of Christ.

> They met on a stated day before it was light, and addressed a form of prayer to Christ, as to a divinity, binding themselves by a solemn oath, not for the purposes of any wicked design, but never to commit any fraud, theft, or adultery, never to falsify their word, nor deny a trust when they should be called upon to deliver it up; after which it was their custom to separate, and then reassemble, to eat in common a harmless meal" (*Letters*, XCVII).[2]

Pliny's statement (that members of the superstition "addressed a form of prayer to Christ, as to a divinity") suggests that Pliny believed Christ to be different from the gods worshiped by other men. Unlike their deities he had lived upon the earth.

Tacitus, an aristocratic historian and contemporary of Pliny, describes the awful fire that engulfed Rome in 64 A.D. Writing about 116 A.D., he points to the possible origin of the fire.

> Consequently, to get rid of the report [which accused him of having set fire to Rome], Nero fastened the guilt and inflicted the most exquisite tortures on a class hated for their abominations, called Christians by the populace. Christus, from whom the name had its origin, suffered the extreme penalty during the reign of Tiberius at the hands of one of our procurators, Pontius Pilatus, and a most mischievous superstition, thus checked for the moment, again broke out not only in Judaea, the first source of the evil, but even in Rome, where all things hideous and shame-

---

[1] See Maurice Goguel, *The Life of Jesus*, tr. Olive Wyon (London: George Allen & Unwin, Ltd., 1933), pp. 61–69, for a more extended treatment.

[2] C. W. Eliot, ed., *Letters and Treatises of Cicero and Pliny*, Harvard Classics, tr. Wm. Melmoth, rev. by F. T. C. Bosanquet (New York: P. F. Collier & Son Corp., © 1937), IX, 406.

ful from every part of the world find their centre and become popular (*Annals*, XV, 44).[3]

Tacitus did not secure his information about Jesus' death from a Christian source. If he had, he would not have treated the nationalistic outbreak in Judea (which provoked the Jewish war) and the simultaneous alleged arson activities of Christians in Rome as part and parcel of the same movement. Neither did he derive his data from a Jewish source, for it would not have called Jesus "Christus." The pagan origin of Tacitus' statements presents solid evidence for the existence of Jesus.

Suetonius, biographer and reporter, wrote his *Lives of the Twelve Caesars* in 120 A.D. In a single sentence he reports that Claudius (41–54 A.D.) "banished from Rome all the Jews, who were continually making disturbances at the instigation of one Chrestus" (XXV).[4] The spelling of Chrestus and the indication that he was present in Rome raises difficulties. Perhaps an unknown Jewish agitator is referred to, but in view of Tacitus' reference to Christus and the Christians' habit of speaking of Christ in the present tense, it is more likely that Chrestus is merely another spelling for Christus.

Although these three Roman writers testify to the existence of Jesus, they tell us practically nothing about his life. The paucity of their knowl-

People's Square, Rome, is dominated by an Egyptian obelisk. The famous Dome of St. Peter's can be seen in the background. In 64 A.D., Rome was engulfed in a terrible fire which Nero blamed on the Christians.

3Moses Hadas, ed., *The Complete Works of Tacitus*, Modern Library, tr. A. J. Church and W. J. Brodribb (New York: Random House, Inc., © 1942), pp. 380–81.
4Suetonius, *The Lives of the Twelve Caesars*, Bohn's Classical Library, tr. A. Thompson, rev. by T. Forester (London: G. Bell and Sons, Ltd., 1911), p. 318.

edge should not perturb us. "Because the birth of Christianity was the most pregnant fact in the whole history of the first century, we find it difficult to realize that its contemporaries did not see its importance. We forget that, for a Pliny or a Tacitus or a Suetonius, and, indeed, for the whole of Roman society in the first century, Christianity was merely a contemptible Eastern superstition. It was ignored, save when it proved the occasion of political and social ferment."[5]

The evidence for Jesus' existence found in Roman sources is supported in Jewish literature. References to Jesus appear in Josephus and the Talmud.

Josephus (38–95? A.D.) was an eminent Jewish historian. He was of priestly descent, but as a young man he became a Pharisee. During the tragic revolt (66–70 A.D.) he switched from the Jewish to the Roman side. At the war's end he went to Rome, retired on a pension, and acquired lasting fame as author of *The Jewish Wars* and *The Antiquities of the Jews*. Since he wished simultaneously to flatter the Romans and favor the Jews, his writings are flavored with strong biases. They are also overladen with Christian additions; consequently, it is not possible to be certain of the exact portions written by Josephus. Two brief quotations concern Jesus. The probable Christian additions have been placed in parentheses.

> Now there was about this time [Pilate's governorship] Jesus, a wise man (if it be lawful to call him a man); for he was a doer of wonderful works, a teacher of such men as receive the truth with pleasure. He drew over to him both many of the Jews and many of the Gentiles. (He was the Christ.) And when Pilate, at the suggestion of the principal men amongst us, had condemned him to the cross, those who loved him at the first did not forsake him; (for he appeared to them alive again the third day; as the divine prophets had foretold these and ten thousand other wonderful things concerning him.) And the tribe of Christians, so named from him, are not extinct at this day" (*Antiquities*, XVIII, 3,3).

> He [Ananus, Jewish high priest] assembled the sanhedrin of judges, and brought before them the brother of Jesus, who was called Christ, whose name was James, and some others; and when he had formed an accusation against them as breakers of the law, he delivered them to be stoned" (*Antiquities*, XX, 9,1).[6]

The Talmud[7] refers to Jesus. Its charge that Jesus was born of an adulteress and a man named Pandera (sometimes identified as a Roman soldier) is a transparent effort to disprove the Christian claims of virgin birth or Davidic descent for Jesus. Joseph Klausner, the distinguished Jewish scholar, after carefully sifting fact from fancy, has settled on the

[5]Goguel, *The Life of Jesus*, p. 98.

[6]*The Life and Works of Flavius Josephus*, tr. William Whiston (New York: Holt, Rinehart and Winston, Inc., n.d.), pp. 535 and 598 respectively.

[7]An encyclopedia of Jewish tradition supplementing the Old Testament. It is primarily concerned with law but it covers a wide range of subjects. It reached final form in the fifth century A.D., although it covers centuries of Jewish life.

following list of reliable Talmudic statements concerning Jesus: he practiced sorcery (performed miracles), led Israel astray, mocked at the words of
the wise, expounded Scripture like a Pharisee, had five disciples, taught
that he had not come to take away from or add to the Law, was hanged
(crucified) as a false teacher on the eve of the Passover, and his disciples
healed in his name.[8]

Neither Roman nor Jewish sources supply us with anything new about
Jesus. They merely confirm what we already know from Christian sources.
In one respect, however, these confirmations are of paramount importance.
They underscore a simple truth: Jesus lived. Even the occasional absurdities
and caricatures embedded in the later Talmudic literature assume that he
was a flesh-and-blood antagonist. Why else would he have been attacked
with such vehemence? The legend of Jesus' unreality conflicts with Klausner's considered conclusion: "It is unreasonable to question . . . the existence
of Jesus."[9]

Boyhood

Legends dealing with Jesus' boyhood abound in the Apocryphal Gospels. "Apocryphal" originally meant hidden or secret and applied to works
confined to an inner circle of believers. In order to gain acceptance apocryphal writings usually masqueraded under the names of worthies like James,
Peter, and Paul. When the claimed authorship was disproved, "apocryphal"
acquired the connotation of false or spurious.

The Apocryphal New Testament contains not only Gospels but Acts,
Epistles, and Revelations. In fact, it includes every class of writing found
in the New Testament. Since it is sometimes said that these writings were
excluded from the New Testament either by accident or arbitrariness, a
peek into some of them is required.

At the tender age of three Jesus was playing one day with a group of
boys.

> And he took a dried fish and put it into a basin and commanded it to
> move to and fro, and it began to move. And again he said to the fish:
> Cast out thy salt that is in thee and go into the water. And it came to
> pass. (Gospel of Thomas, Latin Text, I).[10]

One day, when Jesus was five years old, he was playing at the ford of
a brook.

> He gathered together the waters that flowed *there* into pools, and made
> them straightway clean, and commanded them by his word alone. And

8Klausner, *Jesus of Nazareth*, p. 46.
9Klausner, *Jesus of Nazareth*, p. 20.
10*The Apocryphal New Testament*, corrected ed., tr. M. R. James (Oxford: The
Clarendon Press, 1955), p. 58.

having made soft clay, he fashioned thereof twelve sparrows. And it was the sabbath when he did these things. And there were also many other little children playing with him.

And a certain Jew when he saw what Jesus did, playing upon the sabbath day, departed straightway and told his father Joseph.... And Joseph came to the place and saw: and cried out to him, saying: Wherefore doest thou these things on the sabbath, which it is not lawful to do? But Jesus clapped his hands together and cried out to the sparrows and said to them: Go! and the sparrows took their flight and went away chirping. And when the Jews saw it they were amazed, and departed and told their chief men that which they had seen Jesus do.

But the son of Annas the scribe was standing there with Joseph; and he took a branch of a willow and dispersed the waters which Jesus had gathered together. And when Jesus saw what was done, he was wroth and said unto him: O evil, ungodly, and foolish one, what hurt did the pools and the water do thee? behold, now also thou shalt be withered like a tree, and shall not bear leaves, neither root, nor fruit. And straightway that lad withered up wholly.... (Gospel of James, Greek Text A, II: 1b–III: 3a).[11]

When Jesus was a child of six, his mother, sending him to draw water from the well and bring it into the house,

gave him a pitcher; but in the press he struck it *against another* and the pitcher was broken. But Jesus spread out the garment which was upon him and filled it with water and brought it to his mother. And when his mother saw what was done she kissed him; and she kept within herself the mysteries which she saw him do. (Gospel of Thomas, Greek Text A, XI: 1b–2).[12]

Jesus' father was a carpenter who made ploughs and yokes,

and there was required of him a bed by a certain rich man, that he should make it for him. And whereas one beam ... was too short, and *Joseph* knew not what to do, the young child Jesus said to his father Joseph: Lay down the two pieces of wood and make them even at the end next unto thee. And Joseph did as the young child said unto him. And Jesus stood at the other end and took hold upon the shorter beam and stretched it and made it equal with the other. (Gospel of Thomas, Greek Text A, XIII: 1a–e).[13]

One final illustration will suffice. The Arabic Gospel of the Infancy (XLI–XLII) records that Jesus' playmates made him king. All passers-by were made to stop and salute him. When the parents of a child bitten by a snake approached, they too were halted and forced to honor the king. Jesus

---

[11]James, *The Apocryphal New Testament*, pp. 49–50.
[12]James, *The Apocryphal New Testament*, p. 52.
[13]James, *The Apocryphal New Testament*, pp. 52–53.

then made haste to the snake's nest and commanded the reptile to suck the poison out of the boy. The snake obeyed. It burst asunder. The boy was healed.

Some of the Apocryphal Gospels (Thomas, James) stem from the second century A.D. Others are of a much later origin. With variations they all betray a fascination for the far-out that is not found in their New Testament counterparts. "There is no question of any one's having excluded them from the New Testament: they have done that for themselves."[14] They picture Jesus not as a boy but as Barnum. As folklore they are charming; but they are not a source of edification. They contribute nothing to our understanding of Jesus. The Jesus they portray does not speak with the restrained simplicity and disciplined moral integrity of the canonical Gospels. His words are of the world and his works are of the devil. He acts like a capricious conjurer who uses power for prideful purposes.

Education

If all of the legends about Jesus' education could be believed, he would have been a syncretic sage. One account declares that he received regular training at the hands of Egyptian priests in a temple at Heliopolis. Then they sent him off to preach in Palestine. Another story asserts that Jesus spent six years at the feet of Buddhist monks in India. A third affirms that he was an Essene. It credits the Essene Order with ingenious manipulation of Jesus' activity to make him appear to have supernatural power. It describes his resurrection as a clever deceit. According to this story, Jesus was taken down from the cross not dead but unconscious. Essene physicians nursed him back to normal, and from time to time permitted Jesus to show himself to those who thought him dead.[15]

These legends are alike in one respect; they are the feverish products of hyperactive imaginations. If we want authentic information about Jesus, we shall have to leave the legends and turn to the New Testament and its sources.

[14]James, *The Apocryphal New Testament*, pp. xi–xii.
[15]See Goguel, *The Life of Jesus*, pp. 46–48, for a more complete account.

part 2

The Sources

According to Christian doctrine the world was created ex nihilo, *out of nothing. Not so with man. According to Genesis 2:7, he was formed from the dust of the ground. Ever since that eventful day, whatever man has fashioned has been made as he was—out of something. What could a potter create without clay, a weaver without yarn, a carpenter without wood?*

The New Testament did not suddenly spring into being one day ex nihilo *at the command of the Lord. Like man and his creations, it was made out of something—oral traditions, eyewitness accounts, sermons, personal testimonies, and major and minor written documents. Hundreds of different people contributed to its foundation. Scores of authors composed, copied, edited, and arranged the data. It took a hundred years (50–150 A.D.) to complete the twenty-seven books which now comprise the New Testament.*

The account of how the New Testament came into being is as fascinating as a Sherlock Holmes mystery. Some of the clues conflict. Here and there testimony is suspect. Yet, sufficient evidence is available to enable experts to trace, with reasonable accuracy, the development of the Good News from the spoken word to the written words. The various sources used to form the New Testament provide the foundation on which our knowledge of Jesus rests. Apart from their identification and evaluation, no adequate understanding of his life and work is possible. To this twin task we shall now turn. Primary attention will be focused on the sources of the Gospels since they record the bulk of the data about Jesus.

chapter six

The Growth
of the Gospel

As a member of a modern university faculty, Jesus would be judged a failure. Since he had no Ph.D., he might be compelled to spend his entire teaching career as an instructor. Most likely he would be assigned the task of teaching introductory courses to freshmen; and just how long he would be able to keep this position is uncertain. In many institutions, instructors must publish or perish. Jesus never wrote a book. On one occasion he did write on the ground (Jn. 8:6), but such an effort would scarcely qualify him for advancement.

Oral Gospel (30–50 A.D.)

Jesus entrusted the Good News (Gospel) to his disciples by word of mouth. In so doing he followed a common educational practice. The Jews had erected a monument to memory work. Rabbis discoursed at length to their disciples and then summarized their thoughts in easily-remembered statements or stories. These their disciples repeated until even the dullest knew them by heart. We inherited the habit of writing things down from the Greeks. Their teachers insisted that important pronouncements be recorded, even if students had to use the hems of their garments as a paper substitute.

Jesus spoke to his disciples in Aramaic, the language of the Galilean peasant. No stenographer was present to preserve a verbatim account of his sayings. This would have been contrary to custom and common sense.

Since the kingdom of God was believed to be imminent, the preparation of a permanent record would have been the acme of absurdity.

For twenty years (*c.* 30–50 A.D.) after Jesus' death, the Good News remained in an oral state. Even the traumatic experience of his death did not prompt the recording of Jesus' words and works. His close associates were still on hand to be consulted. His disciples, who survived him by many years, combined intimate knowledge with memory sharpened by emotion to provide a rich storehouse of information for the curious and the concerned. The compelling conviction that Jesus would soon return in judgment obscured any thought of permanent records. Besides, the Christian community already had a Bible. They scanned the Hebrew Scriptures to discern and to declare the significance of Christ.

Jesus' ministry had not been "done in a corner" (Acts 26:26). Our knowledge of it does not rest solely on the recollections of the Twelve. Thousands of people in Galilee and Judea had seen and heard Jesus. Undoubtedly many of them were consulted when the gospel tradition was being formed. Every effort was apparently made to secure reliable firsthand evidence. Judas' successor had to be one who had "accompanied us during all the time that the Lord Jesus went in and out among us, beginning from the baptism of John until the day when he was taken up from us" (Acts 1:21–22). The same stress on eyewitnesses is found in speeches attributed to the apostles in Acts (3:15; 4:20; 4:33; 10:39) and in Paul's account of the resurrection appearances (I Cor. 15:3–8). Luke strikes a similar note in the preface of his Gospel. He states that the things which he writes "were delivered to us by those who from the beginning were eyewitnesses and ministers of the word" (1:2). The fact that the sources of our written Gospels rest ultimately on the testimony of eyewitnesses constitutes the strongest claim for their essential validity.

Paul furnishes us with an example of the attempt to keep firsthand testimony separate from personal opinion in the developing tradition. In the fifties he wrote a letter to the church in Corinth. Among other things he dealt with the subject of marriage: "To the married I give charge, *not I but the Lord,* that the wife should not separate from her husband" (I Cor. 7:10). Here he clearly rested his case on a remembered teaching of Jesus. In the very next paragraph, however, he wrote: "To the rest *I say, not the Lord,* that if any brother has a wife who is an unbeliever, and she consents to live with him, he should not divorce her" (I Cor. 7:12).[1] He later explains why he offers his own views: "I give my opinion as one who by the Lord's mercy is trustworthy" (I Cor. 7:25).

The gospel tradition was assembled to meet the needs of the early Christian community. Jesus' death required explanation, and the Passion Story was the result. Peter had vigorously protested when Jesus had declared at Caesarea Philippi that he must suffer and die. Since Jewish thought held that the Messiah would live forever, a dead Messiah was a contradiction in terms. Gentiles also found it difficult to embrace a man who had

[1]Emphasis added.

been crucified as a common criminal. The cross was "a stumbling-block to the Jews and folly to the Gentiles" (I Cor. 1:23). The Passion Story served as a document for the defense. It brought to a climax the conflict between Jesus and his opponents. It emphasized Jesus' innocence and the perverted justice of Jewish leaders. It grounded the cross in God's foreknowledge as set forth in Scripture. The cross was thus transformed from a stumbling-block into a sign of God's self-giving love.

Along with the Passion Story the gospel tradition came to include incidents which depicted Jesus' consciousness of his divine appointment and favor. The Baptism portrayed the decisive nature of his call and established him as the heir apparent of John's predictions. The Temptation, the Transfiguration, and the Confession at Caesarea Philippi delineated Jesus' sense of mission and destiny. The miracles showed that God had granted him unusual power. Proof-texts from Hebrew Scripture revealed the true Author of the unfolding drama. Although the various collections were originally designed to convince skeptics, a divine dividend lay hidden in the gathered data: the confidence of the Christians themselves was bolstered!

Converts required instruction. They "devoted themselves to the apostles' teaching" (Acts 2:42). The Sermon on the Mount (Matthew 5–7) is a case in point. It contains a large number of Jesus' sayings on issues which confronted the converts. The parables of Jesus served a similar purpose. They answered such questions as, "What is the kingdom of God like?" (Mustard Seed, Leaven, Pearl of Great Price); "Who is my neighbor?" (Good Samaritan); "What is God like?" (Lost Sheep, Lost Coin, Lost Son). Other collections were prompted by questions like the following: "What is the relation between Jesus and Moses, the Gospel and the Law?" "What is the place of possessions in the kingdom?" "Are Gentiles excluded?" "Should a Christian pay taxes to Rome?" "Should he pay taxes to the Temple in Jerusalem?"

Different centers of Christian influence—Jerusalem, Caesarea, Antioch—developed independent collections of gospel material in response to local needs. Some of these collections may have jumped their provincial boundaries to serve the common needs of Christians elsewhere. At any rate the double decade of developing oral tradition was characterized by fluidity and spontaneity. Function was decisive. The various units of the gospel story that eventually found their way into the New Testament were recalled and arranged in usable form.

First Writings (50–65 A.D.)

By mid-century the followers of Jesus were forced to reappraise the need for written records. (1) Eyewitnesses were now either aged or dead, and it was feared that information about Jesus might perish with them. (2) The imminent return of Jesus in judgment had failed to materialize. People who had expected no extended history were forced to take time seriously. (3) Debates about the nature and practice of the faith called for the formulation of authoritative written records. (4) The rapid growth of the fellowship made written records essential. A dramatic shift in the center of interest occurred about this time when Paul took the church from its Judean origin and spread its influence abroad. Ephesus and Rome attained prominence along with Jerusalem and Antioch. Gentiles outnumbered "Jews" in the new religion. A brief for missionary preaching, the instruction of converts, and the defense of the Gospel against its enemies—in a universal language—became a necessity.

It would be folly to assume that the Oral Gospel vanished the moment written records began to appear. There was no sharp break at the year 50 A.D. The two traditions undoubtedly lived side by side for a time. The period of the First Writings simply carried forward the tendencies already existing in the formation of the Oral Gospel. The tradition was amalgamated into larger collections. These latter became, for the most part, the written sources for the canonical Gospels.

Paul provides the first known written witness to Jesus. The two men were contemporaries. The likelihood that Paul did not know Jesus in the flesh does not invalidate his testimony. He was later in touch with many eyewitnesses, including Peter, John, and James, the brother of Jesus (Gal. 2:9). He preached the Gospel in their presence, and they extended to him the right hand of fellowship.

Paul's undisputed letters were written between 50 A.D. and 62 A.D. They contain only scattered and fragmentary information about Jesus. This is not surprising. Paul's chief interest was in the risen Christ who had confronted him and had changed him from a persecutor of "the Way" to a campaigner. Moreover, his readers had already heard and accepted the Gospel. His aim was to supplement their knowledge and to sustain their faith. Yet, there are many more details of Jesus' life in Paul's letters than is commonly assumed.[2] His most valuable testimony concerns the Lord's Supper (I Cor. 11:23–25) and the resurrection (I Cor. 15:3–8).

Q is a hypothetical source. No one in the modern world has ever seen it, but a careful study of Matthew and Luke has prompted scholars to posit its existence.[3] These two Gospels have about 207 verses in common that are not found in Mark.[4] Sometimes the parallel passages (such as the Beatitudes[5]) suggest that different versions of the same source were used. Usually, though, the language is so similar (often identical for many consecutive verses) that a single source is required to explain it. This hypothetical source is commonly called Q (from the German word *Quelle*, meaning "source"). Had an English-speaking scholar first advanced the theory, it might have been called "S."

Q was not a Gospel. It contained no account of the birth, passion, or

---

[2]See Goguel, *The Life of Jesus*, pp. 119–27.

[3]See Theodore R. Rosché, "The Words of Jesus and the Future of the 'Q' Hypothesis," *Journal of Biblical Literature*, LXXIX, Part III (1960), 210–20, where doubt is cast on the need for the Q hypothesis.

[4]Most of the material in Lk. 3:2–4:16; 6:20–7:35; 9:57–10:24; 11:2–12:59; 13:18–35; 17:20–37 and Matthew's parallel accounts. A few of these verses must be excluded. A few scattered parallels are found outside these sections.

[5]Mt. 5:3–12; Lk. 6:20–22.

resurrection of Jesus. Although it may have included an occasional narrative, it was mainly a collection of miscellaneous sayings arranged topically. "Ninety per cent of the document is positive religious and moral teaching."[6] It was probably intended as a manual of instruction on the duties of the Christian life. Just who committed the Q material to writing (around 50 A.D.) is anybody's guess. On the strength of a statement made around 140 A.D. by Papias, Bishop of Hierapolis, it has been suggested that Matthew is the strongest candidate: "Matthew composed his history in the Hebrew [Aramaic] dialect...."[7] This could not have been the immediate source of Matthew and Luke, however, since they almost certainly drew on a Greek document. Q probably ceased to circulate shortly after it was incorporated into Matthew and Luke. The fact that these two Gospels relied so heavily on Q bears witness to the high regard in which it was held by the early church.

L is a symbol for another hypothetical source. Exclusive of the birth stories,[8] there are about three hundred verses in Luke's Gospel which have no parallel elsewhere. The supposition is that they were derived from some independent source. Luke may have collected and recorded the material during Paul's imprisonment in Caesarea (57–59 A.D.), or Philip the Evangelist may have been its "author." At best these are but educated guesses. At any rate L is usually dated about 60 A.D.

L contains both narrative and teaching matter. It is rich in parables, including the Good Samaritan and the Prodigal Son. These stories emphasize God's mercy and Jesus' concern for outcasts. Additional teachings strike the same note. Incidents in the ministry of Jesus are narrated—from the preaching of John the Baptist through the crucifixion, resurrection, and ascension—without much concern for chronological order.

L may actually stand not for a single written source but for several sources. It may also include oral tradition incorporated into the Gospel by its author. It is Luke's fidelity to his sources and his habit of using them in blocks which have caused scholars to refer to his independent tradition as L.

M stands for a third hypothetical source. It is the source of the material peculiar to Matthew. It contains about a dozen proof-texts from Hebrew Scripture, an equal number of narratives (Nativity, Peter Walking on the Water, the Coin in the Fish's Mouth, etc.), and many parables (Wise and Foolish Maidens, Last Judgment), and sayings. The spirit of M is intensely Jewish. It reveals a keen interest in Jesus' relation to Judaism, picturing him as a second Moses. This fact has led to speculation that Jerusalem was the organizing center of the M collection. Its date is about 65 A.D.[9]

[6]T. W. Manson, "The Sayings of Jesus," in H. D. A. Major, T. W. Manson, and C. J. Wright, *The Mission and Message of Jesus* (New York: E. P. Dutton & Co., Inc., © 1938), p. 308. Reprinted by permission of the publishers.

[7]Papias' words have come to us by way of the fourth-century church historian Eusebius, *Ecclesiastical History*, III, 39.

[8]Luke 1–2, which may depend on Hebrew or Aramaic sources.

[9]A representative reconstruction of Q, M, and L, conveniently displayed in full text, may be found in such books as A. M. Hunter, *The Work and Words of Jesus* (Philadelphia: The Westminster Press, 1950) and E. Basil Redlich, *The Student's Introduction*

Final Writings (65–100 A.D.)

When the Jews revolted against Roman occupation in 66–70 A.D., they sealed their fate in blood. Tens of thousands lost their lives, and an even larger number were dispersed. Jerusalem was destroyed. These frightful years had a profound effect on the Christian community also. The church was severed from its Palestinian roots. Eyewitnesses became ever more scarce. Hope for the imminent return of Jesus began to fade. An increasing demand for more adequate records resulted.

Mark was the first extant written Gospel. This conviction is supported by several facts. (1) Matthew reproduces about ninety percent of Mark in his Gospel and Luke about fifty percent. When a passage in Mark is absent from either Matthew or Luke, it is usually found in the other. This destroys the notion that Mark was a later abridgment of Matthew. A better case can be made for the idea that Matthew and Luke abridged Mark in order to make room for their considerable non-Markan material. (2) Matthew and Luke customarily follow the order of Mark. When either departs from it, the other usually remains faithful. (3) Matthew and Luke frequently improve Mark's grammar and refine his style. (4) Matthew and Luke modify or omit phrases in Mark that they consider offensive. In the story of the Stilling of the Storm, Mark's "Teacher, do you not care if we perish?" (4:38b) is reduced to a simple factual exclamation in Luke 8:24 and a plea for help in Matthew 8:25. Mark reports that when the Rich Man addressed Jesus as "Good Teacher," he replied, "Why do you call me good? No one is good but God alone" (10:18). Matthew rewrites Jesus' response to read, "Why do you ask me about what is good?" (19:17). Evidence that Matthew revised Mark's account is furnished by Luke (18:18–19), who faithfully follows Mark's version.[10]

The authorship of Mark is a matter of dispute. The traditional view asserts that the book was written by John Mark. The earliest disciples, it is

---

to the Synoptic Gospels (London and New York: Longmans, Green and Co., 1936). A reconstruction without the text can be found in H. C. Kee, F. W. Young, and K. Froehlich, *Understanding the New Testament*, 2nd ed. (Englewood Cliffs, N.J.: Prentice-Hall, Inc., 1957, 1965), pp. 466–470.

[10]According to Eusebius, *Ecclesiastical History*, IV, 8, Irenaeus held that Matthew was written before Mark. This has remained the official Roman Catholic position until recently. Since *Divino Affiante Spiritu* (1943) and *De Revelatione* (1965), scholars of that faith have been free to interpret the 1911 and 1912 decrees of the Pontifical Biblical Commission providing they respect the teaching authority of the church and do nothing contrary to declared dogma. Most of them today support the priority of Mark and its use by Matthew and Luke. The latest and best Catholic exegetical work, R. E. Brown, J. A. Fitzmyer, and R. E. Murphy, eds., *The Jerome Biblical Commentary*, 2 vols. (Englewood Cliffs, N.J.: Prentice-Hall, Inc., 1968), II, 4–5 and 63, takes this position. The best case for Mark's alleged dependence on Matthew is made by W. R. Farmer, *The Synoptic Problem: A Critical Analysis* (New York: The Macmillan Company, 1964). F. W. Beare's review of the book in the *Journal of Biblical Literature*, LXXXIV, No. 3 (1965), pp. 295–297, is critical and convincing.

said, customarily assembled in his mother's house in Jerusalem (Acts 12:12). He accompanied Barnabas and Paul on their first missionary journey as far as Perga; then he left them and returned to Jerusalem (Acts 13:13). He was later reconciled with Paul and became a useful fellow worker in Rome (Col. 4:10; II Tim. 4:11; Philem. 24). He is referred to in I Peter as "my son Mark" (5:13) and is associated with Babylon (Rome). Papias also links him with Peter and quotes John the presbyter as saying that Mark wrote down what he remembered from Peter's preaching.[11] Irenaeus, bishop of Lyons about 180 A.D., supports the testimony of Papias.[12]

Such solid evidence would seem to establish John Mark's authorship beyond question. But recent studies have become increasingly skeptical of the claim. (1) The statement of Papias is of questionable value. The separate units of Mark cannot possibly stand for the preaching of Peter, as the findings of form criticism demonstrate. On the basis of I Peter 5:13, Papias was probably attempting to give Mark's writing its needed apostolic authority. (2) Nowhere does the Gospel suggest the name of its author. (3) Mark or Marcus was a common Roman name. (4) The Gospel has a definite anti-Jewish bias. (5) Its author is unfamiliar with the geography and topography of northern Palestine (7:31).[13] (6) A Jerusalem Jew would have been better informed regarding Jewish practices (7:3–4; 10:12) and procedures connected with the trial of Jesus, and less dependent on secondary sources. Frederick C. Grant sums up the case as follows: "Mark can hardly be the work of a Palestinian Christian Jew."[14]

Those who reject John Mark's authorship assert that if we must regard the Gospel of Mark as anonymous, a decided advantage results. No longer does it matter that Mark was not a trained historian. The Gospel is not the product of a single literary effort resting on one person's recollections. It is more broadly and securely based. It rests on a widespread social tradition. It is not "history, nor biography, nor even the scattered reminiscences of an apostle, but is a selection from a tradition, set down for the same purpose as that which had hitherto kept the tradition alive, namely, the proclamation of the saving message, the good news, about Jesus Christ, the Son of God."[15]

Rome is often suggested as the place of Mark's composition, but nothing in the Gospel clearly indicates its place of origin. The Roman tradition stems in part from a deduction based upon I Peter 5:13. There "Peter" sends greetings from Mark from "Babylon" (Rome). But since Mark has no connection with Peter, as we have observed, its alleged Roman origin is pure supposition. The author's careful explanation of Aramaic words and

---

[11]Eusebius, *Ecclesiastical History*, III, 39.

[12]*Against Heresies*, III, 1, 1.

[13]He could have acquired his knowledge of events and conditions in Jerusalem from the Passion Story.

[14]Frederick C. Grant, "Introduction and Exegesis, The Gospel According to St. Mark," in George Arthur Buttrick, ed., *The Interpreter's Bible* (New York and Nashville: Abingdon Press, © 1951), VII, 633.

[15]Grant, *The Interpreter's Bible*, VII, 632.

Jewish customs (5:41; 7:3–4,11,34; 15:22) implies Gentile readership, but his use of Latin words transliterated into Greek (5:9; 12:15,42; 15:16,39) no more prove Roman authorship than our use of *hoi polloi* would indicate that this book was composed in Athens. Nor is it a convincing argument that nonapostolic Mark would never have made it into the New Testament without a special Roman connection. Some scholars assert that Mark originated in Syrian Antioch; others favor Alexandria; one has proposed Galilee because of the author's great emphasis on that region.[16] When competent specialists disagree, it is the course of wisdom to refrain from pontificating on such apparently insoluble matters as authorship and place of origin.

The date of Mark is something of an enigma. The apocalyptic discourse in chapter 13 provides the only solid clue. When some disciples asked Jesus when the Temple would be destroyed and the accompanying catastrophes accomplished, his reply included a reference to the destruction of an undesignated holy place (13:14). Matthew's parallel passage indirectly identifies the holy place as the Jerusalem Temple (Mt. 24:15), and Luke's comparable material clearly associates the prophecy with the siege of Jerusalem (Lk. 21:20). Roman armies attacked the Holy City from 67 to 70 A.D. Since Mark's account specifically mentions neither the Temple nor Jerusalem, some scholars argue that it must have been written prior to the siege. They consider the passage to be a genuine prophecy and date Mark in the early sixties. Other experts regard the passage as a "prophecy after the event" and date Mark in the early seventies. They believe that Mark's vague language precludes precise dating, and they assert that the book reflects the apocalyptists' habit of relating historical happenings as though they were still to come. Since Mark was used by both Matthew and Luke, which were probably written in the eighties, it would have had to circulate for some time prior to the eighties. Although the vividness of Mark's account suggests that the event described was close at hand, Luke's more graphic and specific passage seems to have been written in retrospect. It is our conviction, therefore, that Mark was composed between 65 and 70 A.D.

The purpose of Mark, unlike the Gospels of Luke and John, is not explicitly stated. Some of his reasons for writing, though, are not difficult to detect. (1) He wanted to confirm and strengthen the faith of his readers in the face of their impending suffering. That he was writing primarily for Christians is suggested by Mark's use of the technical word "gospel," introduction of characters without explanation, and assumption that the teachings of Jesus are known. (2) He wanted to persuade the faithful that the impending destruction of Jerusalem was a sign of the Consummation of the Age. His eschatological interests frequently appear in the Gospel (4:29; 9:1; 12:1–12), but they are most forcefully revealed in chapter 13. The passage depicts the suffering, persecution, and natural disturbances that will precede the End. After the tribulation, the Son of Man will come in the clouds and send the angels to "gather his elect from the four winds" (13:27).

16Willi Marxsen, *Introduction to the New Testament*, tr. G. Buswell (Philadelphia: Fortress Press, 1970), p. 143.

(3) He wanted to assure his readers that the coming Son of Man and the crucified Christ were identical. Jesus' humiliation and rejection disturbed early Christians, but Mark saw a divine necessity in his death: "For the Son of man also came not to be served but to serve, and to give his life as a ransom for many" (10:45). This Gospel is "a swiftly moving drama of the Cross."[17] The Passion dominates the narrative almost from the beginning.

Mark's sources were many. Whether they were oral or written is disputed, but some of the material was undoubtedly grouped together before it reached the author. His most evident sources were (1) the Passion Story; (2) a collection of teachings, parables, and sayings somewhat akin to Q; (3) stories of conflict between Jesus and his adversaries (2:13–3:6); (4) stories like the death of John the Baptist (6:14–29); and (5) the Little Apocalypse (13:1–37).

Several characteristics of the Gospel of Mark help to distinguish it from the other Gospels. (1) It is the simplest, shortest, and oldest of them all. (2) Its arrangement is sometimes chronological, sometimes geographical, and often topical. (3) It presents the most candid account of Jesus, picturing him at times as one who is limited in knowledge (5:9,30; 6:38; 9:16,21) and power (6:5). Although it clearly views Jesus as the Son of God, it frankly faces his humanity. Jesus hungers, tires, becomes angry, wonders, groans, pities, prays, cries, and dies. (4) It is filled with action. Jesus is pictured as a doer. He calls disciples, collects crowds, disputes opponents, travels, teaches, and touches lepers. (5) It is geared to Gentiles. Roman coins are used (6:37; 12:42; 14:5), and Roman laws are cited (10:12). Jewish customs and Aramaic words are explained (3:17; 5:41; 7:11,34; 15:22). (6) It advances the Messianic-secret motif (which Matthew and Luke follow in part). Jesus' Messiahship, which is never convincingly disclosed to the public, is revealed in five successive stages. (a) Jesus is informed at his baptism (1:11). (b) The demons recognize who he is (1:24). (c) Peter, perhaps speaking for all of the disciples, perceives that Jesus is the Messiah (8:29). (d) Jesus quietly affirms who he is by his symbolic ride into Jerusalem (11:1–10). (e) The climax is reached on the final day of Jesus' life. In a secret session, the High Priest asks Jesus, "Are you the Christ, the Son of the Blessed?" Jesus replies, "I am" (14:61–62).

Mark's structure appears to be clear-cut. His Gospel has traditionally been divided into two almost equal parts. The first division (1:14–8:26) concerns Jesus' Galilean ministry. His conflict with the demons and the religious and civil authorities is accompanied by a corresponding surge of popularity among the crowds. Although the common people hear him gladly, their grasp of his mission and message is minimal. Even his intimate disciples fail to comprehend his teachings and their true significance. The second division (11:1–16:8) describes Jesus' ministry in Jerusalem, the machinations of the power structure that precipitate the crucifixion, and the surprising resurrection. The two divisions are preceded by an introduction (1:1–13) and followed by an ending added by a later hand (16:9–20),

---

[17]Donald T. Rowlingson, *Introduction to New Testament Study* (New York: The Macmillan Company, 1956), p. 66.

and they are linked by Peter's confession, the Transfiguration, and a summary account of the journey to Jerusalem (8:27–10:52).[18]

Mark remained the only Gospel for nearly two decades. Then Matthew and Luke incorporated most of it into their more extensive works. This is convincing proof of how highly prized Mark was in the early church. When Mark was written, it was separated from the death of Jesus by little more than a generation. Its contents help dispel the uncertainty of oral tradition and provide us with invaluable testimony concerning the Man and his Mission. By writing the first Gospel, Mark set a pattern and established a trend. Every known Gospel of early times—canonical (excepting John, perhaps) or heretical—used Mark as a leading source.

Matthew, according to ancient church tradition, was written by the disciple Matthew, a converted tax collector. The tradition rests on the statement of Papias: "Matthew composed his history in the Hebrew dialect...."[19] Similar statements are made by Irenaeus,[20] Origen,[21] Eusebius,[22] and Jerome.[23] But many modern scholars remain unconvinced for several reasons. (1) Matthew was written not in Hebrew (Aramaic) but in Greek. Its author used Greek sources (including Q and Mark) and addressed a predominantly Gentile church. (2) Papias' testimony refers only to the sayings of Jesus, not to the entire Gospel of Matthew. Even so, it is of dubious value since it probably represents an effort to certify church tradition. (3) The substitution of Matthew for Levi in Matthew 9:9 (compare Mk. 2:14 and Lk. 5:27) is not a cryptic indication of authorship. It is better explained by the fact that there is no Levi listed among the disciples in the material beginning with Matthew 10:2. (4) It was customary for Jewish writers to adopt notable names from the past under which they communicated religious truth. (5) Matthew's author reinterprets the ethical teachings of Jesus, codifies them, and applies them to situations that a disciple of Jesus probably would not have lived long enough to see. (6) An eyewitness would not have depended so heavily for his narrative on Mark, who was not a disciple. Sherman E. Johnson concludes: "A careful reading of Matthew... shows that the book cannot have been written by an eyewitness. It is a compendium of church tradition, artistically edited, not the personal observations of a participant."[24]

It has been proposed that the First Gospel in the New Testament is the work not of a single author but of a "school" of Christian scribes who used the Old Testament as a guide to their understanding of Jesus, in a manner reminiscent of the sect at Qumran.[25] Although the theory is an attractive one, it is difficult to produce detailed data in its support.

---

[18]For a different view of Mark's structure see C. E. Faw, "The Outline of Mark," *Journal of Bible and Religion*, XXV, No. 1 (1957), 19–23.

[19]In Eusebius, *Ecclesiastical History*, III, 39.

[20]*Against Heresies*, III, 1,1.

[21]In Eusebius, *Ecclesiastical History*, VI, 25.

[22]*Ecclesiastical History*, III, 24.

[23]*Commentary on Matthew*, Prooem., 5.

[24]*The Interpreter's Bible*, VII, 242.

[25]Krister Stendahl, *The School of St. Matthew* (Philadelphia: Fortress Press, 1968).

If Matthew's authorship of the First Gospel cannot be defended, there is no cause for despair. We can treat it as anonymous, as we must Mark, and see what the Gospel suggests concerning its author. He was a second-generation Christian of Hebrew extraction. His native tongue was Greek, and he used Greek sources. He secured his knowledge of Jesus not from personal recollections as an apostle but from oral and written traditions that circulated in his own community.

The Gospel of Matthew gives no certain indication of its place of origin. Its author, as we have noted, wrote in Greek and used Greek sources. His quotations from the Old Testament were usually taken from the Septuagint, a Greek translation popular among Hellenized Jews. A probable place for Matthew's composition would be a center of Greek-speaking Christians with a Hebrew background. Alexandria, Caesarea, and Pella (in Perea) have been suggested, but scholarly consensus has settled on Syrian Antioch.[26] That city meets the general specifications, and it was there that Matthew was first quoted by Ignatius.

The date of Matthew is also uncertain. The latest possible year would be about 115 A.D., when Ignatius quoted the Gospel. Since he regarded Matthew as authoritative, it must have been in circulation for some time—perhaps from 100 A.D. or sooner. Matthew's use of Mark, on the other hand, makes a date earlier than 65–70 A.D. unlikely. A date later than 70 A.D. is presupposed by Matthew's clear reference to the conquest and burning of Jerusalem (22:7), the addition of the word "desolate" (23:38), the alteration of Mark 13:14 (24:15), and the presence of the phrase "to this day" (27:8). When time is allowed for Mark's circulation and acceptance, the probable date of Matthew's composition falls between 75 and 100 A.D. Matthew's ecclesiastical concerns and his advanced theology indicate 80 to 85 A.D. as the most likely date.[27]

Various purposes have been suggested for the composition of Matthew: (1) to prove that Jesus was the predicted Messiah of prophecy; (2) to win converts from Judaism; (3) to show that Jesus established the church; (4) to supplement Mark, which was deficient in the teachings of Jesus, by adding to Mark's "deeds" sayings of Jesus from Q and other sources; (5) to provide a manual for Christian catechists. Perhaps all of these motives were in the mind of the author when he wrote.

Mark was the most important of Matthew's sources. In reproducing about ninety percent of the earliest Gospel, Matthew made his own book a second edition of Mark, revised and enlarged. From chapter 3 onward, he generally followed Mark's order, but he did not use the earliest Gospel slavishly. He abbreviated it, corrected it, added to it, and omitted from it to suit his purpose. In addition to Mark he used Q (a collection of teachings), M (materials found only in his Gospel), a list of Old Testament quo-

---

[26]See B. H. Streeter, *The Four Gospels: A Study of Origins* (New York: The Macmillan Co., 1925), where each Gospel is assigned to one of the four centers of early Christianity.

[27]Johnson, *The Interpreter's Bible*, VII, 240–41, argues for a date not far from the year 100. Conservative scholars often date Matthew and Luke in the sixties.

tations, a genealogy of Jesus' ancestors, and a nativity narrative. These parts he fashioned into an artistic whole.

Matthew's characteristics are revealed by a thoughtful study of his impressive work. (1) It is a Gospel of discourses. At intervals five large blocks of Jesus' teaching are introduced into Mark's basic structure: the Sermon on the Mount (5–7); Instructions to Disciples (9:35–11:1); Parables of the Kingdom (13:1–53); Offenders and Forgiveness (18:1–19:2); and the Approaching End (24:1–26:2). (2) It is topical in arrangement. What chronology it has is largely due to Mark. (3) It tends to idealize both the disciples and Jesus. References to the disciples' ignorance or bewilderment are deleted (Mk. 9:6,10,32; compare Mt. 7:4–5; 17:9–10,22–23) or diminished (Mk. 8:17–21; Mt. 16:9–12). The crassly self-seeking question concerning special seats in the kingdom is transferred from the mouths of James and John (Mk. 10:35) to their mother (Mt. 20:20). Jesus' sternness (Mk. 1:43), anger (Mk. 3:5; 10:14), and alleged insanity (Mk. 3:21) are omitted. That Jesus *could* do no mighty works in Nazareth (Mk. 6:5) is changed to read that he *did* not do many mighty works there (Mt. 13:58). (4) It pictures Jesus as the Davidic Messiah foretold by Scripture. About 130 times, Matthew quotes or alludes to the Old Testament to prove his point. Twelve times he uses the phrase "that it might be fulfilled" to connect Jesus with the words of a prophet or psalmist. He revises Mark to make it conform to prophetic statements (Mk. 14:10–11; Mt. 27:3–10 and Mk. 15:23; Mt. 27:34). (5) It presents Jesus' ministry as the completion of Israel's sacred history. Jesus did not come to destroy the old but to bring it to its full flower. (6) It evidences a keen interest in numerical arrangements. Its author has grouped his material into threes, fives, sevens, and other numerical schemes for didactic purposes. There are three sections to the genealogy, three temptations, three miracles (leprosy, palsy, fever), three denials by Peter, three parables about the future, three wonders at the crucifixion. There are five major discourses, and five searching questions in one day in Jerusalem. There are seven parables in chapter thirteen. (7) It occasionally magnifies the miraculous. From Jesus' supernatural birth and star-guided visitors to the convulsions of nature and the resurrection of the saints that accompanied his death, readers are alerted to God's power at work in the world. Matthew includes most of the miracle stories found in his sources, abbreviates them, and sometimes heightens their miraculous element (9:18; 20:30). (8) It frequently uses doublets (two versions of the same story from different sources) and repetitions. As in Mark, from which some of them were derived, they establish connections within the Gospel, give it greater unity, and highlight some of Matthew's major concerns. (9) Its style, when compared to Mark, is smooth and flowing. Words like "truly" and "lo" help make it so. Although Matthew compresses Mark's narratives, he also omits ambiguities (Mk. 6:5–6; Mt. 13:58), redundancies (Mk. 1:32; Mt. 8:16; Mk. 4:39; Mt. 8:26b), and tasteless or tortured forms of speech (Mk. 1:12–13; Mt. 4:1).

Matthew's fondness for structure is evident throughout his Gospel. Jesus' genealogy, as we have noted, is artificially arranged into three groups of fourteen ancestors each (1:1–17). Five blocks of teaching material are introduced at intervals into Mark's basic outline. This fivefold pattern has prompted some scholars to conclude that Matthew is consciously imitating the fivefold Torah. He views the Gospel as a new Law (Pentateuch) and Jesus as a second Moses.[28] Each of the extended discourses is introduced by a series of narratives that relate the activities of Jesus, and each is concluded by some such phrase as "And when Jesus had finished these sayings . . ." The first narrative-discourse is preceded by an account of Jesus' birth and infancy, and the fifth is followed by the Passion and resurrection. In the outline of Matthew that follows, the five blocks of teaching material are in italics.

I. Introduction: Nativity Narratives		1:1–2:23
II. Jesus' Life and Law		
Book 1	Baptism and Temptation	3:1–4:25
	Sermon on the Mount	5:1–7:29
Book 2	Jesus' Mighty Works	8:1–9:34
	Instructions to Disciples	9:35–11:1
Book 3	Questions and Controversies	11:2–12:50
	Parables of the Kingdom	13:1–53
Book 4	More Mighty Works and Teachings	13:54–17:27
	On Sin and Forgiveness	18:1–19:2
Book 5	Teachings and Happenings in Judea	19:3–23:39
	The End of the Age	24:1–26:1
III. Conclusion: Crucifixion and Resurrection		26:2–28:20

Matthew quickly pushed Mark out of first place on the Christian best-seller list. It is a wonder that Mark ever survived. Matthew was inclusive. It contained most of Mark and much more. Its convenient sectional arrangement made it an ideal manual for church study and worship. Its free-flowing style excited interest, and its adroit handling of delicate questions (for example, why did Jesus submit to a sin baptism at the hands of an inferior?) erased doubts. Second-century writers quoted Matthew more than any other Gospel. When the four Gospels began to circulate together, Matthew headed the collection, and it has never relinquished that position. There is much about Matthew's masterpiece to justify the extravagant judgment that it is the most important book in the world.

Luke and the Acts of the Apostles were written by the same author. This conclusion of modern scholarship is supported by tradition, the common dedication of the two works to Theophilus (Lk. 1:3; Acts 1:1), the cross reference to the Gospel in Acts 1:1, and the similarity of style and vocabulary. The Gospel ends with Jesus' assurance to his disciples that he will send the promise of his Father upon them, his command that they stay in Jerusalem until they are clothed with power from on high, and an indication of his parting from them (24:49–53). Acts opens with a reminder

[28]See B. W. Bacon, *Studies in St. Matthew* (New York: Henry Holt and Co., 1930). For a critique of Bacon's hypothesis, see W. D. Davies, *The Setting of the Sermon on the Mount* (Cambridge: At the University Press, 1964), pp. 14–93.

of the promise and command, a notation of the disciples waiting at Jerusalem for the promise to be fulfilled, a more elaborate account of Jesus' departure (ascension), and a stirring story of the fulfillment of the promise by the gift of the Spirit at Pentecost (1:1–2:13). Just as the first volume looks ahead to the second, the second looks back to the first. They are two predetermined parts of a single work.

Luke, according to tradition, bears the name of its author, the beloved physician and traveling companion of Paul. The book did not originally carry his name, of course, and Papias does not mention him. Irenaeus, writing about 180 A.D., states that Acts was written by Luke, an attendant of Paul.[29] This view was affirmed by the Roman church in the Muratorian canon near the end of the second century. An ancient introduction to the Gospel, called the anti-Marcionite prologue, identifies Luke as a doctor, a disciple of the apostles, and the author of both Luke and Acts. These conclusions rest primarily on the preface, Paul's references to Luke by name (Col. 4:14; Philem. 24), and the so-called "we" sections of Acts (16:10–17; 20:5–15; 21:1–18; 27:1–28:16), which present a first-person-plural account of travels with Paul.

The identification of Dr. Luke as author is by no means unanimous. Word studies do not support the claim that the author was a physician. A technical medical language did not exist in antiquity. Nearly all of Luke's so-called technical terms were used by nonmedical writers of his age.[30] "It would indeed be equally easy to prove from the number of nautical terms used in Ch. 27 [of Acts] that Luke was a sailor, or that he was a lawyer from the considerable number of legal expressions used in the closing chapters."[31] Yet an undeniable medical interest does permeate the whole of Luke-Acts. Attention is focused on the healing and care of the sick, on cures effected by the apostles (in Acts), and on protection of the good name of the medical profession (Lk. 8:43; compare Mk. 5:26). The author may well have been a physician. Whether he was Dr. Luke, however, is an open question. Everything we know about the author is revealed in his work, and that work (like Mark and Matthew) is best regarded as anonymous.

Luke's place of composition is unknown. Greece (Corinth?), Alexandria, Caesarea, Ephesus, and Rome have been suggested. The multiplicity of possibilities underscores the uncertainty. Perhaps the strongest case can be made for Rome, but it is far from conclusive.

Luke was written about 80–85 A.D. This conclusion is suggested by the combination of several facts. (1) Luke reproduces about fifty percent of Mark, which is dated 65–70 A.D. (2) Jesus had predicted that Jerusalem would be destroyed, and this fateful event occurred in 70 A.D. Luke contains passages indicating that the prophecy has already been fulfilled

---

[29]*Against Heresies*, III, 13,3.

[30]See H. J. Cadbury, *The Style and Literary Method of Luke* (Cambridge: Harvard University Press, 1920), pp. 39–72; and "Lexical Notes on Luke-Acts," *Journal of Biblical Literature*, XLV (1926), 190–209.

[31]G. H. C. Macgregor, "Introduction, The Acts of the Apostles," in George Arthur Buttrick, ed., *The Interpreter's Bible* (New York and Nashville: Abingdon Press, © 1954), IX, 8. See pp. 19–21 for a cogent discussion of the authorship of Luke-Acts.

(19:41–44; 21:20–24). (3) Luke uses no material from Matthew (80–85 A.D.), and Matthew uses none from Luke. Which Gospel was written first is impossible to determine. (4) Luke's author wrote a second volume (Acts) during the last decade of the first century (Acts 1:1–2). (5) Luke betrays no knowledge of the collected letters of Paul, which were in circulation after 100 A.D.

Luke's purposes in writing his Gospel were numerous (1) The preface (1:1–4) states that he wrote to communicate more fully and accurately the truth of the Gospel. If this motive can be taken at face value, then Luke was the first historian of the Christian movement; another (Eusebius) would not appear for three centuries. (2) He wanted to prove that Christianity was not subversive. During the early years of the Christian movement Rome regarded it as a Jewish sect. Since Judaism was a legal religion, Christians profited immeasurably from this identification. They enjoyed freedom from interference and freedom for propaganda. Their movement spread and their numbers multiplied. Rapid growth led to Jewish hostility and repudiation and to Roman suspicion. The church was deprived of the mother faith's immunity. Sporadic local persecution of Christians broke out (as under Nero in 64 A.D.). Luke wanted to forestall further violence. He took special pains to picture such redeeming factors as Jesus' political loyalty, Pilate's belief in Jesus' innocence, and Herod Antipas's failure to find legal grounds for Jesus' death. (3) Luke wanted to show that Christianity was a world religion devoid of racial smugness. He traces Jesus' family tree from Adam (father of the human race) rather than from Abraham (father of the Hebrews). He casts a half-breed Samaritan in the hero's role of one of Jesus' most striking parables. All references to the strictly Jewish mission of Jesus (cf. Mt. 10:5; 15:24) are absent. He alone records Jesus' mission charge to "the seventy," traditional number for all the nations of the earth (10:1–20). (4) Luke wanted to demonstrate that the church had superseded the synagogue as the true eschatological community of Israel and was entitled to the recognition and protection of the Roman state. In order to accomplish this goal, Luke emphasizes that Jesus was the acknowledged Christ of Jewish expectation, who had been resurrected "to give repentance to Israel and forgiveness of sins" (Acts 5:31). Luke stresses that Jesus' early followers were Jews. They worshiped in the Temple and in the synagogues. Paul was an ardent Pharisee who first preached in Jewish synagogues that Jesus was the long-expected Jewish Messiah. It was only when Paul was expelled from the synagogues that he became an apostle to the Gentiles. The stubborn refusal of the Jews to recognize and accept their own Messiah prompted God to form a new community. This community—the church—possessed all of the rights, privileges, and prerogatives that were once held by Judaism.

Luke attributes his material to "eyewitnesses and ministers of the word" (1:2), but scholars believe that he employed three principal sources. He used about one-half of Mark, omitting 6:44–8:26 for no apparent reason. He usually adheres to Mark's order, quoting him at length and interspersing the quoted blocks with other material. Mark's tales are telescoped and his style is refined. Such Semiticisms as Boanerges, Iscariot, hosanna, abba, Gethsemane, and Golgotha are banished. Numerals and adverbs are generally deleted. Specific Semitic terms (scribes, rabbi) are generalized (lawyers, master). Luke also uses Q, which he quotes in relative order and with fine fidelity. About one-third of Luke is derived from a special source, L. It would be brash to conclude that L circulated as a single document. The birth and infancy stories betray a different style and content from Luke's other material. They may well have existed independently. Much of the passion and resurrection data from L probably came from oral tradition. Even the central block of L material lacks homogeneity. Nevertheless, L (like M for Matthew's special source) is a convenient symbol for Luke's special tradition. How poverty-stricken we would be without it! It is rich in parables—seventeen of them—including the Good Samaritan, the Rich Fool, the Pharisee and the Publican, and the Dishonest Steward. Caesarea, a Hellenistic city on the fringe of Palestine, advances the most convincing claim as the place where Luke's special source was collected and preserved. Except for the miracle material, L rivals Q in early origin.

Luke has many characteristics which distinguish it from the other Gospels. (1) Its author was a Gentile. (2) It begins with a formal preface. (3) It is the first volume of a larger work (Luke-Acts). Both books share common interests, purposes, and vocabulary. (4) It is the longest, most complete Gospel. (5) It is a universal Gospel. The kingdom is color-blind, class-blind, and culture-blind. "All flesh shall see the salvation of God" (3:6). (6) It has the best Greek and the most polished style of any Gospel. Its author had a way with words. His pictures are vivid and arresting. His contrasts captivate interest: Martha and Mary, "Dives" and Lazarus, the Pharisee and the Publican, the Priest and Levite and the Good Samaritan. (7) It records the first Christian hymns, best known to us by their Latin titles: Ave Maria (1:28–33), the Magnificat (1:46–55), the Benedictus (1:68–79), the Gloria in Excelsis (2:14), and the Nunc Dimittis (2:29–32). (8) It manifests special interest in certain subjects: prayer, women, the dangers of wealth (the rich fool, the rich ruler, the rich man), concern for the poor and miracles. (9) It stresses the work of the Holy Spirit. Everyone connected with Jesus' supernatural birth is filled with or visited by the Holy Spirit (1:15,35,41,67,80; 2:25). Jesus' ministry is inaugurated by "the Spirit of the Lord" (4:18), and guidance of the Holy Spirit is evident throughout his life and the lives of his followers (10:21; 24:49). (10) It places eschatology on the periphery of Christian concern. Mark envisages an interval of evangelism before the End of the Age (Mk. 13:10). Matthew describes the establishment of the Church, its apostolic authority, and its disciplinary procedure (16:18–19; 18:15–17). Luke mutes passages in Mark that herald the imminence of the End. He views the postponed parousia as providential. It enables the Church to play its necessary role in the divine drama of redemption.

Luke's structure is simple, and it reveals how the author used his sources. The order of Mark and large blocks of his material provide the framework for the book. Q is largely confined to 6:20–8:3 ("the lesser interpolation") and 9:51–18:14 ("the greater interpolation"), although the latter is shared with L. Luke's special source is used exclusively for the first two chapters.

Preface	1:1–4
Birth and Boyhood of John and Jesus	1:5–2:52
John's Mission; Jesus' Baptism and Temptation	3:1–4:13
The Galilean Ministry	4:14–9:50
Journey to Jerusalem	9:51–19:27
Final Days in the Holy City	19:28–24:53

John, according to tradition, was written by the Apostle John, the son of Zebedee. The case for his authorship rests on strong external evidence. From the latter part of the second century and from widely-based sections of the empire (Asia, Gaul, Egypt, Africa, and Rome), a consistent witness attributes the Fourth Gospel to him. This witness includes the anti-Marcionite prologue, Irenaeus, Clement of Alexandria, Tertullian, and the Muratorian canon.

These seemingly unimpeachable witnesses, however, are called into question by other considerations. (1) The Gospel does not identify its author or mention John by name. The assertion in the appendix (21:24) that the beloved disciple (13:23; 19:26; 20:2; 21:7,20) was the author is curiously unspecific. (2) John would not immodestly have referred to himself as the beloved disciple. (3) No witnesses affirm his authorship for nearly a century. (4) Papias mentions two Johns, and there were tombs for two Johns at Ephesus. Moreover, a tradition supports the early martyrdom of the Apostle John. (5) The Apostle would have been of advanced age when the Gospel was written. (6) Ignatius and Justin Martyr are silent regarding the authorship of the book. (7) The Fourth Gospel differs radically in style, characteristics, and order of events from the first three. If they were written by Apostles, as some claim, then it is unlikely that the Fourth Gospel was.

If the Apostle John did not write the Fourth Gospel, who did? Other suggestions include the Elder John, an unknown Jerusalem disciple, and an unknown Greek Christian, but it is best to regard the author as anonymous. Everything we know about him is supplied by the Gospel itself.

Three separate cities vie for John's place of origin—Ephesus, Syrian Antioch, and Alexandria. The theory of an Alexandrian locale is based on the affinities of this Gospel to Hermetic literature and the writings of Philo and on the enthusiasm elicited by John among the Alexandrian Gnostics. Heracleon, who was one of them, composed the first commentary on John. The Antioch hypothesis rests on the close connection between Johannine thought and the letters of Ignatius, Bishop of Antioch. A Syrian fragment, attached to the Armenian translation of Ephrem's commentary on Tatian's *Diatessaron*, states that John wrote his Gospel at Antioch in Greek. Perhaps the most popular theory, though, is that the Fourth Gospel originated in Ephesus. This city had a strong Jewish community, was the reputed home of a John-the-Baptist sect (Acts 18:25), and welcomed countless currents of Hellenistic culture and thought. The diversity of views among scholars, however, should caution us to reserve judgment on the Gospel's place of origin. We believe that John was a Christian of Jewish extraction whose faith had originally been fashioned by the Diaspora synagogue. He was profoundly influenced by Hellenistic (including Gnostic) and Qumran-type speculation as well. But his cultural conditioning, from whatever direction and at whatever place, never got the better of his Christian convictions.

The date of the Gospel of John cannot be later than 130–150 A.D. since it is quoted by the authors of three papyrus fragments composed about that time.[32] Those who stress the Hellenistic nature of the Gospel tend to date it near the close of the first century (90–100 A.D.). Those who accept the Apostle John's authorship and those who find frequent affinities between John and the Qumran Scrolls often advocate an earlier date. But a date prior to Mark confronts seemingly insuperable problems. What circumstances prompted the author to write at such an early stage? Why did he use the Gospel form? Can a convincing New Testament chronology be constructed without assuming the priority of Mark?

We believe that John was written about 100 A.D. Our conclusion is based on the author's possible use of Mark and Luke in their written form. It is supported by the Gospel's emphasis on the presence of Christ and eternal life, and its subordination of the parousia and the consummation of the kingdom. It is also buttressed by the author's attitude toward the Jews and their Law. The hostility between church and synagogue suggests a period somewhat later than Matthew, and the partial shift from conflict over the Law to conflict over the person of Christ and his relationship to God bespeaks a similar time period. The Gentile mission, which is justified from a Jewish perspective and supported by appeals to Israel's sacred writings in the first three Gospels, is no longer an issue in John.

The primary purpose of John is clearly stated: "These are written that you may believe that Jesus is the Christ, the Son of God, and that believing you may have life in his name" (20:31). Aside from this evangelistic mission, the author had definite apologetic interests. He wrote to defend the Gospel against those who would deny, diminish, or destroy its claims. Three groups in particular are singled out—the Jews, the devotees of John the Baptist, and the Docetists. (1) The hostility of "the Jews" (a by-no-means monolithic term in John[33]) toward Jesus is attributed to their ignorance of the Father (5:38; 7:28; 8:39–44,54–55; 15:21; 16:3). Their Law is labeled second-rate (1:17) and made to bear witness to Christ (5:39; 10:34–36). (2) The rivalry of the disciples of John the Baptist is undercut by emphasizing John's subordinate function and status. Twice in the prologue the hymn about the Logos (Word) is interrupted for this purpose (1:6–8,15).[34] (3) Docetic (from *dokein*, meaning "to seem") denials of Jesus' humanity are combatted by the affirmations that "all things were made through" the

---

[32]Papyrus Egerton 2, the Rylands fragment (P52), and Papyrus Bodmer II (P66).
[33]C. Milo Connick, "The Alleged Anti-Jewish Character of the Fourth Gospel" (Doctoral dissertation, Boston University, 1944), pp. 9–32.
[34]See also 1:19–27,29–34; 3:22–30; 4:1–3; 5:36–37; 10:40–42.

Word (1:3); "the Word became flesh and dwelt among us" (1:14); and while incarnate the Word experienced hunger, thirst, weariness, and suffering.[35]

John's sources are not easily isolated. His consummate skill in homogenizing his material may have obliterated them completely. The detective work is so discouraging that one scholar has quipped that if John used documentary sources he must have written them himself![36] Other specialists, however, believe that he probably used independent oral tradition, some material from Mark and Luke (or similar traditions in either oral or written form), a book of "signs," a source for the discourses, a Passion Story, a hymn in praise of wisdom adapted to form most of his prologue, and possibly the collected letters of Paul.

At first blush, John seems to have much in common with the other Gospels. They all introduce Jesus' ministry with an account of John the Baptist. They record the calling of the Twelve and describe Jesus' popular mission in Galilee. The Fourth Gospel repeats familiar stories found in one or more of the other Gospels: the Temple Cleansing, the Feeding of the Five Thousand, the Stilling of the Storm, Jesus' Anointing, the Triumphal Entry, the Last Supper, the Trials, and the Crucifixion. Yet careful examination reveals that John has many characteristics which set it apart. (1) It omits about ninety percent of the material in the other Gospels—including the genealogy, the births of John and Jesus, the Baptism, the Temptation, and the Transfiguration. When it does relate an incident treated in the other Gospels, it often reflects a later stage in the tradition's transmission. (2) It contradicts the first three Gospels regarding the length of Jesus' ministry (four years vs. about one), the place of his main mission (Judea vs. Galilee), and the time of the Temple Cleansing (at the beginning vs. the end of his ministry). (3) It contains no Messianic secret and no parables. Allegories generally expand a series of "I am" sayings. (4) It transforms the very speech of Jesus. The peasant-prophet-Messiah of the first three Gospels is replaced by the preexistent Son of God, a stranger to humility and to limited knowledge. (5) It makes extensive use of symbols (bread, door, vine, way, word, water) and words with double meanings (*anōthen*, 3:3, may be translated either "anew" or "from above"). Hence, scholars are fond of saying that the apparent meaning of this Gospel is seldom the real meaning. (6) It makes use of extended discourses. They appear to flow on spontaneously, but they actually follow a specific pattern. Jesus, Nicodemus, the Samaritan woman, and others employ identical styles of speech. Where one ends and the other begins cannot always be determined. (7) It stresses present eternal life, truth, light, darkness, and glory rather than the coming of the kingdom of God, the need for forgiveness, righteousness, watchfulness, and the End of the Age. (8) It makes effective use of such dramatic devices as artistic form, concentrated action, contrasts (light-darkness, life-death, love-hate), symmetry, variety, and irony.[37]

---

[35]See E. C. Colwell, *John Defends the Gospel* (New York: Willett, Clark and Co., 1936).

[36]Pierson Parker, "Two Editions of John," *Journal of Biblical Literature*, LXXV, No. 4 (1956), p. 304.

[37]See C. Milo Connick, "The Dramatic Character of the Fourth Gospel," *Journal of Biblical Literature*, LXVII, Part II (1948), 159–69.

John's lack of unity is seen in its abrupt transitions, chronological incongruities, and parenthetical comments. These peculiarities have created numerous theories regarding the Gospel's partition, displacement, and redaction.[38] A few illustrations will suffice. (1) The story of the Adulterous Woman (7:53–8:11) is missing in the best manuscripts, and modern editions of John put it in the footnotes. (2) Chapters 5 and 6 are transposed, since 6:1 follows 4:54 more logically than it follows 5:47. (3) The abruptness of 10:1 is diminished by placing 10:1–18 after 10:29. (4) Chapter 12:36–43, beginning with "When Jesus had said this," should follow 12:50 to prevent the interruption of Jesus' speech by the evangelist's reflections.

These and other reconstructions of John presuppose that its author was greatly concerned about chronological sequence and logical thought progression. Although we recognize the existence of editorial additions to the Gospel and the secondary character of its final chapter, we believe that the book possesses an intrinsic unity. Its structure can be easily discerned.

Prologue	1:1–18
Public Ministry of Jesus	1:19–12:50
From the witness of the Baptist to the witness of the Word	
Private Ministry of Jesus	13:1–17:26
Instruction of the disciples	
Passion and Resurrection	18:1–20:31
Epilogue	21:1–25

Other New Testament writings besides those we have considered provide information about Jesus. Acts, Hebrews, I Peter, and Revelation repeat and confirm what we already know from the Gospels and their sources. To treat them individually lies beyond the scope of this study. We need only remember that every New Testament book bears witness to Jesus' life among men and to his lordship of the church.

Sources Evaluated

Are all sources which furnish information about Jesus of equal value, or do some speak with an authority others cannot claim? Not all scholars answer alike. The evaluation which follows may be regarded as a reasonable consensus of source critics.

Paul, who provides the first known written witness to Jesus, does not tell us all he knows about the Nazarene. Where he does give testimony, it can be accepted with general confidence. He wrote early and was in close touch with many eyewitnesses, including Peter, John, and James, the brother of Jesus (Gal. 2:9). His accounts of the Lord's Supper and the resurrection are especially noteworthy.

Q is also of an early date. It is a first-rate source for the sayings of Jesus. Its extensive use by Matthew and Luke confirms this judgment.

---

[38] See W. F. Howard, *The Fourth Gospel in Recent Criticism and Interpretation,* 4th ed., rev. by C. K. Barrett (London: Epworth Press, 1955).

L has high historical value so far as the teachings of Jesus are concerned, but its narratives are of mixed reliability. Although it contains much material of considerable worth (especially in the Passion account), ostensibly historical scenes frequently betray theological or apologetic concerns.

M should be used with critical caution. It undoubtedly contains much valuable material. Nevertheless, it evidences "a considerable amount of adulteration from the Jewish side and from the teaching of John the Baptist. Each piece of teaching must be considered on its merits and in comparison with what is given in the earlier and more reliable source *Q*."[39]

Mark is a source of real value as its early date and its use by Matthew and Luke attest. Yet Mark's material was influenced by its author's purpose and theological perspective and must be evaluated accordingly.

Matthew is a rich source for many of Jesus' teachings, but it is less valuable for the events of Jesus' ministry. This Gospel does give us a glimpse into the many-sided nature of the developing Christian community.

Luke provides valuable teachings of Jesus through the L source, and other parts of this Gospel are to be prized as well. As an accurate record of history, however, it leaves much to be desired. It is controlled by its author's purposes and must be evaluated against the background of other Christian sources and the writings of non-Christian authors. As a theological treatise, Luke (-Acts) knows no peer.[40]

John is extremely difficult to appraise. It handles historical tradition with sovereign freedom in the interest of faith. The earlier Gospels were also written to nourish faith, but John goes much further. Here history and interpretation are inextricably interwoven. John's reported words of Jesus may rest on authentic sayings, but they are recorded in the idiom of the author. He wrote essential biography, portraying the permanent aspects of the mind and the meaning of Jesus. "His portrait combined historical reminiscences with meanings which he had learned from Paul and from his own religious experience with the Living Christ, as well as from speculation about Jesus in terms of Hellenistic thought and Jewish Wisdom ideas.[41] Consequently, we cannot be as sure of finding in John the actual or approximate words and works of Jesus as we can in Matthew, Mark, and Luke. This is not to assert that John is devoid of historical value. Quite to the contrary. In some respects it is superior to the others.[42] While we cannot class John among our main sources, we cannot ignore it either. It can and should be used judiciously.[43]

[39]Manson, in *The Mission and Message of Jesus*, p. 318.

[40]For a discussion of the limitations of Luke as an historian and of his brilliance as a theologian, see C. Milo Connick, *The New Testament: An Introduction to Its History, Literature, and Thought* (Encino, Calif.: Dickenson Publishing Co., Inc., 1972), pp. 232–236.

[41]Rowlingson, *Introduction to New Testament Study*, p. 74.

[42]As in the dating of the crucifixion, topographical references, and the like.

[43]Probably the best commentary on John is R. E. Brown, *The Gospel According to John*, a two-volume work in *The Anchor Bible* (New York: Doubleday & Co., 1966 and 1970). Also noteworthy are C. H. Dodd, *Historical Tradition in the Fourth Gospel* and *The Interpretation of the Fourth Gospel* (Cambridge: At the University Press, 1963 and 1965 respectively). J. L. Martyn, *History and Theology in the Fourth Gospel* (New York: Harper & Row, Publishers, Inc., 1968), is also instructive.

Synoptic Problem and Its Suggested Solutions[44]

The Gospel of John, as we have seen, is a different kind of Gospel from the first three. Matthew, Mark, and Luke "look together" at the mission and message of Jesus. For this reason they are called the Synoptic Gospels. Nevertheless, close scrutiny of the Synoptics reveals not only a great similarity of viewpoint and content but also a remarkable variety. How can the similarities and differences be accounted for? This is the Synoptic Problem. Many solutions have been proposed. They fall into three main groups: those that claim the Gospels rest (1) on oral tradition; (2) on written documents; and (3) on both oral and written sources.

The oral theory, which asserts that the Synoptics are very similar because they had a common *oral* Aramaic source, was once rather popular. It has now generally been discarded. It explains some of the similarities of the Synoptics but none of the differences. It fails to account for the amazing likenesses which can be explained only on the basis of the Greek language. It provides no explanation of Mark's omission of so much teaching material found in Matthew and Luke. (The theory of a *written* Aramaic source faces the same criticisms.) The oral Aramaic theory does call attention to the fact that the Gospel was first known by word of mouth. It does not follow from this, however, that our written Gospels are directly dependent on an oral (or written) Aramaic tradition.

The theory of documentary dependence states that the Synoptics were formed from earlier written documents (or that they were copied from each other). It, too, has known many variations. We shall confine our discussion to those in current favor. While some form of the documentary theory is generally endorsed as the best possible solution to the Synoptic Problem, the reader should realize that "the synoptic problem is a complicated one; it becomes more complicated the more one studies it, and no solution can claim to be complete in its scope or to be any more certain than is that particular hypothesis which is more probable than the alternatives."[45] The work of the form critics, which will be discussed in the following chapter, has served to support the theory that both written and oral traditions were used by the Synoptic authors.

The two-document theory holds that the authors of Matthew and Luke used Q and Mark as main sources. Their use of Q explains the remarkable parallels between the sayings of Jesus in their Gospels, and their use of Mark accounts for the fact that they independently follow Mark's order, polish his style, and together reproduce nearly all of his Gospel. Differences between Matthew and Luke are explained by their authors' departures from

---

[44]We might have discussed this subject at the beginning of the chapter. It seemed better, however, to let the Synoptic Problem emerge naturally out of the description of the gospel tradition. To have dealt with it after our treatment of Luke and before John, where it logically belongs, would have rudely interrupted the march of the sources.

[45]H. J. Cadbury, *The Making of Luke-Acts* (New York: The Macmillan Company, 1927), p. 64.

Q and Mark (or the use of slightly different versions of each) and their use of independent traditions. The two-document theory assumes the priority of Mark,[46] connected Greek sources for the Synoptics, and the non-acquaintance of Matthew and Luke with each other's Gospel. The theory has received the widespread approval of scholars.[47] It is outlined in the diagram below.

The four-document theory has supplanted the two-document hypothesis in the minds of some scholars. The latter seems to them too narrowly based.

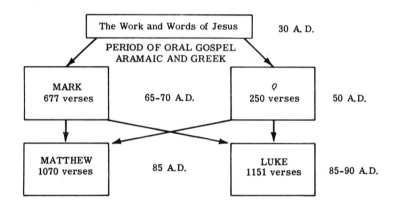

Matthew and Luke contain material not found in *Q* or Mark. Each Gospel has parts peculiar to itself. The learned and resourceful B. H. Streeter studied the special materials and decided that they represented documents. Each of the Synoptic sources he assigned to a special church. Mark was made in Rome. Matthew's special source (M) originated in Jerusalem, Luke's (L) in Caesarea, and *Q* in Antioch. The four (plus a first edition of Luke, called Proto-Luke) were collected and combined in the pattern shown in the following diagram.[48]

---

[46]See page 71.

[47]Notable exceptions are conservative Protestant scholars who hold that each Gospel author, under the control of the Holy Spirit, wrote an independent account which was unrelated to any other Gospel. Their works were based on direct knowledge, oral teachings, and short written records. See H. C. Thiessen, *Introduction to the New Testament* (Grand Rapids: W. B. Eerdmans Publishing Co., 1943), pp. 101–29.

[48]See B. H. Streeter, *The Four Gospels: A Study of Origins* (New York: The Macmillan Company, 1925), pp. 150–81, 485–562.

Proto-Luke has not won significant scholarly support. Streeter noted five sections of Luke (3:1–4:30; 6:12–8:3; 9:51–18:14; 19:1–27; 22:14–24:53) which are wholly or largely independent of Mark. They formed a "Gospel" comparable to Mark in length and scope, consisting of alternating blocks of Q and L materials. Streeter theorized that to this first edition (Proto-Luke), Luke prefixed the birth stories and inserted narratives from Mark to form the Gospel of Luke.

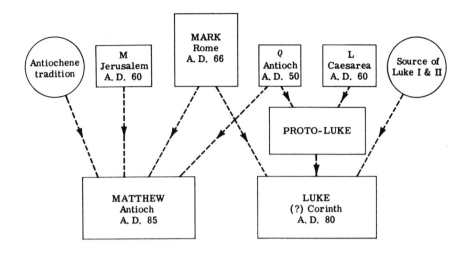

The multiple-document theory developed naturally from the two- and four-document theories. Luke declares in his preface that many tried to compile a narrative of Jesus while eyewitnesses were still around (Lk. 1:1–2). Perhaps there were many written documents used by the authors of the Synoptics. One scholar has isolated seven sources: Syrian, Roman, General (Traditional Petrine narrative), Palestinian-Syrian (Q), Palestinian-Caesarean (L), Palestinian-Judean (Special Passion Story), and Judean (Lucan infancy story).[49]

The number of written sources used by Synoptic authors has probably reached its maximum in the multiple-document theory. In order of decreasing certainty: Matthew's and Luke's use of Mark is demonstrable; Q is a cogent hypothesis which falls somewhat short of certainty; M is attractive but speculative; and L is doubtful in documentary form. It is frightfully difficult to determine in some instances just where oral sources terminate and written ones begin. For this reason we prefer a modified four-*source* theory (Mark, Q, L, and M) to the four-*document* theory. As long as Q is recognized as a source used by both Luke and Matthew, and L and M are regarded as their respective private sources, we are on relatively safe scholastic soil. But to assume that "these bodies of material are coterminous with certain lost documents . . . is taking a step not justified by the evidence. It might indeed be so; but it cannot be demonstrated. We do not know whether Q was one document, or perhaps several. . . . We do not know whether L was one continuous document, including the passion story, or a group of documents, as it came to Luke's hand. . . . And the M material shows rather definitely the diversity of several lines of development. Though considerations of simplicity favor limitation of the number of common sources, the separate sources may have been numerous, and either written or oral."[50] Vincent Taylor's insight is basic: "... It is probable that all the evangelists ... have drawn upon oral tradition to a greater extent than has been commonly recognized."[51]

[50]A. M. Perry, "The Growth of the Gospels," in George Arthur Buttrick, ed., *The Interpreter's Bible* (New York and Nashville: Abingdon Press, 1951), VII, 66.
[51]Vincent Taylor, *The Life and Ministry of Jesus* (New York and Nashville: Abingdon Press, © 1955), p. 24.

chapter seven

Behind the Gospels

After World War I, interest shifted from the written to the oral sources of the Gospels. Decades of painstaking search for the written sources had largely exhausted the possibilities. The question of whether the Gospels could be penetrated to their actual beginnings was answered in the affirmative by some scholars, who subjected the Synoptics to microscopic examination. Their labor only confirmed what previous study had suggested; these accounts are not monolithic. They are made up of separate, unrelated anecdotes and other pieces of tradition. Nearly any one of the paragraphs can be removed from its surroundings and allowed to stand alone, complete and self-explanatory. The evangelists fashioned the fragments into a more or less connected narrative. But each of the authors, aware that the individual units were really independent, did not hesitate to rearrange them to suit his purpose.

The fragmentary and independent nature of the Synoptic material should not surprise us. Extensive, connected accounts bespeak written records. But for twenty years or more the gospel was preserved by word of mouth only. A short, self-contained paragraph is the form most easily committed to memory. The full force of this truth was hammered home by a new trend in scholarship called "form criticism." It received its name from the German word, *Formgeschichte*.

Form Criticism

Form criticism uses the results of folklore study to discover the forms of the gospel material in their early oral stages. It assumes that (1) folk

91

literature develops certain rather fixed forms (like a limerick or conundrum), (2) these forms are transmitted with little alteration, (3) the forms result from the situation in which the tradition was fixed, and (4) the history of the tradition itself can be discovered from the form.

Operating from these assumptions, form critics try to penetrate the Gospels to the oral period. They use the written records as clues in their quest, and they isolate and classify each individual unit (called a "pericope" —a "cutting around," a section) according to its form.[1] They evaluate it historically and attempt to recover the purpose of the people who produced the first stories about Jesus and applied them to their own situation.

Among the first and foremost of the form critics were Martin Dibelius of Heidelberg and Rudolf Bultmann of Marburg. Dibelius set forth the principles of form criticism in 1919.[2] Two years later Bultmann wrote an extensive analysis of the gospel materials.[3] Both attempted to discover the setting in which the gospel tradition developed. Dibelius concluded that the tradition originated in the missionary preaching of the church. This preaching dealt with the kerygma—the proclamation of Jesus as the Messiah and Savior who would soon return. The kerygma created an immediate demand for further information. Who was Jesus? What had he done? Bultmann regarded Dibelius' account of the activity of the church as too narrowly based. He attributed the origin of the forms in the Gospels more to the controversies of the church (especially those between the church and synagogue) and to the need for instruction of converts.

Types of Forms

Most form critics hold that the Passion Story had a connected sequence almost from the beginning. It was vital to the cause of evangelism. It removed "the stigma of the Cross, justifying it as the will of God and the way of salvation."[4] In addition to the Passion Story, form critics find that the independent units (pericopes) exhibit five main forms. Names used to describe the forms vary from expert to expert. We shall follow the terminology of Vincent Taylor.[5]

Pronouncement stories[6] are brief narratives in dialogue form which purport to describe an encounter between Jesus and others. They are frequently of a controversial character and are sometimes connected with a miracle. The setting is charactertstically general and vague. Only minimum

---

[1]The Fourth Gospel contains few of the forms found in the Synoptics. This fact strongly suggests that it was composed at a later date.

[2]Martin Dibelius, *From Tradition to Gospel*, tr. Bertram Lee Woolf (New York: Charles Scribner's Sons, 1935).

[3]Rudolf Bultmann, *History of the Synoptic Tradition*, 2nd ed., tr. John Marsh (New York: Harper and Row, Publishers, Inc., 1968).

[4]Perry, in *The Interpreter's Bible*, VII, 70.

[5]*The Formation of the Gospel Tradition* (London: Macmillan & Co., Ltd., 1933).

[6]Dibelius used *paradigm* and Bultmann *apophthegmata* to describe this form.

Form critics hold that the Passion Story has had a connected sequence almost from the beginning. The number of Passion Plays presented in modern times reveals that the Story still holds a fascination for believers and nonbelievers alike. Shown in this photograph is a scene from the Passion Play, given at Tegelen, Holland, in which Jesus falls beneath the weight of the cross.

details are furnished as background for the distinctive feature of the story —a striking statement by Jesus that can be applied generally. The overriding interest is in Jesus' pronouncement, not in the persons or the details of the incident related. The stories were remembered and transmitted not primarily to perpetuate accounts of past happenings (history) but to provide the Christian community with an authoritative standard for its life in the world. The pericope concerning payment of taxes to Caesar is a good example (Mk. 12:13–17).

Miracle stories[7] are usually longer, more detailed, and more dramatic than pronouncement stories. They generally follow a threefold pattern of development: (1) some difficulty is described, (2) the method used to overcome it is related, and (3) the miracle's effect is reported. The interest of the story is in the display of power. Sometimes narratives seem to be a blend of miracle and pronouncement stories (Mk. 2:3–12), and on one occasion two miracle stories are combined in one narrative (Mk. 5:21–43). A miracle story in its pure form is found in Mark 1:40-45. Although the miracle stories (like the pronouncement stories) originally circulated independently, they may well have circulated in collections during the final phase of the period of oral transmission.

[7]Dibelius calls them *Novellen* and Bultmann *Logia*.

Sayings[8] of Jesus often circulated alone during the oral period. They lacked any narrative framework linking them to their original occasion in Jesus' ministry. Even after many of them had forfeited their independence by joining small collections, some continued on their autonomous way. Proof of this is provided by their floating nature. The same saying is supplied with different contexts in the Synoptics (Lk. 14:11, 18:14; Mt. 23:12). Although some of the collections of sayings may have originated with Jesus himself (Lk. 6:20–22, for example), the great bulk of them stem from the Christian community. Dibelius thinks that they were preserved for the purpose of instructing new converts. A collection exhibiting a common theme is found in Mark 8:34–9:1.

Parables[9] are found in abundance in the Synoptics. The term usually covers the simile (a succinct statement of likeness), the narrative parable (an extended simile), and the example story (such as the Good Samaritan). The primary function of a parable is to compare. It does this by placing a familiar or convincing incident or story alongside something less familiar in order to shed light on the latter. The truth it sponsors is usually singular and independent of the parable itself. Since the original setting of many of the parables was soon forgotten and early Christians delighted in hunting for hidden meanings in Jesus' message, a tendency developed during the oral period to allegorize the parables. The nonparabolic teachings of Jesus are much more difficult to classify according to form. Bultmann sorts them according to wisdom sayings of the proverbial type (Mt. 6:34b; 12:34b), prophetic (Lk. 10:23–24) and apocalyptic (Mk. 13:24–27) utterances, sayings about the Law and its traditional interpretations (Mk. 7:15; 10:11–12), and first-person-singular sayings that suggest Jesus' sense of authority (Mt. 10:16; Lk. 10:19–20).

Stories about Jesus[10] comprise the final class of pericopes according to Taylor. Since this designation does not describe a literary form and includes stories about persons other than Jesus, many critics prefer the terms *legends* and *myths*. The form of legends resembles the stories about saints and holy men in all cultures. Legends usually concern the associates of Jesus and display a distinct biographical interest (Mt. 14:28–33; Lk. 5:1–11; 19:1–10). Their practical value is minimal, and according to the form critics, so is their historical worth. Dibelius includes the Nativity Stories in this category. Luke's account of Jesus at the age of twelve also illustrates the legendary form (2:41–49). Myths are stories in which the agent is superhuman rather than human, such as in the Temptation and Transfiguration (Mt. 4:1–11; Lk. 4:1–13; Mk. 9:2–8). Dibelius finds only a few myths (including such sayings as Mt. 11:28), but Bultmann's list is much longer.[11]

---

[8]Dibelius uses the term *Paranesis* and Bultmann *Wundergeschichten*.

[9]Dibelius and Bultmann use the term *Gleichnis*. Taylor's term is intended to include a wider range of stories of diverse subject matter which do not submit to easy classification under other headings.

[10]Called *Mythen* and *Legende* by Dibelius and *Geschichtserzählung* and *Legende* by Bultmann.

[11]For a concise treatment of form criticism see E. V. McKnight, *What is Form Criticism?* (Philadelphia: Fortress Press, 1969). A. M. Perry, "The Growth of the Gospels," in *The Interpreter's Bible*, VII, 68–72, is also instructive.

Result of Form Criticism

Form critics practically paralyzed the search for the historical Jesus. They proved, at least to their own satisfaction, that the gospel records were made up of a mass of individual, unrelated units. These units resembled pearls on a string. The pearls had "grown in the sea of the early Christian communities but the string had been manufactured by gospel writers. The pearls had been selected, polished and valued, even created at times, in the living environment of the church in the course of its preaching, controversy, teaching, persecution and worship."[12] Since the pearls had been strongly colored and shaped by the practical needs and doctrinal beliefs of the church, they could not furnish authentic information about Jesus' life and work.

One after another of the form critics concluded that the historical task is a vain undertaking. Rudolf Bultmann wrote: "I do indeed think that we can now know almost nothing concerning the life and personality of Jesus, since the early Christian sources show no interest in either, are more-over fragmentary and often legendary; and other sources about Jesus do not exist."[13] G. Bertram embraced a similar skepticism: "The figure of Jesus is not directly accessible to history. It is futile to try to place him within a process of historical development . . . ; not what he was, but what he is, is all that is revealed to the believer; the historian must be content with this statement."[14]

Limitations of the Method

Not all New Testament scholars became eager devotees of form criticism. As time passed, this tool for probing behind the Gospels came in for some searching criticism. (1) The classifications of gospel material proposed by prominent form critics are by no means identical. (2) The classifications are not based solely on considerations of form, but also on the subject matter or the style in which the narrative is told. This fact compromises the claimed objectivity of the form critics. (3) Many pericopes actually have a mixed form. Form critics are hard pressed to point out many pure examples of any form. This difficulty weakens one of the foundation stones of the theory—that form is the decisive or predominant factor in the development of the tradition. (4) The assumption that the forms created the tradition is suspect. Communities are more likely to shape and conserve than to create. (5) A number of unwarranted assumptions regarding the needs and

[12]Dwight Marion Beck, *Through the Gospels to Jesus* (New York: Harper & Row, Publishers, Inc., 1954), p. 56. Reprinted by permission.

[13]Rudolf Bultmann, *Jesus and the Word*, tr. L. P. Smith and E. H. Lantero (New York: Charles Scribner's Sons, 1958), p. 8.

[14]Quoted by Goguel, *The Life of Jesus*, p. 59.

requirements of the early church have been made by the form critics. (6) There has been a tendency to confuse the history of the form with the history of the subject matter. (7) The picture of early church life has been oversimplified by concentrating too much on the function of forms. Many other factors were at work in the growth and control of tradition. (8) The results of literary criticism have often been neglected. (9) The identification of a particular form does not really tell us where that form came from.[15]

Acceptance of the Method

Despite the reservations aroused by form criticism, the new discipline eventually won wide (but not unanimous) scholarly support.[16] The double decade of development between Jesus and the first written records that were incorporated into the Gospels had been surrounded by a wall of silence. The imaginative efforts of the form critics to penetrate that wall and to reconstruct the lost period of the gospel tradition resulted in two major accomplishments. (1) It established the independent and self-contained nature of much of the gospel material. Interpreters could no longer rely on the immediate context of a particular passage or saying, since the context had probably been provided by the author of the Gospel and thus might not reflect its original setting at all. (2) It demonstrated the decisive role the church played in the selection and shaping of the gospel record.

Historical Search Renewed

Although a chastened search for the historical Jesus continued in some circles (especially in Britain) during the peak activity of the form critics, its development among the disciples of Bultmann was quite unexpected. The "New Quest" began on October 20, 1953, when Ernst Käsemann gave a lecture at Marburg on "The Problem of the Historical Jesus" to a re-union of Bultmann students. He asserted that the Easter event cannot be understood apart from the earthly Jesus and that the Synoptic tradition contains pieces which the historian must regard as authentic.[17] An elaboration of this view is contained in Günther Bornkamm's *Jesus von Nazareth,* which appeared in 1956. Bornkamm does not share the extreme skepticism of form critics who hold that "the map of the actual history of Jesus, once

15B. S. Easton, *The Gospel Before the Gospels* (New York: Charles Scribner's Sons, 1928), emphasizes the limitations of form criticism as a historical tool. Vincent Taylor, *The Formation of the Gospel Tradition* (London: Macmillan & Co., Ltd., 1933), offers a more balanced account and acknowledges the usefulness of form criticism as a limited tool.

16C. H. Dodd, T. W. Manson, Vincent Taylor, and others continued the search for the historical Jesus although they readily acknowledged that a complete biography was an impossibility.

17See Ernst Käsemann, *Essays on New Testament Themes,* tr. W. J. Montague (London: SCM Press, 1964), pp. 15–47.

so clearly marked, must . . . be in all honesty left blank."[18] He acknowledges that the gospel materials are seen through the eyes of the post-Easter faith of the church; but he contends that they are not to be dismissed as the mere product of imagination. "The tradition of the Gospels is itself very considerably concerned with the pre-Easter history of Jesus, different though this interest is from that of modern historical science."[19] The tradition "points beyond itself to him whom the Church has encountered in his earthly form and who proves his presence to her as the resurrected and risen Lord. In every layer, therefore, and in each individual part, the tradition is witness of the reality of his history and the reality of his resurrection. Our task, then, is to seek the history *in* the Kerygma of the Gospels, and in this history to seek the Kerygma."[20]

Bornkamm believes that the Gospels tell the story of Jesus in pericopes. "These story scenes give his history not only when pieced together, but each one in itself contains the person and history of Jesus in their entirety. None requires explanation in terms of previous happenings. . . . This way of telling his story has its exact counterpart in the transmission of his words. Here again each word stands by itself, exhaustive in itself, not dependent on context for its meaning. . . ."[21]

Bornkamm grants that "the Gospel tradition, in origin and purpose, is directed to the practical use of the believing Church, to whom mere history as such means very little. Surely the historian is forced thereby to criticise this tradition, which often enough is silent where he seeks an answer, naïvely generalises where he enquires after the individual element in each case, and frequently blurs the distinction between history and interpretation. These are legitimate questions. And yet we must never lose sight of the fact that, precisely in this way of transmitting and recounting, the person and work of Jesus, in their unmistakable uniqueness and distinctiveness, are shown forth. . . . Understood in this way, the primitive tradition of Jesus is brim full of history."[22]

Redaction Criticism

World War II brought a virtual halt to literary activity. After 1945, however, Synoptic research was resumed and a new direction was taken.

[18]Günther Bornkamm, *Jesus of Nazareth*, tr. Irene and Fraser McLuskey with J. M. Robinson (New York: Harper & Row, Publishers, Inc., 1960), p. 10. Reprinted by permission.

[19]Bornkamm, *Jesus of Nazareth*, p. 22.

[20]Bornkamm, *Jesus of Nazareth*, p. 21.

[21]Bornkamm, *Jesus of Nazareth*, p. 25.

[22]Bornkamm, *Jesus of Nazareth*, pp. 25–26. Other significant studies of the period include James M. Robinson, *A New Quest of the Historical Jesus* (Naperville, Ill.: Alec R. Allenson, Inc., 1959); Ernst Fuchs, "The Quest of the Historical Jesus," *Studies of the Historical Jesus* (London: SCM Press, 1964), pp. 11–31. See also C. C. McCown, *The Search for the Real Jesus* (New York: Charles Scribner's Sons, 1940), for a depiction of the quest which occurred earlier in the twentieth century.

Form critics had viewed the authors of the Synoptics primarily as collectors and transmitters of traditions which they had received. The form critics had paid little attention to such questions as the controlling concepts and the unity of individual Gospels. Yet their conviction that the Synoptics were composite works whose individual units had been strung together by their authors like pearls on a string naturally raised certain questions. How did the evangelists connect their individual units? Why did they put them in different places in their respective Gospels? Did they alter their inherited tradition when they incorporated it into their works? What theological motifs were at work in their arrangement and modification of received material?

Although the new direction in Synoptic research came to full flower after World War II, its beginnings reach back to the turn of the century. Wilhelm Wrede's *Das Messiasgeheimnis in den Evangelien* [The Messianic Secret in the Gospels] appeared in 1901.[23] It pulverized the "Marcan hypothesis" (the assumption that Mark was a reliable historical account) by demonstrating that major aspects of the Marcan narratives are not historical but rather are permeated by a theological concept (the Messianic Secret) which originated after Easter. The pioneer studies in form criticism include a chapter on the final composition of the Gospels which deals with their theological patterns, to be sure, but R. H. Lightfoot became the first practitioner of the as-yet-unnamed methodology. In the Bampton Lectures of 1934, he stressed the interpretative nature of Mark, a book that he and others of his generation had been taught was almost wholly historical.[24]

The scholarly silence imposed by the Second World War was broken by three continental specialists. Although they worked independently of each other, they employed the methodology anticipated by Lightfoot many years earlier. One of them, Willi Marxsen, gave the new technique its name, *Redaktionsgeschichte* (redaction criticism), in 1954.[25] The three specialists recognized that the evangelists were not merely collectors and transmitters of traditional material, as the form critics claimed, but redactors (editors and revisers). They arranged and altered the material they had received to express their own theology or that of the church of their day, a theology often quite different from that found in the original. They were, to a very considerable degree, authors in their own right. We shall begin with Bornkamm's study, which appeared first.

Günther Bornkamm wrote a brief article in 1948 about Matthew's account of the Stilling of the Storm (8:23–27), in which he demonstrated how the evangelist functioned not as a mere collector of tradition but as

[23]Göttingen: Vandenhoeck & Ruprecht.

[24]R. H. Lightfoot, *History and Interpretation in the Gospels* (New York: Harper & Row, Publishers, Inc., n.d.), p. 57.

[25]Some other scholars (such as Ernst Haenchen) prefer the term "composition criticism," but no term is altogether satisfactory. We use "redaction cricitism" to refer to the whole range of creative activities which can be discovered in an evangelist by means of which his theology can be discerned. See Norman Perrin, *What is Redaction Criticism?* (Philadelphia: Fortress Press, 1969), pp. 65–67.

an author as well.[26] When Bornkamm compared Matthew's version of the pericope with its parallels in Mark (4:35–41) and Luke (8:22–25), he discovered that Matthew put the story in a different context and presented it in such a way as to give it a new meaning. Matthew placed the story after two sayings about discipleship (8:19–22); in both instances the word "follow" (as a disciple) was used, and this word was repeated in the pericope concerning the storm on the lake (8:23). By prefacing the Stilling of the Storm with sayings about "following," the evangelist endowed the pericope with exemplary significance. The turbulent ride of the disciples with Jesus in the boat and the Stilling of the Storm typified the tribulations of discipleship and the small ship of the church. By placing the pericope in a context different from the one he found in Mark, Matthew became the pericope's earliest known interpreter.

Matthew not only placed the pericope in a different context, but he also altered its substance. Several instances could be cited, but one of Bornkamm's illustrations will suffice. Note the evangelist's choice of the word used by the disciples to address Jesus when they called to him for help. Matthew replaced Mark's "Master" ($\delta\iota\delta\acute{\alpha}\sigma\kappa\alpha\lambda\epsilon$) with "Lord" ($\kappa\acute{\upsilon}\rho\iota\epsilon$). "Lord" is a respectful human title in Mark and Luke, but it is an uncommon form of address in Matthew. There it is a divine predicate of majesty —at once a prayer and a declaration of discipleship.

Bornkamm's interpretation of the Stilling of the Storm did not constitute a repudiation of the principles of form criticism but an endorsement of them. He and subsequent redactionists simply insisted that the form-critical emphasis on individual units should be supplemented by an awareness of the general conception and composition of each Synoptic as a whole. Only the contents of a given Gospel—not that Gospel in its entirety—can be considered composite material. The redaction of a Gospel (its arrangement and composition into a particular framework) is the product of the evangelist. His selection of the traditional material, the order in which he used it, and his alterations of it were dictated by his theology. He was a theological author operating from theological perspectives.[27]

If Bornkamm was the first genuine redaction critic, Hans Conzelmann was undoubtedly the foremost. His monumental work, *Die Mitte der Zeit*,[28] appeared in 1954. Conzelmann compared the text of Luke with that of his sources (mainly Mark) in order to discern the evangelist's editorial activity. The study revealed Luke's theological motivation, which certain texts ap-

[26]Günther Bornkamm, "Die Sturmstillung in Matthäusevangelium," *Wort und Dienst, Jahrbuch der Theologischen Schule Bethel* NF (1948), pp. 49–54; reprinted in G. Bornkamm, Gerhard Barth, and H. J. Held, *Tradition and Interpretation in Matthew*, tr. Percy Scott (Philadelphia: The Westminster Press, 1963), pp. 52–57.

[27]For additional studies by Bornkamm and by several of his students, see Bornkamm, Barth, and Held, *Tradition and Interpretation in Matthew*; H. E. Tödt, *Son of Man in the Synoptic Tradition*, tr. D. M. Barton (London: SCM Press, 1965); Ferdinand Hahn, *The Titles of Jesus in Christology* (New York: World Publishing Co., 1969).

[28]"The Center of Time." The English translation of the book is *The Theology of St. Luke* (New York: Harper & Row, Publishers, Inc., 1960).

pear to summarize. For example, take Luke 16:16, which is based on the same Q source as Matthew 11:12–13 but is farther from the original. In Matthew's version, John the Baptist marked the *beginning* of the new era of violence that foreshadowed the coming of the kingdom. But Luke telescoped and modified the Q saying to show that the Baptist marked the *end* of the period of the law and the prophets. This enabled Luke to divide salvation history into three epochs: (1) the period of Israel—which includes John the Baptist and the early history of Jesus—when the promise of salvation was given by God through the prophets; (2) the ministry of Jesus— "the center of time" when the promised salvation was fulfilled in Jesus' words and works—which terminates with the ascension and is described by the Gospel of Luke; (3) the church and its mission to the world (Acts).

The threefold scheme was created by Luke, according to Conzelmann, in response to the dominant theological problem of his day—the postponed parousia. In the infancy of the church the parousia was expected at any moment, but by Luke's time the continuation of the world was an established fact. Luke saw the theological significance of this unexpected turn of events, and from it he drew two conclusions: (1) the history of Jesus belonged to the past, and (2) Christians should take into account the possibility that the End might not arrive for a long time. Consequently, Luke composed his Gospel as a history of Jesus, and in Acts he put that history in the mouths of the apostles as the substance of their preaching of salvation. Simultaneously, he perceived that the post-Jesus period had its own special meaning. It was the time when the church carried the story of Jesus to all mankind. The writing of Acts as a sequel to the Gospel of Luke constituted a major theological breakthrough. Luke thereby placed the ministry of Jesus at the center of time and underscored the existence of the church as a world-wide witness to that history as the completed redemption of God. His theological perception at once solved the problem of the postponed parousia and placed early Christian eschatology on the periphery of the full history of salvation.[29]

Bornkamm's studies of Matthew and Conzelmann's studies of Luke were followed in 1956 by Willi Marxsen's *Der Evangelist Markus*.[30] Marxsen stresses that redaction criticism is not a mere continuation of form criticism; redaction criticism just began at a later date. Although it presupposes the results of form criticism, redaction criticism differs from form criticism in several significant ways. (1) Form criticism regards the evangelists primarily as collectors of tradition, but redaction criticism views them as authors in their own right. (2) Form criticism is largely concerned with reducing the tradition to small, individual units and discovering how they came into being originally. Redaction criticism deals with the larger units (including the form of the work as a whole) and seeks to learn why those

---

[29]For critiques of Conzelmann's threefold scheme for Luke, see Helmut Flender, *St. Luke: Theologian of Redemptive History*, tr. R. H. and Ilsa Fuller (Philadelphia: Fortress Press, 1967) and Fred O. Francis, "Eschatology and History in Luke-Acts," *Journal of the American Academy of Religion*, XXXVII, No. 4 (1969), 49–63.

[30]Published in English as Willi Marxsen, *Mark the Evangelist*, tr. R. A. Harrisville (New York: Abingdon Press, 1969).

units were formed as they were. (3) The form-critical stress on the individual units and on the evangelists as collectors neglects the innovation of Mark who assembled smaller and larger units of the tradition into something entirely new—a "Gospel." Redaction criticism, on the other hand, has as one of its basic purposes the discovery of the theology that prompted Mark to create the gospel form and the theologies that led Matthew and Luke to adopt and adapt it. (4) Form criticism and redaction criticism deal with different "life situations" of the Synoptic material. If Jeremias's work on the parables is honored,[31] some of the Synoptic material can be traced to a setting in the life of Jesus—the first of three life situations. The form critic seeks to set gospel material in its context in the life of the early church—the second life situation. The redaction critic views the gospel material in its setting in the work and purpose of the evangelist—the third life situation. What really happened (the first life situation) is of no interest to the redaction critic. His concern is how the evangelists used early church tradition (the second life situation) in the composition of their Gospels.

We cannot deal in detail with the four studies which comprise Marxsen's book: the tradition about John the Baptist, geographical references in the gospel narratives, the concept of *euangelion* (Gospel), and Mark 13. A brief review of his treatment of the John the Baptist tradition will illustrate his redaction-critical methodology. He argues that the Baptist tradition in Mark, whatever the form of its previous history, is a composition of the evangelist. It was, so to speak, composed "backwards." Its purpose is to interpret the story of Jesus by means of a reference to John. It tells us nothing about John or baptism per se. It is a commentary about Christ. Moreover, just as the Baptist tradition interprets Jesus, the Old Testament quotations placed in the narrative interpret John. Note the close connection between the Old Testament prophecies about the wilderness in Mark 1:3 and the appearance of John in the wilderness in Mark 1:4. Its purpose is to demonstrate that John is the fulfiller of the prophecies and, as such, is the forerunner of Jesus. Consequently, "in the wilderness" in 1:4 is not a geographical reference but a theological assertion. It provides John with credentials to fulfill prophecy.

A similar understanding is dictated by the time reference in Mark 1:14. Although it assuredly refers to the arrest of John by Herod, it is not intended to indicate that Jesus' ministry began only after John was jailed. The statement is christological. It simply means that John was the forerunner and Jesus the one who follows after, the one awaited. John's story, therefore, has to be terminated before Jesus' story can begin. The details of John's arrest and death are recorded later in Mark, but the notation of his arrest has to appear in 1:14 because the evangelist wants to relate John and Jesus theologically. "Now after John was arrested, Jesus came into Galilee, preaching the gospel of God . . ." (1:14). Mark can start his Gospel with the phrase, "The beginning of the gospel of Jesus Christ," and then launch into an account of John the Baptist because he uses the Baptist

---

[31]Joachim Jeremias, *The Parables of Jesus*, tr. S. H. Hooke (London: SCM Press Ltd., 1963; printed in the U.S. by Charles Scribner's Sons).

tradition as a commentary on Christ. By presenting the Baptist as a fulfiller of prophecy and as the forerunner of Christ he articulates a major
theme of his Gospel—that Jesus is the Christ.

After Marxsen completes his discussion of Mark's use of the Baptist
tradition, he shows how Matthew and Luke make use of Mark's account.
For example, the later evangelists turn Mark's theological reference to the
wilderness into a geographical one. Matthew uses the Old Testament not
only as an interpretative vehicle but as a proof-text—thus relegating the
Old Testament to an earlier time period. The theological relationship between John and Jesus becomes a chronological one. Luke carries the process
even further. He separates the Baptist from Jesus by relegating him to the
period in salvation history just prior to "the center of time" (Lk. 16:16).
John's work is finished. Consequently, Luke records John's arrest (3:20)
before he tells of Jesus' baptism (3:21). John is only a prophet. His eschatological significance, so prominent in Mark, has vanished.[32]

Marxsen's study of the Baptist tradition in the Synoptics (as well as his
other studies) demonstrates that even though the separate accounts betray
only minor literary differences, they express markedly different theological
perspectives. When the work of Bornkamm, Conzelmann, Marxsen, and
subsequent redaction critics is considered, serious questions are raised about
the nature of the Gospels, the possibility or propriety of a quest for the
historical Jesus, and the actual locus of revelation in the Christian faith.

Results of Redaction Criticism

Redaction criticism is a relatively new discipline. Pioneer works, such
as that of Conzelmann, have been enthusiastically received, modified, or
partially rejected. Current practitioners of the methodology are busily engaged in wide-ranging research and writing. It may take a decade or more
before anything like a scholarly consensus can be reached regarding redaction criticism's contribution to Biblical studies. Although it is hazardous to
speculate, certain contributions of the discipline seem relatively assured.

1. Redaction criticism has markedly increased our reservoir of information about the theological history of early Christianity by focusing attention
on the evangelists as ranking theologians. All previous attempts to expound
the subject, as in books on New Testament theology, the history of Christian
doctrine, and the like, must be revised to take into account the discoveries
of the redaction critics.

2. Redaction criticism has made considerably more difficult (some
scholars would say impossible) any kind of quest for the historical Jesus.
Although the seeds of this conclusion were sown and nurtured by the form
critics, their harvest was left for the redactionists. Their conviction that the
material in the respective Gospels reflects the theological perceptions of

---

32See Marxsen, *Mark the Evangelist*, pp. 15–53, to which our treatment is indebted.

the evangelists, editors of the tradition, or preachers and prophets in the early church markedly reduces the amount of material, if any, that can be attributed to Jesus. It also makes imperative, after the history of the tradition has been determined, the establishment of strict standards by which the authenticity of the material can be judged. No longer can it be assumed (if indeed it ever could) that if it "sounds like Jesus" or "is supported by two of the Synoptic sources," it is genuine.

Professors Norman Perrin and Reginald H. Fuller, working independently, have suggested identical standards to be used in determining what gospel material is authentic, although they employ different nomenclatures. We shall use Perrin's designations.[33] (1) *Dissimilarity.* This criterion is the most important. It means that material may be attributed to Jesus if it is dissimilar to known tendencies in Judaism before him or in the church after him. Perrin cites as an illustration the address to God in Luke's version (11:2) of the Lord's Prayer: "Abba" (Father). This intimate form of address was anathema to the Jews, and Matthew's parallel passage (6:9), which reflects the piety of the early church, moves in another direction.[34] (2) *Multiple attestation.* Material may be accepted as coming from Jesus if it is found in numerous sources or forms of tradition—unless, of course, the multiple references are the result of some common church practice such as the Lord's Supper. An example of multiple attestation is Jesus' concern for the religiously disinherited, such as the "tax collectors and sinners." (3) *Coherence.* Material which coheres with already authenticated material may be considered authentic—providing it passes appropriate linguistic and environmental tests. The Greek origin of Mark's interpretation of the parable of the Sower (4:13–20) and the church origin of the commissioning of Peter in Matthew (16:18–19) would disqualify these passages.

The application of such stringent standards as those advocated by Perrin and Fuller does not make the quest for the historical Jesus fruitless, but it does shift the burden of proof to those who make the claims of authenticity. Although redaction criticism has shifted and increased that burden, we do not believe that it has made it unbearable.

3. Redaction criticism has greatly enhanced our understanding of the nature of a "Gospel." Parallels can be found for other types of writing in the New Testament (apocalyptic, letters, general epistles, etc.), but none exists for "Gospel." It is a unique literary creation of early Christianity designed to express a distinctive facet of its faith. This fact surfaced as a result of the work of the redaction critics. They revealed how decisively the theological perspectives of the evangelists or transmitters of tradition influ-

---

[33]Norman Perrin, *Rediscovering the Teaching of Jesus* (London: SCM Press, 1967; printed in the U.S. by Harper & Row Publishers, Inc.), pp. 15–49. Compare Perrin, *What is Redaction Criticism?*, pp. 70–71, to which we are also indebted. Reginald H. Fuller, *A Critical Introduction to the New Testament* (Naperville, Ill.: Alec R. Allenson, 1966), pp. 91–104, uses the terms "distinctiveness," "cross-section method," and "consistency," respectively.

[34]See Joachim Jeremias, *New Testament Theology*, tr. John Bowden (New York: Charles Scribner's Sons, 1971), pp. 61–68.

enced the formation of the gospel material. If redaction criticism is taken seriously, then, a Gospel cannot be considered a history of the mission and message of Jesus during a given time span; it is, rather, a history of Christian experiences at any time. To be sure, a Gospel presents this history of Christian experience in the guise of an account of Jesus' words and works, but the account is actually a combination of historical memories, interpreted tradition, and material created by the evangelists. The evangelists treated their material with such sovereign freedom because of a conviction, shared by the early church, that the historical Jesus and the Exalted Lord were one and the same. Without this conviction, there would have been no "Gospel." With it, a distinctive feature of gospel material comes to light: "The representation of the present [experience of the Exalted Lord] in the form of the past [ministry of the historical Jesus]."[35]

The Gospels were written in retrospect. In them the fine distinctions between past, present, and future to which we are accustomed tended to disappear. What was happening interpreted what had happened. The present experience of the Exalted Lord infused the past *and* the future with new meaning. This is not to say that the historical Jesus was unimportant to the faith of the evangelists. He was important, but he was not the primary concern of their faith. What Jesus had done in the flesh was of less concern to the evangelists than what he would do as the coming Lord/Son of Man. If he had had no past, of course, he would have had no future. But it was the early Christians' hope of the future that gave meaning to their memories. That hope was grounded not so much in reminiscences of a past ministry as in their present experience of the resurrected Christ. "What is unique in Mark," comments Marxsen, "is that he describes the 'Crucified One' of Paul's theology ... by using the tradition of the earthly Jesus which is now proclaimed by the Exalted Lord."[36]

As significant as the contributions of redaction criticism are, the discipline is not without its shortcomings. Chief among them is the incomplete nature of its work to date. For this deficiency, time is the only remedy. Another limitation is the extreme subtlety redaction criticism attributes to the evangelists as authors. It is doubtful that they really thought things out in such infinite detail. Marxsen's restriction of the term "Gospel" to Mark and his identification of Mark's historical situation with Galilee are cases in point.[37]

Literary criticism has customarily dealt with such matters as authorship, date, destination, possible composite nature, and sources of the Gospels. We covered these items in the previous chapter, and on the basis of our findings set forth the nature, purposes, characteristics, and structures of the individual Gospels. We delayed until this chapter the discussion of form

[35]Perrin, *What Is Redaction Criticism?*, p. 78. See also pp. 64–79.

[36]Marxsen, *Mark the Evangelist*, p. 148.

[37]For an excellent review and evaluation of redaction criticism, see Joachim Rohde, *Rediscovering the Teaching of the Evangelists*, tr. D. M. Barton (London: SCM Press, 1968).

criticism[38] and redaction criticism[39] in order to outline the chronological development of Gospel research. The newer methodologies have contributed much to our understanding of the nature of the Gospels, and they require modification of conclusions reached by means of literary criticism alone. As we begin our search for *Jesus: the Man, the Mission, and the Message,* we shall make use of the valid insights provided by all three approaches.

[38]Form criticism attempts to penetrate the sources revealed by literary criticism in order to discover what happened to the Jesus tradition during the oral period.

[39]Redaction criticism examines the smaller units of tradition revealed by the form critics in order to determine how these units were combined to form larger complexes and the individual Gospels. The purposes of redaction criticism are to understand why the evangelists connected and modified the tradition as they did, to discover in their connections and modifications their theological viewpoints, and to expound the theological viewpoints of the individual Gospels as finished products.

part 3

The Formative Years

Until recently, children, like Topsy, "just grew." Their early years were looked upon as a prolonged prologue to personhood. They were "cute," "spoiled," "unruly," or "obedient." Their experiences were thought to have little lasting importance. Parental responsibilities were considered adequately fulfilled when the youngsters were kept safe from harm, clean, well-fed, and out of the way.

Then came modern psychology, and parents learned a new language. It was sprinkled with such fascinating and frightening words as "repression," "sublimation," "frustration," "complex," and "neurosis." The carefree became concerned. Caution encircled the cradle. The sudden awareness that rearing could reap a monster or a missionary was sobering. The formative years acquired new status. Little folks were now seen as pliable pieces of protoplasm whose future lay hidden in the present. No form of determinism was intended, but for the first time the full force of the environment in childhood development was felt.

Jesus was born into an environment. He did not rear himself. He was nursed, weaned, taught, disciplined, and directed by others. He "increased in wisdom and in stature, and in favor with God and man" (Lk. 2:52). A careful examination of the formative factors connected with his birth, boyhood, and youth should prove to be enlightening as well as interesting.

chapter eight

The Virgin Birth

Accounts of Jesus' virgin birth were originally private. They played no part in Jesus' public ministry. Nowhere does the New Testament even hint that he made their acceptance a condition of discipleship. The first preaching about Jesus (the kerygma) does not mention them—nor do Paul, Mark, or the early chapters of Acts. Matthew and Luke include independent records of the virgin birth in their beginning chapters. Had his origin played any part in Jesus' ministry, these authors would undoubtedly have had occasion to refer back to it in later chapters. This they did not do.

According to the records, Jesus' disciples knew about his mission, message, death, and resurrection before they knew about his birth. Only after they had felt the impact of his person, purpose, and position did they make inquiries concerning his origin. Historically and theologically, then, the account of Jesus' birth is later than his own claims and those made by his earliest followers. Chronologically, his birth stands first; and psychologically, the modern student starts with it. So, also, shall we.

The nativity narratives are confined to the first two chapters of Matthew and Luke. The popular mind has merged the separate gospel accounts into a single Christmas Story. Actually Matthew and Luke use different orders of events and record different facts. In order to avoid confusion our treatment will follow a chronological sequence based on both accounts. The reader should bear in mind, however, that there are two different accounts and that the Gospels are not in agreement on the sequence of events.

Genealogy[1]

Our generation has few roots. We are preoccupied with the present. Our sense of history is dulled by other interests—popularity, success, peace, and progress. Most of us would find it impossible to name our great-grandfathers. This was not the case for first-century Jews; they had a well-developed sense of history and a consuming interest in ancestry. They could climb their family tree with ease.

The Jewish God was a God of history. He had spoken to His people in the past (to Abraham, Moses, and the prophets). He had delivered them from their perils (in the Exodus). However, He was not just an echo of the past; He was the Lord of the present. He would speak to His people again. He would speak to them through His Messiah and deliver them from their enemies.

Prevailing opinion held that the Messiah would be a descendant of David, Israel's greatest king. It is not surprising, then, that Matthew and Luke should record the family tree of Jesus. They wanted to establish his credentials, to prove that he was of David's line. What is surprising is that they do not present the same genealogy. Indeed, the genealogies are not merely different; they are in conflict with each other and with the virgin birth of Jesus.

Matthew traces the ancestry from Abraham (Father of the Hebrews) to Jesus, while Luke begins with Jesus and ends with Adam, the son of God (Father of all men).

Matthew contains forty-six names from Abraham to Jesus; Luke has seventy-seven names from Jesus to Adam.

Luke lists Heli (3:23) instead of Jacob as Jesus' grandfather, seven immediate descendants of Zerubbabel (3:26–27) which differ from those in Matthew, Neri instead of Jechoniah as the father of Shealtiel (3:27), and other discrepancies. He traces Jesus' ancestry through Nathan to David (3:31) while Matthew traces it through Solomon (1:6), another son of David.

Matthew departs from normal Jewish practice and includes five women in the genealogy. Three of them (Tamar, Rahab, and Bathsheba) were tainted with sexual irregularities. One of them (Ruth) was a foreigner. The fifth was Mary, the mother of Jesus.

Matthew divides his list of names into three sections of fourteen generations each.[2] Jesus' Davidic descent appears to be deliberately enshrined in this schematic arrangement. The Hebrew alphabet had no vowels. Each consonant possessed a numerical equivalent. Without vowels David would be spelled Dvd. "D" (daleth) had the value of four, "v" (waw) the value of six. D (4) + v (6) + d (4) = 14. Three (a Hebrew number signifying completeness) sections, of fourteen generations each, add up to triple certitude.

---

[1]Mt. 1:1–17; Lk. 3:23–38.

[2]Only thirteen appear in the third section, indicating that a name has been lost.

Luke shows scant interest in Jewish heroes or chronology, He was a Gentile Christian. He does not relate Jesus' genealogy in connection with his birth. He puts it about thirty years later in connection with his baptism and the beginning of his public ministry.

The differences between the genealogies are mild in comparison with the conflicts between the genealogies and the virgin birth. Both Matthew and Luke state that Jesus was born of a virgin. Yet both of them contain genealogies which trace the ancestry of Jesus through Joseph. If Joseph was not the biological father of Jesus, then the family trees are pointless. Their purpose is to prove that Jesus was a descendant of David, hence a person with proper Messianic credentials. There are some indications that Matthew and Luke (or later editors) were aware of the difficulty. Matthew abruptly diverts the ancestral line from Joseph to Mary: "Jacob the father of Joseph the husband of Mary, of whom Jesus was born" (1:16). Luke treats the problem with a parenthetical comment: "Jesus, when he began his ministry, was about thirty years of age, being the son (as was supposed) of Joseph" (3:23). These attempts at reconciliation do not banish the problem. The real purpose of the genealogies is to show that Jesus is a descendant of David *through Joseph.*

The problems presented by the genealogies were recognized early.[3] Three main solutions have been suggested. (1) Matthew gives the genealogy of Joseph; Luke gives the genealogy of Mary. Roman Catholic scholars, Martin Luther, and others have endorsed this idea. But the theory is unlikely. Joseph is designated a son of David in Mt. 1:20 and Lk. 1:27. Nowhere is it indicated that Mary was of Davidic descent. Indeed, if we are to take seriously Luke's suggestion (1:36) that Mary was a relative of Elizabeth, a member of the tribe of Levi, then Mary was probably of priestly descent. For most people, who expected the Messiah to be of Davidic descent, Luke's tracing of Jesus' ancestry through Mary would prove that he was not the Messiah at all. This was hardly Luke's intent. (2) Matthew gives Jesus' legal descent; Luke gives his natural descent. A number of eminent scholars have advanced this view.[4] It leaves unexplained, however, why Luke would make a double departure from tradition and trace Jesus' ancestry through his *mother* who was probably a *Levite.* (3) The two genealogies represent separate traditions which originated in different sections of the church. An increasing number of scholars take this position. It coheres with their concept of the tradition's development and delivers them from the necessity of harmonizing the accounts.[5]

---

[3]See Eusebius, *Ecclesiastical History,* I, 7, where Julius Africanus (?–232 A.D.) accounts for the discrepancies between the genealogies on the basis of the levirate law, by which a dead brother's childless widow might be married to a living brother to raise up children in the name of the deceased. This theory would permit the natural ancestors to differ at several points from the legal ancestors and result in two equally valid genealogies.

[4]See J. G. Machen, *The Virgin Birth of Christ* (New York: Harper & Row, Publishers, Inc., 1930), for the definitive exposition of this position.

[5]See S. MacLean Gilmour, "Exegesis, The Gospel According to St. Luke," in George Arthur Buttrick, ed., *The Interpreter's Bible* (New York and Nashville: Abingdon Press, © 1952), VIII, 80–83.

Promise of the Baptist's Birth[6]

Barrenness was a triple tragedy for a Jewish woman. It shriveled the hopes of her husband for posterity, sparked taunts from other women when she appeared at the village well, and signified her sin. To be barren was to be out of favor with God and man. To be pregnant was to be blessed.

The future parents of John the Baptist (like Abraham and Sarah before them) were childless and advanced in years. Zechariah was a priest, and his wife, Elizabeth, was also of the tribe of Levi. The priests were divided into twenty-four classes. The class of Abijah, of which Zechariah was a member, was the eighth. Each class was responsible for the conduct of Temple worship for one week at semiannual intervals.[7] Twice daily, before the morning and evening sacrifices, a priest offered incense in the Holy Place. The number of priests within each class was so large that the privilege of performing the priestly function was determined by lot. When the lot fell on Zechariah to burn incense, he evidently prayed to the Lord that his childless state be terminated. An angel informed him that his prayer had been heard, his wife would bear him a son, his name should be John, he would be filled with the Holy Spirit, and in the spirit and power of Elijah he would make the people ready for God's rule.

Like the Christians who prayed for Peter's release from prison (Acts 12:1–16), Zechariah couldn't believe his ears. He demanded proof that the promise would be fulfilled. The angel identified himself as Gabriel and sentenced Zechariah to nine months of silence for his lack of faith. The people were astonished at Zechariah's protracted stay in the Temple. They feared that he might incur God's wrath. When Zechariah finally appeared and failed to give the customary blessing to the assembly, they correctly perceived that he had seen a vision. Zechariah's term ended with the next Sabbath. He headed home, Elizabeth subsequently conceived, and for five months she remained in confinement. She waited until it was perfectly obvious that she was going to have a baby before she ventured forth to the village well, the social center of the Near East. She had had enough of the taunts of her fellow townswomen.

Annunciation[8]

Six months after Zechariah's vision in the Temple, Gabriel appeared to a maiden in Nazareth named Mary. Mary was betrothed to Joseph, a man of the house of David. Betrothal was not comparable to our engagement. It was a legal relationship, and it could be dissolved only by the man's giving

[6]Lk. 1:5–25.
[7]Josephus, *Antiquities*, VII, 14,7.
[8]Lk. 1:26–38; compare Mt. 1:18–25.

the woman a writ of divorce. Should the man die during the betrothed state, his betrothed would be considered his widow. Nevertheless, betrothal was distinguished from marriage. Marriage occurred only when the bridegroom took the bride to his home and the relationship was consummated.

Gabriel's greeting to Mary must have startled the young virgin: "Hail, O favored one, the Lord is with you!" (Lk. 1:28). Sensing Mary's troubled state of mind, Gabriel sought to reassure her. He made his greeting explicit: "You have found favor with God. And behold, you will conceive in your womb and bear a son" (Lk. 1:30–31).

No wonder Mary was troubled! (Joseph was disturbed, too, according to Mt. 1:19–21, and would have divorced Mary had the Lord not dissuaded him.) "How can this be," she queried Gabriel, "since I have no husband?" (Lk. 1:34). Mary's question has received varied treatment at the hands of scholars. (1) Some suggest that it was added to the text by a later hand than Luke in the interests of the virgin birth.[9] If this clause were missing, Gabriel's promise could apply to a son whom Mary was to conceive in natural wedlock. (2) Others maintain that the passage was added by Luke himself. This claim is authenticated by almost unbroken manuscript support of the verse.[10] The story of Jesus' supernatural generation was probably already known to Luke. He edited his sources (perhaps not too skillfully) to convey it. (3) Still others hold that Mary's question is an integral part of Lucan material which is based on Aramaic originals. The substance of these originals rests on the only really trustworthy source—Mary herself.[11]

Mary's manifestation of astonishment that she should have a son without Joseph's assistance has given Roman Catholics, Orthodox, and some Protestant believers support for their doctrine of the perpetual virginity of Mary. The phrase, "since I have no husband," it is said, not only declares Mary's present virginal status, but it also indicates that she had made a vow to remain a virgin forever. Moreover, her vow does not conflict with Matthew's remark that Joseph "knew her not *until* she had borne a son."[12] To state that they did not have sexual intercourse until she had produced a child does not imply that they did have it afterwards. These interpretations of the texts, however, do not explain (1) why, in view of her vow, Mary was betrothed to Joseph, and (2) why it is presupposed in Mk. 6:3 and Mt. 13:55–56 that Jesus had brothers and sisters.

The Old Testament knew of many births which resulted from divine intervention, but the birth of Mary's son was different. He had no human father. Matthew found proof of this in the Scriptures (Is. 7:14). "Behold, a virgin shall conceive and bear a son, and his name shall be called Emman-

---

9Streeter, *The Four Gospels*, pp. 267–68. Compare Frederick C. Grant, *An Introduction to New Testament Thought* (New York and Nashville: Abingdon Press, 1950), pp. 230–32.

10H. D. A. Major, "Incident in the Life of Jesus," in H. D. A. Major, T. W. Manson, and C. J. Wright, *The Mission and Message of Jesus* (New York: E. P. Dutton & Co., Inc., 1938), p. 262. Compare Gilmour, *The Interpreter's Bible*, VIII, 36.

11Hunter, *The Work and Words of Jesus*, p. 29.

12Emphasis added.

uel" (Mt. 1:23). Matthew correctly quoted the Septuagint (LXX), a Greek translation of the Hebrew Scripture. The Septuagint itself, however, was inaccurate. It translated the Hebrew word *'almāh*, which means strictly a young woman of marriageable age—without any indication as to whether she is or is not a virgin, by *parthenos*, which normally means a virgin.[13] Other Greek versions properly translate *'almāh* by *neanis* (a young woman). Although it cannot be denied that Matthew is a vigorous advocate of the virgin birth of Jesus, in this instance his supporting evidence is unjustified. Isaiah 7:14, in the original Hebrew, does not predict a virgin birth for him who shall be called Emmanuel.[14]

When Gabriel informed Zechariah that Elizabeth would give birth to a son, Zechariah demanded a sign. He wanted proof that the promise would be fulfilled. Instead of a sign he received an enforced silence. Mary, too, was plagued with doubts when Gabriel addressed her. She did not ask him to authenticate his message, but a sign was given to her anyway: "Behold, your kinswoman Elizabeth in her old age has also conceived a son; and this is the sixth month with her who was called barren" (Lk. 1:36). If aged and impotent Elizabeth had conceived through the power of God, could not the virgin Mary also? "For with God nothing will be impossible" (Lk. 1:37).

Mary's Visit to Elizabeth and the Magnificat[15]

Gabriel's good news concerning Elizabeth's unexpected pregnancy prompted Mary to make an impromptu visit to her kinswoman. Luke is vague about Elizabeth's place of residence—"a city of Judah" in "the hill country." Christian tradition has identified the place as 'Ein-Karem, near Jerusalem, some eighty miles south of Nazareth. When Mary reached the city, she greeted Elizabeth. The unborn John the Baptist leaped in his mother's womb. His prophetic awareness of the presence of the prenatal Messiah was transferred to Elizabeth. The prospective mother of the Forerunner then recognized the prospective mother of the Messiah. Under the inspiration of the Holy Spirit, Elizabeth bestowed a triple blessing on Mary: (1) for her preeminent position among women; (2) for her motherhood of the Messiah; and (3) for her belief in God's promise.

The magnificent Magnificat,[16] which begins in Lk. 1:46, is known throughout the church as the Hymn of Mary. Mary is the acknowledged speaker in all Greek manuscripts and in most translations. Yet Elizabeth, not Mary, is credited with the hymn in the earliest Old Latin manuscripts and by such eminent and erudite Church Fathers as Irenaeus, Origen, and

[13]Sometimes the Septuagint uses *parthenos* to refer to a girl who is no longer a virgin, as in Gen. 34:3.

[14]Moreover, "no trace of a Messianic interpretation of this passage has been found" (Hunter, *The Work and Words of Jesus*, p. 30).

[15]Lk. 1:39–56.

[16]So called from the first word in the Latin versions of the psalm.

According to tradition, the Church of the Visitation, located at 'Ein-Karem ("Spring of the Vineyard"), marks the place where Mary visited Elizabeth (Lk. 1:39). The church is presumably built on the site of the summer house of Zechariah and Elizabeth.

Jerome. Internal evidence strongly supports Elizabeth as the speaker in the original composition. (1) Elizabeth is the one who has just been filled with prophetic inspiration. (2) The Magnificat is closely modeled after the Song of Hannah in I Samuel 2:1–10. Hannah poured out her praise to God after her protracted period of barrenness had been ended by God in response to her prayer. This release from barrenness fits Elizabeth's situation, but it misses Mary's by a country mile. Luke 1:48a ("for he has regarded the low estate of his handmaiden") coheres with sterility but not with virginity. (3) The words which immediately follow the Magnificat ("And Mary remained with *her*"[17]) read as if Elizabeth was the speaker in 1:46. (4) Since by the time the Magnificat was composed, Mary had become the greater of the two women, it is unlikely that any scribe would have changed "Mary" to "Elizabeth." Perhaps, as S. MacLean Gilmour has indicated, the question of who spoke the Magnificat is academic. "Neither Mary nor Elizabeth can seriously be considered as the author of the psalm. Almost every phrase in the Magnificat has its parallel in I Sam. 1:11; I Sam. 2:1–10, or elsewhere in the O. T. [Old Testament]. Luke or his source took a Jewish (or Jewish-

---

[17]Lk. 1:56, emphasis added.

Christian) hymn of praise and fitted it to this situation, possibly by the interpolation of vs. 48."[18]

Mary remained with Elizabeth until the Baptist was born. Then she returned to her home. Whose home? Her parental home, or the one she and Joseph had established? Luke doesn't say. She and Joseph were presumably married before Jesus was born, but there is no indication of when the marriage took place.

Birth of the Baptist and the Benedictus[19]

The neighbors and kinsfolk of Elizabeth and Zechariah rejoiced when their son was born. They even participated in the naming of the child. On the eighth day the infant was circumcised by an expert in keeping with strict rabbinical rules. It was proposed that the boy be named Zechariah after his father. Elizabeth objected: "Not so; he shall be called John" (Lk. 1:60).[20] Zechariah was then consulted. The speechless father reached for a tablet and wrote, "His name is John" (Lk. 1:63). All were astonished. Surely greatness could be expected of a child born under such remarkable circumstances! Zechariah's sentence had now been served, so his speech was restored.

The Benedictus (Lk. 1:68–79) is attributed to Zechariah; but this attribution poses a problem. The song seems to celebrate the birth of the Messiah rather than that of the Baptist. (1) It opens by thanking God for having raised up a horn of salvation "in the house of his servant David" (1:69). This reference would be inappropriate for John, a descendant of Levi; but it would dovetail nicely with the popular expectation that the Messiah would be of the house of David. (2) The child is hailed as the "dayspring" (1:78), the title given the Messiah in Jeremiah (23:5) and Zechariah (3:8; 6:12).[21] (3) The phrase, "to give light to those who sit in darkness and in the shadow of death" (1:79), echoes the Messianic prophecy of Isaiah 9:1–2. "It would seem, therefore, that the *Benedictus* heralds or acclaims the birth of the Messiah, not the birth of His forerunner."[22]

The Benedictus was probably originally a Christian hymn—perhaps even a Jewish one—made up of a collection of Old Testament phrases. Luke (or his source) adopted it and adapted it to his purpose. Christian content is specifically introduced in 1:76–79. The deliverance of the nation from its political enemies is the concern of 1:68–75. But salvation from sins is the

18Gilmour, "Exegesis, The Gospel According to St. Luke," in George Arthur Buttrick, ed., *The Interpreter's Bible* (New York and Nashville: Abingdon Press, © 1952), VIII, 42.
19Lk. 1:57–80.
20A child was usually named at birth, more frequently after his grandfather than his father.
21The same Greek word (*anatolē*) is translated "Branch" in the Septuagint version of the passages from Jeremiah and Zechariah and "dayspring" in the alternate reading of the Revised Standard Version of the Benedictus.
22H. D. A. Major, "Incidents in the Life of Jesus," in H. D. A. Major, T. W. Manson, and C. J. Wright, *The Mission and Message of Jesus* (New York: E. P. Dutton and Co., Inc., © 1938), p. 266.

concern of 1:77. Earlier, Jesus had been given the title "the Son of the Most High" (1:32). Now John is called "the prophet of the Most High" (1:76).

Birth of Jesus[23]

The birth stories of Jesus breathe an atmosphere of mystery, involving wise men, humble shepherds, a directional star, angelic voices, and gifts that would dazzle a king. Their cadence resembles that of pure poetry and reminds one not to impose on them the prose of history. How could such an era-splitting moment be captured by the historian alone? Yet the details of place, time, and people cannot be ignored.

Where was Jesus born? Matthew and Luke say "Bethlehem," a Judean village six miles south of Jerusalem. The three central participants were Mary, Joseph, and Jesus. Beyond these common features the accounts are at odds.

Matthew	*Luke*
Mary and Joseph live in *Bethlehem* (2:1)	Mary and Joseph live in *Nazareth* (2:4)
	The two travel to Bethlehem in connection with Roman census (2:4–5)
Jesus born in *Joseph's house* (2:11)	No room in the inn; Jesus placed in a *manger* (2:6–7)
King Herod learns of Jesus' birth; consults star-guided wise men (2:3–7)	
Wise men from East visit Babe; warned in a dream to take different route home (2:8–12)	*Shepherds* from nearby fields visit Babe (2:8–19)
	Jesus circumcised on eighth day and given name (2:21)
Joseph warned; flight into Egypt (2:13–15)	
Herod slaughters innocent children (2:16–18)	
Herod dies; angel tells Joseph to return (2:19–20)	
Family heads toward Bethlehem; Archelaus' reputation and a dream divert them *to a new home, Nazareth* (2:21–23)	Family *returns* to their home in *Nazareth* (2:22–40)

[23]Mt. 1:18–25; Lk. 2:1–20.

The common witness of Matthew and Luke that Jesus was born in Bethlehem has been questioned. Some scholars are convinced that Nazareth was the place of his birth. (1) Aside from Matthew and Luke, evidence to support the Bethlehem birth is hard to come by. (2) The Gospels speak of Jesus as the Nazarene (Mt. 2:23) and Jesus of Nazareth (Mk. 1:24; Lk. 4:34; Jn. 1:45). Then, as now, a person was identified according to the place of his birth, not his residence. The official Roman inscription on the cross read "Jesus of Nazareth" (Jn. 19:19). His early followers were called Nazarenes (Acts 24:5). (3) When Jesus was rejected at Nazareth, he said, "A prophet is not without honor, except in his own country" (Mk. 6:4). The Greek word for "country" may mean either one's ancestral home or his birthplace. Joseph was a descendant of David, so Jesus' ancestral home was Bethlehem. The only sense in which Nazareth could be called Jesus' "country" would be that he was born there.[24] (4) Jesus was reared in Nazareth, an obscure

A modern pilgrim to Bethlehem can see this street scene in "the city of David," traditional birthplace of Jesus (Lk. 2:4–7).

---

[24]Philo of Alexandria, however, did call Jerusalem his *patris*. See Robert M. Grant, *A Historical Introduction to the New Testament* (New York: Harper & Row, Publishers, Inc., 1963), pp. 276, 303.

village with no Messianic associations. (5) Matthew and Luke have legendary elements in their nativity narratives. (6) The stories that Jesus was born in Bethlehem arose after Jesus had been acknowledged to be the Messiah. They were undoubtedly designed to provide him with the proper credentials. The Scriptures had foretold that the Messiah would come from Bethlehem. (7) A betrothed woman would have lived with her parents. Under no circumstances would she have traveled alone with her intended from Nazareth to Bethlehem.

The arguments for Jesus' birth at Nazareth are impressive. Nevertheless, they have not won the overwhelming support of scholars. It is a serious matter to doubt the double witness of Matthew and Luke. If Jesus was born at Nazareth, no historical credence can be given to the story of the virgin birth and its attendant circumstances. The Nazareth nativity has not caught the fancy of laymen either. In the absence of convincing disproof, most Christians continued to regard Bethlehem as the birthplace of Jesus "of Nazareth."

Just where in Bethlehem Jesus was born is not indicated. Luke states that there was no room in the "inn." The location of this crowded inn is unknown. The place of last resort, in which the baby was laid, was a "manger." Christian imaginations have viewed it as part of a stable or of a house where animals were kept. Actually it was a feeding trough and might have been out in the open air conveniently located for the shepherds

A priest prays before the rock-cut recess under the choir of the ancient basilica in Bethlehem. In the background, according to tradition, is the manger in which the infant Jesus lay. The place of Jesus' birth is marked by a star and bears the inscription (in Latin), "Here Jesus Christ was born of the Virgin Mary."

whose flocks roamed the nearby hills. Second-century tradition focused on a cave as the birthplace of Jesus. Constantine erected a great basilica over the cave in the fourth century. Many alterations were made in the ages that followed. In the twelfth century the church was completely restored by the Crusaders. Today the proprietorship of the Church of the Nativity is shared by the Latin, Greek, and Armenian Communions. The Cave of the Nativity, which is located under the choir of the ancient basilica, contains a rock-cut recess. In the recess modern pilgrims may view the manger believed by many to be the place where the baby Jesus lay.

When was Jesus born? Any Sunday School student knows that it was on December 25 in the year 1. What he doesn't know is that December 25 was first suggested by Hippolytus about 200 A.D. In the early part of the third century, some parts of the church celebrated January 6 as Jesus' birthday, a practice continued by Eastern Orthodoxy today. After long uncertainty the day of December 25 was finally fixed in Rome in the first quarter of the fourth century. It was the date of the winter solstice (according to the Julian calendar) and had long been the occasion of a pagan festival connected with the rebirth of various solar deities. The year 1 A.D., chosen by a Roman monk named Dionysius Exiguus in the sixth century, was based on a miscalculation.

Matthew furnishes three references which help to establish the year of Jesus' birth. (1) Jesus was born "in the days of Herod the king" (2:1). The Herod mentioned is Herod the Great, who died in 4 B.C. (2) Herod, in a vain effort to eliminate the Messiah, "killed all the male children in Bethlehem and in all that region who were two years old or under" (2:16). This would place Jesus' birth sometime during 6–4 B.C. (3) The "star in the East" (2:2) may refer to the close conjunction of Jupiter and Saturn which, according to Kepler and other astronomers, occurred three times in 7 B.C. (The flight into Egypt and the Egyptian residence—2:13–14, 19–21— furnish no help since they are without any indication of time and length.)

Matthew's references have led most scholars to fix the birth of Jesus sometime during the years 8–4 B.C. The picture is clouded, however, by Luke's reference to a census: "In those days a decree went out from Caesar Augustus that all the world should be enrolled. This was the first enrollment, when Quirinius was governor of Syria. And all went to be enrolled, each to his own city. And Joseph also went up from Galilee, from the city of Nazareth, to Judea, to the city of David, which is called Bethlehem, because he was of the house and lineage of David, to be enrolled with Mary, his betrothed, who was with child" (2:1–5).

There is no evidence outside of Luke that an empire-wide census took place near the time of Jesus' birth. Since Herod the Great was a native Jewish ruler, it is unlikely that Augustus would have ordered a census in his territory although he clearly had the power to do so. There was an imperial enrollment in Palestine in 6 A.D. when Quirinius was governor of Syria (6–9 A.D.). But this is too late a date for the birth of Jesus. By then the political conditions had changed markedly. Archelaus had been banished and Judea had been placed under a Roman procurator. The census was resented as an act of imperial tyranny. It sparked a rebellion headed by Judas of Galilee (Acts 5:37). Josephus, our primary authority on this matter, implies that this census was the first enrollment.[24] If there had been one prior to this, the second would probably not have been so bitterly resisted.

Many ingenious efforts have been made to defend Luke's accuracy of dating. The most convincing case has been marshaled by Sir William Ramsay.[25] An inscription, found in 1912, named Quirinius chief magistrate of Antioch. Ramsay dated the inscription 10–7 B.C. Saturninus Varus was governor of Syria from 9–4 B.C. Quirinius, argued Ramsay, held a position of authority in Syria while Varus was governor. It was under Quirinius in 8–6 B.C. that the first enrollment took place. It was not for the purpose of taxation but for enumeration and a pledge of loyalty.[26] Quirinius held office a second time in Syria (this time as governor) in 6–9 A.D. Attractive as Ramsay's arguments are, many scholars hold that they fall short of demonstration.

Who visited the newborn babe in Bethlehem? Luke tells of shepherds who went to Bethlehem to verify the angels' announcement of the Savior's birth (2:8–20). When they publicly made known their experience, all who heard it were astonished, except Mary who had been prepared for all that had happened.[27] Matthew, on the other hand, knows nothing about shepherds but much about "wise men from the East" (2:1–12). These Magi were probably Babylonian astrologers or Zoroastrian priests. Astrology had originated in Babylonia many centuries before Christ. Astrologers "read" the stars and predicted eclipses. They also forecast human events such as the birth and death of princes. That some Babylonian astrologers should conclude from their study that a great personage would be born in Palestine was not at all unlikely. When they informed Herod of their mission, he assembled the Sanhedrin in order to inquire of them where the Christ was to be born. They told him, "In Bethlehem of Judea" (2:5). Herod relayed the message to the Magi and asked them "what *time* the star [had] appeared."[28] His question had astrological significance; and the answer would also enable him to determine the age of the child. The Magi departed with instructions from Herod to bring him word when they had found the child so that he could go and worship him. The star "went before them, till it came to rest over the place where the child was" (2:9).

Some people take the account of the star quite literally. They believe

[24]*Wars*, II, 8,1; VII, 8,1.

[25]Sir William Ramsay, *Was Christ Born at Bethlehem?* (London: Hodder and Stoughton, 1898), pp. 241–47; and Sir William Ramsay, *The Bearing of Recent Discoveries on the Trustworthiness of the New Testament* (London: Hodder and Stoughton, 1915), pp. 222–300. For a critique of Ramsay's position see Samuel Sandmel, "Quirinius," in *The Interpreter's Dictionary of the Bible*, ed. George A. Buttrick (New York: Abingdon Press, 1962), K–Q, 975–77.

[26]A census conducted for the purpose of raising taxes on property would probably have been taken at a man's residence, not at his ancestral home—contrary to Lk. 2:4–6. "The Roman state was interested in a man's property, not in his pedigree" (Gilmour, in *The Interpreter's Bible*, VIII, 50).

[27]If Jesus' mission as "Savior, who is Christ the Lord" was as well attested at his birth as Luke indicates, how can the later attitude of his parents (2:50) and fellow townsmen (4:22) be explained?

[28]Mt. 2:7, emphasis added.

that the beam of light which pulsated from it was so perfectly focused that it illumined the temporary residence of Joseph and Mary and no other. They ground their conviction both in the omnipotence of God and in scientific reckonings. Halley's comet passed over the perihelion in 12 B.C., and Jupiter and Saturn were in close conjunction three times in 7 B.C. Other people discount the star's astronomical behavior and center on its astrological significance for the Babylonian visitors. Still others think of the star as the poet's way of expressing divine guidance.

The gifts the Magi offered the Bethlehem babe were typically eastern—gold, frankincense, and myrrh. No symbolism was intended. They were simply appropriate presents for a king. Later, Christian tradition came to regard the gifts as symbolic. Gold symbolized Christ's royalty, incense his priesthood, and myrrh his death. No mention is made in Matthew of the number or the station of the Magi; but legend quickly filled this void. It limited the Magi to three (inferred from the number of gifts) and crowned them kings—Melchior from Persia, Gaspar from India, and Balthasar from Arabia.[29]

After the Magi had presented their gifts, they were "warned in a dream not to return to Herod" (2:12). The Greek word for "warned" means "to be instructed by an oracle." So they bypassed Herod, departing to their own country another way.

Circumcision, Purification, and Presentation[30]

Eight days after the nativity, the pious parents of the Bethlehem babe had him circumcised in conformity with the requirements of the Law.[31] The sacred rite of circumcision not only put off "the body of flesh"[32] (the lower nature) but also initiated the infant male into the covenant community of Israel. Henceforth he would be the recipient of its blessings and subject to its responsibilities. For a Messiah not to have been thus linked with the people of the promise would have been unthinkable.

The name given to the infant was "Jesus." It was a common name. It was the Greek equivalent of the Semitic name, "Joshua." Both meant "the Lord is salvation." Luke reminds us that the name had actually been given to the child prior to his conception by the angel Gabriel (1:31).

For seven days after Jesus' birth Mary was considered "unclean" (Lev. 12:2). For thirty-three additional days she was required to remain in ceremonial isolation (Lev. 12:4).[33] At the close of the forty-day period of confinement Mary, Joseph, and Jesus left Bethlehem for Jerusalem. They made the journey to enable Mary to participate in a Temple service which would terminate her uncleanness. A wealthy woman was required to bring to the

---

[29]Perhaps the legend was rooted in Is. 60:6 and Ps. 72:10. See S. V. McCasland, "Magi," in *The Interpreter's Dictionary of the Bible,* ed. George A. Buttrick (New York: Abingdon Press, 1962), K–Q, 221–23.

[30]Lk. 2:21–40.

[31]Leviticus 12:3.

[32]Col. 2:11.

[33]The birth of a girl doubled both periods of confinement (Lev. 12:5).

priest a lamb and a young pigeon or turtledove. A poor mother like Mary was permitted to bring two turtledoves or two young pigeons, one for a burnt offering and one for a sin offering.

The reading of Lk. 2:22 ("And when the time came for their purification") has provoked endless comment. Whose purification? Scholars are divided. Some say "Mary and Joseph." This view is said to be justified by the context: "And when the time came for *their* purification ... *they* brought him up to Jerusalem."[34] But why would *Joseph* need to be purified? Others say "Mary and her babe" are plainly implied.[35] But why would *Jesus* require purification? The Jewish ceremony involved only the mother (Lev. 12:6). Evidence for this practice is found in later manuscripts, where the text has been changed from "their" purification to "her" purification. If Jesus was included in the purification ceremony, a serious problem exists for those who hold that the transmission of human guilt (inherited from Adam) was broken for Jesus by the virgin birth.

Luke interrupts the story of the purification with an account of the presentation (2:22b–23). Actually the two rites were separate in Judaism. Like Hannah before her (I Samuel 1), Mary presented her child to the Lord in recognition that it was from the Lord that she had received him. In Israel every first-born male belonged to the Lord (Ex. 13:2). But the child could be redeemed from the Lord by a substitute offering (Ex. 13:13). Luke omits any mention of this. The offering referred to in 2:24 was for Mary's purification. It had nothing to do with the ransom of the first-born.

At the time of the presentation[36] two aged saints, who had been waiting for the Messiah to come to redeem Israel, recognized Jesus through the help of the Holy Spirit. Simeon took the child in his arms, blessed God, and uttered the Nunc Dimittis (Lk. 2:29–32). The psalm expressed his willingness to die, now that he had seen in the babe the salvation intended for all peoples, both Gentile and Jewish.[37] He then blessed the parents and predicted that the babe would separate the righteous from the unrighteous and that Mary would grieve at the tragic fate of her son. Anna also hailed the advent of God's Messiah.

Flight to Egypt, Massacre, and Return[38]

Egypt had once been a refuge, then a house of bondage for the Hebrews. In the first century it was friendly. It included the Sinai peninsula, the nearest part of which was not far from Bethlehem. Only Matthew mentions the flight of Mary, Joseph, and Jesus from Bethlehem to Egypt. It has been suggested that Matthew's story was created to refute Jewish charges

[34]Emphasis added. See Alfred Plummer, *The Gospel According to St. Luke*, 6th ed. (New York: Charles Scribner's Sons, 1903), p. 63.

[35]Major, in *The Mission and Message of Jesus*, p. 269.

[36]"To do for him according to the custom of the law" (2:27) must refer to the rite of presentation, since the child was not involved in the purification ceremony.

[37]The astonishment that Mary and Joseph expressed at Simeon's declaration indicates that (1) they were unaware that their son was to be God's Messiah or (2) they were surprised that Jesus would be the savior of Gentiles as well as Jews.

[38]Mt. 2:13–23.

that Jesus worked in Egypt, learned magic, and later used his acquired skills to support his claim to divinity. The story of the flight acknowledged that Jesus was in Egypt. But it placed him there in response to a divinely initiated dream, and it removed him from the country long before he was old enough to receive instructions from its magicians. Coptic priests in Cairo are far from convinced that the story was manufactured. With pride they point out to pilgrims where the baby Jesus lay.

No indication is given as to how long the family stayed in Egypt. Presumably it was only a matter of months. When Herod died in 4 B.C. an angel instructed Joseph to return with his family to Israel. Matthew's characteristically strong stress on the fulfillment of prophecy prompts him to quote from Hosea 11:1 ("Out of Egypt I called my son") in connection with the family's exodus. But the prophecy was not literally fulfilled by Jesus' return from Egypt. Hosea spoke in the past tense and referred to a past historical event, the Exodus. Israel is often spoken of in the Old Testament as the Lord's "son."

Herod's initial impulse had been to kill Mary's child only. But when he discovered that he had been tricked by the wise men, he resorted to more truculent measures. He killed "all the male children in Bethlehem and in all that region who were two years old or under, according to the time which he had ascertained from the wise men" (Mt. 2:16).

Could Herod have massacred so many children in Bethlehem and its environs? He certainly could. Any man who could murder his mother-in-law, his beloved wife, and three of his sons (and innumerable others) was capable of such a dastardly deed. In a play on Greek words, Augustus remarked that he would rather be Herod's sow than his son. Yet, outside of Matthew there is no historical evidence that any slaughter of babies in Bethlehem took place. Matthew saw the massacre as a fulfillment of Jeremiah's prophecy (31:15) concerning Rachel; however, Jeremiah actually makes no reference whatsoever to the *slaughter* of children. His words concern Nebuchadnezzar's captives from Jerusalem. As they travel along the road past Ramah on their way into Babylonian captivity, Rachel, a mother in Israel, is described as standing by the roadside weeping for her children who are being driven into exile.

When Jesus' parents returned to Palestine, they quickly discovered that Herod's demise was not an unmixed blessing. His cruel and despotic eldest son, Archelaus, now ruled over Judea (4 B.C.–6 A.D.). Fear and faith in a divinely dispatched dream prompted the parents to withdraw to the district of Galilee and to settle down in the city of Nazareth. As Matthew relates the account, no hint is given that Mary and Joseph had ever laid eyes on Nazareth before. They had not (in contrast with Luke's account) gone from Nazareth to Bethlehem before Jesus' birth. Nor were they now *returning* to Nazareth. Matthew apparently assumes that Bethlehem was the native city of Joseph, a descendant of David, and Mary, his wife. The young couple would have returned to Bethlehem from Egypt had Archelaus not been the ruler of Judea. To escape his rule they switched plans and located in Nazareth. This unpremeditated change made possible a fulfillment of prophecy: "He shall be called a Nazarene" (2:23).

Matthew's reference to this Old Testament prediction has caused much difficulty. "There is no Old Testament oracle which affirms that the Messiah, or indeed anyone else, shall be called the Nazarene."[39] Jewish writers were fond of puns. Matthew may have been indulging in a play on words. His allusion may be to Judges 13:5 ("The boy shall be a Nazirite") or to Isaiah 11:1 ("There shall come forth a shoot from the stump of Jesse, and a branch shall grow out of his roots"). In this case, Matthew's meaning would be that the prophecy should be understood as saying *noçrî* (Nazarene) rather than *nâzîr* (Nazirite) or *nēçer* (branch).

Matthew's account of Jesus' escape from Herod, his sojourn in Egypt, and his return to Palestine has a striking parallel in the story of Moses, Israel's greatest son. Moses' birth was also marked by a massacre of babies. Through God's help he escaped the wrath of the vengeful Pharaoh, and after a prolonged sojourn in the wilderness he led his people to the threshold of a new life in Canaan. This parallel between the stories of Jesus and Moses is more than coincidence, for Matthew viewed Jesus as a second and greater Moses.

Manner of Jesus' Birth

At this point in our study we have considered all of the gospel material related to Jesus' nativity. Now we shall summarize the principal data for and against the virgin birth.

For:

1. Both Matthew and Luke report the virgin birth. They not only report Jesus' supernatural generation, but they give the impression that their authors personally believed in the miracle.
2. Christian tradition and belief support the virgin birth. As Matthew and Luke indicate, accounts of the virgin birth circulated at an early date and were widely believed. The virgin birth was incorporated in the Apostles' Creed. For Roman Catholic and Orthodox Christians it is a necessary article of faith, as it is a personal article of faith for many Protestants. Perhaps eighty percent of all Christians believe in the virgin birth.
3. The purification of Mary (and Jesus) described in Luke 2:21–22 was a concession to custom and implied no prior sin or uncleanness for the Virgin Mary or her son.
4. Matthew traces Jesus' *legal* descent, Luke his *natural* descent. Hence the genealogies are not in conflict.
5. The fact that Jesus and early New Testament writers never mention the virgin birth proves nothing. Some of the most profound and deeply-held beliefs are not publicly articulated. The mere fact that they are not proclaimed does not mean that they are not held.
6. All things are possible with God. Surely the Creator and Sustainer of all life could cause a virgin to conceive if He willed to do so.

Against:

1. In the Hebrew, Isaiah 7:14 does not predict that the Messiah will be born of a virgin. Matthew quotes from the Septuagint, a Greek translation of the

[39]Major, in *The Mission and Message of Jesus*, p. 237.

Hebrew. The Septuagint incorrectly translates the Hebrew word *'almāh* (young woman) by *parthenos* (virgin). Other Greek versions translate *'almāh* by *neanis* (young woman).

2. Luke 1:34 ("How can this be, since I have no husband?") was added to the text to avoid conflict with the then current story of the virgin birth.

3. The virgin birth removes the basis for the purification (Lk. 2:21–22).

4. If Jesus was born of a virgin, the genealogies are pointless. Both trace the line of Jesus through Joseph. To trace Jesus' line through Mary would prove to the people that Jesus was not the Messiah, since the Messiah was to be "of David" and Mary was "of Levi" (Lk. 1:36). Moreover, the genealogies are in hopeless conflict. How, for example, can one man be the son of two brothers, Nathan and Solomon?

5. The earliest New Testament writings (Paul's letters) and the earliest Gospel (Mark) do not mention the virgin birth. Jesus did not make belief in it a condition of discipleship. The first preaching about Jesus (the kerygma) does not mention it. Indeed, the nativity narratives are confined to the first two chapters of Matthew and Luke, and neither of these Gospels ever refers back to them. If the twenty-seven books of the New Testament had originally circulated as one book, the failure of twenty-five of them to deal with the nativity would be understandable. But since each book originally circulated independently, it is clear that for the earliest Christians the virgin birth was either nonexistent or unimportant.

6. Supernatural and virgin birth stories abound in the scriptures of other religions. Buddha was a preexistent heavenly being who, in connection with the prophetic dream of a queen, became the queen's first-born child when she was forty-five years old. Zoroaster's mother was supernaturally "glorified" when she was an unmarried woman of fifteen. Mahavira (founder of Jainism), a preexistent being, was supernaturally placed in his mother's womb in fulfillment of fourteen wonderful prophetic dreams. Lao-tze (founder of Taoism) was born a fully-matured and wise philosopher. His mother, who had the longest pregnancy on record, carried him in her womb for seventy-two or eighty-four years (according to different traditions). How does Jesus' virgin birth differ from others?

What, then, can be concluded concerning the virgin birth of Jesus? Was it fact or fancy? In their answers to this question, faithful and informed Christians differ. For many, the virgin birth is entirely congruous with the New Testament portrait of Christ. It was "a fitting preface to a life which was crowned by resurrection from the dead."[40] For others the virgin birth has a basis in spiritual truth but not in physical fact. The manhood of Jesus depended on a normal conception and birth. His sinlessness was unrelated to the manner of his birth; it depended on his decision to conform to the will of God. The supreme miracle "was the actual entrance into the world of one who in his mind and spirit completely expressed and embodied the reality of God."[41] The truth embodied in the virgin birth is the wonderful and mysterious paradox of Christ's simultaneous humanity and divinity.

[40]Hunter, *The Work and Words of Jesus*, p. 30.

[41]Walter Russell Bowie, "Exposition, The Gospel According to St. Luke," in George Arthur Buttrick, ed., *The Interpreter's Bible* (New York and Nashville: Abingdon Press, © 1952), VIII, 39.

chapter nine

Growth Toward Greatness

The early church seems to have been singularly uninterested in the life of Jesus prior to his public ministry. It preserved only one incident connected with his boyhood.[1] Aside from this, the early part of his life was hidden by thirty years of silence. We have seen how later Christians attempted to compensate for this deficiency in the Gospels.[2] They gave free reign to their imaginations to pierce the silence and produce a boy wonder who was at once marvelous and grotesque.

Today information concerning Jesus' early years is not limited to Luke's account of him in the Temple at the age of twelve. Neither is it based on the pious speculation of later legends. A reasonably accurate reconstruction of Jesus' boyhood can be made on the foundation of known facts about life in first-century Palestine. What was Nazareth like? What kind of home life and education prevailed? What languages were spoken? The answers to these questions lead us as close to the boy Jesus as it is possible to come. The place of judicious conjecture in such a reconstruction is acknowledged, since what was true of life in general may not have been true of Mary's and Joseph's family. Nevertheless, a study of the known and carefully conjectured life of Nazareth in the first century will shed valuable light on the boyhood of Jesus and his subsequent mission and message.

[1]Lk. 2:41–52.
[2]Chapter five.

Nazareth, a saucer-shaped depression halfway up the slopes of the Galilean hills, was the city of Jesus' boyhood and youth and the scene of his labor as a carpenter.

City without Hope

Nazareth was a nonentity. It is not mentioned in the Old Testament, in the writings of Josephus, or in the Talmud. Nathanael's contemptuous phrase accurately reflects its reputation in Judea: "Can anything good come out of Nazareth?" (Jn. 1:46). No prophet had ever come from Nazareth, and none was expected from such an unlikely source: "Search and you will see that no prophet is to arise from Galilee."[3] What a strange place for the home of Jesus!

Nazareth, however, did have some positive features. The city lay in a saucer-like depression halfway up the slopes of the Galilean hills, but its isolation was more apparent than real. From the southern rim of the saucer one could see thirty miles in three directions. Below lay the fertile Valley of Esdraelon, a virtual map of Old Testament history. Across Esdraelon, opposite to Nazareth, "there emerged from the Samarian hills the road from Jerusalem, thronged annually with pilgrims, and the road from Egypt with its merchants going up and down."[4] To the north of Nazareth a trail, which could be traversed in thirty minutes, led to the main east-west road

[3]Jn. 7:52. Actually Galilee did have a prophet—Jonah, son of Amittai, who came from Gath-helpher of Zebulon, a short walk from Nazareth on the road to Cana.
[4]George Adam Smith, *The Historical Geography of the Holy Land*, 14th ed. (New York: A. C. Armstrong and Son, 1908), p. 433. Reprinted by permission of Harper & Row, Publishers, Inc.

The Church of Joseph in Nazareth is believed to be on the site of Joseph's carpentry shop, beneath which was "the home of the Holy Family," pictured here.

of Lower Galilee. Barely three miles from this road lay Sepphoris, the Big City of Jesus' boyhood. Sepphoris was destroyed by the Romans when Jesus was a lad of about ten. In his young manhood it was refounded by Herod Antipas as a Greek city and was made the capital of Galilee. Jesus may have been one of the carpenters who helped to rebuild it.

Home

To see what Jesus' home probably looked like, one needs only to visit Nazareth today. Houses there have changed little during the centuries. The Gospels also give us many helpful hints. Houses on the plains might be made from clay dug from a nearby pit and molded into large bricks which were baked in the sun. Clay was inexpensive, and it provided excellent insulation against the heat of summer and cold of winter. In Nazareth, however, the cheapest building material was stone. Rough stones were picked up from the fields and laid on a foundation of slightly squared blocks to form the thick walls of the house. The flat roofs were constructed of poles which were stripped of their bark, covered with branches and leaves, and topped with a layer of mud to shed the rain. A small window or two provided a modicum of fresh air and light, as did the wooden door when open. Houses were one-story with an outside stairway leading to the roof. The roof's flat expanse did triple duty. It served as a fruit-drying furnace in the daytime, a social center in the cool of the evening, and a fresh-air dormitory during the summer nights.

The interior of a Nazareth home was usually one large room constructed on two levels. The upper level was used by the family, and the lower level by the animals. In exchange for the protection provided by the house, the animals furnished heat for the home. This heat was supplemented during the winter months by a small charcoal brazier or open fireplace. Food was cooked outside when the weather permitted. It was served on a wooden platter or metal tray which was set down on the floor or on a low table. In the better homes people reclined on couches to eat, but in the poorer homes they simply squatted on the floor. Their hands and feet were washed before eating. Since fingers substituted for cutlery, their hands required another cleansing afterwards.

Only two meals were eaten daily. Dinner, which corresponded to our luncheon, was served at noon. The main meal was supper. It was eaten after sundown when the day's work had been completed (Lk. 17:7–8). If breakfast was eaten, it was an informal meal consisting only of bread and oil or butter. The foundation food was bread—barley for the poor, wheat for the fortunate. Bread was such an important article of diet that it became a Semitic symbol for all food: "Give us this day our daily bread" (Mt. 6:11). Bread was made from grain grown in the nearby fields. Women ground the grain into flour with a primitive stone mill located in the courtyard. The flour was poured into a stone mixing bowl, water was added, and the contents kneaded into dough. Leaven or yeast was "hidden" in the dough, the dough was covered, put in a warm place, and allowed to ferment "till it was all leavened" (Lk. 13:21). Then the dough was shaped into round, thin, flat cakes, plastered on the side of a large clay oven preheated by coals, and baked into bread.

Other foods served along with the bread were a vegetable or two from the garden, fruit from the orchard (olives, grapes, figs, dates), clabbered goat's milk, perhaps a bit of cheese, and sometimes a relish of fish from the Sea of Galilee. Meat was a luxury restricted to weddings and feast days when mutton, poultry, or goat would be served. Pork was prohibited, of course, except for the heathen. The beverage was ordinarily water from Nazareth's gushing spring. Morning and evening the women walked to the spring and returned with enormous jars of water on their heads. This method of transporting water gave them a magnificent carriage. Wine was also drunk, but sparingly in the poorer homes. It was kept in skin bottles, made brittle from long use. When new wine was poured into them and it began to ferment, they often burst (Mt. 9:17). The wine was made from grapes raised on the slopes and crushed by the feet of youths and maidens in the local winepresses.

Furniture was scant and of simple design. There was a saucer-shaped lamp made of clay, which could give light to all in the house or be hidden under a bushel (meal-tub). Chairs were not needed, since visitors could squat or recline on rugs and piled-up cushions. Bedsteads were uncommon. At night a mat was spread on bright-colored rugs of local manufacture which covered the hard clay floor. Over the mat was placed a quilt, and over the sleeper a covering of wool or skins for warmth. When Jesus commanded the infirm man to "rise, take up your pallet, and walk" (Jn. 5:8), he was not expecting a man who had a moment ago been a cripple to shoulder a western-style bed. This man had only to pick up his bed roll and carry it with him.

Three basic articles of clothing were worn in Nazareth—a coat, a cloak, and sandals. The coat was a long undergarment with sleeves. It was made from cotton, linen, or wool and resembled a modern dressing gown. It was drawn tightly around the body with the edges overlapping each other in front. At the waist it was held in place by a girdle which doubled as a lunch basket and money belt. When its owner was at work or on a journey, the coat would be tucked up into the girdle to permit freedom of movement. A poor man might own several coats. They would be needed to provide for a change. But he would probably have only one cloak. The cloak was a long, loose-fitting outer garment worn open at the front. It was worn over the coat by day and used as a blanket at night. It was sometimes taken as security for a debt; but the Law thoughtfully required that it be returned before sunset: "If ever you take your neighbor's garment in pledge, you shall restore it to him before the sun goes down; for that is his only covering, it is his mantle for his body; in what else shall he sleep?" (Ex. 22:26–27). On festive occasions the wealthy wore a silk robe in place of the cloak. It was this "best robe" that the forgiving father placed on the shoulders of his prodigal son (Lk. 15:22). Sandals of leather or wood were worn. The exposed feet were soon soiled. A good host never failed to provide his guests with water with which to wash their feet (Lk. 7:44).

In some such home as we have described Jesus was reared. It was not, so far as we can tell, smitten by abject poverty. Neither was it rich. It was the kind of home where the discovery of a lost coin brought great rejoicing (Lk. 15:8–9); where clothes were scarce, protected from moths (Mt. 6:19), and plentifully patched (Mt. 9:16); where new wine was an enemy of old wineskins (Mt. 9:17); and where a lad soon learned that if he asked his father for a fish he would not be given a serpent (Mt. 7:10).

Family

When Jesus returned to Nazareth during an early phase of his ministry, according to the Synoptics, his fellow townsmen were astonished at his teaching in their synagogue. They could not comprehend how a local product, lacking in rabbinical training, could speak with such wisdom and perform with such power. Incredulously they asked one another, "Is not this the carpenter's son? Is not his mother called Mary? And are not his brothers James and Joseph and Simon and Judas? And are not all his sisters with us?"[5] According to the Gospels, then, Jesus had four brothers and at least two sisters. He was reared in a family with a minimum of nine people.

The Greek word which is translated "brothers" was not as precise in meaning as we might think. It could include relatives who were beyond the closest blood ties. This fact, combined with the faith of many third- and fourth-century Christians in the perpetual virginity of Mary, produced two explanatory theories: (1) Epiphanius (*c.* 315–403 A.D.), bishop of the eastern Greek church in Cyprus, declared that Jesus' "brothers" were sons of Joseph by a previous marriage; (2) Jerome (*c.* 340 420 A.D.), saintly scholar of the western Latin church and author of the Vulgate, suggested that the "brothers" were cousins, sons of another Mary (Mt. 27:56). Both theories support the perpetual virginity of Mary, but their Biblical basis is suspect.

Jesus was Mary's first-born child (Mt. 1:25). If Mary was not a perpetual virgin, then Jesus' brothers and sisters were younger than he. The brothers did not believe in Jesus during his earthly career, but at least two of them became posthumous followers. James reportedly exercised decisive leadership in the Jerusalem church (Acts 15:13–21), and James and Jude (or Judas) are credited with the authorship of two New Testament epistles.

Jesus' father does not appear in the gospel record after the Temple visit when Jesus was aged twelve. An ancient and well-attested tradition indicates that Joseph died during Jesus' youth. If this was true, then Mary's first-born son became the breadwinner and family head at an early age.

Languages

Hebrew was a dead language for most first-century Palestinians. The rabbis and learned scribes had a practiced command of it. Jesus knew it well enough to read from a Hebrew scroll in the synagogue in Nazareth (Lk. 4:16–19). But the Palestinian's mother tongue was Aramaic, a Semitic language related to Hebrew. So strange had Hebrew become that the Law was read in the synagogues in Hebrew and was then recited in an Aramaic paraphrase (Targum) so the congregation could comprehend it. In addition to Aramaic, Greek was also widely understood. This was especially true in "Galilee of the Gentiles" in which Nazareth was located. Palestinians learned the common Greek of commerce for the same reason that the people of the Middle East learn English today. Bilingualism was an economic necessity in the marketplace. We may confidently conclude, then, that Jesus was trilingual. He read and spoke Aramaic fluently. He knew Hebrew well enough to read it in public. He had a carpenter's command of common Greek.

[5]Mt. 13:55–56. See *Gospel Parallels,* 2nd rev. ed. (New York: Thomas Nelson & Sons, 1957), sections 10 and 89. Many modern commentators have identified his mother and brothers (Mk. 3:32) with "his friends" (Mk. 3:21) and have thus provided a motive for the visit in Mk. 3:31–35.

Education

Joseph provided Jesus with his early education. The Law commanded every pious father to teach his sons the Shema: "Hear, O Israel: The Lord our God is one Lord; and you shall love the Lord your God with all your heart, and with all your soul, and with all your might. And these words . . . you shall teach . . . diligently to your children, and shall talk of them when you sit in your house, and when you walk by the way, and when you lie down, and when you rise" (Deut. 6:4–7).

Did Jesus attend a synagogue school in Nazareth? Some scholars declare that he did. "In the period after the return from the Babylonian exile the synagogue system provided, in every Jewish community of any size, a synagogue school in which all male children were taught the Law."[6] Others deny it. "Jesus could have had no formal education. Public schools for the study of the Bible had . . . been established some decades before his birth, but they were confined to Jerusalem; it was decades after his death before they were extended to the countryside."[7]

Whether at home or in school, Jesus learned the first century Palestinian equivalent of the "three R's" in Aramaic. He also learned Hebrew, not too difficult a task for one who knew Aramaic. He absorbed common Greek by "osmosis." Jesus could not have read his Bible at home. The sacred scrolls of Scripture were scarce and prohibitive in price. It is unlikely that his father could have afforded even a fragment. Jesus' knowledge of his people's Scripture was doubtless acquired by attendance at the synagogue services Sabbath after Sabbath. Like his fellow Galileans he probably depended largely on the Aramaic paraphrases of the Hebrew. Certain Biblical books seem to have spoken to him with peculiar power—Deuteronomy, Psalms, Isaiah, and Daniel. An alert mind and a retentive memory, unspoiled by dependence on written records, enabled him to remember what he heard. In addition to the Bible, he seems to have been acquainted with the wisdom of Ahiqar, Tobit, and the Testaments of the Twelve Patriarchs.[8]

Joseph taught Jesus a trade. Custom decreed that the eldest son should follow the occupation of his father. So Jesus, like Joseph, became a carpenter (Mk. 6:3), as Justin Martyr (*Dialogue with Trypho*, 88) indicates. His tools included a hammer, chisel, saw, and plane. He doubtless made handles for hoes and flails, yoke for oxen, crude plows with small iron shares and single handles (Lk. 9:62), and wooden tables and doors. It is unlikely that all his working hours were spent in the carpenter shop. He probably labored on construction projects in Nazareth and perhaps in

[6]Major, in *The Mission and Message of Jesus*, p. 271. See also Hunter, *The Work and Words of Jesus*, p. 31; Charles M. Laymon, *The Life and Teachings of Jesus* (New York and Nashville: Abingdon Press, 1955), p. 76.

[7]A. T. Olmstead, *Jesus in the Light of History* (New York: Charles Scribner's Sons, 1942), p. 12.

[8]See Olmstead, *Jesus in the Light of History*, pp. 15–20.

nearby communities. In later years the marks of his trade were still with him. His speech was sprinkled with figures from the carpenter shop. He spoke of specks which irritate the eyes and logs that blind them (Mt. 7:5), a house foolishly built on sand and another solidly built on rock (Lk. 6:46–49), the futility of anxiously attempting to add a cubit to one's span of life (Mt. 6:27), and the difference between conduct "when the wood is green" and "when it is dry" (Lk. 23:31).

Jesus was taught by nature. His parables and sayings make this abundantly clear.

> He spoke of grass, and wind, and rain,
> And fig-trees, and fair weather,
> And made it His delight to bring
> Heaven and earth together.[9]

Jesus was taught by human experience. His perceptive and profound insights into human nature did not suddenly spring to life when he was thirty. They were the product of a mind and spirit long attuned to the human scene. The characters that populate his parables were doubtless drawn from the crowds and closets of his youth. In Nazareth and its environs he observed the prideful Pharisee who thanked God he was not like other men, the calculating customer of creature comforts called the Dishonest Steward, the wastrel dubbed the Prodigal Son, and the self-sufficient pagan called the Unjust Judge. These and countless other characters bear convincing witness that Jesus was a straight "A" student in the school of human experience.

Son of the Law[10]

When a Jewish boy reached the age of twelve he became "a son of the Law" (*Ben-Torah*). He was then regarded as a religious adult and counted as one of the ten adult male Jews required to form a synagogue. Henceforth he was expected to discharge his religious duties and to wear the phylacteries as a reminder of his obligation to keep the Law. Among other things the Law required all adult male Jews to present themselves three times a year in the Temple—on the Feasts of Passover, Pentecost, and Tabernacles (Ex. 23:14–17; Deut. 16:6). Since the Dispersion of the Jewish people, however, distance made the requirement impractical. Most Palestinians determined to go at least once a year. Women were not obliged to make the pilgrimage, but they often did, especially at Passover.

Jesus' newly-acquired status as " a son of the Law" apparently coincided with the Feast of the Passover. When he was twelve years old, he accompanied his parents on a journey to Jerusalem. He may well have gone with

[9]Thomas Toke Lynch, in A. M. Hunter, *The Work and Words of Jesus*, p. 32.
[10]Lk. 2:41–52.

The Dome of the Rock (Mosque of Omar) in Jerusalem is located on the approximate site of the ancient Hebrew Temple. The Mosque is beautifully faced with slabs of marble and multicolored mosaics. In the foreground, Moslems are performing washings required by the Koran before worshiping. Inside the Mosque, surrounded by a railing, is a huge sacred rock on which it is said Abraham intended to sacrifice his son, Isaac. (Photograph courtesy of Dr. J. S. Robinson.)

them before, since they went "every year at the feast of the Passover" (Lk. 2:41). But this was the first trip from which he would return as an adult. The Feast of the Passover coincided with the first day of the Feast of Unleavened Bread. Taken together the two occupied a period of seven or eight days. Many pilgrims remained for only the first two days when the principal sacrifices were made. But Luke would have us understand that Mary and Joseph remained for the entire week.

When the Feasts were finished, Mary and Joseph departed for home. They traveled in a caravan made up of Nazareth neighbors. The women started first, and the men followed close behind. Small children traveled with their mothers, older ones with either group. Mary assumed that Jesus was with Joseph. Joseph thought he was with Mary. It was not until the two groups gathered at night around the open campfire near modern Ramallah that Jesus' parents discovered their error. Jesus was not in the caravan. Mary and Joseph spent the next day retracing their steps. On the third day they found Jesus in a hall of one of the outer courts of the Temple. He was busily engaged in discussion with teachers of the Law. Mary was astonished. Her motherly irritation rose quickly to the surface. "Son, why have you treated us so? Behold, your father and I have been looking for you anxiously" (2:48). Mary's words do not fit the Lucan picture of a woman who had given miraculous birth to a son and had been informed of his Messiahship before his conception.

Jesus responded to his mother's reprimand with the unstudied innocence of a twelve-year-old: "How is that you sought me? Did you not know that I must be in *my Father's* house?"[11] Pious Jews avoided all direct reference to God. Never would they have addressed Him as an intimate. The early Christians who preserved the words, "my Father's house," believed that Jesus stood in a unique filial relationship to God. This relationship permitted him to address God in the same familiar way a first-century Jew addressed his earthly father.

The Temple scene we have just described has been painted under the caption, "The Boy Jesus Teaching in the Temple." That Jesus was a perceptive and precocious youngster—a genius—is undeniable. It is doubtful, though, that he arranged the meeting with the rabbis to discover how much they knew, to correct their errors, and to supplement their knowledge from his own omniscience. If the account is regarded as historical, a better caption would be "Son of the Law Learning from the Lawyers." When Jesus returned to Nazareth he behaved as an obedient son. He *"increased* in wisdom [which he could hardly have done had he been all-wise from birth] and in stature, and in favor with God and man" (2:52).[12] Artists have painted a halo around his head, but there is no evidence that he ever wore it in Nazareth. The "hidden years" of his youth must be understood in the context of growth toward greatness. The interest of the evangelist, though, is not historical but theological. For him the setting of the incident (house= Temple) is as significant as the insight (*my* Father=intimate relationship). Both the setting and the insight (which Luke casts in the form of a legend) have symbolic significance. Jesus' awareness of his special relationship with his Father in his Father's house presages his mission. As the Father's Son, he will call the scattered children of God back to their Father's house.

11Lk. 2:49, emphasis added.
12Emphasis added.

chapter ten

Prophetic Predecessor

August 19, 14 A.D., was a portentous day. Caesar Augustus lay dead. Tiberius, his close associate for the past two years, prepared to succeed him as head of the Roman Empire. The emperorship of Tiberius was later immortalized by an obscure author who recounted the stirring story of a new religion: "In the fifteenth year of the reign of Tiberius Caesar. . . the word of God came to John the son of Zechariah in the wilderness" (Lk. 3:1–2). This reference pinpoints the beginning of the career of one of the most prominent personalities in the New Testament, John the Baptist. The "fifteenth year" is equivalent to 28 or 29 A.D.[1] It is the only fixed date in gospel chronology.

Place (1)[2]

The wilderness, scene of John's work, conjures up a false image in modern minds. It was not a region of shifting desert sand, barren rocks, or wild forest; it was a place where shepherds pastured their flocks (Lk. 15:4).

[1]If the "fifteenth year" is reckoned from the regency of Tiberius instead of from the death of Augustus (when Tiberius became sole emperor), then the year would be 26 or 27 A.D.

[2]Numbers in parentheses following the chapter subtitles, parable titles, and miracle stories refer to sections in B. H. Throckmorton, Jr., ed., *Gospel Parallels*, 2nd rev. ed. (New York: Thomas Nelson & Sons, 1957). This chapter is based upon Mt. 3:1–2; 14:1–12; Mk. 1:1–8; 6:17–29; Lk. 3:1–20. Reference to the Fourth Gospel will be made in the body of the text or in footnotes.

It was a solitary place, devoid of human habitation. There were many such isolated spots in southern Palestine.

Matthew locates John in the "wilderness of Judea" (3:1), the traditional Jewish phrase for the howling wasteland east of Jerusalem. This designation is unlikely; John would have encountered insuperable difficulties baptizing his converts there. The Fourth Gospel provides a better clue. It speaks of John baptizing at "Bethany beyond the Jordan" (1:28) and at Aenon near Salim (3:23). Archeological discoveries have made it possible to locate both places with relative certainty. Bethany (Bethabara) was a hamlet in Perea on the east bank of the Jordan not far from where travelers forded the river on their way from Jerusalem (via Jericho) to Rabbath Ammon in Transjordan. Bethany belonged to the territory of Herod Antipas, a fact of no small consequence, as we shall soon see. Aenon ("springs") was located thirty miles to the north on the west bank of the Jordan. Both sites were close to well-traveled routes and amply supplied with water. John's wilderness sojourn did not make of him a peripatetic prophet in "all the region about the Jordan" as Luke's altered source indicates (3:3). It did, however, place him in a location where he was easily accessible to many travelers. With holy hyperbole the Gospel record tells us that *"all* the country of Judea, and *all* the people of Jerusalem" (Mk. 1:5) and *"all* the region about the Jordan" (Mt. 3:5) came to him.[3]

The Monastery of John the Baptist, located in the "wilderness of Judea," marks the traditional but historically improbable place where the Baptist was active.

[3]Emphasis added. See pp. 101–102 and Willi Marxsen, *Mark the Evangelist*, pp. 30–53, where Marxsen regards "in the wilderness" (Mk. 1:4) not as a geographical but as a theological term (which Mt. and Lk. treat geographically). Marxsen believes that the Baptist tradition tells us nothing about John or baptism since it is a commentary not about John but about Christ.

Purpose

What compelled John to become a wilderness wanderer? He was of priestly descent (Lk. 1:5). He would normally have followed in his father's footsteps and become a priest. Such a career would have been dictated not only by family tradition but also by the very nature of the priestly office. God had specifically selected one of the sons of Israel (Levi) and his descendants for this sacred task. Our Gospels do not say why John turned his back on the sacred and the settled to dwell in insecurity and lonely isolation.

It has been suggested that John was in open revolt against the segment of the priestly group that lived in Jerusalem. A sharp cleavage had developed in the first-century priesthood. The Jerusalem aristocracy were addicted to bureaucracy and infected with nepotism. They demanded the lion's share of the offerings of the pious, lived in relative luxury, and looked down on their country cousins who spent most of the year in the small towns of Judea. When John applied at Jerusalem for ordination, his rural rearing would have brought him few rewards. He might well have been regarded as a country bumpkin come to claim his share of the offerings. As such, he would have been a threat to the extravagant living of the Jerusalem priests and the prospective status of their sons. In turn, John may have been repulsed by what he saw—secularized priests bent on achieving an ever higher standard of living. Their conduct could do nothing but bring the wrath of God down on them. It was a sight that would drive a sensitive soul into the wilderness.[4]

This suggestion is an attractive one. Perhaps some such circumstances as described did enter into John's vocational choice. But his drastic decision cannot have been prompted by purely negative factors. His mission and message suggest that he was a man driven by divine necessity. The forebears of his faith had found the supernatural in the wilderness—Moses in the wilderness of Sinai, Elijah in the wilderness under a broom tree (I Kings 19:4–8), Amos in the wilderness of Tekoa. So close was the relationship between the prophet and the wilderness that the dress of the prophet had become the dress of the wilderness-dweller (Zech. 13:4). When John took up residence in the wilderness, he adopted this nomadic dress. Mark, Matthew, and other New Testament writers saw in his mantle and girdle the symbols of his prophetic role and his relation to Elijah. For John the clothing was probably chosen for climatic rather than dramatic reasons. It was the customary clothing for a wilderness sojourn, and it signified no more than did his diet. Locusts and wild honey were simply the available foods in the wilderness. It was what John did in the wilderness that "eventually suggested that his garb had a greater, prophetic significance."[5]

The prophet's kinship with the wilderness was not prompted primarily

---

[4]See Carl H. Kraeling, *John the Baptist* (New York and London: Charles Scribner's Sons, 1951), to which we are indebted in our discussion of the Baptist.

[5]Kraeling, *John the Baptist*, p. 15.

by his yen for solitude. Neither was it caused primarily by his protest against the pattern of his people's lives. It was produced by his compulsive desire to receive insight and understanding in the presence of the Divine. John's solitary sojourn was a conspicuous success. He became what he had not been before—a preacher. His first audience was made up of travelers along the dusty highroads, bent on other missions. What a forbidding figure the bearded, sun-blackened prophet must have presented! In time the passers-by were joined by an ever-increasing company of people who sought John out. They were attracted not by his forbidding appearance but by his faith.

Message (1–3)

John announced the imminence of an event the Jews had long awaited —God's final universal judgment. He proclaimed the coming of a transcendent Messiah who would purge men of evil and destroy the unrepentant. His message was dressed in the fashionable garb of eschatology (the doctrine of the end of the age). He used such phrases as "the wrath to come" (Mt. 3:7) and "the ax is laid to the root of the trees" (Mt. 3:10). He pictured the heavenly Messiah with a "winnowing fork in his hand, to clear his threshing floor, and to gather the wheat into his granary; but the chaff he will burn with unquenchable fire" (Lk. 3:17). Not since the days of Malachi had a message of such fierce foreboding been preached to the people. Lest anyone mistake the prophet for the Messiah, the difference is made crystal clear. John was a mere "voice," unfit even to be a slave (i.e., untie the sandals) of the Mightier One through whom God's judgment would be executed (Lk. 3:16).

What should men do to prepare for the coming crisis? They should (1) repent of their sins and (2) behave ethically. Repentance for the Greek meant a mere change of mind. For the Jew it meant a radical reorientation of the entire person. It involved a turning away from sin and unrighteousness, a wholehearted return to the Lord, and a firm determination to follow His will. Repentance required total commitment.[6]

Repentance was a prominent feature of the Jewish religion. It was taught in every synagogue and assumed in every Temple sacrifice. Why, then, did John make such a fuss about repentance? It was because something new had been added to the religious situation. The final universal judgment of God was imminent. This faith fractured the practice of conventional religion. It made a mockery of the claims to patriarchal descent: "... for I tell you, God is able from these stones to raise up children to Abraham" (Mt. 3:9). No one was exempt from the need for repentance— not even the Jews. Only the repentant could expectantly await the coming of the Mightier One and his judgment.

What kind of behavior did John demand of his converts? Nothing very

---

[6]Only Mt. 3:2 indicates that John spoke of a coming "kingdom of heaven." It is doubtful that he used the phrase. He spoke of the coming judgment of wrath. See Kraeling, *John the Baptist*, p. 67; Hunter, *The Work and Words of Jesus*, p. 34n.

radical. Those who were blessed with surplus clothing and food were instructed to share with the less fortunate. "The poor are to help the destitute."[7] The tax collectors (who were accustomed to collecting all that the traffic would bear above and beyond the requirements of Rome and pocketing the difference) were counseled to collect no more than was appointed them (Lk. 3:13). Soldiers, strongly tempted to abuse their police power, were enjoined to eschew violence, avoid false accusation, and be content with their wages (Lk. 3:14). The blessed were not expected to distribute all of their clothing and food. The tax collectors and soldiers were not asked to abandon their professions. John's teachings mitigated the baser evils of a corrupt system, but they did not transform that system. They constituted a genuine "interim ethic"—one designed to do until the Messiah should come. The sick society was still in need of a physician.

Rite of Baptism (1, 4)

The repentance which John demanded of his converts was consummated by baptism "in the river Jordan, confessing their sins" (Mk. 1:5). The importance of this rite in John's work is emphasized by the fact that he was popularly called "the baptizer" (Mk. 1:4). Just what transpired at the river cannot be determined. Since the converts were baptized "*in* the Jordan" (Mk. 1:5) and then "came up *out* of the water" (Mk. 1:10), it is probable that they immersed themselves in the Jordan under John's direction.[8]

Many attempts have been made to account for John's emphasis on baptism. Some scholars attribute it to non-Jewish influences such as an Iranian myth or the mystery cults. Others have explained it on the basis of Jewish practices. Certainly there were partial precedents in Judaism. Ablutions and baptisms were widespread. The Levitical Law prescribed washings for the purpose of purification. Converts to Judaism were required to submit to baptism. Whatever the source of John's rite, its central characteristics are unmistakable. (1) It was a water baptism. (2) It was predicated on repentance and accompanied by the confession of sins. (3) It was not to be repeated, as were the customary ceremonial washings. (4) It was required of all men, Jews as well as Gentiles. (5) It was preparatory. It anticipated the baptism "with fire" of the Mightier One who would presently appear.[9] When an individual submitted to John's baptism, he pre-enacted his own judgment. He acknowledged God's sovereignty, confessed his sins, and trusted in divine forgiveness and deliverance.

What did John's baptismal rite do for the convert? Was it a sacrament, effectual in and of itself? Probably not. The validity of a rite in Judaism

---

[7]Manson, in *The Mission and Message of Jesus*, p. 545.

[8]Emphasis added.

[9]Mk. 1:8 mentions a baptism "with the Holy Spirit." Mt. 3:11 and Lk. 3:16 copy Mk. and add from the Q source "and with fire." A baptism "with fire" would be more in keeping with John's message. "Fire" was a familiar metaphor for judgment. The phrase "with the Holy Spirit" probably reflects a later Christian understanding of baptism in Christ.

depended on the divine command which initiated it and on the attitude of the people performing it. As an act of self-humiliation before God, John's baptism would have been regarded as an expression of genuine repentance. Repentance was believed to elicit divine forgiveness. John's rite, then, "could mediate forgiveness without conferring it."[10]

Imprisonment and Death (5, 111)

John's career was meteoric. Suddenly he appeared in the wilderness of the Lower Jordan. For a few months, perhaps for a year or so, he preached with prophetic passion. Just as suddenly he was gone. The circumstances of his going are clouded by two conflicting accounts, the familiar one in Mark and the little known one in Josephus.

Mark states that John was jailed to please Herodias,[11] the wife of Herod's brother Philip. John had declared that it was unlawful for Herod to have married his brother's wife. Herodias consequently resented John and wanted to kill him. But Herod, a nominal Jew, had an unholy fear of the holy man. He kept John "safe" in prison and listened to him with mingled joy and perplexity. On Herod's birthday, apparently at his capital city of Tiberias in Galilee, he gave a banquet for his courtiers, officers, and the leading men of Galilee. During the banquet the guests were entertained by the delightful dancing of Salome (whose name we owe to Josephus), daughter of Herodias. Herod was so taken by the performance that he grandiosely promised Salome anything she asked, even half of his kingdom. Salome conferred with Herodias and returned with her wish: "I want you to give me at once the head of John the Baptist on a platter" (Mk. 6:25). The king was dismayed, but he had made a public pledge, and he was not about to lose face in front of his friends. John was beheaded. His faithful disciples came and claimed his body and laid it in a tomb. The grudge of Herodias had been satisfied through her daughter Salome.

Several points in Mark's account are questionable. (1) Herod Antipas was not a king. He was a tetrarch (ruler of a quarter of a kingdom) of Galilee and Perea, as Matthew and Luke correctly observe. (2) Herod was not married to his brother Philip's wife. He was married to Herodias, the wife of another Herod.[12] (3) For Salome, a woman of noble blood who was

---

10Kraeling, *John the Baptist*, pp. 121–22.
11Mk. 6:17–29.
12Herodias was the daughter of Herod Antipas's half-brother, Aristobulus. No disapproval was connected with the fact that Herod Antipas had married his niece. What was disapproved was that Herodias had previously been married to another half-brother, a Herod who lived as a private citizen in Rome. That marriage had produced a daughter, Salome. (It was Salome who was the wife of Herod Philip, tetrarch of the region northeast of Galilee.) The Roman Herod was still living. For Herod Antipas, then, to have married Herodias—even if she was divorced—was clearly contrary to Leviticus: "If a man takes his brother's wife, it is impurity" (20:21). Approval would have been given to such a sister-in-law marriage only if the Roman Herod had died and his marriage to Herodias had been childless.

"already in all probability the wife of the Tetrarch Philip," to appear at an ancient stag dinner is quite improbable.[13] (4) Herod Antipas's promise to Salome of half his kingdom sounds strange. He had no kingdom, and what he did have was not his to give away. (5) It would be contrary to Herod's custom and character to provide John with protective custody and to be "exceedingly sorry" when the stratagem of Herodias led to the demise of one who was popular with the people. (6) The motive for John's imprisonment and death is insufficient. If Herodias had cared as much about John's disapproval as Mark indicates, she could have disposed of the prophet with greater ease and certainty. She was reared in the intrigue of the Herodian courts. She could have contrived to have John meet with a fatal accident. (7) The royal palace at Tiberias on the Sea of Galilee was an unlikely place for John to be imprisoned and executed.

The inaccuracies in Mark's story have prompted scholars to turn to Josephus for clarification. Josephus says that John was imprisoned and executed at the frontier fortress of Machaerus on the shore of the Dead Sea. This accords with John's activity. As long as the prophet preached on the western bank of the Jordan (in Judea or Samaria) he would have been out of reach of "that fox," Herod Antipas (Lk. 13:32). But the Gospel of John asserts that John baptized on the eastern bank of the river "in Bethany beyond the Jordan" (1:28). This Bethany was in Perea, the bailiwick of Herod Antipas. If John was arrested while sojourning in the territory of Herod Antipas, what would be more natural than for John to be taken to the nearby fortress of Machaerus—to be imprisoned and later executed?

Josephus also provides another motive for John's imprisonment. He states that Herod, who "feared lest the great influence John had over the people might put it into his power and inclination to raise a rebellion, (for they seemed ready to do any thing he should advise,) thought it best, by putting him to death, to prevent any mischief he might cause, and not bring himself into difficulties, by sparing a man who might make him repent of it when it should be too late."[14]

The political motive for John's imprisonment is supported by the course of secular events. The Nabataeans were a powerful Arab people in the Near East in Herod's day. They controlled territory that stretched from the borders of Egypt and Palestine in the south through most of modern Jordan to the region of Damascus. The only pockets of independence were the Decapolis, Perea, and the tetrarchy of Philip. Herod Antipas, with an eye to the preservation of Perea as part of his tetrarchy, married the daughter of Aretas IV, king of the Nabataeans. When Herod fell in love with Herodias, he resolved to divorce his Nabataean princess. But the princess learned of the arrangements and asked of Herod permission to visit the fortress of Machaerus, located at the southern end of Perea. From there she reached Aretas. A few years later war broke out between Aretas and Antipas. Antipas' lands were penetrated and his troops defeated. Had it not been for Roman intervention, Herod would have been routed from his tetrarchy. The

13Kraeling, *John the Baptist*, p. 87.
14*Antiquities*, XVIII, 5,2.

defeat of Antipas was regarded by the Jewish people as divine punishment for the murder of John the Baptist.[15]

The marital muddle of Antipas created an unhealthful political climate. The weather was worsened by the sudden appearance in the Jordan Valley and Perea of a powerful prophet. He condemned Antipas, saying: "It is not lawful for you to have your brother's wife" (Mk. 6:18). This denunciation, in addition to increasing the ethical heat and humidity, promised a political tornado. It made possible the alignment of "the pious Jewish inhabitants of Peraea with those of Arabic stock against their sovereign."[16] Against such formidable enemies Herod would have small chance of success. To mitigate the potential danger he acted swiftly. He had the leader of the pious Jewish inhabitants arrested and subsequently executed.

Influence

Whatever political power John possessed perished with him. The same cannot be said of his religious influence. It continued to exert itself in his native land and later in the world at large. The Gospels speak of John's disciples (Lk. 5:33; 11:1; etc.). Paul encounters about a dozen disciples in Ephesus in the middle fifties who knew only "the baptism of John" (Acts 19:1–5). Near the turn of the century the Fourth Gospel reduces John to a mere "voice" and his disciples to belated but eager converts of Jesus (1:23, 35–51). John's early followers probably regarded him as the eschatological prophet whose appearance signaled the start of the New Age. It was only a short step from this estimate for them to conclude that he was both prophet and Messiah who acted in God's stead.[17] Among the Mandaeans, John was considered a genuine prophet in Messianic dress and Jesus was judged to be a false Messiah. These facts lend credence to the contention that followers of John remained independent of the Christian church for many decades. "From a Christian view the sun soon dimmed the moon, but both John and his movement had remarkable significance and even rivalry for beginning Christianity."[18]

The Christian church, which once paradoxically saw in John and his movement a herald and a rival, later made the Baptist a saint and honored him with a feast day. Such recognition would not have come to him, however, if his preaching in the wilderness had not reverberated in the streets of Nazareth. There a young carpenter was so moved by what he heard of John that he journeyed southward. One day he stood with his brethren on the bank of the Jordan. With them he listened intently to John's message of the impending judgment of God. With them he went down into the river and was baptized. Wherever the story of that carpenter is told, John's mission and message are remembered.

[15]*Antiquities*, XVIII, 5,1–3.
[16]Kraeling, *John the Baptist*, p. 91.
[17]See the *Testament of Levi* 8:15–16, where the two roles are merged. In the *Manual of Discipline* ix, II, from Qumran, three eschatological figures are envisaged—prophet, lay Messiah, and priestly Messiah.
[18]Beck, *Through the Gospels to Jesus*, p. 115.

part 4

The Work

High school students are usually encouraged to consider a vocational choice during their junior year. Many have selected their life work by the time they graduate. Those who enter college have a longer period of time to consider their future vocation. At the end of four years, they may either enter their chosen profession or embark upon two to four years of graduate study in preparation for it. Even postgraduate students have normally completed their vocational preparation and become well-established in their professions by the time they are thirty. Major vocational changes do not customarily occur after this age.

Jesus made a radical change in his life work when he was thirty (Lk. 3:23). Prior to this time, he had been a carpenter. Then word reached him concerning John. It was reported that John was preaching in the wilderness and baptizing large crowds in the Jordan river. Jesus left his work to investigate the report. At the Jordan, Jesus submitted to John's baptism, and the course of his career was changed. He never returned to the carpenter's bench. As he came up out of the Jordan, he received an announcement from God which plunged him into the wilderness for a prolonged period of soul-searching. When he emerged, the carpenter had become a campaigner.

Jesus' campaign consisted of powerful words and mighty works. It evoked the extremes of popularity and rejection. It included the choice and training of disciples who would later become leaders in the early church. We shall now turn our attention to the meaning of Jesus' baptism, the nature of his commitment in the wilderness, and the impact of his campaign on the populace.

chapter eleven

The Announcement

Word of the Baptist's powerful preaching reached Nazareth. Jesus, like many of his Galilean countrymen, was intrigued. He resolved to make the sixty-five-mile journey to the Lower Jordan to hear and see John in person. Mark describes the meeting of the two with succinct simplicity: "In those days Jesus came from Nazareth of Galilee and was baptized by John in the Jordan" (1:9).

Sin Baptism (6)[1]

Matthew states that "Jesus came from Galilee to the Jordan to John, *to be baptized* by him."[2] Mark and Luke indicate no prior purpose on Jesus' part. He may have pondered John's message for days after his arrival before he presented himself for baptism. That Jesus was baptized by John cannot be doubted. The Synoptics speak as one on this subject. Surely the church would not have invented an incident that required so much explanation later on. Mark and Luke give no hint that the baptism posed any difficulties. Matthew alone records John's protest: "I need to be baptized by you, and do you come to me?" (3:14).

From a relatively early date Jesus' baptism caused consternation in the church. Followers of the Baptist were then rivals if not opponents. How could Christians explain the embarrassing fact that Jesus had been baptized

---

[1]Mt. 3:13–17; Mk. 1:9–11; Lk. 3:21–22.
[2]Mt. 3:13, emphasis added.

by someone whom they regarded as inferior to him? More bothersome still was the nature of the baptism itself. How could one who was believed to be sinless submit to "a baptism of repentance for the forgiveness of sins"? (Mk. 1:4). Jewish antagonists made much of this point. They charged that Jesus was not only a sinner but a publicly-confessed one. He was unfit, therefore, to be the Messiah.

Matthew resolves the dilemma of a sinless Jesus seeking a baptism for the remission of sins. He reports that Jesus said to John: "Let it be so now; for thus it is fitting for us to fulfill all righteousness" (3:15). In short, Jesus was to be baptized not because he personally needed baptism but because others did. He was to be baptized as an example to Judaism. Matthew's explanation makes sense if John knew that Jesus was the Mightier One whose imminent coming and judgment he proclaimed. But it is doubtful that John possessed this knowledge. When word of Jesus' ministry reached John after his arrest and imprisonment, he sent disciples to Jesus to inquire: "Are you he who is to come, or shall we look for another?" (Mt. 11:3).

Early Christians were stung by the attacks on Jesus' moral status. Jewish opponents persistently impugned his character both during his ministry and after his death. John's followers joined the carping chorus. They argued that the baptism proved Jesus' sinfulness and John's superiority. Jesus' supporters publicly proclaimed their conviction that Jesus was sinless. Matthew took account of this conviction when he recorded John's protest at the prospect of baptizing Jesus. The Fourth Gospel echoed the conviction when its author reported Jesus' query to his adversaries: "Which of you convicts me of sin?" (8:46). The author of I Peter confirmed the tradition when he said of Jesus, "He committed no sin" (2:22). The author of Hebrews did likewise when he declared that in Jesus we have "one who in every respect has been tempted as we are, yet without sinning" (4:15). Jerome's quotation from the Gospel according to the Hebrews states that the mother and brothers of Jesus said, " 'John Baptist baptizeth unto the remission of sins; let us go and be baptized of him.' But Jesus said to them, 'Wherein . . . have I sinned, that I should go and be baptized of him? unless peradventure this very thing that I have said is *a sin* of ignorance.' "[3]

The concept of Jesus' sinlessness did not arise naturally from his goodness, love, courage, and obedience. It was conceived in controversy and born of a particular view of his death. Paul spoke of Jesus as God's great atoning sacrifice: "For our sake he [God] made him to be [the expiation of] sin who knew no sin, so that in him we might become the righteousness of God" (II Cor. 5:21). For the early church the validity of Jesus' Messiahship rested on his sinlessness. A sinner could not be the savior of sinners.

The conviction of the church that Jesus was sinless seems to contrast

---

[3] James, *The Apocryphal New Testament*, p. 6. Günther Bornkamm, in G. Bornkamm, Gerhard Barth, and H. J. Held, *Tradition and Interpretation in Matthew*, tr. Percy Scott (London: SCM Press, 1963), pp. 36–37, thinks that there is nothing in Mt. 3:14–15 to warrant interpreting it exclusively in terms of Jesus' sinlessness. The conversation is a reflection on salvation history. It poses the question of how the Messianic Judge of the world can place himself, through baptism, in a line with sinners. The answer: the Messianic Judge can do this "to fulfill all righteousness."

with his estimate of himself. Nowhere did Jesus teach that he was sinless, save in the latest Gospel, John. When the rich ruler addressed him as "Good teacher," he rejected the appellation with the retort: "Why do you call *me* good? No one is good but God alone."[4] The saying reminds us that saints are the ones most conscious of their imperfections. The followers of Jesus, in their anxiety to refute his critics and to affirm their own faith in him, unwittingly attributed to him the very sin that he later scathingly condemned—the sin of self-righteousness.

Are we to conclude, then, that Jesus approached his baptism as a sinner among a crowd of sinners?[5] Certainly not! He did not sin "after the manner of the frightened throng who went down into the water with him."[6] Was he, then, the sinless sin-bearer who was baptized as an example to his people? Such a view, as we have seen, is predicated on a particular concept of his death. It could hardly have been held by one who was not yet aware of his mission. Jesus was attracted to the Jordan by John's message. He decided to submit to the judgment and forgiveness of God proclaimed by the Baptist. He thus identified himself with the sinful nation and those in Israel who anticipated God's decisive action in the near future. But he was not baptized "as one obsessed by a sense of sin, nor as the sin-bearer of His people, but as one inspired by a great hope."[7] If he had any awareness of personal sin, it was not precipitated by reflections on a misspent youth. It was caused by the recognition that moral and spiritual obligations are infinite. "We can well believe that in the supreme moral and spiritual temptations which beset Him in His Messianic ministry He proved victorious on every occasion: but to believe this is not the same as to believe in the dogma of the sinlessness of Jesus from His infancy until the time when He felt Himself called to the Messianic Office."[8]

Three-phased Proclamation (6)

If the reader had been present at Jesus' baptism, what would he have seen and heard? To what extraordinary phenomena could he bear witness? Not a single thing! According to Mark, what happened to Jesus was purely personal; it was not even shared with John. The divine announcement was presented in three phases. Jesus (1) saw the heavens opened, (2) experienced the descent of the Spirit, and (3) heard a heavenly voice say, *"Thou art my*

[4]Mk. 10:18, emphasis added. Mt. 19:17 is a transparent attempt to tone down Mark's version, as Luke 18:19 indicates.

[5]See J. M. Murry, *Jesus, Man of Genius* (New York: Harper & Row, Publishers, Inc., 1926), p. 22.

[6]W. E. Rollins and M. B. Rollins, *Jesus and His Ministry* (Greenwich, Conn.: Seabury Press, 1954), p. 38.

[7]Major, in *The Mission and Message of Jesus*, p. 23.

[8]Major, in *The Mission and Message of Jesus*, p. 23. The general validity of this quotation can be recognized without necessarily endorsing Major's view of Jesus' Messianic consciousness.

beloved Son; with thee I am well pleased" (1:11).[9] This revelation was given only to Jesus.

Quite a different picture is presented in Matthew and Luke. Matthew makes the revelation a public pronouncement: "*This* is my beloved Son" (3:17).[10] Luke preserves the private nature of the disclosure as recorded in Mark; but he names, objectifies, and materializes the Spirit: "The *Holy* Spirit descended upon him *in bodily form*, as a dove" (3:22).[11] The Fourth Gospel contains no account of the baptism, but it does mention that the Spirit descended on Jesus. The Baptist accepts this as proof of Jesus' Messiahship (Jn. 1:32–34).

If John had seen and believed what is recorded in the Fourth Gospel concerning Jesus' Messiahship, if he had witnessed the material manifestation of the Spirit reported in the Third Gospel, or if he had heard the heavenly voice mentioned in the First Gospel—how could he later have sent disciples from his prison cell to Jesus to ask, "Are you he who is to come, or shall we look for another?" (Mt. 11:3). Clearly the later Synoptics have transformed the Marcan account of Jesus' baptism as a purely personal and private affair into a public experience.

Significance of the Symbols (6)

If the message which came to Jesus at his baptism was "in code," only he could decipher it. Some months later, when he had disciples with whom to share his mission, he chose to relate what had happened to him at the Jordan. He expressed himself in conventional oriental imagery. It is well that he did. The most momentous happenings of life—like "falling" in love or being converted—are the most difficult to communicate. Prose kills them; poetry breathes into them the breath of life. Jesus spoke of opened heavens, the Spirit descending like a dove, and a heavenly voice. These figures did not form the substance of the revelation. They were its symbols. No Jew would have taken them literally.

The Jews received messages from God through many mediums: dreams, angels, miracles, laws, the casting of lots, and the like. They also received messages from the prophets to whom God spoke directly. But God's direct word was believed to have ended with the prophets Haggai, Zechariah, and Malachi. There then arose the thought of a divine voice from heaven (Dan. 4:31). It was later literally called *bath qôl*, "daughter [or "echo"] of the voice [of God]." Rabbis and other saintly men testified that they had heard it. One rabbi declared that it sounded like the cooing of a dove.

The Jews believed that God resided above the heavens. Mark wrote that at his baptism Jesus saw the heavens opened. The way is thus paved for the descent of the Spirit. The Spirit descended upon Jesus "like a dove"

9Emphasis added.
10Emphasis added.
11Emphasis added.

(1:10). The phrase has been variously interpreted. It may mean (1) flying directly to the mark, like a dove to its dovecot; (2) gently as a dove, as in Jesus' injunction to his disciples (Mt. 10:16); or (3) in the spirit of wisdom. Most likely the phrase symbolized (4) the life-giving, creative activity of God. Genesis 1:2 depicts the Spirit of God as hovering like a bird over the chaos, producing life and order.[12] Whatever else it may connote, the Spirit always carries with it the idea of power—power in which God is active. "God anointed Jesus of Nazareth with the Holy Spirit and with power" (Acts 10:38). "Thus only can we explain the manifest note of authority and finality which informs his later words and deeds."[13] Whatever the intended meaning of "the Spirit descending upon him like a dove," we may be sure of one thing. The Spirit was not in the *form* of a dove, not even in Luke. A literal dove at Jesus' baptism is the invention of artists.

After the Spirit had descended upon Jesus, he heard a voice "from heaven." He did not hear it with his physical ear, or the crowd would have heard it also. Neither did he hear it directly. It was the *bath qôl*, an echo on earth of a word uttered by God in heaven. As usual, the voice spoke the language of Scripture: "Thou art my beloved Son; with thee I am well pleased" (Mk. 1:11).

The message is based on a Psalm and a section of II Isaiah, modified to suit the situation. The Psalm celebrates a royal coronation. In it the king speaks of a message received from the Lord on the day of his installation. "You are my son, today I have begotten you" (Ps. 2:7). The words are those used in the legal adoption of a child.[14] "Today" refers to the day the king ascended the throne. The section from II Isaiah was quoted frequently in the early church and interpreted Messianically: "Behold my servant, whom I uphold, my chosen one, in whom my soul delights; I have put my spirit upon him, he will bring forth justice to the nations" (Is. 42:1). The import of the passage is expressed in Mark's words ". . . with thee I am well pleased" (1:11). "Beloved, as used by Mark, does not mean one son who is preferred above all others, but the 'only' son."[15]

The baptism precipitated a crisis, according to the Synoptics, which led to a new career. The carpenter became a campaigner. What happened at the Jordan to cause all this? The heavens split open, the Spirit descended, and a heavenly voice cried out. What was the substance of the symbols? "Thou art my beloved Son; with thee I am well pleased." Did the baptism then mark the birth of Jesus' Messianic consciousness? Not according to the Fourth Gospel. It records no baptism because Jesus knew "in the beginning" who he was (1:1). But what about the Synoptics? The birth stories of Matthew and Luke immediately reveal his Messiahship. Matthew makes the baptism an occasion for the public announcement of Jesus' status: "*This* is my beloved Son" (3:17).[16] In Mark, however, Jesus' Messiahship

---

[12]See Major, in *The Mission and Message of Jesus*, p. 25.
[13]Hunter, *The Work and Words of Jesus*, p. 37.
[14]Code of Hammurabi, 170–71; cf. II Sam. 7:14.
[15]Grant, in *The Interpreter's Bible*, VII, 654.
[16]Emphasis added.

is a secret. The secret is disclosed in five successive stages. (1) Jesus is informed of it at his baptism. (2) The demons recognize him (1:24). (3) Peter perceives the Messiahship of Jesus near Caesarea Philippi (8:29). (4) Jesus quietly affirms it by his symbolic ride into Jerusalem. (5) The climax is reached when Jesus says "I am" before the high priest on the final day of his life on earth (Mk. 14:62).

The Synoptics tell different stories about Jesus' baptism. This fact has caused specialists to hold various opposing opinions concerning the subject of Jesus' Messianic consciousness. (1) There are those who deny that Jesus ever thought of himself as the Messiah. They regard the account of the baptism as an invention of the early church, designed to prove that Jesus was filled with the Spirit of God and chosen by heaven for the office of Messiah.[17] (2) Others deny that "Jesus' baptism marked the birth of his 'messianic consciousness'" but declare that "some experience of divine vocation lay back of Jesus' ministry...."[18] That vocation is often thought of in terms of divine sonship. (3) Still other scholars believe that Jesus was conscious of his Messianic role at his baptism, but that he had no clear idea of the direction it would take. The meaning of his mission was gradually unfolded to him during his ministry.[19] (4) Yet others claim that Jesus was not only conscious of his Messianic role at the baptism, but that he had a clear-cut concept of what that role involved. "Jesus knows that he is the Messiah, but such a Messiah as no Jew has hitherto envisaged, a Messiah who takes upon him the form of a Servant. But the lot of the Servant was more than service—it was...a service that for 'the many's sake' must issue in shame and death. May we not say that as the Messiah began his work there must have fallen across his path the shadow of a cross?"[20]

These four views relative to Jesus' awareness of his Messianic mission at his baptism by no means exhaust the possibilities. Neither do they include the subtle shades of difference which exist among specialists associated with any given point. Yet they serve a useful purpose. They demonstrate conclusively that unanimity concerning Jesus' Messianic consciousness does not exist. Where scholars differ, students should not rush to hasty conclusions. At this point in our study we should be content with the conviction that the baptism stands at the crossroads of Jesus' life. For the Synoptic evangelists the meaning of the baptism is plain. They wrote from the vantage point of Jesus' death and resurrection. From their perspective the baptism was seen as the occasion of Jesus' empowerment by the Spirit as the Messiah/Son of God. In Jesus, God has boldly entered Satan's realm to wrest the world from his grasp. The baptism signaled the beginning of that cosmic struggle by which the Lord would reassert His sovereignty on earth and reclaim that earth for His people. What the baptism meant to Jesus,

---

[17]C. Guignebert, *Jesus*, tr. S. H. Hooke (London: Kegan Paul, Trench, Trubner & Co., Ltd., 1935), p. 155.

[18]Grant, in *The Interpreter's Bible*, VII, 654.

[19]See Manson, in *The Mission and Message of Jesus*, p. 338. Compare Major, in the same book, p. 29.

[20]Hunter, *The Work and Words of Jesus*, p. 37.

if this can be determined, must await a fuller exploration of his mission and message.

Jesus and John (64–65)[21]

The relationship between Jesus and John, as recorded in the Gospels, bristles with difficulties. In his birth stories Luke binds the two together by blood and prophecy. He declares that in their prenatal state the Future Forerunner saluted the Future Messiah. Matthew's birth stories do not connect the families or the births of Jesus and John. But in his account of the baptism he shows that John is fully aware of Jesus' Messianic mission. Later both Luke and Matthew introduce material which is at cross-purposes with their theory. "Now when John heard in prison about the deeds of the Christ [sic], he sent word by his disciples and said to him, 'Are you he who is to come, or shall we look for another?' " (Mt. 11:2–3; cf. Lk. 7:18–19). Such a question is hard to harmonize with blood relationship, prenatal prophetic knowledge, long association, and adult awareness of who Jesus really was. It does, however, fit nicely with Mark's implication that Jesus and John first met at the baptism. It also coheres with the writings of Josephus who in no way connects John with Jesus.[22]

Jesus' answers to John tells us much about both: "Go and tell John what you hear and see: the blind receive their sight and the lame walk, lepers are cleansed and the deaf hear, and the dead are raised up, and the poor have good news preached to them" (Mt. 11:4–5). The indirect reply seems to add up to a qualified yes. The Jews believed that in the Messianic age all sickness would be healed.[23] Jesus, according to the evangelists, saw in his own work the dawning of the new age. But from the Baptist's viewpoint Jesus' answer must have been a resounding no. John had preached that the Mightier One would judge and destroy the wicked. A Good-Physician Messiah must have struck him as being a contradiction in terms. Jesus was apparently aware of what John's reaction might be. He added a beatitude which said, "Blessed is he who is not scandalized by me."[24]

Jesus probably began his ministry in rather close agreement with the thought of John. Perhaps he was even a disciple of the Baptist. The two may have had parallel ministries for a period (Jn. 3:22–24). But sometime between Jesus' baptism and the appearance of John's disciples from his prison cell, there developed striking differences between the two. (1) John sojourned in the wilderness and expected the crowds to come to him; Jesus was an itinerant preacher who carried his message from village to village, from mountaintop to sea. (2) John lived the austere life of a nomad and stressed fasting; Jesus was semi-domesticated, rejected excessive fasting, and acquired the (false) reputation of being a "glutton and wine-bibber."

---

[21]Mt. 11:2–19; Lk. 7:18–35; 16:16.
[22]*Antiquities*, XVIII, 5,2.
[23]Jubilees 23:26–30; Enoch 5:8–9.
[24]The author's translation of Mt. 11:6.

(3) John practiced the rite of baptism; Jesus did not. (4) John looked forward to the impending crisis with fear; Jesus viewed it as an occasion of joy. (5) John demanded an attainable ethic from his hearers; Jesus' ethic was much more stringent. (6) John emphasized God's righteousness and judgment; Jesus emphasized God's love and mercy. (7) For John the day of judgment was future though close at hand; for Jesus the Kingdom was in some sense already present though largely future.[25]

Jesus had a high regard for John despite their differences. After Jesus had justified his way to John, and John's disciples had departed, he justified John to the people: "What," he asked, "did you go out into the wilderness [the place of John's preaching] to behold? A reed shaken by the wind?" (Mt. 11:7). Certainly not! John was no tenderfoot who could be flattened by any wind that blew. "Why then did you go out? To see a man clothed in soft raiment?" (Mt. 11:8). Hardly! John was not a member of the comfort cult. He was akin to Amos. The austerity that he preached was the austerity that he practiced. "Behold, those who wear soft raiment are in king's houses" (Mt. 11:8). John was in the king's prison. "Why then did you go out? To see a prophet? Yes, I tell you, and more than a prophet" (Mt. 11:9).

The verse that follows in Matthew (11:10; compare Lk. 7:27) is perplexing. It is patterned after Malachi 3:1: "Behold, I send my messenger to prepare *the* way before *me*, and the Lord whom you seek will suddenly come to his temple."[26] In Malachi the messenger (Elijah) is the forerunner of God himself. No mention is made of a Messiah. In Matthew (and Luke) the personal pronouns are changed to make the "quotation" refer to the herald of the Messiah (John) instead of the herald of the Lord: "This is he of whom it is written, 'Behold, I send my messenger *before thy face*, who shall prepare *thy* way before *thee.*' "[27]

There were three traditions in rabbinical thought concerning Elijah. (1) Elijah belongs to the tribe of Gad. He prepares the way for God (as in Malachi) and is the redeemer of Israel. (2) Elijah belongs to the tribe of Levi. He is the High Priest of the Messianic Age, a colleague—not a forerunner—of the Messiah. (3) Elijah belongs to the tribe of Benjamin. He is the forerunner of the Messiah; his chief task is to announce the good news of the Messiah's coming.[28] The third view was popular among early Christians. Matthew stresses the identification of John and Elijah. He reports that Jesus said to the crowds: "If you are willing to accept it, he [John] is Elijah who is to come" (11:14). But in John's preaching, while he considered himself to be the herald of the Messiah, there is no hint that he identified himself with Elijah. The Fourth Gospel flatly contradicts such an identification. When emissaries of the Jews ask John if he is Elijah, he replies: "I am not" (1:21).

What may we conclude about Mt. 11:10 (Lk. 5:27)? It is an early

[25]See Kraeling, *John the Baptist*, pp. 146–47, which, for the most part, forms the basis for these comparisons.

[26]Emphasis added.

[27]Emphasis added.

[28]See Manson, in *The Mission and Message of Jesus*, p. 361.

Christian addition.[29] Its removal improves the connection between the previous and following verses. It apparently had a habit of floating from one context to another. It appears in Mark 1:2 (erroneously credited to Isaiah) where it makes no sense. It is probable that the early church linked John with Elijah to silence Jewish objections that the true Messiah must be anointed and announced as such by Elijah.[30]

What did Jesus mean by the phrase Matthew (11:9) and Luke (7:26) attribute to him—that John was a prophet and "more than a prophet"? Prophets proclaimed the word of God. John did that. He announced the imminent coming of the Mightier One in judgment, but that was not all. John was a prophet with a program. He actively prepared his people for the approaching crisis by requiring them to confess their sins, be baptized, and live according to superior ethical principles. He was not merely John the prophet. He was John *the Baptist.* "Among those born of women there has arisen no one greater than John the Baptist" (Mt. 11:11). Abraham, Moses, Elijah—none was greater than John. What a tremendous tribute! Then there follows a comment that seems to curdle the compliment: "Yet he who is least in the kingdom of heaven is greater than he" (Mt. 11:11).

For Mark, the ministry of Jesus begins with the ministry of John. The evangelist treats the ministry of John before he deals with the ministry of Jesus because he regards the Baptist as the forerunner of the Coming One— not because he wishes to present the proper historical sequence. In Mark's view, John rightfully belongs to the Gospel. Matthew introduces a temporal sequence into his accounts of John and Jesus, and Luke (16:16) relegates John to a prior period of salvation history—the period of Israel. John does not belong to the kingdom; he precedes it.[31]

The compliment Jesus pays is not left-handed. John marks a turning point in history. He is the last of the greatest of the Old Order. But he does not belong to the New Order which is now at hand. His record of obedience and devotion is doubtless Olympian. The "least in the kingdom" —who are greater than John—are not greater in what they do for God. They are greater in what God does for them. They excel not in production but in privileges. The real parallel to John in the Old Testament is not Elijah; it is Moses. Moses led the children of Israel to the border of the Promised Land but could not enter himself. John led his followers to the threshold of the New Order proclaimed by Jesus, but he could not enter. "He was the last . . . of the heroes of faith, who looked for 'the city that hath foundations, whose builder and maker is God,' who died without receiving the promises."[32]

Jesus and John may have proclaimed different messages and attracted different followings.[33] But the early Christians never doubted God's wisdom in choosing John to do His work. "Wisdom is justified by her deeds" (Mt.

[29]As evidenced by its presence in Q.
[30]See Justin, *Dialogue with Trypho,* VIII, 49, 110.
[31]See Marxsen, *Mark the Evangelist,* pp. 42–53.
[32]Manson, in *The Mission and Message of Jesus,* p. 362.
[33]At least in part.

11:19). The baptism of John *was* from heaven (Mt. 21:23–27). The early church laid hold of a spiritual truth when it regarded John as the forerunner of Jesus. We often see the providence of God more in retrospect than in prospect. In the light of Jesus' ministry, death, and resurrection, the church could see God at work in John's ministry—pointing to His climactic revelation which would follow. In the providence of God, John's work paved the way for the Good News and was superseded by it.

chapter twelve

The Commitment

Familiar roads sometimes lead to unexpected destinations. The route from Nazareth to the Jordan was such a road for Jesus. Very likely he set out to hear John with the same mixed motives—curiosity and concern—which moved his fellow Galileans. With them he went down into the river to be baptized. To the crowds his baptism seemed no different from the rest. How could they know that it had precipitated a unique experience? The announcement of God was for Jesus' ears alone: "*Thou* art my beloved Son; with *thee* I am well pleased" (Mk. 1:11).[1] From this time forward, Jesus, the carpenter, could never return to his bench in Nazareth.

Temptation (8)[2]

The incident that followed the startling disclosure at the baptism was quite as unexpected as the message itself. Mark relates it with stark simplicity: "The Spirit immediately drove him out into the wilderness. And he was in the wilderness forty days, tempted by Satan; and he was with the wild beasts; and the angels ministered to him" (1:12–13).

Each of the Synoptics treats Jesus' temptation, but each does so in a different way. Mark says that the Spirit drove Jesus (literally, "kicked him out") into the wilderness. Such blunt language abashed Matthew and Luke. They record that the Spirit led Jesus into the wilderness. Mark specifies

[1]Emphasis added.
[2]This chapter is based upon Mt. 4:1–11; Mk. 1:12–13; Lk. 4:1–13.

neither the nature nor the number of the temptations and says nothing about a fast. Matthew and Luke mention Jesus' fast and list the same three temptations, although they record the temptations in a different order. Mark states that Jesus was tempted during a forty-day period. Matthew declares that Jesus was led into the wilderness to *be tempted* (as he had gone to the Jordan *to be baptized*), spent forty days fasting, and then was thrice tempted. Luke appears to combine the two versions. Jesus was tempted for forty days in the wilderness (Mark), during which time he fasted (Matthew), and then the triple temptation commenced.

Background

It was a common concept among the Jews that a man of God should undergo a time of testing. God had permitted such stalwarts as Abraham, Noah, Joseph, Job, and Daniel their trials. The trials had led to triumphs. Why should the Son of God be an exception? Jesus had been fortified by the Spirit at his baptism. Now, during his temptations, he was called upon to wage a war of wit and will against a wily adversary. The wilderness, scene of the testing and training of so many in Israel, was the battlefield.

For forty days the battle raged. Forty is an oriental round number. It represents a considerable but indefinite period of time. Moses fasted "forty days and forty nights" on Mt. Sinai when he received the Ten Commandments (Ex. 34:28). Elijah traveled "forty days and forty nights" to the same

The Mount of Temptations, near modern Jericho, is identified by tradition as the place where Jesus was tempted by Satan. A monastery on the side of the mountain contains a tiny chapel in a cave. It is here that Jesus is said to have spent forty days and nights.

mountain in flight from Jezebel (I Kings 19:8). For forty years the children of Israel wandered in the wilderness under the leadership of Moses (Deut. 1:3).

Satan is the name of the tempter in Mark. Matthew and Luke call him *the devil*, a term usually used in later New Testament writings. Satan plays a minor role in the Old Testament, where he appears seldom and late. In Job he takes the part of the loyal opposition. He roams the earth in search of candidates who will flunk their final exams on faith in the Lord. All of his testing, however, is carried on under the proctorship and in accordance with the protocol of the Lord. Satan has not yet "fallen." In Chronicles he prompts David to conduct a census of Israel. This so displeases God that He sends a plague on the people (I Chr. 21:1–14). It is not until Judaism is influenced by Persian thought (538–333 B.C.) that Satan's status markedly changes. In the literature written "between the Testaments" he becomes an evil deity opposed to God (just as Ahriman is opposed to Ormazd in Persian dualism). The calamities of nature and the depraved impulses of men are attributed to him. In the New Testament Paul pictures him as "the god of this world" who has "blinded the minds of the unbelievers' '(II Cor. 4:4). Satan's assault against the Son of God in the wilderness is no exhibition match. It is a power struggle for high stakes—the control of the world. On its outcome hangs the career of Jesus and the cause of God.

Modern man is chary about accepting the reality of Satan or the devil. He has scientific explanations for earthquakes and psychological ones for sins. He points with pride to the fact that Satan never became an article of faith in the Christian creed. He denies Satan's actual existence by affirming his poetic personification. Yet all the while he is haunted by the secret fear that the devil's power may multiply by denials. As he faces the threat of atomic annihilation and the rising incidence of personality disintegration, modern man is led to wonder. Perhaps the concept of Satan is a realistic assessment of evil. Why of late have theologians and psychiatrists reverted to a vocabulary which includes such a term as "demonic forces"?

In the Bible, Satan has his demons, but God has His angels. They were His attendants in the heavenly court and served to accent the majesty and glory of the Lord. As seen or unseen messengers of God they brought word to men in their dreams or during their waking hours. They guarded men from danger, aided them during death, and were ever alert to defeat the forces of evil. Later Jewish thought held that the Law was mediated by them. Some of their number (Gabriel and Michael) receive personal names in the book of Daniel (8:16; 12:1). In Tobit, Raphael is the wonder-working guide. The Sadducees denied the existence of angels, but the Pharisees believed in them. Angels were not emphasized in Jesus' teaching, but during his temptation they served and supported him.

Judaism was not an ascetic religion, but fasting was an integral part of the religious calendar. It was obligatory on the Day of Atonement (Yom Kippur), New Year's Day (Rosh Hashana), and on the anniversaries of great calamities in Jewish history. Special public fasts were also proclaimed from time to time to avert disaster, such as a prolonged drought or an enemy attack. Many devout Jews went above and beyond the call of public fasting. They practiced private, voluntary fasting as well. The Pharisees fasted twice a week, on Thursday and Monday, the days they believed Moses respectively ascended and descended Mt. Sinai. The disciples of John did likewise. Fasting was thus a well-known discipline to induce spiritual development. Matthew and Luke agree that Jesus fasted during his temptation. This may be a reference merely to the scant amount of available food in the area. It is more likely that it implies a religious act. In either case, fasting and hunger are a necessary prelude to the first temptation.

Satanic Suggestions

Two of Satan's suggestions to Jesus in the wilderness are prefaced with the phrase, "If you are the Son of God." In Jewish thought the term "Son of God" had multiple meanings. It was used to describe (1) the Israelite nation as a whole (Ex. 4:22), (2) the godly and upright in Israel (Hos. 1:10), (3) an anointed king (Ps. 2:7), (4) angels (Job 38:7), and (5) the Messiah. It was never a standard title for the Messiah, however. It was applied to him in only a few apocalyptic books[3] and occasionally in late rabbinical writings. When in the Old Testament it is used to designate an individual or the nation, "it usually calls attention to the moral relationship of love and filial obedience which should exist between a father and his son."[4]

The first temptation[5] comes to Jesus at the close of a considerable period of fasting. He is ravenously hungry. The devil aims at a highly vulnerable point: "If you are the Son of God, command these stones to become bread" (Mt. 4:3). Palestine was a rock collector's paradise. It provided an inexhaustible supply of raw material for one who could convert stones into bread. It was commonly believed that the Messianic Age would be marked by a miraculous abundance of material goods. Jesus was hungry. So were his countrymen. They faced an almost constant threat of famine. If he was the Son of God, why shouldn't he produce one of the promised signs of the Messiah's coming?

Bread is basic. Without it life cannot be sustained. So convinced of this was Jesus that he later included a petition for daily bread in the Disciples' Prayer (Mt. 6:11). But was bread for the body man's deepest need? Certainly not! Man's deepest need was not for bread *from* heaven but for the bread *of* heaven, God Himself. This had been the point of God's dealings with Israel during her wilderness sojourn. He had allowed His people to hunger. Then He had fed them with manna. He had wanted to impress on them the fact that bread does not have top priority. In this experience of his ancestors, Jesus found ammunition which could pierce the armor of the devil. He cited a portion of Deuteronomy 8:3 to this end: "Man shall not live by bread alone, but by every word that proceeds from the mouth of God" (Mt. 4:4).

[3]Enoch 105:2; II Esdras 7:28–29; 13:32,37,52.
[4]Johnson, in *The Interpreter's Bible*, VII, 270.
[5]We shall follow Matthew's order.

The second temptation takes place in Jerusalem. The devil sets Jesus on "the pinnacle of the temple." "Temple" covers the whole complex of buildings within the sacred enclosure. "Pinnacle" suggests the royal colonnade on the south side of the outer court. This cloister overlooked the Kidron valley. To look down from the roof could make one giddy.[6] Jewish tradition held that the Messiah would appear on the roof of the Temple and proclaim deliverance to the people. There was, however, no expectation that he would validate his title by jumping off.

The devil, once wounded by a text from Scripture,[7] tries a text himself: "If you are the Son of God, throw yourself down; for it is written, 'He will give his angels charge of you,' and 'On their hands they will bear you up, lest you strike your foot against a stone'" (Mt. 4:6). The quotation is from Ps. 91:11-12. It is intended to be understood Messianically. The challenge to Jesus is crystal clear: God has made Jesus the Messiah. He has promised the Messiah protection. (It would be no small angelic company that could guarantee an unbruised foot in rocky Palestine.) Why should Jesus not use this insurance policy? For Jesus to jump from the roof to the valley below without injury would be convincing proof to the crowd of his call.[8]

Jesus counters the devil's second suggestion with a quotation based on Deut. 6:16: "You shall not tempt the Lord your God" (Mt. 4:7). The full text in Deuteronomy runs as follows: "You shall not put the Lord your God to the test, as you tested him at Massah." The reference to Massah is explained by Ex. 17:1-7. The people of Israel found fault with Moses because there was no water at Rephidim. As their pressure intensified, Moses cried to the Lord. The Lord instructed Moses to strike a rock with the rod that had turned the Nile red and water would gush out. Moses did so, and he called the place Massah (Proof) and Meribah (Contention) "because of the fault-finding of the children of Israel, and because they put the Lord to the proof by saying, 'Is the Lord among us or not?'" (Ex. 17:7).

For Jesus to jump off the pinnacle of the Temple would be for him to say, in effect, "All right, God. You called me to be Your special Son. You promised me protection. Now validate your promise!" Such language on the lips of Jesus would be unthinkable; and an attitude which would prompt such language would be incredible. For Jesus to test God's word would amount to a confession of his own lack of faith in God. He was not called to command God but to trust and obey Him. "If the way of obedience means leaping over a precipice—or going to the Cross—that is another matter; but to thrust oneself into peril, merely to provide God with the occasion for a miracle, is not faith but presumption."[9]

The third temptation describes how the devil showed Jesus all the kingdoms of the world and their glory. Careful students will detect at once the differences between the accounts of Luke and Matthew. Luke gives no

---

[6]Josephus, *Antiquities* XV, 11,5. On the appearance of the Messiah on the Temple's roof see *Pesikta Rabba* 162a.

[7]Twice in Luke's sequence.

[8]Other motives which have been suggested: (1) to assure Jesus of God's power or (2) to attract attention.

[9]Manson, in *The Mission and Message of Jesus*, p. 337.

inkling of the place. His phrase "in a moment of time" implies a visionary experience. Matthew mentions the summit of a very high mountain. (Of course there is no mountain in the world whose height would permit one to see Palestine, let alone the Roman Empire, which Matthew probably had in mind.) The devil's claim of the sole right to dispose of the world's control is absent from Matthew. The assumption probably struck him as blasphemous.

The third proposal of the devil is not prefaced by the words, "If you are the Son of God."[10] As Jesus takes a panoramic view of the world and its glory, the devil declares, "All these I will give you" (Mt. 4:9). Despite Matthew's failure to mention it there was really no doubt that the devil controlled the world and could dispose of it as he wished (Lk. 4:6). Once the world had been God's alone. But since the Flood men had rejected Him. His full sovereignty was confined to heaven. From time to time His rule was reestablished on earth, as when He became King of Israel. But when Israel sinned, God's kingdom was taken from her. She became subject to heathen nations. Persian dualism produced in Jewish thinking a kingdom of evil as well as a kingdom of God. The devil headed up the kingdom of evil and (except for isolated instances of piety and purpose) ruled the earth. This is why it was necessary to pray, "Thy kingdom come, Thy will be done, on earth as it is in heaven" (Mt. 6:10).

There was some fine print in the devil's contract. Jesus could have control of all the kingdoms of the world *if* he would "fall down and worship" the devil (Mt. 4:9). The prospects were dazzling and the demand reasonable. All Jesus was asked to do was to acknowledge the devil's position, and the devil's possessions would be his. It was a small concession for so consequential a reward. It is so much easier to fall down and worship than to stand up and obey.

Jesus spurns the devil's third suggestion. With a note of finality he declares, "Begone, Satan!" (Later he called Peter "Satan" when the apostle tried to divert him from the will of God.[11]) Then he reaches into his rich storehouse of Scripture texts and pulls forth a telling rebuttal: "You shall worship the Lord your God, and him only shall you serve" (Mt. 4:10).[12] The world desperately needed to be won for God; but it could not be purchased at the price of fellowship with Him. The end does not justify the means; the means determines the end. Therefore, submission to Satan would have shattered Jesus' Sonship. The first and final loyalty of the Son is to the Father.

Jesus' command for Satan to depart was obeyed. But Satan did not remain away for long. Luke states that "he departed from him until an opportune time" (4:13). The wilderness ordeal of the Son of God was no isolated incident. Throughout his life on earth, Jesus was "tempted as we

---

[10]Manson, in *The Mission and Message of Jesus*, p. 335, conjectures that it is not used because if Jesus is the Son of God the things which Satan is about to offer are his by right, the right of the Messiah.

[11]Mt. 16:23.

[12]The quotation is based on Deut. 6:13, modified to meet the situation by (1) changing "fear" to "worship," (2) adding "only," and (3) omitting the last third of the verse.

are" (Heb. 4:15). Satan returned to him again and again with subtle suggestions and attractive offers. Proof of this is found in words Jesus addressed to his disciples at the close of his career: "You are those who have *continued* with me in my trials" (Lk. 22:28).[13] As Jesus' friends forsook him, as his disciples misunderstood him, and as his enemies multiplied in number and strength, Satan undoubtedly stepped up his campaign against the carpenter. The campaign reached its climax during the Passion. Satan waged his final assault in the Garden of Gethsemane in the presence of three sleeping "witnesses." In case he lost that battle, he had taken steps to win the war. Thanks to Judas's cooperation Satan had already laid plans for driving nails into a wooden cross.

It is customary in some circles to generalize the three temptations of Jesus. They are erroneously viewed as the kind of vocational decisions that any young man might make at the brink of his career: (1) the relative importance of the spiritual and the material; (2) the need to authenticate God's call; (3) the role of compromise in achieving desired ends. In other circles the temptations are closely connected with the platforms of specific political and religious parties of the day—the Sadducees, the Pharisees, the "Zealots," and others. Certainly the conflicting platforms of these groups were known to Jesus. He did not entertain and reject Satan's suggestions in a political and religious vacuum. "But the poetic, suggestive account of the three phases of his rejection of Satan is not the kind of allegory that can be decoded into the 'platforms' of three distinct parties."[14]

We shall see the temptations of Jesus in sharper focus if we keep in mind a few fundamental considerations. (1) The temptations were real. They posed live options for Jesus, not absurd and fanciful impossibilities. He was actually *tempted* to say yes. (2) The temptations were prolonged, as the figure of "forty days" suggests. (3) They dealt with three aspects of a single concern. They were not three separate and unrelated experiences. (4) That single concern had nothing to do with Jesus' "longing for some inescapably clear validation of the call that had come in the exalted experience of the Baptism."[15] That call had been heard and accepted at the Jordan. (5) The temptations concerned *the use of power* which the Son of God had received from the Spirit at the baptism.

Historicity

Maurice Goguel, the celebrated French historian, is convinced that "Jesus was in contact with John and that he received baptism at his hands."[16] However, when it comes to the temptation experience of Jesus, an incident equally well documented by the Synoptics, Goguel draws a different conclusion. He does not include the temptation in his knowledge-

---

13Emphasis added.
14Rollins and Rollins, *Jesus and His Ministry*, p. 49.
15Rollins and Rollins, *Jesus and His Ministry*, p. 49.
16Goguel, *The Life of Jesus*, p. 269.

able *Life of Jesus*. In this opinion he does not stand alone. Guignebert declares that "the incident of the temptation is completely legendary."[17] Rudolf Bultmann calls it a Hellenistic-Christian legend concerning the problem of miracle,[18] J. A. T. Robinson sees it as an apology for the church as the true and tested Israel,[19] and Walter Bundy regards it as a Christian creation of legendary nature and mythical form.[20]

What prompts some scholars to relegate the temptation of Jesus to the limbo of legends? (1) The temptation is not authenticated by ecclesiastical embarrassment as was the baptism. John's baptism of Jesus made Jesus appear to be a sinner who was inferior to John. The church would not have preserved such damaging testimony unless the baptism had really happened. (2) The temptation accounts are highly stylized. Each Satanic suggestion is rebutted by a quotation from Scripture. The temptation "is a problem play, the product of study and reflection. It is the work of literary art and probably never existed in oral form."[21] (3) The temptation account is a story born of necessity in the early church. Some explanation was needed to account for Jesus' divergence from popular expectations. The temptation story filled this order, and it also depicted the victory over Satan that Jesus achieved during his ministry.

Other scholars, however, affirm the essential historicity of Jesus' temptation. (1) The experience is well attested by the Synoptics. (2) The temptation is closely linked with the baptism, an incident of high historical probability. (3) The quotations from Scripture in the accounts are not used as verbatim proof-texts (the practice of the church) but as ideational support for a pattern of life (the practice of Jesus). (4) The temptation is not colored by the cross. This would almost certainly have been the case if the church had created the stories. The church viewed the temptations from the vantage point of the passion, death, and resurrection of Jesus. Yet the temptation accounts give no clue concerning the course that lay ahead. (5) To trace the temptation to the early church instead of to Jesus would require a writer who "could abstract these principles from the mass of detailed events [of his ministry], recognize them as temptations, reclothe them in the concrete form of this section, give the whole an accurate psychological background, and (by no means least difficult) abstain from explanatory moralizing. Such a task was beyond the powers of anyone in the apostolic or post-apostolic age."[22]

If the temptation of Jesus was essentially historical, as we believe, what did it mean? Was it Messianic? For many scholars the answer is clear.

[17]Guignebert, *Jesus*, p. 158.
[18]Rudolf Bultmann, *History of the Synoptic Tradition*, 2nd ed., tr. John Marsh (New York: Harper & Row, Publishers, Inc., 1968), pp. 254–57.
[19]John A. T. Robinson, *Twelve New Testament Studies* (Naperville, Ill.: Alec R. Allenson, Inc., 1962), p. 60.
[20]Walter E. Bundy, *Jesus and the First Three Gospels* (Cambridge: Harvard University Press, 1955), p. 64.
[21]Bundy, *Jesus and the First Three Gospels*, p. 64.
[22]Burton Scott Easton, *The Gospel According to St. Luke* (New York: Charles Scribner's Sons, 1926), p. 49.

Hunter declares: "These are not the temptations of Jesus; they are the temptations of the Christ; the temptations not of a private person but of one called to be God's Messiah in the establishment of the Kingdom."[23] Major asserts: "It is quite impossible to explain the Mission of Jesus except on the supposition that He possessed the Messianic Consciousness from the beginning of His Ministry."[24] Jeremias rejects the idea that the substance of the temptation accounts can be traced to the poetic imagination of the early church, and he locates the temptation in the historic ministry of Jesus. He regards Satan's three suggestions as three parabolic versions of a single temptation. This temptation is the enticement to subscribe to a false Messianic expectation. Since the political temptation did not exist for the early church and since Jesus informed his disciples about a conflict with Satan (Lk. 22:31–32), it may be conjectured that underneath the different versions of the temptation stories are Jesus' own words. Perhaps he told his disciples about his own victory over the temptation to offer himself as a political Messiah in order to warn them about succumbing to a similar temptation.[25] Other scholars, however, demur. They claim that Jesus' call was to Sonship and that the temptation concerned Sonship, not Messiahship. Or they assert that Messianic meanings in the temptation are anachronistic. The early church found in the miracles of Jesus one of the principal proofs of his Messiahship. When the church preserved the accounts of Jesus' temptation, it placed the Messianic motif at the beginning of his ministry.

We shall return to the dispute concerning Jesus' Messianic consciousness in a later chapter, after we have accumulated more evidence on which to base a reasonable conclusion. At the present stage of our study two points can be made with considerable assurance. (1) The temptation makes the most sense when it is placed in the context of Jesus' divinely appointed mission to Israel. (2) The temptation experience does not reveal the positive features of Jesus' future work. The dialogue with the devil in the desert allows Jesus to reject several Satanic suggestions. Whatever else God wants Jesus to do, He definitely does not want him to do these. Jesus departs from the wilderness without a master plan of his mission, but with full knowledge of who his Master is.

23Hunter, *The Work and Words of Jesus*, p. 38.
24Major, in *The Mission and Message of Jesus*, p. 29.
25Joachim Jeremias, *The Parables of Jesus*, pp. 122–23.

chapter thirteen

The Campaign

Mark states that after "John was arrested, Jesus came into Galilee, preaching the gospel of the kingdom of God" (1:14).[1] If we had only this Gospel, we might easily conclude that Jesus' public ministry was confined almost exclusively to Galilee. It lasted for about a year[2] and came to an abrupt end when Jesus made his first and final journey to Jerusalem. The Fourth Gospel, on the other hand, presents quite a different picture. Jesus began his ministry before John was put in prison (3:24), alternated his activity between Judea and Galilee (chapter 1–6), but spent the bulk of his time in Judea (the remainder of the book). He campaigned for a period of three or four years.[3]

[1]Alternate reading. Willi Marxsen, *Mark the Evangelist*, p. 40, observes that although the Baptist *may* have been arrested before Jesus began his ministry, this is not necessarily so. Mark's account is topical, not chronological; Matthew and Luke introduce the idea of sequence of events.

[2]It is spring (2:23); it is spring again (14:1), the Passover of the Passion.

[3]Three Passovers are mentioned (2:13; 6:4; 12:1). Ethelbert Stauffer, *Jesus and His Story*, tr. Richard and Clara Winston (New York: Alfred A. Knopf, 1960), p. 6n, argues for about a four-year ministry: "In John 1:29, 41ff., the situation during the Passover is assumed. In John 2:13, 23, we hear of the second Passover. In John 3:24, the Baptist is still active. In John 4:35, it is winter. John does not mention the third Passover. In John 5:1, it is autumn, the Feast of Tabernacles. In John 6:4, the fourth Passover is impending. In John 7:2, it is autumn again; in John 10:22, winter once more, the Feast of Dedication at Jerusalem. In John 11:55, we hear of the fifth Passover feast, the Passover of death." For a trenchant criticism of Stauffer's efforts to write a chronologically historical account of Jesus' life see Hugh Anderson, *Jesus and Christian Origins* (New York: Oxford University Press, 1964), pp. 57–61.

A careful study of Mark and the other Synoptics suggests that they and the Fourth Gospel may not be as far apart on the length of Jesus' ministry as some scholars have assumed. (1) Mark introduces pericopes with a minimum of transitional connections. His statement that after John's arrest "Jesus came into Galilee, preaching," does not exclude prior activity elsewhere; it may actually cover it. (2) The sudden, affirmative response of Galilean fishermen to Jesus' call for disciples becomes more intelligible if they had had some previous knowledge of him before they left all and followed him (Mk. 10:28). (3) Jesus' lament over Jerusalem may imply not one but several appeals to that city: "O Jerusalem, Jerusalem, killing the prophets and stoning those who are sent to you! *How often* would I have gathered your children together as a hen gathers her brood under her wings, and you would not!" (Mt. 23:37).[4] (4) On his final visit to Jerusalem, Jesus had friends there who furnished him with an ass and a guest chamber.

Numerous attempts have been made to construct a chronology of Jesus' ministry by using the data furnished by all four Gospels. Stauffer concludes that the chronological structure found in John cannot be fitted "within the narrow span of the Synoptic account. But it is possible to fit the Synoptic frame into John's structure."[5] In this he may be right. But it is questionable that any fitting of the Synoptic frame into the structure of John would yield a reliable chronology of Jesus' activity. The very nature of the Gospels —the Synoptics as well as John—precludes this. The Gospels are not finely-honed historical instruments. They are literary creations "designed to group together into a coherent whole traditions which formerly had an independent existence."[6]

Message in Miniature (9)[7]

Galilee was made to order for Jesus' message. The people there did not live under the heavy doctrinal thumb of Jerusalem. They were of mixed origin, in closer touch with the outside world, and receptive to new movements. Moreover, Jesus was one of them. Many cities dotted the shore of the Sea of Galilee. Jesus chose Capernaum as his headquarters. It was located on the northwest shore of the Sea, a superb center for the evangelization of the area. Over 100,000 people were within easy reach by boat or on foot.[8] Mark records a threefold summary of Jesus' message (1:15).[9]

"*The time is fulfilled*" refers to the time of the Creator, not to time by the clock. Religious people of antiquity generally held that the course of

---

[4]Emphasis added.

[5]Stauffer, *Jesus and His Story*, p. 7.

[6]Goguel, *The Life of Jesus*, p. 235.

[7]Mt. 4:12–17; Mk. 1:14–15; Lk. 4:14–15.

[8]George Adam Smith, *The Historical Geography of the Holy Land*, 14th ed. (New York: A. C. Armstrong & Sons, 1908), p. 447, states that there were nine cities around the Sea of Galilee with reportedly not less than 15,000 inhabitants each.

[9]The fourth utterance, "... believe in the gospel," is a Christian admonition. Jesus stressed *faith* (in God) not *belief* (in the Good News).

The partially restored synagogue pictured here probably stems from the second century A.D. The colonnade of pillars once supported a balcony used by women worshipers. Jesus made his campaign headquarters in Capernaum (Village of Nahum) "...and immediately on the sabbath he entered the synagogue and taught" (Mk. 1:21).

history, at least at its turning points, is determined beforehand. "The time" in Mark means the time fixed in God's foreknowledge, the time foreseen by the prophets, the decisive moment for the achievement of God's eternal purpose.

The sentence is eschatological. (*Eschatos* means "end." Eschatology is characterized by the conviction (1) that the present world will end and be replaced by a new world and (2) that this transition is imminent.) The devotees of "realized eschatology" make much of the verb in the phrases "*is fulfilled*" (Mk. 1:15) and "*is at hand*" (Mt. 4:17). "Jesus said, 'The Reign of God is here.' His Good News was that the Rule of God was no longer a shining hope on the far horizon but a glad reality, a blessed *fait accompli*. '...What had formerly been pure eschatology was there before their eyes: the supernatural made visible. No longer were they dreaming of the kingdom age: they were living in it. It had arrived.' "[10]

The Greek verb (*ēggiken*, Mk.), however, can hardly mean "has arrived." It means "has drawn near." The kingdom was still approaching. There was still opportunity for repentance which would make one ready for its arrival. But the time was short. Jesus' subsequent "mighty works" were viewed by Mark as evidence of its coming. But even in Mark's day the kingdom had not fully arrived.

[10]Hunter, *The Work and Words of Jesus*, p. 43, with the final sub-quotation from J. S. Stewart, *Heralds of God*, p. 64.

"The kingdom of God" is the central theme of Jesus' teaching. The phrase is not found in the Old Testament. Neither is it frequent in post-Biblical writings. But the idea of God as King is prominent in Jewish Scripture (Is. 43:15; Ps. 103:19; etc.). His kingship was His sovereignty or rule. It was manifested in (1) creation, (2) nature, (3) the control of nations, (4) the history of Israel, (5) the Law, and (6) daily providence over people.

Once God's sovereignty had been supreme. Now it was partial. His purposes had been thwarted by sin, rebellion, and rejection of the Law; but all was not lost. When an Israelite obeyed the Law or recited the Shema (Deut. 6:4–9), God's sovereignty was reasserted. His subject had taken upon himself "the yoke of the kingdom." But as long as sin prevailed, as long as Satan exercised authority, God's reign was incomplete. The hope grew that God would one day achieve complete control. The prophets looked for Him to defeat the forces of evil, judge the evildoers, and establish His reign on earth (Is. 9:7; Zech. 14:9). This He would do either directly or through the instrumentality of the Messiah. Then there would follow the Golden Age when He would reward and bless the faithful. The apocalyptists painted a different picture. They spoke often of a supernatural Messiah and a transformed earth or a transcendental heaven.

Jesus never defined what he meant by "the kingdom of God" or "the kingdom of heaven."[11] Consequently its nature and nearness have become matters of heated dispute. "The kingdom" has been defined, among other ways, as (1) a miraculous new order of God, (2) human society organized by love, (3) a spiritual commonwealth made up of those who do God's will, (4) the rule of God in the hearts of men, and (5) the church. It has been argued that the kingdom (1) was present and realized in the person and performance of Jesus and his followers, (2) was in some sense present in Jesus' words and works but was largely an expected future event, or (3) was a wholly future event.

Although Jesus did not define the kingdom, he did profusely illustrate it by the use of parables. Final conclusions regarding the nature and nearness of the kingdom must await their treatment. In the meantime, several observations concerning the kingdom may prove to be helpful. (1) It is *God's* kingdom. Our English word "kingdom" stands for the realm or sphere of a king. This is not the primary meaning of the Greek word[12] translated "kingdom" in the phrase "kingdom of God." The dominant meaning of that word is God's sovereignty or kingly rule. The stress is not on the kingdom but on the King, not on the subjects but on the Sovereign. Since a king does not rule in a void, and since men may enter or be excluded from the kingdom of God, the phrase is sometimes used to describe the sphere *and* the subjects. Nevertheless, the basic meaning concerns God acting in His kingly power, exercising His sovereignty. (2) Jesus is its herald. (3) The conditions of entrance are not racial or national but moral and religious. (4) The Beatitudes (Mt. 5:3–11) describe the character of kingdom members. (5) Even though the kingdom is established by God, men must

---

[11]The two terms mean the same thing. Matthew merely follows pious Jewish practice in avoiding the use of the divine name by writing "the kingdom of heaven."

[12]*Basileia*; Hebrew, *malkuth*; Aramaic, *malkutha*.

prepare for its coming by moral effort (repentance and living as though they are already in the kingdom). (6) In some sense the kingdom is manifesting itself in the mission and message of Jesus although its full force will be felt in the future. (7) It is of supreme value.

"Repent." Jesus did not merely declare that the time was fulfilled and the kingdom of God was at hand. He demanded that men repent. Repentance was a cardinal concept in Judaism. It involved not only remorse for one's sins but also restitution (as far as possible) and the firm resolution not to commit those sins again. Jesus shared this aspect of his message with John; but unlike John, he did not require baptism. For Jesus, repentance meant not only a change of conduct but a change of character. Repentance did not open the door to the kingdom, but it did prepare men for the day when the door would be fully opened.

Call and Training of the Twelve (11, 53, 58)[13]

Jesus began his Galilean campaign alone. It was not long, though, before he abandoned his solo effort and sought out special disciples. He thus adopted a common Jewish custom. The rabbis called special disciples to follow them. Through intimate daily contact with their teachers, the disciples developed character and learned the Law. After many years of intensive training they might achieve their vocational goal and become scholars. Unlike the rabbis, Jesus gave his disciples only a brief training; he called them to become heralds of the kingdom rather than scholars.

There are only three recorded instances where Jesus issued an invitation to special discipleship. The first two invitations were extended to four fishermen: (1) Simon[14] and (2) Andrew, his brother, (3) James and (4) John, his brother. Their response was immediate, perhaps indicating prior acquaintanceship. "Follow me" refers to the custom of disciples walking in single file behind their teacher when on a journey. It would have been presumptuous for the fishermen to follow without an invitation. Once the invitation had been extended, they lost no time in accepting it. Mark writes that James and John "left their father Zebedee in the boat with the hired servants" (1:20). Since Zebedee owned a boat and could hire workers, he was not poor; but neither was he rich. Any fisherman who owned a boat and some nets might hire workers to help him, especially in a good season.

Jesus' third recorded invitation to special discipleship was extended to Matthew (Mt. 9:9) or Levi (Mk. 2:14; Lk. 5:27).[15] He was a collector of customs for a foreign government. His office was located at the northern end

---

[13]Mt. 4:18–22; 9:9–13; 9:35–10:16; Mk. 1:16–20; 2:13–17; Lk. 5:27–32; 10:1–2.

[14]A Greek name, as was Andrew. Simon's Hebrew name was "Simeon" and his nickname was "Peter" (rock).

[15]In order to harmonize the accounts it has been suggested that his name was Matthew Levi. Or was it "James," as many Marcan manuscripts read? Mark calls the collector a "son of Alphaeus." A certain "James the son of Alphaeus" is found in all Synoptic lists of the Twelve. But neither Mark nor Luke lists "Levi" among the Twelve. Did the author of the First Gospel confuse 'Levi' with "Matthew" and substitute "Matthew" in 9:9 and describe him as a tax collector in 10:3?

Fishing boats are tied to the rocks at Tiberias. Since sudden turbulence of the Sea of Galilee is likely to occur any time between noon and nine in the evening, night fishing is desirable. The light of the lanterns on the boats attracts the fish.

of the Sea of Galilee. It was his job to collect import and export duties on goods that moved between the territories of Herod Antipas and Philip. His work involved constant contact with Gentiles. This made it impossible for him to keep the ceremonial law. Such an official was further pushed beyond the pale of respectability by a widespread and well-documented conviction that he and his kind were dishonest. They were called sinners and robbers. Since they worked for Rome, they were also unpatriotic. How strange that Jesus should call such a one to be an intimate associate! "Those who are well have no need of a physician." he explained, "but those who are sick" (Mt. 9:12).

Jesus doubtless issued other invitations to special discipleship, but they are not recorded. Tradition has fixed the total number of intimates at twelve. The pattern was derived from the original twelve tribes of Israel. The purpose was to define the character of the campaign. It was to be a *national* mission. The four lists of the Twelve in the New Testament are not identical.[16] Torturous efforts have been made to harmonize them.[17] A more satisfactory solution is to regard "twelve" as symbolic and approximate. The number in the inner circle probably fluctuated from time to time. At first there were two ... then four ... then five. ...

[16]Mk. 3:16–19; Mt. 10:2–4; Lk. 6:14–16; Acts 1:13.
[17]For example: Thaddaeus (Mt., Mk.) is said to be Judas the Son of James (Lk.) and Judas not Iscariot (Jn.).

We know very little about the Twelve. Simon (Peter) was impulsive and unpredictable. It took considerable imagination for Jesus to see in him a rock-like nature. James and John had explosive tempers and were dubbed "sons of thunder" (Mk. 3:17; Lk. 9:54). Thomas was a twin with analytical tendencies. Simon ("the Cananaean" in Matthew and Mark[18] and "the Zealot" in Luke and Acts) was determined either to achieve political independence or to observe the Law strictly. Judas[19] was an informer. Simon Peter heads all lists, and Judas always stands at the bottom. Peter, James, and John were the most intimate of the intimates. All of the Twelve were from the ranks of unofficial Judaism. All were Galileans, with the possible exception of Judas. They came from the common walks of life, but Jesus gave them uncommon opportunities and responsibilities.

Mighty Works (12–17, 45–48)[20]

Jesus was a preacher. Mark describes what appears to be a sample Sabbath in Capernaum. Jesus spoke in the synagogue. The people "were astonished at his teaching, for he taught them as one who had authority, and not as the scribes" (1:22). It was the manner, not the matter, of his message that impressed them. He was not fond of footnotes. Unlike the scribes, he made little appeal to precedent and authority. "Underived power rather than novelty in content was probably the impression which Jesus gave in his teaching."[21] He taught as though authority resided in him.

Jesus also performed mighty works. When he had finished preaching in the synagogue at Capernaum, he drove an unclean spirit from a man. Later the same day he cured Simon Peter's mother-in-law of a fever. At sundown "they brought to him all who were sick or possessed with demons. . . . And he healed many who were sick with various diseases, and cast out many demons" (Mk. 1:32,34).

Jesus was up long before daybreak the following morning. A crisis had been created for the Campaigner. The demand for mighty works was multiplying. The helpless cried out for healings. Jesus withdrew to a lonely place and prayed for guidance. He was interrupted by Simon and those with him. "Every one is searching for you," they exclaimed. It was his works more than his words that had aroused them. Jesus replied, "Let us go on to the next towns, that I may preach there also; for that is why I came out" (Mk. 1:37–38). Whatever else may be said about the works of Jesus (we shall discuss their nature and meaning at some length in a later chapter), one thing is clear. They were not deliverable upon demand. Jesus' first and foremost task was the proclamation of the Good News. Mighty works

---

[18]"Cananaean" does not refer to the Land of Canaan but means jealous one or zealot.

[19]"Iscariot" may mean "man from Kerioth" or "the false."

[20]Mt. 7:28–8:17; Mk. 1:21–34, 40–45; Lk. 4:31–41; 5:1–16; 7:1–10.

[21]H. J. Cadbury, *Jesus: What Manner of Man* (New York: The Macmillan Company, 1947), p. 72.

played an important part in that activity, but Jesus did not regard them as crowd-pleasers or ends in themselves. And in this instance, he didn't even think of them as necessary or desirable.

Some scholars have constructed a rather precise itinerary of Jesus' Galilean campaign by following Mark's references to places.

1. Jesus centers his activity in Capernaum (1:21). He makes a journey through Galilee (1:39) and one across the Sea of Galilee and back (4:35; 5:21).
2. Jesus visits Nazareth (6:1) and makes another circuit of Galilee (6:6b).
3. Jesus journeys to Bethsaida (6:45) and returns (6:53).
4. Jesus withdraws to the region of Tyre and Sidon (7:24) and returns by way of the Decapolis (7:31).
5. Jesus visits Dalmanutha (8:10), Bethsaida again (8:22), the villages of Caesarea Philippi (8:27), and a "high mountain" (9:2), and returns through Galilee (9:30) to Capernaum (9:33).
6. Jesus then begins the journey to Jerusalem (10:1) through Transjordan and Jericho (10:46).

We think such efforts are futile. Mark's "chronology," as we have observed, is suspect. Matthew and Luke use the same sources in a different order. The evangelists either had little knowledge of the exact sequence of events or they set little store by it. The background and occasion of most of the parables are suspect. The same is true of the miracles. The Sermon on the Mount (Matthew 5–7) or the Sermon on the Plain (Lk. 6:20–49) represents a summary of Jesus' teachings taken from different periods of his activity.[22] We have, consequently, elected to treat separately in later chapters the parables, miracles, and Sermon and also to deal topically with the other gospel material.

Crowds and Critics (52–54, 69–70)[23]

Jesus' campaign greatly stirred the people of Galilee and beyond. After the successful Sabbath in Capernaum "every one" was searching for him (Mk. 1:37). As he moved from synagogue to synagogue throughout the region, large numbers responded to his words and works. When he withdrew to the Sea of Galilee, "a great multitude from Galilee followed; also from Judea and Jerusalem and Idumea and from beyond the Jordan and from about Tyre and Sidon a great multitude, hearing all that he did, came to him" (Mk. 3:7–8). So great was the clamor of the crowds to hear and to be healed that Jesus told his disciples to have a small boat ready for him "lest they should crush him" (Mk. 3:9). At the height of his popularity with the people Jesus fed five thousand men (Mk. 6:44) plus women and children (Mt. 14:21) in a lonely place (Mk. 6:35). "The movement headed by Jesus of Nazareth was much more widespread than the gospels

[22]In Matthew, especially, the form is a literary device of the author of the Gospel. He arranged the teachings of Jesus in five great discourses.
[23]Mt. 9:1–17; 12:1–14; Mk. 2:1–3:6; Lk. 5:17–6:11.

represent; their interests are those of the church of their time, and their method is selective; they are concerned with the apostles and their relations to Jesus more than with the response of the multitudes to his ministry and message."[24]

The popularity of Jesus with the crowds soon aroused opposition. The growing hostility of the scribes (official teachers of the Jewish religion) and the Pharisees (ardent advocates of the scribal viewpoint) is summarized by Mark in a block of five conflict stories.

Conflict over forgiveness of sins (2:1–12). Jesus was at home in Capernaum. Crowds collected. As Jesus preached, people filled the house, crowded the doorway, and spilled out into the courtyard. Four men approached carrying a paralytic on a pallet. The blocked doorway prevented them from reaching Jesus by the normal route. They ascended the outside staircase to the flat roof. They removed a section of the roof (saplings covered with branches and twigs and topped with clay) and lowered the pallet and the paralytic into Jesus' presence.[25]

When Jesus saw the faith of the four friends,[26] he startled the scribes by saying, "My son, your sins are forgiven" (2:5). Some of the scribes retorted, "It is blasphemy! Who can forgive sins but God alone?" (2:7). The scribes held that only God could forgive sins, and they believed that He forgave the repentant immediately without the need of a human intermediary. Jesus had thus committed a double error. He had usurped the position of God and he had done so without requiring repentance on the part of the paralytic. The penalty for such blasphemy was death by stoning (Lev. 24:16).

Jesus replied to the scribal charge of blasphemy with a question: "Which is easier, to say to the paralytic, 'Your sins are forgiven,' or to say, 'Rise, take up your pallet and walk'?" (2:9). Obviously the deed would exceed the declaration. Sin and suffering were regarded as cause and consequence in the ancient world. "Think now, who that was innocent ever perished?" (Job 4:7). "A sick man does not recover from his sickness until all his sins are forgiven him as it is written [Ps. 103:3] 'who forgiveth all thy iniquities who healeth all thy diseases' " (Nedarim 41a). If Jesus could cure the man's paralysis, that would be proof positive that his sins had been forgiven. As long as the paralysis remained, all talk about the man's sins having been forgiven was speculative and blasphemous. Jesus continued, "But that you may know that the Son of man has authority on earth to forgive sins I say to you [the paralytic], rise, take up your pallet and go home" (2:10–11). The paralytic did as he was commanded; and the amazed crowd glorified God, saying, "We never saw anything like this!" (2:12).

Did Jesus claim that *he* could forgive sins? He did not say to the paralytic, "*I* forgive your sins." He said, "Your sins *are* forgiven." But Mark

---

[24]F. C. Grant, *The Gospel of the Kingdom* (New York: The Macmillan Company, 1940), p. xi.

[25]Lk. 5:19 pictures a Roman roof with tile!

[26]And, presumably, the faith of the paralytic who had probably urged his friends to bring him.

clearly intends his readers to conclude that Jesus did have authority to forgive sins. This was the faith of the church at the time this Gospel was written. If Jesus could cure a paralytic and perform other mighty works, he could also pronounce the divine forgiveness of sins. He did this not as a mere prophet of God or even as the Messiah. He did it as "the Son of man [who] has authority on earth to forgive sins" (2:10).

We have a double theme in Mark 2:1–12—the forgiveness of sins and the healing of the paralytic. It has been suggested that 2:5b–10 (which concerns the forgiveness of sins) represents an insertion into an "old" pericope which narrated a healing. "The whole inserted controversial section (vss. 5b–10) reflects the polemics of the early church."[27] Mark 2:12 gives a common conclusion to a miracle story. It makes no mention of the inserted forgiveness-of-sins theme. Whatever the merits of this suggestion, it does not accord with Mark's purpose. For the writer of this Gospel, the conflict with the scribes in this instance has to do primarily with the forgiveness of sins. William Manson concurs. He designates the inserted material as 2:6–11. He holds that it was Jesus' declaration of the forgiveness of sins (5b) "that raised the man to his feet and restored him to life and power."[28]

Conflict over eating with sinners (2:13–17). A despised tax collector named Levi was on duty at the northern end of the Sea of Galilee. As he sat at his office, Jesus passed by and invited him to become a special disciple. Levi promptly accepted. A dinner followed in Jesus' house.[29] Many tax collectors and sinners were present. The tax collectors were not the great magnates who farmed the taxes of entire provinces (publicans). They were the underlings who administered the vicious system. The privilege of collecting the taxes was sold to the highest bidder. He made his profit by charging as much above his "cost" as the traffic would bear. The sinners were those who were careless about keeping the requirements of the Mosaic Law. Strict Jews lumped tax collectors and sinners together and treated them like Samaritans. It was a scandal to associate with such trash. It was shocking for Jesus to call a tax collector to special discipleship. It was immoral for him to consort with a crowd of tax collectors and sinners in his own home and to act as their host at a feast.

The straight-laced scribes of the Pharisees demanded of Jesus' disciples, "Why does he eat with tax collectors and sinners?" (2:16). Jesus replied for his followers. He did not excuse his conduct. He accepted the label but did not regard it as libel. "Those who are well have no need of a physician, but those who are sick; I came not to call the righteous, but sinners" (2:17).

Conflict over fasting (2:18–22). The disciples of John and the Pharisees were observing a fast. The disciples of Jesus were conspicuous because of

---

[27]Grant, in *The Interpreter's Bible*, VII, 672.

[28]William Manson, *Jesus the Messiah* (Philadelphia: The Westminster Press, 1946), p. 68. For a discussion of omissions and modifications Matthew and Luke make in their accounts see H. J. Held, in *Tradition and Interpretation in Matthew*, pp. 175–78. Held shows that Matthew is much more interested in the controversial question about the forgiveness of sins than in the healing.

[29]Lk. 5:29 states that the feast was given in Levi's house.

their nonparticipation. Since fasting was such an integral part of Jewish religious life, the people logically asked Jesus why he and his disciples did not fast. The question concerned voluntary fasting. The people wanted to know why Jesus and his disciples failed to fast above and beyond the call of duty.

Jesus' reply struck at the heart of the matter. He had nothing against fasting as such. If he had, he would never have said to his disciples, "And *when* you fast, do not look dismal, like the hypocrites" (Mt. 6:16).[30] What he objected to was the timing. Fasting was a sign of sorrow. "Can the wedding guests fast while the bridegroom is with them?" (2:19). Of course not! The kingdom of God was at hand. The forces of evil were being overthrown. It was not a time for mourning but for rejoicing.

Fasting was fashionable in the early church. "You must fast on Wednesday and Friday" (Didache 8:1). Why did Christians fast when Jesus and his disciples had not? They believed that Jesus had predicted, "The days will come when the bridegroom is taken away from them, and then they will fast in that day" (2:20). This saying, however, lacks support. It makes Jesus declare that his followers would be justified in fasting after his death although he and his disciples refrained from voluntary fasting during his ministry. Mark 2:20 was written in the perspective of the crucifixion ("that day"). By then the figure of the bridegroom had been identified with Jesus and influenced by his death. If Jesus told his disciples early in his ministry that "The days will come, when the bridegroom is taken away from them . . . ," they completely failed to grasp his point. At a much later date he plainly told them in private of his certain doom. They were incredulous. Peter rebuked Jesus for entertaining such an absurd and repulsive thought (8:32).

The original context of the twin parables that follow (2:21–22) has been lost. In themselves they seem to teach only the danger of new things. If a piece of unshrunk cloth is used to patch an old garment, it will rip the old cloth at the first washing. If new wine in a state of violent fermentation is poured into an old, hard, dry, nonelastic wineskin, it will soon burst the wineskin. In their Marcan context these parables declare that the mission of Jesus and the forms of Judaism (voluntary fasting) are incompatible.[31]

Conflict over Sabbath observance: reaping grain (2:23–28). Jesus and his disciples passed through grainfields on the Sabbath. The disciples paused and plucked heads of grain. (In Luke 6:1 they not only reaped the grain but they threshed it by rubbing the grain between their hands.) The Pharisees, who were ever so handy, protested: "Look, why are they doing what is not lawful on the sabbath?" (2:24). It was a proper question. The Lord had commanded, "Six days you shall work, but on the seventh day

[30]Emphasis added.

[31]Jeremias, *The Parables of Jesus*, pp. 117–18, points out that wedding, wine, and harvest are common Near East symbols of the New Age, and garment is a symbol of the cosmos. Mk. 2:21 compares the old world (whose time has run out; it is no longer worth patching with new cloth) with the New Age. The same point is made by means of the wine metaphor in Mk. 2:22.

you shall rest" (Ex. 34:21). A person who worked on the Sabbath should be put to death (Ex. 31:14). The written Law had undergone considerable elaboration and refinement at the hands of the scribes. This was especially true of Sabbath observance. Pharisees of the first century honored "the tradition of the elders" as highly as the written Mosaic Law. The tradition prohibited thirty-nine principal classes of work on the Sabbath. Two of these were reaping and threshing (Shabbath 7:2). The right of travelers to help themselves to grain (or grapes) standing in the field was not involved. Passers-by were permitted this privilege to satisfy their hunger (Deut. 23:24–25). The issue with which the Pharisees confronted Jesus was that of approved Sabbath conduct.

Jesus defended the conduct of his disciples by an appeal to Scripture. He recalled the time when David was hungry and asked for bread from the high priest, Ahimelech.[32] There was no bread at hand except "the bread of the Presence." These loaves (one for each of the twelve tribes of Israel) were baked on Friday. They were placed on the holy table early on the Sabbath where they remained until the next Sabbath. Then—and only then —could they be eaten by the priests. In the emergency, however, Ahimelech gave David the holy bread and he and his men ate it (I Sam. 21:1–6). A telling point! If David, who was a paragon of virtue in the eyes of the Pharisees, could eat the bread of the Presence to satisfy his hunger, surely Jesus' disciples were entitled to pluck the grain on the Sabbath to satisfy theirs.[33]

We have in this incident an excellent example of a paradigm or pronouncement story. The controversy culminates in a pithy saying of Jesus: "The sabbath was made for man, not man for the sabbath" (2:27). The Pharisees had embalmed the Sabbath with their "whereases." They had made man a Sabbath slave. This was contrary to God's intent. The Sabbath was not made for man's woe but for his welfare.

According to Mark the argument with the Pharisees was clinched by another pronouncement of Jesus: "So the Son of man is lord even of the sabbath" (2:28). "Son of man" in this verse has been variously interpreted. Following as it does 2:27, we would expect it to mean: (1) Man is master of the Sabbath. But what Jew would say that? God had instituted the Sabbath and was its Lord. Man was its object but not its overlord. (2) The Messiah is master of the Sabbath. This is the sense in which Matthew and Luke (who omit Mk. 2:27) seem to understand the phrase. Jesus, as the Messiah, regulates the Sabbath. (3) The saying has been added to the original story and reflects the theology of Mark and the church of his day. The church identified Jesus with the heavenly Son of Man.

Conflict over Sabbath observance: healing (3:1–6). Jesus was in the synagogue on the Sabbath. A man with a withered (probably atrophied) hand was there. The Pharisees focused on Jesus to see if he would heal the

---

[32]Mark's "Abiathar" is an error.
[33]Mt. 12:5–7 adds another illustration. The priests in the Temple are compelled to break their Sabbath by the necessities of their office. Yet they are accounted blameless.

man. They were eager to file charges against him. Sabbath-breaking was a capital offense. Just how rigidly the Law was enforced, though, is uncertain. There were apparently two schools of thought on the matter—the strict and the lenient.

Jesus was evidently aware of the intent of his enemies. He directed the man with the withered hand to come into his presence. Then he addressed a searching double question to the Pharisees: "Is it lawful on the sabbath to do good or to do harm, to save life or to kill?" (3:4). The Pharisees were silent. Jesus' anger[34] mounted with his grief at their hardheartedness. He commanded the cripple to stretch out his hand. The man obeyed. His hand was healed.[35]

It was contrary to the Law, according to the usual rabbinical interpretation, to heal on the Sabbath. Exceptions were permitted only in cases of dire necessity. The case of the man with the withered hand was obviously no emergency. The healing could easily have been postponed until the next day. The school of Hillel held that it was proper to visit the sick and to pray for them on the Sabbath. This was "to do good," but Jesus went further. He healed on the Sabbath. He asserted that to release a man from sickness on the Sabbath was not contrary to God's Law but consistent with it.

The Pharisees were furious. They rushed out and "held counsel with the Herodians against him, how to destroy him" (3:6).[36] We don't know very much about the Herodians.[37] They may have been fanatical devotees of Herod Antipas, ruler of Galilee. If so, they probably longed for the restoration of the Herodian monarchy. Their political interests and instincts were on the side of law and order. They loved the status quo as dearly as the Sadducees. What strange bedfellows the Pharisees and the Herodians made! The Pharisees generally remained aloof from politics and the Herodians were immersed in it. But many an absurd alliance has been created by the appearance of a common threat.

Mark's five controversy stories accent the hostility of the scribes and Pharisees toward Jesus. The link between the Pharisees and the Herodians in 3:6 has been questioned It seems to depict too decisive an action at too early a stage in Jesus' ministry. But Mark's order is not chronological. The conflict stories (resumed, perhaps, in 3:20–30) are themselves not to be thought of as having occurred in rapid succession. They are intended to illustrate the growth in opposition to Jesus as the seaside story that follows illustrates the surge of Jesus' popularity with the crowds (3:7–12).

34Omitted by Mt. and Lk.

35Mt. 12:11–12 introduces another question by Jesus. It concerns the humane custom of lifting a sheep out of a pit on the Sabbath. Lk. puts the question in another context (14:5). Gerhard Barth, in *Tradition and Interpretation in Matthew*, p. 79, observes that two things stand out in Matthew's positive rule for the behavior of the congregation in 12:12b: (1) it is assumed that the Sabbath is still kept in the congregation and (2) the love commandment is superior to the Sabbath commandment. The former limits the latter.

36"Held counsel" probably means "gave counsel," as B and other manuscripts indicate.

37See Samuel Sandmel, "Herodians," in *The Interpreter's Dictionary of the Bible*, ed. George A. Buttrick (New York: Abingdon Press, 1962), E–J, 594–95.

Dishonorable Discharge (10, 85, 89, 108)[38]

Three incidents are recorded in the Synoptics which indicate that the scribes and Pharisees were not alone in their opposition to Jesus. Many of his friends, relatives, and fellow townsmen thought him mad, rejected his mission, or tried to kill him. These incidents occurred during the Galilean ministry, although we cannot be sure exactly when. Neither do we know their sequence. The Gospels themselves do not agree on this.

The first incident (Mk. 3:19b–21). Jesus was at home in Capernaum. A crowd gathered. The crowd was so large that there was no elbow room. Eating was rendered impossible. When Jesus' friends[39] heard about it, they tried to seize him. "He is beside himself," they declared (3:21). Jesus was in a state of dangerous mental agitation. He needed to be rescued by the stable and secure! The charge was a common one against prophets. Elijah sent one of the sons of the prophets to anoint Jehu. After Jehu had returned from the secret anointing, servants asked him about the prophet: "Why did this mad fellow come to you?" (II Kings 9:11).[40]

The second incident (Mk. 3:31–35). Jesus was seated on the ground in Oriental fashion. A crowd was sitting about him listening to him teach. His mother and brothers approached. He took no notice until it was announced to him that they were present. His response was surprising: "Who are my mother and my brothers?" (3:33). Was he an embarrassment to the family? Had they come with the intention of laying hold on him as a lunatic? Had they come to rescue him from the consequences of his popularity and success and from the hands of his enemies? Many modern commentators identify the mother and brothers with "his friends" in 3:21. Jesus' earthly family played a walk-on role in his ministry. The Synoptics do not picture his mother as an important personage. They do not even place her at the scene of the crucifixion. The Fourth Gospel represents Mary as faithful but without full understanding of her son (Jn. 2:4–5). The brothers did not believe in Jesus during his ministry (Jn. 7:5), although they were later active in the affairs of the early church (I Cor. 9:5).

Whatever the family's intent, for Mark the pericope had but one purpose. It was to introduce the pronouncement of Jesus in 3:35. Jesus looked around on those who sat about him: "Here are my mother and my brothers!" (3:34). The meaning of his statement is clear. The supreme relationship in life is not biological; it is spiritual. The kingdom of God has top priority. All other attachments—even the most intimate and personal[41]—are secondary. "Whoever does the will of God," he declared, "is my brother, and sister,

---

38Mt. 12:22–24,46–50; 13:53–58; Mk. 3:19b–22,31–35; 6:1–6; Lk. 4:16–30; 8:19–21; 11:14–16.

39The Greek words (οἱ παρ' αὐτοῦ, "those with him") may mean "his family."

40See Jn. 10:20.

41See Mk. 10:29–30.

and mother" (3:35). This saying was hard for any Jew, taught to honor his father and mother, to accept; and it was even harder for Christian commentators to expound. What better proof is there of its authenticity![42]

The third incident (Mk. 6:1–6). Jesus then left the vicinity of the Sea of Galilee. With his disciples he paid a visit to his home town, Nazareth.[43] He was invited to take part in the synagogue service on the Sabbath. Synagogue worship consisted in the recitation of the Shema, a prayer, a set reading from the Law, a free-choice reading from the Prophets (with explanation and application of one or both Scriptual passages), and a blessing

According to tradition, the Church of the Synagogue in Nazareth marks the site of the synagogue to which Jesus returned to teach his fellow townsmen—to their astonishment and offense (Mk. 6:1–3).

42Gerhard Barth observes in *Tradition and Interpretation in Matthew*, p. 102, that Matthew's change of the audience for Jesus' saying from "the crowd" (Mk. 3:32, 34) to "the disciples" (Mt. 12:49) indicates that for Matthew discipleship means doing the will of God and the will of God is done in discipleship.

43Mk. and Mt. do not mention Nazareth by name. They speak of Jesus' own *patris* (native place *or* ancestral home). Lk. 4:16, preserving the tradition of Jesus' Bethlehem birth, identifies the place as "Nazareth, where he had been brought up." Mk. and Jn. display no knowledge of the story of Jesus' Bethlehem birth.

or a prayer. The Scripture was first read in Hebrew and was then translated verse by verse into Aramaic. Each synagogue had a hazzan. He was appointed by the elders to direct the services, care for the sacred scrolls (codices or books were nonexistent), and to double as a schoolteacher during the week. There was no official "minister." The ruling elders could invite any competent visitor or layman of the congregation to read and interpret. Whoever was selected stood up to read and sat down to teach.

Jesus accepted the invitation to speak in his home town synagogue. His fellow townsmen were astonished at his teaching. They asked, "Where did this man get all this? What is the wisdom given to him? What mighty works are wrought by his hands! Is not this the carpenter, the son of Mary[44] and brother of James and Joseph and Judas and Simon, and are not his sisters here with us?" (6:2–3). Their questions led to an altogether unexpected turn of events. "They took offense at him" (6:3). Why? Wisdom and eloquence should have evoked local pride, not prejudice and offense. Mark gives us no clue to their behavior. Perhaps it was the natural reaction of home town folks toward one whom they had known in boyhood and early manhood, whom they now found speaking to them authoritatively, "putting on airs." Who did he think he was, anyway?

Luke's account of the incident at Nazareth is more extended. He places it much earlier in the Galilean campaign than does Mark (or Matthew). According to Luke, when Jesus stood up in the Nazareth synagogue to read, the hazzan brought him a scroll of the prophet Isaiah. Jesus unrolled the scroll and found where it was written, "The Spirit of the Lord is upon me, because he has anointed me to preach good news to the poor. He has sent me to proclaim release to the captives and recovering of sight to the blind, to set at liberty those who are oppressed, to proclaim the acceptable year of the Lord" (Lk. 4:18–19).

This quotation, based on the Septuagint, shows considerable latitude in the use of Scripture. It omits a phrase (Is. 61:1), adds a phrase from another place (Is. 58:6), and fails to mention "the day of vengeance" (Is. 61:2). The original wording expressed some postexilic prophet's sense of mission. In Luke's context "he has anointed me" refers to Jesus' baptism, and "the acceptable year of the Lord" refers to the Messianic age.

When Jesus finished reading, he handed the scroll back to the hazzan and sat down to teach. The eyes of all in the synagogue were riveted on him. Then he said, "Today this scripture has been fulfilled in your hearing" (Lk. 4:21). The reaction of the people was one of surprise. "And all spoke well of him, and wondered [were amazed] at the gracious words which proceeded out of his mouth; and they said, 'Is not this Joseph's son?' " (Lk. 4:22). Their astonishment is not mixed with hostility as it is in Mark.

Attempts have been made to use Luke's more detailed account to explain Mark's briefer one. The offense expressed by the people in Mark is

---

44This reading is probably late and made under the influence of the idea of the virgin birth. Mt. 13:55 reads, "Is not this the carpenter's son?" Lk. 4:22 reads, "Is not this Joseph's son?" It is improbable that if Mark's reading were original, Mt. and Lk. would have changed it to their present ones.

accounted for by Jesus' proclamation about himself in Luke (4:18–21). "It was doubtless this Messianic claim," asserts Major, "for it was surely nothing less, made by one who had been the village carpenter which excited hostile and contemptuous comment on the part of the congregation."[45] This conclusion seems unwarranted for two reasons. (1) In Luke the people showed surprise but not hostility at Jesus' proclamation. Their disapproval stemmed from another source as we shall soon see. (2) Luke's record of the Nazareth incident is controlled by a literary purpose. This purpose precludes the use of Luke to fill in the gaps in Mark's account.

Luke makes Jesus' visit to Nazareth the inauguration of his public ministry. "Today this scripture has been fulfilled in your hearing" becomes the first public pronouncement of Jesus' mission. His career is considered the fulfillment of the Old Testament prediction. He is viewed as the Messiah. The Messianic age is at hand. The Sabbath day in Nazareth is used as the prelude to the whole of Luke-Acts, the two-volume work which depicts the development of a Jewish sect into a world religion Many of the main motifs of Luke-Acts appear in this prelude: (1) the Old Testament preparation and prediction, (2) the anointing by the Spirit, (3) the good news preached to the poor, (4) the proclamation of the Messianic age, (5) the hostility of the Jews, and (6) the mission to the Gentiles. The plan of Luke's two-volume work is well served by such a literary device.

Jesus replied to the congregation's question ("Is not this Joseph's son?") with the comment: "Doubtless you will quote to me this proverb, 'Physician, heal yourself; what we have heard you did at Capernaum, do here also in your own country' " (Lk. 4:23). Then he continued, "No prophet is acceptable in his own country" (Lk. 4:24). His words are more explicit in Mark: "A prophet is not without honor, except in his own country [Nazareth], and among his own kin [uncles, cousins, and others], and in his own house [mother, brothers, sisters]. And he *could* do no mighty work there, except that he laid his hands upon a few sick people and healed them. And he marveled because of their unbelief" (6:4–6).[46] Luke omits Mark's plain reference to Jesus' kin and family and to the limitation of Jesus' power. Matthew alters Mark to read, "And he *did* not do many mighty works there, because of their unbelief" (13:58).[47] Mark is correct in recording what Jesus himself so often taught: without faith, healing is hampered.

Luke states that Jesus chose two familiar bits of Jewish history to support his role as a prophet who does no mighty works in his home town (4:25–27). During a dire drought God sent Elijah not to an Israelite but to a Sidonian widow of Zarephath. It was her jar of meal that was not spent and her cruse of oil that did not fail (I Kings 17:14). Likewise, in the days of Elisha, there were many lepers in Israel. But it was Naaman, the Syrian, whom Elisha cleansed.

The congregation was infuriated. They did not want the benefits of Jesus' mission to be given to foreigners. "And they rose up and put him out

45In *The Mission and Message of Jesus*, p. 81.
46Emphasis added.
47Emphasis added.

The Hill of the Precipice, seen in the background of this picture, is
pointed out to modern tourists as the historic "brow of the hill" (Lk. 4:29)
from which infuriated fellow townsmen intended to cast Jesus headlong
(Lk. 4:16–30). Changes in topography since the first century, however,
make it impossible to locate the hill in question.

of the city, and led him to the brow of the hill on which their city was
built, that they might throw him down headlong. But passing through the
midst of them he went away" (4:29–30). Luke's choice of material once more
serves his purpose. "The rejection of Jesus by his fellow townsmen prepares
the reader for the rejection of Christ by the Sanhedrin, and the rejection
of the gospel by the Jewish nation."[48]

Mission of the Twelve (58–63, 109, 139–140)[49]

Mark places the mission of the Twelve after Jesus' rejection at Nazareth.
This has caused some commentators to conclude that the rejection motivated the mission. But Mark declares that Jesus had the mission in mind
at the time of the appointment of the Twelve: "And he appointed twelve,
to be with him, and to be sent out to preach and have authority to cast out
demons" (3:14–15). The mission stands much later than the appointment
in Mark. It directly follows the appointment in Matthew. Luke lists two
appointments (of the Twelve and of the Seventy) and two missions. Jesus
may well have sent the Twelve on many missions. The one listed here may
be regarded as typical.

At one point Matthew refers to the Twelve as *apostles* (10:2). The term
designates those who are *sent* with a commission (*apostellō*). It is used in

    [48]Gilmour, in *The Interpreter's Bible*, VIII, 95–96.
    [49]Mt. 9:35–11:1; 16:24–25; 18:5; 24:9,13; Mk. 6:6–13; 8:34–35; 9:37; 13:9–13; Lk. 9:1–6,
23–24,48; 10:1–16; 12:2–9,51–53; 14:26–27; 21:12–17,19.

the New Testament to describe not only the Twelve but others: Barnabas and Paul (Acts 14:14); Matthias (Acts 1:26); James, the brother of Jesus (Gal. 1:19); and Andronicus and Junias (Rom. 16:7). Matthew's use of the term in 10:2 reflects the late first-century conviction in the church that the Twelve were the first apostles. Elsewhere, Matthew refers to the Twelve as *disciples*, those who are *taught*.

Mark's treatment of the mission of the Twelve is the most primitive. Yet even this account represents a fusion of Jesus' original directives and the practices of the early church. The staff (6:8) and sandals (6:9)—which are clear concessions to a "world" mission—are permitted by Mark but forbidden by Matthew (10:10). Luke forbids the staff (9:3). Neither Matthew nor Luke mentions the anointing with oil (Mk. 6:13). This practice was a common one in the treatment of the sick in ancient times (James 5:14–15), but we have no evidence that Jesus followed it. Mark's reference probably reflects later apostolic practice.

Matthew (ch. 10) adds considerably to Mark's account of the mission of the Twelve. The result is a set of directions better suited to the mission of the early church. The task of the missionaries is to announce the nearness of the kingdom and to perform signs of it by healing the sick, raising the dead, and exorcising demons (10:7–8). The imminence of the End forces the disciples to respond to persecution with confession and to separation with decision (10:17–39).[50] Matthew alone attributes to Jesus the command, "Go nowhere among the Gentiles, and enter no town of the Samaritans, but go rather to the lost sheep of the house of Israel" (10:5). Jesus worked almost exclusively in Jewish territory.[51] Would such a command have been necessary? Would Jesus' disciples have thought of doing otherwise? It is doubtful that the disciples needed to be cautioned against taking with them *gold* or *silver* (10:9). They were not that affluent. Mark mentions only the command to take no copper coin (Mk. 6:8). The injunction to seek out him who is *worthy* in a town (10:11) smacks of later moralism. Most of the instructions in 10:17–39 concern the Christian church rather than the Twelve. Persecutions which plagued first-century Christians prior to the writing of Matthew are suggested by 10:21–22. "You will not have gone through all the towns of Israel, before the Son of man comes" (10:23) is an extraordinary saying on the lips of Jesus. It is found nowhere else. It coheres beautifully with the conviction of the early church that its Lord would return before the church could complete its preaching mission. It clashes thunderously with Jesus' repeated teaching that only God knows the time.

Matthew used both Mark and Q to form his account of Jesus' instructions to the Twelve. Luke used a few details from Q to modify Mark's account (Lk. 9:1–6), but he placed the bulk of the Q material in another context (Lk. 10:1–11). Luke's sole account of the mission of the Seventy

---

[50]See Günther Bornkamm's illuminating discussion in *Tradition and Interpretation in Matthew*, pp. 17–19.

[51]Mk. 7:24–31 and 8:27–9:1 put Jesus on Gentile soil. Luke once places him in the region of Samaria (17:11).

(10:1–20) has produced numerous explanatory theories. (1) It is a doublet, another version of the sending out of the Twelve. (2) Luke intended the Seventy to symbolize the later Gentile mission, just as the Twelve symbolized the mission to the Jews. Seventy[52] is often thought of in Jewish literature as the number of the Gentile nations. But if Luke had this in mind, why did he imply that the missionaries were dispatched only to Jewish or Samaritan centers? And why did they return so soon?[53] (3) Luke mentioned seventy only because it is a round number for a large group (Ex. 24:1; Num. 11:16). (4) The Seventy were messengers Jesus sent ahead to the towns and villages on the route of his journey to Jerusalem. Their mission was to arrange entertainment for the party when they stopped at night. They also saw to it that Jesus had a colt on which he could ride into Jerusalem and an upper room in which he and his disciples could eat the Passover meal.[54]

What may we conclude about the mission of the Twelve? What did Jesus really tell them? Jesus did not make plans for an organized church; neither did he structure a world-wide campaign. Sometime during the Galilean ministry he sent his disciples out on a mission. Its aim was to arouse the nation. Its message was the nearness of the kingdom. Its summons was to repentance. The disciples were to travel in pairs. They were to depend on the hospitality of their hearers for support. They were to cast out demons and heal the sick. They were to remain only where they were welcome. Time was of the essence.

Meal for Many (64, 110–112, 118)[55]

When Jesus sent the Twelve on their mission, they aroused not only Galilee but Galilee's ruler. Herod Antipas was averse to mass movements, which to him spelled trouble. Galilee, which frequently exploded into open revolt, was turbulent enough without them. The Tetrarch had learned to deal ruthlessly with suspected insurrectionists. When John the Baptist's movement mushroomed, Herod pushed the panic button. John had reprimanded Herod for his illicit marriage (Mk. 6:18) and was considered a political threat. Herod removed the prickly prophet from the scene and cast him into prison.[56]

Then came the Carpenter and his campaigners to disturb Herod's precarious peace of mind. Mark tersely reports, "King Herod heard of it; for Jesus' name had become known" (6:14). It would have been strange indeed if Herod had not heard of Jesus. It would have been stranger still if Herod

[52]Or seventy-two.

[53]See Lk. 24:46–49 where the Gentile mission is entrusted to the Eleven and their associates.

[54]See E. J. Goodspeed, *A Life of Jesus* (New York: Harper & Row, Publishers, Inc., 1950), pp. 144–45.

[55]Mt. 11:2–6; 14:1–21; 15:32–39; Mk. 6:14–44; 8:1–10; Lk. 7:18–23; 9:7–17.

[56]Herod's motive was to keep John "safe," according to Mk. 6:20. But it was actually *Herod's* safety that worried Herod, as Josephus indicates.

had not feared him. The crowds flocked to him in increasing numbers to hear his words and witness his works. The rising tide of opposition on the part of religious leaders had slammed the door of the synagogue in Jesus' face. He was now forced to teach along the lakeside and at other outdoor spots. The open-air crowds advertised his popularity even more. Speculation was rife. Some said, "John the baptizer has been raised from the dead; that is why these powers are at work in him" (6:14). Palestinians held that the soul of a man who had met a violent death was fortified in the spirit world. Since John had met such a death, it was natural for some to conclude that Jesus was either John come back to life or one under the control of John's empowered spirit. Others said, "It is Elijah" (6:15). It was a popular expectation that Elijah would return before "the great and terrible day" (Mal. 4:5). Still others said, "It is a prophet, like one of the prophets of old" (6:15). Herod concurred with the first surmise: "John, whom I beheaded, has been raised" (6:16).

The Gospels do not say how long the mission of the Twelve lasted. It may have been terminated by the tragedy of John's beheading. When the disciples did return to Jesus at Capernaum, they "told him all that they had done and taught. And he said to them, 'Come away by yourselves to a lonely place, and rest a while.' For many were coming and going, and they had no leisure even to eat. And they went away in the boat to a lonely place by themselves. Now many saw them going, and knew them, and they ran there on foot from all the towns, and got there ahead of them. As he landed he saw a great throng, and he had compassion on them, because they were like sheep without a shepherd; and he began to teach them many things" (Mk. 6:30–34).

The location of the landing is not specified. Some scholars suggest that Jesus took the boat to the northeastern end of the Sea of Galilee. There he was in the territory of the more tolerant Philip and out of reach of the hostile Herod. The crowds followed the boat around the northern end of the lake and arrived ahead of Jesus and his disciples.[57] This suggestion is attractive, but it makes rapid runners of the crowd or slow rowers of the disciples. Other scholars think that Jesus had not gone very far in the boat when he noticed the crowds in pursuit. He then came ashore on the west side of the lake.[58]

The day is remembered primarily for what occurred at its close. The crowds had been assembled for hours. Jesus had taught them "many things" (Mk. 6:34). They had grown tired and hungry. The disciples suggested to Jesus that he send the crowds into the country and nearby villages. There they could purchase something to eat. Jesus countered with an astounding command: "You give them something to eat" (Mk. 6:37a). The perplexed disciples replied, "Shall we go and buy two hundred denarii worth of bread, and give it to them to eat?" (Mk. 6:37b). They were talking like madmen. Two hundred denarii were equivalent to forty dollars with a purchasing

---

[57] Rollins and Rollins, *Jesus and His Ministry*, p. 76.

[58] T. W. Manson, *The Servant-Messiah* (Cambridge: At the University Press, 1956), p. 70.

The Church of the Multiplication, shown in this picture, marks the traditional site where Jesus multiplied the bread and fish and fed the multitude. Somewhere along the shores of the Sea of Galilee, seen in the background, he called his first disciples.

power many times that amount. Jesus told the disciples to take an inventory: "How many loaves have you? Go and see" (Mk. 6:38). When they had found out, they reported back: "Five, and two fish" (Mk. 6:38).

Jesus commanded the crowds to sit down on the green grass (which suggests the spring of the year) by companies (of fifty or one hundred). Then he took the five loaves and the two fish, "looked up to heaven, and blessed [God for the food], and broke the loaves, and gave them to the disciples to set before the people; and he divided the two fish among them all. And they all ate and were satisfied. And they took up twelve baskets full of broken pieces and of the fish. And those who ate the loaves were five thousand men" (Mk. 6:41–44). Matthew adds "women and children" to the five thousand men (14:21), making a total of perhaps twenty thousand people.

Matthew's treatment of the conversation between Jesus and the disciples highlights the disciples' lack of faith (rather than their lack of understanding, as reported in Mark), and it accents their mediating role in connection with the meal. Matthew omits the audacious counter-question of Mark 6:37b ("Shall we go and buy two hundred denarii worth of bread, and give it to them to eat?"). Perhaps it is because he thinks it unbecoming, but more likely because he sees the disciples' role differently. They do not understand Jesus' command in Mark (a common deficiency in this Gospel), but they do in Matthew. There Jesus says, "They need not go away," because he is not thinking about food to be purchased in the villages; he is thinking about food the disciples already have. Hence the disciples immediately catalog their food supply. Their failure is not the lack of understanding but of faith: "We have only five loaves here and two fish (Mt.

14:17). In Mark and Luke, moreover, Jesus *gives* the loaves to the disciples to *distribute* to the crowds, but in Matthew the disciples' role is magnified. They share in the giving.[59]

This is the only miracle story told in each of the four Gospels.[60] Mark (8:1–9) and Matthew (15:32–38) also record a feeding of the four thousand. All appear to be variant forms of the same tradition. Mark seems to support this conclusion. On one occasion Jesus fed five thousand with five loaves and two fish (6:30–44). Later (8:1–9), when he proposed to feed four thousand, the disciples reacted (8:4) as though they had never heard of the first feeding: "How can one feed these men with bread here in the desert?" (This crowd was fed with seven loaves and a few small fish.) But the real problem is not whether there was one feeding or two. If Jesus could perform the mighty work once, he could do it again and again. The real questions are "How?" and "Why?"

Many theories have been developed to explain the feeding. (1) Some see no problem here. They accept the story as literal fact. Jesus was God incarnate. All things are possible with God. Jesus multiplied the food exactly as described. (2) Others view the feeding as a miracle of sharing. They make much of a small detail added by John: "There is a lad here who has five barley loaves and two fish" (6:9). It was the lad's lunch that made possible the miracle. He offered to share it with others who had come without supplies. His unselfishness was contagious. The foresighted shared with the hindsighted. After the potluck was over, there was food to spare. (3) Still others assert that the crowds were fed with spiritual food. Jesus spoke to his hearers "of the kingdom of God" (Lk. 9:11). They became so full of this kind of food that they forgot about any other. When the story was told, a feast on the Bread of Life was mistakenly reported as a meal of the "staff of life" and a few fish. (4) Some claim that the feeding is modeled after similar stories in the Old Testament. Moses had fed the people with manna during the wilderness wanderings (Exodus 16). Elijah had multiplied "a handful of meal in a jar, and a little oil in a cruse" so that three persons "ate for many days" (I Kings 17:8–16). Elisha had multiplied twenty loaves of barley and some fresh grain to feed a hundred men. "And they ate, and had some left" (II Kings 4:42–44). Now one greater than Moses, Elijah, or Elisha was here (Mt. 12:42). (5) Some say the feeding is the first Lord's Supper. The incident is entirely historical except for the words that there were twelve baskets full remaining.

There is much in the story of the feeding that suggests a Messianic meal. The Synoptics frequently employ the figures of eating and drinking to depict religious realities. More than once they picture the kingdom of God in terms of a banquet (Mt. 22:1–14; Lk. 14:16–24). The similarities between the feeding and the Lord's Supper are striking; for example, the blessing, the breaking of the bread, and the distribution of the bread by the disciples as by the deacons in the early church. The Lord's Supper is certainly an anticipation of the Messianic banquet. For the people who ate

---

[59] See H. J. Held, in *Tradition and Interpretation in Matthew*, pp. 181–84.
[60] Mt. 14:13–21; Mk. 6:30–44; Lk. 9:10–17; Jn. 6:1–14.

the meal in repentance and faith, it was a foretaste of the kingdom which was to come. Indeed, in a sense, they already reveled in its blessings.

This intepretation, though, is not without its difficulties. (1) It does not solve the multiplication problem. Not one of the six narratives of the feeding "states in so many words that Jesus multiplied the food. This is left to be inferred from the statement that 'all ate and had enough,' and that twelve baskets of fragments were taken up."[61] But the inference is plain, and the problem remains. (2) If the feeding was a Messianic meal, the disciples evidently failed to grasp its significance. Mark states that they "did not understand about the loaves" (Mk. 6:52). This lack of understanding is typical of the disciples in Mark, but it has continued for nineteen centuries.

Withdrawal (113–117, 121)[62]

The Meal for Many marked the virtual end of Jesus' Galilean ministry. Shortly thereafter "he arose and went away to the region of Tyre and Sidon" (Mk. 7:24). These cities lay to the north of Galilee on the Phoenician coast of the Mediterranean. What prompted his withdrawal is not indicated. Several theories have been advanced. (1) Some say that he entered the area to conduct a Gentile mission. This is contradicted by his desire for seclusion and his reluctance to heal (Mk. 7:24–27). (2) Others regard the withdrawal as a flight from the hostile Herod. Herod had moved quickly to terminate the work of John. How could he afford to tolerate the greater threat inherent in the campaign of Jesus? Had he not declared that Jesus was "John, whom I beheaded" (Mk. 6:16)? (3) Still others are convinced that the withdrawal was "far more a flight from the dangerous enthusiasm of his friends than from the suspicions and fears of his enemies."[63] Jesus' teachings had aroused the people. The "Messianic meal" had multiplied their enthusiasm. The spirit of revolt against Rome was rife. Roman rule galled the Galileans. Heavy taxation aggravated them. The brutal murder of John the Baptist appalled them. They longed for the restoration of "the kingdom of our father David" (Mk. 11:10). Mark declares that immediately after the feeding Jesus "*made* his disciples get into the boat and go before him to the other side, to Bethsaida, while he dismissed the crowd" (6:45).[64] He apparently believed it would be easier to persuade the crowd to disperse after the disciples had departed; this suggests that the disciples shared the convictions of the crowd. The Fourth Gospel supports the theory that Jesus' withdrawal was a flight from friends. "Perceiving then that they were about to come and take him by force to make him king, Jesus withdrew again to the

---

[61]William Manson, *The Gospel of Luke*, The Moffatt New Testament Commentary (New York and London: Harper and Row, Publishers, Inc., © 1930), p. 104. Used by permission of Hodder & Stoughton, Ltd., London, the British Publishers.

[62]Mt. 14:22–15:31; Mk. 6:45–7:37; 8:22–26.

[63]T. W. Manson, *The Servant-Messiah*, (Cambridge: At the University Press, 1956), p. 71.

[64]Emphasis added.

hills by himself" (Jn. 6:15). Preoccupation with the miracle of multiplication has tended to obscure the real nature of the crisis. "The main interest of the original narrative lay not in the realm of physical miracle but in another quarter."[65] The crisis was not metaphysical but political. This theory is weakened, however, by evidence from the Synoptics themselves. Mark maintains the Messianic secret to the very end. Never does Jesus publicly appeal to his Messianic authority. In the crucial conversation near Caesarea Philippi—when Jesus asked his disciples who men thought he was —several different answers were given. The belief that Jesus was the Messiah was not one of them. This would seem to indicate that Jesus had not acted in such a way as to arouse in the popular mind the idea that his mission was Messianic. (4) Some think Jesus withdrew from Galilee for rest and prayer. (5) Others argue that he withdrew to permit the hostility of his critics to moderate.

Just how long Jesus remained in Phoenician territory is unknown. His stay there is followed in Mark's account by a visit to the Decapolis (another district outside of Galilee) and to Bethsaida and the villages of Caesarea Philippi (still outside of Galilee in the territory of the tolerant Philip).[66]

Peter's Confession (122, 127, 191)[67]

A crucial conversation took place near Caesarea Philippi. Jesus was evidently concerned about the interpretation of his mission by the people of Galilee and by Herod Antipas. He asked his disciples, "Who do men say that I am?" (Mk. 8:27). The answers given by the disciples coincided with the rumors rehearsed in Mark 6:14–16, which we dealt with earlier in this chapter. After the disciples had summarized the results of their latest "public-opinion poll," Jesus asked for their own views: "Who do *you* say that I am?"[68] Peter, perhaps acting as spokesman for the group, replied, "You are the Christ."[69] ("Christ" is derived from the Greek equivalent of the Hebrew word, "Messiah.") Jesus then instructed the disciples "to tell no one about him" (Mk. 8:29–30).

This passage raises a pertinent question. Did Jesus think of his mission in Messianic terms? On this subject scholars are sharply divided. Many, basing their opinion on several different events, hold that he did. The Baptism concerned his appointment. The Temptation concerned his commitment. The Messianic meal was a foretaste of the Messianic banquet. After the Messianic meal, the crowd tried to force Jesus to become a king (Jn. 6:15). Jesus did not deny Peter's confession of his Messiahship near Caesarea Philippi. His command "to tell no one" was dictated by the

---

[65]William Manson, *The Gospel of Luke*, p. 105.

[66]Mk. 7:31; 8:22; 8:27.

[67]Mt. 16:13–23; 17:22–23; 20:17–19; Mk. 8:27–33; 9:30–32; 10:32–34; Lk. 9:18–22, 43b–45; 18:31–34.

[68]Emphasis added.

[69]Mt. (16:16) and Lk. (9:20) add interpretative words.

political connotations the title had in the minds of others. The Triumphal
Entry (Mk. 11:7–10) and the Anointing at Bethany (Mk. 14:3) are definite
Messianic demonstrations. And was not Jesus condemned and crucified as a
pretender to the Jewish throne?

In spite of these arguments, an increasing number of scholars reject the
claim that Jesus thought of his mission in Messianic terms. They contend
that the Messianic interpretation of his life and work belongs to early
Christology. It was the credo of the Christian community read back into
the records. "I am personally of the opinion," observes Rudolf Bultmann,
the distinguished German critic, "that Jesus did not believe himself to
be the Messiah."[70]

The issue of Jesus' Messianic consciousness is too momentous to be
decided by a single saying, even so important a saying as that of Peter.
We shall return to the subject in chapter seventeen where the various titles
applied to Jesus will be considered in some detail. In the meantime, the
reader would be well advised to remember two things. (1) Scholars are
divided on the question of Jesus' Messianic consciousness. (2) "Messiah"
was a multipurpose word. It had been applied to Israel, to patriarchs, to
kings, to prophets, and even to a Persian, Cyrus the Great, who was neither
Jewish nor Christian. It was not a proper noun. It was an adjective. It
meant anointed, consecrated, or appointed by God. It did not become a
proper noun, the exclusive title of a single person, until after the time of
Jesus. Then it became almost a synonym for his last name. "Messiah" or
"Christ" appears seldom in the Synoptics and is never used by Jesus as a
self-designation.

Matthew alone has the disputed passage which follows Peter's confession: "And Jesus answered him, 'Blessed are you, Simon Bar-Jona! For
flesh and blood has not revealed this to you, but my Father who is in
heaven. And I tell you, you are Peter, and on this rock I will build my
church, and the powers of death shall not prevail against it. I will give you
the keys of the kingdom of heaven, and whatever you bind on earth shall
be bound in heaven, and whatever you loose on earth shall be loosed in
heaven' " (Mt. 16:17–19).

The text of this passage is authentic. All Greek manuscripts and ancient
translations contain it. The source of the text, however, is hotly disputed.
Three basic conclusions can be discerned.

Acceptance of the passage as historical. It is Hebraic in language and
thought, akin to other sayings of Jesus in style, and in keeping with the
prominence of Peter found throughout the Synoptics. The basis of Peter's
confession was not humanity ("flesh and blood") but divinity ("my Father").
When Jesus called Simon, son of Jonah, "Peter" (*Petros,*[71] Rock Man), he
gave him a new name. When he said, "And on this rock [*petra*] I will build
my church [*ekklēsia*]," he established the primacy of Peter. The church was
founded on Peter, the man, as a living, perpetual institution ("the powers
of death shall not prevail against it"). When Jesus gave Peter "the keys of

---

[70]Bultmann, *Jesus and the Word,* p. 9.
[71]In Aramaic there would be no separate form to indicate the masculine gender.

the kingdom of heaven" with the power to "bind" and "loose," he made the church synonymous with the kingdom and delegated to Peter the authority to forgive sins and to control the population of heaven and hell. Peter became the first pope at Rome, Christ's first Vicar on earth. He passed on his prerogatives to his successor, who passed them on to his successor, and so forth. The church which Jesus founded on Peter (called the Catholic Church by its members) is the true church. Other churches were man-made —founded by Luther, Calvin, Wesley, and others. Insofar as they depart from the authoritative teachings of the Catholic Church, they are false or separated, a term popularized by the ecumenically-minded Pope John XXIII.

As popular as this position is among Roman Catholics, it is by no means universal. Their experts in dogma differ as to where their Church has spoken authoritatively about the literal sense of Scripture. Vatican I seems to have done so when it insisted that Christ gave Peter primacy among the apostles, but other specialists deny that this is the case. The extent to which the church and the kingdom can be equated is also disputed. Some Catholic exegetes think that the original context of Matthew 16:17–19 was post-ressurectional. They doubt that Jesus ever used the word *ekklēsia* (church). Although they believe that Peter is the rock on which the church is built, they declare that the passage from which this idea is derived does not make clear in what sense he is the foundation. The true-church claim of the Roman Catholic Church remains intact, but the relationship of this claim to the truth claims of other churches such as the Eastern Orthodox and Lutheran is currently undergoing fruitful reexamination.[72]

Conditional acceptance of the passage. It is considered essentially historical, but some of the conclusions reached in the foregoing position are unwarranted and inaccurate. "This rock" does not refer to Peter, the man, who, as any man, would be an uncertain foundation on which to build anything. The reference is either to Jesus himself (according to several early church fathers) or to Peter's affirmation that Jesus is the Christ. That Jesus intended to establish a living, perpetual institution is questionable. The word "church" appears only twice in Matthew and not at all in the other Gospels. It belongs to a time later than Jesus. It was a new and distinctive fellowship which resulted from the resurrection. Jesus did not identify the church with the kingdom. He proclaimed the coming of the kingdom of God. The "keys of the kingdom" are symbols of authority rather than literal

---

[72]See John L. McKenzie, S.J., "The Gospel According to Matthew," in J. A. Fitzmyer and R. E. Brown, eds., *The Jerome Biblical Commentary* (Englewood Cliffs, N.J.: Prentice-Hall, Inc., 1968, II), 91–93; compare 602 and 783–84; E. F. Sutcliffe, S.J., "St. Peter's Double Confession in Matthew 16:16–19," in M. R. Ryan, ed., *Contemporary New Testament Studies* (Collegeville, Minn.: Liturgical Press, 1965), pp. 260–69; Hans Küng, *The Church*, trans. Ray and Rosaleen Ockenden (New York: Sheed & Ward, 1967). L. K. Schmidt, "The Church," in J. R. Coates, ed., *Bible Key Words* (New York: Harper & Row, 1951), pp. 33–50, defends the authenticity of Mt. 16:17–19. Oscar Cullmann, *Peter—Disciple, Apostle, Martyr*, trans. F. V. Filson (Philadelphia: Westminster Press, 1953), a distinguished Protestant scholar, thinks the passage is genuine, but suggests that the Last Supper was the original setting. He believes that Peter was promised authority over the whole church, but the authority ended when he set out on his missionary activity.

power to control entrance to the church or the hereafter. In rabbinical language "to bind" or "to loose" meant to declare certain actions forbidden or permitted. "If one seah of unclean Heave-offering falls into a hundred seahs of clean, the School of Shammai bind [forbid] the entire lot, but the School of Hillel loose [permit] it."[73] "Thus Peter's decisions regarding the Old Testament law (e.g., in Acts 10:44–48) will be ratified in heaven. Later Christian tradition extended this principle to include the power to forgive or retain sins."[74] The primacy of Peter is not established by the passage. Elsewhere the power to loose and bind is given to all the disciples (Mt. 18:18; Jn. 20:23). Other passages suggest that there is no primacy of any disciple. There are twelve thrones of apparently equal importance (Mt. 19:28). When James and John, the sons of Zebedee, ask for special positions in the kingdom, this request is refused. It is not refused on the ground that the primacy belongs to Peter, but on the ground that it is not in the power of Jesus to confer such rank (Mk. 10:35–45). No brief summary could include all possible points of view. Neither could it do justice to denominational differences and emphases. In the main, however, this second conclusion may be regarded as representative of current Protestant thought, and it reflects a segment of Roman Catholic conviction as well.

Rejection of the passage. It is unhistorical—either a composition of Matthew or a reflection of thinking in some section of the early church. The passage is found nowhere else in the New Testament. Since the books of the New Testament circulated individually or in small clusters for centuries before they were combined into one "book," it is indeed strange that such an important pronouncement is found only in a single three-verse passage in Matthew. Its absence from Mark is especially noteworthy if Papias' statement that Mark was an interpreter of Peter is accurate. No amount of modesty would have prevented Peter from proclaiming that the church was built on him. Nor would Mark have been so careless as to have omitted such a significant truth from the reminiscences which he recorded. The word "church" reflects the conditions of a later time. In Mt. 18:17 it refers to the local community. But here (Mt. 16:18) it means the whole church, the great body of which the local groups are but parts. This belongs to the period of Paul and the Acts. The Synoptics, except for the two references in Matthew, speak not of the church but of a group of disciples whom Jesus taught about the coming kingdom of God. The equation of the kingdom of God with the church clashes with Jesus' teachings elsewhere. Paul displays no knowledge of the primacy of Peter. Paul writes that when Peter came to Antioch, "I opposed him to his face, because he stood condemned" (Gal. 2:11). James, not Peter, seems to have been the dominant figure in the Jerusalem Church (Acts 15:13–21). It was to the "Mother Church" in Jerusalem that Paul returned and reported concerning his missionary enterprises. It was to this church that he brought his famous collection for the poor saints. Moreover, if Jesus had given Peter special authority, he would not have called Peter "Satan" (Mt. 16:23); the disciples would not have disputed

[73]Terumoth, 5:4.
[74]Johnson, in *The Interpreter's Bible*, VII, 453.

about who was greatest (Mt. 18:1), nor would they have asked for special treatment (Mk. 10:37); and Peter would never have asked what he would get for following Jesus (Mt. 19:27). This third conclusion is supported by an increasing number of scholars.[75]

Careful analysis of Mark 8:27–33 reveals four constituent parts—Peter's confession, a command to silence, a passion prediction, and Peter's and Jesus' reciprocal rebukes. Since the command to silence is a common theme in Mark, it must be attributed to the evangelist. The passion prediction, as we shall soon see, is a creation of the church. Verse 32a is Mark's connecting link between the passion prediction and the double rebuke. When the contributions of the evangelist and the church are subtracted, there remains a simple pronouncement story:

> *Setting*: Jesus asks the disciples near Caesarea Philippi who they think he is.
> *Action*: Peter replies, "You are the Christ."
> *Pronouncement*: Jesus replies to Peter: "Get behind me, Satan!"

Since "Messiah" was often drawn in David's image as a religious-national leader, Reginald H. Fuller concludes that Jesus rejected the title "as a merely human and even diabolical temptation."[76]

Matthew reworked Mark's account of the confession near Caesarea Philippi, with the result that the one incident became two: the revelation to Peter (16:13–16) and Peter's commission as head of the church (16:17–19). The inserted commissioning broke the close connection between the confession and its subsequent misunderstanding (so characteristic of Mark) and overshadowed Mark's christological concerns by Matthew's ecclesiastical ones. Where Matthew followed Mark's account, two changes are evident. (1) "Who do men say that *I* am?" (Mk. 8:27) becomes "Who do men say that the *Son of man* is?" (Mt. 16:13),[77] and the passion prediction of Mark 8:31 is rewritten to take this into account (Mt. 16:21). This has the effect of making Jesus, who is about to set forth the existence and authority of the church with Peter at its helm, announce himself as the Son of man— a term of ultimate authority in Matthew. (2) "You are the Christ" (Mk. 8:29) has appended to it "the Son of the living God" (Mt. 16:16)—a common confession of the early church. Clearly Matthew's account was written in retrospect of the resurrection (as were, of course, the other Gospels) when Jesus had been identified with the apocalyptic Son of man (I Enoch 37–71) who performs very much like God Himself in Christian thought. "Son of God," which was not a standard title for Messiah in pre-Christian Judaism, has also taken on exalted meaning in Matthew.[78]

Luke (9:18–27) omitted the dispute between Jesus and Peter recorded

---

[75]See T. W. Manson, in *The Mission and Message of Jesus*, pp. 494–97; Johnson, in *The Interpreter's Bible*, VII, 448–49; and Rollins and Rollins, *Jesus and His Ministry*, p. 188.

[76]Reginald H. Fuller, *The Foundations of New Testament Christology* (New York: Charles Scribner's Sons, 1965), p. 109. Used by permission.

[77]Emphasis added.

[78]See H. E. Tödt, *The Son of Man in the Synoptic Tradition*, tr. D. M. Barton (London: SCM Press, 1965); printed in the U.S. by Westminster Press), pp. 144–49.

in Mark 8:32–33. Mark's christological point evidently didn't interest him. He also omitted "in this adulterous and sinful generation" (Mk. 8:38) and "come with power" (Mk. 9:1), and he added "daily" to Mark 8:34. The effect is to replace Mark's note of urgency sounded in the face of persecution preceding the imminent End of the Age with a call for persistent witnessing for an indefinite time.

Three passion predictions in Mark (8:31; 9:31; 10:32–34) follow in relatively rapid order Jesus' charge to the disciples "to tell no one about him" (8:30). Their content is similar. In the first prediction Jesus declares "that the Son of man must suffer many things, and be rejected by the elders and the chief priests and the scribes, and be killed, and after three days rise again." The predictions show that Jesus foresaw his sufferings, rejection and death, and resurrection. From the time of Peter's confession near Caesarea Philippi, Jesus began to prepare the disciples for the tragic and triumphant events which would follow. He taught them "plainly" (Mk. 8:32).

That Jesus realized the dangers that surrounded him seems likely, and that he recognized the calculated risk involved in a journey to Jerusalem is highly probable. But it is a good deal less certain that he foresaw the detailed events which would occur, or that he repeatedly instructed his disciples concerning them. If he did, they must have been dull pupils—an unwarranted reflection on them and the one who had chosen them. Except for Peter's spontaneous outburst (Mk. 8:32), the disciples betrayed no awareness of the predictions. Throughout the Passion they acted as though they had never heard of them. "If Jesus predicted his suffering, death, and resurrection in such explicit terms, it is difficult to see why in the Gospels the disciples are portrayed as crushed by the Crucifixion and surprised by the Resurrection." [79] Moreover, Jesus' own attitude does not seem to support his precise foreknowledge of events. And finally, as F. C. Grant has observed, "the quality of his martyr death is neutralized, and his heroism is made unreal and reduced to the mere histrionic performance of an assigned role, if he foresaw in advance the full details of his passion and the eventual denouement of his career." [80] For these and other reasons many scholars regard the three passion predictions as a literary technique used by Mark to advance his purpose.

Mark composed 8:27–10:52 as an introduction to the passion narrative in order to prepare his readers for its proper understanding. The passage is united by three geographical references—to Caesarea Philippi (8:27), to Galilee (9:30), and to Judea and beyond the Jordan (10:1). Each division has its own passion prediction (8:31; 9:31; 10:33–34). The third one intensifies the stress by its specific reference to Jerusalem, the place of the Passion, toward which Jesus and his disciples are going.

Peter reacted violently to Jesus' prediction of his suffering and death. The reference to the resurrection impressed him not at all. All he could think about was the paradoxical, even contradictory, nature of the pro-

[79]Johnson, in *The Interpreter's Bible*, VII, 454.
[80]In *The Interpreter's Bible*, VII, 767–68.

nouncement: the Messiah would *suffer* and *die!* It was a revolutionary and revolting idea. The Messiah would not suffer. He would rule in triumph and glory. He would not die. He would live forever. So Peter rebuked Jesus, only to be rebuked in turn: "Get behind me, Satan! For you are not on the side of God, but of men" (Mk. 8:33). He was indeed! He had not progressed beyond the popular conception of the Messiah. He thought the Messiah could act only in terms of triumph and glory.[81]

The teachings about discipleship which follow in Mark 8:34–9:1 strongly emphasize persecution and suffering. The disciple must "deny himself and take up his *cross.*" Saving his life only to lose it, or losing his life only to save it "for *my sake* and the *gospel's*" is an ever-present possibility.[82] Although Mark is presumably reporting Jesus' instructions to his disciples, the language ("cross," "my sake," "gospel's") is that of the early church. Indeed, the passage moves with alacrity between the historic ministry of Jesus and the life of the church. Mark is concerned both with the suffering of Jesus and with the prospective suffering of the members of his church. Since Jesus' suffering was a past event when he wrote, Mark's purpose is to prepare his readers for persecution by linking it with the suffering of Jesus. As the Master went, so must the disciple go; as the disciple goes, so will the Master go with him at the End.[83]

Confirmation (124, 125)[84]

About a week after Peter's confession[85] Jesus took his three closest disciples (Peter, James, and John) "and led them up a high mountain apart by themselves" (Mk. 9:2). The location of the unnamed mountain is disputed. Mount Tabor, near Nazareth, has been considered the traditional site since the fourth century; however, this designation is improbable for several reasons. Tabor was in Galilee, a district Jesus now seemed determined to avoid. It was about fifty miles as the crow flies from Caesarea Philippi where Jesus and the Twelve had been a week previous. It was not a "high" mountain, and it was inhabited. The most likely location for the

[81]Norman Perrin, *What is Redaction Criticism?* (Philadelphia: Fortress Press, 1969), pp. 55–56, argues that Mark is here combatting the "divine man" Christology prevalent in the church for which he wrote. The Greek world believed in "divine men"—"sons of God" who revealed the divine reality present in them as substance or power by performing miracles and having ecstatic experiences. Mark places this false Christology on Peter's lips and has Jesus reject it emphatically. Mark's purpose in presenting Peter's misunderstanding of Jesus (and the disciples' misunderstanding schematization throughout his Gospel) is to permit Mark to press for the acceptance of a suffering servant Christology by the church for which he is writing.

[82]Emphasis added.

[83]A paraphrase of a statement in Norman Perrin, *What is Redaction Criticism?* (Philadelphia: Fortress Press, 1969), p. 52.

[84]Mt. 17:1–13; Mk. 9:2–13; Lk. 9:28–36.

[85]"Six days" (Mk. 9:2, followed by Mt. 17:1); "about eight days" (Lk. 9:28). These indications of time were doubtless provided by the evangelists since they were almost certainly not a part of the earliest tradition. No chronology can be derived from such references.

Mount Tabor, near Nazareth, has been considered the site of Jesus' Transfiguration since the fourth century. From its summit, 1,843 feet above sea level, there unfolds a magnificent vista of the Valleys of Esdraelon and Jezreel.

Transfiguration, if the incident is historical, would seem to be somewhere on the slopes of mighty Mount Hermon.

Mark states that on the high mountain Jesus "was transfigured[86] before them, and his garments became glistening, intensely white, as no fuller on earth could bleach them. And there appeared to them Elijah with Moses; and they were talking to Jesus. And Peter said to Jesus, 'Master, it is well that we are here; let us make three booths, one for you and one for Moses and one for Elijah.' For he did not know what to say, for they were exceedingly afraid. And a cloud overshadowed them, and a voice came out of the cloud, 'This is my beloved Son; listen to him.' And suddenly looking around they no longer saw any one with them but Jesus only" (Mk. 9:2–8).

What actually happened on the mountain? The story has been called a myth, a legend, a postresurrection appearance of Jesus read back into an earlier period of his life, an expression of the theology of the early church which forecasts Christ's glory in his second coming, and a vision. Matthew reports that Jesus referred to the experience as a vision (Mt. 17:9). Some visions are worthless. Others are charged with meaning and produce profound consequences. Among the latter are Isaiah's vision of the Lord, Saul's vision of the risen Christ on the Damascus road, Constantine's vision of the

---

[86]*Metemorphōthē* is a technical term in late Greek for the act of metamorphosis. "It means a change of form, an effulgence from within, not a mere 'flood of glory' from without" (Grant, in *The Interpreter's Bible*, VII, 775).

Cross, and Joan of Arc's vision of the Virgin. In each case the one who had the vision was in a state of deep perplexity. And in each case the vision resolved doubts and clothed the person with power and pure purpose. A genuine vision, it should be noted, is not an hallucination induced by phantasy. It is the product of an authentic psychical state preceded by a period of fear, doubt, difficulty, or desire; and as such it is both real and revealing.[87] In Mark the vision (of Peter? the three intimates?) is treated as an epiphany.

What transpired on the mountain is presented in most detail in Luke. The two greatest figures in Israel, Moses and Elijah, appeared in glory. Moses represented the Law and Elijah the Prophets. Taken together, they symbolized the whole of Hebrew Scripture in Jesus' day. They talked to Jesus. The subject of their conversation, recorded only in Luke, is illuminating. It discloses the meaning of the Transfiguration. They "spoke of his departure [death], which he was to accomplish [which awaited him] at Jerusalem" (9:31). The disciples saw Jesus' glory. His altered countenance and dazzling white raiment doubtless reminded them of Moses after he had descended Mount Sinai with the Ten Commandments: "Moses did not know that the skin of his face shone because he had been talking with God" (Ex. 34:29). As Moses and Elijah were about to part from Jesus, Peter made a puzzling proposition: "Master, it is well that we are here; let us make three booths, one for you and one for Moses and one for Elijah" (9:33). The booths he had in mind were those the Jews built at the Feast of Tabernacles and on the flat roofs of their dwellings in the summer season. Peter apparently wanted to prolong the Transfiguration experience.

We turn now to the account in Mark. A luminous cloud, considered by devout Jews to be an ancient symbol of the divine Presence, overshadowed them all. A voice came out of the cloud. It was the *bath qôl* (*daughter* or *echo of the voice* of God) of the baptism. Its message had not changed: "This is my beloved Son; listen to him" (9:7). Suddenly the disciples saw no one save Jesus. As they left the mountain Jesus commanded the disciples to tell no one what they had seen "until the Son of man should have risen from the dead. So they kept the matter to themselves, questioning what the rising from the dead meant" (9:9–10).[88] It was not that they disbelieved that the dead would rise. That was a familiar idea in Judaism. The Pharisees were strong advocates of it. Jesus himself endorsed it. Some even thought Jesus was John risen from the dead. What the disciples couldn't understand was a dead Messiah. That was a contradiction in terms. How could the Messiah come from the grave if it was impossible for him to die?

As the disciples mulled over the problem of a resurrected Messiah, another question formed on their lips, "Why do the scribes say that first Elijah must come?" (Mk. 9:11). The disciples knew about Malachi's prediction that Elijah would appear "before the great and terrible day of the Lord comes" (Mal. 4:5). But he obviously hadn't come. Yet the disciples, according to Mark, believed that Jesus was the Messiah. How could this be? Jesus

87See Major, in *The Mission and Message of Jesus*, pp. 113–14.
88Matthew omits Mk. 9:10.

solved the dilemma by saying that Elijah had come in the person of John
the Baptist, "But I tell you that Elijah has come, and they did to him whatever they pleased" (9:13). How ironic that the Son of Man would soon endure the same fate as that of the Second Elijah!

The Transfiguration story appears to be foreign to its context in Mark.
It breaks the natural connection between 9:1 (where it is indicated that
some will not die before they see the kingdom come) and 9:11–13 (where
the disciples ask, "Why do the scribes say that first Elijah must come?"). The
word "first" clearly refers to the subject matter of 9:1. The Transfiguration
story once existed as a single and separate unit (II Peter 1:17–18). Bultmann
regards it as Mark's interpolation and attributes 9:9–10 to his editing.[89]
Mark connects the Transfiguration with the resurrection in 9:9. The resurrection becomes the key by which the Christian community unlocks the
meaning of Jesus' celestial glory disclosed to the disciples at the Transfiguration. The disciples are not permitted to talk to others about what they
have seen until after the Son of Man rises from the dead. The term "Son
of Man" suggests the sovereignty of the figure who descends from the
mountain to his death. His service through suffering will show forth his
glory at his rising.

Early Christians identified the Baptist as the forerunner of the judge
of the last days (Mt. 3:12; Lk. 3:17–18). Because they made this identification, they also saw John as the forerunner of Jesus. According to their view,
Jesus not only proclaimed God's final judgment, but he would one day
return to execute it. Moreover, the early Christians saw John as the forerunner of Jesus' mission and message. It was only natural that they should
link John's fate and Jesus' suffering. The reason that John did not restore
all things (as the common notion of the forerunner expected) was because
the Jews did to him "whatever they pleased" (Mk. 9:13). The same fate was
in store for the Son of Man (Mt. 17:12b). His sovereignty was not accepted;
so he must suffer. The suffering of the Baptist demolished the scribal objec-
tion recorded in Mark 9:11, and it reminded the Christians of the suffering
of the "mightier one" foretold in Scripture.[90]

The week between Peter's confession and Jesus' Transfiguration, in the
Synoptic setting, must have been charged with tension and turmoil for
the disciples. At its beginning Jesus had defined his mission in terms of the
Servant depicted in Isaiah 53. Never before had the suffering, rejection, and
humiliation of the Servant been applied to the expected Messiah. This
identification was "the most original and daring of all the characteristic
features of the teaching of Jesus."[91] It struck the disciples with the force of
a solid-fueled rocket. (Peter's protest is proof positive.) It confronted them

---

[89]Rudolf Bultmann, *The History of the Synoptic Tradition*, 2nd ed., tr. John Marsh
(Oxford: Basil Blackwell, 1968; printed in the U.S. by Harper & Row, Publishers, Inc.),
pp. 152, 259–61.

[90]See the illuminating discussion in Tödt, *The Son of Man in the Synoptic Tradition*,
pp. 194–98, to which we are indebted.

[91]H. Wheeler Robinson, *Redemption and Revelation* (New York and London:
Harper & Row, Publishers, Inc., © 1942), p. 199. Reprinted by permission of James Nisbet
& Co., Ltd., London.

with a seemingly impossible choice: inspired Scripture or inspiring Messiah? Should they adhere to their Scripture and its prediction of a triumphant Messiah? Or should they adopt Jesus' radical notion of a suffering servant Messiah?

The disciples' dilemma remained unresolved for a week. Then came the Transfiguration. Moses and Elijah appeared. They "spoke of his departure, which he was to accomplish at Jerusalem" (Lk. 9:31). It took two agreeing witnesses to establish a fact in a Jewish court. Could any witnesses match the luster of Moses and Eiljah? Together they represented Hebrew Scripture. Together they confirmed the necessity of Jesus' suffering and death. In addition, the voice out of the cloud confirmed the announcement at the baptism: "This is my beloved Son" (Mk. 9:7).

From a literary viewpoint, the Transfiguration constitutes a continental divide in the ministry of Jesus. From it we can look in two directions. Looking backward, we can see Peter's confession; the Meal for Many; the mission of the Twelve; the rejection by fellow townsmen, family, and friends; the enthusiastic crowds and the caustic critics; the mighty works; the call of the disciples; the message in miniature; the baptism and commitment of Jesus; and the preparatory work of John. Looking forward, we can see the journey to Jerusalem; the entry; the final appeal to the nation; and the betrayal, agony, arrest, trial, crucifixion, and triumph. Before we make the journey to Jerusalem, however, we shall pause to consider Jesus' teachings, his miracles and his titles.

part 5

The Message, Miracles, and Master

Many books have been written about the methods of the Master. Jesus was a skilled teacher. Twenty centuries later pedagogues continue to marvel at his ability to communicate. Our present study, however, is more interested in the matter than in the method of his teaching. What did he say that caused men to become martyrs? What ideas did he sponsor that inspired simple Palestinian peasants and still inspire learned scholars of today? He talked about a wayward son, a helpful neighbor, workers in a vineyard, a loaf of bread. We call these stories parables. A study of the parables reveals much that was at the heart of Jesus' teaching. Other insights are gained from his collected sayings, commonly called the Sermon on the Mount.

Jesus' contemporaries were impressed by his mighty works as well as by his words. Many followed him because he healed the sick, cast out demons, fed the multitudes, and raised the dead. Modern men often refer to these deeds as miracles. It is much easier to name them than to explain them. Did Jesus repeal the laws of nature, or are the miracles merely figures of speech, happy coincidences, or the product of misunderstandings? What did Jesus' works mean to those directly affected, to the bystanders, and to Jesus himself? What significance do they have today?

Jesus was more than a teacher and a doer of mighty deeds. In the Synoptics he is called a prophet, Son of David, Son of man, Son [of God], Lord, and Christ. Which, if any, of these titles did he accept for himself? What did they mean to him?

In this part of our study, we shall deal at length with the message, the miracles, and the Master.

chapter fourteen

The Parables

If there had been a *Who's Who in Palestine,* how would Jesus have been listed? As a carpenter? That was the trade which he had learned and practiced until the age of thirty. Preacher? That was why he "came out" (Mk. 1:38). Healer? He "healed many, so that all who had diseases pressed upon him to touch him" (Mk. 3:10). Teacher? He was indeed! The word is applied to him nearly fifty times in the Synoptics.[1]

The Gospels report that Jesus repeatedly "entered the synagogue and taught" (Mk. 1:21). The Sermon on the Mount begins and ends with the phrase "he taught them" (Mt. 5:2; 7:29). The disciples frequently called him teacher. They asked him to teach them to pray (Lk. 11:1). In a moment of extreme danger, when their boat was buffeted by a strong wind and pounded by mighty waves, they cried out, "Teacher, do you not care if we perish?" (Mk. 4:38). The disciples weren't the only ones; others also called him teacher. For example, the rich young man asked, "Teacher, what good deed must I do to have eternal life?" (Mt. 19:16).

Jesus has been called the world's greatest teacher. His teachings have been declared the highest ethic known to man. These descriptions are doubtless deserved; yet, they often give birth to faulty impressions. Jesus was no latter-day Confucius or Socrates. His teachings were not university lectures prepared for pedagogical purposes. In fact, according to the strict standard of his day he was not a teacher at all. Teaching was a well-established and honored profession. Its members were called "scribes" or "rabbis." Before they could practice their profession, they were required to spend many years

---

[1]*Didaskalos,* from whose root "didactic" is derived.

studying in the schools. They had to learn the dead Hebrew language and acquire a minute knowledge of their "Bible" (the Law and the Prophets) and the oral law as well. Jesus had neither the scribal training nor the scribal viewpoint. He was an artisan. He was called from the carpenter shop not to teach but to preach. To proclaim the imminence of the kingdom of God and the necessity of repentance was his primary task. But such a task involved a good deal more than the mere repetition of the proclamation. Many who heard him had different ideas about the kingdom and its ethic from his own. In order to clarify the nature of the kingdom and the kind of righteousness it demanded, Jesus became a teacher. As a teacher he exhibited extraordinary skills. Nowhere is this more evident than in his use of parables.[2]

Nature and Number

A *parable* is an earthly story with a heavenly meaning. Its basic function is comparison. It places a familiar or convincing story or incident alongside something less familiar in order to shed light on the latter. A parable has been called an extended simile. A *simile* is a succinct statement of likeness. Jesus' parable of the Leaven is representative: "The kingdom of heaven is like leaven which a woman took and hid in three measures of meal, till it was all leavened" (Mt. 13:33). A *metaphor* is a compressed simile. It equates one object with another, or at least it seems to do so. The Fourth Gospel is replete with metaphors: "I am the living bread" (6:51); "I am the door" (10:9); "I am the good shepherd" (10:11); " I am the way" (14:6).

A parable should be distinguished from both a fable and an allegory. The first distinction can be made easily, for whether or not a parable is historical, it is true to life. A *fable* is built on fantasy. It departs from nature and endows animals and even inanimate objects with human capacities and emotions. (See the famous story Jotham told the men of Shechem in Judges 9:7-20.) An *allegory* is a prolonged metaphor or a series of them which makes a continuous narrative. It precisely personifies abstract truth. Every detail in the description of the actors and the action has a parallel meaning. In contrast, the parable usually contains only one idea. It is like a lens "which gathers many of the sun's rays and brings them to a focus upon a single point."[3] The details of the parable have no significance in themselves; they merely serve to advance the comparison which is the point of the parable.

There was a time in the history of the church when Jesus' parables were treated as allegories. The results were fantastic. Augustine, for example, reached into the recesses of his fertile mind and adorned the swift and

[2]For a comprehensive treatment of Jesus' teaching role see H. B. Sharman, *Jesus As Teacher* (New York: Harper & Row, Publishers, Inc., 1935).

[3]G. H. Hubbard, *The Teaching of Jesus in Parables* (Boston: The Pilgrim Press, 1907), p. xvi.

pointed parable of the Good Samaritan (Lk. 10:30–37) with detailed comparisons.[4] The "certain man" who went down from Jerusalem to Jericho was Adam. Jerusalem was the city of peace from which Adam fell. Jericho was man's mortality. The thieves were the devil and his angels, who stripped Adam of his immortality. The priest and Levite represented the bankrupt Old Testament ministry. The Samaritan was Christ. The inn was the church. The innkeeper was Paul. These identifications would have astounded Jesus. The original point of the parable—the need for love without limit—has been completely hidden by a profusion of allegorical embroidery.

It is sometimes questioned whether Jesus ever used the allegory, since it is a tool of the writer rather than the speaker. Moreover, the Synoptics contain few, if any, allegories. But some of the parables betray allegorical signs. The parables of the Pounds (Lk. 19:12–27) and the Wicked Tenants (Mt. 21:33–43; Mk. 12:1–11; Lk. 20:9–18) are illustrations of allegorical parables; and the parable of the Sower might well be called the allegory of the Soils (Mt. 13:3–8; Mk. 4:3–8; Lk. 8:5–8).

In the Septuagint the Greek word for parable translates the Hebrew noun *māshāl*. The root meaning of *māshāl* is "to be like." In Hebrew literature *māshāl* stands for nearly any kind of verbal image—metaphor, simile, allegory, example story, riddle, proverb, taunt. In the Synoptics "parable" covers a similar range of expressions. Generally, however, the word is restricted to three types of utterance: the simile, the narrative parable, and the example story. The simile and narrative parable teach by analogy. The example story teaches directly what is to be imitated or avoided. Example stories are found only in Luke's special tradition: the Good Samaritan, the Rich Fool, the Rich Man and Lazarus, and the Pharisee and the Publican.

Matthew states that Jesus said nothing to the crowds without a parable (13:34). Many of his teachings did not survive the oral period of transmission, and those which did survive cannot easily be classified. How many parables are there in the Synoptics? The number differs from expert to expert, depending on their definition of "parable." Our list, found in Appendix I, is based on the broad meaning of *māshāl*. It could easily be expanded by the inclusion of every figurative expression used by Jesus. It could also be contracted by the elimination of metaphors and similes. As it stands, it should provide the reader with a ready reference.

Purpose (90, 91, 93, 99)[5]

The Hebrews had a penchant for the concrete. They did not speak about the providence of God. They said, "The Lord is my shepherd, I shall not want" (Ps. 23:1). They did not discourse on heredity. They declared, "The fathers have eaten sour grapes, and the children's teeth are set on

---

[4]*Quaestiones Evangeliorum*, II, 19.
[5]Mt. 13:1–15,18–23,34–35; Mk. 4:1–20,33–34; Lk. 8:4–15.

edge" (Ezek. 18:2). They loved "truth embodied in a tale."[6] With a simple story about a rich man's flocks and a poor man's single little ewe lamb, Nathan reproved David for the death of Uriah and the theft of Uriah's wife (II Sam. 12:1–14). Isaiah pricked the conscience of Israel by comparing her with a vineyard which God had planted and tended. God's purpose had been to produce grapes. The vineyard had brought forth wild grapes instead (Is. 5:1–7). Parables were used in Jesus' day to clarify the Scriptures. Many such stories are found in the literature of rabbinical Judaism. Jesus did not invent the technique of teaching by parables. He was much too wise to rely on a new and untested device. He chose a medium of expression which had already been proven.

Mark indicates that Jesus adopted the parabolic method of teaching after his Galilean ministry had been in progress for some time. The hostility of the religious leaders and the pressure of the crowds had prompted Jesus to withdraw from the synagogues and cities and to teach in the open air and in deserted places. After Mark records the parable of the Sower (which seems to show the different ways people responded to Jesus' message), he reports why Jesus spoke in parables. To the Twelve and other followers Jesus said, "To you has been given the secret of the kingdom of God, but for those outside everything is in parables; so that they may indeed see but not perceive, and may indeed hear but not understand; lest they should turn again, and be forgiven" (4:11–12).

Mark's passage suggests that Jesus spoke in parables to perplex rather than to persuade, to conceal rather than to reveal. The citation (given in a fuller form in Mt. 13:13–15) is based on Isaiah 6:9–10. On the surface the Isaiah passage seems to confirm the point the evangelists are trying to make. But Isaiah would hardly have persisted in his preaching had he known from the beginning that it was pointless. These verses represent the results of his ministry. In spite of his heroic efforts to proclaim the word of God, the people stubbornly rejected his message. Years later, as the prophet reflected on his call, he concluded that his work had been foreordained to failure. God had willed it that way.

A similar thought may have been in the mind of Mark. Jesus' teachings differentiated and separated his hearers. The parable of the Sower makes this plain. Some heard with the outer ear only. Others offered a surface response. Still others allowed the kingdom to be one of many interests so that "thorns" soon grew up and choked it. Mark saw the divinely intended result in the consequences of Jesus' teaching. The purpose of teaching in parables was colored by the actual course of events. It was also colored by Mark's theology. In his editorial formulation (4:10–12), designed to connect the parable with its interpretation, he expressed a familiar conviction. God had hardened human minds so that they were unable to comprehend the truth. Only His elect were given the secret of the kingdom, and even they were to be kept from complete understanding until after the resurrection.[7]

---

[6]Alfred Tennyson, *In Memoriam*, st. xxxvi.

[7]Mk. 4:13; 6:51–53; 7:18; 8:17–21; 9:6,10,32; 10:32. Four different interpretations of Mk. 4:11–12 are presented in A. M. Hunter, *The Work and Words of Jesus* (Philadelphia:

We must distinguish, however, between Mark's view and Jesus'. As C. H. Dodd has commented, that Jesus "desired not to be understood by the people in general, and therefore clothed His teaching in unintelligible forms, cannot be made credible on any reasonable reading of the Gospels."[8] Neither can it be made to agree with a later passage in Mark, where it is stated that Jesus spoke the word with many parables "as they were able to hear it" (4:33).

Background

The parables teach us much that was not intended. They open the door of first-century Palestine and invite us to come in. They speak of the baking of bread, the patching of garments, the storing of wine, the sowing of seed, the growth of grain, the harvest, fishing, the barren tree, the unfinished tower, and the lost coin. Their disclosures are not limited to the world of things; they also present a living pageant of people. They introduce us to the preening Pharisee and the pious publican, the privileged priest and the scorned Samaritan, the pompous person who pushes his way to the head table, the love-filled father, the persistent widow and the unjust judge, children at play, the rich fool piling up the perishable, the faithless servant, the indifferent guests, the wise and foolish maidens, the saying and the doing sons, the hardhearted servant, the envy-filled vineyard-workers, the searching shepherd, the wicked tenants, and the solid builder.

In addition to teaching us about things and people in first-century Palestine, the parables also teach us about their narrator. They picture him as a man of many interests. Nothing was too small or common to escape his attention. He had a fascination for the familiar. The ordinary happenings of daily life etched themselves in his memory. As he matured, he was able to draw on a seemingly inexhaustible supply of stored-up experiences. When these experiences passed through his perfectly focused personality, they became matchless parables. Their charm and cutting edge stem from their naturalness. They cling to the mind like burs until their point is made.

Trustworthiness

The parables of Jesus had two historical settings almost from the beginning—the original one of his ministry and the later one provided by the early church. The stories and similes were first delivered in specific situations and directed toward particular audiences. No effort was made to record them. Their content and context were either remembered or forgotten. The remembered parables, the form critics remind us, circulated

---

The Westminster Press, 1950), p. 45. See also Gerhard Barth, in *Tradition and Interpretation in Matthew*, pp. 105–112.

8C. H. Dodd, *The Parables of the Kingdom* (New York: Charles Scribner's Sons, 1936), p. 15.

singly or in pairs. For a double decade they lived in the oral tradition of the church. The church collected the parables, pressed them into service, arranged them according to subject matter, and created a new setting for them.

The parables underwent considerable modification when they were employed by the church in its preaching and teaching mission. Their translation from Aramaic into Greek inevitably resulted in many alterations of vocabulary and hence of meanings. There was also a tendency to substitute the Hellenistic for the Palestinian environment. (Lk. 6:47–48, for example, pictures a house with a cellar, uncommon in Palestine.) Some of the parables were embellished. "From the fig tree learn its lesson" (Mk. 13:28) became "Look at the fig tree, *and all the trees*" (Lk. 21:29).[9] Some were given a different audience. The parable of the Lost Sheep is addressed to Jesus' opponents in Luke (15:3–7). There, in its original setting, it is apologetic. It constitutes a stirring defense of Jesus' ministry to the religiously disinherited. Stress is placed on the joy of the shepherd. In Matthew the parable is directed to the disciples (18:12–14). They are urged to follow the shepherd's example and be faithful pastors to the wayward members of the church. Emphasis is on the shepherd's persistent search. Some parables were made instruments of exhortation. The Defendant (Lk. 12:58–59), originally a parable of crisis, became a call to Christians to become reconciled with an estranged brother. Others were transposed into a different time period. As told by Jesus, the parable of the Wise and Foolish Maidens was a ringing challenge to his audience to prepare for the crisis of the kingdom. In the hands of the church it became a warning about the crisis of its day—the return of Christ (the parousia). Still others (the Weeds, the Net, the Sower) were allegorized. A few were fused. In Matthew, the Wedding Garment (22:11–13), an originally independent parable, was added to the Marriage Feast (22:2–10). At several points Luke's parable of the Pounds (19:12–27) betrays the intrusion of another parable of a man who set out to claim a kingdom. Generalized conclusions were added to some of the parables. Sometimes the conclusions miss the point of the parable, as in Mt. 20:16. Even when they don't, they are secondary.[10]

These facts are deeply disturbing to some, who are loath to admit that the early followers of Jesus could have handled his sacred words in such a way. These people, however, should not be unduly upset. In our own day, in church schools and from pulpits, Jesus' teachings are also used for Christian nurture and edification. To recognize that the parables underwent transformation during their transmission is not to destroy their historicity. Quite the contrary. It makes the recovery of their original content and context possible. In many instances it may be necessary to remove the parables from their second historical setting and to place them in their first. Thanks to the diligent work of the form critics this can be done with reasonable

---

[9]Emphasis added.

[10]The limitation of space does not permit us to describe in detail the fascinating account of the development of the parables from their first to their second historical setting. This has been done elsewhere. Perhaps the most stimulating and suggestive treatment, from which this general outline has been derived, is that by Joachim Jeremias, *The Parables of Jesus*. Our treatment of the parables owes much to Jeremias although we do not follow him at every point.

assurance. The necessarily speculative nature of such a process, of course, cannot yield absolutely certain results; but imaginative, informed, and disciplined speculation—a vital part of all historical inquiry—can produce probabilities. In the judgment of such a capable critic as Jeremias, "the student of the parables of Jesus . . . may be confident that he stands upon a particularly firm historical foundation. The parables are a fragment of the original rock of tradition."[11]

Message

Any search for the meaning of the parables must begin with an awareness of the modifications they have undergone. When these modifications are accounted for, in so far as this is possible, a striking fact appears: many of the parables sponsor the same point. The differences among the parables turn out to be secondary. Apparently Jesus never wearied of expressing his ideas in ever-changing images. His basic concepts were few. The parables cluster around them quite naturally. Taken together, the groupings provide a rather comprehensive summary of his message.

The nearness of the kingdom. The number of parables which reveal the urgency of the situation is great. Again and again Jesus utters cries of warning. When the kingdom comes, it will result in judgment. His hearers can read the Weather Signs (160), but they cannot discern the signs of the times.[12] They are like Children in the Market Place (65).[13] The children cannot agree on a game. Some want to play "wedding." Others want to play "funeral." Neither proposal is mutually acceptable. Quarreling results. Jesus' hearers are similar to the children. They exhaust themselves in idle bickering while their eternal destiny hangs in the balance.

The Budding Fig Tree (220) has a parousia setting in the Synoptics.[14] "From the fig tree," declares Jesus to his disciples, "learn its lesson: as soon as its branch becomes tender and puts forth its leaves, you know that summer is near. So also, when you see these things taking place, you know that he is near, at the very gates" (Mk. 13:28–29). "These things" refers to the "signs of the end" previously described. When the disciples see "these things" taking place, they will know that he (Revised Standard Version, "the Son of man") or it (King James Version, "the end") is near.

The setting is secondary. The questions posed by the disciples in Mark 13:4 and Luke 21:7 refer solely to the destruction of the Temple. Matthew 24:3 alters the second question raised in Mark and Luke (making it refer to the parousia) and adds a third which concerns eschatology. But the internal meaning of the Budding Fig Tree does not fit well with the awful portents which announce the end. The parable points in another direction. The fig tree was a familiar figure in Jewish thought. Unlike the carob,

---

11Jeremias, *The Parables of Jesus*, p. 11.

12Mt. 16:2–3; Lk. 12:54–56.

13Mt. 11:16–17; Lk. 7:31–32.

14Mt. 24:32–33; Mk. 13:28–29; Lk. 21:29–31. Jeremias, *The Parables of Jesus*, pp. 119–20, classifies this parable under the title, "Now Is the Day of Salvation."

olive, and ilex it shed its leaves completely. Then its stark twigs stood for death. But when the sap began to rise, its shoots, bursting with life, announced the approach of summer.

Luke correctly classifies the Budding Fig Tree as a kingdom parable. "When you see these things taking place, you know that the kingdom of God is near" (21:31). On Jesus' lips the parable proclaims that the summer of God's salvation is fast approaching. When it arrives, it will bring new life to those who are ready.

The parable of the Rich Fool (156) has usually been interpreted as a stark warning against greed.[15] More likely it is a parable of "the times." A bumper crop made a prosperous farmer's barns inadequate. In order to accommodate his surplus and to insure himself against future crop failures, he resolved to tear down his barns and build bigger ones. What a fool! He had failed to take God into account. "This night your soul is required of you" (Lk. 12:20). All the while he was making his plans and anticipating the joys of his future leisure, the sword of Damocles was hanging over his head.

The Supervising Servant (158) speaks of one servant, not two.[16] "Who then is the faithful and wise servant, whom his master has set over his household, to give them their food at the proper time? Blessed is that servant whom his master when he comes will find so doing. Truly, I say to you, he will set him over all his possessions. But if that wicked servant says to himself, 'My master is delayed,' and begins to beat his fellow servants, and eats and drinks with the drunken, the master of that servant will come on a day when he does not expect him and at an hour he does not know, and will punish him, and put him with the hypocrites" (Mt. 24:45–51b).[17]

The early church saw a parousia parable in the Supervising Servant. This is clear from its context. The master is the Son of man returning to judge the world (Mt. 24:44; Lk. 12:40). The servant stands for the church members or its leaders (Luke). They are admonished not to betray their trust because the parousia is delayed. Luke, who equates the servant with the apostles, limits the application of the parable to them. They have been placed in a position of authority. They know the master's will better than the others. A more rigorous reckoning will be required of them if they permit the postponement of the parousia to prompt them to abuse their office (Lk. 12:47–48).

When the gospel context of the Supervising Servant is disregarded and its later allegorical features are removed,[18] we are left with the picture of a large household living under tension. The master is away. He may return at any time. Preparedness is the point of the parable. Its subject is the coming of the kingdom. The kingdom is near. Jesus probably delivered the parable as a warning to the religious leaders (the scribes or the high-priestly group).

The parables of the Talents and the Pounds (195) sound a similar

[15]Lk. 12:16–20.

[16]Mt. 24:45–51a; Lk. 12:42–46.

[17]Matthew has changed "the unfaithful" (Lk. 12:46) to "the hypocrites" and added his characteristic "...there men will weep and gnash their teeth" (24:51b).

[18]See Jeremias, *The Parables of Jesus*, pp. 55–58.

warning.[19] This is not divulged by their present context and content in the Gospels. There they are clearly parousia parables. The Lucan version is prefaced with a comment stating that the parable was told by Jesus to refute false expectations that the kingdom would appear immediately (19:11). Another parable has been fused with the original: "A nobleman went into a far country to receive kingly power and then return. But his citizens hated him and sent an embassy after him, saying, 'We do not want this man to reign over us.' When he returned, having received the kingly power, he said, 'As for these enemies of mine, bring them here and slay them before me.' "[20] How strikingly similar is this story to the one told by Josephus concerning Archelaus and his quest for the throne of his father, Herod the Great![21]

Luke's account transforms a "man" (Mt. 25:14) into a "nobleman" and a simple parable into an allegory. The nobleman is Christ. He departs (the ascension) to a distant country (heaven) to receive a kingdom. He entrusts the management of his affairs to his servants (the Christians) while he is away. His citizens (the Jews) reject him as their king (deny his Messiahship). When he has received the kingdom, he returns (the parousia). The return brings rewards for the servants and punishment for the rebels (Final Judgment). Thus the allegory confirms the delay of the parousia and indicates what will happen when it becomes a reality. The point is plain. The followers of Christ must remain faithful during the interim.

It is doubtful that Jesus would have described himself as one who drew out what he had not paid in and reaped where he had not sown (Lk. 19:22). Neither would he have compared himself to a vindictive Oriental despot who gloated over the sight of his enemies slaughtered before his eyes (Lk. 19:27). Matthew's version of the parable is earlier, but even it is not without later additions. The setting is secondary. The parable is placed among the parousia parables. The expressions, "Enter into the joy of your master" (25:21,23), and the command, "cast the worthless servant into the outer darkness" (25:30) are christological. It is no longer "a man" but the Christ of the parousia who speaks. He awards a share in the New Age to some and assigns others to eternal damnation.[22]

When the allegorical and moralistic features are removed from the Talents and the Pounds, a simple parable shines forth. A rich and rapacious employer entrusts a sum of money[23] to each of his three servants[24] before

---

[19]Mt. 25:14–28; Lk. 19:12–27.

[20]See Lk. 19:12,14,15,27.

[21]See p. 38 and *Antiquities*, XVII, 9, 1.

[22]Mt. 25:29 is a floating saying also found in Mk. 4:25; Mt. 13:12; Lk. 8:18. It has been added to the parables as a generalized conclusion. Mt. 25:30, missing in Luke, is also an addition—a typical Matthew touch.

[23]Matthew, who has a liking for large figures, mentions one, two, and five talents. They would be roughly equivalent to $1,000, $2,000, and $5,000, very substantial sums. Luke speaks of ten pounds given to each servant. Ten pounds would be about $200, a more likely figure.

[24]Luke mentions ten servants, but the Greek in 19:20 contradicts this. The original number, as Matthew states, was three. Luke has increased the number of servants and Matthew has magnified the amount of money.

setting out on a long journey. They are to put the money to good use. The employer will require a reckoning of them when he returns. On his return the employer demands an account of his servants' stewardship. The two faithful ones have increased their capital. They are commended and given increased responsibility. The third servant, on whom the spotlight of the story is focused, has carefully hoarded his money for fear of losing it. He returns the sum without increment and is severely censured. The very least he might have done was to have deposited the money with bankers. Then he could have returned the capital with interest. His trust is taken from him and given to one who has been faithful.

To whom was the parable originally addressed? Probably to the scribes, who had failed to make use of the trust that God had given them. They had embalmed the Law with "whereases," thus confining God's revelations to the circle of the learned. This practice was tantamount to defrauding God. He had the right to expect productive results from His revelations. The scribal failure to merit God's confidence was serious at any time. Now it was crucial, since the settling of accounts was fast approaching.

The Watchful Servants (158) and its variant version, the Watchful Doorkeeper (222), are parousia parables in the Gospels.[25] Luke 12:37b is an allegorical addition. It describes what Jesus has done (Lk. 22:27; Jn. 13:4–5) and will do again at his return. No earthly master would gird himself, have his servants sit at table, and serve them. Neither would he expect his whole staff of servants to watch for his return (Lk. 12:36–38). He would command the doorkeeper to be on the alert, as he does in Mark 13:34. Luke's version makes the parable apply to the entire Christian community. Mark's parable is nearer the original, but even it displays two secondary features. (1) "Like a man going on a journey" (13:34) is imported by a later hand from Matthew 25:14. The master has merely gone to a banquet in Luke 12:36. This coheres with the order to the doorkeeper to keep watch during the night (Mk. 13:34–35). It hardly suits a longer journey. That would be of indefinite length and the return would not likely be nocturnal. (2) The transfer of authority to the servants (Mk. 13:34) is unnecesary during such a short absence. This feature is derived from Matthew 24:45 (Luke 12:42).

When the additions to these parables are removed, the original story appears. A certain master, who was about to attend a banquet, commanded his doorkeeper to be on the alert. He was to open the door immediately when his master returned and knocked. It would be well for the doorkeeper if the master found him watching—no matter what time of the night it might be. The warning concerns not the parousia but the advent of the kingdom. The parable was probably spoken to the scribes or other leaders of the Jews.

The parables of the Speck and Log (36),[26] the Blind Guides (76),[27] the Lamp and Bushel (94, 153),[28] the Body's Lamp (153),[29] and the Tree and

---

[25]Lk. 12:35–38; Mk. 13:34–36.
[26]Mt. 7:3–5; Lk. 6:41–42.
[27]Mt. 15:14; Lk. 6:39.
[28]Mk. 4:21; Lk. 8:16 and Mt. 5:15; Lk. 11:33.
[29]Mt. 6:22–23; Lk. 11:34–35.

Fruit (41)[30] were all originally directed at Israel's leaders. The parables score the scribes and Pharisees for their spiritual blindness.[31] They have squandered their time and talent criticizing their fellow men and commending themselves. They have hidden God's revelation from others. They are myopic and unfruitful. So great is their "darkness" that they are completely oblivious of the nearness of the kingdom.

The Savorless Salt (20, 132) varies in content and context in the Gospels.[32] It was probably originally intended as a warning to the nation. Israel, who had once known the saving and savoring knowledge of God, had now lost it. She was as useless as salt which had lost its salinity. The parable of the Barren Fig Tree (162) makes the same point.[33] A man planted a fig tree in his vineyard, a common practice in Palestine. Habitually (for "three years") it bore no fruit. The owner instructed his vinedresser to destroy the tree. The vindresser replied, "Let it alone, sir, this year also, till I dig about it and put on manure. And if it bears fruit next year, well and good; but if not, you can cut it down" (Lk. 13:8–9). The sterile fig tree symbolized Israel. Her time for repentance was short.

The twin parables of the New Cloth and the New Wine (54) are connected with the figure of the wedding in the Synoptics, and both employ traditional metaphors for the New Age.[34] No one sews a piece of new cloth on an old garment. The patch would shrink with the first washing. The resulting tear would be worse than the first. Neither does a person put new wine into old, hard wineskins. Fermentation would cause the nonelastic skins to burst, and the wine would be lost. Wine was often used as a symbol of the time of salvation (Gen. 9:20; Num. 13:23 24), and garment was a common figure for the cosmos. (Heb. 1:10–12; Acts 10:11–12). The Old Age, which is compared to the old garment, has spent itself. It is not worth patching with new cloth. The New Age is at hand.[35]

The Wise and Foolish Maidens (227) is a parousia parable in Matthew.[36] This is shown by "then" of vs. 1 (which relates this parable to the preceding parousia parable, the Supervising Servant) and "Watch therefore" of vs. 13. "Then" is a favorite connective of Matthew. "Watch therefore" contradicts the parable. All the maidens slept—the wise as well as the foolish! What is condemned is not the sleeping but the failure of the foolish maidens to provide a reserve supply of oil for their lamps. What happened to the parable is easy to surmise. When Matthew noted the words, "As the bridegroom was delayed" (vs. 5), he turned what was originally a story about an earthly wedding into an allegory of Christ and his expected return. Christ became the heavenly bridegroom. The ten maidens were the ex-

---

30Mt. 7:16–20; Lk. 6:43–45.

31See Lk. 6:42. Compare Mt. 7:5. "Hypocrite" is never used elsewhere in the Gospels to describe the disciples.

32Mt. 5:13; Mk. 9:50; Lk. 14:34–35.

33Lk. 13:6–9.

34Mt. 9:16–17; Mk. 2:21–22; Lk. 5:36–38.

35See Jeremias, *The Parables of Jesus*, pp. 115–24, who places these parables (as well as the Lamp and Bushel) under the category, "Now Is the Day of Salvation."

36Mt. 25:1–13.

pectant Christians. The delayed bridegroom was the postponed parousia, and the stern rejection of the foolish maidens was the final judgment. The parable thus became a summons to Christians to be ready for the parousia.

A wedding had priority in a Palestinian village. It outranked most other attractions. The participants—including the guests—were relieved of certain religious duties. Scholars forsook the study of the Law to attend. The wedding feast was held at night. There was no ceremony performed by a rabbi. The ceremony began when the bridegroom marched with his friends to the home of the bride to bring her to the feast in his home. The maidens in the parable were the bride's companions,[37] who awaited the arrival of the bridegroom. When he came, they would take him in to the bride and then accompany the couple to the bridegroom's house. They waited with lamps lighted. The oil in the small clay lamps was consumed as the maidens slept. Suddenly at midnight there was a cry, "Behold, the bridegroom! Come out to meet him" (Mt. 25:6). The maidens arose and trimmed their burnt wicks. Five maidens had an extra supply of oil. Five had none. The wise refused to share their supply with the foolish lest they also run short. Instead, they made what appears to be an impractical suggestion: "Go rather to the dealers and buy for yourselves" (Mt. 25:9).[38] While the foolish maidens implemented the suggestion, the bridegroom came. Those who were ready took him to the bride. Then they accompanied the couple to the marriage feast, and the door was shut. When the foolish maidens finally arrived, they were denied admittance.

As Jesus tells it, the parable of the Wise and Foolish Maidens is a crisis parable. The hour of judgment, which precedes the kingdom's coming, is at hand. Are his hearers prepared for it? Have they provided themselves with an abundant supply of the oil of repentance? Or are they like the foolish maidens—inviting the festal door to be shut against them?[39]

Luke's Great Banquet and Matthew's Marriage Feast (205) are variants of an original parable of Jesus.[40] Luke 14:16–21 and Matthew 22:2–5,8–10 represent the substance of what the evangelists found in Q. Matthew turned the parable into a marriage feast for the king's son. This enabled him to add an independent parable, the Wedding Garment (22:11–13), perhaps to correct the impression made by the previous parable that salvation is easy for sinners. The Wedding Garment insists on the need for righteousness (or repentance). The parable in Matthew has been modified so much that it has become an allegory setting forth the plan of salvation. The king is God.

---

[37]Since (1) no mention was made of the bride and (2) the bridegroom was delayed, it has been suggested that the ten maidens were not bridesmaids, but village girls. Their intent was to welcome the bridegroom when he came from his parents' home to his new home for his wedding. See Beck, *Through the Gospels to Jesus*, p. 294.

[38]Where could they buy oil at midnight? Nevertheless, they were successful in their quest.

[39]Luke's parable of the Closed Door (13:24–30) sponsors a similar point. See Jeremias, *The Parables of Jesus*, pp. 95–96, where it is shown that Luke's parable is made up of the conclusion of one parable (Mt. 25:10–12) and three passages (Mt. 7:13–14, 22–23; 8:11–12) related to it by illustrative content.

[40]Lk. 14:16–24; Mt. 22:2–10.

The servants are prophets and apostles whom the Jews have maltreated and murdered. The destruction of the murderers and the burning of their city are thinly veiled references to the capture and burning of Jerusalem by Titus and his Roman legions in 70 A.D.

Luke's Great Banquet stands closer to Jesus, but it is not without its allegorical touches. Lk. 14:21b–22 was added to make vs. 23 refer to the Gentile mission of the church. (Matthew speaks only of a Jewish mission.) Lk. 14:24 equates the banquet of the parable with the Messianic feast. Jesus' original parable, probably addressed to the professedly religious, vindicates his mission and the gospel message. The kingdom is near. ("Come; for all is now ready," the servant is told to proclaim in 14:17.) If the "righteous" will not heed the call of God, those whom they despise as sinners and outcasts will. They will be the ones admitted to the kingdom, and the others will be informed that all seats are taken.

The Wicked Tenants (204) appears to be pure allegory.[41] The vineyard represented Israel, the tenants were Israel's leaders, and the owner of the vineyard was God. The servants sent to collect the fruit (which symbolized righteousness) were the prophets. The heir, whose death represented the crucifixion, was Jesus. The destruction of the tenants symbolized the destruction of Israel's leaders; and the new tenants were the apostles, who managed the Gentile church, the New Israel.

Since Jesus rarely if ever used the form of allegory, the genuineness of the Wicked Tenants has been questioned.[42] But we believe that beneath the allegorical additions an authentic parable can be discovered. Luke's account is garnished the least, but even he cannot refrain from allegorical touches (20:13,15,17–18). The features of a simple story are found in Luke 20:10–12. A different servant was sent three years in succession to collect some of the fruit of the vineyard. The first was beaten. The second was beaten and treated shamefully. The third was wounded. (No hint of allegory is found here. Mark 12:2–5a agrees with Luke that only one servant was sent each of the three times.) Finally, the owner of the vineyard sent his son, who was murdered. This account largely coheres with its parallel in the Gospel of Thomas (65) which is free of allegorical additions. There the story follows the customary folk-tale pattern. The activities of three separate rent-collectors (two servants and the son) build to a climax with the death of the son. The tradition prior to Mark hastened the process of allegorization of the story in two main ways. (1) It inserted 12:5b. This broke the triple formula, popular in such stories, and made the account refer to "many others" who are beaten or killed—an obvious reference to the fate of the prophets.[43] (2) It inserted the prediction of the resurrection in

---

[41]Mt. 21:33–43; Mk. 12:1–11; Lk. 20:9–18.

[42]See Grant, in *The Interpreter's Bible*, VII, 836–38. Compare Hunter, *Interpreting the Parables*, pp. 87–88, 116–18, where the parable's essential authenticity is vigorously defended.

[43]Matthew's version begins with sending out several servants who are beaten, killed, or stoned. They are followed by a larger group who experience the same fate. The two missions represent the earlier and the later prophets as the reference to stoning indicates.

12:10–11 increasing the christological point of the parable. In Matthew's account the story reaches its allegorical zenith.[44]

The early church saw in the slain son the crucifixion of Christ. Matthew (21:39) and Luke (20:15), contrary to Mark (12:8), state that the son was first cast out of the vineyard and then slain. These are clearly christological colorings. They reflect the slaying of Jesus outside the city (Jn. 19:17; Heb. 13:12–13). The quotation from Psalm 118:22–23 (Mt. 21:42; Mk. 12:10–11; Lk. 20:17) was a favorite proof-text in the early church for the resurrection and exaltation of the rejected Christ.

Neither the sending of the servants nor the sending of the son has any allegorical significance in the original parable. The Synoptics indicate that Jesus spoke this parable to members of the Sanhedrin, and this may well be correct. He was not talking to the nation but to its leaders. God's patience was running out. He was about to demand his dues—and to inflict judgment upon the rent-renegers.

Jesus spoke in specific situations. The recovery of those situations is essential for the proper understanding of his message. He was not a mere sponsor of moral principles. The parables which deal with the nearness of the kingdom are crisis parables. Their aim was to shock Israel, to alert her concerning the coming catastrophe. She was rushing headlong to her own destruction, with her leaders accelerating the process. These parables were designed to call her to repentance and to reverse her course.

The inevitability of the kingdom. The twin parables of the Mustard Seed (97) and the Leaven (98) are parables of encouragement.[45] They assure their hearers of the kingdom's coming. The stress is not on the process but on the prospect. The mustard seed's smallness is proverbial. Yet when it is planted in the ground, the results are surprising. It grows to a height of ten or twelve feet and becomes the greatest of all shrubs.[46] The leaven produces similar results. The housewife hides a tiny bit of it in an enormous quantity of meal. (Three measures would feed over 150 people.) She covers the container with a cloth and leaves the mass to stand overnight. In the morning the whole is leavened.

Neither parable supports the idea that the kingdom grows gradually. The mustard seed grows rapidly. The leaven does its work overnight. To the evangelists these parables probably suggested the spread of the gospel and the growth of the church in apostolic times. Jesus' point lies in the contrast between the tiny beginnings and the astonishing ends. God is asserting his sovereignty. The mighty consequences will soon be evident. Nothing man can do will hasten or hinder the kingdom's coming.

The Seed Growing Secretly (95) is another contrast parable.[47] A man

---

[44]See the detailed and resourceful treatment of this parable in Jeremias, *The Parables of Jesus*, pp. 70–77.

[45]Mt. 13:31–33; Mk. 4:30–32; Lk. 13:18–21.

[46]Birds do not normally build nests in it. This is a reference to Dan. 4:20–22, where Nebuchadnezzar's kingdom is likened to a great tree in which birds roost.

[47]Mk. 4:26–29. Some scholars regard vs. 29 as an apocalyptic appendage.

scatters seed on the ground. Then he goes about his daily routine. Without any help from the farmer the seed sprouts and grows: "first the blade, then the ear, then the full grain in the ear" (Mk. 4:28). All the while the farmer is ignorant of how it happens. Suddenly the grain is ripe and ready for the sickle. To Mark and his readers, the parable gave needed assurance that the delay in the kingdom's coming was only temporary. However, a delayed kingdom is farthest from Jesus' thoughts; the parable makes the point of the kingdom's proximity and inevitability.

The Sower (90) strikes westerners as a horrible example of farming.[48] The sower broadcasts his seed indiscriminately—on the path made through the field by the villagers, among the thorns, on the thin covering of soil hiding the limestone underneath, and on good soil. "What kind of harvest should one expect," we ask, "from such prodigal planting?" The question betrays our ignorance. In Palestine sowing precedes plowing. What appears to us as frightful farming is customary and, at least in the parable, fructifying.

In order to grasp the point of the Sower we shall have to disregard the interpretation which transforms it into a Christian allegory (93).[49] According to that interpretation the sower is Christ, the seed is the word, the soils are different kinds of listeners, and the moral is "Take heed then how you hear" (Lk. 8:18, which correctly renders the Aramaic word translated "what" in Mk. 4:24). This interpretation shifts the emphasis from the eschatological to the exhortative. What Jesus really sets forth is another contrast parable. It concerns the coming of the kingdom. First he suggests the manifold frustrations to which the sower's labor is liable—the sun-baked soil, the thorns, the weather, the plundering birds. Then, by way of contrast, he describes the glorious grain standing in the field awaiting the harvest. The yield is unusual. (A return of fortyfold or fiftyfold on wheat sown in the U.S. is considered good. A hundredfold would be phenomenal.) The tripling of the harvest's yield ("thirtyfold and sixtyfold and a hundredfold") suggests the eschatological overflowing of God's goodness. As bystanders watched the sower, much of the labor seemed futile and fruitless. Failures were frequent. But Jesus is confident. He knows that God has made a beginning. In spite of every failure the kingdom will inevitably come.[50]

The inclusiveness of the kingdom. Many of the parables which make this point were originally addressed to Jesus' critics. The Lost Sheep, the Lost Coin, and the Lost Son were spoken to the scribes and Pharisees (Lk. 15:2). The parable of the Two Debtors was directed at the suspicious Simon, the Pharisee (Lk. 7:40). The Pharisee and the Publican was addressed to Pharisees (Lk. 18:9). The Two Sons was spoken to members of the Sanhedrin (Mt. 21:23). The Physician and the Sick was directed toward the

---

[48]Mt. 13:3–8; Mk. 4:3–8; Lk. 8:5–8.

[49]Mt. 13:18–23; Mk. 4:13–20; Lk. 8:11–15.

[50]We are indebted to Jeremias, *The Parables of Jesus*, pp. 77–79; 149–53, for this interpretation. Although a number of scholars acknowledge that the interpretation of the Sower found in the Synoptics is allegorical and late, they hold that the original parable was designed by Jesus to show how different groups responded to his message. See Grant, in *The Interpreter's Bible*, VII, 695–700.

scribes of the Pharisees (Mk. 2:16). While these parables contain the Good News of God, they were addressed to Jesus' opponents rather than to his followers. "Their main object is not the presentation of the gospel, but defense and vindication of the gospel."[51]

The parable of the Physician and the Sick (53) was born at a banquet.[52] Jesus was eating with sinners and tax collectors. These were people who were immoral (adulterers, swindlers), followed dishonorable callings (involving dishonesty or immorality—tax-collecting, tanning, and the like), or otherwise were careless about keeping the Law. The scribes of the Pharisees, who were ultrastrict in observing the food regulations and other requirements of Pharisaism, protested to Jesus' disciples. These scribes avoided all contact with Jews who were lax, lest they themselves should be contaminated. Why did Jesus eat with such people? "Those who are well have no need of a physician," he replied, "but those who are sick; I came not to call the righteous, but sinners" (Mk. 2:17). Of course he was concerned about "the righteous," for he knew that all men are sinners and need to repent. But the kingdom of which he spoke was not confined to the respectable. It was especially interested in those considered to be beyond the pale of Providence.

The Two Sons (203) makes much the same point.[53] Members of the Sanhedrin had apparently complained because Jesus had offered God's kingdom to publicans and prostitutes. To these religious leaders Jesus addressed a parable: "A man had two sons; and he went to the first and said, 'Son, go and work in the vineyard today.' And he answered, 'I will not'; but afterward he repented and went. And he went to the second and said the same; and he answered, 'I go, sir,' but did not go. Which of the two did the will of his father?" They said, "The first." Jesus said to them, "Truly, I say to you, the tax collectors and the harlots go into the kingdom of God before you" (Mt. 21:28–31).

When Israel's leaders judged the characters in this parable, they judged themselves. They were like the second son. They believed that penitence was virtually impossible for publicans and prostitutes. From the leaders' viewpoint, such people could not make the restitution which repentance required. But the publicans and prostitutes were like the first son. They had disobeyed God, but they had shown sorrow and had repented. They would be received into the kingdom.

The Two Debtors (83)[54] is surrounded by the story of a sinful woman, probably a prostitute, who anointed Jesus' feet in the house of Simon, the Pharisee.[55] Jeremias suggests that Jesus may have preached a sermon on

---

[51]Jeremias, *The Parables of Jesus,* p. 124.

[52]Mt. 9:12; Mk. 2:17; Lk. 5:31.

[53]Mt. 21:28–31. Verse 32 has been added. It occurs as an independent saying in Lk. 7:29–30.

[54]Lk. 7:41–43.

[55]Some scholars hold that Luke has fused two independent traditions—the story of 7:36–40, 44–47a and the parable of 7:41–43. The point of the story (one who loves much is forgiven much) contradicts the point of the parable (one who is forgiven much, loves much). Lk. 7:47b is in harmony with the parable but not with the story. Lk. 7:48–50 introduces a new motif.

forgiveness that morning in the synagogue.[56] Simon had invited Jesus to a banquet, since it was considered meritorious to invite a traveling teacher to a Sabbath meal. When Jesus arrived, Simon failed to extend to him the common courtesies—water for a foot bath, a kiss of welcome, and oil for anointing his head. Sometime during the banquet the woman who was a sinner learned of Jesus' whereabouts. She appeared at Simon's house bearing an alabaster flask of ointment. She stood behind Jesus who was reclining on a couch with his feet stretched away from the table. Her tears (produced by grief for her sins and gratitude for Jesus' sermon on forgiveness) fell on his feet. Alarmed at having moistened Jesus with her tears, she forgot where she was. She removed her head-covering and unbound her hair. (This was considered a disgraceful thing for a married woman to do in public.) Then she dried Jesus' feet with her hair, kissed his feet (an act of the deepest gratitude, such as that felt for a person who had saved one's life), and anointed them. Simon was shocked. He had invited Jesus to his home because he had believed him to be a prophet. Jesus' failure to discern the character of the woman was proof that the invitation had been a huge mistake. "If this man were a prophet," Simon said to himself, "he would have known who and what sort of woman this is who is touching him, for she is a sinner" (Lk. 7:39).

The stage was now set for the parable. Jesus replied to Simon's silent criticism. " 'A certain creditor had two debtors; one owed five hundred denarii, and the other fifty.[57] When they could not pay, he forgave them both. Now which of them will love him more?[58] Simon answered, 'The one, I supose, to whom he forgave more.' And he said to him, 'You have judged rightly' " (Lk. 7:40–43). The parable contrasts the great and small debt, the deep and surface gratitude. The greater the debt forgiven, the greater the gratitude. God's goodness is extended to the worst of sinners and matches the depth of their repentance.

The Lost Son (173) is a parable in two parts. The first depicts the joy and love with which a father welcomes home a repentant son (Lk. 15:11–24). The second rebukes the elder brother's criticism of this reception (Lk. 15: 25–32). The second part is not a separate parable. It is tied to the first by the opening verse: "There was a man who had *two* sons" (Lk. 15:11).[59] The entire parable hinges on the contrasting attitudes of the father and the elder brother toward the prodigal. What we have here is a story of *two* lost sons. The elder brother was lost even though he had never left home. The story is a parable, not an allegory. The father is not God; he is a man. "Father, I have sinned against heaven [God] *and* before you" (15:18,21).[60] Yet who would deny that to Jesus the earthly father's love suggested that of the heavenly Father?

56See his perceptive treatment in *The Parables of Jesus*, p. 126.

57About $100 and $10 respectively, with a purchasing power several times these amounts.

58Jeremias, *The Parables of Jesus*, p. 127, states that Jesus' question means, "Which of them will feel the deeper thankfulness?"

59Emphasis added.

60Emphasis added.

In this parable, the younger son asked his father for his share of the property. The first-born son was entitled to a double portion (Deut. 21:17). This would make the younger son's share one-third. His request was extraordinary. He wanted not only the right of possession but also the right of disposal, which normally could be acquired only at the father's death. Nevertheless, the father complied with his request. He divided his property between his sons. A few days later, after the younger son had had time to dispose of his share, he "gathered all he had and took his journey into a far country, and there he squandered his property in loose living" (Lk. 15:13).

After the prodigal son had dissipated his substance, a severe famine struck his adopted country. He was destitute. Forced to seek employment, he took the only job available to him. He became a swineherd, a degrading occupation for a Jew. His new occupation made the habitual practice of his religion impossible. Soon he began to envy the swine. He would gladly have filled his stomach with the carob pods which he fed to them, but the food of swine was repulsive to him. He found no one who would give him anything to eat. Suddenly he saw how foolish he was. He realized that he was perishing while his father's hired servants had plenty to eat. He decided to go to his father and say, "Father, I have sinned against heaven and before you; I am no longer worthy to be called your son; treat me as one of your hired servants" (Lk. 15:18–19).

The prodigal arose and went to his father. While he was still some distance away, his father "saw him and had compassion, and ran [an unusual act for an aged Oriental] and embraced him and kissed him. And the son said to him, 'Father, I have sinned against heaven and before you; I am no longer worthy to be called your son'" (Lk. 15:20–21). The father interrupted his son's carefully rehearsed speech to give three commands to his servants. (1) "Bring quickly the best robe, and put it on him." The robe was a mark of great distinction. When a king wanted to honor an official, he clothed him in a costly robe. (2) "Put a ring on his hand, and shoes on his feet." The ring was a signet ring and signified the granting of authority; the shoes were a status symbol, since they were worn by free men. No longer would the prodigal go about barefoot like a slave. (3) "Bring the fatted calf and kill it, and let us make merry" (Lk. 15:22–23). The slaughter of the fatted calf was the prelude to a feast for the family and servants. The three commands shouted the father's forgiveness and the reinstatement of his son. In a vivid parallelism which explained his readiness to forgive, the father said, "For this my son was dead, and is alive again; he was lost, and is found" (Lk. 15:24). The feast was followed by music and dancing by the men.

When the elder son returned from his day's work in the field, he heard music (loud singing and hand-clapping) and dancing. When he asked one of the servants to tell him the reason for the festivities, he learned of his brother's return and of his father's joy and forgiveness. He was angry and refused to enter his father's house. When his father came out and entreated him, the elder son was so incensed that he failed to use the customary address in replying to his father. When he spoke of his brother, he substituted the contemptuous phrase, "this son of yours." On his father he heaped reproach, saying that although his life of virtue had gone unnoticed, his brother's life of dissipation and vice had been rewarded with a feast. The father's reply to this diatribe began with an unusually affectionate address: "My dear child."[61] The father continued, "You are always with me, and all that is mine is yours. [The prodigal had been forgiven and restored to the family circle, but none of the remaining inheritance would be his.] It was fitting to make merry and be glad, for this *your brother* [a telling rebuke of the elder brother's unbrotherly phrase] was dead, and is alive; he was lost, and is found" (Lk. 15:31–32).[62]

The parable makes a double point. The first part describes the boundless love of God. It was spoken in defense of Jesus' mission to the religiously disinherited. To his critics he said in effect, "I am only doing what God does." The second part rebukes the narrow attitude of the elder brother. Its target was probably the scribes and Pharisees. They behaved like the elder brother. They were offended by the inclusive nature of God's love and Jesus' ministry.

The twin parables of the Lost Sheep and the Lost Coin (172) make the same point as the first part of the Lost Son.[63] The scribes and Pharisees murmured because Jesus ate with sinners (Lk. 15:2). They felt that any man who fraternized with such folk was irreligious and should be shunned. In response to their caustic criticism Jesus told two parables.

Strict Jews classified shepherds with the sinners. They suspected the shepherds of pasturing their sheep in foreign fields and helping themselves to the produce of the flock. This classification did not prevent Jesus from using the figure of a shepherd to illustrate the active love of God. He asked his critics, "What man of you, having a hundred sheep, if he has lost one of them, does not leave the ninety-nine in the wilderness [uncultivated pasture land], and go after the one which is lost, until he finds it? [A hundred sheep constituted a large flock in first-century Palestine. Yet, the loss of a single one was a serious matter.] And when he has found it, he lays it on his shoulders, rejoicing. And when he comes home, he calls together his friends and his neighbors, saying to them, 'Rejoice with me, for I have found my sheep which was lost' " (Lk. 15:4–6).

If the Lost Sheep had a special appeal for men, the Lost Coin would attract the attention of women. "What woman," asked Jesus, "having ten silver coins,[64] if she loses one coin, does not light a lamp [not because it was night, but because Palestinian houses were poorly provided with windows] and sweep the house and seek diligently until she finds it? And when she has found it, she calls together her friends and neighbors, saying, 'Rejoice with me, for I have found the coin which I had lost' " (Lk. 15:8–9). Both

---

61Gk., *teknon.*

62Emphasis added.

63Mt. 18:12–14; Lk. 15:3–7, 8–10.

64The Greek drachma, roughly equivalent to the Roman denarius, was worth about sixteen cents. Its first-century purchasing power was several times that amount. The ten coins could be the life savings of a poor woman. Jeremias suggests that the lost coin may have been part of the woman's headdress and of her dowry (Jeremias, *The Parables of Jesus,* p. 134).

parables end with an indirect reference to the Deity[65] and convey the same message: as the shepherd rejoices over the return of the lost lamb and the woman over the recovery of the lost coin, so God rejoices over the salvation of sinners. His love is inclusive.

The Pharisee and Publican (186) is an example story.[66] It was addressed to those Pharisees "who trusted in themselves that they were righteous and despised others" (Lk. 18:9). It tells about two men who went up into the Temple to pray. One was a Pharisee. He found a conspicuous place and in an undertone gave voice to the vices from which he had habitually abstained. "God, I thank thee that I am not like other men, extortioners, unjust, adulterers, or even like this tax collector" (Lk. 18:11). Then he catalogued his virtues. "I fast twice a week, I give tithes of all that I get" (Lk. 18:12). Both the fasting and the tithing were works of supererogation. Semiweekly fasts were voluntary. The Law required only agricultural products to be tithed.[67]

Not all Pharisees were like the one in the parable. Yet there were enough like him so that the Talmud contains a prayer from a first-century rabbi which bears a striking similarity to the one found here: "I thank thee, O Lord, my God, that thou hast given me a place among those who sit in the House of Study, and not among those who sit at the street corners; for I rise early and they rise early, but I rise early to study the words of the Law, and they rise early to engage in vain things; I labor and they labor, but I labor and receive a reward, and they labor and receive no reward; I live and they live, but I live for the life of the future world, and they live for the pit of destruction."[68]

The other man in the parable was a tax collector. He shared the odium of his occupation. The "righteous" called him a sinner, shunned him, and saw to it that he was shorn of his civil rights. The tax collector took a position "far off" from the altar. He was so overwhelmed by his own unworthiness that his eyes remained riveted on the ground. He could not lift them toward heaven. He smote his breast (really his heart, the seat of sin) and cried out in contrition, "God, be merciful to me a sinner!" (Lk. 18:13) Jesus' concluding words must have shocked his listeners: "I tell you, this man went down to his house justified rather than the other" (Lk. 18:14a).[69] The Pharisees were not yet ready to accept the idea that God welcomes the hopeless, despairing sinner and reproves the self-righteous.

The parable of the Laborers in the Vineyard (190) attempts to vindicate the Gospel against its critics.[70] Jesus spent much of his ministry among the religiously disinherited, for they needed him most. The scribes and

---

[65]"In heaven" (Lk. 15:7) and "before the angels of God" (Lk. 15:10).

[66]Lk. 18:10–14a.

[67]Deut. 14:22–23. Jeremias, *The Parables of Jesus,* p. 112, concludes that the Pharisee tithed everything that he *bought.* He thus was certain that he used nothing that had not been tithed, even though corn, new wine, and oil would already have been tithed by the producer.

[68]Berakoth 28b.

[69]Lk. 18:14b is a floating saying which the evangelist had previously used in 14:11.

[70]Mt. 20:1–15. Vs. 16 has been added. It is a generalized conclusion (see Mk. 10:31; Lk. 13:30) which misses the point of the parable, which teaches no lesson about the *reversal* of rank. All workers receive the same wage.

Pharisees took a jaundiced view of his preaching. The "people of the land" were careless about keeping the Law and the traditions. From the orthodox viewpoint, they were not entitled to special consideration, which should be reserved for those who had earned it. In this parable Jesus justifies his practice and exposes the selfish concern of his critics. The rewards of the kingdom, he declares, are not determined by man's merit. They are the free gift of God's grace extended to whom He wills.

The Jewish working day began at sunrise and ended at sunset. Early one morning an estate owner hired some laborers to work in his vineyard. The wage agreed upon was a denarius, the usual day's wage for a laborer at that time.[71] About nine, twelve, and three o'clock other workers were hired. The owner promised to pay them whatever was right. At five o'clock a final group was employed. When the day's work was done, each worker was paid a denarius. Those who had labored long grumbled. They had expected a bonus because they had borne the burden of the day and the scorching heat. The owner replied to their protest, "Friend, I am doing you no wrong; did you not agree with me for a denarius? Take what belongs to you, and go; I choose to give to this last as I give to you. Am I not allowed to do what I choose with what belongs to me? Or do you begrudge my generosity?" (Mt. 20:13–15).

The parable offends those who find in it a celestial endorsement of a terrestrial system of economics. They claim that strict justice is not served. This is so; but this is not the point of the parable. Even if it were, the burden-bearers would have had small cause for complaint. They received exactly what they had bargained for, a full day's pay. Their grumbling was not grounded in injustice; it sprang from envy. If the five-o'clockers had been given one-twelfth of a denarius, their protest would never have arisen. How fortunate it is that God does not deal with us on the basis of strict justice. If He did, who could stand? "There is such a thing as the twelfth part of a denar. It was called a *pondion*. But there is no such thing as a twelfth part of the love of God."[72] His love includes those who were lightly regarded in Jesus' day.

The Unjust Judge (185) is recorded only in Luke.[73] Its editorial introduction announces that the point of the parable is persistence in prayer (Lk. 18:1). Unfortunately, the editor missed the point of the parable and in addition showed poor technique in story-telling.[74] Jesus never gave away his point in advance. "In a certain city," Jesus said, "there was a judge who neither feared God nor regarded man; and there was a widow in that city

---

[71]About twenty cents, with a first-century purchasing power several times that figure.
[72]T. W. Manson, in *The Mission and Message of Jesus*, p. 512.
[73]Lk. 18:2–5.
[74]See Gilmour, in *The Interpreter's Bible*, VIII, 306–308, for a contrary view. The parable proper is confined to Lk. 18:2–5. Lk. 18:6–8a was added to it in the process of transmission. Still later Lk. 18:8b was added. It reflects a spirit of pessimism which may have been prompted by the growth of heretical groups in the church. Jeremias, *The Parables of Jesus*, pp. 153–60, lists the Unjust Judge and the Friend at Midnight under "The Great Assurance." Both Jeremias and Manson, in *The Mission and Message of Jesus*, p. 559, regard Lk. 18:6–8a as genuine.

who kept coming to him and saying, 'Vindicate me against my adversary' "
(Lk. 18:2–3). Perhaps a debt, pledge, or part of an inheritance was being
kept from her. Her opponent was probably rich and powerful. When she
failed to secure satisfaction from him, she appealed to the court for justice.
The judge refused to hear her case. The widow was too poor to offer him
a bribe. Her only weapon was her persistence, which she employed with a
vengeance. Finally, the judge yielded, saying, "I will vindicate her, or she
will wear me out by her continual coming" (Lk. 18:5). The parable's central
figure is the judge rather than the widow. Its point is produced by a leap
from the lesser to the greater. If an unjust judge can be induced by a de-
fenseless but persistent widow to give justice, how much more can one
expect from a righteous God! The scribes and Pharisees may exclude "publicans and sinners" from God's concern, but God doesn't. He will listen to
them when they call upon him. His love is inclusive.

The Friend at Midnight (147),[75] so far as Luke is concerned, makes the
same point as the Unjust Judge: persistent prayer brings results. But in
their original context both parables stressed God's readiness to respond to
those who call upon him. A vivid picture of life in a first-century Palestinian
village is provided by the Friend at Midnight. Women arose before sunup
to bake the day's supply of bread for the family. Three loaves made a meal
for each person. In the evening the women chatted at the village well. If
anyone had a bread surplus, it soon became common knowledge. When unexpected guests arrived during the night (people often traveled at night to
avoid the scorching heat of the day), a hurried visit was made to those who
had bread to spare. Jesus asks, "Which of you who has a friend will go to
him at midnight and say to him, 'Friend, lend me three loaves; for a friend
of mine has arrived on a journey, and I have nothing to set before him';
and he will answer from within, 'Do not bother me; the door is now shut
[bolted and locked], and my children are with me in bed [the whole family
slept together]; I cannot get up and give you anything'?" (Lk. 11:5–7). It
would be an effort to get up, a nuisance to draw the bolt, and the noise
would awaken the children. The friend's irritation is indicated by the omission of "Friend" in his reply. "I tell you," continued Jesus, "though he will
not get up and give him anything because he is his friend, yet because of his
importunity he will rise and give him whatever he needs" (Lk. 11:8).

The words which introduce this parable ("Which of you") are regularly
used in the Synoptics to raise questions which require an emphatic answer.[76]
Consequently, Luke 11:5–7 should be regarded as one extended rhetorical
question ("Can you imagine . . . ?"). The answer to the question would be,
"Certainly not!" It would be unthinkable for a man to refuse a request
for bread at midnight. If friendship would not avail, persistence would.
The bread-owner would rise and give his petitioner the bread for which he
asked and whatever else he needed. As in the Unjust Judge, the audience is
expected to make the leap from the lesser to the greater. If a human friend
will undergo considerable inconvenience to give a neighbor bread in the

[75]Lk. 11:5–8.
[76]Lk. 12:25; 14:28; 15:4; 17:7; Mt. 7:9; 12:11.

middle of the night, how much more will the divine Friend harken to the cry of the needy!

Jesus associated with the riffraff. Respectable people shunned them, but this did not matter to him. They were sick and needed a physician. They were also responsive. When they heard the Good News, they repented. They experienced the astounding forgiveness of God, and their hearts overflowed with gratitude. The "righteous" objected to Jesus' gospel to the outcasts. The "righteous" wanted to preserve the privilege of walking with God for themselves alone. They had not yet learned that the kingdom is inclusive.

The cost of discipleship. Jesus calls for complete commitment. "If any one comes to me and does not hate his own father and mother and wife and children and brothers and sisters, yes, and even his own life, he cannot be my disciple" (Lk. 14:26). A disciple must "leave the dead to bury their own dead" (Lk. 9:60). Once he has put his hand to the plow, he cannot look back (Lk. 9:62). The kingdom has top priority (Mt. 6:33). It is not for impulsive disciples.

The companion parables of the Tower Builder and the Warring King (171) counsel would-be disciples to count the cost.[77] "For which of you, desiring to build a tower,"[78] asks Jesus, "does not first sit down and count the cost, whether he has enough to complete it? Otherwise, when he has laid a foundation, and is not able to finish, all who see it begin to mock him, saying, 'This man began to build, and was not able to finish.' Or what king, going to encounter another king in war, will not sit down first and take counsel whether he is able with ten thousand to meet him who comes against him with twenty thousand? And if not, while the other is yet a great way off, he sends an embassy and asks terms of peace."[79]

The Empty House (88) contains a similar warning to potential disciples.[80] An "unclean spirit" was a synonym in Jewish thought for "demon." Popular belief held that the desert (a "waterless" place) was a demon's natural home. "When the unclean spirit has gone out of a man," says Jesus, "he passes through waterless places seeking rest, but he finds none. [He has become a domesticated demon. He is no longer content with a nomadic life.] Then he says, 'I will return to my house from which I came.' And when he comes he finds it empty, swept, and put in order [properly prepared for guests]. Then he goes and brings with him seven other spirits more evil than himself, and they enter and dwell there, and the last state of that man becomes worse than the first" (Mt. 12:43–45c). Seven was a Hebrew number for completeness. The "seven other spirits" represent every type of temptation and wickedness. Their alliance with the first demon made a second exorcism unlikely.

[77]Lk. 14:28–32.

[78]The Greek word may mean an expensive building as well as a simple watchtower.

[79]Lk. 14:33 appears to be a later, generalized conclusion.

[80]Mt. 12:43–45c (45d has been added); Lk. 11:24–26. Jeremias, *The Parables of Jesus*, pp. 196–98, lists the Tower Builder and the Warring King and The Empty House under "The Challenge of the Hour."

The point of the parable is inescapable. The expulsion of a demon merely restores the victim to his original state. Conditions are exactly the same as they were before the demon first took possession. Exorcism is not enough. If the demon is to be kept out, the house must not remain empty. A new master must rule there. The house of the demon must become the dwelling place of God (I Cor. 6:19; Eph. 2:22).

The Householder (103) may be Jesus' answer to a scribe who has volunteered to become a disciple and is uncertain as to how his learning will be utilized in his new work. "Every scribe who has been trained for the kingdom of heaven," says Jesus, "is like a householder who brings out of his treasure what is new and what is old."[81] A scribe who becomes a disciple will have the best of two worlds, the Jewish and the Christian. He will wed the wisdom of the Old Order and the New. Thus understood, the parable expresses perfectly the Jewish-Christian ideal. But does it express the thought of Jesus? This is doubtful. It is hard to reconcile it with the parables of the New Wine and the New Cloth, or with the antitheses of the Sermon on the Mount: "You have heard that it was said. . . . But I say to you" (Mt. 5:21–22,27–28, etc.). A sharp cleavage existed between Jesus' teaching and the scribal interpretation of the Law. This is stressed by Matthew more than by any other Gospel. Perhaps the Householder is an unconscious self-portrait of the evangelist.[82]

The Good Samaritan (144)[83] follows the account in Luke of a lawyer's question (143).[84] "And behold, a lawyer stood up to put him to a test [to determine Jesus' qualifications], saying 'Teacher, what shall I do to inherit eternal life?'[85] [The circumstances reveal a radical reversal of roles—a Bible scholar asking a layman about something in the field of the scholar's own specialty! Probably Jesus' teaching had pricked the scholar's curiosity or conscience.] He said to him, 'What is written in the law? How do you [the credentialed expert] read?' And he answered, 'You shall love the Lord your God with all your heart, and with all your soul, and with all your strength, and with all your mind; and your neighbor as yourself.'[86] And he said to him, 'You have answered right; do this, and you will live' " (Lk. 10:25–28).

Jesus and the lawyer were in full agreement. The legatees of eternal life were those who loved God and their neighbor. Loving God was no problem; most Jews did that. The real difficulty was in loving one's neighbor. Where did "neighbor" end and "nonneighbor" begin? All ancient civilizations drew the line somewhere—between Greek and barbarians, Roman

81Mt. 13:52. The "therefore" which introduces the saying in Matthew serves to connect it with the preceding material. Its original context may have been quite different.

82B. W. Bacon, *Studies in Matthew* (New York: Henry Holt & Co., 1930), p. 131.

83Lk. 10:30–37.

84Lk. 10:25–28.

85Luke changed "scribe" (Mk. 12:28) to "lawyer" to suit his Gentile readers. Did he also substitute a question which dealt with a subject appealing to Gentiles (eternal life) for one of interest only to the Jews (the commandment of first importance, Mk. 12:28)?

86This was not a new thought. See *The Testaments of the Twelve Patriarchs*, Issachar 5:1–2.

citizen and foreigner, freeman and slave, or Jew and Gentile. Leviticus 19:18 equated "neighbor" with "fellow Israelite." Yet the term was elastic; it could be stretched to include converts to Judaism, or it could be contracted to exclude "Jews" who neglected or rejected their faith. Obviously "neighbor" needed to be defined. The lawyer asked, "And who is my neighbor?" Jesus answered, "A man was going *down* from Jerusalem to Jericho, and he fell among robbers, who stripped him and beat him, and departed, leaving him half dead. [The seventeen-mile road, with a descent of about 3,300 feet, passed through deserted ravines and by barren cliffs and caves. It was made to order for robbers.] Now by chance a priest was going down that road; and when he saw him he passed by on the other side. So likewise a Levite, when he came to the place and saw him, passed by on the other side. But a Samaritan, as he journeyed, came to where he was; and when he saw him, he had compassion, and went and bound up his wounds, pouring on oil and wine [widely-used healing agents]; then he set him on his own beast and brought him to an inn, and took care of him. And the next day he took out two denarii [worth about forty cents and equal to two days' wages] and gave them to the innkeeper, saying, 'Take care of him; and whatever more you spend, I will repay you when I come back.' Which of these three, do you think, proved neighbor to the man who fell among the robbers?" The lawyer answered, "The one who showed mercy on him." Jesus replied, "Go and do likewise."[87] This parable raises a number of questions.

(1) Why did the priest and the Levite, representatives of professional and lay religion, fail to render aid? Were they utterly callous? Were they reluctant to interfere with God's justice because they shared the belief that misfortune was God's judgment on sin? Did they avoid contact with the victim on Levitical grounds because they believed he was dead? (Lev. 21:1). Or were they on missions which they honestly held to be more urgent?

(2) What was a hated half-breed heretic doing in Jerusalem? The parable suggests that the Samaritan was a merchant who made regular trips to the Holy City and was on good terms with the landlord of an inn. Such behavior hardly accords with our knowledge of the Jewish-Samaritan cold war of Jesus' time. Some interpreters have therefore maintained that the third character in the parable was originally not a Samaritan but a Jew. His conduct was contrasted with that of his religious leaders. But it just could be that Jesus chose an extreme example to set forth the categorical nature of love.[88] An astute Jewish scholar declares, "Whether the Samaritan was original to the parable or not, at all events he is there now, and the conception of the good Samaritan is one which the world will not easily let go."[89]

(3) Does the parable really answer the lawyer's question? He asked, "Who is my neighbor?" He was given an illustration of neighborliness. This was no doubt deliberate. The lawyer's question was unanswerable. "Love does not begin by defining its objects: it discovers them. And failure in the

---

[87]Lk. 10:29–37, emphasis added.

[88]See Jeremias, *The Parables of Jesus*, p. 204.

[89]C. G. Montefiore, *The Synoptic Gospels*, 2nd rev. ed. (London: Macmillan & Co., Ltd., 1927), II, 468.

observance of the great commandment comes not from lack of precise information about the application of it, but from lack of love. The point of the parable is that if a man has love in his heart, it will tell him who his neighbor is."[90] The cost of discipleship is love without limit.

The Sheep and Goats (229) also stresses the centrality of love.[91] Is it a genuine parable of Jesus? Its opening verse reminds us of Matthew 16:27 and 19:28. Matthew's favorite connective ("then") appears six times in the parable. References to "the righteous" (25:37), "the devil and his angels" (25:41), and "eternal punishment" (25:46) also seem to betray his hand. Despite signs of the evangelist's style, however, many scholars subscribe to the parable's substantial authenticity. "It certainly contains features of such startling originality that it is difficult to credit them to anyone but the Master Himself."[92]

The principal characters in the parable are the Son of man, all the nations, the King, the King's Father, the Lord, and the King's brethren. The specific identity of some of the characters is in doubt. The King's Father surely represents God. God is not the judge in this parable, as He was in common Jewish expectations. The King, then, is Christ,[93] who pronounces the judgments. The King is also called "Lord" and "Son of man."[94] The people who receive judgment are "all the nations" (25:32). They are the Gentiles, according to Matthew's usage. Who, then, are the King's brethren? Not the disciples. To confine "my brethren" to the disciples in view of the reference to the Gentiles "would be to assume a world-wide mission to the remotest nations, a conception which does not correspond with the outlook of Jesus."[95] The King's brethren are the needy and the afflicted.

The parable probably arose in response to the question, "By what standard will the heathen be judged?" The gist of Jesus' reply is: those who have shown love to the needy ("the least of these my brethren," 25:40) have shown it to the Christ. At the Last Judgment, they will be granted a share in the kingdom. Those who have not loved the needy will have no part in it.

The Unmerciful Servant (136) warns disciples that they must learn to forgive.[96] When a certain king called his servants (high government officials) to present their accounts for audit, one servant showed a deficit of 10,000 talents. (This was a colossal figure, equal to about $10,000,000 with a purchasing power many times that amount.[97] It was probably deliberately

---

[90]Manson, in *The Mission and Message of Jesus*, pp. 553–54.

[91]Mt. 25:31–46.

[92]Manson, in *The Mission and Message of Jesus*, p. 541.

[93]The resurrected Christ or the heavenly figure described in Enoch? This problem will be discussed at length in a later chapter. Here, it should be noted, Jesus does not *explicitly* identify himself with the heavenly figure.

[94]Some scholars hold "Son of man" is a collective term (as in Dan. 7:13) and here refers to the King and his brethren. See Manson, in *The Mission and Message of Jesus*, pp. 541–42.

[95]Jeremias, *The Parables of Jesus*, p. 207.

[96]Mt. 18:23–34.

[97]The yearly tribute of Galilee and Perea in 4 B.C. was only 200 talents—or one-fiftieth of the sum named here!

chosen to heighten the contrast with the figure to follow.) When the servant could not pay, the king ordered that he, his family, and his substance be sold. (Even so drastic a measure, of course, would provide only a token payment on so monstrous a debt.) The servant pleaded for patience until he could repay the debt. The king went far beyond the plea. He forgave the debt.[98] But his generosity was lost on his servant. The servant soon met a fellow servant (a colleague in the royal service) who owed him the equivalent of twenty dollars—a trifling sum compared to the debt that had been forgiven. When the fellow servant could not pay, his plea for patience was ignored. He was put in prison. Colleagues of the imprisoned servant were indignant. They reported the disgraceful incident directly to the king. The king was angry. He upbraided the hardhearted creditor for his lack of mercy and turned him over to the torturers until his original debt was paid. The moral for disciples is summed up in the secondary and concluding verse, "So also my heavenly Father will do to every one of you, if you do not forgive your brother from your heart" (Mt. 18:35).

The City on a Hill (20) is intended to encourage Jesus' disciples.[99] The cost of following him is considerable. The parables we have just dealt with make this clear But prospective citizens of the kingdom need not be afraid, for they have the Gospel; and this is all they need. God has put them in a place of prominence. Their role is to illumine. If they have faith—even as little as a grain of mustard seed—nothing will be impossible for them. "A city set on a hill cannot be hid" (Mt. 5:14b).

The supreme value of the kingdom. This is the point of the twin parables of the Hidden Treasure and the Precious Pearl (101). "The kingdom of heaven," said Jesus, "is like treasure hidden in a field, which a man found and covered up; then in his joy he goes and sells all that he has and buys that field. Again, the kingdom of heaven is like a merchant in search of fine pearls, who, on finding one pearl of great value, went and sold all that he had and bought it" (Mt. 13:44–46).

The Hidden Treasure can be readily reconstructed. People often hid their wealth (garments, hangings, rugs, coins) in their houses or fields— "where moth and rust consume and where thieves break in and steal" (Mt. 6:19). One day while a day laborer was plowing, his ox sank into a hole. Quite by accident a treasure, probably hidden and forgotten by a previous owner of the land, was unearthed. Quickly the laborer covered it up. Then he sold all that he had and bought the field.

No importance should be attached to the method of discovery in these parables. Just because a man stumbles on his wealth in one case and searches for it in the other, we should not conclude that the parables reveal "Jesus' awareness that it is often by very different roads that men come to the Kingdom."[100] Neither should we be concerned about the morality of

---

[98]"Debt" here literally means "loan." Perhaps the debtor had been working with capital loaned for that purpose. If so, his deficiency could be called embezzlement.

[99]Mt. 5:14b.

[100]A. M. Hunter, *Interpreting the Parables* (London: SCM Press Ltd., © 1960), p. 65. Printed in the U.S. by the Westminster Press.

the plower's action although it was apparently technically proper.[101] These are parables, not allegories. As parables, they promote a single point. When one finds something of supreme value, he sells all to possess it.

In the parables of the Hidden Treasure and the Precious Pearl, scholars frequently find Jesus' call for complete self-surrender. Jesus did make such calls, but not in these parables. When the man behind the plough discovered the buried treasure, he did not sit down and calculate the cost of purchasing the field. He hid the treasure and in his joy went and sold all that he had so that he could buy the field. The stress in the story is on what the man found, not on what he gave up. He found (to paraphrase Manson) wealth that devalues all other currencies.[102]

The challenge of the kingdom. The hour is late. God's patience is nearly exhausted. The ax is about to fall on the unfruitful fig tree. God's will is soon to be realized. The parable of the Defendant (161) graphically pictures the human predicament.[103] The setting is the Sermon on the Mount in Matthew. There the parable reads like common-sense counsel to Christians concerning their controversies with opponents. They are advised to make a settlement before they reach the courts. Luke's parallel passage is placed in a more probable context—one dealing with the end of the age. Jesus directs the attention of his hearers to their lack of spiritual perceptivity. In other areas they are razor-sharp. When they see a cloud rising over the Mediterranean, they know a shower is coming. When they feel a wind blow from the southern desert, they know there will be a scorching heat. When their creditors threaten them with jail unless they pay their debts, they know it is time to settle out of court. What they don't seem to realize is that they are already on their way to the court where they must give account of their lives. The time to be reconciled to God is now.

The Dishonest Steward (174) echoes a similar thought.[104] A certain rich man had a steward (an estate manager) who was charged with wasting his master's goods. The steward was subsequently dismissed. The thought of losing his position plunged him into a period of panic. He was too weak to do manual labor. He was too proud to beg. He had to live by his wits, so he concocted a clever plan. He would show kindness to his master's debtors. Then they would be obligated to entertain him when he was put out of his present position. So he summoned his master's debtors one by one and instructed them to falsify their accounts.[105] The first debtor owed a hundred measures of oil (about 875 gallons). He was told to reduce the bill to fifty measures. The second debtor owed a hundred measures of wheat (nearly 1,100 bushels). He was instructed to write eighty measures. (The fact that the steward was squandering his master's substance in order to establish his

[101]*Baba Bathra* 4:8–9.

[102]Manson, in *The Mission and Message of Jesus*, p. 488. Jeremias, *The Parables of Jesus*, pp. 198–201, lists these two parables under "Realized Discipleship."

[103]Mt. 5:25–26; Lk. 12:58–59.

[104]Lk. 16:1–8.

[105]Were the debtors (1) tenants who had signed agreements to pay their land rent in kind or (2) wholesale merchants who had given promissory notes for goods received?

own security did not seem to bother him.) When the master learned of the steward's conduct he "commended the dishonest steward for his prudence; for the sons of this world are wiser in their own generation than the sons of light" (Lk. 16:8).

Why did Jesus use a parable in which a disreputable character is praised? Jesus' ethical judgment of the steward is found in his description. He is a dishonest steward. He is praised not for his rascality but for his resourcefulness. There is a world of difference between applauding the clever steward because he is dishonest and applauding the dishonest steward because he is clever.[106]

The parable constitutes a challenge to Jesus' listeners to see clearly their own situation. Like the dishonest steward they are threatened with imminent disaster; but their crisis is much more acute. The dishonest steward was prudent. He acted unscrupulously, to be sure, but boldly and resolutely to make a new life for himself. Will the sons of light do the same—in a better way and for better ends?

The parable ends with vs. 8. The sayings which follow (vss. 9–13) have only a topical likeness to the parable and were not originally a part of it. Verse 9 indicates that by disposing of worldly wealth in a proper way one will have treasure in heaven. It has authentic parallels (Mt. 6:19–20; Mk. 10:21; Lk. 12:33–34), but this parable is not one of them.

The Rich Man and Lazarus (177) falls into two parts. The first concerns a rich man and a poor man and the reversal of their fortunes in the next life (Lk. 16:19–26). The second part deals with the petition of the rich man that the poor man be sent to the rich man's five brothers to warn them lest they end up as he has (Lk. 16:27–31). The second part of the parable may have been prompted by a demand that Jesus produce a sign to prove that there is a future life. The description of the rich man (often called "Dives" from the word with which the Vulgate translated the adjective "rich") suggests a Sadducee. He was wealthy as were the Sadducees; and he was clothed in purple, the color of royalty. The Sadducees were the aristocratic party in Judaism. The rich man lived luxuriously as did the Sadducees. He anticipated no life beyond this one; the Sadducees also repudiated belief in a future life.

The life of Lazarus stands in sharp contrast. Prostrate and ulcerated, he was dependent on crumbs ("pieces of bread with which the guests wiped their hands and then threw under the table"[107]). He was so weak he couldn't defend himself against the vagrant dogs which nosed around him and licked his sores. Dogs, like swine, were considered unclean animals. Their unwelcome ministrations climaxed the poor man's miseries. Lazarus[108] (Helped of God) was appropriately named. He received no help from men.

Death brought a radical reversal of roles. Lazarus was carried by the

---

[106]T. W. Manson, in *The Mission and Message of Jesus*, p. 584.

[107]Jeremias, *The Parables of Jesus*, p. 184.

[108]The Grecized form of the Hebrew name "Eleāzār." This is the only time a proper name is used in one of Jesus' parables.

angels to Abraham's bosom, a place of honor in Paradise. The rich man, probably after a lavish funeral as was befitting to one of his station, was buried; and that was the end of the matter. The Sadducees believed man's final end to be Sheol, a dumping ground for human beings, a place devoid of distinctions, where death was the great leveler.[109] But Hades provided a rude awakening for the rich man. It contained features of Gehenna or hell, including anguish and flame. In torment the rich man looked about for help. He saw Abraham far off and Lazarus with him. He called Abraham "Father," a claim he could make as a son of the covenant. He asked Abraham to send Lazarus, whose needs he had callously ignored on earth, to quench his thirst. The petition was denied. "Son, remember that you in your lifetime received your good things, and Lazarus in like manner evil things; but now he is comforted here, and you are in anguish. And besides all this, between us and you a great chasm has been fixed, in order that those who would pass from here to you may not be able, and none may cross from there to us" (Lk. 16:25–26). Had the rich man shown mercy, things would have been different. Now it was too late. The roles were reversed and the reversal was irrevocable.

In the second part of the parable, the rich man began to think of his brothers. They were living as he had lived, believing what he had believed. Unless they were persuaded to believe in a future life, they would join him in torment. So he directed a second petition to Abraham. He asked that Lazarus be sent to warn the brothers. Abraham replied, "They have Moses and the prophets; let them hear them" (Lk. 16:29). The rich man doubted that Scripture would suffice, since it hadn't persuaded him. He felt that if his brothers could see someone from the dead, they would repent. "If they do not hear Moses and the prophets," concluded Abraham, "neither will they be convinced if some one should rise from the dead" (Lk. 16:31).

The parable showed that the rich man's request for a sign to convince his brothers was futile. The request also evidenced a lack of faith. If men will not submit to the Word of God, their situation is hopeless. If they do submit, they will believe in a future life and act mercifully toward the needy.

The Wedding Garment (205) follows the Marriage Feast in Matthew.[110] The sequence has long troubled commentators. Why should a man who had been hustled off the street to attend a wedding be expected to appear in a wedding garment?[111] Why is the parable missing in Luke? Why the abrupt

---

[109]This primitive view of Sheol was modified after the Exile. The ideas of resurrection and retribution transformed Sheol into a waiting place for both sinners and righteous before final judgment. But the Sadducees remained loyal to the original idea of Sheol.

[110]Mt. 22:11–13. See pp. 207, 213–14.

[111]The suggestion that wedding garments were issued to guests invited on the spur of the moment is unconvincing on two counts. (1) The complaint against the offender in vs. 12 is not that he refused to wear an offered garment but that he came without one. (2) There is no evidence that special garments were provided for festive occasions. The "wedding garment" may have been a newly-washed garment. Even so, the question is germane. Why should a man from the street be expected to appear at a wedding in newly-washed clothes?

change from "servants" (*douloi*, vss. 3, 4, 6, 8, 10) to "attendants" (*diakonoi*, vs. 13)? Clearly the Wedding Garment is an independent parable. Matthew placed the parable after the Marriage Feast to avoid a misunderstanding of the promiscuous invitation in vs. 9. This verse seemed to suggest that the conduct of the called was unimportant, that the church took into its fold "both bad and good" (vs. 10). In the context of the verse, the gospel of the free grace of God might be interpreted to relieve its members of moral responsibility. The Wedding Garment attached to the Marriage Feast served as a corrective. It stressed the need for righteousness (or repentance).[112]

The original point of the Wedding Garment may have been quite different. A rabbinical parallel suggests that the man without a wedding garment was neither rude nor uninvited. He was a fool. His summons to the marriage feast came sooner than he had expected, and he was caught unprepared. Jesus challenged his hearers to be on constant alert lest they find themselves in a like predicament concerning the coming kingdom.[113]

The parable of the Places at Table (169) seems to say that modesty is the best policy.[114] This teaching was not new. Proverbs 25:6-7 had made the point centuries before. Did Luke merely take a familiar rule of etiquette and attempt to spiritualize it by attaching the saying in vs. 11? Perhaps, but more likely it was Jesus who turned it into a parable of the kingdom. The real point of the parable has a close affinity with the message of the Laborers in the Vineyard and Jesus' response to the request of the sons of Zebedee (Mk. 10:35-45).

The parable was spoken during some table talk between Jesus and the Pharisees. Jesus had observed how feverishly fond some of the guests were of the places of honor. He warned his hearers, "When you are invited by any one to a marriage feast, do not sit down in a place of honor, lest a more eminent man than you be invited by him [the most important guests— distinguished by reason of age or social standing—usually arrived last]; and he who invited you both will come and say to you, 'Give place to this man,' and then you will begin with shame to take the lowest place [since all the other seats will have been taken in the meantime]. But when you are invited, go and sit in the lowest place, so that when your host comes he may say to you, 'Friend, go up higher'; then you will be honored in the presence of all who sit at table with you" (Lk. 14:8-10). The following verse might appear to be a secondary generalized conclusion, but the rabbinical parallel to the parable has convinced Jeremias that Luke 14:11 is genuine. It speaks of God's eschatological activity, the humbling of the proud and the exalting of the humble. Jesus' hearers were expected to see in the parable hints of an impending heavenly banquet—and to renounce self-righteousness and humble themselves before God.[115]

The parable of the Servant's Duty (181) issues a similar call for humility

---

[112]Vs. 14 may be a genuine saying, but it doesn't belong here. It fits neither vss. 2-10 nor 11-13. In the former, many are called and none chosen. In the latter, many are called and all but one are chosen.

[113]See Jeremias, *The Parables of Jesus*, pp. 187-89.

[114]Lk. 14:7-11.

[115]Jeremias, *The Parables of Jesus*, pp. 191-94.

(Lk. 17:7–10). It is unconnected with the preceding material in Luke. It was probably originally directed toward the Pharisees' preoccupation with merit. Jesus says in effect that a farmer never fusses over a slave when the slave returns from a dawn-to-dusk day in the field under the blazing sun. Instead, the farmer orders the slave to prepare the farmer's evening meal. He does not thank the slave for the service. It is his duty. No rights stem from responsibilities fulfilled. This is true also of the faithful followers of Jesus. No matter how diligently they labor, they can never store up merit sufficient to put God in their debt. They can never demand reward. They owe all they are capable of doing—and more! "What we receive from God is grace and goodness, and not reward."[116]

The Two Foundations (43) forms a finale for the Sermon in Matthew and Luke.[117] "Every one then who hears these words of mine and does them," says Jesus, "will be like a wise man who built his house upon the rock; and the rain fell, and the floods came, and the winds blew and beat upon that house, but it did not fall, because it had been founded on the rock" (Mt. 7:24–25). The wise man prepared for certainties. Rains, floods, and winds occurred every year in Palestine, but the wise man outwitted the forces of nature by building on a sure foundation. "And every one who hears these words of mine and does not do them," continues Jesus, "will be like a foolish man who built his house upon the sand" (Mt. 7:26). The house he built was as substantial as that of the wise man. The only difference was in the foundation. In place of rock, the foolish man chose the smooth, inviting sand of a river bed. When the rain fell and the floods came and the winds blew, he wished he had built on the rock.

This parable sums up the challenge of the kingdom. Action is the keynote. "How happy are they," says Jesus in effect, "who build their lives on the firm foundation of hearing and heeding my words! They will be ready when the kingdom comes."

The climax of the kingdom. God's full sovereignty had once prevailed everywhere. Because of man's sin and rebellion this was no longer true. God's rule was largely confined to heaven. But the day would soon come— and Jesus viewed his words and works as a prelude to that day—when God's will would "be done, on earth as it is in heaven" (Mt. 6:10). Evil would be banished. The living and the dead would be judged. The final separation would be made.

Not all people were content to leave to God the task of separation. The Pharisees considered those who were ignorant of the Law to be accursed. They remained aloof from their fellow Jews and regarded themselves as the true people of God. The Essenes went one step further. If at all possible, they withdrew from the normal life of man and established a pure community apart. Some unknown, ardent advocate of separation—perhaps a Pharisee shocked by Jesus' concern for outcasts—asked Jesus why he did not separate the sinners from the saints. Jesus responded with a pair of parables.

---

[116]Montefiore, *The Synoptic Gospels*, II, 543.
[117]Mt. 7:24–27; Lk. 6:47–49.

The Weeds (96)[118] is one of the two separation parables. The other one
is the Net. The Weeds is followed by an obvious interpretation (100).[119]
(The only other parable with such an explanation is the Sower.) The interpretation is clearly allegorical and secondary. It misses the point of the
parable (the need for patience). It contains expressions which Jesus could
hardly have used (such as "the field is the world," Mt. 13:38). It is permeated
with the stylistic characteristics of Matthew ("then," etc.).[120] A number of
scholars claim that the Weeds itself is secondary,[121] that it is an allegory
suited to the situation of the early church. Should the church purge itself
of unfaithful members? Certainly not. It should let both the faithful and the
unfaithful grow until the harvest. In spite of this attractive suggestion, the
Weeds may be considered an authentic parable. A similar story is reported
from modern Palestine. The Weeds may have been grounded in an actual
happening.[122]

The "weeds" are usually identified as the poisonous darnel (*lolium
temulentum*). Darnel grows to the height of about two feet, is closely related to bearded wheat botanically, and produces grain of a similar size but
of a dark color. In their early stages of growth darnel and wheat are difficult
to distinguish. But "when the plants came up and bore grain, then the
weeds appeared also" (Mt. 13:26). They could be distinguished by their
darker color and perhaps by their lesser height. When the servants reported
the condition of the field to the householder (there was probably a profusion of weeds), the householder attributed the misfortune to the work of
an enemy. (Is this not a human trait?) The suggestion of the servants that
the field be weeded was vetoed. "No," the householder declared, "lest in
gathering the weeds you root up the wheat along with them. Let both grow
together until the harvest; and at harvest time I will tell the reapers, Gather
the weeds first and bind them in bundles to be burned, but gather the wheat
into my barn" (Mt. 13:29–30). The wheat was not harmed at harvest since
the weeds were not pulled up by their roots. As the reapers cut the grain
with their sickles, they cut the weeds to fall in a different direction. The
weeds were then bound into bundles probably to be dried and used as fuel
(compare Mt. 6:30). The parable is concerned with the climax of the kingdom. Disciples must patiently wait for God's separation.

---

[118]Mt. 13:24–30.

[119]Mt. 13:36–43.

[120]Jeremias, *The Parables of Jesus*, pp. 81–85, lists 37 examples.

[121]Mt. 13 reproduces all of Mk. 4 except vss. 21–25 (for which Mt. has other
parallels) and 26–29. A careful linguistic study suggests that Mt. 13:24–30 is an allegorical
expansion of the cryptic parable found in Mk. 4:26–29. "The ground" (Mk. 4:26) is
changed to "his field" (Mt. 13:24). Any field might have a certain amount of weeds.
The "enemy" (Mt. 13:28) is not needed in the story. It is inserted as an allegorical allusion to the devil. Servants do not normally ask permission to gather the weeds, nor are
the weeds usually gathered first. The reapers and the servants seem to be different. Yet
in real life, while the farmer might employ extra help during the harvest, his regular
servants also did their share. See Johnson, in *The Interpreter's Bible*, VII, 414–15;
Manson, in *The Mission and Message of Jesus*, pp. 484–85.

[122]Jeremias, *The Parables of Jesus*, pp. 224–25.

Near the shore of the Sea of Galilee, fishing nets are strung on ropes between eucalyptus trees to dry in the early morning.

The Net (102)[123] is clearly connected by content with the Weeds. Like its twin, it is followed by an allegorical interpretation (Mt. 13:49–50). In this instance the interpretation is not so obvious. It is a shortened version of Matthew 13:40b–43 and plainly reflects Matthew's style.[124] The evangelist has turned the parable into something quite different from the original. He has made it a description of the Final Judgment; and in the process, he has virtually obscured Jesus' plea for patience.

The "net" was large. Sometimes it was dragged between two boats; sometimes it was placed in the water by a single boat with one end of the net fastened to the shore by long ropes. When such a net was brought to shore, it contained "fish of every kind" (Mt. 13:47). The kingdom of God is not compared in the parable to a net which catches and keeps fish of every kind. It is compared to the sorting which follows the fishing. The fishermen "sorted the good into vessels but threw away the bad" (Mt. 13:48). The bad were unclean fish (those without "fins and scales," Lev. 11:10) and inedible creatures. This parable, like the Weeds, is eschatological. It con-

---

[123]Mt. 13:47–48. Only vs. 47 is considered original by some scholars. See Rudolf Otto, *The Kingdom of God and the Son of Man*, rev. ed., tr. Floyd V. Filson and Bertram Lee-Woolf (Boston: The Beacon Press, 1943), p. 127, and Manson, in *The Mission and Message of Jesus*, p. 489.

[124]Jeremias, *The Parables of Jesus*, p. 85, lists six examples.

cerns the Final Judgment which will usher in the kingdom of God. Those who desire the separate community of the holy on earth are urged to wait patiently for the climax of the kingdom.

Why did Jesus stress the need for patience? The Weeds and the Net suggest two reasons. (1) Men are unable to do the separating efficiently and accurately (Mt. 13:29). The true and false disciples, like the wheat and the weeds, closely resemble each other in their early stages. Since men cannot know what goes on in one another's hearts, they are likely to make errors of judgment and root up good wheat with the weeds. (2) The kingdom is God's. He has fixed the time of separation. That time has not yet arrived (Mt. 13:48). Opportunity for repentance has not yet run out (Lk. 13:6–9). "Till then, all false zeal must be checked, the field must be left to ripen in patience, the net must be cast widely, and everything else left to God in faith, until his hour comes."[125]

We have now completed our efforts to recover the original significance of the parables. They were the primary tool by which Jesus proclaimed the central theme of his ministry—the kingdom of God. They stressed:

1. the nearness of the kingdom,
2. the inevitability of the kingdom,
3. the inclusiveness of the kingdom,
4. the cost of discipleship,
5. the supreme value of the kingdom,
6. the challenge of the kingdom,
7. the climax of the kingdom.

Not everything that Jesus taught about the kingdom was expressed in parables. The Sermon on the Mount provides us with another rich source of information. To that source we shall now turn our attention.

[125]Jeremias, *The Parables of Jesus*, pp. 226–27. See his full treatment of these two parables, pp. 81–85, 224–27, to which our interpretation is indebted. Dan O. Via, *The Parables: Their Literary and Existential Dimension* (Philadelphia: Fortress Press, 1967) takes issue with the Dodd-Jeremias treatment of the parables. Via thinks that the parables proper are genuine works of art whose basic meaning is not to be limited to their original proclamation.

chapter fifteen

The Sermon

The Sermon on the Mount (Matthew 5–7) contains only 107 verses. Consequently, it is commonly assumed to have been delivered by Jesus at a single sitting. Its structure, however, suggests otherwise. The Sermon actually contains summaries of scores of sermons. It was the habit of rabbis first to discourse at length on a subject, and then to shorten their thoughts into easily remembered statements, which they repeated to their disciples until the latter knew them by heart. Jesus evidently emulated the rabbis in this regard.

The parallel material found in Luke (6:20–49) is called the Sermon on the Plain. The two versions begin with the Beatitudes and end with the Two Foundations. They differ markedly, however, in length. Luke contains only 30 verses to Matthew's 107. The following conclusion is inescapable. The Sermon on the Mount consists of a collection of summaries of Jesus' teaching over an extended period. Matthew took these summaries, supplemented them by his own interpretative comments, and fashioned the whole into a marvelous mosaic, which he placed in a mountain setting. It was intended to parallel Moses' reception of the Law on Mount Sinai. The Old Order (Judaism) finds its fulfillment in the New Order (the kingdom of heaven) which is at hand.[1]

---

[1]Although Matthew's paralleling of Moses and Jesus is clearly evident, it is erroneous to conclude that the Sermon is New Law and Jesus is a New Moses. The kingdom constitutes the completion of Israel's sacred history—God's final statement of his will for which Israel's teaching was necessary and valid preparation. See W. D. Davies, *The Setting of the Sermon on the Mount* (Cambridge: At the University Press, 1964), pp. 93–108.

Beatitudes (19)[2]

In Matthew the Beatitudes describe the characteristics of kingdom members—followers of Jesus in any age ("Blessed are *the poor*").[3] The Beatitudes constitute a fitting introduction to the author's code for Christian discipleship (chapters 5–7). They are not candid camera shots of eight different kinds of character. They present one character in eight different ways—like so many facets of a diamond. The character described bears a striking similarity to Jesus himself. The first clause in each Beatitude sets forth the condition, the kind of character required. The second clause describes the consequence. Matthew's eight Beatitudes (if 5:11–12 is seen as a duplicate of 5:10) are paralleled by only four in Luke 6:20–23. Each of these is matched by a corresponding woe (Lk. 6:24–26). Luke's Beatitudes are addressed to the multitude ("Blessed are *you*"), and the emphasis seems to be on the concrete situation and the notion of social change.[4]

"Blessed are the poor in spirit, for theirs is the kingdom of heaven" (Mt. 5:3). "Blessed" was an honored term in the Hebrew heritage. It meant "How happy!" and was often used to express warmest congratulations. It signified the well-being which results when people enjoy God's favor. Those who have this well-being are to be congratulated. In Luke "the poor" seems to stand for the poverty-stricken, and such an identification accents a well-attested emphasis in Jesus' teaching. Matthew, sensing that happiness and poverty are strange bedfellows, added the words "in spirit" to clarify the meaning and designate the area under consideration. It was a spiritual rather than an economic status, according to Matthew, which Jesus had in mind. This usage goes back to the Psalms (9:18; 10:9; 12:5; 34:6) where poor and pious were used interchangeably. The poor were the faithful, the religious, or the saintly. They were keenly aware of their spiritual need. Opposite to them stood the rich. Heaven's blessing was not withheld from the rich because of their wealth. Their predicament was caused by what wealth had done to them. It had caused them to grow self-satisfied and self-sufficient. It had prompted them to declare their independence from God and to establish a do-it-yourself movement.

"The kingdom of heaven," a shorthand expression for God's rule and its benefits, belongs to the poor in spirit. The present tense of the verb cannot be stressed. Jesus spoke in Aramaic and would have used no verb. In some sense the kingdom was an exciting reality at the very moment he spoke; consequently, those who were acutely aware of their spiritual need could enjoy its benefits in advance. Full citizenship, however, lay in the future. The kingdom was partly a possession, but primarily a promise.

[2]Mt. 5:3–12; Lk. 6:20–23.
[3]Emphasis added.
[4]Emphasis added. See M. L. Mowry, "Beatitudes," in G. A. Buttrick, ed., *The Interpreter's Dictionary of the Bible*, A–D, 369–71.

Not far from Capernaum, overlooking the Sea of Galilee, is a mountain called the Mount of the Beatitudes. Tradition has it that here Jesus preached the famous Sermon on the Mount (Mt. 5–7) and chose his twelve disciples (Lk. 6:12–16). The convent and round church shown in the picture belong to the Italian Franciscan nuns.

"Blessed are those who mourn, for they shall be comforted" (Mt. 5:4). This Beatitude seems to contradict what we know about woe. We do not find many happy mourners, and good grief is a mere figure of speech. "Those who mourn" may mean those who are sorry for personal or national sins or those who weep over the woes which precede the Messiah's coming. It may also include those whose sorrow comes from other sources— loss of position, power, possessions, virtue, or loved ones. "They shall be comforted" should not be confused with "they shall be comfortable." The Greek verb for comfort means "to strengthen much." The mourners are not disaster-proof. They sin and suffer as do other men. They differ only in the way they respond to their situation. When they sin, they seek forgiveness and experience the comfort that comes with confession. When others sin, they grieve for them. When trouble torments the mourners, they bear it with courage, confident of strength to see it through. They are fortified from above.

"Blessed are the meek, for they shall inherit the earth" (Mt. 5:5). The word "meek" has undergone a metamorphosis. Today it calls to mind Casper Milquetoast and Uriah Heep, spineless characters startled by their own shadows. But to Biblical writers, it had an altogether different meaning. Moses is described as "very meek, more than all men" (Num. 12:3). Yet, he defied the mighty Egyptian Pharaoh and liberated his people from slavery. The clue to the term is found in its object. Meekness concerns a man's attitude toward God rather than toward men. Moses was bold and authoritative when dealing with men. But in the presence of God he was as pliant as a willow. Opposite to the meek stand the proud, who pray, *"My will be done"* and expect God to adjust His will to their convenience.

That the meek "shall inherit the earth" seems unbelievable. That they might find a foremost place in the kingdom of heaven seems reasonable; but that they should inherit the earth—Palestine or a part of it—taxes our credulity. We think of the earth as belonging to the strong and aggressive. If by some miracle the meek should inherit the earth, the hustlers would soon take it away from them. This Beatitude echoes the Old Testament. God made a promise to Abraham that his descendants would occupy the land stretching from the Nile to the Euphrates (Gen. 15:18–21). The promise was not a will or testament which automatically went into effect no matter what the intended beneficiary should do. The promise was a covenant. Covenants become operative only when the intended beneficiary meets the obligations imposed by the terms of the covenant: God chose Israel to be His people; Israel chose Him to be her God. When Israel remained faithful to God, then she would possess the land. Originally, the statement, "The meek shall possess the land" (Ps. 37:11), was taken quite literally, as promising a real-estate reward for righteousness. However, Jesus and his followers were standing on the promised real estate. Jesus did not offer his followers what they already had. When he declared that the meek "shall inherit the earth," he was speaking poetically. He meant that they would enjoy the blessings of the kingdom.

"*Blessed are those who hunger and thirst for righteousness, for they shall be satisfied*" (Mt. 5:6). As in the first Beatitude, Luke's reading is nearer the original. It seems to stress a physical condition. Matthew adds "for righteousness" to clarify the meaning. "Hunger and thirst" had long been used to symbolize intense spiritual longing. Amos had declared that God would send a famine on the land, "not a famine of bread, nor a thirst for water, but of hearing the words of the Lord" (Amos 8:11). The righteousness" referred to is the subject of the entire Sermon—the character and conduct of God. To long intensely for the reign of God is not to experience "the gnawing of starvation, or the fruitless hunger of the prodigal in the far country."[5] It is to have a hearty appetite at the Father's table. The satisfaction of that appetite is guaranteed.

"*Blessed are the merciful, for they shall obtain mercy*" (Mt. 5:7). Mercy is sympathetic lovingkindness, the nearest thing to love expressed in the Beatitudes. It includes pity, compassion, forgiveness, willingness to suffer, and active concern. It may be expressed by feelings, words, and deeds. It was not a popular subject in first-century Palestine. Many people believed that all suffering was the result of sin; consequently, they hesitated to be helpful because they did not want to obstruct justice. They believed that men were poor because they had broken God's law; women were barren because they lacked His favor; and the plight of the sick, the lame, the halt, and the blind was not accidental but consequential. These people were sowers reaping their wild oats. The Romans were contemptuous of mercy. They believed the practice of mercy showed weakness in the presence of

---

5Hugh Martin, *The Beatitudes* (New York: Harper & Row, Publishers, Inc., 1953), p. 49. Reprinted by permission of the Student Christian Movement Press, Ltd., London.

subject peoples. The Stoics tended to view mercy as a vulgar emotion. Priests and Levites were sometimes too preoccupied to express it. Some Pharisees, simmering in their self-righteousness, showed little mercy for those who did not practice their brand of religion. But Jesus pronounced "the merciful" blessed.

The merciful "shall obtain mercy." From whom? Will they obtain it from men? We tend to believe that sympathy breeds sympathy, concern calls forth concern, and kindly judgments evoke judgments in kind. However, there are exceptions, which merely prove the rule; the most merciful man in history was murdered. The benediction of this Beatitude comes not from merciful men, but from Merciful Heaven. The merciful obtain mercy from God. Mercy is part of His nature. It falls alike on the merciful and the unmerciful. Only the merciful, however, can receive it. God can forgive the unforgiven. He cannot forgive the unforgiving. The very heart of forgiveness is restored fellowship. "Unless forgiveness flows out of a man's heart, there is no room in it for the forgiveness of God."[6]

"Blessed are the pure in heart, for they shall see God" (Mt. 5:8). The "pure" are not the physically clean. Neither are they the ceremonially cleansed. Ceremonial cleansing was a vital necessity for the Jews. They believed that when they worshiped in the Temple they appeared before God. Many kinds of bodily defilement—such as contact with Gentiles and with the dead—disqualified them for this experience. So they meticulously undertook the purifications prescribed by the Law. Only thus could they be sure of seeing God as they worshiped. Jesus, however, showed little sympathy for this kind of purity; and he showed even less for the mere absence of evil. "In heart," as "in spirit" in the first Beatitude, defines the area of discussion. The pure are the sincerely single-minded, whose aim is to love God and to serve Him wholeheartedly. They allow nothing to divert them from this purpose.

Those who are focused on God shall "see God." Seeing Him is "not a matter of optics but of spiritual fellowship."[7] It is "to be near him, and to know him, and to rejoice in him, in one."[8] The privilege is a present one for the pure in heart even though at best they "see in a mirror dimly." But the day will come when they shall see God "face to face" (I Cor. 13:12).

"Blessed are the peacemakers, for they shall be called sons of God" (Mt. 5:9). It is the peacemakers who are praised, not the peacelovers. Their assets are frozen. Peace doesn't happen. It is made. Although the other Beatitudes imply activity, this one demands it. Peace without end was a part of the prophetic program (Is. 9:7). Under the heel of Rome, peace prospects were not popular in seething Galilee; but this did not deter Jesus from praising the peacemakers. They not only attempt to avoid war; they constantly try to overcome enmity with good will. They "seek peace,

[6]Martin, *The Beatitudes*, p. 59.

[7]Archibald M. Hunter, *A Pattern for Life* (Philadelphia: The Westminster Press, 1953), p. 35.

[8]Montefiore, *The Synoptic Gospels*, II, 38.

and pursue it" (Ps. 34:14). They "make up quarrels and reconcile enemies."[9] But they do not wait for conflicts to arise. They deal with causes
as well as cures. Their aim is peace, and their method is peaceful. They
"abstain from provocation, move with gentleness, and plead in love."[10]

The peacemakers shall be called "sons of God." In the Hebrew idiom
"sons of" may refer not only to shared descent but also to shared nature as
in "sons of wisdom." The seventh Beatitude follows naturally the sixth.
Those who are focused on the Father enjoy His fellowship; they also share
His nature. He is the God of peace. His son is the Prince of Peace. His
command is "On earth peace!" (Lk. 2:14).

*"Blessed are those who are persecuted for righteousness' sake, for theirs
is the kingdom of heaven"* (Mt. 5:10).[11] What a peculiar pronouncement!
How happy are "the persecuted"! A distinguished Jewish scholar thinks it
is unique. "To tell them [the disciples] that they ought positively to be glad
and rejoice in their misfortunes struck a new note—a note of great significance and power, a note which was to have great consequences of far-
reaching importance."[12] "For righteousness' sake" was added by Matthew
to relieve the ambiguity. Not every persecution promotes happiness; it
depends on the motive. If persecution is unworthily invited—say for self-
glory—it does not qualify. It has to be for righteousness' sake. For the Jew,
righteousness meant obedience to the Law.[13] This Beatitude teaches that
those who experience hardship, suffering, or persecution while performing
for God are the happy ones.

Those who are persecuted for righteousness' sake belong to "the kingdom of heaven." God is King. His kingdom is where His rule is obeyed.
Those who are persecuted because they follow the will of God are His
subjects. They know present happiness because they are approved by God;
and in the life to come their happiness will be made complete.

The eschatological character of the Beatitudes is acknowledged by many
New Testament scholars.[14] Six of the eight Beatitudes express their promises
in Greek with a future tense. Even where the present tense is used (Mt.
5:3, 10), the future reference is not excluded. There would have been no

---

[9]Manson, in *The Mission and Message of Jesus*, p. 443.

[10]George A. Buttrick, ed., "Exposition, The Gospel According to St. Matthew," in
The Interpreter's Bible (New York and Nashville: Abingdon Press, © 1951), VII, 286.

[11]Mt. 5:11–12 is an expanded duplicate of vs. 10. "Falsely," omitted by some Western
authorities and by Luke, is probably an addition. Lk. 6:22–23 differs from Matthew's
account without affecting the general sense. Luke lists four kinds of persecution—hatred,
isolation or excommunication, reproach, and slander.

[12]Montefiore, *The Synoptic Gospels*, II, 44.

[13]Matthew was disturbed by the discrepancy he observed between doctrine and deed
in his opponents and by their misunderstanding of the original intent of the Law, but
he never repudiated the Law itself. His understanding of the Law in principle did not
vary from that of Judaism. See Günther Bornkamm, in Bornkamm, Barth, and Held,
Tradition and Interpretation in Matthew, pp. 24–32.

[14]See Martin Dibelius, *The Sermon on the Mount*, tr. Carl H. Kraeling (New York:
Charles Scribner's Sons, 1940), pp. 22, 61; Hans Windisch, *The Meaning of the Sermon
on the Mount*, tr. S. MacLean Gilmour, © 1951 by W. L. Jenkins (Philadelphia: The
Westminster Press, 1951), pp. 113, 168.

verb at all in Aramaic. To state that the reward of the "poor" and the "persecuted" is the kingdom of heaven leaves unanswered when that reward is to be received. It all depends on when the kingdom comes. The form of the Beatitudes in Luke 6:21 (and the corresponding "woes" in 6:25) stresses more sharply the future character of the promised rewards: "Blessed are you that hunger *now*, for you *shall* be satisfied [at the eschaton]."[15] Nevertheless, as our interpretation has pointed out, it is not only in the future that the people of the Beatitudes will be happy. They are, in some measure at least, happy now. Perhaps a reason for their present happiness is the prospect of their future reward; but their present happiness also stems from the nature of their character and commitment.

Law and Kingdom (21)[16]

The Beatitudes describe life in the kingdom of God. Disciples are urged to live that life openly before the world (Mt. 5:13–16). Now life in the kingdom is compared with life as it was understood and lived under the Law. The words of Matthew 5:18–19 "stick in the throat."[17] It is unlikely that Jesus ever uttered these verses. They teach that the Law is true and permanent in its minutest detail—down to the last dotted *i* and crossed *t*. Gerhard Barth thinks that these verses (excepting 5:18c) were taken over by Matthew from a church conflict concerning the validity of the Law. When the evangelist adopted them and introduced them by his own words (5:17), he aligned himself with the conservatives in his church and against those who wished to abolish the Law.[18] Jesus had not come to abolish the Law but to actualize it in word and deed. If Barth's analysis is correct, then Matthew did not merely transmit the teachings about the Law (5:18–19), but he commented on them (5:17) and incorporated them into his total plan of salvation history (5:18c).[19]

Matthew 5:20 serves as a heading for 5:21–48: "Unless your righteousness exceeds that of the scribes and Pharisees," declared Jesus, "you will never enter the kingdom of heaven." "There was no finer standard of righteousness in the ancient world than the Pharisaic, with its emphasis on personal holiness and social responsibility."[20] Why then did Jesus exhort his hearers to exceed it? According to Matthew, he did so because the scribes and Pharisees sometimes misinterpreted the Old Testament commands. Jesus articulated their proper meaning and encouraged their actualization. When he did this, of course, he contradicted part of the Rabbinic tradition and some of the Old Testament commands themselves—

15Emphasis added.

16Mt. 5:17–20.

17Montefiore, *The Synoptic Gospels*, II, 46.

18Gerhard Barth, in Bornkamm, Barth, and Held, *Tradition and Interpretation in Matthew*, pp. 64–71.

19Gerhard Barth, in Bornkamm, Barth, and Held, *Tradition and Interpretation in Matthew*, pp. 70–71.

20Johnson, in *The Interpreter's Bible*, VII, 293–94.

as our study of the six contrasting statements which follow in Matthew will demonstrate.[21]

Six Contrasts

Matthew imposed the antithetical form on the three sayings he found in *Q* (those that begin at 5:31, 5:38, and 5:43), but the other three were presumably in antithetical form when he received them. A simpler set of sayings lies behind Matthew 5:21–48. Matthew has added his own comments and other sayings of Jesus. The kernel of the original sayings probably consisted of six terse contrasts.[22] We shall treat them by subject matter.

Murder (22).[23] The common people were generally illiterate. They could not read the Law themselves but came to know it by hearing it read in the synagogues. When Jesus said, "You shall not kill," they would at once recognize it as the sixth commandment delivered to Moses on Mt. Sinai (Ex. 20:13; Deut. 5:17). The commandment concerned murder, not killing. A murderer was liable to trial and judgment before a duly constituted authority. In Jesus' day that authority was probably the local Sanhedrin composed of twenty-three members. If convicted, the murderer was put to death (Ex. 21:12; Lev. 24:17).

The words, "but I say to you," remind us of the prophetic formula: "Thus says the Lord" (Amos 1:3,6,9). The rabbis cited authority. But Jesus dispensed with formulas and footnotes. He spoke on his own authority. The saying, "every one who is angry with his brother," contrasts act with anger. The Law restrained the end of sin (murder) but not its beginning (anger). Jesus was concerned about causes as well as consequences. He saw anger as incipient murder; and he taught that any one angry with his brother would be "liable to judgment." It is the divine judgment that anger brings. Human courts address themselves to the overt act. They would have to declare the angry man's case "without jurisdiction." Jesus was concerned with motives. They are known only to God.

Adultery (23).[24] The seventh commandment prohibited adultery (Ex. 20:14; Deut. 5:18). This commandment was supplemented by the tenth commandment which forbade a man to desire another's wife (Ex. 20:17). Taken together, they went far toward preserving the peace and purity of the Palestinian home. The Law limited adultery to sexual intercourse with the wife or the betrothed of a Jew. It did not include fornication (all sexual relations not between husband and wife or betrothed). Men had a higher legal status than women. They could divorce their wives, but their wives could not divorce them. (Mark 10:12, which suggests that a woman

[21]Montefiore, *The Synoptic Gospels*, II, 47.
[22]Vss. 21a and 22a; 27–28; 31–32; 33a and 34a; 38–39a; 43a and 44a.
[23]Mt. 5:21–26.
[24]Mt. 5:27–30.

could divorce her husband, was evidently written under Roman influence.)
An unfaithful married man did not commit adultery against his wife but
against his lover's husband. An unfaithful married woman, however, committed adultery against her husband.

Jesus declared that "every one who looks at a woman lustfully has already committed adultery with her in his heart." What is the lustful look?
It is persistent purposing. It is not the consummation (adultery) or the
consideration (glance, thought, desire) but the commitment (conscious
choice, will). According to Moses, a man on a deserted island could not
commit adultery. Jesus said he could, if his persistent purpose was to treat
a woman as a passing pleasure rather than as a person. No woman need
be present for a man to commit adultery with her in his heart.

Divorce (24).[25] There was no controversy about the principle of divorce
in first-century Palestine. The two leading rabbinical schools of Shammai
and Hillel approved it. Their difference concerned the proper grounds for
divorce. Shammai and his followers were the stricter. They allowed divorce
only in the case of some serious moral offense like adultery. Hillel and his
disciples permitted divorce for nearly any indecency, such as a wife letting
her husband's food burn.

It was no idle question which the Pharisees one day put to Jesus: "Is it
lawful for a man to divorce his wife?" (Mk. 10:2). Did the new teacher side
with Shammai or Hillel? Jesus countered with a question: "What did Moses
command you?" (Mk. 10:3). They replied that Moses permitted divorce
providing the husband should give his wife a written certificate. The certificate was intended to define and protect the woman's status. After it had
been delivered to her, the husband would have no further claim on her.
She would be a free agent. She could marry again. Jesus labeled Moses'
permission a concession to the hardheartedness of the people. He indicated
that marriage was intended to be permanent. "What therefore God has
joined together, let not man put asunder" (Mk. 10:9).

Matthew based his account on the one in Mark, but between the two
there is a striking difference. Matthew indicates that Jesus did find one
valid reason for divorce—"on the ground of unchastity" (5:32). Most
scholars attribute this exception to Matthew. (1) It was not Jesus' habit to
make exceptions. He used "strong, brief, unqualified assertions to drive
home unfamiliar or unwelcome truths."[26] (2) Mark, Luke, and Paul knew
nothing about the exception (I Cor. 7:10–16). (3) In Matthew 19:9, where
the exception also occurs, Matthew clearly inserted it in his source. (4)
Unchastity, viewed from the perspective of Jesus' total teachings, would not
in itself be an adequate ground for divorce. What if the guilty party repented and resolved to live by the higher righteousness henceforth? Jesus
would have men forgive seventy times seven. Matthew's exceptive phrase
reflects the serious disagreement which prevailed among early Christians.

25Mt. 5:31–32; 19:9; Mk. 10:11–12; Lk. 16:18. Compare Mk. 10:2–9.
26Alexander Balmain Bruce, "The Synoptic Gospels" in W. Robertson Nicoll, ed.,
The Expositor's Greek Testament (Grand Rapids: Wm. B. Eerdmans Publishing Company,
n.d.), I, 110.

Jesus had taught that marriage is permanent. His followers attempted to translate this principle into precepts. It was rough going. Love does not lend itself to legislation. Some found the teaching too rigorous. So, one by one, exceptions were made to it. The first was "on the ground of unchastity." As the centuries passed others were added.

Oath-taking (25).[27] "You shall not swear falsely" has no exact parallel in the Old Testament. It summarizes the thought of the third and ninth commandments (Ex. 20:7,16). The Law did not censure swearing, but its misuse, perjury. Oath-taking was not obligatory. But once an oath had been made, it had to be kept.[28] "Do not swear at all" is an emphatic statement. Oaths imply a double standard of truth-telling. If one is obligated to be honest while under an oath, it is suggested that some freedom from this necessity exists when he is not. Moreover, an oath binds one to what he regards as truth at the moment. Further revelation might prove him wrong. He would then be committed to falsehood by his oath.

Jesus' saying is supported by related teachings. All oaths are included in the ban, not just the old and solemn ones which mention the Lord's name. "Heaven . . . earth . . . Jerusalem" imply a reference to God. Heaven is His throne. Earth is His footstool. Jerusalem is His city. To swear by them is to swear by God. One should simply say yes or no. Anything else is superfluous. An honest man's word cannot be fortified. Such an attempt "comes from evil," the evil of untruthfulness.

Retaliation (26).[29] Retaliation was unlimited in the infancy of the human race. Might made right. But necessity eventually gave birth to a new law—"an eye for an eye." The Hebrews did not invent it. It was at least as old as the twentieth century B.C. It is found in the Code of Hammurabi, the great Babylonian ruler. Limited retaliation was a tremendous advance over unlimited retaliation. It put an end to interminable blood feuds by precisely defining the amount of revenge permitted. No longer could one repay injuries at compound interest.

The command, "Do not resist one who is evil," slays the past. It replaces unlimited retaliation and limited retaliation with no retaliation. Jesus' followers are told not to protect themselves, not to resist one who is evil. The saying is a hard one, and it has provoked endless debate—often at the expense of the spirit it was intended to sponsor. We should keep in mind several considerations. (1) Jesus spoke about personal wrong done to a personal enemy. He did not pontificate about the proper response to police power or the mass destruction of modern warfare. (2) His saying cannot be understood in isolation. By itself it may be nothing more than an endorsement of negative goodness. Taken in connection with the next contrasting statement in the series, which has to do with loving one's enemies, it becomes a necessary prelude to a positive principle. (3) The

---

27Mt. 5:33–37.

28"But shall perform to the Lord what you have sworn" (5:33b) has been added. It concerns vows, promises to God. Oaths are not performed to the Lord but to men. God is witness to an oath but not its recipient.

29Mt. 5:38–42; Lk. 6:29–30.

teaching involves risk. It is not a substitute for casualty insurance. It is to be followed not because it is prudential but because it is Paternal. It is the way our Heavenly Father acts. (4) The illustrations which follow the saying cannot be taken literally. They are borrowed by Matthew from other teachings of Jesus and are clothed in figurative language.[30] Just think what would happen if a person forced you to go with him one mile—and wanted you to go with him only that distance—and you insisted on going with him two! (5) Jesus did not discard justice with this saying; instead, he commanded responses which replace hostility with helpfulness.

Love's limit (27).[31] Leviticus enjoined Jews to "love their neighbor" (Lev. 19:18). Neighbor meant fellow-Israelite. The rabbis later stretched the term to cover converts and resident aliens. From the time of Ezra, however, the spirit of Judaism became increasingly hostile toward foreigners. Love became largely confined to national limits. The command, "and hate your enemy," has deeply offended Jewish commentators. Small wonder. It is unhistorical. It can be found nowhere in the Law. On the contrary, Exodus (23:4–5) and Proverbs counsel concern for one's enemy: "If your enemy is hungry, give him bread to eat" (Prov. 25:21). The offensive command played no part in Jesus' teaching. It clashes with the succinct phrasing of the other sayings in the series: "You shall not kill," "You shall not commit adultery," "An eye for an eye and a tooth for a tooth."

The command, "Love your enemies," climaxes the contrasts. Love is a word with many meanings. In the Greek language it had three. (1) *Eros*, ascending love, is love of an adorable object. It is sexual love. We derive the word erotic from it. (2) *Philia*, horizontal love, stands for friendship. It rests on reciprocity. Philadelphia (love of brother), philanthropy (love of man), and philosophy (love of wisdom) stem from it. (3) *Agape*, descending love, is unmerited love. He who has *agape* loves the unlovable. When Matthew reported Jesus' saying, he used *agape* rather than *eros* or *philia*. Jesus did not counsel marriage or friendship by his saying. (How could a moral person be a mate or a friend of a Herod or a Hitler?) He did not ask his followers to like their enemies. He commanded them to love them. Someone may protest, "But a man like Herod or Hitler doesn't deserve to be loved." Precisely! Jesus did not recommend reasonable reciprocity among friends. He did not laud love of the lovable. He called his disciples to love the unlovable—those who merit no consideration whatsoever. He asked them to do to others what God has always done. God's love is perfect. He *correctly understands* the Law, and He *acts* in accordance with it. He makes his sun rise on the evil and on the good and sends rain on the just and on the unjust. The disciples should be perfect as God is perfect.

The six contrasting statements in Matthew are directed against the Old Testament. Although the teachings about murder, adultery, and oath-taking provide only for an internalization and intensification of the pro-

---

[30]The fourth illustration is really two in one. Neither the beggar nor the borrower has anything to do with retaliation. Neither normally injures his victim. Luke's illustrations are briefer and strategically placed in the section on love of enemies.

[31]Mt. 5:43–48; Lk. 6:27–28,32–36.

hibitions, this is not the case with the teachings about divorce and re-taliation. If the saying about divorce does not annul the Old Testament injunction, it considerably restricts it; and the teaching on retaliation actually overthrows the Old Testament teaching on "an eye for an eye." The teaching about love expands and deepens certain Old Testament commands and grounds them in the character of God.

Current Practices Condemned

When Jesus contrasted life in the kingdom with life as it was under-stood and lived under the Law (Mt. 5:21–48), he dealt with man's relations with man. When he contrasts life in the kingdom with current practices, his attention shifts to man's relations with his Maker (Mt. 6:1–18). The theme is found in the first verse: "Beware of practicing your piety before men." Piety for publicity is contrasted with true worship by illustrations in three areas: (1) almsgiving (vss. 2–4), (2) praying (vss. 5–6), and (3) fasting (vss. 16–18). To the teaching on prayer, Matthew attached other sayings of Jesus. They concern (1) how not to pray (vss. 7–8), (2) how to pray (vss. 9–13), and (3) prayer for forgiveness (vss. 14–15).

Almsgiving (28).[32] Almsgiving was a primary duty in Judaism. It was a means of salvation as well as a form of worship. It delivered one from death and took away one's sin (Tobit 12:8–9). "Blessed is he," said the psalmist, "who considers the poor" (Ps. 41:1). "Sound no trumpet" is usually taken figuratively to mean "Don't advertise your altruism!" It may, however, refer to an actual Jewish custom. The "hypocrites" are actors who play a part, giving in order to gain attention. Their reward is in keeping with their motivation. "Do not let your left hand know what your right hand is doing" is a vivid Arab proverb. It means "Don't let even your best friend know about your charitable deeds." "Your Father who sees in secret" is a Greek translation which misses the point of the original Aramaic phrase meaning "your Father who sees what is secret." The un-publicized gift, unknown to man, is seen by God; He will reward the giver with His approval.

Praying (29).[33] Devout Jews had set times for prayer. In addition to attendance at regularly scheduled Temple and synagogue services, they prayed at 9 a.m., 12 noon, and 3 p.m. daily. From the time of Ezra, their prayer routine had become increasingly mechanical. The hypocrites were pleased when the hour of prayer overtook them in a well-frequented place. Indeed, they probably planned it that way. They loved to stand in the synagogues where men congregated for worship. They were fond of the street corners where men conversed and conducted business. Either place would insure a sizable audience. (The hypocrites wanted to be alone with

32Mt. 6:1–4.
33Mt. 6:5–8.

God—at Broadway and 42nd Street!) They craved the attention of men. They received only what they craved.

"But when you pray, go into your room." "Room" first meant a store-chamber, then any place of privacy. Any place will do if it permits the whole man to be focused on God. Jesus did not condemn public prayer. He and his disciples attended synagogue services and prayed in public with regularity. Jesus simply insisted that all prayer be directed to God instead of to the galleries. "Pray to your Father who is in secret" should probably read, "Pray in secret to your Father and your Father who sees what is secret will reward you." "Do not heap up empty phrases"—a warning against imitating Gentiles—is now added to the one about aping actors. Pagan prayer was characterized by repetition. The prophets of Baal, in their famous contest with Elijah on Mt. Carmel, shouted from morning until noon: "O Baal, answer us!" (I Kings 18:26) They believed that the babble might weary their god into granting their request. But "the kingdom of God does not consist in talk but in power" (I Cor. 4:20). "Your Father knows what you need before you ask him." Why then pray at all? We pray not to fill the void of God's ignorance, nor to make God change his mind. "Prayer is not overcoming God's reluctance; it is laying hold of his willingness."[34]

Fasting (31).[35] Fasting was an integral part of the religious calendar. In addition to the required public fasts many devout Jews practiced private, voluntary fasting. The Pharisees fasted twice a week (Lk. 18:12), and so did the disciples of the Baptist (Mt. 9:14). "And when you fast" (not "if you fast") suggests that Jesus' disciples also fasted voluntarily although not with regularity. Originally fasting had nothing directly to do with food and water. It came about naturally as a result of a deep feeling of grief. The death of a loved one (I Sam. 31:1–13) or the oppressive burden of sin caused sorrow. Sorrow affected the appetite or the appearance. In time, the external evidences of sorrow (going without food, water, and washings) were mistaken for the real thing. Fasting became more a matter of fashion than of faith.

"Do not look dismal, like the hypocrites." Put-on piety, like theatrical make-up, is for professional actors. It has no place in pure religion. The hypocrites "disfigure their faces that their fasting may be seen by men." The translation obscures an adroit play on words in the Greek. No literal rendering does it justice. "They make their faces *disappear* that they may *appear*." And how was this sleight of hand accomplished? They smeared ashes on their faces and looked sanctimonious or let their faces disappear behind an accumulated deposit of dirt. Either way the disappearance of their faces made them conspicuous. Voluntary fasting provided them with a perfect stage on which to parade their piety. "Anoint your head and wash

---

[34]Archbishop Trench, quoted in Horace T. Houf, *What Religion Is and Does*, rev. ed. (New York and London: Harper & Row, Publishers, Inc., 1945), p. 181. Used by permission.

[35]Mt. 6:16–18.

your face." Anointing was the symbol of joy, the opposite of sorrow. Washing was the symbol of cleanliness, the opposite of dirt. Ashes advertise
piety, and dirt attracts attention. Disciples are to hide their fasting, avoid
external signs. They are to let fasting be what it was originally—a spontaneous, inner feeling of sorrow. Then they will be approved by God, not
applauded by men.

Disciples' Prayer (30)[36]

The most famous prayer in history consists of only fifty-four words,
forty of which are monosyllables. It can be repeated in twenty seconds. It is
simple enough to have meaning for a five-year-old. Yet it is so profound
that it exhausts the intelligence of the perceptively mature. It is private
enough to be used in a closet. It is public enough to serve many faiths in
corporate worship. It is commonly called the Lord's Prayer. Actually it is a
prayer fashioned for disciples.

Matthew and Luke preserve different versions of the Disciples' Prayer.
The striking differences between them have provoked disturbing questions.
Why are there two versions? Which version is authentic? Which setting is
proper? Why wasn't the Prayer preserved as Jesus gave it? How original is
the Prayer? On these questions scholars are in sharp disagreement. We can
only suggest some probable answers here.[37]

Neither Matthew's nor Luke's version reproduces the Prayer precisely
as Jesus worded it. Once it may have consisted of only three petitions: (1)
for the coming of the kingdom, (2) for daily bread, and (3) for forgiveness
of sins. The artistry, poetic character, and sevenfold form of Matthew's
account suggest that it was designed for public worship. But its setting in
Matthew is clearly secondary. It interrupts the movement of the discourse
in which it is placed, as does the entire passage (vss. 7–15). The passage is
not directly related to hypocrisy, the subject of vss. 1–6 and 16–18. It mars
the symmetry of the three illustrations of almsgiving, praying, and fasting.
Matthew evidently placed the Disciples' Prayer here because it bears a
topical relationship to the sayings in 6:5–8. Luke, who placed the Prayer
much later in his account, indicated that the disciples were once present
with Jesus while he prayed. When he had finished, one of them said to
him, "Lord, teach us to pray, as John taught his disciples" (11:1). By way
of answer, Jesus gave them the Disciples' Prayer. It was customary for
prominent teachers to create special prayers for their followers. John had
evidently followed the practice. Jesus' disciples wanted a prayer which
would faithfully reflect their Master's teaching. The disciples were not
neophytes. They knew how to pray. What they wanted was a prayer custom-
made for the kingdom. What Jesus gave them was best preserved by Luke.
Matthew's amplified and polished account resulted from the worship needs
of the early Christian community.

[36]Mt. 6:9–13; Lk. 11:2–4.
[37]See Connick, *Build on the Rock*, pp. 103–107, for a summary discussion.

The Church of Pater Noster, located on the Mount of Olives, is built on the traditional site where Jesus taught his disciples "The Lord's Prayer." The church has the Prayer inscribed on its walls in thirty-six different languages.

Matthew's version consists of seven clauses: the address, plus two groups of three petitions each. From his viewpoint, it is the perfect pattern for prayer.

Our Father	(The address)
Thy name Thy kingdom Thy will	(Petitions centered on God)
Our bread Our debts Our temptations	(Petitions centered on human needs)

Our Father. Jesus did not invent the term Father. It was used in the Old Testament (usually to mean Father of the nation) and in other religions (usually in the biological or philosophical sense). In the Apocrypha, as later among the rabbis, men spoke of God as Father of the individual. What others vaguely sensed or occasionally stated, Jesus made central. "Our" is missing in Luke; in Matthew it suggests the community consciousness of the worshiping congregation. "Our Father" (like "our daily bread" and "our debts") reminds us also of the social nature of the prayer. When a first-century Jew addressed his earthly father, he used the Aramaic word *abba* (father). It was the familiar and intimate form of address. Propriety precluded its being used to describe another man's father, and piety prevented its being applied to God. Jesus abolished the latter distinction. He used *abba* when he addressed God and instructed his disciples to do the same. For him God was not a cold and impersonal power, process, or principle. He was a loving, concerned, responsive, redemptive person whom Jesus knew intimately. "Who art in heaven" indicates the postal address customarily assigned to God in a pre-scientific age. Men prayed standing, with hands outstretched and eyes lifted toward the sky. This crude conception gradually gave way to a growing sense of God's presence everywhere. Then, "in heaven" came to denote God's separateness, His majesty. The address, or invocation, prepares the way for the petitions which follow. The petitions are not merely requests made of God; they are affirmations of faith in Him. "He is holy!" "His kingdom is coming!" "His way will prevail!"

Hallowed be thy name. The ancients thought that the personality of a man was inextricably bound up with his name. When a man's name was spoken, the man himself was affected. It was not permissible to speak the sacred name of God. "The whole name was known only to the High Priest, who uttered it once a year when he stood before God in the Holy of Holies. God himself was in his name."[38] "Hallowed" echoes Isaiah: "Holy, holy, holy is the Lord of hosts" (Is. 6:3). To hallow God's name is to make it holy. Men do this when they accept his revelation and live in accordance with his will.

Thy kingdom come. The thought is eschatological. The kingdom is not here. If it were, it would be foolish and futile to pray for it to come. The kingdom is near ("at hand," Mt. 4:17). The seed which has been sown must be allowed to ripen. When the harvest comes, there will be a separation of the weeds from the wheat (Mt. 13:30) and a sorting of the fish (Mt. 13:48). God has fixed the time of the separating and the sorting. That moment, while near, has not yet arrived. When it does come, the first petition—which probably has a present as well as future reference in the Prayer —will be finally fulfilled. God's name will be hallowed.

Thy will be done, on earth as it is in heaven. This petition is absent from Luke. Its genuineness has been questioned. It simply repeats the second petition. Where God's will is done, His sovereignty is acknowledged and active. The third petition both parallels and expounds the second. The first half of the Disciples' Prayer is now complete. The three petitions which center on God are followed by three which are centered on man's needs.

[38]E. F. Scott, *The Lord's Prayer* (New York: Charles Scribner's Sons, 1952), p. 87.

Give us this day our daily bread. The bread mentioned here should not be thought of in the Fourth-Gospel sense as a figure for Jesus. Neither should it be taken as a hidden reference to sacramental bread which is given for spiritual nourishment. The Greek word means ordinary bread, the basic element in a Palestinian's diet. It stands as a symbol for all necessary food and, by implication, for everything essential to physical welfare. The petition is for bread, however, not for dessert. "Daily" is ambiguous. Matthew added "this day" and Luke added "each day" in an effort to clarify its meaning. When the petition is prayed in the morning, it means bread for the day at hand. When used at night, it asks for bread for the morrow. The disciples are to ask God from day to day for sufficient provision to perform their tasks. They are not to stockpile bread for the future. They are to live their lives in daily dependence on God.

> Back of the loaf is the snowy flour,
>   And back of the flour the mill,
> And back of the mill is the wheat and the shower,
>   And the sun and the Father's will.[39]

Forgive us our debts. The fifth petition is closely related to the fourth. "Give" is followed by "forgive." Both express human hungers. Bread is basic. It is just as basic to have the barrier of sin between oneself and God removed. Both sin and hunger are daily occurrences. We need to ask for forgiveness day by day, just as we need to ask for daily bread. Luke's version of the petition has "sins" for Matthew's "debts." Debt was a common Jewish metaphor for sin. God was viewed as the great Creditor. To Him all of man's service is due. His forgiveness is the gracious remission of debt. The sinner is obligated to make amends. He is not free until he has fulfilled this obligation—paid his debt. But "debts" would have made little sense to Luke's Gentile readers. Consequently, he substituted for the original the more intelligible term "sins." Both words stand for anything that mars man's relationship with his Maker: omissions, dispositions, and deeds which are contrary to His will.

As we also have forgiven our debtors.[40] This part of the petition is un-Jewish, and some Jewish scholars have protested it. Is God's forgiveness conditional? Does He forgive us only to the extent that we have forgiven others? Certainly not! His forgiveness is not limited *to* our forgiving, it is limited *by* it. "An unforgiving spirit in us shuts the door in God's face, even though his compassions still surround the house. He is ready to forgive, but we are not ready to be forgiven."[41] Man's recalcitrance should not be mistaken for God's reluctance.

39Reprinted from *Thoughts for Everyday Living* by Maltbie D. Babcock (New York: Charles Scribner's Sons, 1901).

40Matthew uses the present perfect tense (action completed before the present), "As we also *have* forgiven" (6:12b). Luke employs the present tense, "for we ourselves *forgive*" (11:4b). Emphasis added.

41Buttrick, in *The Interpreter's Bible*, VII, 314.

For the love of God is broader
Than the measure of man's mind.

Jesus' intended meaning is preserved by Luke. "Forgive us . . . for we ourselves forgive" (11:4). The sentence is both an appeal for God's generosity and an affirmation that the one praying is generous toward others. It serves a double purpose. In the very act of praying for his own forgiveness, the petitioner is prompted to forgive others.

We do pray for mercy,
And that same prayer doth teach us all to render
The deeds of mercy.[42]

Lead us not into temptation, but deliver us from evil. The sixth and final petition is preventive. It seeks protection from future failures, while the fifth sought pardon for past ones. Luke has nothing corresponding to "but deliver us from evil." This is not a separate petition as some have held.[43] It stands in poetic parallelism to the first half of the sentence, repeating its thought in different words. Its sole purpose is to round out the form of the Prayer.

The petition poses a perplexing problem. What does it mean to be tempted? The Greek word translated "temptation" may mean (1) enticement to sin or (2) trial of a man's fidelity. But God does not induce men to sin. "Let no one say when he is tempted, 'I am tempted by God', for God . . . tempts no one; but each person is tempted when he is lured and enticed by his own desire" (James 1:13–14). Clearly it is the second meaning of temptation which Jesus had in mind. God does put men on trial. He tested Abraham when He asked the Patriarch to sacrifice his only son, Isaac (Gen. 22:1–13). He tested Job when He permitted Satan to afflict Job until he despaired of his life (Job 1:1–3:26). He even allowed Jesus his trials on the Mountain (Mt. 4:1–11) and in the Garden (Mt. 26:36–46). God tests, but He does not entice. His objective is not man's seduction but his salvation.

Every testing involves a calculated risk. A man might succumb to sin. If this were not so, he could not develop moral fiber. "Lead us not into temptation" voices a natural human shrinking from difficult encounters. It also doubles as a cry for help when taxing tests do come—as come they must. Perhaps the petition is less a principle of logic than a plea of the soul, although there is much logic in it. Man cannot play his own providence.[44] When tests come, his strength is insufficient. Logic demands that he declare his dependence. God will not let him be tempted beyond his strength "but with the temptation will also provide the way of escape" (1 Cor. 10:13). The petition may be helpfully paraphrased: "Spare us trials that will severely test our faith, but if we must be tested, give us strength to live through the trials victoriously."

[42]Shakespeare, *The Merchant of Venice*, Act IV, Scene I, lines 195–97.
[43]Scott, *The Lord's Prayer*, p. 107.
[44]Buttrick, in *The Interpreter's Bible*, VII, 315.

In its familiar form the Disciples' Prayer ends with a doxology: "For thine is the kingdom and the power and the glory, forever. Amen." Why is this not found in the Revised Standard Version? Because it is missing in the three most important manuscripts and also in Luke's version. It was apparently unknown to early Church Fathers (Tertullian, Cyprian, Origen). Where it does appear, the text varies. It was undoubtedly not a part of the original Prayer. When the Prayer came to be used liturgically in the various churches, a doxology was added. It was a happy addition. It served to end the Prayer as it had begun—with thought about God's sovereignty.[45]

Four Persistent Problems

The characteristics and compensations of kingdom members have been set forth (Mt. 5:3–16). Life in the kingdom has been contrasted with life as it was understood and lived under the Law (Mt. 5:17–48). Current religious practices have been condemned (Mt. 6:1–18). Now the Sermon turns the spotlight on four persistent human problems: possessions, anxiety, judgment, and prayer (Mt. 6:19–7:12).

Possessions (32).[46] Most people in first-century Palestine had few possessions; but their poverty did not prevent them from dreaming. They dreamed of owning expensive rugs and garments, of eating at elegant banquets, and of enjoying the air-conditioned comfort of a fig tree's shade. They dreamed and they schemed to catch up with the Herods. The comfort cult was so communicable that Jesus felt it necessary to warn his followers about the folly of piling up the perishable.

"Do not lay up . . . treasures on earth." People hid their wealth in their houses or fields. Since some of the treasures were fabrics (garments, hangings, rugs), they were under a triple sentence of perishability. (1) Moths and worms[47] could devour them with impunity. (2) Thieves could break in through the mud walls of the house and make off with them. (3) Even if possessions should survive the first two hazards, death would soon separate them from their owners anyway.

"Lay up . . . treasures in heaven." Beatitude treasures are mothproof. No thief on earth can steal them. Death puts a period to the perishable, but it becomes a comma to heavenly treasures. Earthly treasures depreciate. Heavenly treasures appreciate. "For where your treasure is, there will your heart be also." A man's interests are where his investments are. If his goal is to make a million, he will devote his time, talent, and thought to that end. He may, if he is industrious and lucky, succeed when half of his mature years have been spent. Then he will spend his remaining years

[45]At the close of the Prayer, Matthew misplaced a teaching of Jesus on forgiveness (6:14–15). It is really related to the fifth petition.

[46]Mt. 6:19–21; Lk. 12:33–34.

[47]The alternate Revised Standard Version reading. The Greek word means "eating." It is a general term which covers a whole class of agents that attack vegetables.

protecting his investment. The possessor becomes the possessed. What started out as a search for security ends in insecurity. The world's goods do not remove anxiety. Instead, they are a source of anxiety, for they are perishable and cry out to be preserved.

Anxiety (35).[48] Jesus encouraged forethought: "For which of you, desiring to build a tower, does not first sit down and count the cost, whether he has enough to complete it?" (Lk. 14:28). What he deplored was anxious forethought. Anxiety is fear-laden, born of distrust. It is not to be confused with eagerness which is fearless. "About your life" refers to natural life, not the life of the spirit or soul. It is the kind of life preserved by food and drink and kept comfortable by clothing.

In two compelling illustrations dealing with wild birds and wild flowers, Jesus prescribes trust in God as the antidote for anxiety. "The birds" do not exhaust themselves providing for their future needs. They are carefree and happy. Every now and then they pause in their work and pour out their heart in song. God gives them life, and he provides for them. If these little creatures are cared for, why should God's children be careworn? Are they not of more value than the birds? Anxiety cannot "add one cubit to their span of life." A cubit is about eighteen inches, the length of a forearm. To add inches to the length of one's life would seem to be a mixed metaphor. So some commentators take the Greek word translated "span" to mean "stature." This is the meaning in Luke 19:3. The question then becomes, "Which of you by being anxious can increase his height?" More likely the Greek should be translated "span." In papyrus usage it commonly means "age." Linear measurements of age also appear in the Psalms: "Behold, thou hast made my days a few handbreadths" (Ps. 39:5). So the question becomes, "Which of you by being anxious can prolong his life?" Man may desire a long life, but worry won't bring it. Anxiety is a friend of morticians.

"The lilies" are wild flowers, probably the purple anemone. On state occasions, Solomon dressed in gorgeous attire. Yet even his royal purple robes were no match for the delicate beauty of the lilies. Wild "grass" replaces wild flowers as the figure of speech. Today the grass is green. Tomorrow it is fit only for fuel. It is thrown into a round, earthenware pot and ignited. Dough is spread on the sides of the pot, and the burning grass is reduced to ashes. If God lavishes his love on the short-lived plant, how much more will He care for His children! His children have no need to worship the Gentile trinity: food, drink, and clothing. Their Father knows their need. If they "seek first his kingdom," their needs will be met. Anxiety is unnerving, unnecessary, and unprofitable. More to the point, it is unbecoming. It is tantamount to a vote of no confidence in God. It shouts that the God who creates life will not provide for its continuance, and therefore men must be anxious about their life. Trust is "for the birds."

48Mt. 6:25–34; Lk. 12:22–31. This is the longest single teaching (except those in parable or story form) ascribed to Jesus in the Synoptics. Its length militates against original oral composition and transmission. Mt. 6:27, 33, and 34 appear to break the flow of thought.

Well, look at the birds! Consider the lilies! God cares for them. Let go—
and let God! Trust is the perfect antidote for anxiety.

Judgment (36).[49] Jesus knew that "appraisals are a stock in trade of the
mind."[50] Without them, morals would become merely mores. The bedrock of the ethical life is the power to discriminate. When he said, "Judge
not, that you be not judged," Jesus did not prohibit judgments. His teaching echoes the Mishnah: "Do not judge your fellow until you are in his
position" (Aboth 2:5). "When you judge any man weight the scales in his
favor" (Aboth 1:6). What Jesus prohibited by his command was unloving
judgments. It is a fundamental principle of the moral order that like
begets like: lies beget lies; philandering begets philandering; censoriousness begets censoriousness. Likewise, honesty begets honesty; fidelity begets
fidelity; love begets love. Jesus said, "Judge not [unlovingly] that you be
not [unlovingly] judged" (Mt. 7:1). Is it only human judgment that he has
in mind? The use of the passive ("that you be not judged"), a standard
Jewish circumlocution to avoid mentioning the name of God, suggests that
reference to Final Judgment is also intended.

The point is hammered home in the parable of the Speck and the Log.
The picture is purposely grotesque. The Eastern imagination was prone to
use hyperbole. The "speck" stands for any small, dry object—chaff, chip of
wood, tiny twig. It can be so microscopic as to avoid detection by another
and yet cause excruciating pain. Any decent chap would willingly render
first-aid to a fellow in a speck of trouble. The "log" is a beam or joist used
in building. That it could be in one's eye is a natural impossibility. In the
parable, it serves as a monstrous symbol of a common fault. The compul-
sion to correct others, coupled with complacency concerning one's own
shortcomings, is hypocrisy. Reformation should be a home-grown product.
Certain it is that Mr. Log-Eye is in no position to help Mr. Speck-Eye
until he has had a log-rolling session with himself.

Prayer (38).[51] This passage is unrelated to its context in Matthew. In
Luke it fittingly follows the Disciples' Prayer and the Friend at Midnight.
"Ask . . . seek . . . knock." Notice the progression. It is easy to ask—and
necessary. Asking reveals a need and a feeling of dependence. But "we
must not be panhandlers, merely asking."[52] We must also seek—seek as for
a lost object. It is no accident that great saints were called seekers. We
must knock—knock as at a locked door. What an appropriate figure to
follow the Friend at Midnight (Lk. 11:5-8)! The triple exhortation is followed by the triple promise: "Receives . . . finds . . . it will be opened."
The emphasis is on the exhortation. God does not grant every wish. Jesus
himself prayed, "My Father, if it be possible, let this cup pass from me"
(Mt. 26:39). The wish was denied. The teaching is purposely hyperbolic.
It stresses the need for persistence in prayer. God knows what is good for

---

[49]Mt. 7:1-5; Lk. 6:37-38,41-42.
[50]Buttrick, in *The Interpreter's Bible*, VII, 324.
[51]Mt. 7:7-11; Lk. 11:9-13.
[52]Buttrick, in *The Interpreter's Bible*, VII, 328.

men. They should trust His wisdom, power, and love. If they ask, seek, and knock, He will answer their requests to their benefit—both now and in the age to come.

"Bread . . . stone"; "fish . . . serpent." Notice the similarity of shape in each pair of contrasts. No earthly father worthy of the name would give his son a stone when he asked for bread or a serpent when he asked for fish. "You who are evil" is not a certification of man's depravity. It is simply a recognition that when a man is compared to God, his sinfulness is self-evident. If persistent petition can move a sleeping Palestinian peasant to give bread (Lk. 11:5–8), how much more will it avail with a loving heavenly Father! Disciples can knock at the door of His kingdom with perfect confidence.

Golden Rule (39)[53]

The Sermon reaches its summit at this point. The teaching is found in a variety of forms and in widely divergent places—Jewish and Gentile, prior to Jesus and after him. "What thou hatest, do to no man" (Tobit 4:15). When Hillel was asked to summarize the Law, he quoted Tobit 4:15 and added, "this is the whole law and the rest is commentary." Hindu, Confucian, and Zoroastrian writings also contain the teaching expressed negatively. Aristotle put the thought positively but restricted its application to the circle of one's friends. Lao-Tze, the founder of Taoism, was the only one other than Jesus to state the idea both positively and universally. Although the positive form of the teaching may be preferable to the negative, the uniqueness of Jesus' saying lies not in its content but in its context. Jesus based his thought on the character and conduct of God Himself: "Love your enemies and pray for those who persecute you, so that you may be sons of your Father who is in heaven; for he makes his sun rise on the evil and on the good, and sends rain on the just and on the unjust" (Mt. 5:44–45). Apart from this context the saying becomes little more than a piece of prudential secular wisdom, which it probably was originally.

Epilogue

The Sermon proper is over. Life in the kingdom has been described (Mt. 5:3–16), contrasted both with life understood and lived under the Law and with current practices (Mt. 5:17–6:18), and applied to several disturbing human problems (Mt. 6:19–7:12). Now, in a kind of epilogue (Mt. 7:13–27), listeners are challenged to acknowledge the kingdom's coming and to redirect their lives in accordance with the divine pattern.

Two Ways (40).[54] Matthew combines the familiar Jewish figure of the two ways with that of the narrow and wide gates. Luke's version follows a question put to Jesus by someone who wanted him to calculate the com-

[53]Mt. 7:12; Lk. 6:31.
[54]Mt. 7:13–14; Lk. 13:23–24.

position of heaven. " 'Lord, will those who are saved be few?' And he said to them, 'Strive to enter by the narrow door; for many, I tell you, will seek to enter and will not be able' " (13:23–24). Here the metaphor is a door instead of a gate. There is only one door and the question is which side of it a person is on. "The reply of Jesus begins by asserting that the way of salvation is a door which God opens and man enters. The entry cannot be made without God. The gate of heaven opens only from the inside. But also man has to make his own way in, once the door is opened. And this is not easy. The entrance is narrow, and it is a case of struggling through rather than strolling in."[55]

Perhaps Jesus' original point was: "How hard it is to enter the kingdom of God!" (Mk. 10:24). Matthew took the saying as it came to him, structured it antithetically,[56] and combined it with the well-known teaching that there are two ways.[57] One leads to life and the other to death. Life, of course, is life in the kingdom.

Tree and Fruit (41).[58] This passage is introduced in Matthew without a connecting particle and without any topical relationship to the preceding material. It probably formed no part of the original sermon. The warning about "false prophets" (vs. 15) could hardly refer to the Pharisees and Sadducees. They were men of tradition and laid no claim to prophecy. The false prophets were men of Matthew's own day, men in the church who confessed Jesus as Lord and prohesied and performed mighty works in his name (7:22). They failed to do God's will (and hence bore bad fruit, 7:17) because they were antinomians (ἀνομιαν)—doers of lawlessness (7:23). Matthew was so firmly opposed to them that he surrounded the Sermon on the Mount with condemnations of their thought and practice (5:17–18; 7:15–16) and expounded the entire Sermon in relation to the Law. The antinomians appeared to be sheep. This made it easy for them to enter the sheepfold (the church). Once inside, they were in a perfect position to undermine the faith of the flock.

As it stands, Matthew 7:16–20 is poorly arranged. Probably the original parable of the Tree and Fruit was as follows:

16b Are grapes gathered from thorns, or figs from thistles?
18 A sound tree cannot bear evil fruit,
    nor can a bad tree bear good fruit.[59]

"Lord, Lord" (42).[60] A good disciple not only says "Lord, Lord"; he does the will of the Father. Luke's saying is nearer the original: "Why do you call me 'Lord, Lord,' and not do what I tell you?" (6:46). The thought now shifts to the future. "On that day" refers to the Day of Judgment. Those who have come before the Court of Last Resort have prophesied,

---

[55]Manson, in *The Mission and Message of Jesus*, p. 417.
[56]See Manson, in *The Mission and Message of Jesus*, p. 467.
[57]Deut. 11:26; Jer. 21:8; Ps. 1:6; Didache 1:1; Barnabas 18:1.
[58]Mt. 7:15–20; Lk. 6:43–45.
[59]Verse 17 is a positive proposition from another source. Verse 19 is a teaching imported from the Baptist (Mt. 3:10; Lk. 3:9). Verse 20 is a generalized conclusion.
[60]Mt. 7:21–23; Lk. 6:46; 13:26–27.

cast out demons, and performed miracles in Jesus' name. "I never knew you," a mild rebuke in rabbinical thought, falls on the ears of the do-gooders with a painful thud. They expect praise, not blame. Their fault, according to Matthew, is a double one: they have neither properly under-stood nor practiced the Law. Their disposition has been to deceive. They have claimed that they were acting in Jesus' behalf and with his authority, but they have possessed neither his insight into the Law nor his ability to actualize it. So they are classified not with the true but with the false.

Two Foundations (43).[61] The series of exhortations to do God's will, started in Matthew 7:13, is climaxed by this parable. "Then" (Mt. 7:24) refers not only to the teaching immediately preceding it (Mt. 7:21–23) but to the entire collection of teachings. As we have seen,[62] the keynote is action. They are wise who build their lives on the firm foundation of hear-ing and doing the words of Jesus as found in the Sermon. They will be ready when the kingdom comes.

Sermon and Eschatology

A sharp cleavage exists among scholars concerning the extent of escha-tology in the Sermon. Dibelius thinks that it pervades the whole. "True, an explicit reference to the eschatological expectation is missing in some groups of sayings; in the prohibition of anger and invective, of oaths and of divorce. . . . Some critics might therefore question the eschatological back-ground of these sayings in general, but it seems to me that such a criticism would be wrong for two reasons. (1) It is legitimate to suppose that the whole message of our Lord has an eschatological background. . . . (2) The Sermon on the Mount in its introduction bears witness to its eschatological orientation."[63] Windisch, on the other hand, holds that Matthew has heightened the eschatological elements in the Sermon. "One can go so far as to lay down the rule: pericopes and logia in which the nearness of the judgment and the eschatological rule of God are not expressly articulated do not need to be directly referred by exegesis to the eschatological situ-ation."[64] A more moderate position is taken by Harvey K. McArthur. He concludes that "about 40 per cent of the Sermon is directly dominated by eschatology, another 40 per cent is without any explicit eschatological reference, and the remaining 20 per cent is debatable."[65] In none of the numerous references to the eschaton does he find emphasis on its immi-nence. The note of imminence, if such exists, must be supplied from the general tenor of Jesus' proclamation. Whether one agrees with Dibelius,

[61]Mt. 7:24–27; Lk. 6:47–49.

[62]See p. 233.

[63]Martin Dibelius, *The Sermon on the Mount* (New York: Charles Scribner's Sons, 1940), pp. 60–61. See also p. 65.

[64]Hans Windisch, *The Meaning of the Sermon on the Mount*, tr. S. M. Gilmour (Philadelphia: The Westminster Press, 1951), pp. 29–30.

[65]Harvey K. McArthur, *Understanding the Sermon on the Mount* (New York: Harper & Row, Publishers, Inc., 1960), p. 91. Used by permission of the author.

Windisch, or McArthur, he can hardly escape the conclusion that eschatology played a significant—if not decisive—role in the Sermon on the Mount.

Eschatology and Ethics

Was the Sermon's ethic conditioned by Jesus' eschatology? Did he proclaim here (and elsewhere) a kind of crash program to be carried out in the short interim before the eschaton? Would his ethical demands have been different had he expected the world to continue for two millenniums? If so, are his modern followers freed from the stringent imperatives of the Sermon?

Nearly every conceivable answer has been given to these and related questions. McArthur presents twelve "versions and evasions" of the Sermon.[66] The twelve are not mutually exclusive. An advocate of one interpretation may endorse other approaches in a different context.

The absolutist view is taken by those who hold that the commands of the Sermon are to be taken literally and applied absolutely and universally. Even here, however, there is a recognition that some passages (like Mt. 5:29–30) contain a symbolic element. This was the position of Augustine, St. Francis, the Anabaptists, and Tolstoi.

The modification view is held by those who qualify the Sermon by inserting phrases or interpretations which lack historical or theological support. Matthew added "except on the ground of unchastity" (5:32; compare 19:9) to Mk. 10:11. Luther interpreted Mt. 5:42 to mean that one should give to him who begs if he is a genuine seeker and not a vagrant or tramp.[67]

The hyperbole view is based on the conviction that Jesus used exaggeration to dramatize his demands. While the form of the demands is absolute, their application must be relative. If they were taken literally, social life would be impossible.

The general-principles view points out that while many of Jesus' commands refer to specific situations, their intent was to teach general truths through the individual illustrations. Mt. 5:39b, for example, does not cover blows received on the right cheek only; all forms of personal injury are included. So held Augustine, Chrysostom, and others.

The attitudes-not-acts view declares that Jesus' real concern was not with deeds but with dispositions (attitudes, motivations). The Law condemned adultery (the act). Jesus condemned the lustful look (the persistent purpose). Augustine often stressed Jesus' emphasis on attitudes. Wilhelm Herrmann made this the basis of his interpretation of the entire Sermon.[68]

---

[66] McArthur, *Understanding the Sermon on the Mount*, pp. 105–27, to which our discussion is indebted.

[67] See Jaroslav Pelikan, ed. and tr., *Luther's Works* (St. Louis: Concordia Publishing House, 1956), XXI, 115–18.

[68] See Wilhelm Herrmann, "The Moral Teachings of Jesus" in Adolf Harnack and Wilhelm Herrmann, *The Social Gospel*, tr. G. M. Craik (New York: G. P. Putnam's Sons, 1907).

The double-standard view is embraced by the Roman Catholic tradition. A distinction is made between the precepts and the counsels of the Gospel. Obedience to the precepts is necessary for salvation. Obedience to the counsels is essential for perfection. Such obedience is also regarded as a surer way of gaining salvation. Only those who separate themselves from the common life of the laity by taking the vows of poverty, chastity, and obedience can achieve perfection. Thus the radical nature of the Sermon's ethic is reserved for the few.

The two-realm view, a double standard of a different order, appears in Protestantism. Luther did not divide the church into two groups—one obligated to obey the precepts and the other the precepts and the counsels. He divided humanity into two spheres—the spiritual and the secular. The Christian lives in both. In the spiritual sphere, he must obey all the commands of the Sermon. But in the secular sphere, this is not so. "According to his body and property, he is related by subjection and obligation to the emperor, inasmuch as he occupies some office or station in life or has a house and home, a wife and children; for all these are things that pertain to the emperor. Here he must necessarily do what he is told and what this outward life requires. If he has a house or a wife and children or servants and refuses to support them or, if need be, to protect them, he does wrong."[69]

The analogy-of-Scripture view interprets the demands of the Sermon in relation to other teachings in the New and Old Testaments. Augustine, for example, insisted that Mt. 5:22c ("Whoever says, 'You fool!' shall be liable to the hell of fire") should be interpreted so as not to conflict with Gal. 3:1 ("O foolish Galatians!"). This approach, also taken by Luther and Calvin, assumes a single ethical level throughout the Bible. It also frequently results in a marked modification of the Sermon's radical nature.

The interim-ethic view insists that Jesus expected the imminent end of history. This expectation accounted for the radical nature of his ethic. His commands constituted a program to be carried out in the short interim still allowed human history. They were not designed for a future ideal human society or for the divine society itself. Consequently, attempts to build a civilization based on them are irrelevant. The interim-ethic emphasis, first made by Johannes Weiss, was popularized by Albert Schweitzer.[70]

The modern dispensationalist view divides Scripture into a series of radically different periods of time. In each period, the obedience of men is tested with respect to some specific revelation of God's will. According to *The Scofield Reference Bible*[71] there are seven dispensations: (1) Innocency, which ended with man's expulsion from the Garden of Eden, Gen. 3:24, (2) Conscience, Gen. 3:23, (3) Human Government, Gen. 8:20, (4) Promise, Gen. 12:1, (5) Law, Ex. 19:8, (6) Grace, Jn. 1:17, and (7) Kingdom,

---

[69]Pelikan, *Luther's Works*, XXI, 109.

[70]Albert Schweitzer, *The Mystery of the Kingdom of God*, tr. Walter Lowrie (London: A. & C. Black, 1925).

[71]See p. 5, note 5 of *The Scofield Reference Bible*. Oxford University Press, New York, now publishes this Bible. It was edited by the Rev. C. I. Scofield and first appeared in 1909. It has been widely used throughout American fundamentalism.

Eph. 1:10. The ethical demands of the Sermon, also found elsewhere in Jesus' teaching, were intended for the kingdom dispensation. They have only secondary application for contemporary Christians, since they live in the dispensation of grace. Dispensationalists take the absolutist view of the Sermon, but they relegate the Sermon's radical requirements to the final dispensation.

The repentance view holds that the primary purpose of the Sermon is to awaken in men an awareness of their sinfulness so that they will repent. The Lutheran tradition, along with others, has stressed this function. (If repentance is regarded as a substitute for obedience, then the demands of the Sermon are seriously weakened. If repentance is regarded as a preliminary step toward obedience, the problem of how the Sermon can be fulfilled in daily life remains.)

The unconditioned-divine-will view asserts that the Sermon sets forth the absolute will of God. It declares what God demands of men at all times. But its complete fulfillment cannot come until the kingdom comes. In the meantime, men must make their own adjustments in the light of earthly limitations. Although the eschatological expectation created the occasion for the proclamation of God's will—making men free to understand what it is—it did not create an interim ethic. The ethic of the Sermon is eternal. The most persuasive proponent of this position has been Martin Dibelius.[72]

We now return to one of the concerns which prompted this survey of the interpretations of the Sermon. Did Jesus proclaim a crash program to be carried out in the short interim before the eschaton? A careful study of the Sermon indicates that he did not. The imminence of the end is not stressed in the Sermon or in the ethical demands outside of it. Jesus surely believed that the time was short. The nearness of the end undoubtedly accentuated the urgency of the crisis. But the imminence of the eschaton did not account for the stringency of his demands. It provided the occasion for them. When, for example, he rejected the Mosaic concessions concerning divorce, he did not do so because the end was near. He defended his teaching on the ground that "from the beginning of creation" God had intended marriage to be permanent (Mk. 10:6).

The twelve different approaches to the Sermon's ethic cannot be conveniently classified as either true or false. Most of them contain some truth. None of them is altogether adequate in itself. The Sermon is a composite. Different parts of it demand different methods of interpretation. Indeed, a single passage may require two or more approaches for its explanation.[73] It is beyond the scope of our study to evaluate in detail each of the twelve views outlined above. This has been ably done elsewhere.[74] Here we shall simply highlight those which have made the greatest contribution. The

---

[72]Dibelius, *The Sermon on the Mount*.

[73]"If any one forces you to go one mile, go with him two miles" (Mt. 5:41) may require for its interpretation an appeal both to the hyperbole and general-principles views.

[74]McArthur, *Understanding the Sermon on the Mount*, pp. 128–48, on which our evaluation is based.

absolutist is right in stressing that the commands of the Sermon are to be taken seriously. When this is done, we are led to *repentance,* although this is probably not the Sermon's primary purpose. Repentance is not an end in itself. It prompts us to ask how we should live. The Sermon gives us direction but not directions. If we are to appropriate its meaning, we shall need to recognize that it contains *hyperboles,* that its specific injunctions are less important than the *general principles* which they illustrate, that the stress is on *attitudes* as well as *acts,* and that the Sermon presents the *unconditioned divine will.* We must adjust in the human situation as best we can—never mistaking our conditioned response for God's unconditioned will.

chapter sixteen

The Miracles

The Gospels do not contain the word "miracle." Miracle is a modern term. It describes a happening which is contrary to the known laws of nature. But the evangelists wrote in a prescientific age. They did not think of occurrences as being either coherent with nature's laws or contrary to them. How could they? They knew nothing about most of the laws. The Gospels speak of "powers" (*dunameis*), "wonders" (*terata*), "mighty works" (*dunata erga*), and "signs" (*sēmeia*). A happening sometimes seemed strange. People watched it and wondered. They interpreted it as a special manifestation of God's activity. ("Power" was another name for God, as Mark 14:62 indicates.) Strange happenings testified not only to God's presence but also to his purpose. Thus understood, miracle is altogether Biblical.

Number

Nearly one-third of Mark is devoted to miracles. Matthew and Luke report most of Mark's miracles and add a few others. In all, the Gospels list about thirty-five. Some of them are described in considerable detail (Mt. 8:28–34; 14:13–21). Others are given the briefest treatment (Mt. 8:14–15; 9:32–33). A great number of miracles are not described at all. They are merely mentioned in a general way. Jesus healed "every disease and every infirmity among the people" (Mt. 4:23). At Peter's house, "he cast out the spirits with a word, and healed all who were sick" (Mt. 8:16). He healed "the lame, the maimed, the blind, the dumb, and many others" (Mt. 15:30).

From the wealth of references to miracles in the Gospels, three things are evident. (1) The evangelists practiced a remarkable restraint in their reports of Jesus' mighty works. They could easily have multiplied the miracles by developing such pregnant statements as he "healed all who were sick" (Mt. 8:16). Striking deeds impress people and are readily remembered. The evangelists must have had a rich memory bank from which to draw. Yet they allotted much less space to Jesus' mighty works than to his sayings and teachings. (2) Jesus' healing ministry was an integral part of his mission and not just an accidental appendage. (3) The case for the cures which Jesus reportedly wrought is broadly based. It rests on the relatively small number which are described and also on hundreds of others which are merely mentioned.

Records

Five main stages in the development of the miracle material have been distinguished. (1) In most cases there was an actual happening in which Jesus participated. (2) The happening was interpreted by those who witnessed it. (3) The story of the happening was used by the church in its evangelistic, educational, and polemic endeavors. (4) The story appeared in its first written forms. (5) The story was included in the gospel records. We shall discuss stages two, three, and five in reverse order.

Mark's accounts of the miracles are lifelike, individualized, and detailed. Matthew condenses Mark's stories at the expense of their individuality. At the same time that Matthew telescopes Mark's materials, he adds to them. The end result is a shift in emphasis and sometimes in form. Mark's miracle stories are retold not because they have value in themselves but because of the message they contain. The form of Mark's healing miracles in Matthew is conversational. The miracles are still reported, but the stress is on the striking sayings of Jesus which the miracles occasioned. Matthew's modifications of Mark's material are not arbitrary. They are made in the interests of theological themes he wishes to highlight (faith, discipleship, Christology), and they are based on important points in the narrative before him. If a narrative does not contain such points (Mk. 7:31–37; 8:22–26), it is omitted. Luke usually follows Mark more closely, but he also condenses, adds to, and omits Marcan material.

The miracle material came under the influence of the same tendencies to which any story is subjected during a period of oral transmission (stage three). Vincent Taylor lists these tendencies as follows: (1) the addition of explanatory or inferential points at the same time the story is being shortened; (2) the substitution of indirect for direct speech; (3) the elimination of personal and place names; (4) the rounding out of the story and the dropping of details; (5) the retention, in the main, of the story's substance. When Taylor examines the gospel accounts in the light of these observations, he concludes that the shorter and more conventional stories passed through many more hands before they were recorded than the longer and more colorful ones.[1]

The eyewitnesses (stage two) to the strange happenings in which Jesus participated were not seasoned journalists from the Jerusalem *Times* or the Galilean *Gazette*. Neither were they court stenographers or tested historians. Least of all were they graduates of Hebrew University with its modern scientific and philosophical orientation. Objective reporting in any age is difficult if not impossible. So much depends on the training, experience, and viewpoint of the observers. The witnesses of Jesus' wonders were first-century Palestinians—farmers, fishermen, artisans, and day laborers. Many were illiterate and superstitious. Most of them believed in a three-storied (heaven, earth, hell), geocentric "universe." They attributed mental illness to demon possession and physical deformity to sin.

These facts do not invalidate the testimonies which make up the gospel records. They do, however, place those testimonies in a world radically different from our own. It is in the framework of that world—not ours—that they must be understood. When people watched Jesus calm a madman, they did not rush home to their relatives and neighbors with a candid-camera exposure or with a psychiatric analysis. They joyously declared that Jesus had driven out the demons. When a herd of swine grazing nearby plunged down the steep bank into the sea and was drowned as the madman was calmed, the witnesses did not conduct an inquest. They assumed that the two incidents were related as cause and effect. What could be more logical? Did not demons always seek embodiment? Once they had been exorcised from the madman, the demons entered the swine and incited them. If a twentieth-century historian had been on hand, he might have concluded that the cries of the demented and the gathering of the crowd had frightened the excitable swine and had caused them to stampede.[2]

It would be just as foolish to ignore the possible misinterpretation on the part of eyewitnesses as it would be to force all of the miracles into a modern mold. A story reported from a modern classroom highlights the importance of the frame of reference of observers. "Out in Yellowstone Park there's a geyser called Old Faithful that blows off every 70 minutes. Now you are standing there, watch in hand, waiting for the old man to shoot. You know he's due to blow his top in just two minutes. About this time you hear a yell, and you see a wild Indian coming, running like mad, and chased by a huge grizzly bear which is gaining on him. Now the Indian doesn't know anything about the geyser. Just as the bear almost grabs him, he leaps right over the geyser and rushes on. An instant later Old Faithful, right on the dot, shoots the works and blows the bear sky-high. Well, now, to the

---

[1]Taylor, *The Formation of the Gospel Tradition*, pp. 124–26 and Appendix B. It should be noted, however, that a long and detailed story does not always indicate antiquity. The narratives in the Fourth Gospel are lengthy and detailed, but they are so because of the author's literary and doctrinal interests.

[2]This was not the viewpoint of the evangelists, of course, nor the reason why they incorporated the story in their Gospels.

Indian, it is a miracle, to the bear it is death, and to you, watch in hand, it is just a coincidence. It's all in how you look at it."[3]

Technique

Any treatment of the techniques used by Jesus in performing miracles must be based on the gospel records. These records are incomplete and at times incoherent. Where details are present, they cannot be pressed. The same miracle, when given in different Gospels, may exhibit different techniques. In some instances, such as in the feeding of the five thousand, the technique sheds no light on the happening itself. In all cases the method is of secondary significance.

The methods used by Jesus in performing mighty works were varied. (1) Sometimes he merely spoke. He "rebuked the wind, and said to the sea, 'Peace! Be still!'" (Mk. 4:39). (2) Once he touched a sufferer and said nothing (Lk. 22:51). (3) Frequently he touched the sufferer and spoke some words. He took Jairus' daughter "by the hand" and said to her, "Little girl, I say to you, arise" (Mk. 5:41). He touched a leper and said to him, "I will; be clean" (Mk. 1:41). (4) At times it was sufficient that he be touched. A woman with a hemorrhage touched him and "immediately the hemorrhage ceased" (Mk. 5:29). "And all the crowd sought to touch him, for power came forth from him and healed them all" (Lk. 6:19).

Types

Jesus' miracles are recorded in the Synoptics in two of the various forms distinguished by form criticism.[4] The pronouncement story provides a context for an important saying of Jesus. The saying is as important as the miracle itself, if not more so. Examples of this type are the case of the man with the withered hand (70)[5] and the man with dropsy (168).[6] Many of the stories, however, are told as independent units in which the main interest is in the miracle story proper.

Another way to classify the miracles is by subject matter. They fall rather naturally into four groups: exorcisms (casting out demons), healings, resuscitations, and nature wonders. The first three groups concern unusual changes in people. The fourth group reports unusual changes in nonhuman objects, such as bread and water. For the most part, the evangelists recorded typical examples of Jesus' many mighty works. We shall do likewise.

[3]Chester Warren Quimby, "Straight from the Class Room," *The Journal of Bible and Religion*, XXI, No. 1 (1953), 62.

[4]See Dibelius, *From Tradition to Gospel*, pp. 70–119. Compare Taylor, *The Formation of the Gospel Tradition*, p. 30, whose terminology we have adopted.

[5]Mt. 12:9–14; Mk. 3:1–6; Lk. 6:6–11.

[6]Lk. 14:1–6.

Exorcisms cannot always be sharply distinguished from healings in the Synoptics (12, 106, 116, 126).[7] The activity of demons was associated with all kinds of abnormality—moral evil, mental derangement, physical disorders, and even destructive storms. Generally, however, "casting out demons" refers to the relief of mental disorders and "healing" to the cure of physical disease. Mark records four stories (1:23; 5:2; 7:25; 9:17) in which the demons were defeated by Jesus. We shall focus our attention on the second story.

The Gerasene Demoniac (106) raises a number of questions. (1) How many demoniacs were cured by Jesus? Mark and Luke say one. Matthew doubles the number. (2) Where did the exorcism take place? Mark and Luke state in "the country of the Gerasenes" while Matthew says it was in "the country of the Gadarenes." Gerasa was over thirty miles southeast of the Sea of Galilee, and Gadara was not "opposite Galilee" but seven miles southeast of the Sea. Gergesa, which has manuscript support in Luke, was preferred by Origen. Its location, perhaps halfway down the eastern coast of the Sea, is uncertain. (3) Were the demons transferred by Jesus from the demoniac(s) to the swine, or did the witnesses misinterpret two coincidental happenings? (4) Why did Jesus depart from his usual custom and instruct the healed demoniac to proclaim the miracle? (5) Why did Jesus fail to teach among the Gerasenes?

These and other questions have caused many critics to doubt the factual nature of the account. They regard the story as "a folk tale current in a pagan neighborhood but a folk tale about Jesus and his restoration of a notorious and dangerous demoniac, the man with the thousand devils."[8] On the other hand, the unusual detail of the story has convinced many commentators that the account is primitive. Whatever its origin, the story appears in the Synoptics as an illustration of the faith of the church in Jesus' ability to free men from the power of Satan. Four features of the story are found in other exorcisms recorded in the Gospels. (1) The condition of the demoniac is described. (2) The demon recognizes who Jesus really is. (3) Jesus speaks to the demon and commands him to come out. (4) The onlookers are afraid or astonished.

The demoniac lived among "the tombs," the dwelling place of demons in ancient tales. One whom they possessed would naturally live there, too. Palestine was plentifully supplied with caves or caverns hewn out of rock. They provided an appropriate place of refuge for societal misfits. The graphic details of the demoniac's life are ghastly and true to life. Chains and fetters could not hold him. No one had the strength to subdue him. He cried out constantly and bruised himself with stones. When he saw Jesus, the man (as mouthpiece of the demon) shouted that Jesus was "Son of the Most High God." He feared Jesus' supernatural power and sought to subvert it in two ways. (1) He revealed Jesus' true name, which was unknown among

---

[7]Mt. 8:28–34; 15:22–28; 17:14–20; Mk. 1:23–28; 5:2–20; 7:25–30; 9:14–29; Lk. 4:33–37; 8:27–39; 9:37–43a.

[8]Grant, in *The Interpreter's Bible*, VII, 712.

sane men. It was a common belief that to speak a man's name was to exercise control over him. (2) He adjured Jesus (commanded him as if under oath) not to torment him.[9] (We are told belatedly in Mark 5:8 that Jesus had already begun the exorcism.)

Jesus responded to the subversive sayings by asking the man his name. (To control a demon, an exorcist would have to know his name.) The man replied that his name was Legion. (A Roman legion usually numbered five or six thousand soldiers. Since the severity of an affliction was popularly believed to be proportionate to the number of demons which had caused the disorder, this man's case should be considered critical.) Now that his name was known, the demoniac admitted defeat. He parleyed for the best possible terms. As servile spokesman for the spirits, he begged Jesus not to send the demons out of the country which was their natural habitat. They had to seek embodiment somewhere. In desperation they urged Jesus to send them into the swine. Thus they would be able to remain in the country. Jesus complied with their request. But the demons were duped. They failed to see the catastrophic consequences of their request. The two thousand swine rushed down the steep bank and were drowned in the Sea.

No one saw the demons pass from the sufferer into the swine. The transfer was inferred by the witnesses from the conversation between Jesus and the demoniac and from the crazy conduct of the herd. Was the inference accurate, or were the swine merely alarmed by the madman's behavior?[10] There was no doubt in the minds of the herdsmen as to what had happened. They fled and sounded the alarm. When the aroused Gerasenes came to investigate, they found the demoniac "clothed and in his right mind." They were afraid—more afraid of the exorcist than of the demoniac. Jesus' awesome power might be used again. They could ill afford to lose two thousand swine every time he warred with the demons. So they begged him to depart from their neighborhood. When the man who had been restored to mental health asked to accompany Jesus, he was refused. Jesus told him to return home and tell his friends how much the Lord had done for him.

The exorcisms of Jesus have been variously viewed. (1) Some accept the stories without reservation. (2) Others take the stories literally but declare that the world has changed. Demons no longer possess people as they did in Jesus' day. (3) Still others assert that the stories describe authentic experiences which were mistakenly interpreted. Demon possession was the first-century equivalent of mental illness. (4) Not a few consider demon possession and its cure to be an unsolved problem on which modern psychology sheds helpful light. (5) Some look upon the stories as pious fabrica-

---

[9]Mark's adjuration is turned into a request in Luke 8:28: "I beseech you." Matthew's sharply condensed version of Mark omits the adjuration and any word about the healing or the healed. His focus is on the person of Jesus, and he puts on the lips of the demons a christological question: "Have you come here to torment us before the time?" (8:29). According to Matthew, Jesus *has* come to turn the demons over to torment prior to the "time" when God's sovereignty would be fully established. This christological emphasis pushes the miracle into the background.

[10]Critics of the latter theory point out that the demoniac grew calm—not excited— in the presence of Jesus.

tions.[11] Increasingly, however, emphasis is shifting from an attempt to explain exorcisms to an attempt to understand the first-century world view and the meaning of exorcisms for the people who lived then.

Healings abound in the Synoptics. The variety of physical (or functional) disorders whose cures are recounted is astonishing. Included are fever (13), leprosy (45, 182), paralysis (52), dumbness (57), atrophy (70), hemorrhage (107), deafness and speech impediment (117), blindness (121, 193), epilepsy (126), infirmity (163), dropsy (168), and a severed ear (240).[12] The list contains characteristic examples of countless cases of healing covered by the frequently repeated statement that Jesus healed "every disease and every infirmity among the people" (Mt. 4:23). Each disease and its reported cure merit individual study. We shall consider only the healing of a leper.

The Healing of a Leper (45) raises a question: what was leprosy?[13] Biblical leprosy included several kinds of skin disorders (variously identified as contagious ringworm, psoriasis, leucoderma, and vitiligo) and even mildew on walls and in culinary vessels. Since it was believed to attack clothing (Lev. 13:47) and walls (Lev. 14:34), it may often have been caused by a fungus. "The disease now called leprosy, Hansen's disease, or *Elephantiasis Graecorum* was perhaps known in ancient Egypt, but is not referred to here."[14] "Leprosy" was a rather common disease in Palestine. The entire tractate Negaim in the Mishnah is devoted to it. The rabbis generally held that leprosy was a direct punishment for serious sins. Although the Law presupposed that it could be cured, its healing was said to be as difficult as raising the dead. Victims were shunned for two reasons: (1) the fear of contagion and (2) the ritualistic uncleanness which resulted when the holy people of Israel came in physical contact with the diseased. Consequently, the afflicted were required to dwell apart from normal society, wear torn clothes and loose hair, and with covered mouth cry out the warning, "Unclean, unclean" (Lev. 13:45–46). They remained unclean until they were pronounced cured by a priest and their sacrifices were performed.

Mark presents a vivid account of the leper's cleansing. No date or place is recorded. The story is related as an example of Jesus' activity on his tour throughout all Galilee. The leper approached Jesus.[15] "If you will," he declared, "you can make me clean" (1:40). The evangelist clearly understood the words, "make me clean," to involve a miracle, as in the story of Naaman (II Kings 5). The evangelist did not think in terms of a mere certification of a cleansing that had already happened, as have some modern commentators. The certification was the prerogative of the priests. Jesus, moved by

---

[11]See S. Vernon McCasland, *By the Finger of God* (New York: The Macmillan Company, 1951), pp. 1–11.

[12]Mt. 8:1–4,14–15; 9:1–8,20–22,32–33; 12:9–14; 17:14–18; 20:29–34; Mk. 1:29–31,40–45; 2:1–12; 3:1–6; 5:25–34; 7:31–37; 8:22–26; 9:14–27; 10:46–52; Lk. 4:38–39; 5:12–26; 6:6–11; 8:43–48; 9:37–42; 13:10–17; 14:1–4; 17:11–19; 18:35–43; 22:49–51.

[13]Mt. 8:1–4; Mk. 1:40–45; Lk. 5:12–16.

[14]Johnson, in *The Interpreter's Bible*, VII, 338.

[15]Mt. 8:2 and Lk. 5:12 indicate that the leper addressed Jesus as "Lord," a name rare in Mark (7:28). "Lord" ranged in meaning from "Sir" to "God." It was widely used in the early church to suggest the exalted relationship of Jesus to his followers.

compassion, disregarded ceremonial defilement and possible contagion. He stretched out his hand, touched the leper (a familiar gesture of healing), spoke to him, and immediately cured him. This immediate cleansing—a puzzle to the modern mind—signified the supernatural.

Abruptly the emotional climate worsened. Jesus' compassion turned to active anger. He "sternly charged him"[16] and promptly sent him away. Why the sudden shift of sentiment? At what was Jesus resentful? (1) The Leper's audacious and illegal approach to him? (2) His presumptuous demand—"if you will"—implying a possible refusal? (3) Or the foreknowledge of what the man would do next? (Contrary to Jesus' command he talked freely. Consequently, Jesus' ministry was hampered by hordes of people hungry for healings.) Whatever the cause, Jesus instructed the cured leper to "say nothing to anyone; but go, show yourself to the priest." The purification ceremony was performed only in Jerusalem. There the officiating priest, who doubled as a health officer, would examine him. If he should be declared clean, then "what Moses [had] commanded" would be offered—two birds, one of which would be slain and the other released as part of the disinfection ceremony (Lev. 14:4–7). This ceremony would constitute "proof to the people" that the leper was healed; and he would then be accepted back into society. But the man acted contrary to Jesus' charge. He "spread the news" of what Jesus had done for him. It had been Jesus' intention to preach in the surrounding villages (Mk. 1:38), but now he could no longer openly enter a town because of the man's disobedience. He was confined to the country where "people came to him from every quarter"—presumably to be healed rather than to hear the Good News.[17]

The longing to be healed persists. Today people flock to Protestant faith groups, Christian Science midweek meetings, and Roman Catholic shrines in search of dramatic cures for minor and major illnesses. Not a few testify to their success. Some experience relief from apparently hopeless afflictions. The capacity of the body to respond to mental states is not fully known. If informed medical estimates are correct, fifty to seventy percent of our modern hospital beds are occupied by people who display symptoms which have no known organic cause. Doubtless many who claim to have been cured at religious services fall into this category.

Many of Jesus' healings may also be explained on a functional basis. The evangelists did not distinguish between functional and organic diseases; nor did the eyewitnesses on whose testimony their accounts are ultimately based. Even if such data could have been given, they would have been

[16]The Greek literally means "being very angry with him" (1:43). Matthew omits and Luke modifies Mark's record at this point.

[17]Matthew, who omits anything in Mark which suggests a limitation of Jesus' power, does not include Mk. 1:45, which speaks of Jesus' inability to show himself in the Galilean towns at this time. His omission of the descriptive material in Mark highlights the conversational character of the healing. His termination of the story with the command that the healed fulfill the Mosaic requirements makes his account less a miracle story and more a christological affirmation: Jesus came not to destroy the Law but to fulfill it! Luke reproduces Mark quite faithfully and even supplements his account by stating that Jesus spent the period of consequent seclusion in prayer.

The tomb of Lazarus in Bethany is the traditional place from which Jesus resurrected his friend.

inimical to the spirit and purpose of the Gospels. The Gospels offer a Savior whose power to save was not contingent on such distinctions. The evangelists present the mighty works as proof of God's power in Jesus.

Resuscitations are rare in the Gospels. There are only two in the Synoptics and only one in John. Mark, followed by Matthew and Luke, records the raising of Jairus' Daughter (107), Luke the raising of the Widow of Nain's Son (80), and John the raising of Lazarus.[18] The first two might conceivably be classed as extreme cases of physical healing. This can scarcely be said of the third. Lazarus had been dead for four days. The only kind of resuscitation which could apply to his case would be a "raising from the dead." The story is full of difficulties as well as devotional treasures. Why is such an impressive miracle not found in the Synoptics? Why did Jesus

[18]Mt. 9:18–26; Mk. 5:21–43; Lk. 7:11–17; 8:40–56; Jn. 11:17–44.

delay for two days before going to see Lazarus? Could a man who had been dead for four days have been restored to physical life? Could he have walked with his hands and feet tightly bound and face wrapped with a cloth? Some commentators regard the narrative as a dramatic allegory.[19] Its central thought is expressed in Jesus' words to Martha: "I am the resurrection and the life; he who believes in me, though he die, yet shall he live, and whoever lives and believes in me shall never die" (Jn. 11:25–26).

Jairus' Daughter (107) has been selected to illustrate resuscitations in the Synoptics.[20] Since the story is interrupted by the healing of the Woman with a Hemorrhage, it has been suggested that we have here an example of Mark's telescoping of narratives and his artistry in indicating the passage of time between the arrival of Jairus and Jesus' entrance into Jairus' house. It is possible, though, that the two incidents occurred just as Mark relates them.

The scene is set in Jewish territory. Jesus had just crossed the Sea of Galilee by boat. A great crowd had gathered about him on the western shore. Then Jairus, "a ruler of the synagogue" (probably a lay president chosen to preside over the services and business), spied him. Jairus fell at Jesus' feet and declared that his "little daughter[21] [was] at the point of death."[22] He implored Jesus to "come and lay [his] hands on her" (a common method of spiritual healing in the early church and since) that she might be made well and live. Jesus responded affirmatively. On the way to Jairus' house, Jesus paused when the woman with the hemorrhage touched his garment. While he was speaking to her, word arrived from the ruler's house that the child was dead. There was no need to trouble the Teacher further. But Jesus reassured Jairus: "Do not fear, only believe" (Mk. 5:36). Since no raising of the dead had previously been reported in Mark, great faith was required of the father.

Jesus dismissed the crowd before he reached the ruler's house.[23] He allowed no one to accompany Jairus and him except his three intimates—Peter, James, and John. These were the three who later witnessed the Transfiguration (Mk. 9:2) and sleepily shared the experience in Gethsemane (Mk. 14:33). When they reached the house, a public wake was in process. Personal and professional mourners were weeping and wailing loudly. Jesus declared that their sorrow was premature. "The child is not dead but sleeping" (Mk. 5:39). From this statement some commentators have concluded that the miracle Jesus performed was one of diagnosis and not resurrection from the dead. The bystanders believed that the child was dead, but Jesus knew better. He discerned that she was in a coma. He roused her from her cataleptic state. What appeared to be a miracle was merely a natural re-

[19]See C. J. Wright, "Jesus: the Revelation of God," in H. D. A. Major, T. W. Manson, and C. J. Wright, *The Mission and Message of Jesus* (New York: E. P. Dutton & Co., Inc., 1938), pp. 832–47.

[20]Mt. 9:18–26; Mk. 5:21–43; Lk. 8:40–56.

[21]Luke states that she was an "only" daughter (8:42), an inference from Mark's "little daughter" (5:23).

[22]Mt. 9:18 declares that she "has just died," and Lk. 8:42 that she "was dying."

[23]In Lk. 8:51 the crowd is dismissed at the door.

covery. The conjecture is an attractive one. There were many cases in the ancient world of the hasty burial of an apparently dead person who, as a subsequent opening of the grave revealed, awakened from a coma to a living death. If Jesus hadn't arrived in time, Jairus' daughter might have suffered a similar fate.

Whatever merit this theory may have, it overlooks several facts. (1) When Jesus declared that the child was not dead but asleep, he had not yet entered the death chamber (Mk. 5:40). He had made no diagnosis. He could have had no knowledge that the little girl was in a coma. All he knew was that she had been reported to be dead. (2) Jesus showed no interest in analyzing illnesses, and the evangelists do not present him as an expert diagnostician. They understood the story to describe an act of resurrection from the dead. (3) Sleep was a common euphemism for death among the Jews and early Christians. Jesus may have described the child as "sleeping" to suggest that her death was temporary.

The crowd knew that Jairus' daughter was dead. They took Jesus' words quite literally and laughed at him. "He put them all outside" as did Elijah and Elisha when they restored the dead.[24] A similar procedure was practiced in pagan parallels. Was it so that unbelievers would not see the miracle? The rabbis held that God raised the dead through the instrumentality of righteous men. Jesus took the child's parents and his intimates and entered the death chamber. He took the child by the hand and commanded her to arise. Her response was immediate; she got up and walked. The crowd was amazed. Jesus commanded that the child be fed. This was natural enough. Food was what she needed. But in the story it provided convincing testimony that the dead had come back to life.[25]

Matthew noticeably abbreviates Mark's account and increases the daughter's difficulty. She is dead—not at the point of death (Mk. 5:23). He does this to magnify not the miracle itself but the faith required of the ruler. This judgment is confirmed by the setting of the miracle. The double story (Mt. 9:18–26) is placed alongside the healing of two blind men (9:27–31). All three illustrate the same point: "According to your faith be it done to you" (9:29). They are examples to be emulated by the church of Matthew's day.

Luke rather faithfully reproduces Mark's story, but he adds some details (the daughter was an "only" child) and explanations (the woman "declared in the presence of all the people why she had touched him," 8:47b; "and she shall be well," 8:50; "knowing that she was dead," 8:53; "and her spirit returned," 8:55) which increase the miraculous character of the occurrence.

Did Jesus raise Jairus' daughter from the dead? Did he rouse her from a coma? Or is a far more probable source for such a story "to be found in the similar tales long told of Elijah and Elisha"?[26] "To all appearance

---

[24]See I Kings 17:19; II Kings 4:33. Compare Acts 9:40.

[25]Mark (5:43), followed by Luke (8:56), contains the impossible command that no one should be told about the resuscitation. This is in keeping with Mark's theory of the Messianic secret.

[26]Morton Scott Enslin, *The Prophet from Nazareth* (New York: McGraw-Hill Book Company, Inc., © 1961), p. 154. Used by permission.

The Sea of Galilee may become quite rough when sudden storms are provoked by cold air currents from the west. This photograph was taken from Capernaum.

the girl was dead; on the other hand, medicine knows of cataleptic states which can be mistaken for death. Since we have no way of investigating the event, we shall do well to avoid overconfident theorizing."[27]

Nature wonders, like resuscitations, appear infrequently in the Gospels. They are called nature wonders because the objects in which changes are wrought are nonhuman. The Synoptics relate the Stilling of the Storm (105), the Feeding of the Five Thousand (112) and its variant, the Feeding of the Four Thousand (118), the Walking on the Water (113), and the Cursing of the Fig Tree (199).[28] John contains the Changing of Water into Wine (2:1–11). We shall examine the first Synoptic story.

The Stilling of the Storm (105) in Mark is full of concrete details.[29] On the evening of the day that Jesus had preached his parables from his pulpit on the Sea to the congregation on the shore, he urged his disciples to go with him across to the other side. They left the crowd and took him with them in the boat. While they were on the Sea a great storm of wind arose. The waves beat into the boat and it began to fill with water. The description is dramatic and realistic. The Sea is hemmed in on the east and west by mountains. The summer's sun beats down on the basin with un-

[27]Johnson, in *The Interpreter's Bible*, VII, 358.
[28]Mt. 8:18,23–27; 14:13–33; 15:32–39; 21:18–19; Mk. 4:35–41; 6:30–52; 8:1–10; 11:12–14; Lk. 8:22–25; 9:10–17.
[29]Mt. 8:18,23–27; Mk. 4:35–41; Lk. 8:22–25.

mitigated fury. Without warning cold air currents from the west frequently pounce on the superheated depression and provoke sudden storms. Just as suddenly the storms may subside.

Jesus, exhausted by his teaching, was in the stern, asleep on the cushion. The frightened disciples rudely roused him with a stupid question: "Teacher, do you not care if we perish?"[30] Jesus awakened. He "rebuked the wind and said to the sea, 'Peace! Be still!'" (4:39).[31] "Be still!" or "Be muzzled!" is recorded by Mark as having been used by Jesus when he addressed the demoniac in the synagogue at Capernaum (1:25). It has been suggested that Jesus was addressing the demon of the storm in Mark 4:39. This "would be appropriate enough if commenting on an incident in the *Arabian Nights*," writes Major, "but it presupposes that Jesus held a view of the operations of Nature which is without support in His teaching record in the Gospels."[32] If Jesus' words were from a formula of adjuration used for binding a demon, he certainly did not mean them in the magical sense— a formula effective in and of itself. Jesus' rebuke is expressed in the singular. It could just as properly be addressed to a frantic and voluble disciple as to the wind. The "waves" (Lk. 8:24; compare Mt. 8:26) would seem to have required the plural. "The wind ceased, and there was great calm." The great calm corresponds to the state of the healed demoniac in the next story (Mk. 5:15). Jesus asked the disciples why they were afraid. They were apparently more frightened by the calm than by the storm. Jesus asked them, "Have you no faith?" (Mk. 5:40). Don't you trust in God? The disciples were filled with awe. They wondered who Jesus was that even wind and sea should obey him. Mark's answer is implied. He is the supernatural Son of God!

The Stilling of the Storm has been classified as a nature wonder. Major suggests that this classification is unfortunate and unnecessary. "May we not assume that this wonder-story grew out of a remarkable coincidence. The rebuke administered by Jesus to a voluble and cowardly disciple, coinciding as it did with the subsidence of the storm, was interpreted by His wonder-loving disciples as a rebuke administered to the storm itself."[33] But such a natural explanation calls forth the condemnation of Enslin. "More difficult of explanation than the sudden staying of wind and wave would be the antics of the folk in the boat, several of whom presumably were experienced fishermen. Their amazement at what would seem a far from unusual experience on a valley-skirted lake is surpassed by their standing up and moving around in the boat. Similarly Jesus' ability, not to stay the wind, but to stand up in a tossing boat, is a feat not to be minimized. In a word, the story, as it now stands, seems far from a first-hand account from folks accustomed to fishing trips on Galilee's lake, and attempts to account 'rationally' for certain details in a story where all the other details are equally

---

[30]Mk. 4:38. The caustic query bears no mark of an invention. The reverence felt at a later date would have modified it, as it did in Mt. 8:25 and Lk. 8:24. What better proof of the account's essential historicity?

[31]"Peace! Be still!" is omitted by Matthew and Luke.

[32]Major, in *The Mission and Message of Jesus*, p. 73.

[33]Major, in *The Mission and Message of Jesus*, p. 73.

perplexing would seem a thankless task. Nor is it at all necessary. A far more
ready-to-hand explanation of the story is to be found in the numerous
poetic accounts of the Lord's prowess in this particular sort of act."[34]
Enslin suggests that Psalm 107:23–30 is a likely source of the story.

> Some went down to the sea in ships,
>   doing business on the great waters;
> they saw the deeds of the Lord,
>   his wondrous works in the deep.
> For he commanded, and raised the stormy wind,
>   which lifted up the waves of the sea.
> They mounted up to heaven, they went down to
>   the depths;
>   their courage melted away in their evil plight;
> they reeled and staggered like drunken men,
>   and were at their wits' end.
> Then they cried to the Lord in their trouble,
>   and he delivered them from their distress;
> he made the storm be still,
>   and the waves of the sea were hushed.
> Then they were glad because they had quiet,
>   and he brought them to their desired haven.[35]

Mark's account of the Stilling of the Storm is the first in a cycle of three
miracle stories (4:35–5:43). Each is an example of Jesus' mighty works, and
each bears the marks of a typical miracle story. The word "disciples" does
not appear in the first story, and the brash question (4:38) ill befits people
of their persuasion.

The context and content of the Stilling of the Storm in Matthew are
quite different. Matthew inserts between 8:18 and 8:23 (Mk. 4:35 and 4:36)
two scenes which have to do with discipleship. They are irrelevant to a
journey by sea, are placed in another context by Luke (9:57–60), and are
first attached to the storm by Matthew. He understands the storm story as
a story about discipleship. The sea journey is begun by a command of Jesus.
The change of the call to discipleship from the beginning of the scene (Lk.
9:59) to the second part (Mt. 8:22) suggests that for Matthew the call has
already occurred (8:18). Its renewal in 8:22 is of a different nature. It is no
longer concerned with the *original* decision in favor of discipleship but with
the *repeated* demands for commitment required by members of the church
in Matthew's day. Modifications of the narrative also enable him to accomplish his purpose.[36] Mark reports the Stilling of the Storm first and
the rebuke addressed to the disciples second. Matthew reverses the order,
puts the conversation between Jesus and the disciples at the center, and
causes the Stilling of the Storm to become a postscript. The theme is no

[34]Enslin, *The Prophet from Nazareth*, p. 156.
[35]Compare Ps. 89:9.
[36]See pp. 176–77.

longer Jesus and the storm but Jesus and the disciples—and discipleship in the church.[37]

Rational Explanations

The miracles attributed to Jesus posed no problem for early Christians. They accepted his mighty works as a matter of course, since they believed he and his immediate disciples were possessed of unusual powers. When the New Testament achieved its final form, there occurred a further strengthening of the Christian conviction concerning mighty works. Canonicity ensured historicity. The stories recorded in the Gospels and Acts were divinely attested and guaranteed. They thus differed from similar stories found in secular literature and in the sacred writings of other religions. The New Testament accounts underscored the uniqueness of Jesus. To deny them was to reject him.

The Renaissance fostered individualism, empiricism, and rationalism. These, in turn, formed the foundation stones of modern science. When scientists studied the world, they discovered a universe—a universe undreamed of by the evangelists. Scientific and critical methods were applied to the study of religion. A caustic climate encircled the wonders of Jesus. The evangelists, it was held, sincerely believed that they were recording miracles. Their error stemmed from their ignorance of the laws of nature. Seventeenth- and eighteenth-century rationalists quickly removed this ignorance. They advanced common-sense explanations of the miracles. Their approach is not dead.[38] Neither are their explanations. Distinguished contemporary scholars employ some of them.

It is quite possible to place a question mark after many of the miracles. Even conservative scholars have felt compelled to do this. The rush of the swine into the Sea as Jesus healed the Gerasene demoniac may have been coincidence (106). The leper who approached Jesus may have had an arrested skin disease which Jesus certified (45). The recovery of Peter's mother-in-law (13) and the centurion's servant (46) may be explained on the basis of crises whose favorable outcome would have occurred anyway. The cases of paralysis (52), dumbness (57), atrophy (70), hemorrhage (107), deafness and speech impediment (117), blindness (121, 193), and infirmity (163) may have been functional disorders which readily responded to faith. It may be that Jairus' daughter (107) and the son of the widow of Nain (80) were not really dead but in a coma. The resurrection of Lazarus may be accounted for by the symbolic and allegorical nature of the Fourth Gospel. Since storms arise and terminate suddenly on the Sea of Galilee, the stilling of the storm may

37See the excellent study by H. J. Held, "Matthew as Interpreter of the Miracle Stories," in Bornkamm, Barth, and Held, *Tradition and Interpretation in Matthew*, pp. 165–299, to which our interpretation of the miracles is indebted.

38See J. M. Thompson, *Miracles in the New Testament* (London: E. Arnold, 1912), which attempts to find a rationalistic explanation of each alleged miracle.

have been a remarkable coincidence (105). Jesus' walking on the water (113) may have been in reality walking by the water or through the shoals. (Each interpretation of this incident is permitted by the Greek preposition and by the context.) The cursing of the fig tree (199, 201) may have been based on an original parable (compare Lk. 13:6–9).[39]

Few responsible scholars accept all of the miracles attributed to Jesus exactly as they stand. The evangelists themselves do not always agree as to what took place. (Did the cursed fig tree wither immediately or sometime later?[40]) Some of the "miracles" may in fact be allegories. Some may be the product of mere coincidences. Some may be based on psychological and spiritual factors. Some may reflect holy hyperbole. However, the wholesale reduction of Jesus' mighty works to a rational basis by any or all of these explanations is surely unwarranted. If, for example, some of his healings are being duplicated today by the application of newly discovered psychological laws, we must remember that Jesus lived nearly two thousand years ago. His was an age of simple people and widespread superstition. His anticipation of modern psychiatric therapeutics—if such it was—must in itself be classified as a miracle requiring explanation. "Explanations which are harder to credit than the difficulties which they seek to explain are to most academic disciplines suspect."[41]

No scientist or historian can categorically decide today precisely what powers Jesus exercised. Neither can he determine exactly what happening lies behind a given miracle story. He is too far removed from the scene. "It is better to leave the stories as they stand, recognizing that whereas miracle stories are now often more of a burden than a support to faith, in the ancient world they possessed evidential value. At the same time they were not looked upon as contraventions of a universal system of natural law, and hence were not quite so stupendous to those who experienced or reported them as they would be to us. In fact, granted the possibility of divine intervention in the 'constitution and course of nature,' miracles were only natural; and hence the center of interest in such stories ... was not really in the miracle, as it would be for us, but in what it proved: the presence, the power, the saving purpose of God."[42]

Role of Faith

Faith played a vital role in the mighty works performed by Jesus. He expected to find or to induce an appropriate psychic state in those who approached him to be healed. When it was lacking, as it was in Nazareth, he

39The incident "seems petty and pointless [since it was not the season for figs, Mk. 11:13] and wholly out of character, and the shock of it brings into bold relief the totally different quality of the bulk of the Gospel material." (Rollins and Rollins, *Jesus and His Ministry*, p. 144n).

40Compare Mt. 21:19 and Mk. 11:20.

41Enslin, *The Prophet from Nazareth*, p. 158.

42Grant, in *The Interpreter's Bible*, VII, 711.

"could do no mighty work there, except that he laid his hands upon a few sick people and healed them" (Mk. 6:5). Jesus had the power to heal (Lk. 5:17), but faith and expectancy in the victim were required to activate it. "According to your faith," Jesus declared to the blind men, "be it done to you" (Mt. 9:29). Sometimes, as in the case of the woman with the hemorrhage, faith and expectancy were present without Jesus' knowledge. Then power went forth from him, and the healing took place. Even so, the catalytic agent is clear: "Daughter, your faith has made you well" (Mk. 5:34). The centurion's servant was not required to be present (46). The paralytic benefited not only from his own faith but also from the faith of the four men who carried him to Jesus (52). But faith was not always present as a subjective condition. It would have been impossible in the instances of those who were raised from the dead—even if they were only in a deep coma.

A "hidden" factor in Jesus' power to perform mighty works was undoubtedly his own vibrant faith in God. This aspect of the healing process is largely obscured in the Gospels. The reason is not difficult to find. By the time the records were written, Jesus himself had become such an object of faith that the evangelists mainly stressed faith in him. They did not explicitly treat his own faith, a faith which enabled him to become a channel of power, in connection with his mighty works. They focused attention on the necessary faith of the sufferers. They even showed us how Jesus deepened the faith of the father of the epileptic boy and permitted us to hear the father's poignant reply: "I believe; help my unbelief!" (Mk. 9:24). But implicit in this and every other miracle story in the Gospels is the decisive role played by faith in the life of the one who required it of others.

Jesus' View

It is not surprising that the evangelists picture Jesus as a miracle worker. He lived at a time when miracles were common. Miracle stories clustered like grapes about the stem of historical personages. Their aim was to inflate the personal status of the hero. It was even considered legitimate to manufacture miraculous tales for this purpose. Splendid examples of Greek miracle stories may be found in the *Life of Apollonius of Tyana*,[43] written in the third century A.D. by Philostratos. It narrates the journeys of a famous Greek philosopher, traveler, and wonder-worker of the first century. Rabbinical stories may be read in the Mishnah and in the Soncino Talmud.[44] It is little wonder then that Jesus disclaimed being the sole wonder-worker.

---

[43]See the Loeb Classical Library.

[44]Miracle stories are also told about the founders of the world's great religions. Buddha healed the sick by a look and fed 500 people without previous supplies. Zoroaster cured diseases, counteracted wolves, and liberated rain. Mohammed wrought many miracles. See R. E. Hume, *The World's Living Religions*, rev. ed. (New York: Charles Scribner's Sons, 1947), especially pp. 264–65.

"If I cast out demons by Beelzebub," he inquired of the Pharisees, "by whom do your sons [disciples] cast them out?" (Mt. 12:27).

Although the miracle stories found in the Gospels resemble the popular tales in many ways, they exhibit a rugged independence in others. (1) They are devoid of magical formulas. (2) They do not make use of sacred objects to bring about the desired cures.[45] (3) They repeatedly emphasize the need for faith on the part of the sufferer—a stress which is usually lacking in the secular parallels. (4) They present the miracles as manifestations of the power of God. They are not ends in themselves but signs of the kingdom's coming. Although they are told to glorify Jesus, this is not their exclusive end, as is so often the case in the popular parallels.

Jesus' attitude toward mighty works differed markedly from that of many of his contemporaries. (1) He condemned faith which rested on miracles. He refused to use miracles to prop up his pronouncements or to enhance his status. When scribes and Pharisees demanded a sign of him, he classified them as part of an evil and adulterous generation. (The press for physical proof of God's power fractures faith. Karl Barth has rightly insisted that a God who can be proved cannot be believed in.) Jesus called to mind the Ninevites. They repented not because of the miracles of Jonah but because of his preaching. Jesus pointed to the Queen of Sheba. She was convinced not by the wonders of Solomon but by his wisdom. Now something greater than either Solomon or the Queen of Sheba was here (Mt. 12:38–42). In the Rich Man and Lazarus (177), Jesus asserted that if men would not hear Moses and the prophets, neither would they be persuaded if someone should rise from the dead (Lk. 16:31). (2) He consigned miracles to an important but secondary place in his mission. This fact is implicit in his condemnation of faith resting on miracles and is explicit in a striking Capernaum statement. At the end of a strenuous day of teaching and healing Jesus found himself surrounded by a horde of sufferers expecting to be healed. He responded to their needs and healed many who were sick and cast out many demons. The next morning, long before daybreak, he sought out a secluded spot for soul-searching prayer. Simon (and others) discovered his whereabouts and informed him that every one was searching for him. The searchers' strongly-implied purpose was to induce Jesus to resume the healings and exorcisms which had occupied so much of the previous day. But Jesus replied, "Let us go on to the next towns, that I may preach there also; for that is why I came out" (Mk. 1:38). (3) A compelling motive for his mighty works was his deep love for people. He was "moved with pity" (Mk. 1:41; compare Mt. 20:34). He had "compassion" (Mk. 8:2; Lk. 7:13). To overlook this basic factor in the miracles would be inexcusable. Here as elsewhere in his mission Jesus acted to relieve suffering. (4) Jesus saw his miracles as evidences of the power of God at work. When scribes accused him of casting out demons by the power of Beelzebub, the prince of demons, Jesus attempted to show them the idiocy of the charge. How futile it would be for evil to assault evil! He then reminded the scribes that "no one can

[45]The use of spittle, which was popularly held to have curative powers, might be considered an exception (Jn. 9:6).

enter a strong man's house and plunder his goods, unless he first binds the strong man" (Mk. 3:27). The *Q* source includes in this episode another saying: "But if it is by the Spirit of God that I cast out demons, then the kingdom of God has come unto you" (Mt. 12:28; Lk. 11:20).

Church's View

When the early church collected and conserved knowledge about Jesus, it assigned a significant place in the Gospels to his mighty works. The church cherished the miracle stories for many reasons. The stories had evidential value. For the evangelists they constituted evidence of Jesus' Messiahship or of his unique Sonship. The Synoptic writers viewed the miracles as a means by which Jesus defeated the demons and offered solace to the suffering and the oppressed. Matthew frequently modified the miracle tradition to make it transport christological concerns and teachings about faith and discipleship aimed at the church of his day. The author of the Fourth Gospel saw the miracles as signs to evoke belief in Jesus as the preexistent, incarnate Son of God. The stories revealed God's purpose and power. They showed his compassion. The Hebrew mind did not "dwell upon the *Being* of God, but rather upon *His Activity*."[46] Through His Anointed One, God had acted to release and restore His children. The merciful acts of Jesus were not merely good deeds; they were God's deeds. They demonstrated His purpose of salvation and His power to triumph no matter how entrenched evil might be. The stories symbolized God's continuing concern for His people. This concern had once been expressed through Jesus in his exorcisms, healings, resuscitations, and nature wonders. Now the days of his flesh were finished; but he had told his disciples in his resurrected state, "Lo, I am with you always" (Mt. 28:20). Jesus' stilling of the storm, his walking on the water to his distressed disciples, and his other mighty works served to remind the early Christians that the Power which had been at work in Jesus was not spent!

Conclusion

It is a long leap from the first to the twentieth century, a leap which requires a radical revision of viewpoints. The man-centered world of the Mediterranean has expanded into a universe that is "finite but unbounded." Demon possession has given way to mental illness. Mighty works have been replaced by mighty drugs, spittle by sulfa, healers by physicians, astrologers by astronomers, evangelists by historians, and an open system by law and order.

The informed observer cannot stand in the twentieth century and draw

[46]Alan Richardson, *The Miracle Stories of the Gospels* (London: SCM Press, 1941), p. 5. This book is distributed in the U.S. by Alec R. Allenson, Inc., Naperville, Ill.

infallible conclusions about what took place in the first. Allowances must be made for errors of interpretation on the part of eyewitnesses, for the modifications of the material during the oral period, and for the inconsistencies of the gospel records. When such allowances have been made, there still remains abundant evidence of Jesus' unusual power. The most striking fact about this power was its strict subordination to his purpose, the proclamation of the kingdom of God.

chapter seventeen

The Messianic Question

The popular picture of Jesus assumes his Messiahship. For many years, according to this view, he lived the simple life of a carpenter in Nazareth. Suddenly one day, at the age of thirty, he was catapulted to prominence by means of his startling proclamation. He announced to his Galilean country-men that he was the long-awaited Messiah of the Jews. He performed miracles to prove his point and called on his hearers to accept his claims and conform to his commands.

This picture is partly predicated on the Fourth Gospel. In that masterful mosaic there is no question about Jesus' Messiahship. From the very be-ginning it is evident to the reader who Jesus really is. His debates with the Jews center about his claims concerning his own person. He speaks re-peatedly of his saving significance.

The Synoptic portrait is markedly different. It depicts Jesus going through the towns and villages of Galilee preaching the gospel of God, saying, "The time is fulfilled, and the kingdom of God is at hand; repent" (Mk. 1:15). His proclamation does not concern himself. He stirs the entire area with his mighty works; but his miracles are not signs performed to convince and convert the incredulous. At synagogue services, in houses, in a boat by the seashore, or on a mountaintop, he proclaims the coming of the kingdom. He entices, persuades, and warns his hearers to be ready. But in all his preaching he never clearly states his title, his authority, or his place in the divine plan.

The early church soon decided who Jesus was. The church called him "Christ," "Son of God" (Mk. 1:1), "Lord" (Mt. 7:21), "Savior" (Lk. 2:11), "Word" (Jn. 1:14), and "High Priest" (Heb. 7:26). These titles are interesting and informative, but they do not tell us what Jesus thought of himself. Before we consider those titles in the Synoptics which are said to be Jesus' self-designations, we shall pause to present a brief history of Hebrew hopes.

Hebrew Hopes

"Messiah" translates a Hebrew word which means "anointed." It appears in Greek as "Christos" and in English as "Christ." The term is often misunderstood. In the Old Testament it is used as an adjective rather than a noun. It modifies a noun which is either expressed or implied. The usual phrase is "anointed of the Lord." "Messiah" is not a term reserved for one specific person. It is applied to many figures through whom God asserts his sovereignty—priests, patriarchs, prophets, kings, the nation, and even Cyrus, the potentate of Persia.

The use of "the Messianic hope" to describe the future expectations of blessedness to which pious Jews looked forward in Jesus' day is doubtful for two reasons. (1) It suggests that there was only *one* such expectation. The truth is that there were many. They ranged from one end of the spectrum to the other—from a fanatical nationalism which looked for a political restoration of Israel with a descendant of David seated on an earthly throne, to the less precise conviction that in the future all men would acknowledge Israel's God to be supreme. (2) It thrusts into undue prominence the figure of the Messiah. Many forms of the Jewish hope did not involve a Messiah at all. God Himself, it was thought, would be King in the new age. In addition to the numerous traditional hopes of the Jews, there was the apocalyptic expectation of a cataclysmic end of the present age. It featured a supernatural figure who would descend from heaven with the clouds to institute the Final Judgment. It is misleading to lump together all of these diverse and often discordant opinions about the future under one simple and singular term, "the Messianic hope."

Different segments of the Hebrew community sponsored different expectations simultaneously. A hope prominent in one period might be peripheral in another. There were doubtless many Hebrews who had no hope at all. In times of relative peace and prosperity they were content with the world as it was. It is therefore impossible to present a concise, coherent, and chronological account of the history of Hebrew hopes. We must be satisfied with a treatment of the main lines of Hebrew thought concerning the future.

Hebrew hopes were anchored in heaven. The Hebrews believed that God had made a covenant with Abraham. He had promised the Patriarch that his descendants would be numerous and would occupy the land from the Nile to the Euphrates (Gen. 15:18). Abraham's descendants multiplied. In Egypt they were enslaved, and under Moses they were liberated. At Sinai God offered them a covenant. "Now therefore, if you will obey my voice and keep my covenant, you shall be my own possession among all peoples; for all the earth is mine, and you shall be to me a kingdom of priests and a holy nation" (Ex. 19:5–6a). Then God appeared to Moses and gave him the laws which were to be binding on the covenant people (Ex. 19:9–20:20). From that time onward, devout Hebrews (now called Israelites) were convinced that they were assured future blessings. They were the chosen people of God. He would be faithful to His covenant. This hope was grounded in God and was prior to all other hopes.

The conquest of Canaan and the period of the Judges laid the foundation for the United Kingdom. This was Israel's Golden Age. For a century she enjoyed remarkable power, prestige, and prosperity under the leadership of "the Lord's anointed"—Saul, David, and Solomon. After Solomon, the kingdom was divided. Eventually, Israel fell to the Assyrians and Judah to the Babylonians. But God had not confined his covenants to Abraham and Israel. He had also made one with David and his descendants.

> Once for all I have sworn by my holiness;
>   I will not lie to David.
> His line shall endure for ever,
>   his throne as long as the sun before me.[1]

In times of distress and deportation, later generations looked back to the days of David. They saw them as a pledge for the future. Hosea (3:5) and Amos (9:11–12) envisaged the renewed glory of the house of David and the reunion of the twelve tribes—not the coming of the Messiah.[2] Jeremiah dwelt on the restoration of a succession of kings—not one preeminent king of David's line (Jer. 17:25; 22:4).

Attention was focused on a single descendant of David in some prophecies. Isaiah pleaded with Ahaz, Judah's king, to cancel his plan to ask for Assyrian help on behalf of his besieged country. The prophet felt that the Lord would overthrow the Syro-Israelite attackers. Ahaz thought otherwise. Isaiah declared that the Lord would confirm his word by any sign the king might choose. But Ahaz, who had apparently already decided on another course of action, declined to put the Lord to a test. The prophet replied that the Lord would provide a sign anyway. The sign promised was the birth of a child who would be called Immanuel ("God [is] with us"). The language of Isaiah 7:14 presupposes that the mother was already pregnant (or soon would be) and that the child would be born in the near future. (How else could the child have had significance for Ahaz?) Before the child would reach the age of choice, the Syro-Israelite alliance would be broken up and Assyria would bring havoc on Judah (Is. 7:1–17).

The sign given to Ahaz was the child himself. The manner of his birth was incidental. The child would be born to a particular family. The definite article is used in the Hebrew: "*The* woman shall conceive." Some scholars have suggested that the woman was the queen and the child was the future king of Judah, Hezekiah. Be that as it may, the prophet certainly had a son of the house of David in mind. In contrast to Ahaz, the faithless

---

[1]Ps. 89:35–36.
[2]The passage from Amos is probably from a later hand.

king, he predicted the advent of a child-king who would in time faithfully perform the tasks of government. At first the child would live in a time of woe (the Assyrian invasion). But once that domination had been removed, the child would ascend the throne as the agent of God's rule. Then the meaning of his name—Immanuel—would be self-evident.

> For to us a child is born,
>   to us a son is given;
> and the government will be upon his shoulder,
>   and his name will be called
> 'Wonderful Counselor, Mighty God,
>   Everlasting Father, Prince of Peace.'
> Of the increase of his government and of peace
>   there will be no end,
> upon the throne of David, and over his kingdom,
>   to establish it, and to uphold it
> with justice and with righteousness
>   from this time forth and for evermore (Is. 9:6–7).

This prophecy passed from Isaiah "into the stream of prophetic tradition and eventually was transposed into a higher key in the Christian gospel (see Matt. 4:15–16)."[3]

The Babylonian Exile dashed Israel's hopes for a glorious future. Separated from the Holy Land and the Holy Temple, she even despaired of worship. But the prophet Ezekiel convinced her that the Lord could be worshipped in a pagan land and prophesied her eventual resurrection as a nation. Near the end of the Exile, II Isaiah appeared. This prophet proclaimed good news. Israel had paid double for her sins. Now a New Exodus awaited her. From first to last, II Isaiah's words (Isaiah 40–55) were permeated by a triumphant hope. "It is as if the hell and the horror had been left behind, and one is moving up a high, sun-drenched summit to the very doors of the Kingdom of God. There is good news to tell (40:9–11; 52:1–12): the night of humiliation has ended, a glorious future lies ahead."[4]

A broad universalism pervades the message of II Isaiah. Israel's redemption is a part of the redemption of all nations. From her, blessings will come for all the families of the earth. As the Lord's Servant, Israel will not merely restore the preserved of Israel; she will be a light to the nations so that His salvation shall reach to the end of the earth (Is. 49:6). Several times the prophet makes mention of "the servant of the Lord." In at least four passages the Servant is described but never clearly identified (Is. 42:1–4; 49:1–6; 50:4–9; 52:13–53:12). At times the Servant is clearly Israel: "And he said to me, 'You are my servant, Israel, in whom I will be glorified' " (Is. 49:3). At other times—indeed, in this same poem—the Servant is not Israel; instead, the Servant has a mission to Israel: "And now the Lord says, who formed me from the womb to be his servant, to bring Jacob [all

---

[3]Anderson, *Understanding the Old Testament*, p. 274.
[4]John Bright, *The Kingdom of God* (New York and Nashville: Abingdon Press, 1953), pp. 137–38.

Israel] back to him" (Is. 49:5). Perhaps here the Servant is the ideal Israel, the righteous remnant which has remained faithful. In still other instances, the wording (especially the concrete description of the Servant in Isaiah 53) suggests that the prophet has an individual in mind. Does II Isaiah view the Servant in a collective sense (either as the covenant community or as the righteous remnant) or as an individual? Does he think the work of the Servant will take place in his own day or in the Messianic future (the "last days")? On these questions there is no scholarly consensus.

The unusual nature of the Servant's task is set forth by II Isaiah. "He will not cry or lift up his voice, or make it heard in the street [as did the prophets]; a bruised reed he will not break, and a dimly burning wick he will not quench" (42:2-3). Gently, quietly he will persist until he has established justice in all the earth. The Lord has hidden him like an arrow in a quiver until the appointed time when he will be sent forth to accomplish his universal mission (49:1-6). His close fellowship with God will enable him to sustain the weary and submit to gross afflictions—the lash of the smiters, the sting of the beard-pluckers, and the spit of the contemptuous (50:4-9).

The Servant will be exalted through suffering. This startling idea reaches a thundering climax in the fourth Servant poem (52:13-53:12). The contrast between his present appearance—"marred beyond human semblance"—and his ultimate triumph will astonish the nations (52:13-15). The Servant has grown up "like a root out of dry ground." He has no beauty. He is despised and rejected by men. Men hide their faces to avoid his ugliness. The kings, speaking for their people, are astounded to discover that such a revolting figure is the chosen agent of God (53:1-3). They thought the Servant was suffering for his own sins. Not so! He was suffering in their stead. His suffering was for the nations. "But he was wounded for our transgressions, he was bruised for our iniquities; upon him was the chastisement that made us whole, and with his stripes we are healed" (53:5).

The Servant does not protest his afflictions. He is judged, executed, and buried in a criminal's grave (53:7-9). But God himself is at work in the Servant's career. "The Servant is not a victim, but a victor."[5] His mission will end in triumph and exaltation. He will have posterity and a long life. The Servant will look with satisfaction on the successful result of his suffering (53:10-12).

The idea of the Servant's sacrifice described so movingly in II Isaiah has had a tremendous influence on Christian theology. Christians today cannot read the prophet's poetry without remembering many New Testament passages. Mark 10:45, one of Jesus' familiar sayings, serves as an example: "For the Son of man also came not to be served but to serve, and to give his life as a ransom for many." Jewish thought, however, did not usually conceive of the Messiah in terms of the suffering Servant. It is possible—as a number of New Testament scholars have asserted—that Jesus found the model for his mission in the thought of II Isaiah. For this reason,

---

[5]Anderson, *Understanding the Old Testament*, p. 425.

we have included this prophet in our discussion of "the Messianic hope." Whether or not the prophecy was Messianic, it did express an important hope of the Hebrews, and it was used Messianically later on—perhaps in the Qumran community at the beginning of the Christian era, possibly by Jesus, certainly by the early church.

The conviction of II Isaiah that Hebrew captives in Babylonia would shortly be released was soon validated. Cyrus, king of Persia, the Lord's "anointed" (Is. 45:1), defeated Babylonia and freed the exiles. Those who returned to Jerusalem discovered a desolate city. Even the construction of the Temple failed to bring the promised prosperity. Decades later Nehemiah and Ezra lamented the ruined state of Jerusalem and urged their comfort-loving brethren in Babylon to help rebuild the fallen fortunes of their native land. In the minds of those who responded, dreams of the glorious kingdom proclaimed by the prophets loomed large. The dreams were doomed to disappointment. Palestine lay prone under Persian domination for over two centuries (538–330 B.C.). Finally the Persian Empire crumbled, but instead of freedom, the Jews received a new master, the Greeks. After the Greeks, the Egyptians ruled the Jews for over a century (320–198 B.C.). The Egyptians were succeeded by the Syrians.

Continuous domination by pagan powers evoked a profound pessimism among the Jews, and their prolonged contact with the Persians provided them with a view of the universe tailored to their mood. According to Zoroastrianism, the religion of Persia, the world was the battleground of two opposing spiritual forces. The evil in the world was due to the activity of demonic forces headed by the god of evil. Some day in the future, declared the Persian priests, God would destroy the devil and his angels, the dead would be raised and judged, the wicked would be punished, and the righteous would be revived and rewarded with life in the new age.

As pious Jews meditated on their miseries, they increasingly saw in Persian dualism the explanation for their misfortunes. The postponement of paradise was not due solely to God's delay in punishing Babylonia, Persia, and Syria. (Israel had already paid double for her sins.) The postponement was due to the cosmic conflict which raged behind visible phenomena. This conflict was carried on between God and evil spirits who were under the banner of Satan. The present age was controlled by Satan. At a predetermined time God would destroy Satan; then the day of deliverance and reward would come. However, just prior to that glorious day a period of trial and calamity would prevail. The forces of evil would make their final move—a malignant outburst against God and his followers.

The development of Jewish thought under the influence of Persian dualism is called apocalypticism. The book of Daniel provides the first Biblical example. The Syrian overlord, Antiochus Epiphanes (175–164 B.C.), zealously persecuted the Jews because they resisted his determined efforts to Hellenize them. Judas Maccabeus, son of a Jewish priest, and his brothers opposed this attempt with vigorous military action. It was a dark hour; the prospect for victory seemed slight. It appeared that only God could save the Jews. This thesis was supported by Daniel's visions. Several awesome beasts passed before him. The beasts represented the evil nations which had thwarted Hebrew hopes. The doom of the evil nations was sealed. Daniel looked up to heaven and saw what was to come. The old order had been judged; now the new era was beginning. The figure who symbolized the new era was in human form in contrast with the beasts which represented the former kingdoms.

> I saw in the night visions,
> and behold, with the clouds of heaven
>   there came one like a son of man,
> and he came to the Ancient of Days [God]
>   and was presented before him.
> And to him was given dominion
>   and glory and kingdom,
> that all peoples, nations, and languages
>   should serve him;
> his dominion is an everlasting dominion,
>   which shall not pass away,
> and his kingdom one
>   that shall not be destroyed (Dan. 7:13-14).

Some see this passage as pointing to an individual figure. Most scholars, however, regard the reference to "one like a son of man" as being collective in character—the new Israel, ideal and glorified. This seems to be the view presented in Daniel 7:17-18: "These four great beasts are four kings who shall arise out of the earth. But the saints of the Most High [God] shall receive the kingdom, and possess the kingdom for ever, for ever and ever." Men are symbolized by beasts in apocalyptic tales, but a celestial being is symbolized by the human form. Here we are to think of a celestial being (or beings) in contrast to the terrestrial nature of the beasts. The kingdom given to "one like a son of man" or "the saints of the Most High" is God's kingdom—His answer to a situation which appeared hopeless by all earthly standards of judgment.

Nearly a century after Daniel was written, another apocalyptic work appeared. It is commonly called the Parables (or Similitudes) of Enoch.[6] It speaks frequently of the Son of Man, usually with the demonstrative—*this* or *that* Son of Man (46:4; 48:2; 69:9,14; 63:11; 69:26; 70:1). In the Parables of Enoch, "*that* Son of Man" does not symbolize the saints of the Most High (Dan. 7:13,18);[7] it is a title—the definite designation of the personal Messiah (Enoch 48:10; 52:4). This Messiah is unlike any (priest, king, righteous remnant) known before in Judaism. He is a preexistent

---

[6] I Enoch 37-71. See R. H. Charles, ed., *The Apocrypha and Pseudepigrapha of the Old Testament* (Oxford: The Clarendon Press, 1913), II, 170-71, where a date between 94-64 B.C. is assigned to the Parables. Some scholars argue for a first century A.D. date or later. See Reginald H. Fuller, *The Mission and Achievement of Jesus* (London: Student Christian Movement Press, Ltd., 1954), p. 98. This book is distributed in the U.S. by Alec R. Allenson, Inc., Naperville, Ill.

[7] Emphasis added.

heavenly being. As the Elect One (40:5; 45:3–4; 49:2,4; 51:3) and the Righteous One (38:2; 53:6) he has been hidden with God from before the creation of the world (48:6). He will remain hidden, too, until the end. Then he will come to judge the world and rule over it (51:1–5). The judging of the world is a function never assigned to the Messiah in earlier Jewish writings. This was to be an activity reserved for the Most High Himself. Clearly in the Parables of Enoch the concept of that Son of Man has "an inclusiveness, finality, and ultra-national range and transcendence belonging to none of the earlier forms of the Messianic idea."[8]

A few years after the Parables of Enoch appeared, a writing of a markedly different viewpoint was penned. That writing is the so-called Psalms of Solomon, and it is usually dated about the middle of the first century B.C. Four passages in particular (8:27–30; 11; 17; 18) set forth the leading ideas of this collection in the simplest and clearest manner—the corruption within Israel, the punishment of Israel by God at the hands of the Gentiles, and the restoration of Israel by God at the hand of His "anointed." The Messiah pictured in these Psalms (17:36; 18:6,8) is endowed with divine gifts. But he is a man and nothing more, and he springs from the house of David. Excerpts from the seventeenth Psalm of Solomon contain the message in miniature.

> Thou, O Lord, didst choose David (to be) king over Israel,
> > And swaredst to him touching his seed that never should his kingdom fail before Thee.
> But, for our sins, sinners rose up against us. . . .
> > They laid waste the throne of David in tumultuous arrogance (vss. 5–6a,8).
> Behold, O Lord, and raise up unto them their king, the son of David,
> > At the time in which Thou seest, O God, that he may reign over Israel Thy servant.
> And gird him with strength, that he may shatter unrighteous rulers,
> > And that he may purge Jerusalem from nations that trample (her) down to destruction. . . .
> And he shall gather together a holy people, whom he shall lead in righteousness,
> > And he shall judge the tribes of the people that has been sanctified by the Lord his God. . . . (vss. 23–25,28)
> So that nations shall come from the ends of the earth to see his glory,
> > Bringing as gifts her sons who had fainted,
> > And to see the glory of the Lord, wherewith God hath glorified her.
> And he (shall be) a righteous king, taught of God, over them,
> And there shall be no unrighteousness in his days in their midst,
> > For all shall be holy and their king the anointed of the Lord (vss. 34–36).[9]

Sometime during Jesus' life another apocalyptic writing appeared—the Assumption of Moses. In this work, the kingdom was to be ushered in by a day of repentance (1:18). Israel's national enemies would be punished, and

[8]W. Manson, *Jesus the Messiah*, p. 145.
[9]The Psalms of Solomon, tr. G. B. Gray, in R. H. Charles, ed., *The Apocrypha and Pseudepigrapha of the Old Testament*, II, 648–50.

she would be exalted to heaven—from whence she would see her enemies in Gehenna (10:8–10). God would intervene "alone" (10:7) in Israel's behalf. No Messiah was mentioned. From the time of the Psalms of Solomon (about 48 B.C.) to the Jewish national catastrophe (70 A.D.), no rabbinic writing about the Messiah or the Messianic age has been preserved.[10]

The early prophets looked forward to the establishment on earth— usually in Palestine—of a kingdom in which the Hebrews would receive compensation for their former misfortunes. But a sharp separation between the present age and the age to come was introduced in the book of Daniel. There for the first time the hope of a resurrection of the dead was clearly expressed. Participation in the coming rule of God would not be limited to the last generation. Many would be raised from the dead to join in it. The acceptance of this idea in the two centuries prior to Jesus led to a strikingly different conception of God's kingly rule. The apocalyptists looked forward to paradise, a heavenly Jerusalem, or some other transcendental salvation. At the very least they dreamed of a transformed earth. After the destruction of Jerusalem, the rabbinic teaching which has been preserved agrees with the apocalypses of IV Ezra (II Esdras) and II Baruch. A double form of hope is presented. Between the present age and the age to come (separated by the resurrection and the judgment) fall the "days of the Messiah." These days are sometimes referred to as "the Jewish good time." This hope constitutes a compromise between the national dreams of power and glory and the conceptions of salvation unhindered by earthly limitations.

In summary, we may say that all Hebrew thought about the future was grounded in God and His covenants. Some hopes involved a Messiah. Others held that God Himself would be King in the new age. Even when a Messiah was expected, there was no uniform picture of the Coming One. Would he be one person (Isaiah); one among a succession of kings (Jeremiah); a Servant—and if so, the nation or a righteous remnant (II Isaiah); "one like a son of man"—"the saints of the Most High" (Daniel); a preexistent, supernatural savior from heaven (Parables of Enoch); or a second and greater David (Psalms of Solomon)? Incomplete as it is, our treatment of Hebrew hopes must now be terminated. It will have served an invaluable purpose, however, if it has firmly established in the mind of the reader the conviction that Hebrew expectations were many and varied. We shall now turn to those titles in the Synoptics which are said to be Jesus' self-designations.

---

[10]For lucid and nontechnical discussions of the Messianic hopes which stirred the Qumran community, see Millar Burrows, *The Dead Sea Scrolls* (New York: The Viking Press, 1955), pp. 264–72, and Frank Moore Cross, Jr., *The Ancient Library of Qumran and Modern Biblical Studies* (New York: Doubleday & Company, Inc., 1958), pp. 162–73. The Scrolls· speak of *two* Messiahs—a priestly Messiah of Aaron and a kingly Messiah of Israel (I QS 9:10–11). The kingly Messiah is subordinate to the priestly Messiah (I QSa 12–17), but this may be due to the priestly interests of the community and the fact that the passage is found in a description of a ritual meal—at which a priest would naturally preside in order to say the blessing.

Prophet

Jesus reportedly referred to himself as a prophet. "A prophet is not without honor," he declared to his fellow townsmen of Nazareth, "except in his own country, and among his own kin, and in his own house" (Mk. 6:4). When friendly Pharisees informed Jesus that Herod intended to kill him, he replied, "I must go on my way today and tomorrow and the day following; for it cannot be that a prophet should perish away from Jerusalem" (Lk. 13:33). Revealing words are imbedded in Luke's story of the sinful woman who anointed Jesus' feet. The host Pharisee was horrified and said to himself, "If this man were a prophet, he would have known who and what sort of woman this is who is touching him, for she is a sinner" (7:39). Why did the Pharisee say, "If he were a prophet"? It was because Jesus claimed to be a prophet and was considered to be one by others.

The crowds called Jesus a prophet. After he had raised the son of the widow of Nain, fear "seized them all; and they glorified God, saying, 'A great prophet has arisen among us!' " (Lk. 7:16). The disciples informed Jesus that men believed that he was John the Baptist, Elijah, or "one of the prophets" (Mk. 8:28). Near the close of his mission—when he entered Jerusalem to the shouts of "Hosanna to the Son of David!"—the crowds said, "This is the prophet Jesus from Nazareth of Galilee" (Mt. 21:11). When the chief priests and the Pharisees tried to arrest Jesus, "they feared the multitudes, because they held him to be a prophet" (Mt. 21:46). Some of the rabble demanded that he prophesy (Mk. 14:65). The conviction of the crowds was shared by the two who traveled toward Emmaus and talked with an unknown pedestrian about recent happenings. " 'Are you the only visitor to Jerusalem," Cleopas asked the Stranger, "who does not know the things that have happened there in these days?' And he said to them, 'What things?' And they said to him, 'Concerning Jesus of Nazareth, who was a prophet mighty in deed and word before God and all the people' " (Lk. 24:18–19).

Some of the passages cited are doubtless of secondary origin. Luke 7:16 ("a great prophet") was probably intended christologically. Luke 7:39 and Matthew's editorial additions (21:11,46) to Mark are likely creations of the church. Most of the verses which report that Jesus was an Old Testament prophet raised from the dead are suspect,[11] but the passages which indicate that Jesus was John the Baptist or Elijah raised from the dead are on firmer ground. They are found in a primary source (Mk. 6:14–15; 8:28). Since the early church never viewed Jesus as John or Elijah raised from the dead (but did think of John as Elijah raised from the dead, Mk. 9:13), it would seem reasonable to regard Mark 6:14 and 8:28 as authentic.

In two instances (Mk. 6:4 and Lk. 13:33) Jesus reportedly compared his fate with that of a prophet, but in neither case did he specifically

[11]Note how Luke (9:8 and 9:19) modifies Mark (6:15 and 8:28 respectively) and Matthew (16:14) adds "Jeremiah" to Mk. 8:28.

identify himself as a prophet. Nevertheless, many scholars think that he intended to do so indirectly and that he acted like a prophet throughout his ministry. C. H. Dodd, for example, has discovered fifteen prophetic characteristics in the content and style of Jesus' mission and message.[12]

Professor Enslin comments, "In the years following the crucifixion, title after title came to be applied to him [Jesus] as his followers sought to answer the question: 'Who then was he?' But that the identification of him as a prophet is to be seen as one of these later accolades is most improbable. Instead, the tendency appears to have been in precisely the opposite direction—namely, to minimize, without flatly denying, this estimate and to substitute for it others which seemed more significant and worthy."[13]

Enslin (and other scholars who share his views) may be right. Jesus may have had no Messianic consciousness. He may have thought of himself simply as a prophet called to proclaim the coming kingdom. This conclusion cannot be embraced, however, prior to a careful examination of other titles used by Jesus.

Son of Man

The term "Son of Man" appears about eighty times in the Gospels. It is found in each of the five sources isolated by scholars—Q, Mark, M, L, and John. Its presence in the Gospels is as conspicuous as its absence from the remainder of the New Testament. Outside the Gospels it is found only in Acts 7:56 and Hebrews 2:6.[14] In the Gospels "Son of Man" is used by no one except Jesus. From the beginning of his public ministry (Mk. 2:10) to the end (Mk. 14:62) it is one of his favorite expressions. He uses it more frequently than any other title of authority. His disciples, followers, petitioners, and opponents refer to him by many names; but they never call him "Son of Man." In the early creeds of Christendom the term is not encountered a single time. From these facts Stauffer reasons that "the primitive church found the idea of the Son of Man imbedded in the oldest traditions . . . [and] treated it as a taboo designation that Jesus Christ had reserved for himself, much as the synagogue treated God's designation of himself (Yahweh).[15]

"Son of Man" is a translation of the Semitic term *ben adam* (Hebrew) or *bar nasha* (Aramaic). It originally meant "man" in the general sense of *anthrōpos* (Greek) and *homo* (Latin). Old Testament examples of this usage abound. Psalm 8:4, a perfect pattern of synonymous poetic parallelism in which the second line of the couplet restates the thought of the first, is a case in point.

> What is *man* that thou art mindful of him,
>   and the *son of man* that thou dost care for him?[16]

[12]C. H. Dodd, in *Mysterium Christi*, eds. G. K. A. Bell, A. Deissmann (London: Longman, 1930), pp. 56–66.

[13]In Enslin's aptly titled book, *The Prophet from Nazareth*, p. 58.

[14]Rev. 1:13 and 14:14 contain the term "one like a son of man."

[15]Stauffer, *Jesus and His Story*, p. 163.

[16]Emphasis added.

In Ezekiel, the term is used scores of times to emphasize the prophet's humility and humanity in contrast with God: "Son of man, stand upon your feet" (Ezek. 2:1). In no sense is "Son of Man" filial as might be suggested by the rendering "son of."

In the book of Daniel a transition takes place. "One like a son of man" is used to describe "the saints of the Most High" (Dan. 7:13,18). Many scholars have concluded from this that "one like a son of man" is a collective term for God's elect rather than a title for a single eschatological figure.[17] Although the author of Daniel assuredly uses the term in a corporate sense, other specialists argue that the poem is from an earlier source in which the term denoted an individual eschatological figure. Daniel's author, it is alleged, does not forsake the original singular understanding of the figure, but he expands it to represent "the saints of the Most High" over whom he rules.[18]

In the Parables of Enoch "Son of Man" no longer means man in the general sense of Psalm 8:4 or Ezekiel. It stands for "*that* Son of Man"—a hidden heavenly being who will come on the clouds to execute the Final Judgment and rule in the New Age (Enoch 51:1–5).[19]

The Son-of-Man sayings in the Synoptics are by no means uniform. Some describe the present activity of the Son of Man, others speak of the impending suffering of the Son of Man, and a third group concerns the future coming of the exalted and glorified Son of Man. The sayings can be grouped as follows:

Present Activity

Mark 2:10,28; 10:45a
Q   Mt. 8:20 = Lk. 9:58; Mt. 11:19 = Lk. 7:34; Mt. 12:32 = Lk. 12:10
M   Mt. 13:37
L   Lk. 19:10
Editorial   Mt. 16:13; Lk. 6:22

Impending Suffering

Mark 8:31; 9:12,31; 10:33,45b; 14:21,41
L   Lk. 22:22; 24:7
Editorial   Mt. 26:2; Lk. 17:25

Future Coming

Mark 8:38; 9:9; 13:26; 14:62
Q   Mt. 12:40 = Lk. 11:30; Mt. 24:27 = Lk. 17:24; Mt. 24:37 = Lk. 17:26;
        Mt. 24:44 = Lk. 12:40
M   Mt. 10:23; 13:41; 19:28; 24:39; 25:31
L   Lk. 17:22,30; 18:8
Editorial   Mt. 16:28; 24:30; Lk. 12:8[20]

---

[17]See T. W. Manson, *The Teachings of Jesus* (Cambridge: At the University Press, 1935), pp. 211ff.

[18]See Reginald H. Fuller, *The Foundations of New Testament Christology* (New York: Charles Scribner's Sons, 1965), pp. 35–36.

[19]Emphasis added.

[20]This arrangement of representative sayings is based on Fuller, *The Mission and Achievement of Jesus*, pp. 96–97.

An analysis of these sayings reveals some interesting facts. The sayings which concern the present and the future activities of the Son of Man are solidly grounded in the earliest and most reliable sources, Q and Mark. The sayings which deal with the suffering of the Son of Man are found almost exclusively in Mark. The exceptions may well be editorial. Q is strangely silent about the suffering Son of Man. The "suffering" sayings stem from prophecies of the Passion and the Passion Story itself. They are never fused with the sayings which announce the future coming (parousia) of the Son of Man.

The "present" sayings all occur in the public teaching of Jesus, whereas the "suffering" sayings are given privately to the disciples. "The "present" sayings include those words which stress the authority of the Son of Man.

> But that you may know that the Son of man has authority on earth to forgive sins... (Mk. 2:10).
>
> So the Son of man is Lord even of the Sabbath (Mk. 2:28).
>
> Foxes have holes, and birds of the air have nests; but the Son of man has nowhere to lay his head (Mt. 8:20; Lk. 9:58).
>
> The Son of man came eating and drinking (Mt. 11:19; compare Lk. 7:34).
>
> And whoever says a word against the Son of man will be forgiven (Mt. 12:32; compare Lk. 12:10).

Scholarly opinion on the authenticity of the "present" sayings is sharply divided. Bultmann contends that the "present" sayings are authentic but not Messianic. "Son of Man" on the lips of Jesus is simply an Aramaic circumlocution for "man" or "I."[21] Bornkamm asserts that the "present" sayings are not authentic. He thinks it is highly unlikely that Jesus made use of an ambiguous secret name which could be taken either as a Messianic title or as "the man" with no Messianic implications whatsoever. He rejects the idea that Jesus used "Son of Man" in a Socratic sense to stimulate his hearers to arrive at their own conclusions. "I consider it probable that the historical Jesus never used the title 'Son of Man' for himself."[22] Tödt asserts that the majority of the "present" sayings were formed by the church.[23]

Some of the "present" sayings, such as Mark 2:10 and 2:28, reflect the concerns of the Palestinian church. But the Q sayings found in Matthew 8:20 ("The Son of man has nowhere to lay his head") and 11:19 ("The Son of man came eating and drinking") are so compatible with the life situation of Jesus' ministry that they cannot be rejected out of hand. Yet such sayings cannot be found in Jewish apocalyptic writings because there the Son of Man is a transcendent figure who will come with the clouds of heaven. Small wonder that scholars have been impaled on the horns of this dilemma! Is there a way of escape? There are several. Affirm the authenticity of the "present" sayings at the possible expense of the "future"

---

[21]Rudolf Bultmann, *Theology of the New Testament*, tr. K. Grobel (New York: Charles Scribner's Sons, 1951), I, 30–31.

[22]*Jesus of Nazareth*, p. 230.

[23]H. E. Tödt, *The Son of Man in the Synoptic Tradition*, tr. D. M. Barton (London: SCM Press, 1965; published in the U.S. by Westminster Press), p. 139.

ones. Or affirm the "future" sayings at the expense of the "present" ones. Or assert that Jesus borrowed "Son of Man" from Jewish apocalyptic writings, markedly modified it, and applied it to himself. Each solution has been advanced—with its attendant strengths and weaknesses.

The "suffering" sayings play no part in the Galilean ministry of Jesus. Immediately after Peter's affirmation at Caesarea Philippi, according to Mark 8:31, Jesus began to teach his disciples "that the Son of man must suffer many things, and be rejected by the elders and the chief priests and the scribes, and be killed, and after three days rise again." This theme occurs again and again in Mark.

> And how is it written of the Son of man, that he should suffer many things and be treated with contempt? (9:12).
>
> The Son of man will be delivered into the hands of men, and they will kill him; and when he is killed, after three days he will rise (9:31).
>
> Behold, we are going up to Jerusalem; and the Son of man will be delivered to the chief priests and the scribes, and they will condemn him to death, and deliver him to the Gentiles (10:33).

The "suffering" sayings and the "future" sayings have been identified as separate and distinct groups. "The difference between the two groups of sayings is obvious," Bornkamm comments. "As much as the one [the "future" sayings] lacks references to the suffering and resurrection of the Son of man, so little does the other [the "suffering" sayings] refer to his coming. They also differ as to their sources: the second group belongs exclusively to Mark's tradition, not to Q."[24]

Some of the "suffering" sayings seem to be the creation of the early church. The three stylized predictions of the Passion (Mk. 8:31; 9:31; 10:33–34) read like summaries of the church's kergyma rather than genuine predictions by Jesus. They relate in some detail who will cause Jesus to suffer, the circumstances under which he will die, and when he will be resurrected. Bornkamm believes that they reveal too precise a foreknowledge of the details of the earthly distress of the Son of Man prior to his resurrection to be authentic. "Even if we do not doubt that Jesus reckoned on his violent death, these prophecies of his suffering and resurrection can hardly be considered to be Jesus' own words."[25] Such considerations have led an increasing number of scholars to conclude that the "suffering" sayings stem from the early church under the influence of the Passion.[26] Other scholars, however, think that it is too arbitrary to deny that any of the "suffering" sayings originated with Jesus. If some are suspect, others

[24]Bornkamm, *Jesus of Nazareth*, p. 229. Fuller, *The Mission and Achievement of Jesus*, p. 104, asserts that the "absence of suffering Son of Man sayings from Q is partly accounted for by the fact that Q was not a gospel, and did not contain a Passion narrative." Moreover, he declares that "although there are no direct predictions of the suffering of the Son of Man in Q, there is an indirect one" (Mt. 8:20; compare Lk. 9:58).

[25]*Jesus of Nazareth*, p. 229.

[26]Bultmann says that the "suffering" sayings are the invention of Mark (*Theology of the New Testament*, I, 30–31).

have a higher claim to authenticity. Neither Mark 9:12 (". . . and how is it written of the Son of man, that he should suffer many things and be treated with contempt?") nor Luke 17:25 ("But first he [the Son of Man] must suffer many things and be rejected by this generation") detail the circumstances of Jesus' death. Indeed, they don't directly mention his death at all; they speak only of suffering and contempt or rejection. Although the setting of Luke 17:25 is editorial, the saying itself may have originated with Jesus.[27] Other sayings which do not contain the Son-of-Man term (Mk. 10:38; Lk. 12:50) indicate that Jesus foresaw both his death and his participation in the kingdom. The suffering Jesus referred to in the "suffering" sayings was his own, and "Son of man" was a self-designation. Jewish thought had never before linked suffering and Son of Man. This was evidently Jesus' original contribution.[28]

The "future" sayings, like the "present" ones, are solidly grounded in the earliest sources, Q and Mark. Yet Branscomb regards them as unauthentic. He believes that they quite likely originated in the Christian community after the resurrection. Two forces were at work to establish the Son-of-Man concept in Christian circles. (1) The disciples had believed that Jesus was going to reveal himself as the Messiah. In this they had been disappointed. The resurrection suggested a different interpretation of their hope. (2) John the Baptist had described a heavenly figure who would come to execute the Final Judgment. John's influence was strong in the early church. Just as John's use of the rite of baptism was adopted after Jesus' death, so his teachings of the heavenly judge helped the church find its way to its new faith. "To the early Church the resurrection was the starting-point of a new theology. It overshadowed and wiped out the crucifixion. The Church's interest was Christ's return for judgment, which was now possible."[29]

The Synoptics seem to support Branscomb's position. Again and again they thrust the Son-of-Man theology into sayings of Jesus in which it did not exist originally.

> Truly, I say to you, there are some standing here who will not taste death before they see *the kingdom of God* come with power (Mk. 9:1, followed by Lk. 9:27).
>
> Truly, I say to you, there are some standing here who will not taste death before they see *the Son of man* coming in his kingdom (Mt. 16:28).
>
> [Near Caesarea Philippi] . . . he asked his disciples, "Who do men say that *I am?*" (Mk. 8:27, followed by Lk. 9:18).

[27]See W. G. Kümmel, *Promise and Fulfillment* (London: SCM Press, 1957), p. 71.

[28]See John W. Bowman, *Jesus' Teaching in Its Environment* (Richmond, Va.: John Knox Press, 1963), pp. 99–103; A. M. Hunter, *The Work and Words of Jesus* (Philadelphia: The Westminster Press, 1950), pp. 84–87.

[29]B. Harvie Branscomb, *The Gospel of Mark*, The Moffatt New Testament Commentary (New York and London: Harper & Row, Publishers, Inc., n.d.), p. 147. See also pp. 146–59. Used by permission of Hodder & Stoughton, Ltd., London, the British Publishers. Compare Norman Perrin, *Rediscovering the Teaching of Jesus* (London: SCM Press, 1967; printed in the U.S. by Harper & Row, Publishers, Inc.), pp. 154–99.

[Near Caesarea Philippi]...he asked his disciples, "Who do men say that *the Son of man is?"* (Mt. 16:13).

Blessed are you when men revile you and persecute you and utter all kinds of evil against you falsely *on my account* (Mt. 5:11).

Blessed are you when men hate you, and when they exclude you and revile you, and cast out your name as evil, on account of *the Son of man!* (Lk. 6:22).[30]

Since it can be shown that the early church introduced the Son-of-Man theology into these and other sayings, a cloud of suspicion hovers over the rest of Jesus' sayings.

Tödt's assessment of the "future" sayings is far less skeptical. On the basis of his redaction-critical studies he asserts the probable authenticity of Matthew 24:27 and parallels; 24:37, 39 par. (Q); Luke 17:30, all comparison sayings; Luke 11:30, the menace-saying; Matthew 24:44 par. (Q), the warning-saying; and Luke 12:8-9 par. (Mark 8:38 par.), the promises. His analysis of Mark 8:38 and Luke 12:8-9 is illuminating. He regards Mark 8:38 as a developed form which has been subject to apocalyptic and Christian influences: "For whoever is ashamed of me *and of my words* in this adulterous and sinful generation, of him will the Son of man also be *ashamed,* when he comes *in the glory of his Father* with the holy angels."[31] "And of my words" mars the parallelism and reflects the church's interest in the teachings of Jesus. The concept of being "ashamed" is Pauline (Rom. 1:16) and may have been employed in the evangelistic work of Hellenistic Christianity. "In the glory" is an apocalyptic touch, and "of his Father" is a Christianization—since God was not called "Father" in Jewish apocalyptic.

Tödt contends that the Q form of the saying found in Luke 12:8-9 is closer to the original.

> Everyone who acknowledges me before men,
>   the Son of man also will acknowledge
>   before the angels of God;
> but he who denies me before men
>   will be denied before the angels of God.

In this, as in all other "future" sayings, Jesus does not explicitly identify himself as "Son of man." Indeed, if the words are taken at face value, the opposite is true: he carefully distinguishes between himself and the Son of Man. Yet in Luke 12:8-9 (Mark 8:38), argues Tödt, there is a soteriological (salvation) continuity (but not a christological identity) between Jesus and the Son of Man. "To be ashamed" (Mk. 8:38) stands for "to deny" (Lk. 12:9; Mt. 10:33). The notion of denying is contrasted with the concept of confessing (acknowledging). Confessing and denying presuppose a previous relationship. Mark 8:38, located among sayings dealing with discipleship, suggests that the previous relationship is fellowship with

30Emphasis added in each quotation.
31Emphasis added.

Jesus. If a follower of Jesus is ashamed of or denies the loyalty and obedience implicit in discipleship, he thereby forfeits his future redemptive fellowship with the Son of Man. Conversely, if he confesses (acknowledges) Jesus before men, the Son of Man will confirm his fellowship with Jesus "before the angels," probably originally a circumlocution for the name of God. Here Jesus makes a claim no prophet had ever made: people should confess him before men. There is no hint of lowliness or suffering; he speaks with supreme authority. Fellowship with him is not only for "time" but for "eternity." Those who confess him before men will have this fellowship confirmed by the Son of Man when he comes with heavenly power.[32]

Fuller agrees with Tödt's judgment as to which "future" sayings are authentic, with one exception. He thinks that Matthew 19:28 should not be considered a church creation in its entirety. He acknowledges that the Greek word translated "new world" is Hellenistic, that "Son of man" is missing in the Lucan parallel (22:28–30), that "his glorious throne" is an apocalyptic addition, and that the Son of Man is an advocate who does not have the function of "judging" or "ruling" (*krinein*) in the authentic sayings. Yet Fuller finds it difficult to attribute to the church (which identified Jesus with the Son of Man and created the "present" and "suffering" sayings to depict this identification) a saying which distinguishes between Jesus and the Son of Man. The form-critical method requires that Matthew 19:28 in some way be certified. Consequently, according to Fuller, Jesus' view of the future Son of Man must be enlarged to include his function as ruler in the kingdom of God.

Tödt's views are challenged at yet another point, the nonchristological character of Luke 12:8–9. Fuller argues that these verses indicate that a person's acceptance of Jesus and the salvation that he brings constitutes a passport to participation in the final kingdom of God. If a person rejects Jesus and the proffered salvation, he is excluded. The distinction between Jesus and the coming Son of Man, then, is akin to the difference between the incipient kingdom breaking through in Jesus and its ultimate consummation. The salvation being imparted in Jesus during his ministry is a salvation which will be certified at the End by the Son of Man. Jesus could not call himself "Son of man" during his ministry, of course, since that figure would not appear until the End. But the ultimate meaning of Jesus' words, Fuller asserts, is not merely soteriological (Tödt) but implicitly christological.[33]

Christ

Q does not contain a single instance of Jesus using "Christ" as a self-designation. This usage is found in Mark only once (9:41). The saying is

---

[32]H. E. Tödt, *The Son of Man in the Synoptic Tradition*, pp. 32–47.

[33]R. H. Fuller, *The Foundations of New Testament Christology*, pp. 119–125. For differing assessments, see also H. W. Teeple, "The Origin of the Son of Man Christology," *Journal of Biblical Literature*, LXXXIV, No. 3 (1965), 213–250; W. O. Walker, Jr., "The Origin of the Son of Man Concept as Applied to Jesus," *Journal of Biblical Literature*, Vol. 91, No. 4 (1972), 482–490.

clearly of secondary origin, as a comparison with its counterpart in Matthew 10:42 will show.

In addition to the Marcan saying already cited, there are two passages in which Jesus is offered the title "Christ" and in which his response is indicated.

Mark 8:27–33 contains Peter's confession to Jesus, "You are the Christ.[34] The confession is followed (8:30) by a common theme in Mark, the Messianic secret, which must be assigned to the Gospel's author. Then come the secondary passion prediction (8:31) and a connecting link (8:32a) between the passion prediction and Jesus' rebuke of Peter. When these questionable features are removed, there remains a simple, three-part pronouncement story:

Question:	"Who do you say that I am?" Jesus asks his disciples near Caesarea Philippi.
Answer:	"You are the Christ," Peter responds.
Pronouncement:	"Get behind me, Satan!" Jesus rebukes Peter.[35]

The natural meaning of the rebuke would seem to be, "No, Peter. I am *not* the Christ!" But supporters of the view that Jesus regarded himself as the Christ demur. They claim that he was simply rejecting a particular meaning of the title—the Davidic model with strong nationalistic overtones.

Mark 14:61–62 describes a preliminary interrogation of Jesus before the Sanhedrin.[36] The High Priest asks Jesus,

> "Are you the Christ, the Son of the Blessed?" And Jesus said, "I am; and you will see the Son of man sitting at the right hand of Power, and coming with the clouds of heaven." And the high priest tore his mantle, and said, "Why do we still need witnesses? You have heard his blasphemy. What is your decision?" And they all condemned him as deserving death (Mk. 14:61b–64).

The meaning of Jesus' answer in Mark appears to be obvious—an unmistakable, unqualified affirmative. But the meaning is not so self-evident when we turn to the parallel passages in the Synoptics:

> "You have said so. But I tell you, hereafter you will see the Son of man seated at the right hand of Power, and coming on the clouds of heaven" (Mt. 26:64).

> "If I tell you, you will not believe; and if I ask you, you will not answer. But from now on the Son of man shall be seated at the right hand of the power of God." And they all said, "Are you the Son of God, then?" And he said to them, "You say that I am" (Lk. 22:67b–70).

Cullmann suggests that the corresponding Aramaic of Jesus' reply in Matthew "by no means indicates a clear affirmation. It is rather a way of

---

[34]See our treatment on pp. 189–94.

[35]See R. H. Fuller, *The Foundations of New Testament Christology*, pp. 109–111, to which this interpretation is indebted.

[36]See our discussion on pp. 376–78.

avoiding a direct answer and can even mean a veiled denial."[37] Moreover, the sentence Jesus adds to these words contains an idea contrary to the common picture of the Messiah. The Son of Man is a heavenly being, not an earthly king who will conquer Israel's enemies and exercise earthly sovereignty. "The sentence begins with the conjunction πλήν, 'But I tell you, hereafter you will see the Son of man seated at the right hand of Power, and coming on the clouds of heaven.' πλήν means an emphasized 'but', which sets one statement over against another which is rejected. It suggests that the preceding answer of Jesus was probably negative. . . . And then follows characteristically not a statement about the Messiah the Jews expected, but a statement about the Son of Man, with whom Jesus openly identified himself."[38] The parallel passage in Luke is believed by Cullmann to support the view that Matthew preserved a literal translation of the Aramaic. "Luke clearly preserves the memory that Jesus refuses to answer directly. He evades the high priest's question and, as in Matthew's report, continues with an explanation not about the Messiah but about the Son of man. . . . Jesus knows that the specific ideas relating to the Jewish Messiah are of a political nature, and nothing is more foreign to his conception of his calling. In order to prevent all misunderstanding from the very beginning, he purposely avoids the title Messiah. But in order to make it clear that he does not thereby give up his conviction that he has to fulfill in a special sense God's plan of salvation for his people and therefore for all humanity, he adds immediately the sentence about the 'Son of Man.' Since he is a heavenly being, the Son of Man is actually more closely related to God than the Messiah. Jesus' rejection of the Messiah title, therefore, by no means indicates a rejection of his claim to an elevated position."[39]

F. C. Grant, on the other hand, finds it extremely difficult to accept Mark 14:61b–64 "as an authentic record of a trial. *The Son of the Blessed* is only a quasi-Jewish equivalent of *the Christ*, and ought to read: 'Are you the Messiah? Are you the Son of the Blessed?' (i.e., do you claim to be?) since Jews did not view the Messiah as 'Son of God.' But both the question and the answer presuppose the Christian view, according to which the Christ *was* the Son of the Blessed One (i.e., God) and was *also* the Son of man who should come with the clouds of heaven. This synthesis is the climax of Mark's Christology, but it was also the faith of the church. Furthermore, such a claim . . . did not amount to *blasphemy* save on the Christian assumption of practical identity of Jesus with God (cf. John 10:33); it would not be blasphemy in the eyes of a Jewish court."[40]

If Cullmann is correct in his contention that Jesus' response is either a way of avoiding a direct answer or a veiled denial, it would have to be a denial to be consistent with his pronouncement near Caesarea Philippi. Mark 14:62b, which identifies Jesus with the coming Son of Man, is doubt-

[37]Oscar Cullmann, *The Christology of the New Testament*, tr. Shirley C. Guthrie and Charles A. M. Hall (London: SCM Press, Ltd., © 1959; published in the U.S. by The Westminster Press, Philadelphia, 1959), p. 118.

[38]Cullmann, *The Christology of the New Testament*, p. 119.

[39]Cullmann, *The Christology of the New Testament*, pp. 120–21.

[40]Grant, in *The Interpreter's Bible*, VII, 890.

less a product of the church. It is possible, of course, that Jesus simply remained silent when the High Priest asked him if he was the Christ. He had done this for the previous question (Mk. 14:60–61), and he would do it before Pilate (Mk. 15:2–5). But the silence syndrome may have been an echo of Isaiah 53:7:

> He was oppressed, and he was afflicted,
> yet he opened not his mouth;
> like a lamb that is led to the slaughter,
> and like a sheep that before its shearers is dumb,
> so he opened not his mouth.

In any case, Mark 14:62 is sandy soil on which to build a case for Jesus' acceptance of the title "Christ."

As impressive as the arguments are that Jesus did not consider himself to be the Christ, a considerable number of scholars continue to maintain that he did. They rest their case on two main factors. (1) Jesus' Messianic consciousness is implicit in a large part of the Synoptic record where no explicit Messianic claim is advanced. It may be that the evangelists have read this element into the story at places where originally it was not present. Nevertheless, there are altogether too many incidents and sayings where the Messianic authority and mission furnish the clue to the understanding of the passage for it to be dismissed. The Messianic claim is inherent in the stories of the Baptism, Temptation, Peter's Confession near Caesarea Philippi, the Transfiguration, and the Entry into Jerusalem. If Jesus regarded himself only as a prophet, why did he enter Jerusalem in a manner so highly suggestive of the Messianic prophecy of Zechariah 9:9? If these Messianic elements are all the invention of the disciples and the early church, the historicity of the Synoptics is virtually nil.[41] (2) Jesus was accused before Pilate of being an insurrectionist against Rome (Lk. 23:2), and he was crucified as "The King of the Jews" (Mk. 15:26; compare Mt. 27:37 and Jn. 19:19). Harvie Branscomb's comment concerning these facts is trenchant. "To accuse a simple Galilean peasant who had never raised his arm in civil disturbance, who had specifically enjoined the payment of taxes to Caesar, and who had confined himself to religious and ethical teaching, of leading an insurrection against Rome and claiming to be king of the Jews would have been the height of absurdity had he not given certain grounds for the accusation. It is the clear evidence of all the sources that the basis of the charge against Jesus was a Messianic claim which he himself admitted."[42] Rudolf Otto declares, "He was crucified as a Messianic claimant, and without the Messianic claim the crucifixion of Christ is meaningless."[43] "Nevertheless," concludes A. M. Hunter, "there

---

41Hunter, *The Work and Words of Jesus*, pp. 80–90.

42Harvie Branscomb, *The Teachings of Jesus* (New York and Nashville: Abingdon Press, © 1931), p. 343.

43Rudolf Otto, *The Kingdom of God and the Son of Man* (Boston: Beacon Press, 1957), pp. 228–29. Reprinted by permission.

was 'a messianic secret.' If Jesus knew Himself to be the Messiah, He did not blazon the fact abroad. He deliberately veiled it (recall His answer to the Baptist), and silenced all who would have sent the messianic rumor flying through Galilee. . . . He had good reasons. For one thing, Jesus knew that He was not the Messiah whom the people expected. . . . Moreover, if Jesus, or His disciples, had published His Messiahship abroad, the claim would have been construed . . . in a political sense, and Rome, with her 'Argus-eye' ever open for movements of this kind, would have taken her own swift way of suppressing it."[44]

Son [of God]

The term "Son of God" had multiple meanings in Jewish thought. It was used to describe the Israelite nation as a whole (Ex. 4:22), the godly and upright in Israel, an anointed king (Ps. 2:7), angels (Job 38:7), and the Messiah. It was not, however, a standard title for the Messiah. It is used of him in only a few apocalyptic books (Enoch 105:2; IV Ezra 7:28–29; 13:32,37,52) and occasionally in late rabbinical writings. When it is used in the Old Testament to designate an individual or the nation, it usually stresses the moral relationship of love and filial obedience which should exist between a father and his son. Christians early applied the title to Jesus. Paul uses it frequently (Rom. 1:3–4, etc.). It marks the metaphysical relationship between God and His incarnate Word in the Fourth Gospel (Jn. 1:1–18). In the Synoptics, "Son of God" is applied to Jesus by the evangelist (Mk. 1:1), the voice from heaven at the Baptism and Transfiguration (Mk. 1:11; 9:7), the demons (Mk. 3:11; 5:7), the high priest (Mk. 14:61), and the centurion at the cross (Mk. 15:39).[45]

The evidence that Jesus used "Son of God" in the Synoptics as a self-designation is meager indeed. Other people used the title without hesitation to address him, but only twice does he seem to use it of himself. Each time "of God" is implied. The first passage has the flavor of the Fourth Gospel.

> All things have been delivered to me by my Father; and no one knows the Son except the Father, and no one knows the Father except the Son and any one to whom the Son chooses to reveal him (Mt. 11:27; compare Lk. 10:22).

The style of this saying stands out in sharp contrast to the other sayings of Jesus in the Synoptics. It dovetails beautifully with the words of Jesus in John. This view is supported not only by the Father-Son emphasis but also by the reciprocal use of the verb "to know." Scholars often refer

---

[44]*The Work and Words of Jesus*, p. 82.

[45]Jesus is not explicitly identified with the son in the Wicked Tenants (204), although the identification is no doubt implied (Mt. 21:33–43; Mk. 12:1–12; Lk. 20:9–18). See pp. 214–15.

to the saying as a thunderbolt from the Johannine sky. Bornkamm lists an impressive group of specialists who agree "that this passage can hardly be called a saying of the historical Jesus."[46]

The second Son-of-God saying is above suspicion so far as Johannine style and thought are concerned. In it, Jesus disclaims any knowledge on the part of the Son as to the date of the End.

> But of that day or that hour no one knows, not even the angels in heaven, nor the Son, but only the Father (Mk. 13:32; compare Mt. 24:36).

Bornkamm believes even this saying shows traces of the Christology of the early church, especially in the use of the title "the Son." "Infrequently though the Messianic title Son (of God) is found in the references to himself of the historical Jesus, the more its use can be explained from the Credo of the Church in which it has its own secure place—based on Ps. ii. 7."[47] Just why the church would insert "the Son" into such a saying is hard to understand. The saying was scandalous. It declared that there was something the Son did not know. The verse was soon subject to change. Many manuscripts of Matthew—a Gospel used more frequently in the church than Mark—omit "nor the Son." Luke omits the entire verse (see after 21:33). Is it not strange that the church would create a saying which would cause it so much embarrassment, a saying which it would later seek partially or wholly to erase from the record?

Jesus' sense of Sonship can be supported quite apart from the attributions of others and the two questioned passages in which he may have claimed Sonship for himself. The Synoptics reveal that he called God "Father" in a new and daring way. In the Garden of Gethsemane Jesus addressed God in Aramaic as "Abba."

> Abba, Father, all things are possible to thee; remove this cup from me; yet not what I will, but what thou wilt (Mk. 14:36).

Some have suggested that the prayer is a composition of the church, since the witnesses were beyond earshot and, at least part of the time, asleep. These limitations, however, do not pertain to the Lord's Prayer in which Jesus addressed God as "Father" (Lk. 11:2). Matthew's "our" is secondary, as is his "who art in heaven" (6:9). The Aramaic-speaking Jew called God *'ābhi* (my Father) and his earthly progenitor *'ăbbā'* (father). When Jesus addressed God as "Abba," he did what no Jew had done before. He used an intimate and familiar term—one reserved for a man's human father and no other—for God. The usage implies not only his unique view of God but also his own uniqueness as Son.

Jesus doubtless discovered the pattern for his Sonship in the Old Testament. "Israel is my first-born son," the Lord said to the Pharaoh through

---

[46] *Jesus of Nazareth*, p. 226.

[47] *Jesus of Nazareth*, p. 226. Fuller, *The Foundations of New Testament Christology*, p. 114, believes that this saying originally probably referred to the "Son of man."

Moses, "and I say to you, 'Let my son go that he may serve me'" (Ex. 4:22b–23a). Through Hosea's lips God declared, "When Israel was a child, I loved him, and out of Egypt I called my son" (Hos. 11:1). Israel became the Son by the choice of God in the Exodus experience, and Sonship required the response of filial love and obedience. The Q accounts of the Baptism and Temptation suggest that in Israel's experience Jesus' own Sonship was prefigured. God chose Jesus to be His Son at the Baptism. The significance of the choice became clear to Jesus during the Temptation. From the beginning of his ministry, in filial love and obedience, Jesus proclaimed the coming of the kingdom and the necessity for repentance.

Servant of the Lord

Although Jesus never uses the actual words, in the opinion of many "the title 'Servant of the Lord' often trembles on His lips."[48] A number of scholars believe that Jesus found the key to his mission in the figure of the suffering Servant of Isaiah 53.[49] Only in Luke 22:37 is this Servant passage quoted directly by Jesus: "For I tell you that this scripture must be fulfilled in me, 'And he was reckoned with transgressors.'" However, the prophecies of the Passion, suffering, rejection, death, and exaltation seem to be paralleled by the ideas expressed in Isaiah 53.

> And he began to teach them that the Son of man must suffer many things, and be rejected by the elders and the chief priests and the scribes, and be killed, and after three days rise again (Mk. 8:31; compare 9:31 and 10:33–34).
> Elijah does come first to restore all things; and how is it written of the Son of man, that he should suffer many things and be treated with contempt? (Mk. 9:12).
> For the Son of man also came not to be served but to serve, and to give his life as a ransom for many (Mk. 10:45).
> This is my blood of the covenant, which is poured out for many (Mk. 14:24).
> But first he [the Son of man] must suffer many things and be rejected by this generation (Lk. 17:25).

Are not these sayings indebted to the Prophet of the Exile?

> He was despised and rejected by men; a man of sorrows, and acquainted with grief (Is. 53:3).
> Surely he has borne our griefs and carried our sorrows; yet we esteemed him stricken, smitten by God, and afflicted (Is. 53:4).

48Hunter, *The Work and Words of Jesus*, p. 80.
49See Taylor, *The Life and Ministry of Jesus*, pp. 148–51; T. W. Manson, *The Servant-Messiah*, p. 73; Hunter, *The Work and Words of Jesus*, p. 87; Cullmann, *The Christology of the New Testament*, pp. 51–82; Joachim Jeremias, *New Testament Theology*, tr. John Bowden (New York: Charles Scribner's Sons, 1971), p. 299.

By oppression and judgment he was taken away (Is. 53:8).

Yet it was the will of the Lord to bruise him; he has put him to grief (Is. 53:10).

He poured out his soul to death, and was numbered with the transgressors (Is. 53:12).

The vicarious element in Mark 10:45 ("a ransom *for many*") and Mark 14:24 ("my blood . . . which is poured out *for many*")[50] has its parallel in "He was wounded for our transgressions" (Is. 53:5), "The Lord has laid on him the iniquity of us all" (Is. 53:6), "When he makes himself an offering for sin" (Is. 53:10), "By his knowledge shall the righteous one, my servant, make many to be accounted righteous" (Is. 53:11), and "Yet he bore the sin of many, and made intercession for the transgressors" (Is. 53:12).

Are the sayings in Mark genuine? Do they reflect the thought of Jesus or that of the early church? Clarence Tucker Craig declares that Isaiah 53 "was not given a messianic interpretation in first-century Judaism. Furthermore, Jesus never called himself 'the servant of the Lord,' nor did he quote from the chapter in any genuine passage. Allusions to other passages in Isaiah which modern criticism includes among the 'servant songs' cannot be adduced to substantiate the claim that Jesus had Isa. 53 in mind."[51]

Bornkamm believes it altogether proper that Isaiah 53 be considered one of the essential passion texts of Christianity. "But, however much the text may say to interpret the secret of Jesus' death as a substitutionary atonement, this interpretation strangely enough does not appear at the beginning of the Christian tradition. We find it for the first time in Acts 8:32ff.; Rom. 4:25; I Peter 2:22–25; Heb. 9:28 and in later documents. Even in the passion narrative we meet . . . only a few scattered echoes of Is. 53 . . . but many more of the Suffering Psalms. From the words of Jesus which have been handed down, we can only name one which makes use of Is. 53. 'For the Son of Man also came not to be served, but to serve, and to give his life as a ransom for many' (Mk. 10:45). We must, however, along with many recent exegetes regard this saying, especially since Luke transmits it in simpler form (Lk. 22:27), as a homiletical saying of the primitive Church in Palestine, which interpreted Jesus' life and death in the sense of Is. 53."[52]

---

[50]Emphasis added.

[51]Clarence Tucker Craig, "The Proclamation of the Kingdom," in George Arthur Buttrick, ed., *The Interpreter's Bible* (New York and Nashville: Abingdon Press, 1951), VII, 149. See also Craig's article, "The Identification of Jesus with the Suffering Servant," *Journal of Religion*, XXIV (1944), 240–45. The contention of W. Manson, *Jesus the Messiah*, pp. 140–43, 155, and other scholars that an actual synthesis of the Son-of-God, Servant-of-the-Lord, and Son-of-Man figures had already taken place in pre-Christian Judaism has not received substantial support.

[52]*Jesus of Nazareth*, p. 227. Bultmann, *Theology of the New Testament*, p. 29, had many years earlier reached the conclusion that the passion prophecies in Mark were "prophecies after the event." Tödt, *The Son of Man in the Synoptic Tradition*, pp. 141–221, holds that the alleged dependence of the passion predictions on Isaiah 53 can better be explained as dependence on Ps. 118:22. Although Mk. 10:45a does allude to Is. 53:11, 10:45b is a secondary elaboration of 10:45a which was originally a "present" saying.

Son of David

The title "son of David" is found in Jesus' own words in only one instance in the Synoptics. While in the Temple teaching, Jesus asked,

How can the scribes say that the Christ is the son of David? David himself, inspired by the Holy Spirit, declared, 'The Lord said to my Lord, Sit at my right hand, till I put thy enemies under thy feet.' David himself calls him Lord; so how is he his son? (Mk. 12:35–37a; compare Mt. 22:41–45; Lk. 20:41–44).

This is a difficult saying. Bultmann denies its authenticity and declares that it is an interpolation of the early church.[53] Enslin holds that it is "primitive in essence. It may also evidence an early Christian answer to the Jewish gibe: 'He cannot be the anointed, for he is not of Davidic lineage,' by the counter-retort: 'Davidic lineage is far from being a *sine qua non* [a necessity].' "[54] Those who accept the saying as genuine often see in it not a denial of Jesus' Davidic descent but a declaration that Davidic descent was not decisive. What really mattered was spiritual not physical origin. The Christ is not from man at all, but from God.[55]

Quite apart from the genuineness of this saying, it is generally agreed that Jesus vigorously rejected the idea of a political kingship connected with the title "son of David." His answer to the cleverly cruel question, "Is it lawful to pay taxes to Caesar, or not?" (Mk. 12:14) is revealing. If he had said no, he would have been arrested and convicted of treason. If he had said yes, he would have been judged unpatriotic. His reply was as specific as the delicate situation would permit. "Render to Caesar the things that are Caesar's" (Mk. 12:17) could have meant nothing less than "Pay the taxes." By his answer Jesus repudiated the position of the superpatriots who longed to slit every Roman throat. His repeated injunctions against retaliation and violence are well established. His followers were to go the second mile and turn the other cheek. If they were unaware that "all who take the sword will perish by the sword" (Mt. 26:52), it was no fault of his. He was clearly uninterested in the reestablishment of David's throne and never dreamed of attempting to mount that throne himself. In his hope of the future, sons of David had no preferential place.

The kindred titles "King of Israel" (Mk. 15:32) and "King of the Jews" (Mk. 15:2) are applied to Jesus in the Synoptics, but they are never found on his lips. When Pilate asked Jesus, "Are you the King of the Jews?" Jesus replied, "You have said so."[56] The evangelists understood Jesus' reply to mean "Yes." Pilate thought the answer noncommittal. If he had understood

[53]*Theology of the New Testament*, Vol. I, p. 28. See also Branscomb, *The Gospel of Mark*, pp. 222–25; Fuller, *The Foundations of New Testament Christology*, p. 111. Compare Bornkamm, *Jesus of Nazareth*, p. 228.

[54]*The Prophet from Nazareth*, p. 136.

[55]Cullmann, *The Christology of the New Testament*, p. 131.

[56]Mt. 27:11; Mk. 15:2; Lk. 23:3.

Jesus to have replied in the affirmative, he would have ended the hearing then and there. There could be no king but Caesar. In the name of Rome he would have had to punish anyone making such a claim to power and position. Instead, Pilate continued his interrogation as though Jesus' reply was no reply at all: "Have you no answer to make?" (Mk. 15:4). "You have said so" may have been spoken ironically. It may have been phrased as a question. But if Pilate's reaction can be trusted, it did not mean "yes."[57]

Lord

The word "Lord" translates the divine names "Yahweh" and "Adonai" in English versions of the Old Testament. Its Greek form (*kyrios*) serves the same purpose in the Septuagint and the Greek New Testament. The Greek word, however, has a wide range of meanings. In addition to a name for deity (Acts 2:34), it is used of an angel (Acts 10:4), of Jesus (Lk. 10:1), and of earthly masters (Acts 16:19, where it is translated "owners"). Often it is used as a substitute for "Rabbi" or "Sir" (Mt. 8:6). But at times it constitutes a full confession of faith. Thomas, speaking to the resurrected Jesus, exclaims: "My Lord and my God!" (Jn. 20:28).[58]

Beare thinks that when the word "Lord" was applied to Jesus it implied nothing more than a simple "Sir." It did not connote any religious meaning in the vocative. Jesus was not usually addressed by the title in the Synoptic tradition. When he was (and this is mostly in Luke), these exceptions should be regarded as reflections of later church practice. In the church, "Lord" was a title of worship prompted by the resurrection.[59]

Other scholars maintain that the church's use of "Lord" reflects an honorific title by which Jesus was addressed during his ministry. To be sure, the vocative *kyrie* is found only in Mark 7:28, where it was used by the Syrophoenician woman. But that it was also used by Jesus' disciples is established by the Q sayings in Luke 6:46: "Why do you call me 'Lord, Lord,' and not do what I tell you?" Why would Jesus ask such a question unless he had been called "Lord" and the term meant more than a simple "Sir"? He clearly demanded that what he said should be done. "To call Jesus *mar* [the Aramaic equivalent of *kyrios*]," concludes Fuller, "means not only to accord him an honorific title [such as Rabbi], but to recognize the authority of his enunciation of God's final, absolute demand."[60]

[57]The two instances in which Jesus is offered the title "Son of David" in Mark (10:47–48; 11:10) are church formations. See Fuller, *The Foundations of New Testament Christology*, pp. 111–14.

[58]See S. E. Johnson, "Lord (Christ)," in G. A. Buttrick, ed., *The Interpreter's Dictionary of the Bible* (New York: Abingdon Press, 1962), K–Q, p. 151.

[59]F. W. Beare, *The Earliest Records of Jesus* (New York: Abingdon Press, 1962), pp. 68–69.

[60]R. H. Fuller, *The Foundations of New Testament Christology* (New York: Charles Scribner's Sons, 1965), p. 119. Used by permission. Compare Cullmann, *The Christology of the New Testament*, pp. 195–237; Tödt, *The Son of Man in the Synoptic Tradition*, p. 289; see also pp. 288–92.

Jesus' Self-understanding

We have consulted a score of scholars concerning the question, "What did Jesus think of himself?" A bewildering variety of answers has emerged. Distinguished specialists are sure that Jesus considered himself to be the Messiah. Equally distinguished specialists deny this. Competent critics assert that Jesus identified himself with the Suffering Servant of II Isaiah. Equally competent critics repudiate the assertion. If we had space to examine the work of a second score of scholars, the diversity of thought would be increased. It ranges from one end of the theological spectrum to the other—from prophet to preexistent Son of God. Perhaps the diversity of opinion stems from the fact that "there is not enough record of sayings of Jesus about Jesus to make it possible for independent studies to arrive at the same conclusion."[61]

Despite the paucity of Jesus' sayings about himself and the conflicting conclusions of acknowledged experts on the subject, we are not left entirely in the dark. We can with reasonable certainty make some statements concerning Jesus and his role.

The regular theme of Jesus' sayings was the kingdom, not himself as king. He was so dominated by the desire to proclaim the nearness of the kingdom and the need for repentance that he devoted scant attention to talk about himself. This failure to speak frequently and forthrightly about himself—if, indeed, it can be called a failure—tells us much about Jesus. He thought far more about God than he did about himself.

Jesus possessed a unique sense of authority. Occasionally, as at Nazareth, he spoke of himself as a prophet. He was a prophet. He shared the prophet's stance and the prophet's sense of inner authority. But he was much more than a prophet. He superseded the tradition of the elders and interpreted the Law with sovereign freedom. These interpretations he set forth not as opinions to be examined, but as commands to be obeyed as the will of God. He performed mighty works "by the finger of God" (Lk. 11:20). He summoned men to follow him and pronounced in advance that if they did, their fellowship with him would be confirmed by the Son of Man at the End (Lk. 12:8–9). He was not, then, simply one of a series of prophets proclaiming the eventual coming of the End. He was *the* eschatological prophet—the bearer of God's *final* offer of salvation and judgment. Men who confessed him had their salvation guaranteed. It was, so to speak, proleptically present. No prophet had ever before made such an audacious claim.

Jesus went to Jerusalem, as he had previously gone to Galilee and its environs, to force a decision concerning the impending crisis—the coming of the kingdom. He doubtless understood the dangers involved although the passion predictions are too precise to be considered his exact words.

61Ernest Cadman Colwell, *An Approach to the Teaching of Jesus* (New York and Nashville: Abingdon Press, © 1947), pp. 74–75.

He may even have expected to be repudiated. Nevertheless he went, fully confident that no matter what his fate, God would ultimately vindicate him. This confidence—conceived at his baptism, born in his ministry, and tested in his crucifixion—was confirmed by his resurrection.

The early church viewed Jesus' life and death from the vantage point of his resurrection. It saw his Messianic mission "*in* his words and deeds and *in* the unmediatedness of his historic appearance."[62] The church was not content, however, to call Jesus "Messiah" in the usual Jewish sense. It transposed the term into a higher key. "Messiah" came to express "the faith that he would return and exercise a universal kingship in the age to come, and it gathered into itself all that they [the early Christians] believed about his relationship to God and man."[63] In Mark 1:1 "Christ" is no longer an adjective or a title. It is the last name of Jesus. To it is appended the title "the Son of God." Jesus may well have used "Son" as correlative to "Father." It expressed the fullness of his own personal consciousness of his intimate relationship to God. But to Mark "Son of God" meant much more than this. It "was the title above all others which expressed the growing thought of Greek-speaking Christianity, moving steadily in the direction of Nicaea, Constantinople, and Chalcedon with their monumental affirmations of the doctrine of the Incarnation."[64]

"What becomes of our Christian faith," the reader may ask, "if Jesus and his disciples did not regard him as Messiah?" Johnson's reply is cogent and convincing. "The answer is that the gospel tradition shows that he was conscious of a unique vocation, so great and transcendent that none of the religious terms then in use was capable of expressing it. He knew that he was commissioned, with an authority greater than that of any prophet or king, to teach and lead the people of God. He expected his disciples to obey and follow him, no matter what the cost, not so much for his own sake as for the sake of God and his kingdom. We observe this in the attitudes of Jesus and the disciples more than in any single thing that he said. Furthermore, he regarded his own death as a sacrifice which would avail for the salvation of his people, and at the Last Supper he symbolized this by a solemn ceremony. If Jesus had come making explicit claims and definitions of his nature and authority, the result would have been to restrict man's faith, for no language could express fully how he was related to God and to mankind. As it was, the [New Testament] writers used a great variety of terms, each of which pointed to one aspect of Jesus' person and work, and each of these words in turn took on the coloration of his unique personality. We must also remember—though it is difficult for us to do so—that the question did not have the same interest for Jesus that it has for us. *We* wish to clothe with appropriate language our faith in God in Christ. *He* was far more concerned to do the will of God and to lead men to God than to be praised and worshiped. Even the Fourth Evangelist recognized that Jesus did not seek glory for himself (John 7:16–18; 8:50,54); and this in itself is the hallmark of his character."[65]

[62]Bornkamm, *Jesus of Nazareth*, p. 178.
[63]Johnson, in *The Interpreter's Bible*, VII, 448.
[64]Grant, in *The Interpreter's Bible*, VII, 643.
[65]Johnson, in *The Interpreter's Bible*, VII, 448.

part **6**

The Work Resumed

The ministry which followed Jesus' Baptism and Temptation created great excitement. The essence of the Galilean's message was set forth in the words, "The time is fulfilled, and the kingdom of God is at hand; repent, and believe in the gospel" (Mk. 1:15). Jesus chose twelve disciples, trained them, and sent them out to spread the Good News. He performed mighty works and acquired a reputation as a healer. So great was his popularity that he found it necessary to escape from those who hungered for healings. "Let us go on to the next towns," he said, "that I may preach there also; for that is why I came out" (Mk. 1:38).

Jesus' popularity aroused opposition among the scribes and the Pharisees, the established religious leaders. His friends and relatives viewed his mission with alarm and embarrassment. At the height of his opponents' fury, Jesus withdrew from Galilee. There followed a period of seclusion which is climaxed in the Synoptic records by Peter's Confession and the Transfiguration. Somewhere in the environs of Caesarea Philippi, the disciples are said to have recognized who Jesus really was—the Messiah. A week later, at the Transfiguration, some of them perceived a faint flicker of what this meant—a flicker which Jesus would soon fan into a flame by repeated teaching. His Messiahship would lead to his suffering and death.

When Jesus resumed his public ministry, the scene of his activity shifted. He set his face toward Jerusalem. His purpose was to present his message at the seat of the nation's religious life. We shall now travel with Jesus and his disciples to Jerusalem, examine the attendant teachings, and observe their fateful consequences.

chapter eighteen

The Journey to Jerusalem

Shortly after Peter's Confession and the Transfiguration, Jesus set out for Jerusalem with his disciples. Mark states, "They went on from there [Caesarea Philippi] and passed through Galilee" (9:30). They traveled in secret in order that Jesus could continue to teach the Twelve concerning the coming cross. (Other suggested reasons for secrecy are fear of Herod and danger of a nationalistic uprising.) They halted briefly at Capernaum (9:33). Then they went "to the region of Judea and beyond the Jordan" (10:1), where Jesus taught the crowds as was his custom. An allusion is made to the journey in 10:17 and again in 10:32: "And they were on the road, going up to Jerusalem, and Jesus was walking ahead of them." Finally we are told that Jesus and his disciples passed through Jericho (10:46) and approached Jerusalem by way of Bethphage and Bethany (11:1). Mark's account is succinct and summary, grossly lacking in detailed information. The trip was not so much a journey as a forced march. The pace was rapid, and the purpose was clear. The Master was marching to martyrdom.

Luke's long section (9:51–19:27) at first glance seems to fill in the details left out by Mark. It begins with the comment, "When the days drew near for him to be received up, he set his face to go to Jerusalem" (9:51). Further references to the journey are found in 13:22, 17:11, 18:31, and 19:11. (Luke 9:51–18:14 is a "great insertion" into the framework of Mark's narrative, sometimes called the "travel document.") Closer inspection of the material does not sustain the initial impression. The whole section is composed of numerous separate incidents, parables, and sayings. Many of them may well belong to the Galilean campaign. Their connection is editorial, not historical. Luke, too, it would appear, had scant information about the journey to Jerusalem. The deficiency is not surprising. The last days in the life of Jesus were so tragic and central for the early church that the period preceding them—from the Transfiguration to the Triumphal Entry—was soon reduced to a bare skeleton.

Traveling Teacher

Since the writers of the Synoptics lacked precise geographical and chronological information, they arranged Jesus' stories and sayings topically. It is therefore impossible to give a day-to-day account of the journey to Jerusalem without heavy reliance on pious imagination. It is the total story —not the continuity of the narrative—which has been preserved in the early tradition. As Jesus journeyed, he doubtless experienced many interruptions. At least on occasion he resumed public teaching. We have already considered many of the teachings assigned to this period in the Synoptics. We shall now turn our attention to the principal teachings and incidents which remain.

The Blessing of the Children (188) is a story of singular beauty.[1] The children ("infants" in Luke 18:15) were probably brought to Jesus by their parents. It was a common Jewish custom for rabbis to place their hands on the heads of children or disciples. The blessing was believed to convey actual aid, not just good wishes. In this instance the parents wanted Jesus to touch their children even as he had touched the sick. The disciples were perturbed. They rebuked the children. No reason is given for their action. Did they object to the annoyance? Did they think the kingdom too precious for little ones? Did they want Jesus' blessing reserved for the righteous? No matter! The rebuke provoked Jesus to indignation (omitted by Matthew and Luke) and prompted him to reply: "Let the children come to me, do not hinder them; for to such belongs the kingdom of God. Truly, I say to you, whoever does not receive the kingdom of God like a child shall not enter it" (Mk. 10:14-15). Children are examples of dependence and receptiveness. They trustfully receive from those on whom they depend. "And he took them in his arms and blessed them, laying his hands upon them" (Mk. 10:16). It is small wonder that this scene was soon used to justify infant baptism.[2]

The Rich Young Ruler (189) derives its title from a merging of data found in Matthew ("young," 19:20) and Luke ("a ruler," 18:18, who is "very rich," 18:23).[3] As Jesus was setting out on his journey, Mark informs us, a young man ran and knelt before him. He knelt in sincerity, not flattery.

---

[1]Mt. 19:13–15; Mk. 10:13–16; Lk. 18:15–17.

[2]Mark may have inserted one of the discipleship sayings (vs. 16; compare 9:36) into the anecdote. Matthew omits Mk. 10:16 in his account. Since Mk. 10:14 seems to prize children for their own sake rather than as examples of possessing something which will make kingdom entrance possible, some scholars think that this verse is a separate saying which contradicts 10:15. See F. W. Beare, *The Earliest Records of Jesus* (New York: Abingdon Press, 1962), p. 193.

[3]Mt. 19:16–22; Mk. 10:17–22; Lk. 18:18–23.

He probably hoped Jesus would invite him to become a disciple. " 'Good Teacher," he said to Jesus, "what must I do to inherit eternal life [enter the kingdom]?' And Jesus said to him, 'Why do you call me good? No one is good but God alone' " (10:17–18). Jesus' response underlines the authenticity of the story which later theology found embarrassing. Jesus' goodness soon led his followers to affirm his sinlessness. Matthew, aware of this, altered Mark's account of Jesus' words to read, "Why do you ask me about what is good?" (19:17). But Mark's version (followed by Lk. 18:19) is to be preferred. The perfect goodness of God was a universal doctrine of Judaism. Jesus' humble humanity prompted him to reply as would any pious Jew: "No one is good but God alone."

Jesus remarked that the man knew the commandments. Then Jesus listed five of them and added another one which forbade fraud.[4] The man declared that he had kept them all from his youth—probably from his bar mitzvah about the age of twelve when he became a son of the Law and reached religious adulthood. "And Jesus looking upon him loved him [a rare statement of affection which is omitted by Matthew and Luke—perhaps because the man later refused to become a disciple], and said to him, 'You lack one thing;[5] go, sell what you have, and give to the poor, and you will have treasure in heaven; and come, follow me.' At that saying his countenance fell, and he went away sorrowful, for he had great possessions" (Mk. 10:21–22). To give "to the poor" was a religious duty in Judaism. To "sell what you have" for that purpose was not. The rich were expected to give alms but not to give all. Jesus did not normally demand that prospective disciples dispose of their wealth; yet in this instance he did. He evidently perceived a deep-seated defect in the "rich young ruler." He preferred his possessions to the priceless kingdom.

The Danger of Riches (189) is driven home by the words Jesus spoke as the young man departed.[6] "How hard it will be for those who have riches to enter the kingdom of God! . . . It is easier for a camel to go through the eye of a needle than for a rich man to enter the kingdom of God" (Mk. 10:23,25).[7] Various attempts have been made to emasculate the teaching. (1) Some sources read "rope" or "ship's cable" (kamilos) instead of "camel" (kamēlos).[8] It is therefore argued that Jesus never mentioned the difficulty of a camel going through the eye of a needle, but rather that of a rope or ship's cable—as if it would be substantially easier to thread a rope or cable through a needle's eye! (2) It is also argued that the needle's eye symbolized a gate, a small postern entrance beside the large city gate, used after dark.

---

[4] Matthew omits "Do not defraud" and adds "You shall love your neighbor as yourself" (19:19).

[5] Matthew has "If you would be perfect" (19:21) which may imply a double standard —one for the ordinary person and another more rigorous one for the saint. For a convincing refutation of this idea see Gerhard Barth, in G. Bornkamm, G. Barth, and H. J. Held, Tradition and Interpretation in Matthew, tr. Percy Scott (London: SCM Press, 1963), pp. 95–101.

[6] Mt. 19:23–26; Mk. 10:23–27; Lk. 18:24–27.

[7] Mk. 10:24 is a colorful variant omitted by Matthew and Luke.

[8] Cyril of Alexandria, a few late Greek manuscripts, and the Armenian version.

It could be entered by a loaded camel only on its knees. The implication is that only thus can a rich man enter the kingdom. Grant's comment is germane: "But such a gate was far too small for a camel, loaded or unloaded; and who ever saw a camel crawl on its four knees!"9 (3) The later manuscripts of Mark 10:24 read "how hard it is *for those who trust in riches* to enter the kingdom of God!"10

The disciples were astonished at Jesus' hard saying. "Then who can be saved?" they asked (Mk. 10:26).11 They evidently shared the view that riches were a mark of righteousness. If the righteous—that is, blessed by God and therefore rich—cannot enter the kingdom, who can? "With men it is impossible," replied Jesus, "but not with God; for all things are possible with God" (Mk. 10:27). It is not impossible for a rich man to enter the kingdom. But he runs greater risks. He is tempted to become wedded to his wealth, to become the servant of his substance instead of the servant of the Lord. Nevertheless, God, in his infinite mercy, can invite him to come in. The story of Zacchaeus is proof that a penitent person of wealth can be saved (Lk. 19:1–10). Jesus' warning about wealth is dressed in hyperbole. He did not intend it to be visualized or vitiated but to be taken seriously.12

Jesus and the Sons of Zebedee (192) indicates both the giver and the ground of greatness.13 The story in Mark falls naturally into two parts (10:35–40 and 41–45), each of which is composite. James and John moved abreast of Jesus on the road and made a childlike request: " 'Teacher, we want you to do for us whatever we ask of you.' And he said to them, 'What do you want me to do for you?' And they said to him, 'Grant us to sit, one at your right hand and one at your left, in your glory' " (10:35–37). Matthew (20:20–22), apparently to protect the good name of the disciples, transfers the question to the mouth of their mother. Jesus' reply, though, is addressed to the brothers. The right hand and the left were positions of greatest honor in a monarch's court. The evangelists had the age to come in mind. "Your glory" originally stood for the glory of God (Mk. 8:38) which would surround the supernatural king of the future. James and John appear to hope that Jesus would enter Jerusalem, expel the Romans, and rule in glory. If so, their request was for chief cabinet seats in the new monarchy.

Jesus' response was immediate. "You do not know what you are asking. Are you able to drink the cup that I drink, or to be baptized with the baptism with which I am baptized?' [The cup stands not for joy and success

---

9Grant, in *The Interpreter's Bible*, VII, 807.

10Emphasis added.

11Luke states that Jesus spoke to the rich man (18:24) and the astonishment was in the crowd rather than in the disciples (18:26).

12The verses which follow (Mt. 19:27–30; Mk. 10:28–31; Lk. 18:28–30; 22:28–30) are permeated with interests of the early church. Mt. 19:28, not found in Mk. or Lk., is an early church saying patterned after Jesus' authentic Son-of-Man utterances. See H. E. Tödt, *The Son of Man in the Synoptic Tradition*, tr. D. M. Barton (London: SCM Press, 1965), pp. 62–64. Such phrases as "for my sake and for the gospel" (Mk. 10:29) and "with persecutions" (Mk. 10:30) are clearly secondary.

13Mt. 20:20–28; Mk. 10:35–45; Lk. 22:24–27.

(Pss. 23:5; 116:13) but for suffering (Pss. 11:6; 75:8; Is. 51:17; Mk. 14:36). The baptism stands for the disaster (Pss. 42:7; 69:2; Is. 43:2; Lk. 12:50) which he will undergo.] And they said to him, 'We are able.' And Jesus said to them, 'The cup that I drink you will drink; and with the baptism with which I am baptized, you will be baptized; but to sit at my right hand or at my left is not mine to grant, but it is for those for whom it has been prepared' " (Mk. 10:38–40). James was martyred under Herod Agrippa about 44 A.D. (Acts 12:2). John's early death is not certain but probable. It is supported by Jesus' prediction (which Mark and Matthew would hardly have stressed if both James and John had not been martyred), a tradition ascribed to the second-century writer Papias, the Syrian church calendar, and other sources. Against it are the traditional interpretation of John 21 and the story of John's death in Ephesus. "But to sit at my right hand or at my left . . ." is not for Jesus to grant. This fateful decision has been determined ". . . by my Father" (Mt. 20:23).[14]

The ten other disciples were indignant that James and John had stolen a march on them. But Jesus dealt as skillfully with the ten as he had with the blatantly ambitious two: "You know that those who are supposed to rule over the Gentiles lord it over them, and their great men exercise authority over them. [This is a caustic comment. The words "rule" and "lord it over them" lay bare the manners and morals of earthly rulers. Perhaps Mark had seen the seamy side of Roman rule under Nero, and Palestine had experienced similar indignities under Pontius Pilate during Jesus' ministry.] But it shall not be so among you; but whoever would be great among you must be your servant, and whoever would be first among you must be slave of all" (Mk. 10:42–44). The word translated "servant" is *diakonos* from which the term "deacon" is derived. "Slave" (*doulos*) denotes one who is called by God to a special service (Josh. 1:1; Jer. 7:25; Rom. 1:1). In poetic parallelism, Jesus proclaimed that the ground of greatness is service.

As final proof that service is the ground of greatness, the Son of Man is cited as one who "came not to be served but to serve, and to give his life as a ransom for many" (Mk. 10:45). This famous saying is often taken as a reiteration by Jesus of his Servant role and as the first clear-cut pronouncement of the purpose of his death. "Ransom" (*lutron*) was a word with multiple meanings. It was (1) the price paid to free a slave or to compensate for a crime, (2) the price Hebrews gave to the Lord to prevent a plague (Num. 3:51), (3) the price paid in place of the sacrifice of the first-born (Num. 18:15), and (4) the offering of the Suffering Servant who "poured out his soul to death" and "bore the sin of many" (Is. 53:12). Since the idea of ransom is rare in the Synoptics, and since Luke's version of the saying (22:27) contains no reference to "a ransom for many," not a few scholars have concluded that this interpretation of Jesus' death stems from the early

---

[14]Scholars who regard Mk. 10:38–40 as secondary point out how naturally vs. 41 connects with vs. 37. Others regard vss. 38–39 as secondary, but they may have a better claim to authenticity than vs. 40, which appears to be a drastic revision of an earlier saying. The composite nature of 10:35–45 can be seen by the different answers in vs. 38 and vs. 40 and by the latter's contradiction of the teaching of 10:41–45.

church. Other scholars maintain that the idea that the death of the righteous atoned for others was a rabbinical doctrine. Jesus employed it at the Last Supper: "This is my blood of the covenant, which is poured out for many" (Mk. 14:24). "So primitive, so Jewish, so scriptural . . . , so non- (if not pre-) Pauline a phrase [as the final clause of Mk. 10:45] is likely to be pre-Marcan as well, and should be understood in as simple and figurative . . . a sense as possible, rather than with a fully developed theological meaning. If so understood, it may well be accepted as authentic. Jesus is aware of his impending destiny. A divine necessity confronts him . . . , and he is prepared to accept it. But his destiny . . . has a meaning; that meaning is one which stands in closest relation to the purpose of God for his people—the 'many' were the nation, then the world, then the church of God called out of many races and tongues. This saying does not formulate a theology of the Atonement, but it is one of the data upon which any theology of the Atonement must inevitably rest."[15] The sudden shift in thought, however, from that of service (10:45a) to that of sacrifice (10:45b) strongly suggests that the latter is a secondary theological comment. Although Jesus offered himself as a model for service, he did not offer himself as a model for ransom. His followers subsequently lay down their lives for him and the Gospel, but their martyr's deaths were not "a ransom for many."[16]

The Blind Bartimaeus (193) received his sight at Jericho.[17] This city was on Jesus' route to Jerusalem by way of the Jordan Valley. It stood in striking contrast to Jerusalem—3,300 feet lower in altitude, hemmed in by the jungle of the Jordan to the north, the flat mountains of Moab to the east, the sparkling Dead Sea to the south, and the Judean highlands to the west. Herod the Great had built a magnificent winter palace there, and residents could boast of a hippodrome, a theater, and swimming pools. Fertile, irrigated fields—filled with balsam and palm groves—surrounded the villas of the rich.

The Bartimaeus story is the last example of Jesus' healing ministry in Mark. It may have been placed at this point in the tradition for a purpose. Mark's other story of the healing of a blind man (8:22–26) is recorded just prior to Peter's Confession—when Peter's eyes were opened—and the Transfiguration. The Bartimaeus narrative also involves a confession of Messiahship, and it is located immediately before the great events of the Triumphal Entry, Temple Cleansing, Crucifixion, and Resurrection. The story reads like an eyewitness account. Jesus departed from Jericho with his disciples and a great crowd.[18] Bartimaeus, a blind beggar, was sitting by the roadside. When rumor reached him that Jesus of Nazareth was passing by, he shouted an appeal for help: " 'Jesus, Son of David, have mercy on me!' And many rebuked him, telling him to be silent ["Son of David" was a Messianic

---

15Grant, in *The Interpreter's Bible*, VII, 819.

16See Tödt's excellent analysis of Mk. 10:45 in *The Son of Man in the Synoptic Tradition*, pp. 202–211.

17Mt. 20:29–34; Mk. 10:46–52; Lk. 18:35–43.

18Luke 18:35 places the story at the time of the entrance of Jesus into Jericho, perhaps to make room for the account concerning Zacchaeus which is to follow.

title with potent political connotations—it could arouse revolutionary hopes in the Jews and repressive measures by the Romans]; but he cried out all the more, 'Son of David, have mercy on me!' [Until this point in Mark only demoniacs had recognized Jesus by this name, and they had been silenced. Here the title received no rebuke for it would soon be proclaimed in Jerusalem.] And Jesus stopped and said, 'Call him.' And they [who had previously rebuked Bartimaeus] called the blind man, saying to him, 'Take heart; rise, he is calling you.' And throwing off his mantle he sprang up and came to Jesus. And Jesus said to him, 'What do you want me to do for you?' ["As a good teacher and pastor he encouraged others to express their wishes, hopes, aspirations, and gave opportunity to them to express their faith, upon which he could then act and build."[19]] And the blind man said to him, 'Master, let me receive my sight.' And Jesus said to him, 'Go your way; your faith has made you well.' And immediately he received his sight and followed him on the way" (Mk. 10:47–52).[20]

The Story of Zacchaeus (194) is found only in Luke (19:1–10). Zacchaeus, "the pure one," was a wealthy tax collector in Jericho, one of the richest districts in Palestine. Indeed, he was a chief tax collector. Jericho, with its balsam trade and traffic from the eastern to the western side of the Jordan, required many collectors. As Jesus passed through the city, Zacchaeus made repeated efforts to see him.[21] But he was frustrated by the density of the crowd and by his own small stature. So he ran on ahead of the crowd, climbed a sycamore tree, and awaited the procession. "And when Jesus came to the place, he looked up and said to him 'Zacchaeus [how he knew his name is not explained], make haste and come down; for I must stay at your house today.' So he made haste and came down, and received him joyfully. And when they saw it they all murmured [the disciples as well as the crowd], 'He has gone in to be the guest of a man who is a sinner.' [Although Zacchaeus was a Jew, he was judged a sinner because of his business. Since he was a chief tax collector, he was regarded as a great sinner—utterly unfit to be Jesus' host.] And Zacchaeus stood and said to the Lord, 'Behold, Lord, the half of my goods I give to the poor [the present tense is used to express purpose for the future, not past practice]; and if I have defrauded any one of anything, I restore it fourfold.'[22] [The Law required stolen sheep to be returned fourfold and stolen money or goods to be doubled (Ex. 22:1–7). In effect then Zacchaeus declared that henceforth he would be a good Jew.] And Jesus said to him, 'Today salvation has come to this house, since he also is a son of Abraham. For the Son of man came to seek and to save the lost' " (Lk. 19:5–10). Jesus did not invite Zacchaeus to become a disciple as he had invited Levi. Neither did he demand that

---

[19]Grant, in The Interpreter's Bible, VII, 822.

[20]Matthew reports that two beggars were cured. Perhaps he wanted (1) to magnify the miracle or (2) to make up for omitting Mark's earlier one (8:22–26) by combining the two accounts.

[21]The Greek verb translated "sought" is imperfect, which indicates continuous effort.

[22]If Zacchaeus could give half of his goods to the poor and have enough left to make multifold restitutions, his exactions must have been minimal.

he give all of his goods to the poor as he had in the case of the Rich Young Ruler. He simply declared that salvation had come to him and his family. Popular prejudice against this publican was passé. He was no longer to be treated as a social leper but as a true son of Abraham. "Salvation" is a word not found elsewhere in Jesus' teaching. Its meaning here is found in the mission of the Son of Man to seek and save the lost such as Zacchaeus.[23]

Entry into Jerusalem (196)[24]

Although there is little to justify such a description, the entry of Jesus into Jerusalem is commonly called triumphal. Jesus drew near to Bethphage (House of Figs) and Bethany (House of Dates). The geographical details are confusing. Matthew mentions only Bethphage (of uncertain location), a little-known suburb of the Holy City. Medieval tradition placed it midway between Bethany and Jerusalem. This would make Mark's order incorrect. Bethany was a village about two miles southeast of Jerusalem. According to the Fourth Gospel, it was the home of Lazarus and his sisters, Mary and Martha (Jn. 12:1–3).

Jesus instructed two of his disciples to go "into the village opposite you, and immediately as you enter it you will find a colt tied, on which no one has ever sat; untie it and bring it. If any one says to you, 'Why are you doing this?' say, 'The Lord has need of it and will send it back here immediately' " (Mk. 11:2–3). "The Lord" is an unusual designation for Jesus in Mark, but it was an integral part of the language of the early church. Perhaps Jesus had arranged for the animal in advance, and "the Lord has need of it" was the password. Maybe the owner was a friend. Possibly the account is intended to emphasize Jesus' omniscience. Gilmour asserts that "to interpret the mysterious details of these verses as an indication that the entry had been prearranged is an unwarranted rationalization of the narrative."[25] Newness had a quality of sacredness to the Semites. The first fruits, the new moon, the first-born son, the first year of marriage were all honored. The colt "on which no one has ever sat" had a similar significance for the evangelists. A sacred animal must bear the Messianic king. Matthew, apparently misreading Messianic prophecy, doubled the animals (21:2). In perfect poetic parallelism (in which the second line of a couplet expresses the same idea as the first) Zechariah had spoken of only one animal.

23There are striking parallels between the story of Zacchaeus and the story of Levi (Mk. 2:13–17; Lk. 5:27–32; compare Mt. 9:9–13). Both concern tax collectors. Both show how Jesus shocked the Jews by accepting the hospitality of an outcast. Both lead up to a saying which is essentially the same. Consequently, some scholars think the Zacchaeus narrative is a variant of the Levi story. See Gilmour, in *The Interpreter's Bible*, VIII, 320–26. The charming detail of the short Zacchaeus climbing the sycamore tree is unlikely. The narrow streets of the town would have had no room for trees. Perhaps the incident took place outside the town.

24Mt. 21:1–9; Mk. 11:1–10; Lk. 19:28–38.

25Gilmour, in *The Interpreter's Bible*, VIII, 336.

Rejoice greatly, O daughter of Zion!
  Shout aloud, O daughter of Jerusalem!
Lo, your king comes to you;
  triumphant and victorious is he,
humble and riding on an ass,
  on a colt the foal of an ass.[26]

Matthew not only doubled the animals ("the ass and the colt") but he had Jesus perform the difficult feat of riding on both of them at once (21:7).

When the two disciples returned, "they brought the colt to Jesus, and threw their garments on it; and he sat upon it. And many spread their garments on the road, and others spread leafy branches which they had cut from the fields" (Mk. 11:7–8). These were Oriental acts of homage. Luke omits all reference to vegetation. Matthew speaks of branches which were cut from the trees (21:8). John alone mentions the great crowd which came out from Jerusalem with "branches of palm trees" to meet Jesus (12:12–13).[27] "And those who went before and those who followed cried out, 'Hosanna! ["Save now!" The ejaculation is found in the Hallel (Ps. 118:25) which was sung at the Feasts of Tabernacles and Passover. It was addressed to a king (II Sam. 14:4) or to God on behalf of a king (Ps. 20:9).] Blessed is he who comes in the name of the Lord! [This is found in Ps. 118:26. It originally referred to the pilgrim on his way to the festival, but Mark understood it to refer to Jesus, the Messiah.] Blessed is the kingdom of our father David that is coming!' " (Mk. 11:9–10). This last verse, omitted by Matthew and Luke, turns the pilgrimage into a Messianic demonstration.

The entry of Jesus into Jerusalem has been variously viewed. (1) Some see it as prophecy transformed into history by the early church. Zechariah had long ago predicted that the Messiah would enter the Holy City riding on an ass, and he had summoned the people to offer him homage. The early church, convinced that Jesus was the Messiah, constructed the entry into Jerusalem to meet the requirements of Zechariah's prophecy. (2) Others hold that the entry is an actual fulfillment of Zechariah 9:9 which Jesus carried out in accordance with a preconceived plan. He knew that he was the Messiah—either from the beginning, from the Baptism, or as the result of a gradual awakening. This knowledge he tacitly confirmed near Caesarea Philippi but insisted that it be kept secret. As he approached Jerusalem, he cast caution to the winds. He mounted the arranged-for animal and entered the Holy City to the Messianic acclaim of the disciples and other pilgrims. The entry was a deliberate symbolic act by which Jesus publicly proclaimed the real nature of his Messiahship. He was not a mighty military ruler rid-

---

[26]Zech. 9:9, emphasis added. Mt. 21:5a is actually taken from Isaiah 62:11. In the quotation from Zech. 9:9, Matthew follows the Septuagint exactly through "your king is coming to you." Then he omits "just and a savior." This enables him to stress the following word, "humble." The lowliness and humiliation of Jesus are frequent themes in Matthew. See Gerhardt Barth, in *Tradition and Interpretation in Matthew*, pp. 129–31.

[27]Since palm trees do not grow in the vicinity of Jerusalem, these branches must have been brought up from Jericho for festive purposes.

The Mount of Olives overlooks the Holy City. At the extreme left is the Garden of Gethsemane, with the Church of the Agony (Church of All Nations) to the right. A Russian Orthodox Church is seen in the picture just to the left of center. Both the road on the left and the one on the right lead to Bethany, whence Jesus entered Jerusalem. In the foreground, out of the picture, is the Dome of the Rock, built on the approximate site of the Jewish Temple.

ing on a horse but a humble man of peace astride an ass. (3) Still others maintain that the entry is the product of both fact and interpretation. The theory that the entry is an invention based on Zechariah 9:9 is not convincing. Why would the early church choose this particular prophecy, which played no significant role in earlier Messianic speculation, from which to spin a legend? From what source did the church get such details as the cutting of the foliage and the particular shouts of the crowd recorded in Mark? They are not found in Zechariah. The theory that Jesus prearranged the entry and patterned it after Zechariah 9:9 is equally unconvincing. Would Jesus have resorted to such a dramatic demonstration of his mission? If so—and if the manner of the entry was obviously Messianic—why was not this fact presented at the trial as proof of Jesus' treasonable ambitions? "Probably Jesus did enter Jerusalem astride an ass—not an uncommon method of journeying—accompanied by exultant and expectant pilgrims who were looking for the speedy inauguration of the kingdom of God. At a later time messianic elements were imposed on the account under the influence of the prophecy in Zech. 9:9. An [Old Testament] passage helped to shape the narrative as we have it, but did not create it."[28]

[28]Gilmour, in *The Interpreter's Bible*, VIII, 335.

Number of Visits

The Synoptic Gospels mention only one visit of Jesus to Jerusalem during his public ministry. This occurred at the close of his career and was terminated by the crucifixion. Mark's chronology, which differs at points from that in Matthew and Luke, is clearly discernible.

Sunday ("Palm"): Entry into Jerusalem and return to Bethany (11:1–11)

Monday: Cursing of the fig tree and cleansing of the Temple (11:12–19)

Tuesday: Parables, controversy stories, and other teachings (11:20–13:37)

Wednesday: Anointing at Bethany and Judas' betrayal (14:1–11)

Thursday: Passover preparation, Last Supper, prayer in Gethsemane, arrest, trial before Sanhedrin (14:12–72)

Friday: Trial before Pilate, condemnation, crucifixion, burial (15:1–47)

Saturday: Jesus in the tomb

Sunday (Easter): Resurrection (16:1–8)

The Fourth Gospel, on the other hand, suggests that Jesus made four or five visits to Jerusalem during his ministry.[29] The Synoptics themselves seem to support a Jerusalem ministry by Jesus prior to the last week. (1) Jesus' lament over Jerusalem implies not one but several appeals to that city: "O Jerusalem, Jerusalem, killing the prophets and stoning those who are sent to you! *How often* would I have gathered your children together as a hen gathers her brood under her wings, and you would not!"[30] (2) Jesus had friends in and near Jerusalem—Mary and Martha in Bethany (Lk. 10:38–42), the provider of the borrowed colt (Mk. 11:1–6), Simon the leper in Bethany (Mk. 14:3), and the owner of the house where the Last Supper was held (Mk. 14:12–16). (3) Opposition to Jesus was already far advanced. It is difficult to explain the bitter hostility of the Jerusalem authorities if this brief visit were his first. (4) While Jesus was no lover of the letter of the Law, he was a Jew. Jews were accustomed to attend the principal feasts in Jerusalem. It is unlikely that Jesus and his disciples completely disregarded this religious practice. (5) After the resurrection the church originated in Jerusalem—not Galilee where Jesus had had his main ministry. According to Acts 1:15, about 120 disciples assembled prior to Pentecost. Although the group probably included many Galileans besides the apostles, there were doubtless more than a few Jerusalemites among them.

Numerous efforts have been made to reconstruct the ministry of Jesus from the Transfiguration to the "Triumphal" Entry. Perhaps the most con-

---

[29]See p. 165.
[30]Mt. 23:37; Lk. 13:34. Emphasis added.

vincing work has been done by Maurice Goguel.[31] Goguel argues that Jesus left Galilee with his disciples shortly before the Feast of Tabernacles in September or October (compare Jn. 7:2). He taught in Jerusalem until the Feast of Dedication in December (compare Jn. 10:22). Soon afterwards he retired across the river Jordan into Perea (compare Jn. 10:40; 11:54). There he remained until shortly before the fateful Passover. Then he returned for the final Entry (Mt. 21:1; Mk. 11:1; Lk. 19:28-29; Jn. 12:1) which quickly led to his arrest and execution.

Goguel's hypothesis is predicated on the historicity of numerous statements in the Fourth Gospel. Scholars are increasingly recognizing that there is history in the Fourth Gospel in addition to its interpretative elements. Unfortunately Goguel's bare outline cannot be filled in with much certainty because of the special characteristics of the Fourth Gospel and the paucity of information in the Synoptics. It may be, as Vincent Taylor suggests, that we are justified in fitting into Goguel's larger framework some of the controversy stories found in Mark 11:27–33 and 12:13–17—especially those concerning authority, the resurrection, and David's son.[32] But it is well to keep in mind that "the units of the gospel tradition at one time circulated independently of one another. The church did not often recall when and where a given saying was first spoken."[33] Although the theory of an extended Jerusalem ministry for Jesus is well supported by data found in all four Gospels, the precise reconstruction of that ministry remains a matter of conjecture. Our subsequent treatment of it will be based mainly on the Synoptic account.

[31]*The Life of Jesus*, pp. 400–428.
[32]*The Life and Ministry of Jesus*, p. 167.
[33]Johnson, in *The Interpreter's Bible*, VII, 500.

chapter nineteen

The Jerusalem Ministry

As pilgrims rounded the shoulder of the Mount of Olives, the Holy City broke into view across the Kidron Valley. Just inside the city wall, the Temple—goal of their journey—stood silhouetted against the western sky. Its gleaming, gold-encrusted stones reached heavenward as did clouds of smoke from the great altar. Nearby rose the tower of Antonia, and beyond it, at the edge of the city, stood Herod's Palace and the Citadel. Jerusalem was a city of incredible beauty and vibrant memories.

Jesus was a Jew. He shared his people's pride in the Holy City. The Psalmist had cried, "If I forget you, O Jerusalem, let my right hand wither! Let my tongue cleave to the roof of my mouth, if I do not remember you, if I do not set Jerusalem above my highest joy!" (Ps. 137:5-6). Yet Jerusalem reminded Jesus of frustrated efforts to arouse the city and the nation. "Would that even today," he declared, "you knew the things that make for peace!" (Lk. 19:42). Like Jeremiah, he heard the alarms of war resounding in his ears long before the days of actual conflict. He pictured the fate of his people as their enemies would surround the city on every side and dash the Temple to the ground, leaving not one stone upon another (Lk. 19:43–44). Twoscore years later, the Romans grimly fulfilled his prediction.

Cursing the Fig Tree (199, 201)[1]

According to Mark, Jesus went into the Temple as soon as he entered Jerusalem. When "he had looked around at everything, as it was already

[1]Mt. 21:18–22 (6:14); Mk. 11:12–14,20–25.

late, he went out to Bethany with the twelve. On the following day, when they came from Bethany, he was hungry. [Does this suggest an early hour or the failure to secure provisions because of the press of pilgrims?] And seeing in the distance a fig tree in leaf [a promise of figs?], he went to see if he could find anything on it. When he came to it, he found nothing but leaves, for it was not the season for figs. And he said to it. 'May no one ever eat fruit from you again.' And his disciples heard it" (11:11–14). As they passed by the next morning, "they saw the fig tree withered away to its roots" (11:20). Matthew states that the fig tree withered "at once" (21:19) after Jesus addressed it. Luke makes no mention of the incident, but he does record the parable of the Barren Fig Tree (13:6–9).

This is a curious story for several reasons. (1) The teachings concerning faith and prayer, valid as they are, do not fit the situation here. Both Matthew (17:20) and Luke (17:6) make use of them in other contexts. (2) Jesus is out of character when he curses a fig tree. (3) Matthew and Mark disagree as to when the tree withered. No doubt the evangelists tell the story to illustrate Jesus' marvelous power, but power used in such a way hardly coheres with his purpose or practice.

Theories concerning the "cursing" abound. (1) It is a developed form of the parable of the Barren Fig Tree (Lk. 13:6–9), which Luke omits because he has already recorded the original. The ancients told such stories to drive home lessons. They did not ask whether they were true to life. The rabbis held that any curse, especially that of a righteous man, might be effective. The sterile fig tree symbolized Israel. If she did not soon bear fruit, she would be destroyed. This theory may be correct, but if the "cursing" developed from the original parable, the point has been destroyed along with the tree. The original parable stressed that Israel's time for repentance was short, not that she could never bear fruit again. (2) The "cursing" actually occurred. Jesus acted out a parable to demonstrate to the disciples that barren lives bring condemnation. But if this were the case, would not the point of such a "parable" have been treasured more than its setting? (3) The disciples mistook a natural phenomenon for a miracle. Jesus' words to the tree were not a curse but a poetic observation after the manner of the prophets. The "curse" may actually have been based on a careful scrutiny of the tree's condition. "The fig tree's barrenness suggests some weakness [Since the fig tree was in full leaf, as Mark states, figs might normally be expected on it, though not ripe ones]: a hard frost on a cold night in the early spring, followed by hot sunshine, might naturally have accomplished its decease."[2] The next day Peter made an erroneous deduction. When he saw the withered fig tree, he remembered Jesus' words of the day before and concluded that they had caused the tree to wither. "Jerusalem is some 4,000 feet [actually about 3,300 feet] above the level of Jericho and as a consequence the Jericho season is several weeks ahead of that of Jerusalem. When in the Jordan valley Jesus had probably eaten figs and may not have realised that the season for figs had not yet come in Jerusalem."[3] (4) The

[2]Major, in *The Mission and Message of Jesus*, p. 144.
[3]Major, in *The Mission and Message of Jesus*, p. 144.

actual incident is lost. "It is wise in such a situation to confess our inability to discover from the fragmentary evidence what the original facts in the case were."[4] As the story now stands, it contains no moral or religious value for modern readers.

Cleansing the Temple (200)[5]

When Jesus entered the Temple he "looked round at everything" (Mk. 11:11). We may profitably do likewise, using as our guide the plan of the Temple area on p. 330. A great court encircled the entire sanctuary. It was called "The Mountain of the House" (J) or "The Court of the Gentiles." While this area belonged to the Temple, it was not considered holy ground. Gentiles, and Jews who had defiled themselves by contact with corpses, were permitted here. So were the sellers of wine and sacrificial animals. Their booths surrounded the inner courts on three sides. Here money-changers set up their tables during the week of Adar 25–Nisan 1. A wall separated the Court of the Gentiles from the sacred precincts. In front of the wall was a low balustrade which Jews called the *soreg* (hedge). Between the hedge and the wall was a space (the *peribolos*) which contained stone tablets warning visitors to be wary: "Let no gentile enter within the hedge and the *peribolos* around the sanctuary. Whoever is caught shall have himself to blame for his consequent death."[6] Beyond the balustrade, up a dozen steps, and through a gateway, lay the Court of the Women (G). Women were not permitted to advance beyond this area. The court's four corners contained chambers for the storage and inspection of wood (for worms), for the storage of wine, for the inspection of lepers who claimed to be cured, and for the purification of those who had failed to follow through on Nazarite vows. Beyond the Court of the Women, on a raised terrace separated by a high wall, was the holy area of the actual sanctuary. Only a narrow strip on the east side was open to laymen. It was called the Court of Israel (F). West of it was the Court of the Priests (E). Three steps and a ramp led to the Altar (C). West of the Altar, and separated from it by an open space, was the House (A), the Temple proper. The House had a high Porch (B) with pillars. From its steps, priests gave the benediction connected with the morning and evening sacrifices. Behind the Porch could be seen the great curtain (Mt. 27:51) which separated the Holy Place from the Holy of Holies where God "resided" and into which only the High Priest could enter, and he but once a year.

When Jesus had "looked round at everything," states Mark, "as it was already late, he went out to Bethany with the Twelve" (11:11). On the following day he returned from Bethany, "cursed" the fig tree on the way,

[4]Branscomb, *The Gospel of Mark*, p. 201.

[5]Mt. 21:12–13; Mk. 11:15–19; Lk. 19:45–48.

[6]This warning, written in Greek, is from one of the tablets which has been preserved. It is quoted from *Bible Atlas*, by Emil G. Kraeling, p. 400. Copyright © 1956 by Rand McNally & Company, publishers, N.Y. We are indebted to Kraeling's description of the Temple area.

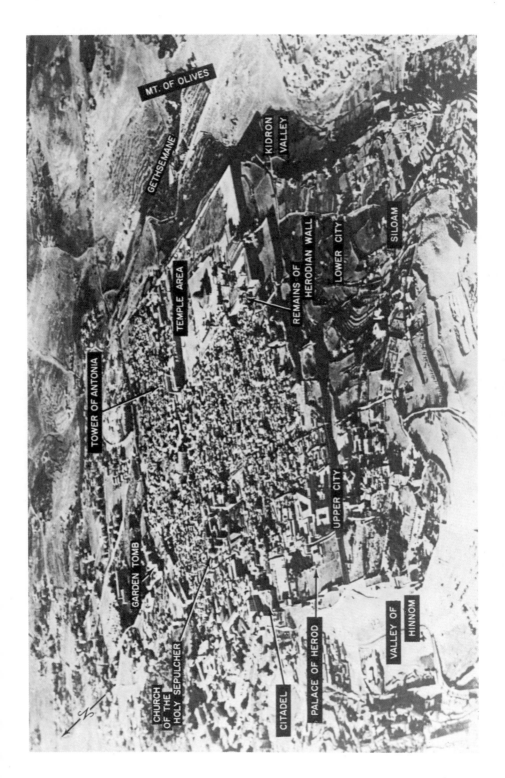

MT. OF OLIVES

GETHSEMANE

KIDRON VALLEY

SILOAM

REMAINS OF HERODIAN WALL

LOWER CITY

TEMPLE AREA

TOWER OF ANTONIA

GARDEN TOMB

CHURCH OF THE HOLY SEPULCHER

UPPER CITY

CITADEL

PALACE OF HEROD

VALLEY OF HINNOM

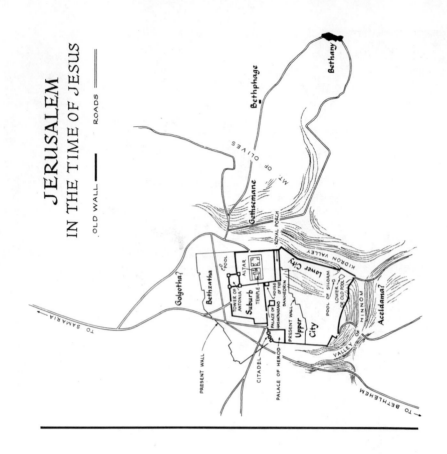

JERUSALEM
IN THE TIME OF JESUS

OLD WALL ——— ROADS ———

TO SAMARIA

PRESENT WALL

Golgotha

Bethzatha

Pool

ALTAR

TOWER OF
ANTONIA

TEMPLE

Suburb

HOUSE OF
CAIAPHAS

PALACE OF
HASMONEANS

SANHEDRIN

PRESENT WALL

Upper
City

CITADEL

PALACE OF HEROD

POOL OF SILOAM

LOWER
OLD POOL

Lower City

KIDRON VALLEY

VALLEY OF HINNOM

Aceldama?

TO BETHLEHEM

ROYAL PORCH

Gethsemane

MT OF OLIVES

Bethphage

Bethany

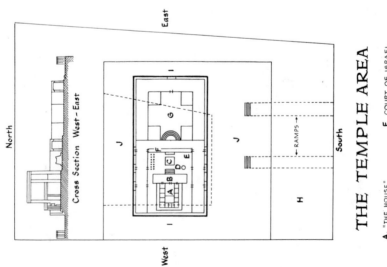

North

Cross Section West – East

West

East

South

J

J

G

F
C
A B
D
E

I

H

← RAMPS →

THE TEMPLE AREA

A. "THE HOUSE"
B. PORCH
C. ALTAR
D. LAVER
E. COURT OF THE PRIESTS

F. COURT OF ISRAEL
G. COURT OF WOMEN
H. ROYAL PORCH
I. SURROUNDING WALL
J. MOUNTAIN OF THE HOUSE

and "entered the temple and began to drive out those who sold and those who bought" (11:15). Matthew (21:12) and Luke (19:45) evidently find it difficult to imagine Jesus calmly looking about the Temple on Sunday and returning in the white heat of anger on Monday. They place the Temple Cleansing on the same day as the Entry. Moreover, for Matthew, a Monday Cleansing would be contrary to a literal fulfillment of prophecy. Malachi, who condemned the priesthood, declared: "Behold, I send my messenger to prepare the way before me, and the Lord whom you seek will *suddenly* come to his temple; the messenger of the covenant in whom you delight, behold, he is coming, says the Lord of hosts. But who can endure the day of his coming, and who can stand when he appears?"[7] In the Fourth Gospel the Cleansing occurs on the occasion of Jesus' first visit to Jerusalem prior to the opening of the Galilean campaign (2:13–22).

It is unlikely that there were two Temple Cleansings. The details are substantially the same in all accounts, and no Gospel records more than one such event. Which dating then is to be preferred—the one in the Synoptics or the one in John? Such a "rebuke of, and challenge to, the authorities seems to belong more naturally and reasonably to the later stage of Jesus' work than to its beginnings. The stories of the Galilean ministry reveal an attitude of suspicious interest on the part of the Jerusalem officials, rather than one of implacable opposition such as must have followed this assumption of leadership and authority."[8] The position of the Temple Cleansing in John can be accounted for on dramatic and doctrinal grounds.

If the Temple Cleansing occurs too early in John, it is placed too late in the Synoptics according to some scholars. Branscomb argues that ordinary money-changers did not conduct business in the Temple. An annual tax of a half shekel for the support of the Temple was required of every adult male Jew. It had to be paid in the silver coinage originally made in the town of Tyre. The work of changing common money to the officially recognized coinage was not done by the ordinary money-changers who conducted business for pilgrims of many lands. It was carried on by special money-changers. The half shekel tax was due by Nisan 1, two weeks before the Passover. From Adar 17 to 27 (the month before Nisan), the money-changers set up their tables in all the towns. From Adar 25 to Nisan 1 they set up their tables in the Temple. It was these tables which Jesus overturned. The Temple Cleansing took place during the week of Adar 25–Nisan 1, two or three weeks before the Passover.[9] Goguel favors an even earlier date. He attaches great importance to Jesus' saying regarding the destruction of the Temple. This saying is found in John (2:19) and in the Synoptic account of the trial before the Sanhedrin (Mt. 26:61; Mk. 14:58). He believes that because of this utterance Jesus was compelled to withdraw from Jerusalem to Perea and in the end was condemned to death. Goguel places the Temple Cleansing just prior to Jesus' withdrawal.[10]

---

[7]Mal. 3:1–2; emphasis added.
[8]Branscomb, *The Gospel of Mark*, pp. 202–3.
[9]Branscomb, *The Gospel of Mark*, 203–4.
[10]*The Life of Jesus*, pp. 412–19.

According to Mark, Jesus did four things in the Court of the Gentiles. He (1) began to drive out the merchants, (2) overturned the tables of the money-changers and the seats of the pigeon-sellers, (3) prohibited people from carrying anything through the Temple, and (4) proclaimed that the Temple should be a house of prayer instead of a den of robbers (11:15–17). The other Gospels omit the reference to the use of the Temple as a short-cut. Only John relates that Jesus made a "whip of cords" (possibly rushes) with which to drive the money-changers, merchants, and animals out of the Temple (2:14–16). In the Synoptics, Jesus seems to enforce his point by quoting Isaiah 56:7 ("My house shall be called a house of prayer for all peoples.") and complaining with Jeremiah that the Temple has become "a den of robbers" (Jer. 7:11). The tables of the money-changers may have been overturned in the general confusion, or Jesus may have upset them deliberately as a means of gaining the attention of the crowd. In either case, no violence to the persons of the money-changers is implied.

Both the money-changers and the animal merchants were in the Temple Court for the convenience of their customers, since worshipers were required by the Law to change their money into proper coinage and the faithful could not bring ritually clean and unblemished animals for sacrifice to Jerusalem from long distances. It is often assumed that all Temple commerce involved graft. This may have been the case, but we have no evidence that the Jewish people protested the money-changers. There is damaging evidence, however, against the sellers of sacrificial animals. Not many years after Jesus' death, a rabbi denounced the exorbitant price of doves and brought their price down by changing the law concerning these offerings. The Temple sales organization was undoubtedly controlled by the Sadducean priests who are cursed in the Talmud for their greed. The priesthood was powerful and wealthy, hated by the people, and rebuked by the scribes and Pharisees for their avarice and rapacity. The family of Annas, the former high priest who appears in the gospel story of John 18:13, ran markets for the sale of sacrificial animals somewhere near the Temple. These markets were destroyed by a popular movement in 67 A.D. When Jesus drove out the sellers of pigeons, he may well have been protesting against extortion.

Jesus gained control of the Temple for a brief period, but he remained only long enough to complete his demonstration. Surely he realized that the money-changers and the pigeon-sellers would be back the next day doing business as usual. He could hardly have hoped for a popular uprising which would put an end to the priestly group and their supporters. Jesus' protest was not against the Temple. Neither was it against the simple selling of animals nor the sacrificial system as such. He moved within the framework of Judaism. As he accepted the Law, so he accepted the Temple and its worship. As long as they fulfilled their intended purpose of bringing people into humble, obedient fellowship with God, they were immune from attack. He condemned them only when they blocked this basic aim.

What did Jesus hope to accomplish by the Temple Cleansing? Answers vary according to the interpreter's understanding of Jesus' self-estimate.

(1) Those who look upon Jesus as a prophet see in the Cleansing a prophetic act. Prophets before and after Jesus resorted to visual aids to reinforce their message. Isaiah went naked and barefoot for three years (Is. 20:1–6). Jeremiah buried his waistcloth (Jer. 13:1–11) and wore a yoke around his neck (Jer. 28:10). Agabas bound his feet and hands with Paul's belt (Acts 21:11–12). So Jesus cleansed the Temple of its abuses. As he executed judgment against the priesthood, so God would judge the people unless they repented. Time for repentance was short since the kingdom was close at hand. (2) Those who attribute to Jesus a Messianic consciousness view the Cleansing as a deliberate symbolic act by which he set forth an aspect of his Messianic office—the purging of contemporary Judaism of its commercialism and materialism. (3) Since the Cleansing took place in the Court of the Gentiles, some claim that it reflects Jesus' concern for the Gentile world and presages the call of the Gentiles and the extension of Christianity to all mankind.

It is not surprising that from the time of the Temple Cleansing in the gospel story, the priests are pictured as actively plotting Jesus' destruction. He had boldly attacked their authority and prestige, if not their pocketbook. Since they could not retaliate directly because of Jesus' extraordinary popularity with the populace, they hatched an alternative with "the scribes" (Mk. 11:18) and "the principal men of the people" (Lk. 19:47). They decided to persuade the Romans to get rid of him. Each night Jesus and his disciples withdrew from the city. This move was made for two reasons, to take precaution against priestly scrutiny and to avoid the crowded housing in the Holy City at the Passover season.

A series of five controversy stories follows the Temple Cleansing in Mark. The questions put to Jesus by his adversaries are designed to trap him into an admission which could be fashioned into a charge deserving the death penalty. The charge would then be placed before the Roman procurator.

Source of Authority (202)[11]

While Jesus campaigned in Galilee, his opponents were the scribes and Pharisees. The Sanhedrin, the supreme religious body of the Jews, no doubt noticed his activity and viewed it with some suspicion. As long as Jesus remained in the northern province, however, he was under the jurisdiction of Herod Antipas and the Sanhedrin was powerless to take any direct action against him. But as soon as Jesus entered Judea, he came into the sphere of the Sanhedrin's surveillance. On the day following the Temple Cleansing, according to Mark, "the chief priests and the scribes and the elders" came to Jesus while he was walking in the Temple. Since the three groups mentioned comprised the Sanhedrin, those who confronted Jesus were that body's representatives. "By what authority," they asked the Carpenter, "are you doing these things [driving out the money-changers and the animal

11Mt. 21:23–27; Mk. 11:27–33; Lk. 20:1–8.

merchants], or who gave you this authority to do them?" (Mk. 11:28). The question did not imply that Jesus had any authority. Quite the contrary! The chief priests themselves were the recognized legal authorities in matters dealing with the Temple. The purpose of the double-barreled question was to wring from Jesus some statement that could be used against him in court.

Jesus answered the question by asking another. Rabbinical debates were often conducted in this fashion. "I will ask you a question: answer me, and I will tell you by what authority I do these things. Was the baptism of John from heaven or from men?" (Mk. 11:29–30). The remaining verses, which describe the uncertainty of the priests and Jesus' answer to them, are probably secondary. Jesus' answer is really given in the counterquestion concerning John (11:30). The Jerusalem authorities did not regard John as inspired, but the people did. It is probable that Jesus "intended to do more than impale his opponents on the horns of a dilemma. He wished to suggest that there was a close connection between his ministry and John's and that his own authority also came *from heaven*. This in itself does not necessarily imply a messianic consciousness on his part."[12]

Tax to Caesar (206)[13]

The Jerusalem authorities sent some of the Pharisees and some of the Herodians to trap Jesus in his talk.[14] These two groups usually went their separate ways. The Pharisees were political quietists who probably suspected that Jesus was a revolutionary. Certainly the Temple Cleansing gave them cause for such a view. The Herodians were partisans of Herod Antipas. They hoped to put Herod on the throne instead of a Maccabean descendant. So they carefully cultivated Roman favor and doubtless supported payment of the tax under discussion.

The Pharisees and Herodians began their thrust with flattery. "Teacher, we know that you are true, and care for no man; for you do not regard the position of men, but truly teach the way of God. Is it lawful to pay taxes to Caesar, or not?" (Mk. 12:14). This was a burning question in Judea. The tax referred to was a head tax or a poll tax, not a tax on property or customs. It was paid into the emperor's treasury (the *fiscus*) and was required of adult males under direct Roman rule. It had been instituted in Judea, Samaria, and Idumea in 6 A.D. when Archelaus was deposed and Roman procurators took over the administration of the territory. A census

12Gilmour, in *The Interpreter's Bible*, VIII, 345.

13Mt. 22:15–22; Mk. 12:13–17; Lk. 20:20–26.

14Luke substitutes "spies," suggests Pharisees in the phrase "who pretended to be sincere," and omits any reference to the Herodians (20:20). Compare Mk. 3:6. David Daube, "Four Types of Question," in *The New Testament and Rabbinic Judaism* (London: Univ. of London, 1956), pp. 158–69, argues that the incident about tax payment and the three that follow (Mk. 12:18–27, 28–34, and 35–37) correspond to a fourfold rabbinical pattern of question and answer used in the Haggadah of the Seder, the Passover eve service.

taken at the same time (Lk. 2:2) to determine the resources of the country for the purpose of taxation provoked a storm of protest. Judas of Galilee led a revolt (Acts 5:37) which was suppressed with some difficulty (Josephus, *Antiquities* XVIII, 1, 1; *Wars* II, 8, 1). Popular resentment of taxes, and of the Roman rule which they represented, remained.

The head tax was not a pressing problem in Galilee, where Jesus resided, since it was not under direct Roman rule. Galilee was governed by Herod Antipas, not by a procurator. Nevertheless, Jesus was a popular teacher and leader. He would be expected to hold pronounced views on such an issue. Of course Jesus' questioners had no intention of enlisting his support either for or against Rome. Their purpose was to trick him, and their question was craftily designed to achieve this purpose. If Jesus should advise payment of the tax, it would be considered a betrayal of the national cause. Anyone who would recommend such a course of action would surely lose the support of the crowds. If he should repudiate the payment, it would be tantamount to treason in Roman eyes.

Jesus' answer began with a question, included a visual aid, and was completed by a declaration. " 'Why put me to the test? Bring me a coin, and let me look at it.' [Evidently Jesus did not have the required coin himself. The tax was paid with a silver denarius which was minted by the Romans and worth about twenty cents. It was not a heavy tax, but it symbolized subservience. Moreover, the coin in which it was paid bore the "likeness and inscription" of the emperor (Mk. 12:16). The reproduction of the head of Augustus or Tiberius shocked Jewish sensibilities and violated the commandment against graven images. The commoner currency of Judea was made of copper and bore such inoffensive symbols as olive trees or palms.] And they brought one. And he said to them, 'Whose likeness and inscription is this?' They said to him, 'Caesar's.' Jesus said to them, 'Render to Caesar the things that are Caesar's, and to God the things that are God's' " (Mk. 12:15–17).

The entire incident is an excellent example of a paradigm or pronouncement story. Everything points to the final, climactic saying in vs. 17 for the sake of which the story is told. The declaration has had an enormous influence. It has often been used to support particular theories concerning the proper relationship between church and state. Jesus' answer has been viewed in a variety of ways. Some see it as a clever evasion. The answer "was primarily intended to be non-committal."[15] Jesus was really anti-Roman, but he refused to get caught on either side of the question before him. This view can hardly be correct. Jesus clearly asserted that the tax should be paid. Coins with Caesar's image on them belonged to the emperor. He had a perfect right to demand them. Others see the answer as advice which caught the testers. They had Caesar's idolatrous coin in hand. Of course they were obligated to return it to him. It was his property. Still others view the answer as an endorsement of the Roman head tax comparable to the advice Jesus gave Peter to pay the Temple tax (Mt. 17:24–27). Some think Jesus

---

[15]Montefiore, *The Synoptic Gospels*, I, 278.

simply reaffirmed the Jewish position of loyalty to God and the government except when the latter demanded apostasy. Apostasy could not have been at issue in this story since sacrifices for the emperor were offered twice daily in the Temple. Others argue that Jesus approved the double obligation to God and government, but he left to the individual the determination of the proper claims of each.

When Jesus added to "render to Caesar" the injunction, "render to God," he was probably speaking to the "Zealot"-minded. They contended that Jews could not pay taxes to Caesar and still honor God as Ruler and King. The Pharisees, on the other hand, accepted Roman rule and were fully prepared to abide by all of its lawful regulations as long as it did not infringe on their religious rights and duties. They never doubted that God was supreme even in Caesar's realm, but they waited patiently for the day when he would assert his power. When that happened, the payment of taxes to Caesar would be an academic question. God's rule would end all others. Jesus evidently sided with the Pharisees. For him it was not a matter of "either-or" but "both-and." Of course Caesar had a right to collect the head tax. Was not his likeness and inscription on the required coin? But God outranked Caesar. To pay tribute to God—to render Him repentance, obedience, and worship—was the primary obligation. How could it have been otherwise for one who preached the coming of the kingdom?

One fact is frequently overlooked in treating the taxes-to-Caesar issue. It was necessary to ask Jesus what his position was on the Roman question. Evidently his views on this subject were not well known. "Nothing could better demonstrate His absorption in the religious problem.... His thought was above the political struggles of the hour, fixed on a vision of obedience in spirit and purpose to the will of God. To all who rendered this obedience salvation would come soon."[16] It is a mistake to read into Jesus' words the position later advanced by Paul. Paul declared that Caesar and all duly-appointed authorities were ordained of God and acted as His agents. To resist them was to resist God Himself (Rom. 13:1–2). It is utter folly to foist on Jesus the medieval idea of the two empires, the secular and the sacred, or the modern ethical dichotomy, the political and the religious. While Jesus was preoccupied with the proclamation of the kingdom's coming, he was not oblivious of man in his total environment. Jesus held the widest possible view of God's rule.

Resurrection of the Dead (207)[17]

The Sadducees are infrequently mentioned in the Gospels, but they turned out to be Jesus' most formidable enemies. The high priest and his friends belonged to this party, and they were the ones who denounced Jesus

---

[16]Branscomb, *The Gospel of Mark*, p. 215.
[17]Mt. 22:23–33; Mk. 12:18–27; Lk. 20:27–40.

before Pilate. The Sadducees were political and social conservatives and Biblical literalists. They followed the written Law but rejected the oral "tradition of the elders." They denied the resurrection of the body, future rewards and punishments, and (according to Acts 23:8) the existence of angels and spirits. The Pharisees, on the other hand, were staunch defenders of these doctrines. No doubt the Sadducees were disappointed at the failure of the Pharisees and Herodians to trap Jesus in his talk, but they probably felt a secret satisfaction at the defeat of their crafty rivals.

The Sadducees seemed to know that Jesus believed in the resurrection. They approached him with a peculiar problem. "Teacher, Moses wrote for us that if a man's brother dies and leaves a wife, but leaves no child, the man must take the wife, and raise up children for his brother" (Mk. 12:19). The Sadducees referred to the so-called levirate law (from the Latin *levir* or husband's brother) found in Deuteronomy 25:5–6. It required the brother of a dead man to marry the widow. The first-born son would then bear the name of the deceased brother. Thus the family name would survive and the property holdings would be kept in the family. The law was probably not enforced in the first century, but it was still practiced occasionally. It continued to be a matter of debate for centuries.

After the Sadducees had set the stage, they spun their story. "There were seven brothers; the first took a wife, and when he died left no children; and the second took her, and died, leaving no children; and the third likewise; and the seven left no children. Last of all the woman also died. In the resurrection whose wife will she be? For the seven had her as wife" (Mk. 12:20–23). It was an unlikely story, the prototype, so to speak, of *Arsenic and Old Lace*. By the time three or four of the brothers had died, one might suppose that the remainder would have hesitated to enter such a fatal union. The picture of the future life in which the woman is surrounded by the seven brothers—each hoping to claim the family heirloom—is a rollick. But the Sadducees were not indulging in cheap humor. They were trying to demonstrate that Moses did not envisage a resurrection. Indeed his "levirate" law made the idea of resurrection absurd.

Jesus again turned the tables on his opponents. "Is not this why you are wrong, that you know neither the scriptures nor the power of God? For when they rise from the dead, they neither marry nor are given in marriage, but are like angels in heaven" (Mk. 12:24–25). The Sadducees had assumed that Jesus held a crass and materialistic view of the resurrection. Not so! Earthly conditions would no longer prevail. Marriage was an institution necessary for the propagation of the race. In the resurrected state, where death would not prevail, marriage would be obsolete. People would be like the angels who were considered to be sexless (I Enoch 15:6–7).

Another saying is added to the one in Mark 12:24–25. Some scholars think it is a separate teaching which has become attached to the previous one.[18] The argument Jesus presents is a purely linguistic one similar to a number which appear in various tractates of the Talmud. Jesus cites the

---

[18]See Johnson, in *The Interpreter's Bible*, VII, 522.

most famous passage in Sadducean Scripture (entitled "The Bush," Ex. 3:6) to prove that the dead are raised. "And as for the dead being raised, have you not read in the book of Moses, in the passage about the bush, how God said to him, 'I *am* the God of Abraham, and the God of Isaac, and the God of Jacob'? He is not God of the dead, but of the living; you are quite wrong" (Mk. 12:26–27).[19] When God spoke to Moses concerning the patriarchs, they had been buried for centuries. Yet he referred to them in the present tense. They were not dead, as the Sadducees supposed, but alive. "The living God" was a distinctive title in Israel. God is not the God of the dead but of the living.

This argument in behalf of the resurrection has limited value although it was quite fashionable and forceful in the first century. Fortunately for us Jesus did not rest his case solely upon one idea; his answer as a whole was based on the nature of God. While he rejected the notion that the next world is a carbon copy of this one, he did not stress the nature of the resurrected dead. He stressed the power of God and the character of God—apart from which any talk about a future life is nonsense.

First Commandment (208)[20]

A scribe who had overheard Jesus' discussion with the Sadducees—and who had apparently been deeply impressed by Jesus' incisive handling of the situation—approached him and asked, "Which commandment is the first of all?" (Mk. 12:28).[21] The tone of this incident differs markedly from that of the previous ones. Here there is no conflict. The scribe is a questioner, not a critic.[22] Perhaps Mark wished to show that Jesus' previous arguments had been effective.

The scribe's question was a familiar one. It had often been raised in professional religious circles. It was not a question of which commandment men were most obliged to observe. They were obliged to observe them all. What the scribe wanted to know was which commandment provided a basic principle for the rest. The Law was loaded with commandments. One rabbi

---

19Emphasis added. Note the remarkable variations in Luke's account (20:34–36, 39–40) and compare their Pauline parallels as given by Major, in *The Mission and Message of Jesus*, p. 150. Rudolf Bultmann, *The History of the Synoptic Tradition*, 2nd ed., tr. John Marsh (Oxford: Basil Blackwell, 1968), p. 26, regards the whole discussion as a reflection of the theological activity of the church.

20Mt. 22:34–40; Mk. 12:28–34; Lk. 10:25–28.

21A "lawyer," a synonym for "scribe," asks the question in Matthew and Luke. Luke uses the incident as an introduction to the parable of the Good Samaritan and omits the narrative from his report of Jesus' last days in Jerusalem. The lawyer asks Jesus about eternal life, not about the first commandment. Beare, *The Earliest Records of Jesus*, p. 159, thinks that Luke's account comes from Q (which he shared with Matthew), that Matthew conflated Mark/Q accounts, and Luke's story may be closer to the original.

22Contrast the lawyer's attitude in Matthew and Luke.

said there were 613. Numerous attempts had been made to set forth the heart of the Hebrew religion. "David" listed eleven items (Ps. 15:2–5), Isaiah six (33:15), Micah three (6:8), and Habakkuk (2:4) and Hillel[23] one each. If the scribe could find out from Jesus which commandment was fundamental to the rest, he would then have a succinct summary of the Law.

Jesus' answer to the scribe is a masterpiece. "The first is, 'Hear, O Israel: The Lord our God, the Lord is one;[24] and you shall love the Lord your God with all your heart, and with all your soul, and with all your mind, and with all your strength.'[25] The second is this, 'You shall love your neighbor as yourself.' There is no other commandment greater than these" (Mk. 12:29–31).

This famous answer, whether by Jesus (Matthew, Mark) or by the lawyer (Luke), united two Old Testament injunctions.[26] The command to love God came from Deuteronomy (6:5) and the command to love one's neighbor was derived from Leviticus (19:18). The combination was not original. It had appeared in the Testaments of the Twelve Patriarchs of the preceding century (Issachar 5:2; 7:6; Dan 5:3). The saying sprang from the heart of Jewish ethical religion.

The scribe repeated Jesus' words and stressed their theological implications (Mk. 12:32–33). "And when Jesus saw that he answered wisely, he said to him, 'You are not far from the kingdom of God' " (Mk. 12:34). This delightful interlude—in which the scribe was deeply appreciative of Jesus' teaching and Jesus warmly commended the insight of the scribe—is absent from Matthew and Luke. They picture the scribe as hostile. He put the question to Jesus to trap him. Their omission, like their failure to record Mark's statement that Jesus loved the Rich Young Ruler, is pointed. The Christians of their day had suffered too much at the hands of the scribes to be able to believe that a scribe had once appreciated Jesus and vice versa. Mark concludes his account with the observation that "after that no one dared to ask him any question" (12:34)—a comment which Luke places at the end of the preceding section (20:40) and Matthew shifts to the end of the following one (22:46).

The way Matthew modifies the material he received, especially in 22:40, enables him to emphasize a familiar theme of his Gospel—that the love commandment is the criterion by which "all the law and the prophets" are to be interpreted. Held has demonstrated that this principle of interpretation is shown in several ways. (1) The content of the conduct required by the Law is determined by love. What one does on the Sabbath, for example, is conditioned by love (12:12). (2) The conception of God is determined by the love commandment. He is merciful, gracious, loving (9:13; 12:7). (3) The

---

[23]"What is hateful to thyself, do not to thy neighbor; this is the whole law, the rest is commentary."

[24]This quotation from the Shema (Deut. 6:4) is omitted by Matthew and Luke.

[25]Matthew contains a threefold expression of this command (22:37).

[26]It is unlikely that the evangelist would have attributed the response to the scribe/lawyer if his source had attributed it to Jesus.

obligation to practice love is prompted by the love which has already been received.[27]

Woes (210)[28]

At the close of the five conflict stories Mark declares that a great throng heard Jesus gladly (12:37b). Then the evangelist reports that Jesus condemned the scribes for their intense desire for special privileges, their exploitation, and hypocrisy. The Gospels contain several collections of sayings in which Jesus denounced his adversaries. Mark 12:38b–40 is the shortest of the collections. Luke 20:45–47 contains the verses found in Mark, and the Third Gospel also preserves a much longer collection (Lk. 11:39–54) from another source. Matthew combines the material in each and adds to it material from his special source (M). The whole, which he has freely rewritten and fitted together, forms all of chapter 23 of his Gospel. He has placed the chapter here not only because it is where Mark has it (after the question about the Messiah's descent), but also because (contrary to Luke 11:42–52) he considered it an appropriate place to put the "woes." They constitute the first part of the fifth and final "book" or main collection in his Gospel, and they are followed by the Apocalypse (ch. 24) and three parables dealing with the Last Judgment (ch. 25).

The Gospels reached their final form during a period of acute conflict. The church and the synagogue were at loggerheads. Matthew 23 tells us much more about the attitude of the early church toward the Pharisees than about Jesus' attitude. Sometimes, as we have seen, Jesus was in complete agreement with the Pharisees (Mt. 22:15–33). At other times he doubtless denounced individual Pharisees for their externalism, legalism, ostentation, and hypocrisy. However, it is highly unlikely that he made a wholesale condemnation of the entire party. After the destruction of Jerusalem in 70 A.D., the Pharisees were the only important influence left in Judaism. It may well be that the gospel tradition contains denunciations of them which were originally intended for others. These polemic passages need to be tempered. The passages themselves sometimes support this position. Matthew 23:2–3 affirms that the teaching of the Pharisees is altogether trustworthy, but Matthew 23:4,16–22,25–26 vigorously criticize their teaching! To acknowledge that the attacks on the Pharisees in the Gospels have been sharpened in the course of transmission is not to blunt the responsibility of the Pharisees. As good, conscientious, and devoted as they were, it cannot be ignored that many of them contributed to the crucifixion of Jesus and

---

27See Gerhard Barth, in *Tradition and Interpretation in Matthew*, pp. 75–85, to which we are indebted. The fifth question in the conflict series (209) is raised by Jesus himself (Mt. 22:41–46; Mk. 12:35–37a; Lk. 20:41–44). It concerns the Messiah's descent. We have dealt with this incident in another context. Refer to pp. 309–310 for a treatment of the material.

28Mt. 23:1–36; Mk. 12:37b–40; Lk. 11:39–54; 20:45–47.

bitterly persecuted the early church. No less a figure than Paul, a Pharisee of Pharisees, bears witness (I Thess. 2:15–16).

There are seven "woes" against "scribes and Pharisees" in Matthew and six "woes" in Luke—three directed against "Pharisees" and three against "lawyers" (scribes). Matthew 23 begins with a general criticism of the scribes and Pharisees (vss. 1–12), is followed by the seven "woes" (vss. 13–33), and ends with a threat and lament (vss. 34–39). Before we discuss the "woes," we shall deal with the general criticism of the scribes and Pharisees.

Jesus condemned the scribes and the Pharisees because they were hypocritical, heartless, and ostentatious (Mt. 23:2–12). (1) They sat on Moses' seat, the stone chair in the synagogue reserved for the most learned teacher of the Law. (Such a practice, of course, was unthinkable while the Temple was still standing and the powers of the priesthood remained intact.) The Law of Moses, which was expounded by the scribes, was the supreme authority. But the scribes did not always practice what they preached (Mt. 23:2–3). (2) They placed heavy burdens on their followers by insisting that they keep the oral as well as the written Law. The oral Law ("the tradition of the elders") consisted of interpretations and applications of the Law of Moses which had developed since Ezra's time. They were committed to writing in the Mishnah in the second century A.D. The scribes and the Pharisees would reduce ("move . . . with their finger") none of these regulations (Mt. 23:24).[29] (3) They did "all their deeds to be seen by men, [made] their phylacteries [leather boxes which contained Scripture[30]] broad and their fringes long, [loved] the place of honor at feasts and the best seats in the synagogues,[31] and salutations in the market places [often a ceremonious affair in the Near East], and being called rabbi ["my great one," an honorific title for scholars] by men" (Mt. 23:5–7).

This picture of the scribes and the Pharisees is a caricature. There were hypocrites among them, and their pretense was condemned by the rabbis. But everything we know about the Pharisees indicates that hypocrisy was not their primary characteristic. Unfortunately, no religious group, past or present, is altogether free from this vice. The Pharisees did bind heavy burdens on their followers, but many of them accepted these burdens willingly and obeyed them joyously. The restrictions provided a hedge against transgression. The hardheartedness of the Pharisees is exaggerated. They relaxed numerous rules of the written Law which the common man found nearly impossible to fulfill. No doubt some scribes and Pharisees loved the limelight. It is human nature to love the place of honor at feasts and the best seats in synagogues or at banquets. The title "rabbi," "doctor," or "professor" (especially if the one addressed is a lowly instructor) displeases few. But it would have been unholy hyperbole for Jesus to have castigated a whole class of people because some had misbehaved. He would not have declared that the scribes and the Pharisees "do *all* their deeds to be seen

---

[29]This teaching is a "woe" against lawyers in Lk. 11:46.
[30]Worn in literal obedience to the commands of Ex. 13:16; Deut. 6:8; 11:18.
[31]This teaching is a "woe" against the Pharisees in Lk. 11:43.

by men" (Mt. 23:5).[32] Such broad brushes were wielded by the early church while it was locked in mortal conflict with the synagogue.[33]

The "woes" may be conveniently summarized.

Mt. 23:	13	kingdom closed	Lk. 11:	42	tithes
woes	15	proselytes[34]	woes against	43	best seats
against	16	oaths[34]	Pharisees	44	unseen
scribes	23	tithes			graves
and	25	cleanliness	against	46	burdens
Pharisees	27	whitewashed tombs	lawyers	47	prophets'
	29	prophets' tombs			tombs
				52	key of
					knowledge

1. "But woe to you, scribes and Pharisees, hypocrites! because you shut the kingdom of heaven against men; for you neither enter yourselves, nor allow those who would enter to go in" (Mt. 23:13). This "woe" provides the climax to Luke's list (11:52); Luke presents the lawyers as having taken away the key of knowledge. Matthew's wording is more primitive. He pictures the scribes and Pharisees as having shut the kingdom against men. By their legalistic pedantry, they made knowledge of the Law so difficult and incomprehensible that neither they nor others could come to God.

2. "Woe to you, scribes and Pharisees, hypocrites! for you traverse sea and land to make a single proselyte, and when he becomes a proselyte, you make him twice as much a child of hell as yourselves" (Mt. 23:15). In the first century, Judaism was a missionary religion; but the wars with Rome and the conflicts with Christianity eventually prompted the abandonment of missionary efforts. In Jesus' day, however, converts were not only welcomed but sought, especially by the school of Hillel. Gentiles became Jews by accepting the Law, submitting to baptism and circumcision (for males), and by making an offering in the Temple. After performing these prerequisites, they possessed all of the privileges and prerogatives of "birthright" Jews and exhibited all of the zeal which characterizes new converts. The point of this "woe" is that enthusiastic proselytes become more masters of the miscellaneous than their converters and thus miss the goal of religion —God.

3. "Woe to you, blind guides, who say, 'If any one swears by the temple, it is nothing; but if any one swears by the gold of the temple, he is bound by his oath.... If any one swears by the altar, it is nothing; but if any one swears by the gift that is on the altar, he is bound by his oath' " (Mt. 23:16,18). Oaths were a serious matter. They were made to men, but God was their witness. The rabbis attempted to discourage people from taking oaths because they should be taken seriously and observed scrupulously. The common people, however, were addicted to oath-taking. The rabbis

---

[32]Emphasis added.

[33]Mt. 23:8–10 are words of a Christian prophet or teacher, vs. 11 stresses service, and vs. 12 (found also in Lk. 14:11; 18:14) may have been a secular proverb.

[34]This passage appears in only one Gospel.

were gradually forced to regulate oath-taking and to draw distinctions. From Jesus' viewpoint the rabbinical distinctions were absurd. They misled men into thinking that some pledges did not matter. Not so! He who swore by the Temple, swore by the gold of the Temple. He who swore by the altar, swore by the gift on the altar. He who swore by heaven, swore by the throne of God and by God Himself (Mt. 23:17,19–22). In Matthew 5:33–37 Jesus prohibited oath-taking altogether.[35]

4. "Woe to you, scribes and Pharisees, hypocrites! for you tithe mint and dill and cummin, and have neglected the weightier matters of the law, justice and mercy and faith; these you ought to have done, without neglecting the others" (Mt. 23:23). Deuteronomy prescribed that grain, wine, and

Gehenna (the Greek form of the Hebrew "Gehinnom," Valley of Hinnom) is referred to as "hell" in the second "woe" in Matthew (23:15). The valley, shown in the photograph, is located southwest of Jerusalem. It stretches from the foot of Mt. Zion eastward to the Kidron Valley. In Old Testament times, little children were sacrificed there to Moloch. The Jews began to abhor the place. They cast into it all kinds of refuse—even the dead bodies of animals and of unburied, executed criminals. Fires were kept burning to consume the refuse and to keep the air from becoming tainted. Thus, the place came to be called "Gehenna of fire."

[35]See p. 246.

oil should be tithed (Deut. 14:22–23). The rabbis added vegetables, fruits, and nuts. Dill and cummin were included by the Mishnah, but mint was exempt (Maaseroth 4:5; Demai 2:1). Jesus surely believed that the tithe law of Deuteronomy should be kept. What he opposed was the Pharisaic elaborations. He thought it "absurd to spend time on the tithing of trifles; one who does so may shift the center of religion and distort it so that the most important things [justice, mercy, and faith] are forgotten."[36]

"You blind guides, straining out a gnat and swallowing a camel!" (Mt. 23:24) is a separate saying with a similar point. It was customary to strain wine through a cloth or fine wicker basket. Both gnat and camel were unclean animals (Lev. 11:4,41). Jesus' saying pillories the elaborate precautions taken by the scribes and Pharisees concerning minor matters and their carelessness about major ones. In their eagerness to avoid a microscopic defilement, they swallowed a macroscopic one. The language is humorous and hyperbolic.[37] The "strain at" in the King James Version is a printer's error.

5. "Woe to you, scribes and Pharisees, hypocrites! for you cleanse the outside of the cup and of the plate, but inside they are full of extortion and rapacity" (Mt. 23:25). Ritual ablutions before meals were not prescribed by the Law, but the Pharisees observed the elaborate oral legislation of the scribes. They kept a supply of water on hand to purify their bodies and the vessels they used. The tractate Kelim of the Mishnah expounds the rules respecting the cleanliness of the cup and the plate. The Pharisees were particular about ritual purity, but they neglected spiritual purity. They were "full of extortion and rapacity"—a phrase that better describes the Sadducean priesthood to which it may have been directed originally. Jesus taught that effective cleansing must begin from within (Mt. 23:26).

Luke's parallel material is not a "woe" but a criticism of the Pharisees (Lk. 11:39–41). Luke adds the thought that God created the outer world as well as the souls of men. "But give for alms those things which are within" (11:41) is a curious command. Perhaps the Greek translator mistook the Aramaic verb "to purify" for that "to give alms." As the verse now stands in the Greek, the meaning is obscure.

6. "Woe to you, scribes and Pharisees, hypocrites! for you are like whitewashed tombs, which outwardly appear beautiful, but within they are full of dead men's bones and all uncleanness" (Mt. 23:27). The tombs were whitewashed in the spring (Adar 15). The purpose was not to improve their appearance but to protect the people—especially the priests and pilgrims at Passover—from accidental defilement. To touch a tomb rendered a person unclean for seven days (Num. 19:16). Of course, the whitewashing did give the tombs a smart appearance. The contrast between their covering and their content would then be more striking. The scribes and Pharisees were likened to the whitewashed tombs—outwardly beautiful but inwardly unclean (Mt. 23:28). Luke compared them to unmarked graves which give

---

[36]Johnson, in *The Interpreter's Bible*, VII, 536.
[37]Compare Mt. 7:3–5; 19:24.

no warning of their true nature. Men who associated with them were unwittingly corrupted (11:44).

7. "Woe to you, scribes and Pharisees, hypocrites! for you build the tombs of the prophets and adorn the monuments of the righteous, saying, 'If we had lived in the days of our fathers, we would not have taken part with them in shedding the blood of the prophets.' Thus you witness against yourselves, that you are sons of those who murdered the prophets" (Mt. 23:29–31). Past prophets had been murdered when they had tried to reform Israel. The scribes and Pharisees condemned their ancestors who had been responsible and commended the virtues of those who had been slain. The prophets were now canonized, and woe betide anyone who dared to venture beyond the lines marked out by them. The scribes and Pharisees were quick to champion causes already won and to defend reputations already approved. What they didn't seem to realize was that the prophets had been put to death because they had challenged the accepted beliefs and practices of their day. The prophets' heresies were now orthodoxy. The scribes and Pharisees defended this new orthodoxy as tenaciously as their wicked ancestors had defended what was orthodox for them. "The very spirit that leads scribes and Pharisees to build the tombs of the old prophets will make them dig the graves of new prophets."[38] "Many an Independence Day orator who eulogizes Lincoln or Washington would have been a bitter opponent of these men if he had lived in their days."[39]

Semitic wisdom assumed that sons would pattern their lives after their fathers. The scribes and Pharisees were true sons of their persecuting ancestors. "Fill up, then, the measure of your fathers" is bitter irony (Mt. 23:32). Destroy the messengers of God as did your forebears. Then Israel's cup of iniquity will be full and God's judgment will be swift. Matthew 23:33 is an imitation of John the Baptist's saying (Mt. 3:7; Lk. 3:7). Matthew 23:34–36 makes no mention of the "Wisdom of God" (A lost Jewish apocryphal book? The risen Christ speaking through a Christian prophet? God in his wisdom?) found in Luke 11:49. Johnson suggests that the original oracle was delivered between 42–50 A.D. against the background of the martyrdom of James and the flight of Peter and other apostles.[40]

The "woes" in Matthew and Luke are barbed and brutal. Their edges were finely honed by the intense pressures exerted after the fall of Jerusalem in 70 A.D. on Jews who had become Christians. Jewish leaders attempted to impose a pattern of Pharisaic conformity on the nation in a desperate effort to recover from the catastrophe. Nonconforming Christians felt the brunt of this effort. The resultant strife between the synagogue and the church colored the report of Jesus' words in the Gospels. Indeed, the quarrel created as well as colored Jesus' words. Nevertheless, behind the "woes" raged a real conflict. Jesus' enemies did not drive him to the cross because of his soothing words and feeble actions.

[38]Manson, in *The Mission and Message of Jesus*, p. 530.
[39]Johnson, in *The Interpreter's Bible*, VII, 538.
[40]In *The Interpreter's Bible*, VII, 539.

Lament over Jerusalem (211)[41]

Jesus' lament has a different context in the two Gospels. Luke indicates that it took place while Jesus was on his way to Jerusalem. Matthew locates it during Jesus' last days in the city. The Scriptures do not support the view that many prophets were murdered in the Holy City. "O Jerusalem, Jerusalem, killing the prophets and stoning those who are sent to you!" (Mt. 23:37) cannot be taken literally. Jerusalem, as the capital, stands for the whole nation. The figure of the bird gathering her brood under her wings is a familiar one in the Old Testament (Deut. 32:11; Pss. 17:8, 36:7). The phrase, "How often would I have gathered your children together" (Mt. 23:37) suggests frequent visits by Jesus to Jerusalem, but it may express longings rather than actions. "Behold, your house is forsaken and desolate" (Mt. 23:38) may be a reference to the Temple. Against this view, it is argued that in the Old Testament the Temple is almost invariably God's house and no one else's. "For I tell you, you will not see me again, until you say, 'Blessed is he who comes in the name of the Lord' " (Mt. 23:39) is much disputed. What does "until you say" mean? In Luke, these words may be a forecast of the Entry into Jerusalem, but when the Entry is made, it is the disciples (not the populace of Jerusalem) who acclaim Jesus. Matthew, who inserts the word "again," interprets these words as a prediction of Jesus' return as the glorified Son of Man. Some scholars regard the saying as a Christian addition.[42]

Widow's Coins (212)[43]

It is a relief to move from the crucible of conflict to the inspiring story of the widow and her coins. Mark (followed by Luke) doubtless placed the incident here because of the reference to widows in the preceding verse. Matthew omitted it, probably because it is unrelated to the theme of the approaching judgment with which he began chapter 24. Jesus "sat down opposite the treasury, and watched the multitude putting money into the treasury" (Mk. 12:41). The treasury was probably a section or room in one of the porticoes of the Court of the Women. In the treasury there were thirteen trumpet-shaped receptacles for the receipt of money. Each receptacle

41Mt. 23:37–39; Lk. 13:34–35.
42See Gilmour, in *The Interpreter's Bible*, VIII, 250. Contrast Manson, in *The Mission and Message of Jesus*, pp. 419–20. Bultmann, *The History of the Synoptic Tradition*, pp. 114–15, thinks that Mt. 23:39 has to be understood in terms of the myth of divine Wisdom. Tödt, *The Son of Man in the Synoptic Tradition*, pp. 83–84, thinks that Luke does not point to the coming Son of Man because he is concerned with the beginning of the Age of the Church. Matthew, however, is concerned with the End which has been fixed by the attitude of Jewish leaders. Hence he points to the coming of the Son of Man.
43Mk. 12:41–44; Lk. 21:1–4.

was for a different purpose. The offerings were voluntary and were used for the support of the Temple. The treasury was under the supervision of priests. Donors were required to state the sum they were offering and the ritualistic purpose which it served. The priests thus ascertained if the amount which was brought corresponded with the requirements set forth in the Law and if the proper coins were in hand. A person who sat nearby could discover the amount of the gift from the conversation which resulted.

Many rich people contributed large sums to the treasury. "And a poor widow came, and put in two copper coins, which make a penny" (Mk. 12:42). The two coins (*lepta*) were the smallest in circulation among the Jews. They were equal in value to about half a cent, with a purchasing power of approximately two cents. It was unlawful to contribute less to the treasury. When Jesus learned of the widow's gift, he called his disciples to him and said, "Truly, I say to you [an expression used to impress hearers with what is to follow], this poor widow has put in more than all those who are contributing to the treasury. For they all contributed out of their abundance; but she out of her poverty has put in everything she had, her whole living" (Mk. 12:43–44). The scribes preyed on the poor widows (Mk. 12:40), but this poor widow put into the treasury "everything she had, her whole living." The sum was small—probably what she needed in order to buy her next meal. But the greatest gift is measured by its cost to the giver rather than by its value.

Destruction of the Temple (213)[44]

As Jesus came out of the Temple, one of his disciples exclaimed, " 'Look, Teacher, what wonderful stones and what wonderful buildings!' And Jesus said to him, 'Do you see these great buildings? There will not be left here one stone upon another, that will not be thrown down' " (Mk. 13:1–2). Jesus was not the first to forecast such an awful fate for the house of God. Micah had envisaged the destruction of the first Temple as a consequence of the people's refusal to repent. "Jerusalem shall become a heap of ruins, and the mountain of the house a wooded height" (Micah 3:12). Many years later his prediction, not yet materialized, had been echoed by Jeremiah. The prophet, speaking for the Lord, had declared, "I will make this house like Shiloh, and I will make this city a curse for all the nations of the earth" (Jer. 26:6). The Babylonians under Nebuchadnezzar had made Jeremiah's words come true. Now Jesus proclaimed that the Temple would be destroyed. Some scholars think that this prediction is a "prophecy after the event." (The Temple was burned by the Romans in 70 A.D.) But this judgment hardly seems justified. The prophecy, in a garbled form, was used against Jesus during his hearing before the Sanhedrin (Mk. 14:58).

The scene now shifts (except in Luke) from the Temple court to the Mount of Olives. It was on this mountain, according to Zechariah, that the

44Mt. 24:1-3; Mk. 13:1-4; Lk. 21:5-7.

Lord would appear on "the day of the Lord" (Zech. 14:4). Here, too, according to popular expectation, the Messiah would be revealed. Privately Jesus' three intimate disciples plus Andrew asked him a twofold question. (All of the disciples asked the question in Matthew.) "Tell us, when will this be, and what will be the sign when these things are all to be accomplished?" (Mk. 13:4). The first half of the question is clear. It refers solely to the predicted destruction of the Temple. The second half of the question in Luke 21:7 deals with the same subject. (In apocalyptic writings, contrary to Jesus' teaching,[45] signs would precede the end, and the date of the end could be inferred from the signs.) But in Mark the second half of the question ("What will be the sign when *these things* are all to be accomplished?") refers not so much to the destruction of the Temple as to the series of catastrophic events of which the Temple's destruction would be a part.[46] It thus serves to introduce a long apocalyptic discourse, the subject of the rest of the chapter. Matthew 24:3 expands Mark's introduction and makes it more explicit: "Tell us, when will this be [the Temple's destruction], and what will be the sign of your coming [the parousia] and of the close of the age [eschatology]?"

Apocalyptic Interlude (214–223)[47]

The discourse which appears in Mark 13 is unique. (1) Nowhere else does the evangelist dwell so long on a single theme. (2) While the introductory words concern the destruction of the Temple, the remainder of the chapter says nothing about this subject. It deals with the end of the age and the parousia of the Son of Man. (3) False Christs are the beginning of the woes in verses 6–8, but in verses 21–22 they appear in the middle of them. (4) Through verse 31, the discourse purports to reveal the signs of the end of the age and its time of occurrence. Verse 32 declares that "of that day or that hour no one knows, not even the angels in heaven, nor the Son, but only the Father." (5) In verse 14 Jesus refers to "the reader" when he is supposed to be speaking to his disciples. (6) Contrary to verse 3, the discourse appears to be addressed to Christians in general rather than to intimate disciples.

These facts, among others, have led many scholars to conclude that Mark 13 is composite. It includes material of an apocalyptic nature together with sayings which stem from Jesus himself. The apocalyptic material is rather easily identified—vss. 6–8, 14–20, 24–27, and possibly 31. These sections are commonly called the "Little Apocalypse."[48] Many scholars equate

---

45Lk. 17:20–24.

46Mk. 13:4, emphasis added.

47Mt. 24:4–36,42; 25:13–15b; Mk. 13:5–37; Lk. 12:38,40; 17:23–24,37; 19:12–13; 21:8–36.

48Strictly speaking, the passages are not an "apocalypse" like Daniel or Revelation in which the secret knowledge is mediated by dreams, visions, or auditions. See the excellent redaction-critical study of Mk. 13 by Willi Marxsen, *Mark the Evangelist,* tr. R. A. Harrisville (New York: Abingdon Press, 1969), pp. 151–206.

it (or the whole of chapter 13) with the "oracle" which circulated among Jewish Christians in Jerusalem shortly before the siege and destruction of the city in 70 A.D. The oracle impelled the Christians to flee from Jerusalem to Pella, east of the Jordan. There they remained in safety during the terrible Roman war in Palestine (Eusebius, *Ecclesiastical History* III, 5). Mark, who apparently considered the apocalyptic warning genuine, included the writing at this point in his Gospel because it seemed to follow vss. 1–2.

This theory is an attractive one. Although it cannot be proved, it does go a long way toward accounting for passages in Mark 13 which sharply challenge Jesus' own teaching. Just when the Little Apocalypse originated is uncertain. Despite its interest in Judea (vs. 14), it makes no reference to the actual events connected with the fall of Jerusalem. This would suggest that it was composed sometime prior to 70 A.D. The most favored date is about 40 A.D. It was then that Gaius Caesar (Caligula) ordered that his statue be set up in the Temple in Jerusalem. This order caused great excitement and agitation among the Jews; and a revolt was avoided only by the death of the emperor and the rescinding of the order (Josephus, *Wars* II, 10, 1–5). The prospect of Caligula's statue being set up in the Temple might well have revived interest in the prophecy of Daniel and stimulated the creation of such writings as the Little Apocalypse. Daniel had foretold that "upon the wing of abominations shall come one who makes desolate" (Dan. 9:27). His words were a veiled reference to the outrageous act of Antiochus Epiphanes, the Syrian overlord who sacrificed a pig to Zeus on the altar of the Lord in the Temple about 168 B.C. Could not Caligula's crude effort have prompted a writer of his time to produce the Little Apocalypse in which he spoke of the emperor's act as "the desolating sacrilege"? (Mk. 13:14). Daniel's figure was repeatedly reinterpreted. By the time Mark used the phrase it may have acquired another meaning. Roman armies, already victorious in Galilee, were marching toward Jerusalem.

How much of Mark 13, if any, can be attributed to Jesus is uncertain. Major believes that vss. 30–37, like the Budding Fig Tree (vss. 28–29) which precedes it,[49] "are very primitive and have strong claims to be regarded as utterances of Jesus, although not necessarily uttered on this occasion or in answer to the question about the destruction of the Temple."[50] Branscomb asserts that genuine sayings of Jesus may be contained in Mark 13, but "the identification of these in the midst of a document which must be regarded as the product of Christian hope and prophecy is highly conjectural."[51] Bornkamm calls attention to the graphic picture of the church depicted in Matthew 24:9–14. It is a suffering church. Its members undergo the fate of Jews among the Gentiles. It is plagued with apostasy, hatred, betrayal, subversion by false prophets, multiplied wickedness, and love grown cold. Yet those who endure will be saved, and the Gospel will be preached to the whole world. Then the End will come. The church has not broken with Judaism. It adheres to the Law, shares the fate of the nation,

---

[49]See pp. 208–209.
[50]In *The Mission and Message of Jesus*, p. 160.
[51]*The Gospel of Mark*, p. 233.

the destruction of the Temple, and the traumas of flight.[52] The close connection in the Synoptics between the apocalypse and the destruction of the Temple is significant. It indicates that Christians regarded the fall of Jerusalem as an eschatological event—a sign that the End was near.

Mark 13 sounds strange to our ears. We have been trained to think of history as a long and unbroken process. We believe that men have lived on earth for many millenniums. But the first readers of Mark honored a markedly different heritage. The prophets had preached about "the day of the Lord" which would bring punishment for evildoers and rewards for the righteous on earth. Centuries of foreign domination had paved the way for apocalypticism. A supernatural world was envisaged which would realize the deferred hopes of the present one. The new age, which would be established by God or his Messiah, was painted in glowing imagery. It was predicted that this new era would come suddenly at the conclusion of a series of woes with a climax of supernatural signs and conflicts with evil powers. The Final Judgment was expected to result in the condemnation of the wicked and the commendation of the righteous. To the earlier hope of a son of David who would reign over the restored Jewish nation was added a mysterious heavenly Son of Man who would come in power and glory. The hopes, as we have seen (chapter seventeen), were many and varied; but they were all based on the belief that God would end the present age and inaugurate a new one. The early readers of Mark intensely believed in the imminent end of the present age (eschatology) and in the return of Jesus (parousia). The apocalyptic return of Jesus formed a part of the message of Paul and, so far as we know, of all the early apostles. It was Jesus' return in power and glory, these Christians felt, which would validate their faith in him and secure their triumph over their Jewish and pagan persecutors, not to mention Satan and his servants.

But what did Jesus teach about the end of the age and his return in glory? The answer to this question cannot be found in Mark 13, a chapter permeated by the theology of the early church. We must turn to the sayings and stories of Jesus which are generally considered authentic. Although not always clear and seldom if ever comprehensive, these sayings and stories seem to support several conclusions. (1) Jesus shared the eschatological view of history which prevailed among his people. He believed in the supremacy of God. He believed that God had created the world, which was "very good" (Gen. 1:31) until man soiled it by sin. He believed that God, at a time of his own choosing, would bring history to an end. The present age would be replaced by a permanent order of righteousness and bliss—the kingdom of God. The new age would come only by God's direct action, not by chance or human effort. In his own ministry, Jesus performed deeds which pointed to the kingdom's nearness and indicated that, in some sense, salvation was not merely a promise but a present possession. (2) Jesus disavowed any unique knowledge of the precise plan of events which would precede the

[52]Günther Bornkamm, "End-Expectation and Church in Matthew," in Günther Bornkamm, Gerhardt Barth, and H. J. Held, *Tradition and Interpretation in Matthew*, tr. Percy Scott (London: SCM Press, 1963), pp. 21–22.

end. His interest was not in timetables and blueprints. At this point he parted company with the apocalyptists. The detailed predictions in Mark 13 would have held no fascination for him. His concern was for perpetual preparedness; his teachings emphasized the fact that men should be ready at any time to meet their Maker (Mt. 24:43; Lk. 12:39). Jesus "accepts the eschatological world view but uses it only as a stimulus to moral effort."[53] (3) Jesus had supreme confidence that God would one day triumph and that with that triumph, his own mission and message would be vindicated. He looked forward to a joyous reunion with his loyal disciples after his death. It cannot be confidently asserted, in our judgment, that he believed in his Second Advent as an apocalyptic Messiah. That the early church held such a view is clear. But when decade after decade (and century after century) passed and her hope failed to materialize, one of three things happened. For a few the hope faded, for many it was postponed to the indefinite future, and for many more it was spiritualized. Jesus' second coming was associated with the coming of the Holy Spirit at Pentecost (Acts 2). The writer of the Fourth Gospel presents Jesus' Second Advent as a divine spiritual indwelling in the lives of his disciples.

[53]Johnson, in *The Interpreter's Bible*, VII, 542.

part 7

The Rejection and Resurrection

No part of the gospel story evoked as much interest and wonder in the early church as did Jesus' death and resurrection. Why was the Christ crucified? A single answer could not be given. A whole series of events was involved. When Jesus entered Jerusalem, his enemies lay in wait for him. Their plot was hastened to fruition by the treacherous cooperation of one of the Twelve. Jesus was arrested, hauled before the authorities, and confronted with false witnesses. Both Jewish and Roman officials seemed indifferent to justice. As a result, Jesus was condemned to death and executed as a common criminal. Then he was laid to rest in a borrowed tomb.

Life for the disciples disintegrated at Jesus' death. One of them had already defected. The others undoubtedly felt afraid and ashamed. They had hoped that Jesus would be the one to redeem Israel. Obviously their hope had been misplaced. They were too stunned by the present to face the future. The enigma of Jesus' crucifixion haunted them.

In the depth of their despair, the disciples heard an amazing rumor. It alleged that Jesus was not dead but alive. As soon as the report was verified, the disciples' hope revived. They no longer had to suffer the sting of humiliation at the thought of the murder of their Master. He had triumphed over death. Now they could tell the story of his crucifixion. It was the prelude to life rather than the end.

We now turn our attention to the tragic and triumphant events of Jesus' rejection and resurrection.

chapter twenty

The Conspiracy

Most of the sayings and stories found in the Gospels circulated as small independent units for many years before they were placed in a chronological framework. The passion narratives appear to be an exception. They contain a unity and a wealth of detail which previous gospel material plainly lacks. These characteristics have been accounted for by Mark's residence in Jerusalem and by the possibility of his participation in some of the events. A more likely reason, however, is the nature of the material itself. The mystery of Jesus' death and resurrection could not be communicated in pithy sayings and isolated incidents. History as profound as this event had to be related as a connected whole.

It is scholarly consensus that the passion narratives were the first part of the Gospels to achieve a relative fixed form, first in the oral tradition and later in the written record. Their authentic parts, therefore, constitute the bedrock of the Gospel. Yet, even the passion accounts were subject to changes, rearrangements, and additions. The importance of the events depicted—not to mention their controversial nature—made them the objects of reflection, interpretation, and development. Modifications of the written material may be easily recognized by comparing Mark 14–15 with the parallel material in Matthew and Luke. Many more changes must have taken place during the oral period. Several factors seem to have been at work. (1) The Scriptures were used as a proof-text. Christ's death was depicted as a fulfillment of prophecy. In the process of demonstration, proof-text and happening tended to coalesce. (2) An apologetic interest arose. In order to protect the church against further persecution, it became necessary to show that, although Jesus had been crucified by Roman soldiers, he had not been a rebel against Rome. (3) The conflict between the church and the synagogue inevitably affected the account of Jesus' trial. (4) The theology of the early church, especially its interpretation of the death of Jesus, influenced the story at points. "The result is that while there is greater circumstantiality and continuity [in the passion narratives], the interpretative elements are the more easily recognizable, particularly by comparing the several Gospels."[1]

Form critics have attempted to penetrate Mark's Passion Story in order to recover its original form. They have also tried to determine what additions were made to the story before it reached Mark. The additions generally assigned to Mark or his predecessors are: (1) the anointing at Bethany (14:3–9) which interrupts the sequence of 14:1–2 and 10–11, and which Luke uses in a markedly different form and in an altogether different context (7:36–50); (2) the preparation for the Passover (14:12–16) which seems to echo 11:1–6; (3) perhaps the Son-of-Man saying in 14:21; (4) the saying in 14:28, the prophecy of Peter's denial (14:30–31), and its occurrence (14:54,66–72); (5) the incident in Gethsemane (14:32–42); (6) the test question at the Jewish trial (14:61b–62); (7) the tearing in two of the Temple veil (15:38); and (8) the women at the cross (15:40–41,47).[2] To identify these passages as "additions" is not to suggest that they are "fictitious and therefore to be discarded; that is no more the case here than in that of the Lukan, Matthaean, Johannine additions, transpositions, or modifications of the narrative. Each passage must be dealt with by itself and on its own merits."[3]

Chronological Conundrum (231, 234)[4]

The determination of Jewish leaders to destroy Jesus (mentioned previously in Mk. 3:6 and 12:8) was intense. The chief priests and the scribes were alarmed at his provocative teaching and his popularity with the people. Every attempt they had made to trap and discredit him had failed. Their only resource was action, and the action had to be swift. The crisis was acute; the feast of the Passover, during which no action could be taken, was fast approaching. The action also had to be secret, since any disturbance of public order, such as an open arrest would provoke, would bring the religious leaders in conflict with the Roman authorities. Jewish leaders knew that such a conflict was to be avoided at all costs.

The Passover was a feast of prehistoric origin.[5] Perhaps it originally

[1]Branscomb, *The Gospel of Mark*, p. 242.

[2]See Frederick C. Grant, *The Earliest Gospel* (New York and Nashville: Abingdon Press, 1943), pp. 175–83.

[3]Grant, in *The Interpreter's Bible*, VII, 866.

[4]Mt. 26:1–5,17–19; Mk. 14:1–2,12–16; Lk. 22:1–2,7–13. Compare Jn. 12:1–8; 13:1.

[5]See W. J. Moulton, "Passover," in *A Dictionary of the Bible*, ed. James Hastings (New York: Charles Scribner's Sons, 1923), III, 684–92; J. C. Rylaarsdam, "Passover and Feast of Unleavened Bread," in *The Interpreter's Dictionary of the Bible*, ed. G. A. Buttrick (New York: Abingdon Press, 1962), K–Q, 663–68.

concerned the sacrifice of the first-born. Israel apparently had observed it prior to the Exodus. At the time of the Exodus, however, the feast took on new meaning. Moses destroyed the Pharaoh's opposition to his liberation movement with the tenth plague—the death of the first-born. The Lord passed over the homes of the Hebrews because they had smeared their houses with blood. Only the first-born of the Egyptians were smitten (Ex. 12:1–30). After the Exodus, the ancient feast came to be associated with this Passover. Later, in Canaan, the Passover was connected with the agricultural festival of Unleavened Bread. The Feast of Unleavened Bread was probably originally the opening festival of the harvest season. If so, the use of unleavened bread can be explained on the basis of the use of new grain, hastily prepared for food in the busy time at the beginning of harvest. For the later Israelites, however, the use of unleavened bread signified their hasty departure from Egypt. Since they had had no time to let their dough rise, they had baked and eaten their bread in the unleavened state.

Mark begins the account of Jesus' preparation for the Passover with a curious statement. "And on the first day of Unleavened Bread, when they sacrificed the passover lamb, his disciples said to him, 'Where will you have us go and prepare for you to eat the passover?'" (14:12). The Passover lamb was sacrificed on the afternoon of Nisan 14. The Passover meal, the central feature of which was the roasted flesh of the lamb, was eaten after sunset of Nisan 14 (or at the beginning of Nisan 15 by Jewish reckoning, since the Jewish day began at sunset) and continued into the night. Nisan 15 marked the first day of the seven-day Feast of Unleavened Bread. Strictly speaking the Passover was not part of, but preceded, the Feast of Unleavened Bread. This distinction is clearly preserved in Jewish writings. "On the fourteenth day of the first month [Nisan] is the Lord's passover. And on the fifteenth day of this month is a feast; seven days shall unleavened bread be eaten" (Num. 28:16–17). Luke follows Mark's wording, but Matthew omits "when they sacrificed the passover lamb" (Mk. 14:12), although he retains the notion that a Passover meal was being prepared. Mark may have written with the Roman day in mind, followed a growing Jewish tendency to treat the two feasts as one, or simply shifted to a different source. In any case, Mark's meaning is clear. It is the Passover meal which Jesus instructs his disciples to prepare (14:12–16).

This fixed date for the Last Supper (after sunset of Nisan 14, which is the beginning of Nisan 15, the first day of Unleavened Bread, the day of the Passover meal) controls the chronology of the Synoptics. Jesus (by Jewish reckoning) ate the Passover meal, was arrested late the same night, was condemned to death in the early morning, was crucified, and died on the cross before sunset the same day—Nisan 15, the day before the Sabbath (Mk. 15:42). The Fourth Gospel, on the other hand, presents a different chronology. It puts everything twenty-four hours earlier. In the Fourth Gospel, the Last Supper is not considered to be the Passover meal (13:1). On the morning of the trial before Pilate, the Jews did not enter the praetorium "so that they might not be defiled, but might eat the passover" (18:28). This was "the day of Preparation for the Passover" (19:14). Jesus died on the cross on Nisan 14 at the time when the Passover lamb was being slain. He thus became "the Lamb of God, who takes away the sin of the world!" (1:29). Nisan 14 was the day before the Sabbath (19:31). John and Mark agree, therefore, that the crucifixion was on Friday, the day before the Sabbath. They disagree as to whether Friday was Nisan 14 (when the Passover lamb was slain) or Nisan 15 (the first day of Un-leavened Bread).

Which chronology is correct—the one in John or the one in the Syn-optics? No easy answer can be given, since two factors cloud the issue. First, we don't have as much precise information about the customs in first-century Judaism as we should like; and second, we cannot be sure what an unscrupulous and violent hierarchy, intent on murder, might do contrary to ritual regulations. Although scholars are sharply divided on the chrono-logical question, most of them favor the Johannine dating. We shall briefly summarize the evidence.

The chief priests and the scribes intended to do away with Jesus before the feast (Mk. 14:1–2). No alteration of this intent is mentioned later. (Actually Mark's statement—which clashes with what finally happens in his Gospel—simply says that the authorities did not want to arrest Jesus *during* the feast. It might mean that they would wait until the feast was over.)

It is unlikely that Jews would engage in so much activity on the night of the Passover meal and the first day of Unleavened Bread. Jesus and the disciples journeyed from the Upper Room of Gethsemane (Mk. 14:15,26). Those who came to arrest Jesus carried swords as did two of the disciples (Mk. 14:43; Lk. 22:38). The Sanhedrin met in full session (Mk. 14:53,55). Simon of Cyrene "was coming in from the country" (Mk. 15:21). (This argument is cogent but not altogether convincing. The walk to Gethsemane would not have exceeded the Sabbath-day's journey permitted on a feast day. The law against carrying arms on a feast day would not have applied to the police who made up at least part of the arresting party. The rule that celebrants of the Passover must remain in the house until morning was not always observed. The comment that Simon of Cyrene was coming from the country does not necessarily mean that he had been at work.)

Paul declares that "Christ, our paschal lamb, has been sacrificed" (I Cor. 5:7). His words, written some time near the Passover season, strongly reflects the ideas connected with the feast. No mention is made of the Pass-over in Paul's description of the Last Supper—a strange omission if it oc-curred on that day. He simply states that "the Lord Jesus on the night when he was betrayed took bread" (I Cor. 11:23). (Although Paul's evidence tends to support the Johannine dating, "Christ, our paschal lamb" may merely mean that Jesus' death occurred at the Passover season.)

Several special features of the Passover meal are not mentioned in the Synoptics. (1) No reference is made to the roasted lamb, the chief article of food at the Passover meal, or to the bitter herbs, or to the attire of the participants (prescribed in Ex. 12). (2) Only one cup is spoken of (from which they all drank), whereas in the Passover ritual each person had his own cup and drank from it four times during the meal. (3) Ordinary bread (*artos*) was used instead of unleavened bread (*azuma*) which was required at Passover. (Some features of the Last Supper, however, do suggest the Passover meal. (1) It is held within the precincts of Jerusalem by special arrangement with one of the city's householders. The Passover had to be eaten within the city limits, and residents were expected to provide quarters for pilgrims for this purpose. (2) The hymn sung at the close of the meal was probably the Hallel. The six thanksgiving Psalms (113–118) were sung in Jewish households at the Passover meal in celebration of the deliverance from Egypt. (3) The bowl or dish into which the disciples dipped with Jesus may have contained the sauce (*charoseth*), compounded of dates, raisins, and vinegar, into which the bitter herbs and (unleavened) bread were dipped.)

The Lord's Supper was celebrated weekly, if not more frequently, in the early church. If it had originally coincided with the Passover meal (an annual affair), would not the early church have observed the Lord's Supper on an annual basis?

The Talmud contains a tradition that Jesus suffered on the eve of the Passover (Sanhedrin 43a).

The second-century Quartodeciman Christians of Asia Minor held that the crucifixion occurred on Nisan 14.

All of the preceding parenthetical data may be marshaled on behalf of the Synoptic dating of the Last Supper. In addition, two important considerations should be kept in mind. (1) People sometimes act contrary to their most sacred traditions and their later better judgment. Fear and hatred might have prompted the religious authorities to move against Jesus on the Passover. Perhaps they felt that their action—far from desecrating such a sacred day—would actually contribute to its sacredness and solemnity by ridding the world of a dangerous heretic. (2) The placing of the crucifixion on the day before the Passover conveniently coheres with John's theology. He was a symbolist and a mystic. He saw Jesus as "the Lamb of God, who takes away the sin of the world!" (1:29). He is the Passover Lamb (who died as the Passover lambs were being slain) whose bones could not be broken (19:32–33). We know that John handled Synoptic material with sovereign freedom. If dramatic and dogmatic reasons prompted him to place the Temple Cleansing prior to the Galilean Campaign, perhaps they also caused him to advance the date of the crucifixion twenty-four hours and to substitute the Foot-Washing for the Lord's Supper.

Many attempts have been made to account for the differences between the Synoptics and John. It is argued that the Pharisees and the Sadducees observed the Passover on different days or that they differed in their reckoning of the calendar. It is also claimed that Galilean Jews rightly conformed to Exodus 12:1–14 and began the Passover with the slaying of the lamb and the eating of the meal on the eve of Nisan 14, while the Jerusalemites followed the current and continuing practice of celebrating the Passover by eating the meal on Nisan 15. There is little chance, however, of erasing the contradictions between the Synoptics and John. We are forced to make a choice; and our decision, based on the available data, is made in favor of John. If the Last Supper was not the Passover meal, what was it? Was it a special kiddush meal designed to usher in and sanctify the sacred day? Or was it a solemn banquet akin to those held by a religious brotherhood? We do not know. The nearness of Passover "gave a tone and emphasis as well as a meaning to the observance which led to some kind of identification of the supper with the paschal meal; but it was chiefly the death of Christ which interpreted both the new supper and the ancient festival, in Christian eyes."[6]

Anointing at Bethany (232)[7]

The story of the anointing of Jesus by a woman is found in all four Gospels. Matthew takes his material from Mark with virtually no changes. John's account also follows the main lines of Mark, with only a few important differences. In the Fourth Gospel, the house where the anointing occurs is that of Lazarus (not Simon the leper) and the woman who performs the anointing is Mary, the sister of Martha and Lazarus (not an anonymous woman). Luke's narrative, however, differs at practically every point. Jesus is at dinner in the house of a Pharisee. The woman who does the beautiful deed is a notorious sinner. The criticism lodged against Jesus concerns his lack of prophetic perception rather than the wanton waste of a precious substance. Clearly Luke has preserved an independent story.[8] The fact that similar traditions often tended to coalesce and transfer details could account for Jesus' Pharisaic host being addressed as "Simon" in Luke.

The use of unguents in the Near East is well known. The anointing of the body, or parts of it, with olive or vegetable oils was a routine made necessary by the climate. Oils were also used for medical and cosmetic purposes. Jesus' host at Bethany, according to Mark, was Simon the leper. The reference must be to a former illness, since the Law isolated lepers. Perhaps Simon had previously been healed by Jesus. As Jesus "sat at table, a woman came with an alabaster jar of ointment of pure nard, very costly, and she broke the jar and poured it over his head. But there were some ["the disciples," Mt. 26:8; "Judas," Jn. 12:4–5] who said to themselves indignantly, 'Why was the ointment thus wasted? For this ointment might have been sold for more than three hundred denarii [equal to a year's wage], and given to the poor.' And they reproached her. But Jesus said, 'Let her alone; why do you trouble her? She has done a beautiful thing to me. For you always have the poor with you, and whenever you will, you can do good to them; but you will not always have me'" (Mk. 14:3–7).

At this point, according to the form critics, the original story ends. The oral tradition usually preserved a striking saying at the conclusion of an episode. Here it is found in "Let her alone. . . . For you always have the poor with you. . . ." Verses 8 and 9 are amplifications of the saying in the light of later events. After Jesus' death, his friends and followers were dis-

---

[6]Grant, in *The Interpreter's Bible*, VII, 876.
[7]Mt. 26:6–13; Mk. 14:3–9. Compare Lk. 7:36–50; Jn. 12:1–8.
[8]See pp. 217–18.

tressed because his body had not been anointed for burial in the proper manner (Mk. 15:46; 16:1). This lack of preparation for burial could hardly have been known before the crucifixion. The comment that the woman's act would be told in memory of her "wherever the gospel is preached in the whole world" is clearly editorial. As the story stands in Mark, though, it is a self-contained anecdote. Since it interrupts the account of the conspiracy and Judas' stealthy conduct, it must be considered an interpolation —perhaps by Mark himself.

Some scholars believe that the woman anoints Jesus as the Messiah. The evangelists say nothing of her purpose, but if this is the case, Jesus "does not accept the acclamation and says, somewhat wryly, that it is an anointing for burial, not kingship."[9] Major, on the other hand, believes that the story of the anointing "possesses a distinction and quality of significant form, which reflects, not the creative imagination of primitive Christian teachers, but the actual reminiscences of eye-witnesses."[10] Jesus' ministry was about to end. The woman's act was an expression of its infinite worth.

Betrayal (233, 243)[11]

The Gospels unanimously assert that Jesus was betrayed to his enemies by one of his intimate disciples. Although we may find the betrayal difficult to understand, we have no valid reason to doubt it. It is hardly the kind of story the early church would have invented. Mark states that Judas Iscariot "went to the chief priests in order to betray him to them. And when they heard it they were glad, and promised to give him money. And he sought an opportunity to betray him" (14:10–11). These verses are really a continuation of verses 1–2. The plot of the chief priests and the scribes to destroy Jesus was given unexpected assistance by Judas.

What was it that Judas betrayed? Two main theories have been advanced. (1) Judas betrayed the Messianic secret. By informing the chief priests that Jesus definitely claimed to be the Messiah, he furnished them with evidence that could be fashioned into a capital charge. To claim to be "the king of the Jews" was treason in Roman eyes. Anyone who made such a claim would undoubtedly be executed. This hypothesis falters, however, because of one fact. Judas did not appear as a witness at Jesus' trial (2) Judas betrayed the place where Jesus slept. Jesus did not remain in the city at night. (Was the city too crowded? Was he too poor? Did he want to avoid arrest?) The authorities could not arrest Jesus during the day because of his popularity with the crowds; and it would have caused considerable commotion for them to have sought him after dark amid the vast multitude of pilgrims encamped outside of Jerusalem. They needed a guide who would

---

[9]Johnson, in *The Interpreter's Bible*, VII, 568.
[10]In *The Mission and Message of Jesus*, p. 166.
[11]Mt. 26:14–16; 27:3–10; Mk. 14:10–11; Lk. 22:3–6. Compare Jn. 12:4–6; 18:2–3; Acts 1:18–19.

take them to the exact spot, in order that they might apprehend Jesus quickly, with a minimum of disturbance. All of our sources, including Acts 1:16, indicate that Judas acted as a guide to the officials who arrested Jesus after dark.

Why did Judas betray Jesus? Many motives have been suggested. (1) Judas loved money. He betrayed Jesus, as Matthew plainly suggests, for thirty pieces of silver (26:15). John agrees and indicates that Judas was dishonest as well as avaricious (12:6). Greed is also the motive presented in the famous Passion Play at Oberammergau. Cupidity in itself would hardly have caused an intimate and trusted disciple to betray Jesus. It might, however, have been mixed with other motives. If Judas received money from the high priests, it was probably because the authorities wished to bind the bargain. Matthew's mention of thirty pieces of silver is patterned after the prophecy in Zechariah which told of a shepherd whose hire was weighed in thirty shekels of silver (Zech. 11:12). Matthew "has again been led astray by his conviction that the Old Testament oracles have higher historical value than the Marcan document."[12] Matthew later relates that after Jesus had been arrested and condemned, Judas brought the thirty pieces of silver to the chief priests and the elders. They refused to accept them. Judas then flung the coins down in the Temple and went and hanged himself. The chief priests bought the potter's field with the money (27:3–10). Thus a second prophecy of Zechariah was fulfilled: "So I took the thirty shekels of silver and cast them into the treasury in the house of the Lord" (Zech. 11:13).[13] According to Luke, Judas bought a field with the "blood money," and his death was either accidental or the result of a punitive miracle (Acts 1:18). (2) Judas was malicious. He was filled with jealousy and hatred of the other disciples. They were all Galileans. Judas was a Judean. Sectional rivalry and Peter's displacement of Judas as leader of the Twelve prompted him to turn Jesus over to his enemies. This theory is farfetched. It is based on the dubious belief that Iscariot meant "man of Kerioth," a Judean hamlet. More likely Iscariot meant a left-wing "Zealot" (*sicarius*). Moreover, alleged dissension among the disciples on sectional or leadership grounds is utterly unsupported by the records. (3) Judas shared the Sadducean point of view. He resented the Temple Cleansing and other challenges to authority. He feared that Jesus would lead his nation to a futile and bloody insurrection. (4) Judas was mistaken but not malicious. He had joined the Jesus movement because he believed that Jesus would one day declare his kingship of Israel and lead a revolt against the Romans. While there was much in Jesus' words and works which disappointed Judas, he lived in hope. That hope was fanned into a raging flame by the Temple Cleansing. When Jesus failed to follow up this deed with a declara-

---

12Major, in *The Mission and Message of Jesus*, p. 162.

13Matthew (27:9) wrongly attributes the prophecy to Jeremiah, but it is really a free paraphrase of Zechariah 11:13. "Treasury," the probable original reading in Zechariah, was changed to "the potter" in the Masoretic Text. Matthew uses both ideas: the money was cast into the treasury, and it was also given to the potter to buy the field. Thus a double prophecy is fulfilled. From this passage, we derive the term "potter's field," a cemetery for paupers.

tion of his Messiahship, Judas decided to force Jesus' hand. He "betrayed" Jesus to the chief priests confident that when they attempted to arrest him, Jesus would openly declare his Messiahship, assert his authority, win the support of the nation, and drive the Romans into the Mediterranean. Judas never dreamed that his act would lead to the crucifixion of Jesus. When it did, Judas "repented," returned the "blood money," and hanged himself (Mt. 27:3–5). (5) Judas hoped that the arrest would place Jesus in protective custody and thus prevent his assassination. (6) Judas was not a free agent. Luke states that Satan entered Judas before he conferred with the religious authorities (22:3–4). John echoes Luke's thought (13:2). But these statements are less an indication of teleological cause than theological consequence. They conflict with Mark who implies that Judas went to the chief priests entirely on his own initiative (14:10).

The simple truth is that no convincing reason is advanced in the Synoptics as to why Judas betrayed Jesus. Avarice and Satan are suggested. Apparently the motive for the betrayal was not known by the early church, and Christians were puzzled then as now. They finally fell back on the explanation that the deed was foretold in the Scriptures.

Preparation for the Passover (234)[14]

Jesus, according to Mark, sent two disciples ("Peter and John," Lk. 22:8) into Jerusalem to make preparation for the Passover. The directions given them were evidently intended to preserve the secret of the precise place where they would eat. This was doubtless in order to prevent a nocturnal arrest. The evangelist indicates earlier that while Jesus taught in the Temple by day he withdrew to Bethany each night (11:11,19). Matthew repeats the tradition (21:17). The instructions have an Oriental quality about them. " 'Go into the city, and a man carrying a jar of water [a distinctive sign since in the Near East women bear water jars and men carry waterskins] will meet you; follow him, and wherever he enters, say to the householder, "The Teacher says, Where is my guest room, where I am to eat the passover with my disciples?" And he will show you a large upper room furnished and ready; there prepare for us' " (Mk. 14:13–15). Matthew omits the incident of the man with the jar of water. In his account the disciples are sent directly to the householder. The incident is doubtless legendary. Many interpreters equate this Upper Room with the one mentioned in Acts 1:13 and locate it in the house of John Mark's mother. Acts 12:12 indicates that her home served as a meeting place for Jesus' followers after the crucifixion. The "man carrying a jar of water" is identified as John Mark and the "householder" as John Mark's father. Careful commentators, however, find many a weak link in this chain of inferences.

The Upper Room may not have been in regular use by the householder. For the Passover period, however, it would be "furnished and

14Mt. 26:17–19; Mk. 14:12–16; Lk. 22:7–13.

These steps lead to the room which Christian tradition considers to be the Upper Room.

ready"—provided with rugs and cushions and a low table. "And the disciples set out and went to the city, and found it as he had told them; and they prepared the passover" (Mk: 14:16). Their preparation involved the purchase, slaughter, and roasting of the Passover lamb and the provision of unleavened bread, bitter herbs, and wine. General preparation for the Passover began at the middle of the preceding month (Adar). Roads and bridges were repaired, tombs were whitewashed, purifications were undertaken, and household utensils were carefully cleaned. On the evening of Nisan 13 the head of the family searched the house for leaven. It had to be burned or scattered to the winds by noon of Nisan 14 when nearly all work stopped. All able-bodied, ceremonially-pure men within a radius of fifteen miles were required to appear before the Lord in the Temple with an offering. The regular evening sacrifice was advanced in order to make room for the Passover sacrifice. Companies of ten to twenty persons were organized. At the appointed hour their representatives, each provided with a lamb not less than eight days old or more than a year, were assembled into three divisions. Each division was admitted successively to the Temple court. When priests thrice blew the silver trumpets, each Israelite in the division just admitted killed his lamb. The blood was caught by the priests who stood in two rows. One row had gold and the other silver bowls. The bowls were then passed to the priests nearest the altar who dashed the contents on its base. The lambs were hung on nails, and their fat was removed and offered on the altar. All the while the Levites sang the Hallel (Pss. 113–118).

The lambs were then taken to the homes where they were roasted whole on a wooden spit. Pomegranate wood was used so that no sap would exude. Under penalty of scourging, no bone of the animal could be broken. If the lamb's flesh came in contact with any foreign substance, that part was cut away. Nothing was eaten after the evening sacrifice until the Passover meal which ended at midnight. Participants dressed in their best garments. Wine, which was not required by the Law, was regarded as an indispensable part of the feast. Each person was provided with four cups of red wine even if it had to be paid for from charitable funds. A sauce (*charoseth*), although not obligatory, was usual. The essential elements of the meal were the bitter herbs, unleavened cakes, free-will offering, and Passover lamb. The supper opened with the blessing, which was pronounced by the head of the family over the first cup of wine which was then drunk. Then came a hand-washing and an accompanying prayer. Then the bitter herbs were dipped into the sauce and passed around. After the second cup of wine was poured, the son (or his spokesman) asked what the feast meant (Ex. 12:26). The father's explanation was followed by the first part of the Hallel (Pss. 113–114). After the third cup of wine, grace was said. The fourth cup of wine was followed by the rest of the Hallel (Pss. 115–118). After the Temple was destroyed in 70 A.D., the sacrifice of the lamb was terminated. The festival continued as a home meal and ceremony (Seder) with a much developed story from Exodus.[15]

Last Supper (235–237)[16]

In the evening of the same day that Jesus sent two disciples to prepare for the Passover (actually the next day, Nisan 15, by Jewish reckoning), he assembled in the Upper Room with his disciples. During the meal he declared that one of his table companions would betray him. When pressed further, he asserted, "It is one of the twelve, one who is dipping bread in the same dish with me" (Mk. 14:20). At any meal, the group would dip into a common dish. If this was the Passover, the reference would be to the sauce into which the bitter herbs were dipped. In Luke, Jesus merely says that "the hand of him who betrays me is with me on the table" (22:21). Matthew goes so far as to have Judas ask, "Is it I, Master?" Jesus replies, "You have said so" (26:25). John makes Jesus' identification of Judas as the betrayer explicit: " 'It is he to whom I shall give this morsel when I

[15]See Moulton, in *A Dictionary of the Bible*, III, 690–91, for a more extended treatment. Our reconstruction is dependent on that account.

[16]Mt. 19:28; 20:25–28; 26:20–29; Mk. 10:42–45; 14:17–25; Lk. 22:14–38.

have dipped it." So when he had dipped the morsel, he gave it to Judas, the son of Simon Iscariot" (13:26).

It is quite likely that Jesus knew who it was who would betray him. He may have had definite information from friends and supporters about visits Judas had made to the religious authorities. Or he may have discerned Judas' intention from his demeanor. Some scholars have concluded that Matthew interprets Jesus' answer "You have said so" to mean "Yes," since Matthew uses the same words in 26:64 as a substitute for Jesus' affirmative response in Mark 14:62. It is more reasonable to consider Jesus' answer noncommittal. It is unbelievable that Jesus could have specifically identified his betrayer without the rest of the disciples making some effort to prevent Judas from carrying out his plan. It was the grossest kind of perfidy to betray a companion after eating with him. Would not as impulsive a person as Peter have drawn his sword and severed Judas from his scheme? The development of Jesus' prediction by Matthew and John must be considered "prophecy after the event."[17]

It was in this Upper Room, according to tradition, that Jesus ate the Last Supper with his disciples.

---

[17]Since Mk. 14:18 is patterned after Ps. 41:9 (as the fuller citation in Jn. 13:18 suggests), many scholars think the entire incident stems from the Psalm. See F. W. Beare, *The Earliest Records of Jesus* (New York: Abingdon Press, 1962), p. 224.

The Last Supper is known by many names. The early church called it the Eucharist (*éucharistēsas*, "when he had given thanks," Mk. 14:23). The Roman church named it the Mass. Protestants commonly refer to it as Holy Communion or the Lord's Supper. The extraordinary development and significance of the sacrament in the church stand in striking contrast to the short and simple story in Mark. In the midst of the meal Jesus "took bread, and blessed [God for the bread], and broke it, and gave it to them, and said, 'Take; this is my body.' And he took a cup, and when he had given thanks he gave it to them, and they all drank of it. And he said to them, 'This is my blood of the covenant, which is poured out for many. Truly, I say to you, I shall not drink again of the fruit of the vine until that day when I drink it new in the kingdom of God' " (Mk. 14:22–25).

Matthew, probably mirroring meanings discovered by the early church, magnifies Mark's record. Jesus tells the disciples to eat the bread and "drink" the wine, that his blood is poured out for many "for the forgiveness of sins," and that he will not again drink wine until he drinks it "with you" in the kingdom of God. Luke places Jesus' words about the future first, reverses the order of bread and cup, implies that only the disciples partook of the wine, and omits any reference to the blood of the covenant or to the forgiveness of sins.[18]

Paul furnishes us with the earliest written account of the Last Supper (I Cor. 11:23–25). He indicates that he received it "from the Lord" (I Cor. 11:23). By this phrase he does not mean "from Jesus' lips" or "by Jesus' inspiration" but "from the Lord through the apostles." Three distinct ideas are found in his letter. (1) The Lord's Supper is an *institution*. Jesus' followers are to repeat ("Do this") the rite. (2) The Lord's Supper is a *memorial* to Jesus. The Passover was a remembrance and a renewal of sacred ties. Christians are to recall Jesus, especially his death, when they celebrate the Supper. "Do this in remembrance" (*anamnēsis*) means "perform" or "practice" this, not "make this sacrifice" (*mnēmosunon*). (3) The Lord's Supper is the *new* covenant. It is a fulfillment of Jeremiah's prophecy. "Behold, the days are coming, says the Lord, when I will make a new covenant with the house of Israel and the house of Judah, not like the covenant which I made with their fathers . . . which they broke. . . . I will put my law within them, and I will write it upon their hearts; and I will be their God, and they shall be my people. . . . I will forgive their iniquity, and I will remember their sin no more" (Jer. 31:31–34).

These three ideas are lacking in Mark and Matthew.[19] They are lacking, also, in the parallel passage in Luke (22:17–19a), often referred to as Luke's shorter version. They are present, however, in Luke's longer version (which includes 22:19b–20), as the following comparison demonstrates.

---

[18]Mark gives the explanation concerning the wine after the disciples drink it without instruction.

[19]Did Mark assume that his readers were aware that the Supper was celebrated regularly? Did he fear that its mention might arouse the Romans to persecution? Or was the command, that the supper be repeated, not given by Jesus, since he expected the imminent end of the world?

Luke 22:19b–20	*I Cor. 11:23–25*
which is given for you	which is for you
do this in remembrance of me	*do this in remembrance* of me
and likewise the cup after the supper, saying,	in the same way also the cup, after supper, saying,
This cup which is poured out for you is the *new* covenant in my blood	This cup is the *new* covenant in my blood[20]

Luke's longer version of the Last Supper is much disputed. It receives strong manuscript support, but the manuscripts are copies dated 250 years after Paul and Luke. Many modern translators favor the shorter text of Luke on the grounds that the longer version is derived from Paul and that its inclusion would mean that the cup was given twice. Did the ideas found in Paul originate with Jesus? The prevailing view is that they are Pauline additions.

Jesus conformed to Jewish custom when he blessed God and broke bread with his disciples. Table fellowship played a prominent role among the people of his day. But the words which he spoke during the meal in the Upper Room were new. According to Mark they symbolized Jesus' approaching death, his shared life with the disciples, and his farewell— combined with the confident expectation that he would participate in the new and coming kingdom of God beyond the bounds of death. Covenant blood was an ancient and honored symbol. When Moses received the Law from God, he sealed the pledge of his people to obey it by sprinkling them with "the blood of the covenant" (Ex. 24:8). This act established a permanent bond between God and Israel. Jesus' use of the phrase, "my blood of the covenant . . . poured out for many," calls to mind the death of the Suffering Servant (Is. 53:11–12). The action and words of the Galilean suggested that as the disciples partook of the bread and wine, they also shared his life. The single cup (in view of the fact that each Passover participant had his own cup) stressed their unity with him. His closing words pointed to the future. The Passover served to remind Israel of God's great deliverance in the past. It also prompted her to look ahead. God would deliver His people again. This hope was often visualized in the form of a Messianic banquet. Although Jesus realized that his last meal was before him, he looked forward with confidence to a new life in God's coming kingdom. The original ideas of the Last Supper were altered under the influence of Jewish sacrificial beliefs. Paul and John identified Jesus with the Passover lamb since the Last Supper occurred at the Passover season.

But what was the meaning of the Last Supper for Jesus? It was not the Lord's Supper of the Christian church. The church, which resulted from the resurrection, had not yet been born. Neither was the Last Supper, in our view, the Passover meal with Messianic overtones found in the Syn-

[20]Emphasis added.

optics[21] or Jesus' preenacted memorial service as envisaged by Paul. Some have regarded it as a special kiddush meal intended to usher in and sanctify the sacred day. But it was more likely a solemn eschatological banquet similar to those celebrated by religious brotherhoods.[22] Common meals had served to cement the bonds between Jesus and his disciples as they had proclaimed the kingdom's coming and the need for repentance. When they gathered for their final meal, they were exhilarated by a joyful feeling of eschatological expectation. Although Jesus' declaration that he would not again drink wine until he drank it new in the kingdom (Mk. 14:25) may at first have signaled sorrow, its central thrust was not lost for long. The relationships that his impending death would rupture were renewable. The kingdom of God would soon be consummated.[23]

Luke indicates that Jesus concluded his words at the table with statements about his betrayal, the greatest among them, a prophecy of Peter's denial, and the disciples' need for preparedness. The first two topics have been covered before, and the third occurs at the Mount of Olives in Mark and Matthew. The words about preparedness were intended to steel the disciples for the dangers which lay ahead. In earlier days they had been cordially welcomed and entertained during their mission.[24] Now the situation had changed. The attitude of the community was hostile. They must take with them a purse and a bag. "And let him who has no sword sell his mantle and buy one" (Lk. 22:36).[25] To this the disciples replied, " 'Look, Lord, here are two swords.' And he said to them, 'It is enough' " (22:38). The disciples took Jesus quite literally and "any hypothesis that they were mistaken," declares Gilmour, "is too subtle to be probable."[26] Perhaps so, but "It is enough" is a peculiar way to speak of two swords. Moreover, two swords would hardly be adequate to protect the Twelve, much less to wage a war against Rome. In Mark 14:41–42, where the same expression is used,[27] it serves to terminate Jesus' agony and the disciples' slumber: "Are you still sleeping and taking your rest? It is enough; the hour has come; the Son of man is betrayed into the hands of sinners. Rise, let us be going; see, my betrayer is at hand." It is better to regard "It is

[21]The view of Joachim Jeremias, *The Eucharistic Words of Jesus*, rev. ed., tr. A. Ehrhardt (Oxford: Basil Blackwell, 1966).

[22]Compare the Qumran writing, *Rule of the Future Community*, II, 17–21.

[23]For a stimulating discussion of the distinction between the Last Supper as a Passover celebration and as an eschatological celebration, see Hans Lietzmann, *Mass and Lord's Supper* (Leiden: E. J. Brill, 1953). Other helpful writings on the Last Supper include Wm. Manson, *Jesus the Messiah* (London: Hodder and Stoughton, Ltd., 1945), pp. 134–46; Jeremias, *The Eucharistic Words of Jesus*; Vincent Taylor, *Jesus and His Sacrifice* (London: Macmillan & Co., 1939), pp. 114–42; 175–86; 201–217.

[24]Luke overlooks the fact that he has included these specific instructions ("no purse or bag or sandals," 22:35) in his account of the mission of the Seventy (10:4), not of the Twelve (9:3).

[25]Verse 37 echoes Is. 53:12. The quotation has little connection with what precedes and follows it. It may not have been part of the present passage originally.

[26]Gilmour, in *The Interpreter's Bible*, VIII, 387.

[27]The Greek is different but the meaning is probably the same, as the translations indicate.

enough" as a Semitism, meaning "Enough of this!" Jesus' metaphor of a sword was misunderstood by the disciples, and he abruptly dismissed the subject. "The future bulged with danger and Jesus wanted his disciples forewarned in mind rather than in money and might."[28]

Prediction of Desertion and Denial (238)[29]

In the late evening, Jesus and his disciples sang a hymn, probably one of the Psalms (115–118) used to end the Passover. Then they left the Upper Room in Jerusalem and crossed the brook Kidron to the Mount of Olives. According to Mark (followed by Matthew), Jesus announced that the disciples would desert him.[30] He cited a passage from Zechariah 13:7 to underscore the prediction. The citation is probably a Christian reflection. Jesus then continued, "But after I am raised up, I will go before you to Galilee" (Mk. 14:28). This verse (as the one to which it points, Mk. 16:7) is an interpolation. It breaks the continuity. The narrative proceeds in verses 29–31 as though verse 28 had not been uttered.[31] Peter ardently asserted his fidelity. Jesus replied, "Truly, I say to you, this very night, before the cock crows twice,[32] you will deny me three times" (Mk. 14:30). Peter vehemently declared that he would risk death but would not deny Jesus. The other disciples joined him in his stand. Luke reports that Jesus told Peter that Satan had demanded to have him, but Jesus had prayed for him that his faith would not fail. When Peter "turned again," he was to strengthen his fellow disciples (22:31–32).

Peter's experience served as a constant reminder to church members faced with persecution. If such a preeminent apostle could deny Jesus, ordinary followers would have to exert extra effort in order to remain faithful. If they should falter, however, they could take comfort in the fact that Peter had been restored to favor after he had renounced his Master. The incident gave no support to those who harbored an unforgiving attitude toward backsliders.

28Beck, *Through the Gospels to Jesus*, p. 307. Beare, *The Earliest Records of Jesus*, pp. 228–29, who acknowledges that this passage is the despair of commentators, thinks that our interpretation is erroneous. He suggests that some stray Zealot phrases have found their way into the text.

29Mt. 26:30–35; Mk. 14:26–31; Lk. 22:31–34,39.

30Luke and John place the prediction at the Last Supper.

31The same holds for Mk. 16:7 which also concerns Jesus' postresurrection Galilean appearance. Verse 8 proceeds as though verse 7 did not exist. The terrified women remain terrified, and they say nothing to any one—in flat disobedience to the angel's command. In Matthew they do exactly the opposite (28:8).

32"Cockcrow," according to Roman reckoning, was the third watch of the night—from about midnight to three o'clock. Mark's mention of two cockcrows would indicate a period of about thirty hours. Some good manuscripts of Mark omit "twice," as do Matthew and Luke. If the omission is authentic, then "before early in the morning" is meant.

Prayer in Gethsemane (239)[33]

On the Mount of Olives, Jesus went with his disciples to a place called
Gethsemane ("oil press"). He asked eight of them to sit while he prayed.
Then he took with him Peter, James, and John (omitted by Luke), and he
"began to be greatly distressed and troubled" (Mk. 14:33). These are
strong words. They stand in striking contrast to the attitude of calm born
of foreknowledge which usually characterizes Jesus in Mark. Even before
he left Galilee, according to the evangelist, Jesus had disclosed to the disciples that he would be put to death and be resurrected. The strong feelings
expressed in Gethsemane must have been prompted not only by the
prospect of death, but by the realization that his own people had rejected
him. His mission and message had been a failure from every human viewpoint. "And he said to them [the three intimates], 'My soul is very sorrowful, even to death; remain here, and watch [for my approaching enemies?
share my vigil?].' "[34]

When Jesus had gone some distance from Peter, James, and John ("a
stone's throw," Lk. 22:41), "he fell on the ground and prayed that, if it
were possible, the hour [an astrological term which Matthew and Luke
omit] might pass from him. And he said, 'Abba, Father, all things are possible to thee; remove this cup from me; yet not what I will, but what thou
wilt'" (Mk. 14:35–36). Since the disciples were out of earshot and asleep

In this picture are shown the Garden of Gethsemane and the Church of
the Agony on the Mount of Olives.

[33]Mt. 26:36–46; Mk. 14:32–42; Lk. 22:40–46. Compare Jn. 18:1–2.
[34]Mk. 14:34. Luke omits Mk. 14:33–34, condenses much of the rest of the story, but
adds 22:43–44. Matthew follows Mark quite faithfully.

The rock in the foreground marks the traditional spot in the Church of the Agony where Jesus prayed while Peter, James, and John slept "a stone's throw" away (Lk. 22:41).

for part of the time, at least, and since Jesus had no opportunity later to tell them of the content of his prayer, it has been argued that the whole scene is an invention of the early church. It is based either on the Disciples' Prayer (especially the petitions, "Thy will be done" and "Lead us not into temptation," Mt. 6:10,13), or on Old Testament passages (such as Pss. 40-52) which deal with the righteous man surrounded by his enemies. There can be little doubt that the entire episode in Mark bears the dramatic and religious marks of the early Christian community. The three times of prayer and the three returns to the disciples (omitted by Luke) match Peter's three denials and Jesus' three days in the tomb. The prayer does remind one of the Disciples' Prayer. "My soul is very sorrowful" echoes "My soul is cast down within me" of Ps. 42:6. We cannot insist on the verbal accuracy of the Gethsemane prayer. But the episode seems to express Jesus' authentic spirit; "Not what I will, but what thou wilt." Its emphasis on the humanity, indecision, and limited knowledge of Jesus is hardly the invention of the church! John omits the scene altogether. It does not cohere with his image of how a divine being would act. "The whole story," concludes the distinguished Jewish scholar, Joseph Klausner, "bears the hallmark of human truth: only a few details are dubious."[35]

35*Jesus of Nazareth*, p. 332.

Luke alone mentions the appearance of an angel and Jesus' agony during his period of prayer. "And there appeared to him an angel from heaven, strengthening him. And being in an agony he prayed more earnestly; and his sweat became like great drops of blood falling down upon the ground" (22:43–44). These verses are omitted in Codex Vaticanus and a number of other important manuscripts. They probably represent an embellishment of Luke's text by a Christian scribe.

Three times, according to Mark and Matthew, Jesus returned from prayer and found the disciples asleep. Some have wondered how they could have slept at such a time. They were probably exhausted by the emotional strain of recent days. They had just eaten a heavy meal. It was their regular resting place (Lk. 21:37; 22:39) and the hour was late. Under these circumstances their sleeping, although lamentable, is understandable. But the double repetition of the experience (omitted by Luke) and the command to watch and pray cannot be considered historical. They are Christian reflections on the difficulties of the spiritual life, designed to show that early Christians exposed to temptation should "watch and pray" lest they be found wanting as were the original disciples. Support for this view is found in Mark itself. In 14:41 (and perhaps in 14:37,40), the reference to Jesus finding "them" sleeping pertains to the eleven disciples, not to the three intimates only. This suggests that 14:33 was added to an earlier narrative by Mark in keeping with his view that Peter, James, and John had a closer fellowship with Jesus than the rest.[36]

"Are you still sleeping," Jesus asked the disciples, "and taking your rest? It is enough; the hour has come; the Son of man is betrayed into the hands of sinners. Rise, let us be going; see, my betrayer is at hand" (Mk. 14:41–42). Mark and Matthew contemplate "the hour" with awe. How could it be that the heavenly Son of Man, who would come again in power and glory, was betrayed into the hands of sinners?

Arrest (240)[37]

Jesus saw—or foresaw—Judas approaching. With him came "a crowd with swords and clubs, from the chief priests and the scribes and the elders" (Mk. 14:43). It was a hastily armed, motley company, according to the Synoptics, apparently from the household of the high priest. They came armed because they regarded Jesus as a revolutionary. Their precautions against possible resistance proved to be partly justified (Mk. 14:47). John indicates that the arresting party was composed in part of Roman soldiers under the command of an officer (18:12). In all probability the group consisted of a detachment of Temple police dispatched by the chief priests. Judas served as guide to the group (Acts 1:16; Jn. 18:2). He had arranged to identify Jesus to the arrestors by giving him a kiss. Some form of identifi-

---

[36]If this theory is correct, then the words "greatly distressed and troubled" in verse 33 were derived from "My soul is very sorrowful, even to death" in verse 34.
[37]Mt. 26:47–56; Mk. 14:43–52; Lk. 22:47–53. Compare Jn. 18:3–11.

cation was desirable since the light was dim at best and a mistake could easily be made. Time was of the essence if a disturbance was to be avoided. A kiss (on the head, not the face) was a clever camouflage. It was the usual way a disciple greeted his master.[38] Once Judas had kissed Jesus, the traitor's responsibility had been discharged. It was then up to the armed band to deliver Jesus to the high priest.

When Jesus was seized, "one of those who stood by drew his sword, and struck the slave of the high priest and cut off his ear" (Mk. 14:47). The literary development of this incident can be easily traced. New details were added to the story, and in Luke's tradition it was transformed into a miracle. The unnamed bystander in Mark was identified as a disciple in Matthew (26:51). He struck off an ear of an unnamed slave (Mk. 14:47; Mt. 26:51). Matthew added to the account a rebuke to the disciple by Jesus (26:52–54). Luke identified the severed appendage as the "right" ear, declared that Jesus "touched his ear and healed him," and inserted another version of Jesus' rebuke to the sword-wielder (22:50–51). John omitted the miracle of healing, retained the "right" ear, and identified the anonymous bystander or disciple as Simon Peter and the anonymous slave as Malchus (18:10–11). It has been suggested that the miracle in Luke is a result of a mistranslation of his Aramaic source. Jesus' command to restore the sword to its sheath (Mt. 26:52) was mistakenly understood to refer to the ear. The twelve legions of angels upon whom Jesus could call for help in Matthew are contrasted with the twelve disciples who will shortly forsake him (26:53,56).

Jesus turned to those who had come to arrest him[39] and declared, " 'Have you come out as against a robber [a word used by Josephus, *Antiquities* XX, 8, 5, to describe revolutionaries who combined banditry and violent nationalism], with swords and clubs to capture me? Day after day I was with you in the temple teaching [where he could have been apprehended peacefully—had it not been for his popularity with the people!], and you did not seize me. But let the scriptures be fulfilled.' And they all forsook him and fled" (Mk. 14:48–50). The part of the Scriptures referred to is not specified; perhaps Isaiah 53 and Psalms 22 and 69 were meant. The desertion of the disciples literally fulfilled Mark 14:27, contrary to their conviction at the time.

A curious story, omitted by the other evangelists, concludes Mark's account of the arrest. "And a young man followed him, with nothing but a linen cloth about his body; and they seized him, but he left the linen cloth and ran away naked" (14:51–52). The young man, perhaps mentioned again in 16:5, is often identified as Mark. This incident, which would hardly have rated inclusion in the record unless it was autobiographical, becomes

---

38Luke indicates that Judas' intention was anticipated and frustrated by Jesus' question, "Judas, would you betray the Son of man with a kiss?" (22:47–48). Compare Mt. 26:50.

39To "the crowds" in Mt. 26:55 and to "the chief priests and captains of the temple and elders" in Lk. 22:52. It is highly improbable that Luke is correct in stating that the chief priests and elders participated personally in such a nocturnal and clandestine affair. Note how severely Luke has abbreviated the Marcan account.

"the artist's signature in the corner of his painting," and paves the way for innumerable conjectures. The Last Supper was held in Mark's mother's house (Acts 12:12). Mark slept during the Supper. Judas first brought the arrestors there, but they arrived after Jesus had left. The traitor then took them to Gethsemane. Mark dashed from the house, just as he was, to warn Jesus. He arrived too late. When he was noticed, he was seized. He managed to escape by wiggling out of his cloak (an outer garment worn over the coat by day and used as a blanket at night) and running away in his coat (a long undergarment).[40] This hypothesis is romantic but not realistic. (1) The "sentence structure indicates that the writer of the Gospel is here following a written source, rather than drawing upon his recollection."[41] (2) If the author had been involved in the incident, would he not have furnished further details as to how he came to be present, the condition of his clothing, and where he hid from his pursuers? (3) Papias states that Mark neither heard nor followed Jesus. Perhaps the incident is another detail which was suggested by the Old Testament. Amos had declared that "he who is stout of heart among the mighty shall flee away naked in that day" (Amos 2:16).

There are many differences of detail among the Gospels as to what happened in Gethsemane. It is clear that the accounts have been influenced by prophecy and the religious interests of the Christian community. But it is arbitrary and unwarranted to deny their essential historicity.[42] That Jesus was arrested at night in a secluded spot in Gethsemane while his disciples were with him seems assured. The tradition of anguish and inner struggle which he experienced before he was able to accept the cruelty of the cross as the will of God must rest on a recollection to this effect by some of the disciples. The Gethsemane experience goes a long way toward explaining the serenity and resignation with which Jesus faced his fate in the final hours. It was in Gethsemane rather than on the cross "that the full surrender was made by Jesus to the Father's Will. . . . The self-restraint and heroic courage with which He faced His accusers and judges were secured by His prayer and self-surrender in Gethsemane."[43]

[40]See Mt. 5:40.

[41]Branscomb, *The Gospel of Mark*, p. 270.

[42]When the probable additions to the account in Mark are removed, a simple, unified story of the arrest is found in Mk. 14:43,45–46,50.

[43]Major, in *The Mission and Message of Jesus*, p. 176.

chapter twenty-one

The Condemnation and Crucifixion

When information in all four Gospels is considered, it would appear that Jesus' condemnation moved through four successive stages. (1) He was first taken before Annas, former high priest and father-in-law of the current high priest, Joseph Caiaphas (18–36 A.D.).[1] Annas made a preliminary examination of Jesus (Jn. 18:12–14,19–24). (2) Jesus was then bound and taken before Caiaphas (Mt., Mk., Lk., Jn.). When morning came, the Sanhedrin met in full session (Mt., Mk., Lk.). (3) The Sanhedrin delivered Jesus to Pilate, the procurator (Mt., Mk., Lk., Jn.). (4) Pilate sent Jesus to Herod Antipas. Herod Antipas questioned Jesus at some length and then returned him to Pilate (Lk. 23:6–16). Mark and Matthew mention only two examinations—the one before the Sanhedrin and the one before Pilate. Only John indicates that Jesus appeared before Annas, and only Luke describes the scene before Herod Antipas.

Authority of the Sanhedrin

Mark indicates that Jesus was taken directly from Gethsemane to the supreme court of the Jewish people, the Sanhedrin. The purpose of the trip was to secure Jesus' condemnation and execution. "Now the chief priests and the whole council sought testimony against Jesus to put him to death"

[1]Paul Winter, *On the Trial of Jesus* (Berlin: Walter de Gruyter & Co., 1961), pp. 31–43, believes that the earliest form of Luke and John and the earliest chapters of Acts mistakenly identify the high priest as Annas. He was probably Ananus II.

(14:55). Did the Sanhedrin at this time have the right to try a capital case for a violation of the Jewish Law, to pronounce sentence, and to carry it out? Or had this authority been removed from the Sanhedrin by the Romans? Scholars are not agreed. The data are meager and conflicting.[2] "It is not lawful," the Jews declared before Pilate, "for us to put any man to death" (Jn. 18:31). Their remark is supported by a statement in the Palestinian Talmud that "forty years before the destruction of the temple [that is, about the time of Jesus' death] the right of capital punishment was taken away from the Jews" (Sanhedrin I, 1). On the other hand, Josephus can be quoted in support of the view that under the procurators the Sanhedrin acted as the official legislative and judicial body of the Jews and carried out the death penalty (*Wars* VI, 2, 4; *Antiquities* XIV, 9, 3).

Some limitation of the Sanhedrin's power in capital cases seems likely. Perhaps such offenses could be tried with the approval of the procurator. More likely he had to confirm the Sanhedrin's verdict. Although the resolution of this problem is of intense historical interest, it is not of primary importance to us. Jesus was not put to death by the Sanhedrin on the charge of blasphemy. He was condemned by Pilate on the charge of high treason. He was not stoned to death by the Jews, but crucified by the Romans.

Jesus before Caiaphas (241)[3]

Jesus' appearance before Caiaphas is often called the "Jewish trial." Mark states that "the chief priests and the whole council [the Sanhedrin]" were present and that "they all *condemned* him as deserving death" (14:55,64).[4] There is much about this "trial" which does not merit the title. Nearly every known rule of Jewish judicial procedure was broken. As many as fourteen violations have been counted. We shall mention only a few. (1) It was held at night. (2) It occurred during a festival. (3) Under these circumstances, it was probably held without a full quorum of twenty-three. (4) No witnesses were called for the defense. (5) The condemnation and execution occurred on the same day. (6) The penalty (death by crucifixion) did not fit the "crime" (blasphemy).

All of these procedures—and many more—are in sharp disagreement with the rule prescribed by the tractate Sanhedrin of the Mishnah. Capital cases had to be tried in the daytime. A verdict of conviction could not be reached until the following day. No trial could be held on the eve of a Sabbath or of a festival. Blasphemy required the mention of the divine name. (The claim to be the Messiah or to sit on the right hand of "Power" would not have sufficed.) The argument that the tractate reflects later practice is

[2]See Branscomb, *The Gospel of Mark*, pp. 271–75, for a succinct summary.
[3]Mt. 26:57–75; Mk. 14:53–72; Lk. 22:54–71.
[4]Emphasis added. Matthew, with some abbreviation, follows Mark's account with few changes. Luke, however, makes major rearrangements of the materials and introduces substantive differences. There is no meeting of the Sanhedrin or appearance of the high priest at night, Peter's denial is introduced immediately, there is no account of false witnesses, etc.

dubious. Sanhedrin was made up largely of traditional material based on earlier practice.[5]

Some scholars insist that the entire account of the "Jewish trial" is an invention. When Jesus was brought before Pilate, no mention was made of a previous Jewish trial. The false witnesses who had testified before the Sanhedrin were conspicuous by their absence. The charge of blasphemy was replaced by the charge of sedition. The penalty was not the Jewish one of stoning but the Roman one of crucifixion. In John, as we have noted, there is no reference to a trial by the Sanhedrin. Jesus was merely examined by Annas and then by Caiaphas.

Some elements in the narrative (such as the false witnesses, the charge of blasphemy, and the final condemnation) do appear to be later developments. It is unreasonable, however, to view the whole story as an invention. The Synoptic reports of Jesus before the Sanhedrin represent "a popular Christian version of what took place between the arrest and the trial by Pilate."[6] These reports reflect the cold war between the early church and the synagogue. They form part of the effort of the Synoptics "to shift the responsibility for the death of Jesus from Roman to Jewish shoulders, or at least to deepen the guilt of the Jewish authorities and lighten that of the procurator."[7] It is altogether likely that after his arrest Jesus was brought before the Jewish religious leaders. This would have been an informal examination by the high priest and his advisers rather than a formal trial before a full session of the Sanhedrin. Its purpose would have been to prepare for the proceedings before Pilate in the morning.

What happened behind the closed doors of the high priest's house in the middle of the night cannot be ascertained. No disciples were present. Two principal points have been preserved in the tradition. (1) A garbled account of Jesus' prophecy of the destruction of the Temple was used as evidence against him. "We heard him say, 'I will destroy this temple that is made with hands, and in three days I will build another, not made with hands' " (Mk. 14:58). Such a charge, reinforced by the recent incident of the Temple Cleansing, would have deeply offended the guardians of the Temple. It would have underscored their suspicion of Jesus' revolutionary purpose. Jesus made no answer to the accusation. Perhaps he regarded any defense as futile. Perhaps his silence was patterned after Isaiah 53:7. (2) The high priest asked Jesus, "Are you the Christ, the Son of the Blessed?" (Mk. 14:61). The form of the question betrays Christian reflection. Caiaphas would not have spoken of "the Christ" but of "the Messiah." "Son of the Blessed" is a Jewish circumlocution for "Son of God," an important item in Mark's theology. Since Jesus' alleged Messiahship was the basis of the charge later pressed before Pilate (Mk. 15:2), it is reasonable to suppose that the essence of the question was addressed to him in the presence of Caiaphas.

Jesus' answer to the question concerning his Messiahship varies from

[5]See the incisive study by Winter, *On the Trial of Jesus*, to which our discussion in this section is partially indebted.

[6]Branscomb, *The Gospel of Mark*, p. 278.

[7]Grant, in *The Interpreter's Bible*, VII, 887.

Gospel to Gospel. Only Mark reports that he said, "I am" (14:62). Matthew's account ("You have said so," Mt. 26:64) and Luke's version, where the question is divided and the answer is twofold ("If I tell you [that I am the Christ], you will not believe; and if I ask you, you will not answer," 22:67–68, and "You say that I am [the Son of God]," 22:70) do not add up to affirmations. They are either noncommital replies or veiled denials. If they are consistent with Jesus' pronouncement near Caesarea Philippi, they would have to be denials.[8] After Jesus said, "I am," he continued, "and you will see the Son of man sitting at the right hand of Power [God], and coming with the clouds of heaven" (Mk. 14:62).[9] At this point the high priest tore his mantle, a proper act when one heard blasphemy. The blasphemy did not consist in Jesus' claim to be the Messiah; it consisted in his prediction, as the high priest understood it, that Jesus would sit at the right hand of Power (God). Since the sacred name of God had not been used, this was not blasphemy punishable by death. Nevertheless, "they all condemned him as deserving death" (Mk. 14:64). Verse 62 cannot be considered a verbatim report. The last part of the verse is a composite of Psalm 110:1 and Daniel 7:13. For Mark, the verse constituted the summit of his Christology. Jesus was the "Christ, the Son of God," (1:1) and also the Son of Man who would come with the clouds of heaven.

After Caiaphas had completed his examination of the prisoner, some of the group spit on Jesus, covered his face, and demanded that he prophesy. Mark suggests that those who engaged in the mockery and vilification were members of the Sanhedrin. It is unlikely that these aristocrats mingled with their servants in such indignities. The authorities probably retired to their beds for a rest after they had turned Jesus over to the band which had arrested him. The guards are reported to have struck him with blows (14:65).

Tragedy overtook Peter, according to the Synoptics, on the night that Jesus was examined by Caiaphas.[10] Peter was the only disciple with courage enough to follow Jesus to the house of the high priest. He got no farther than the courtyard. There he sat with the guards, warmed himself by the fire, and waited while Jesus was examined in an upstairs room. The light of the fire revealed Peter to one of the maids of the high priest. " 'You also were with the Nazarene, Jesus.' But he denied it, saying, 'I neither know nor understand what you mean' " (Mk. 14:67–68). Peter then went out into the gateway. The maid, her suspicions aroused, pursued him. To the bystanders she declared, " 'This man is one of them.' But again he denied it" (Mk. 14:69–70). Then the bystanders took up the charge, saying, " 'Certainly you are one of them; for you are a Galilean.' [Matthew states that Peter's accent betrayed him, 26:73.] But he began to invoke a curse on him-

---

[8]Note that Lk. 22:69 does not speak of the *coming* of the Son of Man since Luke is concerned with the Age of the Church—not the parousia. Matthew introduces the word "hereafter" (26:64), which separates Jesus and his present claims from the future sovereignty of the Son of Man, his coming, and (by implication) his judgment. See H. E. Tödt, *The Son of Man in the Synoptic Tradition*, tr. D. M. Barton (London: SCM Press, 1965), pp. 82–84.

[9]See pp. 302–305.

[10]Matthew states that Judas committed suicide a few hours later. See pp. 361–62.

self and to swear, 'I do not know this man of whom you speak'" (Mk. 14:70–71). Jesus had condemned such curses and oaths (Mt. 5:33–37) and for good reason. As Peter proved, they do not guarantee the truth of a statement. When Peter heard the cock crow "a second time," he remembered Jesus' prediction of his denials, and he "broke down and wept" (Mk. 14:72).

The Gospels present different accounts of Peter's denials. Did they occur before (Lk.) or during (Mk.) Jesus' examination? Was Jesus a witness (Lk.) or not (Mk.)? By whom was each accusation made? Where did each denial take place? Did Peter curse himself (Mk.) or not (Lk.)? How many times did the cock crow? The differences in details and the highly stylized nature of the accounts have led some scholars to deny the historicity of the story. Goguel holds that the story stems from a saying of Jesus which blamed Peter for his presumption and hinted at his defection. According to this view, the church, unable to believe that what Jesus had foreseen had not come to pass, conceived the idea that Peter had denied Jesus. Although "the historicity of the saying of Jesus may be retained . . . that of the denial [must be] rejected."[11] It is unlikely, however, that the church would have fabricated such a derogatory story about its honored apostle. The conflicting details in the narratives may be explained as literary elaborations. The differences are not sufficient to discredit the essential historicity of the accounts. Indeed, if they were all in exact verbal agreement, their validity would be suspect. As they are, we have no evidence of collusion.

Jesus before Pilate (242, 244)[12]

Mark says, "As soon as it was morning the chief priests, with the elders and scribes and the whole council held a consultation" (15:1). The accounts of Matthew (27:1) and Luke (22:66) concur.[13] If, as is probable, Jesus was questioned by his enemies during the night of his arrest, then the morning meeting of the Sanhedrin is intended to give a semblance of legality to the night's proceedings. That a "trial" took place in the morning is most unlikely. The Jewish authorities "took counsel" against Jesus (Mt. 27:1). They made no attempt to carry out any sentence. They apparently relinquished their jurisdiction over him and decided what charge they would bring against him before the Roman court. Then they bound Jesus and delivered him to Pilate.

Pilate was the fifth procurator of Judea. He was appointed to that office by the emperor in 26 A.D. His capitol was at Caesarea, but he came to Jerusalem during the great festivals to supervise the preservation of order. The

---

[11]Goguel, *The Life of Jesus*, p. 492. See also pp. 485–91. Consult Branscomb, *The Gospel of Mark*, pp. 281–82, for a refutation.

[12]Mt. 27:1–2,11–14; Mk. 15:1–5; Lk. 22:66; 23:1–5. Compare Jn. 18:28–40; 19:1,4–16.

[13]Luke, as we have noted, does not mention a nocturnal meeting of the Sanhedrin. He places Mark's account of that event on the following morning. John makes no reference to a "trial." In John's account, Jesus is merely brought before Annas and then Caiaphas for questioning during the night.

Jews considered him to be cruel, avaricious, and inflexible. From time to time he shocked their sensibilities—as when he smuggled military insignia bearing the emperor's image into Jerusalem by night or when he seized Temple funds to build an aqueduct. His brutality in putting down a small uprising in Samaria led to his removal from office in 36 A.D. (Josephus, *Antiquities* XVIII, 3, 1–2; 4, 1–2).

Jesus' trial before the Roman procurator was a public affair (Mk. 15:16; Jn. 19:13; compare Josephus, *Wars* II, 14, 3). It followed soon after Jesus' arrest. Matters must have been arranged in advance. Pilate probably needed little nudging to move against a popular leader whom the Jewish authorities considered to be dangerous. The charge pressed against Jesus is not stated in Mark and Matthew. It can easily be inferred, however, from subsequent events. Pilate asked Jesus, "Are you the King of the Jews?" (Mk. 15:2). After the trial, the soldiers mocked Jesus by placing on him a purple cloak and a crown of thorns, both symbols of royalty. They gave him an imperial salute, struck him with a reed (scepter), and knelt down before him in homage (Mk. 15:16–19). Over the cross the placard, which customarily contained the charge against the condemned, read, "The King of the Jews" (Mk. 15:26). This phrase occurs again and again in the story of the trial and execution (Mk. 15:9,12,32). There can be no reasonable doubt that this was the charge on which Jesus was condemned. The fact that its leader was crucified by the Romans on the charge of high treason proved to be an embarrassment to the early church; consequently, the church would not have created such a political charge as the reason for Jesus' execution. One of the functions of the passion narrative was to mitigate this embarrassment as much as possible.

Mark indicates that the chief priests accused Jesus "of many things" (15:3). Luke expands Mark's phrase into three specific indictments. Jesus (1) perverted the nation, (2) prohibited the payment of taxes to Caesar, and (3) proclaimed that he was "Christ a king" (23:2). Since Luke previously records Jesus' teaching about the head tax (20:25), it is obvious that he intends his reader to regard the second charge as a deliberate falsehood. The first charge is also fallacious. Although Jesus had a popular following, he had given no one legitimate cause to conclude that he was engaged in seditious activity. In Luke, as in the other Synoptics, Pilate's interest is excited by the charge that Jesus claimed to be "Christ a king." Since the political implications of this popular expectation were serious, the chief priests undoubtedly pressed these political features in the presence of the procurator.

Pilate asked Jesus point-blank, "Are you the King of the Jews?" (Mk. 15:2). In view of the strong affirmative with which Jesus reportedly had answered a similar question put to him earlier by Caiaphas (Mk. 14:62), he would be expected to reply here also, "I am." But he didn't. The Synoptics are agreed that he answered Pilate with the words, "You have said so" (Mt. 27:11; Mk. 15:2; Lk. 23:3). What do these words mean? Jesus used them in three different situations. (1) He used them to reply to Judas' question as to whether it was he who would betray him (Mt. 26:25). Here the words did not constitute a denial. Neither were they an affirmation since the other disciples made no effort to prevent Judas from carrying out his plan. They must be considered noncommittal. (2) Jesus used the words again to reply to Caiaphas (Mt. 26:24; Lk. 22:70). What happened after Caiaphas' response ("Why do we still need witnesses?" Mt. 26:65) indicates that he understood Jesus' reply to be an affirmative. But the response of Caiaphas may well have been to the second part of Jesus' reply: "But I tell you, hereafter you will see the Son of man seated at the right hand of Power" (Mt. 26:64). Moreover, we must remember that the examination before Caiaphas was behind closed doors, and no disciples were present. The verbal accuracy of the conversation cannot be stressed. (3) Jesus used the words to reply to Pilate's question (Mt. 27:11; Mk. 15:2; Lk. 23:3). Here the context requires that they be regarded as noncommital. Otherwise Pilate's reaction ("Have you no answer to make?" Mk. 15:4) would be meaningless as would his subsequent insistence (if historical) that Jesus was innocent.

Jesus' noncommittal answer puzzled Pilate. Most men protest their innocence whether they are innocent or guilty. Why was it that even after added prodding by the procurator "Jesus made no further answer" (Mk. 15:5)? Perhaps it was because the question could not be answered. Jesus could not accept his enemies' definition of his mission and message. He was no pretender to the Maccabean throne. Nothing in his words or works suggested that he was. Yet he could not deny that God had anointed him to proclaim the coming of the kingdom and the need for repentance. Consequently, he remained silent. In this silence before his accusers, early Christians saw another fulfillment of prophecy: "He was oppressed, and he was afflicted, yet he opened not his mouth" (Is. 53:7).

Pilate then said to "the chief priests and the multitudes, 'I find no crime in this man.' But they were urgent, saying, 'He stirs up the people, teaching throughout all Judea [a synonym here for the whole of Palestine], from Galilee even to this place'" (Lk. 23:4–5). Luke's account of Jesus' trial before Pilate contains several variations from Mark 15:1–15. These variations include (1) the accusations against Jesus by the Sanhedrin (23:2), (2) the threefold protest by Pilate of Jesus' innocence (23:4,14,22), (3) Pilate's referral of Jesus to Herod Antipas (23:7), and (4) the mocking of Jesus by Herod and his soldiers rather than by the Roman soldiers (23:11). These differences have often been used as evidence that Luke had access to a special source. But Mark's version is basic to Luke's account, and Luke's additions serve to accomplish one of the principal purposes of Luke-Acts— the shifting of the responsibility for Jesus' death from the Romans to the Jews. It was common knowledge when Luke wrote that Jesus had been crucified as a subversive. Roman officials naturally concluded that his followers were also seditious. In his writings Luke took special pains to refute the notion. In his Gospel he pictured Pilate as convinced of Jesus' innocence and making repeated efforts to free him—only to be foiled by malevolent Jews. Throughout Acts, Luke depicted the Roman authorities as unusually solicitous in protecting Paul and his associates from the machinations of the mobs.

Jesus before Herod Antipas (245)[14]

When Pilate heard that Jesus had been active in Galilee, he asked if the prisoner was a Galilean. "And when he learned that he belonged to Herod's jurisdiction, he sent him over to Herod, who was himself in Jerusalem at that time" (Lk. 23:7). Although Herod, a native Jewish ruler, was no saint, he did rather carefully observe Jewish religious customs. There is nothing improbable then in his presence in Jerusalem at the Passover season. Pilate may have (1) wanted Herod to dispose of Jesus' case, (2) wished to show Herod a courtesy (since Jesus was Herod's subject), or (3) wanted to secure his advice. Mark relates nothing of Jesus' encounter with Herod. Indeed if Mark 15:25 is correct in stating that the crucifixion took place at "the third hour" (about 9:00 A.M.), there would not have been time for the meeting of the Sanhedrin, the trial before Pilate, the trip to the tetrarch, the return to Pilate, the sentence of death, the mocking by the soldiers, and the journey to Golgotha. It is not likely, either, that a Roman procurator acting in his own jurisdiction would have sent a prisoner to a non-Roman ruler of a neighboring area. Acts 4:27–28 indicates that Jesus' appearance before Herod and Pilate constituted a fulfillment of one of the Psalms: "The kings of the earth set themselves, and the rulers take counsel together, against the Lord and his anointed" (Ps. 2:2). It may be that Luke's story was suggested by such exegesis. Whatever its source, since Herod was a Jew and Pilate was a Roman, the story served to heighten Jewish and minimize Roman responsibility for Jesus' death.

Herod was delighted to see Jesus. He had heard much about the Galilean and had long nursed a desire to see him. The tetrarch's interest was prompted by curiosity rather than by piety. He wanted Jesus to perform a miracle. When Jesus refused to answer the ruler's questions, Herod's curiosity turned to contempt. He and his soldiers clothed Jesus in gorgeous robes to ridicule his alleged kingship. (This mockery constitutes Luke's parallel to the mockery of Jesus by the Roman soldiers in Mark. Since it is unlikely that the mockery took place twice, Luke's incident has little historical worth.) Then Herod sent Jesus back to Pilate, and the two former enemies became fast friends because of their common opposition to the Carpenter.

Death Sentence (245, 246)[15]

Pilate interpreted Herod's contemptuous dismissal of Jesus as tantamount to an acquittal. The procurator called together the chief priests and the rulers of the people and for the second time declared his conviction that the prisoner was innocent. " 'Behold, nothing deserving death has been

---

[14]Lk. 23:6–12.
[15]Mt. 27:15–26; Mk. 15:6–15; Lk. 23:13–25. Compare Jn. 18:38b–40; 19:1,4–16.

done by him; I will therefore chastise him [a substitute for the scourging which precedes the crucifixion in Mk. 15:15] and release him.' But they all cried out together, 'Away with this man, and release to us Barabbas'—a man who had been thrown into prison for an insurrection started in the city, and for murder" (Lk. 23:15–19).

Mark (followed by Matthew) indicates that it was the crowd which clamored for Barabbas. The crowd was aided and abetted by Pilate's practice of releasing a prisoner at the feast (Mk. 15:6–8). The granting of amnesty at festival times is well known. The Romans practiced it at the lectisternium (Livy V, 13). A Talmudic rule, that a Passover lamb may be slaughtered for one who has been promised release from prison, may reflect Jewish practice in Jesus' time.[16] But there is no evidence outside of the Gospels to indicate that the Roman procurator regularly released a prisoner at the Passover and permitted the crowd to name the one to be released regardless of the nature of his offense. Up to this point, the crowds had been favorably disposed toward Jesus. The chief priests had had to operate by stealth lest Jesus' arrest cause an uproar. Yet suddenly the chief priests were able to stir up the crowd to demand the release of Barabbas in the place of Jesus (Mk. 15:11). Pilate, who could find no crime in Jesus, was coerced by the crowd to condemn him to death. Since (1) the shift in sentiment of the crowd seems implausible, (2) Pilate's behavior was more lenient than Roman administration usually tolerated, and (3) extra-Gospel support for the practice of the release of a prisoner at the Passover is wanting, the historicity of the Barabbas incident has been questioned. Branscomb comments that it looks like "the familiar tendency in the Passion narratives to exonerate the procurator and to throw the blame for Jesus' death on the Jews."[17] On the other hand, the release of a prisoner at the Passover may have been a local custom which Pilate observed in order to placate the Jews. "It is scarcely necessary," concludes Grant, "to brand the incident here as fictitious."[18]

We know nothing about Barabbas ("son of [the] father") except what is disclosed in the Gospels. He is described as "a notorious prisoner" (Mt. 27:16), a rebel "who had committed murder in the insurrection" (Mk. 15:7), and a "robber" (Jn. 18:40). The "insurrection" is sometimes identified with the one hinted at in Luke 13:1. This is pure conjecture. Revolts were common in Judea, and we have no idea which one resulted in Barabbas' imprisonment. In some manuscripts of Matthew, the name of the insurrectionist is "Jesus Barabbas" (27:16–17). The wording of the Greek in Mark 15:7 suggests that "Jesus Barabbas" once stood there, too. Jesus was a common Jewish name in the first century. But early Christians could not permit a man like Barabbas to bear the revered name of their Lord; it was soon dropped from the records. The original choice of the crowd, though, was probably between Jesus Bar-Joseph and Jesus Barabbas. The chief priests

---

[16]See C. B. Chavel, "The Releasing of a Prisoner on the Eve of Passover in Ancient Jerusalem," *Journal of Biblical Literature*, LX (1941), 273–78.

[17]*The Gospel of Mark*, p. 289.

[18]In *The Interpreter's Bible*, VII, 895.

doubtless had mixed motives in inciting the crowd to call for Jesus Barabbas. They secretly sympathized with an insurrectionist against Rome, and they feared the leadership of Jesus.

When Pilate asked the crowd what should be done with the one whom they called the King of the Jews (a sarcastic comment which shows that Pilate did not take the charge seriously), they cried out, " 'Crucify him.' And Pilate said to them, 'Why, what evil has he done?' But they shouted all the more, 'Crucify him.' So Pilate, wishing to satisfy the crowd, released for them Barabbas; and having scourged Jesus, he delivered him to be crucified" (Mk. 15:13–15). Scourging was a gruesome Roman custom inflicted on condemned men preliminary to their crucifixion. A leather whip, with pieces of metal and bone set in it, was used. In the Fourth Gospel, Pilate scourged Jesus in an unsuccessful effort to prevent the crucifixion (19:1).

Matthew alone relates two extraordinary events in connection with Jesus' second appearance before Pilate. (1) While Pilate was sitting on the judgment seat, his wife sent word to him. "Have nothing to do with that righteous man, for I have suffered much over him today in a dream" (27:19). (2) As a result of this message (when the people persisted in the demand that Barabbas be released and Jesus be destroyed, and it appeared that a riot might be brewing), Pilate "took water and washed his hands before the crowd, saying, 'I am innocent of this man's blood, see to it yourselves.' And all the people answered, 'His blood be on us and on our children!' " (27: 24–25).

It is difficult to view these incidents as historical. How could Pilate's wife learn about the sudden early morning trial in time to dream about Jesus, suffer much, and make a report to her husband? How could Pilate, imbued with the principles of Roman justice, abdicate his responsibility for passing sentence and cower in the presence of colonials? And how could the people accept the responsibility for Jesus' death for themselves and their children? Matthew's independent stories are doubtless the product of dramatic imagination. They stem from the strained relations which existed between the church and the synagogue at the time the Gospels were being written. Christians considered the awful bloodshed of the Roman-Jewish war, which culminated in the destruction of Jerusalem in 70 A.D., to be God's judgment on the Jews for the crucifixion of Christ. At approximately the time when the Gospels were being written, the Jews added a curse on heretics to the synagogue service, and Christians were excommunicated (Jn. 9:34; 16:2). The consequences of excommunication were severe. Gone were the privileges which Christians had enjoyed as members of a legal religion (Judaism). Now that their meetings were illegal, they became objects of persecution. Under such circumstances it is not strange that they stressed loyalty to the emperor and sought to show that their Christ had been wrongly condemned by the Jewish leaders. The apocryphal Gospel of Peter (written about 150 A.D.) carries this tendency still further. It transfers blame to the Jews wherever possible and virtually whitewashes Pilate.[19] In the Abyssinian Church, Pilate was canonized as a saint for his insistence on

19See James, *The Apocryphal New Testament*, pp. 90, 92.

Jesus' innocence, and his wife was made a saint in the Greek Church because of her dream.

Who was really responsible for Jesus' death? Certainly not the Jewish people as a whole. Most of them knew nothing about his condemnation and crucifixion until after it had happened. Some of the scribes and Pharisees, in their bitter opposition to Jesus' teaching, contributed to a climate in which more determined enemies could operate successfully. The high-priestly group arranged for Jesus' arrest, and they preferred charges against him before Pilate. They were mostly Sadducean politicians concerned with the preservation of the sacrificial system and their special privileges. Some of the leaders of the Sadducees must bear part of the blame for Jesus' death. But the person most at fault was Pilate. It is sometimes argued that he had a duty to preserve order and to safeguard the steady flow of tribute to Caesar. However, he also had a duty to uphold justice. Instead of honoring this obligation, he chose to pacify the populace in order to protect his own position. His was a common fault. "Human beings continually acquiesce in slaying the innocent in order to protect their own privileges, or to maintain what they think is the right social order, or because the forthrightness of prophets offends their self-righteousness."[20] Pilate had previously mingled the blood of Galileans with their sacrifices (Lk. 13:1). Probably one more Galilean didn't seem important. Little did he realize that by his action he "would carve his name enduringly in the hall of infamy."[21]

Mocking (247)[22]

Pilate's sentence of death is not recorded in the Synoptics, but the succession of events shows that it was given. After the sentence was pronounced, Jesus was scourged and then turned over to Roman soldiers to be crucified. As a condemned criminal he had no rights. The soldiers could do with him as they pleased. They took him into the praetorium, the government house of the procurator during his visits to Jerusalem. It may have been the Castle of Antonia, located at the northwest corner of the Temple enclosure. More likely it was Herod's Palace on the southwest side of the city. There the soldiers engaged in some crude and brutal horseplay. They summoned the whole battalion, perhaps six hundred in all. When they learned that Jesus had been condemned to death for claiming to be the Emperor of the Jews, they proceeded to mock him. The "purple cloak" (Mk. 15:17) with which they clothed him was probably a "scarlet robe" (Mt. 27:28), part of their own uniform. The "crown of thorns" (Mk. 15:17) was not a crown (worn by Oriental monarchs) but a wreath—an imitation of the laurel wreath worn by the emperor, as any Roman coin shows. The wreath was woven from some thorny-looking plant. Its presence on Jesus' head, contrary to the traditional image, would not have caused him to bleed. The soldiers

---

[20]Johnson, in *The Interpreter's Bible*, VII, 599.
[21]Beck, *Through The Gospels to Jesus*, p. 316.
[22]Mt. 27:27–31; Mk. 15:16–20. Compare Jn. 19:2–3.

gave Jesus an imperial salute, struck him with a reed (scepter), and knelt down before him in homage. Then they put his own clothes on him and led him away to be crucified.[23]

While the mocking was taking place, Jesus uttered not a word of protest. The early Christians saw in his bearing and the soldiers' brutality the fulfillment of II Isaiah's prophecy: "I gave my back to the smiters. . . . I hid not my face from shame and spitting. . . . He was despised and rejected by men; a man of sorrows, and acquainted with grief. . . . He was oppressed, and he was afflicted, yet he opened not his mouth" (Is. 50:6; 53:3,7).

Crucifixion (248, 249, 250)[24]

Crucifixion had been practiced by the Romans since the Punic Wars of the third and second centuries B.C. It was a punishment reserved for rebels, slaves, and criminals of the lowest classes. Roman citizens were exempt from its torture. It was customary to crucify prisoners in groups. The method of execution varied in details, but the general procedure is clear. The condemned person was first scourged, a brutally painful experience in itself. As part of his punishment he was forced to carry the heavy crossbeam (*patibulum*), which weighed about eighty or ninety pounds, to the place of execution. The picture of Jesus burdened by the entire cross is an artist's invention.

The place of execution was as public as possible, usually by some well-traveled road. It thus served as a grim warning to witnesses not to provoke "the governing authorities" (Rom. 13:1). When the condemned reached his destination, he was stripped of his clothing. His hands were nailed or tied to the ends of the crossbeam. Then he was lifted up and fastened to a permanent upright pole or post. His body was supported on the pole by a block, his legs were lashed out in an unnatural position, and his feet were nailed or his ankles tied to the upright post so that they were a few inches off the ground. Exposure, loss of blood, maltreatment by sadistic spectators, torture by insects, and impaired circulation caused excruciating pain. Death was normally welcomed as a friend after about twelve hours, but men sometimes suffered for much longer periods. Several days after the fall of Jerusalem, Josephus found three of his friends who had been crucified. He arranged with Titus to have them removed from their crosses and given the greatest care, "yet two of them died under the physician's hands, while the third recovered" (*Life* 75).

A centurion was in charge of the Roman soldiers who escorted Jesus to the place of execution. Mark states that "they *compelled* a passer-by, Simon of Cyrene, who was coming in from the country, the father of Alexander and Rufus, to carry his cross. And they *brought* him to the place called

---

[23]Luke has already described the mocking of Jesus by Herod and his soldiers (23:8–11) so he omits the incident here.
[24]Mt. 27:32–56; Mk. 15:21–41; Lk. 23:26–49. Compare Jn. 19:17–30.

Golgotha (which means the place of a skull)."[25] The word "compelled" is of Persian origin. It refers to the forcing of civilians to perform official duties.[26] It is found in the saying of Jesus, "If any one forces you to go one mile, go with him two miles" (Mt. 5:41). Cyrene was a city with a large Jewish population; it was located west of Alexandria in North Africa. Simon, as his name suggests, was a Jew. Whether he had returned to Jerusalem as a Passover pilgrim or as a permanent resident is not indicated. Since his sons, Alexander and Rufus, were well known to the members of the early church, Simon may later have become a Christian. His widow and his son, Rufus, may be the ones referred to in Romans 16:13.

Why did the soldiers force Simon to carry the crossbeam when it was part of Jesus' punishment that he should carry it himself? Certainly they were not prompted by pity. The verb translated "they brought" in Mark 15:22 may be rendered "they carried." While Simon carried the crossbeam, the soldiers carried Jesus. He was in a state of physical collapse induced by a night of no rest, grueling examinations, the trial before Pilate, and the bloody scourging. This interpretation is supported by the tradition that Jesus fell under the burden of the cross and by the short period of time he was on the cross before he died. The entire incident, however, is contradicted by the Fourth Gospel. There it is flatly stated that Jesus carried his own cross to Golgotha. Basilides, in the early part of the second century, used the Synoptic version to support the Docetic claim that Simon had been crucified in place of the divine Christ. Perhaps the author of the Fourth Gospel was making a defense against this heresy when he wrote that Jesus "went out, bearing his own cross" (19:17).[27]

The way to the cross cannot be determined with certainty. The traditional Stations of the Cross (which originated about the middle of the fourteenth century) begin in the Via Dolorosa—one of the main east-west streets of ancient Jerusalem—at the barracks near the Chapel of Flagellation (scourging) and the Convent of the Sisters of Zion. An ancient pavement has been discovered at the Antonia, the site of which lies between the Chapel and the Convent. It is sometimes identified with "The Pavement" where Pilate passed judgment on Jesus (Jn. 19:13). From the barracks, the stations continue west and south to the Church of the Holy Sepulcher. If, however, the praetorium was located at Herod's Palace rather than at the Antonia, the original Way of the Cross began on the other side of the city.

The traditional location of Golgotha (Aramaic) or Calvary (Latin) is at

25Mk. 15:21–22, emphasis added.

26See Connick, *Build on the Rock*, pp. 84–85.

27Luke asserts that a great multitude of people and of women followed Jesus to Golgotha (23:27). The comment may have been suggested by Zech. 12:10–14. In Luke's thought only the women were grief-stricken. The crowd came from curiosity. The following verses (23:28–31) are reminiscent of 19:41–44 and may have been taken from the same source. The saying in 23:31, which may have been proverbial, appears to be inappropriate as a comparison of the crucifixion with the destruction of Jerusalem in 70 A.D. Verse 32 is an editorial correction of Mk. 15:27 where the two robbers are mentioned only after Jesus' crucifixion is related.

the site of the Church of the Holy Sepulcher. This tradition goes back to 327 A.D. when, under Constantine's direction, a number of holy places were designated. Unfortunately the tradition cannot be traced back any further. According to Jewish law, no one could be buried within the precincts of the Holy City. The author of Hebrews wrote that Jesus "suffered outside the gate" (13:12). The Church of the Holy Sepulcher is situated far within the present walls of the Old City, but it may be outside the location of the second wall of Jerusalem which stood in the first century. This Church "is the only site for Golgotha and the sepulchre which has any archeological basis."[28] The pilgrim, however, may find that "Gordon's Calvary" and the "Garden Tomb," located north of Herod's Gate, provide a more convincing picture of what these places probably looked like. During the siege of Jerusalem in 68–70 A.D., the whole area was denuded of trees. The Romans built a huge ramp against the northern wall. Later destruction and reconstruction in the neighborhood only served to complicate the situation. Today it is virtually hopeless to attempt to locate Golgotha. About all that can be said is that it was probably near one of the city gates on the northern or western side of the city close to a public road. (Mark 15:29 informs us that "those who passed by" scoffed at Jesus.) It is usually assumed that it was called Golgotha ("the place of a skull") because it was a knoll shaped like a human head. A less likely theory is that it derived its name from the fact that it was littered with the skulls of executed criminals.

When Jesus reached Golgotha, the soldiers offered him "wine mingled with myrrh" (Mk. 15:23). It was a pious custom for Jerusalem women to prepare unmixed wine or wine with an opiate and to send it to the condemned. The practice was both humane and Scriptural. "Give strong drink to him who is perishing, and wine to those in bitter distress" (Proverbs 31:6). Jesus refused the wine. He had promised at the Last Supper not to drink again of the fruit of the vine until he drank it in the kingdom. He may also have desired to keep a clear head until the very end. Matthew changes Mark's myrrhed wine into wine "mingled with gall" (27:34) in the belief that Psalm 69:21 was fulfilled.

The evangelists write of Jesus' agony with remarkable restraint: "And they crucified him" (Mk. 15:24). No effort is made to arouse the feelings of their readers. This would have been unnecessary. People of the first century were well acquainted with the horrors of crucifixion. Apparently the clothes of the condemned were the perquisites of his executioners. The soldiers "divided his garments among them, casting lots for them, to decide what each should take" (Mk. 15:24). Early Christians saw in this a fulfillment of prophecy: "They divide my garments among them, and for my raiment they cast lots" (Ps. 22:18). By the time the Fourth Gospel was written, it was noticed that the psalmist had made a distinction between the garments (which were divided) and the raiment (for which lots were cast). Consequently, in this Gospel, the soldiers divided Jesus' garments into four parts, but they cast lots for his seamless tunic (19:23–24).

A placard made of wood and covered with white gypsum was either

28Johnson, in *The Interpreter's Bible*, VII, 602. See also p. 601.

hung around the criminal's neck or carried before him to the place of execution. On it was written in black the crime so that all might know why he had to die. At the place of crucifixion, the placard was affixed to the upright pole above the victim's head. It was nine o'clock in the morning when Jesus was crucified (Mk. 15:25).[29] (Jn. 19:14 indicates that it was about noon.) The inscription on the placard above Jesus' head differs slightly in form from Gospel to Gospel, but its substance is the same—"The King of the Jews" (Mk. 15:26). John indicates that the inscription was written in Hebrew, Latin, and Greek, the languages of religion, empire, and culture, respectively (19:20). The charge was that of high treason. It was a travesty of Jesus' mission and message, and it furnishes proof positive that he was tried, sentenced, and executed by the Romans.

Two robbers were crucified with Jesus, one on either side. Josephus frequently uses "robber" as a synonym for "revolutionary," and that is the probable meaning in Mark. More insults and mockery were added to those inflicted on Jesus at the high priest's house and in the praetorium. Passers-by ridiculed him, saying, " 'Aha! You who would destroy the temple and build it in three days, save yourself, and come down from the cross!' So also the chief priests mocked him to one another with the scribes ["and elders," Mt. 27:41], saying, 'He saved others; he cannot save himself. Let the Christ, the king of Israel, come down now from the cross, that we may see and believe.' Those who were crucified with him also reviled him" (Mk. 15:29–32). Some scholars regard these details as secondary, derived from such prophecies as Isaiah 53 and Psalm 22.[30] The scene, it is said, lacks realism and is constructed out of material already familiar to us. References to the destruction of the Temple and Jesus' kingship of Israel stem from the trials. The aristocratic high priests would not have behaved so unseemly in public against a popular hero. Their conduct echoes the Psalm: "All who see me mock at me, they make mouths at me, they wag their heads; 'He committed his cause to the Lord; let him deliver him, let him rescue him, for he delights in him!' " (Ps. 22:7–8). The taunts may be secondary, since fulfillment of prophecy was a favorite theme of the early church. But Jesus' crucifixion was neither the first nor final time that the sight of suffering has called forth sadism.

Luke alone mentions the repentant criminal. When one of those crucified with Jesus railed at him, he was rebuked by the other. " 'Do you not fear God, since you are under the same sentence of condemnation? And we indeed justly; for we are receiving the due reward of our deeds; but this man has done nothing wrong.' And he said, 'Jesus, remember me when you come in your kingly power.' And he said to him, 'Truly, I say to you, today you will be with me in Paradise' " (23:40–43). Paradise was a word borrowed from the Persians. To them it signified a royal park—well-watered, richly wooded, and generously stocked with game. When the word found its way into the Old Testament, it was often taken quite literally. In the Septuagint, it became the name of the Garden of Eden. In the New Testament,

---

[29]The time indications in Mark (the third, the sixth, and the ninth hour) appear to be literary constructions.

[30]See Branscomb, *The Gospel of Mark*, p. 295.

the word was transposed into a higher key. The paradise of the past was replaced by the paradise of the future, a scene of rest and recompense for the righteous after death. When Jesus told the repentant criminal, "Today you will be with me in Paradise," he promised the criminal more than he had asked. Because the condemned man had feared God, confessed his sin, and recognized Jesus' coming kingship, Jesus pronounced that his happiness would not be postponed until the advent of the kingdom. It would begin that very day in paradise.[31]

Strange portents accompanied the crucifixion. (1) There was darkness over the land from noon until three o'clock. Luke attributes this phenomenon to an eclipse (23:45), an astronomical impossibility during the full moon of the Passover. Others think it was caused by unusually heavy clouds. Still others think it was suggested by the Old Testament. Amos had predicted that on the Day of Judgment God would "make the sun go down at noon, and darken the earth in broad daylight" (Amos 8:9). (2) The curtain of the Temple was torn in two from top to bottom.[32] The "curtain" was doubtless the one which separated the Holy of Holies from the surrounding area. It would not have been visible from outside the Temple, of course, let alone from Golgotha. The curtain was lifted only once a year by the high priest when he entered the presence of God to make sacrificial propitiation for the sins of the people. For the Christian community the tearing of the curtain symbolized the uninterrupted access to God made possible by Jesus' death (Heb. 9:11–12; 10:19–22), the breaking down of the wall between the Jews and the Gentiles, or the Temple's destruction. (3) According to Matthew, an earthquake rent the rocks in the neighborhood of Jerusalem, and dead saints came forth from their tombs and appeared to many people in the Holy City (27:51b–53). Matthew's account is a curious one. No mention is made of what happened to the saints. Was their new life temporary or enduring? Matthew's context strongly suggests that the saints were resurrected at the time of Jesus' death, when the curtain of the Temple was torn. Yet in the following verse the evangelist plainly states that the saints did not come out of their tombs until after Jesus' resurrection. Perhaps Matthew wanted to stress the fact that Jesus was the first to be resurrected. This fact would have been at odds with the prior resurrection of the saints.

Portents at the death of great men were commonly reported in the ancient world. When Caesar died, the sun was veiled, Pompey's statue spouted blood, and the dead walked the streets of Rome. It would have been strange indeed had not similar stories circulated in connection with the death of "Jesus Christ, the Son of God" (Mk. 1:1). It is hardly necessary, however, to regard these unusual incidents as historical. They express the terror and the mystery which surrounded the death of Jesus. Man was awestruck. Nature was convulsed.

What Jesus said while he was on the cross is not altogether clear. Mark

---

[31]Scholars are not agreed as to whether paradise in Jesus' thought meant "heaven" or "the happy side of Sheol" where the righteous dead awaited resurrection.

[32]Since Mk. 15:38 interrupts the sequence, some scholars think it is secondary. See Grant, in *The Interpreter's Bible*, VII, 908.

and Matthew report one utterance, Luke lists three different ones, and John records three others. The church took the total tradition and wove it into a devotional pattern of "seven last words" for Good Friday.

My God, my God, why hast thou forsaken me? (Mk. 15:34; Mt. 27:46).

Father, forgive them; for they know not what they do (Lk. 23:34).

Today you will be with me in Paradise (Lk. 23:43).

Father, into thy hands I commit my spirit! (Lk. 23:46).

Woman, behold your son! [Then he said to the disciple,] Behold your mother! (Jn. 19:26–27).

I thirst (Jn. 19:28).

It is finished (Jn. 19:30).

All seven sayings cannot be considered historical. Luke omits Mark 15:34 and substitutes for it a more appropriate utterance (23:46). John omits them both and substitutes still another saying (19:30). Luke's first saying ("Father, forgive them [the Jews? the Roman soldiers?]; for they know not what they do," 23:34) is omitted by a number of important manuscripts. If it was not a part of the original Gospel, the scribe who inserted it surely understood the spirit of Jesus.

How the seven sayings could be known constitutes a problem. Mark (14:50) and Matthew (26:56) state that the disciples had forsaken Jesus and fled. Luke omits Mark's statement. Perhaps Luke thought that the disciples were present at the crucifixion and included them in the phrase "all his acquaintances" (23:49). If so, the disciples and the "women" (mentioned also in Mark and Matthew) "stood at a distance" (Lk. 23:49). They were presumably out of earshot. But no problem exists in the Fourth Gospel. The women (including Jesus' mother) and at least one of the disciples were "standing near" (19:26).

One word from the cross calls for special comment: "My God, my God, why hast thou forsaken me?" Mark and Matthew report this as the only saying from the cross. It is often thought to be secondary, an interpretation of the "loud cry" of Mark 15:37 under the influence of Psalm 22:1. Luke (23:46) and John (19:30), as we have noted, make substitutions for it.[33] But many scholars wonder why the church would have fabricated a saying which it found so hard to explain. If the utterance is genuine, what did it mean? (1) Some of the bystanders supposed that Jesus was calling on Elijah for help. According to Jewish belief Elijah was the rescuer of the faithful in their time of need. But, it is argued, the Roman soldiers would not have known about Elijah, and the Jews would not have mistaken words so dissimilar in the Aramaic as "Elijah" and "My God." It is possible, however,

---

[33]See F. W. Beare, *The Earliest Records of Jesus* (New York: Abingdon Press, 1962), pp. 238–40, who thinks that there are solid grounds for calling the whole account into question.

that intense pain and prolonged fatigue had conspired to make Jesus' words indistinct. (2) Gnostic heretics held that Jesus was calling on the Aeon, Christ, who left him at that moment. According to their view the Aeon, Christ, had entered Jesus at the Baptism. (3) Christians generally believed that Jesus was calling on God. What prompted Jesus to make the appeal? Did he feel deserted by the Father? Calvin thought so, but this is a dubious hypothesis. Mark and Matthew wrote to multiply faith, not to mock it. They would not have reported Jesus' cry had he died in despair. While Jesus hung on the cross, he probably repeated verses from the Psalms. Psalm 22 was recited by pious Jews in times of adversity much as Christians repeat the Lord's Prayer. Under the circumstances, that Psalm would naturally have come to mind. It begins with a complaint—the very words attributed to Jesus: "My God, my God, why hast thou forsaken me?" It ends with compliments: "I will tell of thy name to my brethren. . . . Posterity shall serve him [the Lord]; men shall tell of the Lord to the coming generation, and proclaim his deliverance to a people yet unborn, that he has wrought it" (vss. 22, 30–31).

From the Christian perspective, then, he who recited Psalm 22 on the cross was not a victim but a victor. When he had finished, he gave a great shout—not a cry of despair, or relief, or the final protest of a failing organ, but a victor's shout. Surely this is what Mark intended his readers to conclude. Matthew (27:50) altered Mark (15:37) in order to indicate that Jesus' life was not taken from him by his crucifiers; he yielded it up on his own accord.

Mark indicated that at this point a certain centurion proclaimed, "Truly this man was the son of God" (15:39). Christians came to regard the soldier's words as the first confession of faith in Jesus after his death. For Matthew the centurion (and those who were with him) uttered the saying not because of the victor's cry but because of the effects of the earthquake. Luke (23:47) changed the centurion's exclamation to "Certainly this man was innocent!" The change was not intended to diminish the force of the confession of faith but to underscore once again a frequent refrain of Luke's Gospel: the Romans realized that Jesus was innocent.

Burial (251, 252, A 1)[34]

Jewish law required that crucified criminals be buried on the day of their impalement (Deut. 21:22–23). Roman law was less rigid. It permitted the crucified to remain on their crosses until their bodies rotted away. In Palestine, however, the Romans were doubtless sensitive to Jewish religious feelings—especially during an important religious festival when the Holy City was crowded with "fanatics." The authorities, in order to avoid possible riots, probably permitted the bodies of the crucified to be removed before sunset. Such a concession to Jewish scruples must often have entailed

---

[34]Mt. 27:57–66; 28:11–15; Mk. 15:42–47; Lk. 23:50–56. Compare Jn. 19:38–42.

the violent death of the crucified at the hands of their executioners. John relates that the soldiers broke the legs of those who were crucified with Jesus in order to hasten their death (Jn. 19:32). Otherwise they could have survived on the cross for several days.

Jesus died at midafternoon on Friday, the day of preparation for the Sabbath. Swift burial was a necessity since the Law decreed that a body could not remain on the cross after sunset. John indicates that it was a special offense for bodies to remain on the cross on the Sabbath (19:31). Joseph of Arimathea went to Pilate and asked for Jesus' body. Arimathea has often been identified with Ramathaim-zophim (I Sam. 1:1), about fifteen miles east of Joppa. Nothing is known about Joseph except what the Gospels disclose. No previous mention is made of him; and there are no references to him in the subsequent stories of the resurrection and the beginnings of the church. Mark states that he was "a respected member of the council" (15:43). Luke understood this phrase to mean that Joseph was a member of the supreme council in Jerusalem which had judged Jesus. In order to relieve Joseph of this responsibility, Luke declares that he "had not consented to their purpose and deed" (23:51). This statement conflicts with Mark's assertion that "they all condemned him as deserving death" (14:64). Perhaps Joseph was a member of one of the smaller Sanhedrins which administered the affairs of the Jewish communities. Such a position would have made him a man of some distinction and importance. Mark further describes Joseph as one who "was . . . looking for the kingdom of God" (15:43). Luke's parallel ("a good and righteous man," 23:50) conveys a similar meaning. But Matthew (27:57) and John (19:38) call Joseph a "disciple." The fact that Joseph does not appear in the subsequent Christian story—even though he was closely connected with the central event—suggests that Mark's description is correct. Joseph was not a disciple but a devout Jew.[35] It was a praiseworthy deed to provide burial for the dead. Joseph's act requires no further justification. It was natural, however, that the early church should come to regard him as a disciple, since he gave final care to the body of the Lord. Matthew alone reports that Joseph was "rich" (Mt. 27:57). This may have been an influence of prophecy. It had been written of the Suffering Servant that "they made his grave with the wicked and with a rich man in his death" (Is. 53:9).

It took considerable courage for Joseph of Arimathea to petition Pilate for Jesus' body. Pilate was surprised that Jesus had suffered so short a time, about six hours according to Mark and three hours according to John. The procurator summoned the centurion and asked him if Jesus was already dead. When Pilate learned that he was dead, he granted the body to Joseph. Joseph bought a linen shroud, removed Jesus' body from the cross, wrapped it, laid it in a tomb hewn out of rock, and rolled a stone against the opening.[36] John indicates that the tomb was in a garden near the place of

---

[35]Notice how similar Mark's description of Joseph is to Luke's description of Simeon (2:25), who blessed the baby Jesus in the Temple.

[36]John adds. that Nicodemus accompanied Joseph and assisted in the burial (19:39–40).

The traditional Tomb of Jesus is located underneath the large dome of the Church of the Holy Sepulcher.

crucifixion (19:41–42). Matthew states that it belonged to Joseph of Arimathea (27:60). Matthew (27:60), Luke (23:53), and John (19:41) report that it was new. Mark does not mention this detail. Since it was later forbidden to bury a criminal in a tomb with one's fathers (Sanhedrin 46–47), the newness of the tomb can be considered authentic. To the Semite newness suggested sacredness.

The description of Jesus' burial place inspires confidence. The Jews buried their dead in family tombs rather than in cemeteries. The tombs, usually hewn out of a rock cliff, were located outside the city walls. A chamber was cut into the rock and recesses were cut on either side in which the bodies were placed. A round, flat, heavy stone was used to close the opening of the tomb and to prevent easy entrance. The stone was rolled in a rock groove cut in front of the doorway. The women did not think they were strong enough to remove the stone from the entrance of Jesus' tomb on the first Easter Sunday (Mk. 16:3). Joseph was probably assisted by servants when he rolled the stone into place after Jesus' burial.

Mark states that two women, Mary Magdalene and Mary the mother of Joseph (who had also witnessed the crucifixion, 15:40) saw where Jesus was laid (15:47). They waited until the sabbath was past before purchasing spices with which to anoint Jesus' body (16:1). In Matthew they sat "opposite the tomb" (27:61). Luke indicates that "the women" who had come with Jesus from Galilee "saw the tomb, and how his body was laid; then they returned, and prepared spices and ointments. On the Sabbath they rested according to the commandment" (23:55–56). They made no effort to anoint Jesus' body on Friday. The burial was a hurried one due to the nearness of the Sabbath. John, on the other hand, describes a permanent burial on Friday in which about a hundred pounds of myrrh and aloes were used (19:39–40).

Some critics have questioned the whole story of the entombment. They assert that the body of Jesus, like that of the prophet Uriah (Jer. 26:22–23), was cast into the grave of the common people. Their assumption contradicts the unanimous witness of the four Gospels. In connection with the burial of Jesus, two incidents are related (the guard at the tomb and the bribing of the soldiers) which bear the marks of manufacture. Matthew reports that on the next day (the Sabbath) the chief priests and the Pharisees went to Pilate and said, "Sir, we remember how that imposter said, while he was alive, 'After three days I will rise again.' Therefore order the sepulchre to be made secure until the third day, lest his disciples go and steal him away, and tell the people, 'He has risen from the dead,' and the last fraud will be worse than the first" (27:63–64). Pilate gave them a guard, presumably of Roman soldiers, and ordered the soldiers to make the tomb as secure as possible. The soldiers then went and sealed the tomb and set a guard. On the following morning (Sunday), when the two Marys went to the tomb, a great earthquake occurred. An angel from heaven rolled back the stone and frightened the guards who became like dead men. The angel informed the

The "Garden Tomb," located north of Herod's Gate, is situated outside the walls of the Holy City. It is believed by some English authorities to be the authentic sepulcher of Jesus. Although archeological support for this view is lacking, the Tomb does provide a convincing picture of what Jesus' burial place probably looked like. Inside the Tomb, visitors are shown a two-room cave hewn out of the rock. Note the trough cut in front of the entrance in which a round, flat stone was rolled to cover the opening.

Gordon's Calvary is named after General Gordon, the hero of Khartoum, who endeavored to prove the authenticity of this site as Golgotha ("the place of a skull"). The "Garden Tomb" is at the foot of this hill, which vaguely resembles the outline of a skull.

women that Jesus had risen and showed them the empty tomb (27:65 28:6). Some of the guards went into the city and told the chief priests all that had happened. The chief priests assembled with the elders and took counsel. Then they gave a sum of money to the soldiers and said, "Tell people, 'His disciples came by night and stole him away while we were asleep.' And if this comes to the governor's ears, we will satisfy him and keep you out of trouble" (28:13–14). The soldiers took the money and did as they were directed.

There are many aspects of the stories of the guard at the tomb (27:62–66) and the bribing of the soldiers (28:11–15) which prompt scholars to suspect their historicity. (1) The accounts are found only in Matthew. (2) The Jewish authorities were strict observers of the Sabbath. It is not likely that they would have gone to Pilate on that sacred day. (3) It is improbable that the Jewish authorities were aware of the prediction that Jesus would rise on the third day. Matthew 27:63 presupposes that the predictions of suffering and resurrection which Jesus made privately to his disciples (16:21; 17:23; 20:19) were known to the general public. But even if these predictions were known, it is doubtful that the chief priests and the Pharisees would have taken them seriously. (4) Would Pilate have granted the request of the Jewish authorities after they had opposed his wish to free Jesus?

(5) Probably not all of the Roman soldiers would have slept on duty. (6) Even if all of the soldiers had slept, they would not have confessed to it for any sum of money, since the penalty for such a dereliction of duty was death. (7) Would the guards have believed that the Jewish authorities were able or willing to protect them from the consequences of their slumber? (8) Would the testimony of sleeping guards be considered valid? (9) Matthew omits Mark's statement (16:1) that the women intended to anoint the body of Jesus. It would have conflicted with Matthew's story of the guards at the tomb who surely would not have allowed the women access to the body.

The first followers of Jesus met many skeptics when they proclaimed the resurrection. To prove their claim they pointed to the empty tomb. Jewish antagonists countered with the charge that the disciples had stolen the body of Jesus from the tomb in order to propagate the falsehood of the resurrection. Christians refuted the Jewish argument with the two stories which are recorded in Matthew. These stories, which are found in a more developed form in the Gospel of Peter 8:29–11:49,[37] are no more historical than the slander which caused their creation.

[37]See James, *The Apocryphal New Testament*, pp. 92–93.

chapter twenty-two

The Resurrection

Jesus' death spelled disillusionment and despair for his disciples. He had come "to his own home, and his own people [had] received him not" (Jn. 1:11). The disciples "had hoped that he was the one to redeem Israel" (Lk. 24:21). Their hope had been misplaced. When the Master was murdered, they felt that he could not be the Christ, for they believed the Christ could not be crucified.

The gloom which enveloped the disciples continued until Sunday. Then a strange event was reported by some women who had gone to Jesus' tomb early in the morning. They had found the stone which covered the opening rolled away. An angel had informed them, "He is not here; for he has risen" (Mt. 28:6). They had rushed to tell the disciples. On the way, they had been met by Jesus himself (Mt. 28:8–10). The disciples were incredulous. The women's words "seemed to them an idle tale, and they did not believe them" (Lk. 24:11).

The doubts of the Eleven were soon changed to belief. They, too, saw their risen Lord. Defeat and despair vanished. In their place came courage and conviction. Faith in the resurrection turned the tragedy of the tomb to triumph. It also turned the world upside down. It made possible the rapid rise and spread of Christianity. It brought about a new day of worship (Sunday) and a new Holy Book (the New Testament). It created the radiant confidence in life after death which permeated the early Christian community. Indeed, the resurrection became the foundation belief of the church. "If Christ has not been raised," Paul wrote to his converts at Corinth, "your faith is futile and you are still in your sins" (I Cor. 15:17).

The consequences of belief in Jesus' resurrection have been far-reaching and decisive. But what about the belief itself? Is it solidly based? If so, what kind of a body did Jesus have, and what became of it? Or does the resurrection belief rest on the wrought-up imaginations of a handful of hysterical women? In a search for answers to these questions, we must turn to the New Testament.

Paul's Witness

The earliest and most comprehensive written account of the resurrection of Jesus has come down to us from Paul. About the middle of the fifth decade the great apostle wrote to his converts at Corinth. In his letter he included information of primary importance which he had previously preached to them in person and which he may have received from the Jerusalem apostles only a few years after the crucifixion.

> I delivered to you as of first importance what I also received, that Christ died for our sins in accordance with the scriptures, that he was buried, that he was raised on the third day in accordance with the scriptures, and that he appeared to Cephas, then to the twelve. Then he appeared to more than five hundred brethren at one time, most of whom are still alive, though some have fallen asleep. Then he appeared to James, then to all the apostles. Last of all, as to one untimely born, he appeared also to me (I Cor. 15:3–8).

The passage prompts several comments. (1) Jesus appeared first to Peter. This assertion coheres with the strategic role Peter played in the circle of the Twelve and with the prediction that Peter would rally the community after Jesus' death (Lk. 22:32). It also coheres with the words found in Luke 24:34: "The Lord has risen indeed, and has appeared to Simon!" This was the statement with which the Eleven and others in Jerusalem greeted the two travelers who had conversed with the resurrected Jesus on the Emmaus road (Lk. 24:13–35). Matthew, however, indicates that Jesus first appeared to the women who visited the tomb (28:9). (2) No indication is given as to where the appearances took place. Did they occur in the vicinity of Jerusalem or in Galilee? Some have argued that only in Galilee would Jesus have had over five hundred followers ready to receive such experiences. If they took place there, they must have happened nearly a week after the crucifixion. (3) No mention is made of the empty tomb or of the appearance to the women. (4) No reference is made to an ascension which forty days after the resurrection put an end to the appearances for a time (Acts 1:9; compare Lk. 24:50–53). (5) Paul includes his own Damascus road "vision" (Acts 26:19) of Jesus with the other appearances.

Our third point calls for special comment. Why was Paul silent concerning the empty tomb? Was he unaware of the tradition, or did he regard the story as unimportant? Hunter maintains that although Paul did not mention the empty tomb, he did imply its existence. "What otherwise is

About the middle of the first century, Paul wrote to his converts at Corinth the earliest and most inclusive account of the resurrection of Jesus. The acropolis of Corinth is shown in the background of this picture.

the point of mentioning the burial? 'Died, buried, raised'—these words are unintelligible unless they mean that what was buried was raised."[1] The argument is cogent, but it cannot be sustained apart from Paul's total thought. Paul regarded Jesus' resurrection as "the first fruits of those who have fallen asleep" (I Cor. 15:20). It signaled the coming of the End and was the guarantee and prototype of the resurrection of "those who belong to Christ" (I Cor. 15:23). Some Palestinians taught that at the resurrection the very same body would be restored (II Baruch 50:2). Paul repudiated this thought in no uncertain terms. Jesus had taught that life after death would be lived under radically different conditions from those which prevailed on earth (Mk. 12:24–25). Paul picked up the thought and elaborated it in terms similar to the later words in the Fourth Gospel about a grain of wheat falling into the earth (Jn. 12:24). Both a body and a seed are placed in the ground, but in each case something different comes out of it. God gives to both a new body (I Cor. 15:36–41). Paul followed his argument by analogy with direct statements concerning the nature of the resurrection body. "What is sown is perishable, what is raised is imperishable. It is sown in dishonor, it is raised in glory. It is sown in weakness, it is raised

[1]Hunter, *The Work and Words of Jesus*, p. 124.

in power. It is sown a physical body, it is raised a spiritual body. . . . Flesh and blood cannot inherit the kingdom of God, nor does the perishable inherit the imperishable. . . . We shall not all sleep [that is, "die," since Paul expected the parousia soon], but we [who are still alive] shall all be changed. . . . The dead will be raised imperishable, and we shall be changed" (I Cor. 15:42b–44b,50,51,52c).

Paul did not define precisely what he meant by the "spiritual body." His reasoning, though, makes perfectly plain that the "spiritual body" is something markedly different from the "physical body." The "spiritual body" is imperishable, glorious, and powerful. It is not an achievement of man but a gift of God. The "physical body" which is placed in a tomb is raised in a transformed condition. It is not a resuscitated corpse (as some Jews thought) or a disembodied spirit (as the Greeks believed). It is a *new* body. Paul did not endorse the idea that man's body, like that of John Brown in the familiar old song, "lies moulderin' in the grave, but his soul goes marching on." Neither did he regard the future life as a continuation, under improved circumstances, of life as he knew it. Between these two extremes, he advanced the idea of the "spiritual body."

The phrase "spiritual body" stressed man's essential unity. Modern medicine uses "psychosomatic" to describe diseases which produce physical symptoms whose origin is mental. The term is a transliteration of two Greek words—*psyche* (soul) and *soma* (body)—which Paul used to form "physical body." Although we continue to speak of body and mind as though they were separate and distinct entities, we know this is not the case. The real man is not merely a physical organism. Neither is he a soul which can be abstracted from the body. He is body and soul in their inter-relatedness. This concept is closely akin to the New Testament idea of man as a unity. When Paul described the state of the resurrected, he did not write of the physical body any more than he wrote of the resurrection of the flesh (*sarx*). He wrote of the resurrection of "the dead." He retained *soma* (body) to indicate that man is resurrected in wholeness. He replaced *psyche* (soul) with *pneuma* (spirit). He believed the dead would be "given" a spiritual body (*pneumatikon soma*).

Paul's Corinthian correspondence strongly suggests that the earliest Christians pointed to the appearance of Jesus rather than to the empty tomb as proof of his resurrection. This suggestion receives further support from the Acts. There it is stated that Jesus "presented himself alive after his passion by many proofs, appearing to them [the apostles] during forty days, and speaking of the kingdom of God" (Acts 1:3). Mark declares that the women who visited the tomb "said nothing to any one, for they were afraid" (16:8).

We now return to the question which prompted our excursion into Paul's thought about the resurrection. Why was Paul silent about the empty tomb and Jesus' appearance to the women? No dogmatic answer can be given. It is possible that Paul knew the women's story in the form in which Mark records it. He may even have dated the resurrection on the third day because of it, although this detail could have been derived from

Hosea 6:2.[2] If Paul was aware of the witness of the women, he made no use of it. Perhaps the witness of the women was unknown (as Mark 16:8 suggests) or disregarded (as Luke 24:11 states) until after Jesus' resurrection had been established on other grounds. After the disciples had declared that Jesus had appeared to them, the women came forward with their story of the empty tomb—or their story was then accredited by the disciples. In time, it was believed not only that the women had discovered the tomb to be empty (Mk. 16:6), but also that Jesus had appeared to them (Mt. 28:9; compare Jn. 20:14), and that they were the first witnesses to the resurrection. These developments, however, occurred after Paul's time. In his day the resurrection was proved not by the empty tomb and the appearance to the women but by the appearances to "Cephas," "the twelve," the "more than five hundred brethren," "James," and "all the apostles" (I Cor. 15:5–7). To "Paul's trained mind an empty tomb was not proof of the resurrection, and he rests his case on firmer ground."[3]

Empty Tomb (253)[4]

Burial rites among the Jews called for washing and anointing the body with fragrant spices. Since there were no undertakers, these acts were usually rendered by relatives or friends. Despite Mark 15:46, which gives every appearance of a permanent burial, Mark intends his readers to conclude that Jesus was hastily buried because the Sabbath was imminent. When the Sabbath was over (at sunset on Saturday), three women bought spices so that they might anoint Jesus' body. The women were Mary Magdalene, Mary, the mother of James, and Salome. All three had witnessed the crucifixion (Mk. 15:40), and the two Marys had seen where Jesus was buried (Mk. 15:47). Early the next morning, just after sunrise, the three made their way to the tomb. They wondered who would roll away the heavy stone which covered the entrance. When they looked up (perhaps an indication that the tomb had been hewn on a hillside), they discovered to their astonishment that the stone had already been rolled back. They stepped inside and saw a young man dressed in a white robe. They were amazed (Mk. 16:1–5).

Much speculation has centered around the identity of this young man. Was it the same youth who followed Jesus on the night of his arrest? (Mk. 14:51). The evangelist uses the same word (neaniskos) in these two instances only. If so, perhaps the young man was Mark himself. Perhaps it was he who had rolled away the stone. Perhaps Jesus had first appeared to him. All this is highly conjectural. Angels were commonly described as young men (II Maccabees 3:26,33; Antiquities V, 8, 2) who wore white robes (Rev. 7:13–14). Matthew interprets Mark's "young man" to be an

---

[2]"After three days" (emphasis added) occurs in Mk. 8:31; 9:31; 10:34. Compare Jonah 1:17 and Mt. 12:40.

[3]Branscomb, The Gospel of Mark, p. 309.

[4]Mt. 28:1–10; Mk. 16:1–8; Lk. 24:1–11. Compare Jn. 20:1–18.

angel (28:5). Luke's "two men . . . in dazzling apparel" appear to be angels, too (24:4).

The angel, as one would expect, possessed supernatural knowledge of the women's purpose: "Do not be amazed; you seek Jesus of Nazareth, who was crucified. He has risen, he is not here; see the place where they laid him" (Mk. 16:6). The angel thus disclosed the fact and the place of the resurrection. The time of the resurrection is not mentioned. It is implied that Jesus rose before the sun—sometime during the night between Saturday and Sunday. "But go," the angel continued, "tell his disciples and Peter that he is going before you to Galilee; there you will see him, as he told you" (Mk. 16:7). This verse interrupts the sequence (as does its cognate, Mk. 14:28). In the following verse the women ignored the angel's command. They did not bear the message to the disciples but, trembling and astonished, they fled from the tomb. They said nothing to anyone because they were afraid. Both Luke and Matthew imply that Mark 16:7 is impossible. Luke (who omitted Mk. 14:28) completely rewrites it: "Remember how he told you *while he was still in Galilee*. . . ." (24:6, emphasis added). The women remembered Jesus' words about betrayal, crucifixion, and resurrection (not his promise to appear in Galilee), and they returned to the disciples and others and made their report (24:7–9). Matthew retains the prediction of Jesus' Galilean appearances, but he has the women run to the disciples with glad tidings.[5]

Matthew's account of the empty tomb differs at many points from Mark's.[6] Only the two Marys visited the tomb. They went just before dawn. No mention is made of their intent to anoint the body. Presumably the guard at the tomb (27:62–66) would have prevented this. A great earthquake—like the one at Jesus' death—took place. An angel descended from heaven and rolled away the stone and sat on it. So awesome was the angel that the guards trembled and became like dead men. His message to the women was the same as in Mark except that they were urged to go "quickly" to tell the disciples, and there was no special mention of Peter. The women ran with fear and great joy. Jesus met them on their way and greeted them. As they worshiped him, he calmed their fear and repeated the message for the disciples to see him in Galilee (28:1–10). This incident is followed by the story of the bribing of the guards (28:11–15).

John reads as though Mary Magdalene were the only woman to visit the empty tomb. From Mary's words, "*We* do not know where they have laid him,"[7] it may be inferred that others were present. Mary went to the tomb while it was still dark. When she saw that the stone had been removed, she ran to Peter and the other disciples. It never occurred to her that Jesus had been resurrected. "They have taken the Lord out of the tomb," she reported, "and we do not know where they have laid him" (20:2). Peter and another disciple ran to the tomb. The linen cloths were

---

[5]If Mark did not end at 16:8, as some scholars maintain, then verse 7 may have been inserted into the narrative prior to the writing of Matthew and Luke, presumably in the interest of a Galilean resurrection appearance which Mark contained.

[6]Most of Luke's important differences have been mentioned.

[7]Jn. 20:2, emphasis added.

inside, and the napkin which had been on Jesus' head was rolled up in a place by itself. The two disciples returned home, but Mary remained. As she was weeping outside the tomb, she looked in and saw two angels. They asked her why she was weeping. She told them it was because Jesus' body had been removed. Then she turned around and saw someone whom she mistook for the gardener. " 'Sir,' she addressed him, 'if you have carried him away, tell me where you have laid him, and I will take him away.' Jesus said to her, 'Mary.' She turned and said to him in Hebrew, 'Rabboni!' (which means Teacher). Jesus said to her, 'Do not hold me, for I have not yet ascended to the Father; but go to my brethren and say to them, I am ascending to my Father and your Father, to my God and your God' " (20:15–17). Mary went to the disciples and told them that she had seen the Lord and what he had said to her.

Mark's Ending (C)[8]

In the two most reliable codices (*Vaticanus* and *Sinaiticus*), the Gospel of Mark ends with *ephobounto gar*, "for they [the women who visited the empty tomb] were afraid" (16:8). The copies of Mark which Matthew and Luke used doubtless ended at 16:8. The ending has impressed many with its abruptness. It seems that something was intended to follow as in 11:18 or Lk. 22:2. One theory is that the original ending was accidentally mutilated. Since Mark knew of the resurrection, it is argued, the climax of his Gospel would have contained an appearance of Jesus. Attempts to reconstruct the "lost ending" from the concluding sections of Matthew and Luke (or even from John and Acts) have been made.[9] The results, however, have not met with widespread acceptance. Mark may have felt that the previous promises of the resurrection (8:31; 9:31; 10:34) were sufficient and that the fitting climax to the truth of the resurrection was an amazed reverence. Parallels have been found to his "abrupt ending," and an increasing number of scholars are persuaded that "for they were afraid" marked the original ending of his work. This conclusion is upheld by Eusebius, the most widely-read Christian scholar of antiquity.[10]

Mark 16:8 may have been the original ending of the First Gospel, but it was not the final one. To some early Christian scribes, this Gospel appeared to be incomplete. Two different endings were added. The Longer Ending (16:9–20) probably dates from the second century. It is found in most of the existing manuscripts of Mark and in all of the ancient versions. Its style and vocabulary differ markedly from Mark, and its content is derived

---

[8]Mk. 16:8,9–20, and the Shorter Ending.

[9]See Major, in *The Mission and Message of Jesus*, pp. 208–11.

[10]See the illuminating discussion of Mark's ending in Marxsen, *Mark the Evangelist*, pp. 75–92. He thinks that the author of Mark inserted 16:7 into its present context, that it refers not to the appearance of the resurrected Jesus in Galilee but to the expected parousia. By the insertion, the resurrection takes on a provisional character which will be consummated by a greater event, the parousia in Galilee.

from data found in the other Gospels and Acts.[11] Three appearances of Jesus are recorded—to Mary Magdalene, to the two walking in the country, and to the Eleven. In spite of these appearances, the disciples remained doubtful. Jesus upbraided them for their incredulity and hardheartedness. He commanded them to preach the Gospel to the whole creation and promised them miraculous power to cast out demons, speak in tongues, handle serpents, drink deadly poison without harm, and heal the sick. Finally he ascended into heaven to sit at God's right hand, and the disciples went forth and preached everywhere. The Lord worked with them so that their message was confirmed by signs.

The Shorter Ending of Mark may be nearly as old as the Longer Ending. It is found in a few manuscripts—sometimes immediately following 16:8 and at other times following 16:9–20. Even an untrained reader can tell that its style and vocabulary are not from the original Mark: "But they reported promptly to those around Peter all that they had been told. And after this, Jesus himself sent out by means of them, from east to west, the sacred and imperishable proclamation of eternal salvation."

Appearances in Luke (B 1, 2, 3)[12]

According to Luke, the women at the tomb did not see Jesus. Neither did the angels announce the resurrection to them. The angels simply asked, "Why do you seek the living among the dead?" and reminded the women that Jesus had predicted his resurrection (24:4–7). The first appearance recorded by Luke is to the "two" on their way to Emmaus, a village of uncertain location about seven miles from Jerusalem. The "two" were not members of the Twelve but of "all the rest" mentioned in 24:9. One of them was named Cleopas. As they journeyed, they discussed all the things that had happened. Jesus joined them, but they did not recognize him. Their senses were either supernaturally dulled, or they were blinded by intense preoccupation. Jesus asked them the subject of their conversation. They halted and looked sad. Then Cleopas expressed astonishment. " 'Are you the only visitor to Jerusalem who does not know the things that have happened there in these days?' And he said to them, 'What things?' And they said to him, 'Concerning Jesus of Nazareth, who was a prophet mighty in deed and word before God and all the people, and how our chief priests and rulers delivered him up to be condemned to death, and crucified him. But we had hoped that he was the one to redeem Israel. Yes, and besides all this, it is now the third day since this happened. Moreover, some women of our company amazed us. They were at the tomb early in the morning and did not find his body; and they came back saying that they had even seen a vision of angels, who said that he was alive. Some of those who were with us went to the tomb, and found it just as the women had said; but

11See Major, in *The Mission and Message of Jesus*, pp. 206–7.
12Lk. 24:13–53. Compare Acts 1:1–11.

him they did not see' " (24:18–24). Then Jesus taught them how to interpret the Scriptures which dealt with the suffering of Christ.

The climax of the story came when the three drew near to Emmaus. Jesus acted as though he would go farther. The two constrained him. " 'Stay with us, for it is toward evening and the day is now far spent.' So he went in to stay with them. When he was at table with them, he took the bread and blessed, and broke it, and gave it to them. And their eyes were opened and they recognized him; and he vanished out of their sight" (24:29–31). The two travelers were humiliated. They now knew that they should have recognized Jesus by his moving exposition of Scripture. Instead, their recognition came only when he broke the bread. The presence of Christ in the breaking of the bread became one of the most convincing assurances to Christians that death was no victor over their Lord.

Despite the lateness of the hour and the length of the journey, the two hurried back to Jerusalem to share their good news with the larger company—only to be told by those assembled that the Lord had indeed risen and had appeared to Simon. Then the two related what had happened on the road to Emmaus and how Jesus had been made known to them in the breaking of the bread.

This Lucan account is a highly polished literary product permeated by the theology and linguistic characteristics of its author. It features two main ideas—that the suffering of Christ is the central theme of the Old Testament and that the assurance of his resurrection is closely connected with the celebration of the Eucharist. His appearance to Peter is introduced almost as an afterthought.

The Emmaus story belongs to a tradition which asserts that Jesus appeared to his followers in a nonmaterial form. To this story Luke adds an account which presupposes a physical resurrection. As the two·reported to the disciples and others what had happened on the road and in Emmaus, Jesus stood in their midst. They were frightened at first, for they thought they saw a spirit. This thought, however, was quickly dispelled. "See my hands and my feet, that it is I myself; handle me, and see; for a spirit has not flesh and bones as you see that I have" (24:39–40). And then, as if piling proof upon proof of his physical presence, he asked, "Have you anything here to eat?" (24:41). They gave him a piece of broiled fish. He took it and ate it before them. The apologetic nature of this episode has often been noted. The stress on the physical nature of the resurrection body, it is asserted, was designed to counter charges that those who claimed that they had seen the risen Jesus had seen only a spirit. Such a response was the initial one of the apostles themselves (Lk. 24:37).

The resurrected Jesus spoke some final words to those present. Everything written about him in the Law, Prophets, and Psalms must be fulfilled. "Thus it is written," he declared, "that the Christ should suffer and on the third day rise from the dead, and that repentance and forgiveness of sins should be preached in his name to all nations, beginning from Jerusalem. You are witnesses of these things. And behold, I send the promise of my Father upon you; but stay in the city, until you are clothed with power from on high" (24:46–49).[13] The outpouring of the Spirit ("the promise of my Father") is foretold in Joel 2:28–29 and is later described by Luke in Acts 2:1–4. Jesus led his listeners out as far as Bethany, blessed them, and parted from them. The words "and was carried up into heaven" are missing from important manuscripts. There is, however, no adequate ground for doubting that this is the story of the Ascension which Luke later elaborates in Acts 1:6–11.

Luke's report of the appearances of Jesus is striking. (1) All of the appearances take place in or near Jerusalem. Matthew lists one appearance (to the women who visited the tomb) near Jerusalem and another (to the Eleven) in Galilee. John 20 records three appearances—to Mary Magdalene, to the Ten (Thomas being absent), and to the Eleven (eight days after the resurrection). All of these appearances are in or near Jerusalem. Only in the Epilogue (John 21) is an appearance in Galilee mentioned. (2) Jesus' appearance to Simon is unique in the Gospels, excepting, of course, the account in the Epilogue of John. (3) Also unique is the promise of "power from on high" for the disciples. (4) All of the appearances occur on the day of resurrection. This creates problems. The two on the way to Emmaus recognized Jesus at the evening meal when he broke bread. They then made the seven-mile walk to Jerusalem. They were told about Jesus' appearance to Simon. Then they related their own experiences. Jesus appeared to the assembled group, instructed them, and then made the two-mile walk to Bethany. This would place the Ascension late at night. But in Acts (1:3,9), we are told that Jesus' appearances continued for a period of forty days before the Ascension took place. Luke's interest, however, was christological rather than chronological.

Great Commission (A 2)[14]

Matthew's Gospel begins with a Jewish Messiah: "The book of the genealogy of Jesus Christ, the son of David, the Son of Abraham" (1:1). It ends with a cosmic Christ—the universal Savior, Lord of heaven and earth: "Now the eleven disciples went to Galilee, to the mountain to which Jesus had directed them. And when they saw him they worshiped him; but some doubted. And Jesus came and said to them, 'All authority in heaven and on earth has been given to me. Go therefore and make disciples of all nations, baptizing them in the name of the Father and of the Son and of the Holy Spirit, teaching them to observe all that I have commanded you; and lo, I am with you always, to the close of the age'" (28:16–20).

[13]Luke's failure to reproduce the Galilee appearances of Jesus and his transfer of the appearances to Jerusalem may stem from Old Testament prophecies. Isaiah (2:3) and Micah (4:2) had declared that "out of Zion shall go forth the law, and the word of the Lord from Jerusalem." Marxsen, *Mark the Evangelist*, p. 83, thinks that the inserted Mk. 16:7 (to which all subsequent tradition can be traced) is the only basis of the Galilee appearances.

[14]Mt. 28:16–20.

Matthew thought of the commission in rabbinical terms. The disciples were to make converts, baptize, and teach. Jesus had carried on his earthly ministry only in Palestine and almost exclusively to Jews. He had taught, lived with his disciples in a closely-knit fellowship, and sent the disciples on missions. But nowhere in the Synoptic records is it suggested that Jesus practiced or commanded baptism or gave a threefold formula to be used with it.[15] A few decades after his death, however, his Jewish followers believed that Jesus had (1) received universal authority from God, (2) commissioned them to make converts of the nations—baptizing them in the name of the Trinity and teaching them all of his commandments, and (3) remained with them and would continue to remain with them until the End of the Age. Clearly these convictions stemmed from the appearances of the risen Christ, and they were reflected in the practices of the church in Matthew's day.

Faith in the Resurrection

No one saw Jesus' resurrection, but many saw the resurrected Jesus. Evidence for his appearances is abundant. Paul testifies that Jesus appeared to Cephas (Peter), the Twelve, more than five hundred brethren, James, and all of the apostles. To this impressive list, he adds Jesus' appearance to himself. Paul, writing about the middle of the fifth decade, based his witness on information he may have received from the apostles themselves. Mark mentions no appearances of the risen Jesus. The angel announces the resurrection, however, and the predictions and the empty tomb imply it. Matthew reports appearances of Jesus to the women who visited the tomb and to the Eleven sometime later in Galilee. Luke includes appearances to the two on the Emmaus road, Simon, and the Eleven. John 20 records appearances to Mary Magdalene, the Ten (Thomas being absent), and the Eleven.

Exactly what happened on the first day of the week is difficult to determine. (1) How many women visited the tomb? One (John), two (Matthew), three (Mark), or a larger number (Luke)? (2) When was the visit made? While it was still dark (John), toward the dawn (Matthew), at early dawn (Luke), or after the sun had risen (Mark)? (3) Why was the visit made? To anoint the body (Mark, Luke) or for some other reason (Matthew, John)? (4) Who was found there? One angel (Mark, Matthew) or two (Luke, John)?[16] (5) Where did the appearances take place? In Luke, they are all in or near Jerusalem. This is also the case in John, except for the incident in the Epilogue (21:1–14). Matthew places one appearance in the Jerusalem area and another in Galilee. Paul does not indicate where the appearances took place. (6) For how long did the appearances continue? For one day (Luke), for several days (Matthew, John), or for forty days (Acts)?

[15]Contrast Jn. 3:5,26; 4:1–3.

[16]Our phrasing of this question assumes that Mark's "young man" and Luke's "two men" were angels.

The empty tomb is a negative witness. Paul made no use of it. Neither, apparently, did other early Christians (Acts 1:3). These facts about the empty-tomb story together with the conflicting details concerning the appearances have turned many a potential believer in the resurrection into a skeptic. Innumerable theories have been advanced as to what actually occurred. (1) Jesus was not buried at all. He was thrown into a pit or left for animals to eat. This explanation hardly accords with the well-known respect Jews had for the human body or with the Law which decreed that convicted criminals must be buried on the day of their execution. (2) The body was removed from the tomb—by Joseph of Arimathea, the Romans, the Jews, the disciples, or grave robbers. Joseph, it is alleged, placed the body in the tomb only temporarily because the Sabbath was imminent. When the Sabbath was over, he moved the body so his family tomb would not be defiled. Would it not already have been defiled? Would not the permanent burial place have become known? If the Romans or the Jews had removed the body from the tomb, they could have later produced the body and refuted the Christians' claim that Jesus had been resurrected. We are driven to the conclusion that they did not produce the body because they could not. To suppose that the disciples themselves stole the body and then went forth to risk their lives preaching a risen Christ whom they knew to be dead taxes our credulity. The astute Jewish scholar, Joseph Klausner, declares that "the nineteen hundred years' faith of millions is not founded on deception."[17] If grave robbers had claimed Jesus' disfigured body, what earthly use would they have made of it? They might have been interested in the linen shroud, or the huge quantity of myrrh and aloes (Jn. 19:39), but the shroud, at least, they left behind. (3) The Galilean women, strangers in Jerusalem, went to the wrong tomb. There were many rock-cut tombs in the area, and it would have been difficult to distinguish one from another without careful notes. But it is doubtful that eyewitnesses of the burial would have made such a mistake. If they had, Joseph of Arimathea would surely have corrected them. He would not have needed notes to find his family tomb. (4) Jesus did not die on the cross. He hung there for a relatively short time. Then he swooned, was taken down for dead, and was buried. He was revived by the spices which had been inserted in the folds of the burial clothes. When his disciples saw him, they thought he had been resurrected from the dead. He left Jerusalem and went into hiding, became an Essene, etc. But how did he escape from the tomb? Who rolled away the stone? What spices could have revived a crucified man so that he appeared to be perfectly normal? And who can imagine Jesus of Nazareth living out the remainder of his days in contemplative isolation? Back to the Temple and back to the people he most surely would have gone. (5) The empty tomb was a later inference from the appearance of Jesus. If so, this would account for the empty tomb but not for the appearances. (6) The appearances were hallucinations. In the half light of early morning, taut and grief-stricken, the women thought they saw an empty tomb. They related their experience to the disciples. Upon hearing the women's story, the disciples, who had heard

17*Jesus of Nazareth*, p. 359.

Jesus predict his resurrection and confidently expected that he would rise from the dead, had false intimations of his presence. Hallucinations, however, are usually quite temporary. Time shows them to be unreal. The disciples, far from expecting Jesus' resurrection, were plunged into grief at his death. When they first learned of the resurrection, they thought it was "an idle tale" (Lk. 24:11). (7) The resurrection reports are based on Old Testament ideas such as that found in Hosea 6:2. The prophet promised that God would raise up his people on the third day. (8) The resurrection faith was based on a vision imparted by God to help the hopeless disciples.

Despite their rather easy refutation, these theories reflect a skepticism which is not altogether without merit. The empty tomb *is* a negative witness, and the records *are* at odds. But would we not be highly distrustful if discrepancies did not exist? Nothing shouts invention so loudly as witnesses who recite in harmony. Wellington, Ney, and Napoleon related markedly different accounts of what happened at Waterloo. Yet no sane man would deny that a battle was fought there. Neither need a Christian reject the resurrection of Jesus because the reports of the first witnesses are not harmonious. Four compelling data support the resurrection claim. (1) The existence of the Christian church. If Jesus' mission and message had ended with his crucifixion, it is difficult to see how the church could have come into existence. It is harder still to explain how it could have continued for so long. (2) The existence of the New Testament. Who would have written the twenty-seven books which comprise this remarkable work if Jesus had ended his career as a crucified criminal? Each writer firmly believed that God had raised Jesus from the dead. (3) The existence of Sunday as the day of worship. Jesus was a Jew. He "went to the synagogue, as his custom was, on the sabbath day" (Lk. 4:16). The tremendous importance of that day for the Jewish people is abundantly established by Jewish legal and rabbinical writings. Yet Jewish followers of Jesus changed their sacred day from the seventh (Saturday) to the first (Sunday) day of the week (Acts 20:7; I Cor. 16:2). What reason would they have had for such a radical departure from tradition other than a radical event? All the Gospels agree that Jesus' resurrection occurred on the first day of the week. (4) The existence of the Lord's Supper as an early Christian rite. It commemorates Jesus' death, but it is not a mournful rite. It is dominated by a spirit of joy and gratitude as the word Eucharist (thanksgiving) suggests.[18]

Form of the Resurrection

If evidence for the resurrection is substantial, the same cannot be said for its *form*. The data, which are conflicting and confusing, have produced varying explanations. We shall confine our treatment to four.

[18]Wolfhart Pannenberg, *Jesus—God and Man* (Philadelphia: The Westminster Press, 1968), pp. 53–114, argues for the historicity of Jesus' resurrection. For a critique of Pannenberg's argument, see Herbert Burhenn, "Pannenberg's Argument for the Historicity of the Resurrection," *Journal of the American Academy of Religion*, XL, No. 3 (1972), 368–79.

Jesus had a physical body. The body that was buried was resurrected. It retained the actual marks of the crucifixion. There is much prima-facie evidence in the Gospels to support this view. Jesus ate, talked, walked, showed his wounds, and was not in the tomb visited. Probably most Jews would have required a physical resurrection in order to be convinced of its reality. But Paul's account, which is the earliest we have, clashes with this interpretation. If Jesus' body was resurrected, we are left with the problem of its disposal. Luke translates it into the sky. This was doubtless an altogether acceptable solution for first-century Palestinians; for post-Copernican Christians, however, it leaves much to be desired. Moreover, if God is a Spirit, what need would there be for a physical body in heaven?

Jesus had a spiritual body. His physical body was transformed. This was Paul's view. "Lo! I tell you a mystery. We shall not all sleep [die], but we shall all be *changed*, in a moment, in the twinkling of an eye, at the last trumpet. For the trumpet will sound, and the dead will be raised *imperishable*, and we [who are still alive] shall be *changed*" (I Cor. 15:51–52).[19] In another letter, Paul declared that the Lord Jesus Christ "will change our lowly body to be like his glorious body" (Phil. 3:21).

Paul's view of the resurrection body was evidently shared by the author of the Fourth Gospel. What conviced Peter and "the other disciple" of the resurrection was the discovery of the undisturbed grave clothes in the empty tomb (Jn. 20:6–9). Only a spiritualized body could have come forth from them without disturbing them. Only a spiritualized body could have entered a room through closed doors (20:19). Only a spiritualized body could have appeared and disappeared at will, made itself visible or invisible, recognizable or unrecognizable (Lk. 24:13–53).

"There is much to commend this *mode* as appropriate to the Resurrection," Major wryly comments, "except the evidence for it."[20] But evidence for it does appear in the records, and impartial observers must take account of it. Surely God could provide such a body if He willed it. If He provided such a one for Jesus, we cannot hope to understand it. We can only conclude with Paul that it was indeed "a mystery."

Jesus appeared in a form similar to that in which discarnate spirits of the dead manifest themselves today. His body was not physical. Neither was it a physical body transformed into a spiritual body. Yet it was real. Jesus' alleged affirmations that his body was composed of flesh and bones are the product of the primitive Christian-Gnostic controversy. The Gnostics, who regarded matter as evil, affirmed that Jesus had no real human body. He was a celestial being uncontaminated by matter. In an effort to refute the Gnostic heresy—which denied the incarnation—defenders of the faith produced the stories of Jesus' physical resurrection. If he had a physical body in his resurrected state, he obviously had had that kind of body before the crucifixion. Proponents of the psychical form of the resurrection argue that the resurrection was first reported in the psychical form. All the appearances listed by Paul are introduced by the Greek word *ōpithē*. This word is appropriately used for psychical experiences.(Moses and Elijah "appeared" at the Transfiguration, Mk. 9:4.) Paul spoke of Jesus' appearance to him in exactly the same way as he did Jesus' appearances to the apostles and others. Clearly Paul's experience was psychical. He later reportedly called it a "vision" (Acts 26:19).

The psychical explanation of Jesus' resurrection has merit, no doubt, but it also has limitations. It does not account for the empty tomb. The attribution of all the "materialism" in the Gospels to the Gnostic controversy is questionable. Jesus' appearance to more than five hundred brethren at once creates a psychical problem of considerable magnitude. And how well authenticated are the alleged psychical appearances in the modern world?

Jesus' resurrection appearances were psychological and subjective. No objective experience of a resurrected Jesus need be posited. Those who had become Jesus' disciples had done so because of the influence of his personality. That influence was so strong that death could not eradicate it. Although he had been crucified, God could not let him die. He was alive and available to his own. No resurrection took place—physical, spiritual-body, or psychical. It was the power of Jesus' personality which persuaded his followers that he was the Messiah and that death was but a prelude to his permanence—as head of their fellowship and a celestial being seated at the right hand of God.

"To me," writes Professor Enslin, "there appears . . . not a changed Jesus, but changed disciples. Jesus was the same. He had sown his seed, had lived his life, had built himself into the lives of those with whom he had lived and worked. . . . The change was not in any physical transformation of the body he had tenanted, but in the outlook and convictions of the men and women whom he had touched. . . . At the time of his arrest the disciples had fled in panic back to Galilee. . . . The bottom had dropped from life. Their house of cards had collapsed. . . . Then something happened. In the place of bleak despair there was a new and victorious confidence. . . . They 'saw the Lord.' Indeed yes: but was it the one with nail-pierced hands, or was it the one with whom they had lived and labored? . . . Back in these familiar scenes, everything spoke of him. As they sat at table, he was with them 'in the breaking of bread'. . . . Had not Jesus built himself . . . into them so completely that he was even then living in them? To think that after such a fellowship they could have remained untouched, unchanged, appears to me absurd. It would have been a greater miracle had they not seen him. . . . The real Jesus was not the flesh and the blood and the bone and the skin, but that something which had the power to reproduce itself in them, that lived in them. . . . God had sent him for a task. God could not be stayed. He was now with God but would soon return. Their task was to carry on. In his constant reference to the one who would come at any moment to consummate the history of the world, to usher in the new age, he had not, as they had blindly thought, meant another. He had, instead, meant himself. God's prophet was none other than God's final judge."[21]

21Enslin, *The Prophet from Nazareth*, pp. 209–13.

Professor Enslin writes with simple and appealing eloquence. Yet the psychological and subjective interpretation of the resurrection, which he and others champion, raises serious questions. Does it accord with the New Testament sources? Most scholars would reply negatively. Jesus' "compelling personality" is not the subject of the earliest kerygma. Is the explanation adequate to account for the rise and rapid spread of a new religion? Again, most scholars do not think it is. Something more than a psychological memory is required.

The Living Faith

The records clearly indicate that there was no single understanding of the resurrection in the early Christian community. An extraordinary event produced varied impressions. Not one of the witnesses long disputed the resurrection; they accorded it first importance. Nothing less can account for the tremendous transformation wrought in them. After the arrest, they were reported to be running. Their hopes had turned to ashes. Soon they were risking mobs, beatings, and imprisonment for the sake of Jesus who had been raised from the dead. Apart from the resurrection, they would never have told the story of the crucifixion.

The resurrection is not readily accepted in a scientific age. We long for positive proof, and our longing is unsatisfied. We cry out for impartial records, and our cry echoes. The records were based on the testimony of believers; they were written by believers; and they were preserved by believers. From the very first word which Jesus uttered on his mission, from the very first work which he performed—fact (what he said or did) was mingled with interpretation (what others thought he said or did and what he meant). The resultant records are biased. In this respect, they do not differ significantly from other historical documents. Every witness sees things from a given point of view. Every witness interprets. All history is partial.

Millions of modern Christians are convinced that their spiritual ancestors did not place their lives on the altar of sacrifice for a noble Nazarene whose life ended at Golgotha. They believe that God freed Jesus from the limitations of space-time and made him accessible to all men. They do not claim to know exactly how this took place. But since their lives have been vitalized by the living Christ, they see nothing strange in the testimonies of the first Christians. Of doubting latter-day Agrippas, they ask with Paul (Acts 26:8), "Why is it thought incredible by any of you that God raises the dead?"

chapter twenty-three

The Living Lord

A remarkable aspect of the story of Jesus is that it has no end. The disciples thought the crucifixion was the end, but they were mistaken. Three days after the crucifixion came the resurrection, followed by Jesus' appearances to many. According to Luke, Jesus then ascended into heaven. Even this event did not break his bond with his followers. They discovered him afresh within their fellowship. He was not a mere memory. He was a continuing presence. This experience gave rise to the Christian community. Jesus, the teacher, who had required faith of his followers, became the object of their faith. They called him "Lord" and cherished the conviction that he was deeply concerned with their welfare.

The story of Jesus, then, is a continuous one. It begins in the Gospels. It is continued in the rest of the New Testament, in the annals of church history, and in the contemporary Christian community. In this book, we have dealt only with the beginning. A hasty glance into the continued and continuing story is now called for. It can do little more than whet the reader's appetite for further investigation.[1]

The Acts

At the Feast of Pentecost, which followed the resurrection, the followers of Jesus experienced the coming of the Holy Spirit. In a sermon in-

---

[1]For a more extensive account of the development of the church, see C. Milo Connick, *The New Testament. An Introduction to Its History, Literature, and Thought* (Encino and Belmont, Calif.: Dickenson Publishing Company, Inc., 1972), pp. 199–423.

tended to explain the event, Peter asserts that it was Jesus himself who sent the Spirit: "Being therefore exalted at the right hand of God, and having received from the Father the promise of the Holy Spirit, he has poured out this which you see and hear" (Acts 2:33).

Jesus' continued presence and work in the Christian community is seen in such incidents as the healing of a lame man at the gate of the Temple. The man had been lame from birth. When he saw Peter and John, he asked them for alms. Peter refused. Instead, he commanded the man to walk in the name of Jesus. To the astonishment of the crowd the man leaped to his feet and walked. There was no doubt in Peter's mind who was responsible for the healing. "The faith which is through Jesus has given the man this perfect health in the presence of you all" (Acts 3:16).

The living Jesus was a compelling reality to Stephen, the first Christian martyr. He was one of seven set aside by the apostles to serve the needs of poor widows (Acts 6:1–6). In the synagogues frequented by Hellenists, he became such a skilled advocate of Jesus that disputes arose. He was haled before the Sanhedrin on the charge of speaking against the Temple and the Law. In the course of his defense he accused the Sanhedrin of putting Jesus to death. Mob violence resulted. Stephen was cast out of the city. He looked up into heaven "and saw the glory of God, and Jesus standing at

Today this entrance to Jerusalem is called St. Stephen's Gate. In Jesus' day it was called "The Sheep Gate." After Stephen was stoned to death near this point, the name was changed to honor him.

the right hand of God" (Acts 7:55). As his enemies stoned him, he addressed Jesus as "Lord," asked him to receive his spirit, and prayed, "Lord, do not hold this sin against them" (Acts 7:60). In death, as in life, the committed had the exalted Jesus as a constant companion.

The Epistles

The foremost campaigner for Christ in the early church was the apostle Paul. He began his career as a persecutor of those who followed Jesus. But after Paul's conversion experience he changed from a persecutor to a campaigner. Years later, he described his call to "preach Jesus" among the Gentiles as a revelation of Jesus initiated by God (Gal. 1:13–16).

Throughout his campaigns Paul had an abiding sense of Jesus' presence in his life. So closely did he associate the Spirit and the Risen Christ that at times they were identical. "Now the Lord is the Spirit, and where the Spirit of the Lord is, there is freedom" (II Cor. 3:17). This close relationship stemmed from the fact that the early Christians experienced no discontinuity in their fellowship with Jesus once the resurrection appearances had ended. He was still present with his people. The Spirit which he sent was at work. What God had begun in Jesus was continued by the Spirit.

The new life which Paul lived after his conversion is vividly described in Galatians. The apostle speaks not of the past but of the present, not of the historical Jesus but of the contemporary Christ. "I have been crucified with Christ; it is no longer I who live, but Christ who lives in me; and the life I now live in the flesh I live by faith in the Son of God, who loved me and gave himself for me" (2:20).

Hebrews

The Letter to the Hebrews was written near the end of the first century during the reign of Domitian. It was addressed to a community of Christians in danger of drifting away from the faith it had once embraced. The anonymous author sought to strengthen the faith of his readers and to save them from apostasy. He pictured Christ as the great High Priest and compared his work with that of the Levitical priesthood. Like the Levitical priests, Christ was human. He was tempted as were other men. He was thus able to sympathize with human weakness and to help men in time of need (4:14–16). Such a message was peculiarly relevant to the readers addressed. Both Christ and the Levitical high priest were appointed by God to act on behalf of men in their relations to God (5:1). Just as the Levitical high priest offered sacrifices for sins, so did Christ. The difference was that the Levitical high priest was beset by human weakness. He was a sinner. He had to offer sacrifices for himself as well as for others (5:2–3). Although Christ was fully human, he did not sin (4:15). He did not need to make sacrifices for himself. "Although he was a Son, he learned obedience through what he suffered; and being made perfect he became the source of eternal salvation to all who obey him" (5:8–9). The Levitical priests were prevented by death from remaining in office. But Christ's priesthood is permanent. "Consequently he is able for all time to save those who draw near to God through him, since he always lives to make intercession for them" (7:25). As the eternal High Priest he continues the ministry he began on earth. His followers look to him as they draw near to God.

Revelation

The book of Revelation bears the marks of a concentration camp. The persecution which had earlier threatened the Christians was now a reality. Domitian had insisted that he be worshiped. A provincial priesthood had actively supported his claim in Asia Minor. Since Christians could not countenance such an idolatrous practice, they soon felt the heavy hand of the Roman state. A prophet by the name of John, according to tradition, was banished to the island of Patmos in the Aegean Sea. He shared "the tribulation" with those on the mainland. One day, while he was in a state of prophetic ecstasy, a voice told him to write what he saw in a book and to send it to the seven churches in Asia Minor (1:11). This writing became the book of Revelation. It is a clarion call to Christians to remain steadfast in their faith in the face of persecution and death. The language is highly symbolic, but to readers steeped in apocalyptic thought, it conveyed the author's message with singular clarity.

No book in the New Testament affirms the lordship of. Jesus as unabashedly as does Revelation. He is the "King of kings and Lord of lords" (19:16), the divine agent of God in the judgment of wicked men and nations, the victorious foe of the Antichrist (17:14). He is worshiped as God is worshiped—by the church on earth and by the angelic hosts of heaven. As the slain lamb, he ransoms men for God "from every tribe and tongue and people and nation" (5:9).

Despite the exaltation of Jesus in the New Testament, the status of God is never threatened. The Son always remains subordinate to the Father. Paul declares that at the end of the age, when all things are subjected to Christ, "then the Son himself will also be subjected to him [the Father] who put all things under him, that God may be everything to every one" (I Cor. 15:28). Jesus' exaltation does, however, raise pressing questions about his precise relationship to the Father and to the sons of men. Answers are provided by the creeds which Christians have formulated and refined.

Beyond the New Testament

The end of the New Testament does not mark the end of the lordship of Jesus. He continues to be a vital presence in the life of the church—

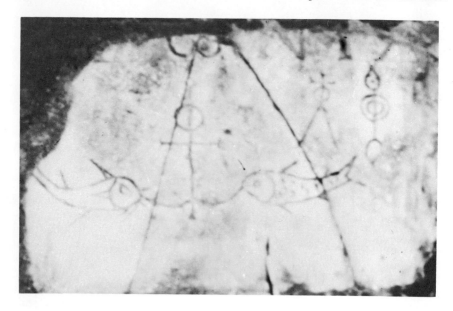

Christians sought safety in the catacombs during the Roman persecutions. On the walls they carved the figure of a fish. The Greek word for fish was *Ichthus*. It is composed of the first letters of the words *Jesous Christos Theou Huios Soter*, "Jesus Christ, God's Son, Savior."

ancient, medieval, and modern. It would take us far afield to explore his influence throughout the centuries. It must suffice to say that in his call as Lord, men and women find a demand for unmatched loyalty. They are prompted to question accepted standards of conduct, criticize their culture, and modify their own behavior. Most followers remain in the world and attempt to change it—often identifying the best in society with Jesus' demands. Some withdraw from the world into monastic orders in an effort to achieve perfection. But whether in the world or out of it, concerned for the transformation of society or the transformation of self, the devout are moved by one overriding conviction—the authoritative presence in their midst of Jesus Christ, their living Lord.

The Parables

Common to	Matthew	Mark	Luke
SAVORLESS SALT	5:13	9:50	14:34–35
LAMP AND BUSHEL	5:15	4:21	8:16
PHYSICIAN AND SICK	9:12	2:17	5:31
NEW CLOTH	9:16	2:21	5:36
NEW WINE	9:17	2:22	5:37–38
SOWER	13:3–8	4:3–8	8:5–8
MUSTARD SEED	13:31–32	4:30–32	13:18–19
WICKED TENANTS	21:33–43	12:1–11	20:9–18
BUDDING FIG TREE	24:32–33	13:28–29	21:29–31

Common to	Matthew	Luke
DEFENDANT	5:25–26	12:58–59
BODY'S LAMP	6:22–23	11:34–35
SPECK AND LOG	7:3–5	6:41–42
TREE AND FRUIT	7:16–20	6:43–45
TWO FOUNDATIONS	7:24–27	6:47–49
CHILDREN IN MARKET PLACE	11:16–17	7:31–32
EMPTY HOUSE	12:43–45c	11:24–26
LEAVEN	13:33	13:20–21
BLIND GUIDES	15:14	6:39
WEATHER SIGNS	16:2–3	12:54–56
LOST SHEEP	18:12–14	15:3–7
SUPERVISING SERVANT	24:45–51a	12:42–46

Peculiar to Matthew	*Matthew*
CITY ON HILL	5:14b
WEEDS	13:24–30
HIDDEN TREASURE	13:44
PRECIOUS PEARL	13:45–46
NET	13:47–48
HOUSEHOLDER	13:52
UNMERCIFUL SERVANT	18:23–34
LABORERS IN VINEYARD	20:1–15
TWO SONS	21:28–31
MARRIAGE FEAST	22:2–10
WEDDING GARMENT	22:11–13
WISE AND FOOLISH MAIDENS	25:1–13
TALENTS	25:14–28
SHEEP AND GOATS	25:31–46

Peculiar to Mark	*Mark*
SEED GROWING SECRETLY	4:26–29
WATCHFUL DOORKEEPER	13:34–36

Peculiar to Luke	*Luke*
TWO DEBTORS	7:41–43
GOOD SAMARITAN	10:30–37
FRIEND AT MIDNIGHT	11:5–8
RICH FOOL	12:16–20
WATCHFUL SERVANTS	12:35–38
BARREN FIG TREE	13:6–9
PLACES AT TABLE	14:7–10
GREAT BANQUET	14:16–24
TOWER BUILDER	14:28–30
WARRING KING	14:31–32
LOST COIN	15:8–10
LOST SON	15:11–32
DISHONEST STEWARD	16:1–8
RICH MAN AND LAZARUS	16:19–31
SERVANT'S DUTY	17:7–10
UNJUST JUDGE	18:2–5
PHARISEE AND PUBLICAN	18:10–14a
POUNDS	19:12–27

appendix two

Chronological Chart

	Roman Emperors	Judean Procurators	Christian Writings	Outstanding Christian Events	Jewish Writings	Outstanding Jewish Events
						Maccabean Revolt, 168 B.C.
					Testaments of the XII Partriarchs, 109–106 (?) B.C.	Dead Sea Sect at Qumran, 105 B.C. (?)–66 A.D.
					I Enoch, 94–64 (?) B.C.	Pompey captures Jerusalem, 63 B.C.
	Augustus, 27 B.C.–14 A.D.				Psalms of Solomon, 48 (?) B.C.	Herod the Great (King of the Jews, Mt. 2:1,19), 37 B.C.–4 B.C.
				Birth of Jesus, 8–4 B.C.	Wisdom of Solomon, 50 B.C.–10 (?) A.D.	Herod Antipas (Tetrarch of Galilee, Mt. 14:1), 4 B.C.–39 A.D.
					Fragments of a Zadokite Work, 18–8 (?) B.C.	Herod Archelaus (Ethnarch of Judea, Mt. 2:22), 4 B.C.–6 A.D.
					Assumption of Moses, 7–29 (?) A.D.	
1 B.C. → 1 A.D.		Coponius, 6–9 A.D.			IV Maccabees, 63 B.C.–38 (?) A.D.	
					First century, A.D. II Enoch	

	Roman Emperors	Judean Procurators	Christian Writings	Outstanding Christian Events	Jewish Writings	Outstanding Jewish Events
10 A.D. →	Tiberius, 14–37 A.D.	Ambibulus, 9–12 A.D. Annius Rufinus, 12–15 A.D.			I, II, III Baruch Martyrdom of Isaiah Books of Adam and Eve	Herod Philip (Tetrarch of Iturea), 4 B.C.–34 A.D.
20 A.D. →		Valerius Gratus, 15–26 A.D.		Preaching of John the Baptist, 27–29 (?) A.D.	IV Ezra (II Esdras)	
30 A.D. →		Pontius Pilate, 26–36 A.D.		Ministry of Jesus, 29–33 (?) A.D. Crucifixion, 30–33 A.D. Conversion of Paul, 33–35 (?) A.D.		Caiaphas, High Priest, 18–36 A.D.
40 A.D. →	Gaius Caligula, 37–41 A.D. Claudius, 41–54 A.D.	Marcellus, 36–37 A.D. Marullus, 37–41 A.D. Cuspius Fadus, 44–46 A.D. Tiberius Alexander, 46–48 A.D.		Peter imprisoned by Herod Agrippa, 41–44 (?) A.D. Martyrdom of James, son of Zebedee, 44 A.D. Paul in southern Galatia, 47–49 (?) A.D.		Theudas' revolt, 40 (?) A.D. Herod Agrippa I (King of the Jews, Acts 12:1-2), 41–44 A.D.

Roman Emperors	Judean Procurators	Christian Writings	Outstanding Christian Events	Jewish Writings	Outstanding Jewish Events
50 A.D. →	Ventidius Cumanus, 48–52 A.D. M. Antonius Felix, 52–60 (?) A.D.	I and II Thessalonians, 50 A.D. I and II Corinthians, 54–55 A.D. Galatians, 56 (?) A.D. Romans, 56–57 A.D. Colossians (?), Philippians, Philemon, 61–62 A.D.	Paul in Corinth, 50–51 A.D. Paul in Ephesus, 52–54 A.D. Paul arrested in Jerusalem, 56 A.D.		Jews banished from Rome by Claudius, 49 (?) A.D.
Nero, 54–68 A.D.					
60 A.D. →	Porcius Festus, 60–62 (?) A.D. Albinus, 62–64 (?) A.D. Gessius Florus, 64–66 A.D.		Paul in Rome, 60 A.D. Death of James, brother of Jesus, 62 A.D. Flight of Christians to Pella, 66–67 A.D.		War With Rome, 66–73 A.D.
Galba, 68–69 A.D. Otho, Vitellius, 69 A.D. Vespasian, 69–79 A.D.		Mark, 65–70 A.D.			Temple and Holy City destroyed 70 A.D.
70 A.D. →					
80 A.D. →		Matthew, 80–85 A.D. Luke-Acts, 85–90 A.D.			
Titus, 79–81 A.D. Domitian, 81–96 A.D.					

	Roman Emperors	Judean Procurators	Christian Writings	Outstanding Christian Events	Jewish Writings	Outstanding Jewish Events
90 A.D. →	Nerva, 96–98 A.D.		(Ephesians, 90 [?] A.D. James, 80–100 A.D. I, II, III John, 100–110 A.D. Hebrews, Revelation, I Peter, I Clement, 90–112 (?) A.D.			The so-called Council of Jamnia, 90 (?) A.D.
100 A.D. → 110 A.D. →	Trajan, 98–117 A.D.		John, 100 (?) A.D. Didache, 100–130 (?) A.D. I and II Timothy and Titus, 100–130 (?) A.D. Shepherd of Hermas, 100–140 (?) A.D.			
120 A.D. →	Hadrian, 117–138 A.D.		Epistles of Ignatius, 110–117 (?) A.D.	Martyrdom of Ignatius, 117 (?) A.D.		
130 A.D. →			Jude, 125 (?) A.D. II Peter, 150 (?) A.D.			Fall of Jerusalem, 134 A.D.

Suggestions
for Further Reading

General

CLASSIC WORKS

A detailed analysis of historical problems and source materials with a brief but excellent section on Jesus' message has been presented by the distinguished French scholar, M. Goguel, *The Life of Jesus*, tr. O. Wyon (London: George Allen & Unwin, Ltd., 1933). Also of great merit is the combined labor of three English scholars, H. D. A. Major, T. W. Manson, and C. J. Wright, *The Mission and Message of Jesus* (New York: E. P. Dutton & Co., Inc., 1938). Two penetrating Jewish specialists who have placed readers in their debt are J. Klausner, with his *Jesus of Nazareth*, tr. H. Danby (New York: Macmillan Company, 1925) and C. G. Montefiore, *The Synoptic Gospels*, rev. ed., Vols. I and II (London: Macmillan & Co., Ltd., 1927). C. Guignebert, *Jesus*, tr. S. H. Hooke (London: Kegan Paul, Trench, Trubner & Co., 1935) and W. E. Bundy, *Jesus and the First Three Gospels* (Cambridge: Harvard University Press, 1955), both reputable and exhaustive works, often arrive at "radical" conclusions. Only Bundy's book takes into consideration the insights of form criticism, and none is based upon redaction criticism.

POPULAR ACCOUNTS

Among the popular accounts anchored in the scholarship of their day are W. R. Bowie, *The Master* (New York: Charles Scribner's Sons, 1929); A. T.

Olmstead, *Jesus in the Light of History* (New York: Charles Scribner's Sons, 1942); E. J. Goodspeed, *A Life of Jesus* (New York: Harper & Row, Publishers, Inc., 1950); M. Dibelius, *Jesus*, tr. C. B. Hedrick and F. C. Grant (Philadelphia: The Westminster Press, 1949); Rudolf Bultmann, *Jesus and the Word*, tr. L. P. Smith and E. H. Lantero (New York: Charles Scribner's Sons, 1934, 1958); H. E. Fosdick, *The Man from Nazareth* (New York: Harper & Row, Publishers, Inc., 1949); S. M. Gilmour, *The Gospel Jesus Preached* (Philadelphia: The Westminster Press, 1957); A. M. Hunter, *The Work and Words of Jesus* (Philadelphia: The Westminster Press, 1950); and D. T. Rowlingson, *Jesus the Religious Ultimate* (New York: Macmillan Company, 1961). Four other books from diverse viewpoints call for special comment. V. Taylor, *The Life and Ministry of Jesus* (New York: Abingdon Press, 1955) combines "realized" and "futuristic" eschatology. E. Stauffer, *Jesus and His Story*, tr. R. & C. Winston (New York: Alfred A. Knopf, Inc., 1960) presents the conservative conclusions of a continental scholar. Much material is drawn from Jewish and Roman sources, and more reliance is placed on the Fourth Gospel than in most works. M. S. Enslin, *The Prophet from Nazareth* (New York: McGraw-Hill Book Company, Inc., 1961) strips Jesus of the theological robes placed on him by the early church and permits him to stand forth as a prophet whose compelling personality produced changed disciples after the crucifixion and prompted them to proclaim the resurrection. G. Bornkamm, *Jesus of Nazareth*, tr. I. and F. McLuskey with J. M. Robinson (New York: Harper & Row, Publishers, Inc., 1960) is a book in the Bultmann tradition which renews the quest for the historical Jesus. The work has received widespread acclaim here and abroad.

COMMENTARIES

The Moffatt New Testament Commentary, ed. and tr. J. Moffatt (New York: Harper & Row, Publishers, Inc. n.d.), furnishes a fine popular handling of the Gospels. It avoids excessive word analysis and specialized vocabulary. At the same time it provides needed background information and makes clear the meaning of the text. T. H. Robinson covers Matthew, B. H. Branscomb deals with Mark, W. Manson expounds Luke, and G. H. C. Macgregor treats John. *Harper's New Testament Commentaries*, ed. H. Chadwick (New York: Harper & Row, Publishers, Inc., 1958–   ), represent excellent work in the popular vein. They are based on fresh translations of the Greek text by front-ranking scholars who reward readers with the fruit of up-to-date critical thought. Matthew is treated by F. V. Filson, Mark by S. E. Johnson, Luke by A. R. C. Leaney, and John by J. N. Sanders. A somewhat more technical treatment is offered in *The Interpreter's Bible*, ed. G. A. Buttrick, Vols. VII and VIII (New York: Abingdon Press, 1951–1957). Both the King James and Revised Standard texts are included. Exegesis is by S. E. Johnson (Matthew), F. C. Grant (Mark), S. M. Gilmour (Luke), and W. F. Howard (John). Volume VII contains background articles of considerable value.

The two books published so far dealing with the Gospels in *The Anchor Bible*, eds. W. F. Albright and D. N. Freedman (Garden City, N.Y.: Doubleday & Co., Inc.), are of uneven quality. R. E. Brown's two-volume study of John (1966) is excellent, but the study of Matthew (1971) by W. F. Albright and C. S. Mann is disappointing. The latter rejects the contributions of both form and redaction criticism.* *The Jerome Biblical Commentary*, II, eds. J. A. Fitzmyer, S.J., and R. E. Brown, S.S. (Englewood Cliffs, N.J.: Prentice-Hall, Inc., 1968), is the latest and best Roman Catholic commentary. Exegesis is by E. J. Mally (Mark), J. L. McKenzie (Matthew), and Carroll Stuhlmueller (Luke).

DICTIONARIES AND ATLASES

A Dictionary of the Bible, ed. J. Hastings (New York: Charles Scribner's Sons, 1898–1904), a five-volume work, is a classic in the field. Even though much of the material is out-of-date, this reference work cannot be ignored. *The Interpreter's Dictionary of the Bible*, ed. G. A. Buttrick (New York: Abingdon Press, 1962), written by 253 scholars from fifteen countries, does for the second half of our century what Hastings' work did for the first. M. S. and J. L. Miller, *Harper's Bible Dictionary* (New York: Harper & Row, Publishers, Inc., 1952) is perhaps the best single-volume work. *The Westminster Historical Atlas to the Bible*, rev. ed. (Philadelphia: The Westminster Press, 1956), ed. G. E. Wright and F. V. Filson, contains choice colored maps and a helpful discussion of history and geography. E. G. Kraeling, *Bible Atlas* (New York: Rand McNally & Company, 1956) is also very useful.

A beautifully illustrated introduction to archeology is G. E. Wright, *Biblical Archaeology* (Philadelphia: The Westminster Press, 1957). C. C. McCown, *The Ladder of Progress in Palestine* (New York: Harper & Row, Publishers, Inc., 1943) and M. Burrows, *What Mean These Stones* (New Haven: American Schools of Oriental Research, 1941) are also valuable. An excellent treatment of the history of the ancient Near East as it bears upon the Bible is J. Finegan, *Light from the Ancient Past* (Princeton: Princeton University Press, 1946). *The Biblical Archaeologist*, ed. G. E. Wright and F. M. Cross, Jr., a quarterly published by the American Schools of Oriental Research at New Haven, is the best source of current archaeological information.

PERIODICALS

The *Journal of Biblical Literature* is the leading periodical in English dealing with the study of the Bible. Its technical nature makes it most suitable for advanced study. Of a more general nature, but with important articles on Biblical subjects and often with penetrating reviews of current books,

*For a critique of the Albright-Mann book see Robin Scroggs, "A New Old Quest?," *Journal of the American Academy of Religion*, XL, No. 4 (1972), pp. 506–512.

are the *Journal of the American Academy of Religion, Journal of Religion, Religion in Life, Journal of Theological Studies, The Harvard Theological Review,* and *Interpretation.*

Readings Chapter By Chapter

CHAPTER ONE: *The Legacy*

The best introductory book on the Old Testament is B. W. Anderson, *Understanding the Old Testament,* 2nd ed. (Englewood Cliffs: Prentice-Hall, Inc., 1966). The author is a reputable scholar, has a lively style, and does a superb job of interweaving literary, historical, and theological approaches. Other books of genuine worth are H. K. Beebe, *The Old Testament, An Introduction to Its Literary, Historical, and Religious Traditions* (Belmont, Calif.: Dickenson Publishing Co., Inc., 1970), and Walter Harrelson, *Interpreting the Old Testament* (New York: Holt, Rinehart, and Winston, Inc., 1964). R. H. Pfeiffer, *Introduction to the Old Testament,* rev. ed. (New York: Harper & Row, Publishers, Inc., 1949) is the fullest introduction in English and features literary criticism. It is rather technical and ponderous but of first rank. The general reader will prefer the abridged form, *The Books of the Old Testament* (New York: Harper & Row, Publishers, Inc., 1957). Elias Bickermann, *From Ezra to the Last of the Maccabees* (New York: Schocken Books, 1962), Nigel Turner's "Hasmoneans," in G. A. Buttrick, ed., *The Interpreter's Dictionary of the Bible* (New York: Abingdon Press, 1962), E–J, 529–535, and Werner Foerster, *From the Exile to Christ: A Historical Introduction to Palestinian Judaism,* tr. G. E. Harris (Philadelphia: Fortress Press, 1964) are instructive.

CHAPTER TWO: *The Land*

The definitive work on Palestine is G. A. Smith, *The Historical Geography of the Holy Land,* 14th ed. (New York: A. C. Armstrong, 1908). The reader will find pp. 45–104 of special usefulness. The author's style is graceful and graphic and his knowledge encyclopedic. Because many changes have occurred in Palestine since the book was written, some of the material needs to be updated. D. Baly, *The Geography of the Bible* (New York: Harper & Row, Publishers, Inc., 1957) is a more recent although less comprehensive work. G. Dalman, *Sacred Sites and Ways,* tr. P. Levertoff (New York: Macmillan Company, 1935), pp. 1–14, is also helpful. N. Glueck, *The River Jordan* (Philadelphia: The Westminster Press, 1946) is masterful. Also see Bible Dictionaries and Atlases.

CHAPTER THREE: *The Law*

The political conditions of Palestine just prior to and during Jesus' lifetime are vividly portrayed in J. Klausner, *Jesus of Nazareth* (New York: Macmillan Company, 1925), pp. 135–73. The rule of the Romans from 63 B.C. to 66 A.D. is succinctly summarized by R. H. Pfeiffer, *History of New Testament Times* (New York: Harper & Row, Publishers, Inc., 1949), pp. 24–40. E. Schürer, *A History of the Jewish People in the Time of Jesus Christ* (Edinburgh: T. & T. Clark, 1885–1890), Divisions I, 370–99, 416–39, and II, 1–87, is invaluable. Josephus, *Antiquities* XIV–XIX and *Wars* I–II provide early and useful data. M. S. Enslin, "Palestine," in *The Interpreter's Bible*, Vol. VII, 100–113, is also instructive.

CHAPTER FOUR: *The Life*

The economic and religious conditions of the Jews during the time of Jesus are cogently covered in J. Klausner, *Jesus of Nazareth* (New York: Macmillan Company, 1925), pp. 174–228. F. C. Grant, *The Economic Background of the Gospels* (London: Oxford University Press, 1926) is also most helpful. G. F. Moore, *Judaism in the First Centuries of the Christian Era* (Cambridge: Harvard University Press, 1927), in two volumes, is the definitive work on this subject. The religious history is briefly covered in R. H. Pfeiffer, *History of New Testament Times* (New York: Harper & Row, Publishers, Inc., 1949), pp. 46–59. M. S. Enslin, *Christian Beginnings* (New York: Harper & Row, Publishers, Inc., 1937), pp. 78–143, provides a helpful treatment. S. E. Johnson, *Jesus in His Homeland* (New York: Charles Scribner's Sons, 1957) is simply and accurately written. The sections which cover the relation of the Essenes to early Christianity (pp. 23–47) and to Jesus (pp. 48–67), and those which cover Jesus' relation to the Pharisees (pp. 10–16) and to the revolutionists (pp. 89–110) are especially instructive. Informative articles on these and related subjects are found under appropriate headings in G. A. Buttrick, ed., *The Interpreter's Dictionary of the Bible* (New York: Abingdon Press, 1962). Louis Finkelstein, *The Pharisees* (Philadelphia: The Jewish Publication Society of America, 1962), 2 vols., is excellent. A comprehensive collection of ancient Jewish and pagan writings appears in C. K. Barrett, *The New Testament Background: Selected Documents* (New York: The Macmillan Co., 1957). A convenient collection of translated sources for Jewish religion is S. W. Baron and J. L. Blau, eds., *Judaism: Postbiblical and Talmudic Period* (New York: Liberal Arts Press, 1954). L. E. Toombs, *The Threshold of Christianity* (Philadelphia: The Westminster Press, 1960) gives a nontechnical coverage of intertestamental literature. S. Angus, *The Environment of Early Christianity* (New York: Charles Scribner's Sons, 1915) gives a general treatment of the ancient world which stresses Christianity as coming in the "fullness of time." Henri Daniel-Rops, *Daily Life in the Time of Jesus*, tr. Patrick O'Brien (New York: New American Library of World Literature, 1962) is also useful. Two balanced and readable books concerning the Dead Sea Scrolls and their implications are M. Burrows, *The Dead Sea Scrolls* (New York: Viking Press, 1955) and F. M. Cross, Jr., *The Ancient Library of Qumran and Modern Biblical*

Studies (New York: Doubleday & Company, Inc., 1958). A. Dupont-Sommer, *The Essene Writings from Qumran* (New York: Meridian Books, 1961) provides a fine translation of the documents, but his conclusions are often questionable. Krister Stendahl, *Introduction to the Scrolls and the New Testament* (New York: Harper & Row, 1957), Geza Vermes, *The Dead Sea Scrolls in English* (Baltimore: Penguin Books, 1962), and Theodor Gaster, *The Dead Sea Scriptures* (Garden City, N.Y.: Doubleday & Co., 1956) are useful collections. Helmer Ringgren, *The Faith of Qumran* (Philadelphia: Fortress Press, 1961) is a choice work, and J. C. Trever, *Untold Story of Qumran* (Westwood, N.J.: Fleming H. Revell Co., 1965) is a handsomely illustrated first-hand account of the discovery of the Scrolls and the intrigue that surrounded their purchase and publication.

CHAPTER FIVE: *The Legends*

Various theories about Jesus' existence and education, the sources of these theories, and the non-Christian and Christian evidences against them (exclusive of the Gospels) are found in M. Goguel, *The Life of Jesus* (London: George Allen & Unwin, Ltd., 1933), pp. 37–133. Legends concerning Jesus' boyhood are found in M. R. James, *The Apocryphal New Testament* (Oxford: Clarendon Press, 1953), a corrected edition, the best collection of English translations together with introductory remarks.

CHAPTER SIX: *The Growth of the Gospel*

F. C. Grant, *The Growth of the Gospels* (New York: Abingdon Press, 1933) provides an excellent and rather detailed survey. F. V. Filson, *Origins of the Gospels* (New York: Abingdon Press, 1938) gives a somewhat more popular treatment. B. H. Streeter, *The Four Gospels*, 4th ed. (London: Macmillan & Co., Ltd., 1930) is a standard work on the Synoptic problem. Briefer accounts of the development of the Gospels are D. T. Rowlingson, *Introduction to New Testament Study* (New York: Macmillan Company, 1956), pp. 57–78, and A. M. Perry, "The Growth of the Gospels," in *The Interpreter's Bible*, Vol. VII, pp. 60–74. Articles which introduce the different Gospels in *The Interpreter's Bible*, Vols. VII and VIII, and in *Harper's New Testament Commentaries* are instructive. Innumerable studies of individual Gospels are also available. F. C. Grant, *The Earliest Gospel* (New York: Abingdon Press, 1943); C. Beach, *The Gospel of Mark* (New York: Harper & Row, Publishers, Inc., 1959); R. M. Lightfoot, *The Gospel Message of Mark* (Oxford: At the Clarendon Press, 1952); J. M. Robinson, *The Problem of History in Mark* (Naperville, Ill.: A. R. Allenson, Inc., 1957); Ernest Best, *The Temptation and the Passion in Mark* (Cambridge: At the University Press, 1965); D. M. and G. H. Slusser, *The Jesus of Mark's Gospel* (Philadelphia: The Westminster Press, 1967). The best redaction-critical study is Willi Marxsen, *Mark the Evangelist*, tr. R. A. Harrisville (New York: Abingdon Press, 1969). B. W. Bacon, *Studies in St. Matthew* (New York: Henry

Holt & Co., 1930) is a difficult but rewarding work. G. D. Kilpatrick, *The Origin of the Gospel According to St. Matthew* (Oxford: At the Clarendon Press, 1946), treats introductory problems. Krister Stendahl, *The School of St. Matthew* (Philadelphia: Fortress Press, 1968), argues for community authorship of Matthew. Günther Bornkamm, Gerhard Barth, and H. J. Held, *Tradition and Interpretation in Matthew* (Philadelphia: The Westminster Press, 1963), is a redaction-critical work of great merit. An older but useful study of Luke is H. J. Cadbury, *The Making of Luke-Acts* (New York: The Macmillan Co., 1927). Hans Conzelmann, *The Theology of St. Luke*, tr. Geofrey Buswell (New York: Harper & Row, Publishers, Inc., 1960), is a path-breaking redaction-critical study. L. E. Keck and J. L. Martyn, *Studies in Luke-Acts* (New York: Abingdon Press, 1966), is also informative. The best work on the Fourth Gospel is R. E. Brown, *The Gospel According to John*, 2 vols., *The Anchor Bible* (Garden City, N.Y.: Doubleday & Co., Inc., 1966). Other valuable studies are W. F. Howard, *The Fourth Gospel in Recent Criticism* (London: The Epworth Press, 1945); C. H. Dodd, *The Interpretation of the Fourth Gospel* and *Historical Tradition in the Fourth Gospel* (Cambridge: At the University Press, 1965 and 1963 respectively); J. L. Martyn, *History and Theology in the Fourth Gospel* (New York: Harper & Row, Publishers, Inc., 1968); Ernst Käsemann, *The Testament of Jesus*, tr. Gerhard Krodel (Philadelphia: Fortress Press, 1968); E. L. Titus, *The Message of the Fourth Gospel* (New York: Abingdon Press, 1957); and E. C. Colwell and E. L. Titus, *The Gospel of the Spirit* (New York: Harper & Row, Publishers, Inc., 1953).

CHAPTER SEVEN: *Behind the Gospels*

The works of two pioneer form critics are of paramount importance—M. Dibelius, *From Tradition to Gospel*, tr. B. L. Woolf (New York: Charles Scribner's Sons, 1935), and R. Bultmann, *The History of the Synoptic Tradition*, tr. John Marsh (Oxford: Basil Blackwell, 1963). B. S. Easton, *The Gospel before the Gospels* (New York: Charles Scribner's Sons, 1928), evaluates form criticism from a conservative viewpoint. V. Taylor, *The Formation of the Gospel Tradition* (London: Macmillan & Co., Ltd., 1938), presents a balanced view. E. B. Redlich, *Form Criticism* (London: Duckworth, 1934), is also helpful. Classic essays on the subject can be found in R. Bultmann and K. Kundsin, *Form Criticism*, tr. F. C. Grant (New York: Harper & Row, Publishers, Inc., 1962). F. C. Grant, ed., *Form Criticism* (New York: Harper & Row, Publishers, Inc., 1962), and E. V. McKnight, *What is Form Criticism?* (Philadelphia: Fortress Press, 1969), are instructive.

For studies in redaction criticism see the books by Marxsen, Conzelmann, and Bornkamm, Barth, and Held listed in suggested readings for chapter six. Norman Perrin, *What is Redaction Criticism?* (Philadelphia: Fortress Press, 1969), is also helpful. Perhaps the best review and evaluation of redaction criticism is Joachim Rohde, *Rediscovering the Teaching of the*

Evangelists, tr. D. M. Barton (London: SCM Press, 1968; printed in the U.S. by The Westminster Press).

CHAPTER EIGHT: *The Virgin Birth*

The classical controversy concerning the virgin birth of Jesus raged between 1890 and 1910. A brilliant group of British scholars (Gore, Sanday, Ramsay, Orr) stoutly defended the tradition with their considerable skill and learning. Opposition to the tradition centered mainly, although not exclusively, in Germany. The extreme position was taken by some (Usener, Schmiedel) and a more moderate stance by others (Lobstein, Harnack, J. M. Thompson). Both sides pressed their arguments to the limit and perhaps beyond. Later works of the same mind-set were (on the traditional side) J. G. Machen, *The Virgin Birth of Christ* (New York: Harper & Row, Publishers, Inc., 1930); and (from the critical viewpoint) E. Worcester, *Studies in the Virgin Birth of the Lord* (New York: Charles Scribner's Sons, 1932). The most moderate and persuasive defense of the tradition is G. H. Box, *The Virgin Birth of Jesus* (London: I. Pitman, 1916). V. Taylor, *The Historical Evidence of the Virgin Birth* (Oxford: Clarendon Press, 1920), is the most dispassionate treatment of the subject available. In recent years, greater attention has been paid to the virgin birth as kerygmatic truth than as historical fact. See Thomas Boslooper, *The Virgin Birth* (Philadelphia: The Westminster Press, 1962). F. W. Beare, *The Earliest Records of Jesus* (New York: Abingdon Press, 1962), pp. 29–35, is instructive.

CHAPTER NINE: *Growth toward Greatness*

Helpful reconstructions of life in Nazareth in the first century are found in A. T. Olmstead, *Jesus in the Light of History* (New York: Charles Scribner's Sons, 1942), pp. 1–27, and H. K. Booth, *The World of Jesus* (New York: Charles Scribner's Sons, 1939), pp. 76–97. Other works which present accounts of Jesus' childhood and youth are C. Guignebert, *Jesus* (London: Kegan Paul, Trench, Trubner & Co., 1935), pp. 133–44; J. Klausner, *Jesus of Nazareth* (New York: Macmillan Company, 1925), pp. 229–38; E. Stauffer, *Jesus and His Story* (New York: Alfred A. Knopf, Inc., 1960), pp. 43–62.

CHAPTER TEN: *Prophetic Predecessor*

The finest work in English on the prophetic predecessor of Jesus is C. H. Kraeling, *John the Baptist* (New York: Charles Scribner's Sons, 1951). Briefer treatments are available in J. Klausner, *Jesus of Nazareth* (New York: Macmillan Company, 1925), pp. 239–50; T. W. Manson, *The Servant-Messiah* (Cambridge: Cambridge University Press, 1956), pp. 36–49; M. Goguel, *The Life of Jesus* (London: George Allen & Unwin, Ltd., 1933), pp. 264–79. W. H. Brownlee, "John the Baptist in the New Light of Ancient Scrolls," in K. Stendahl, ed., *The Scrolls and the New Testament* (New York: Harper & Row, Publishers, Inc., 1956), pp. 33–53, is instructive. Willi

Marxsen, *Mark the Evangelist*, tr. R. A. Harrisville (New York: Abingdon Press, 1969), pp. 30-53, argues that the Baptist tradition tells us nothing about John since it is really a commentary about Christ. W. F. Beare, *The Earliest Records of Jesus* (New York: Abingdon Press, 1962), pp. 36–40, is helpful.

CHAPTER ELEVEN: *The Announcement*

What happened at the baptism of Jesus is ably discussed at appropriate places in the commentaries listed near the beginning of this bibliography. The various "lives" of Jesus provide added interpretations. Relevant passages in H. D. A. Major, T. W. Manson, and C. J. Wright, *The Mission and Message of Jesus* (New York: E. P. Dutton & Co., Inc., 1938), are enlightening. A suggestive treatment is found in F. W. Beare, *The Earliest Records of Jesus* (New York: Abingdon Press, 1962), pp. 40–42. W. E. Bundy, *Jesus and the First Three Gospels* (Cambridge: Harvard University Press, 1955), pp. 53–57, traces the literary development of the story of the baptism. A skeptical view of the historicity of the story is advanced by C. Guignebert, *Jesus* (London: Kegan Paul, Trench, Trubner & Co., 1935), pp. 145–58. Relevant passages in Günther Bornkamm, Gerhard Barth, and H. J. Held, *Tradition and Interpretation in Matthew* (London: SCM Press, 1963), and Willi Marxsen, *Mark the Evangelist* (New York: Abingdon Press, 1969), should also be consulted.

CHAPTER TWELVE: *The Commitment*

In addition to the commentaries and "lives" of Jesus, H. D. A. Major, T. W. Manson, and C. J. Wright, *The Mission and Message of Jesus* (New York: E. P. Dutton & Co., Inc., 1938), should be consulted. F. W. Beare, *The Earliest Records of Jesus* (New York: Abingdon Press, 1962), pp. 42–43, is suggestive. A brief account is presented in D. M. Beck, *Through the Gospels to Jesus* (New York: Harper & Row, Publishers, Inc., 1954), pp. 127–32. Goguel omits the temptation from *The Life of Jesus*. C. Guignebert, *Jesus* (London: Kegan Paul, Trench, Trubner & Co., 1935), p. 158, and W. E. Bundy, *Jesus and the First Three Gospels* (Cambridge: Harvard University Press, 1955), p. 64, regard the temptation as legendary. J. Jeremias, *The Parables of Jesus*, tr. S. H. Hooke (London: SCM Press, 1963), pp. 122–123, locates the temptation in the historic ministry of Jesus.

CHAPTER THIRTEEN: *The Campaign*

A brisk and readable outline of Jesus' campaign from a critically conservative viewpoint is presented in A. M. Hunter, *The Work and Words of Jesus* (Philadelphia: The Westminster Press, 1950), pp. 41–53. A more extensive treatment is given in F. W. Beare, *The Earliest Records of Jesus* (New York: Abingdon Press, 1962), pp. 43–54, 69–145. J. Klausner, *Jesus of Nazareth* (New York: Macmillan Company, 1925), pp. 259–303, and M. Goguel, *The*

Life of Jesus (London: George Allen & Unwin, Ltd., 1933), provide valuable insights. A detailed account of relevant passages is found in D. M. Beck, *Through the Gospels to Jesus* (New York: Harper & Row, Publishers, Inc., 1954), pp. 133–63, 226–35. The commentaries are invaluable guides to the meaning of the text and should be consulted in connection with individual passages. H. D. A. Major, T. W. Manson, and C. J. Wright, *The Mission and Message of Jesus* (New York: E. P. Dutton & Co., Inc., 1938) and C. G. Montefiore, *The Synoptic Gospels*, rev. ed., Vols. I and II (London: Macmillan & Co., Ltd., 1927), are also choice sources. E. Stauffer, *Jesus and His Story*, tr. Richard and Clara Winston (New York: Alfred A. Knopf, 1960), attempts (unsuccessfully, we think) to write a chronologically historical account of Jesus' life. Relevant passages in Günther Bornkamm, Gerhard Barth, and H. J. Held, *Tradition and Interpretation in Matthew* (London: SCM Press, 1963), Willi Marxsen, *Mark the Evangelist* (New York: Abingdon Press, 1969), Hans Conzelmann, *The Theology of St. Luke*, tr. Geoffrey Buswell (New York: Harper & Row, Publishers, Inc., 1961), and H. E. Tödt, *The Son of Man in the Synoptic Tradition*, tr. D. M. Barton (London: SCM Press, 1965), are vital to understanding the events discussed in this chapter. Also of considerable value are Oscar Cullmann, *The Christology of the New Testament*, tr. S. C. Guthrie and C. A. M. Hall (London: SCM Press, 1959), R. H. Fuller, *The Foundations of New Testament Christology* (New York: Charles Scribner's Sons, 1965), J. Jeremias, *New Testament Theology*, tr. John Bowden (New York: Charles Scribner's Sons, 1971), and Eduard Schweizer, *Jesus*, tr. D. E. Green (London: SCM Press, 1971).

CHAPTER FOURTEEN: *The Parables*

The first major book in English to harvest the fruits of critical scholarship was A. B. Bruce, *The Parabolic Teaching of Christ* (New York: A. C. Armstrong, 1892). This was soon followed in Germany by A. Jülicher, *Die Gleichnisreden Jesu* (Leipzig: J. C. B. Mohr, 1888–99), a two-volume work which put an end to the allegorization of the parables. The next significant advance came with C. H. Dodd, *The Parables of the Kingdom* (New York: Charles Scribner's Sons, 1936) a path-breaking work. The climax was reached with J. Jeremias, *The Parables of Jesus*, 3rd rev. ed., tr. S. H. Hooke (London: SCM Press, 1972), the finest work in any language, first published in 1947. Dodd and Jeremias stripped the parables of their secondary places in the Gospels and recovered, in large part at least, their original settings. All worthwhile subsequent works are deeply indebted to these scholars. Critical of the Dodd-Jeremias position is D. O. Via, *The Parables: Their Literary and Existential Dimension* (Philadelphia: Fortress Press, 1967), who views the parables proper as genuine works of art whose primary meaning is not to be limited to their original proclamation. Popular treatments of the parables abound. Among those with a more conservative orientation than Jeremias is A. M. Hunter, *Interpreting the Parables* (Philadelphia: The

Westminster Press, 1960). Norman Perrin, *The Kingdom of God in the Teaching of Jesus* (London: SCM Press, 1963), gives a fine résumé of thought about the kingdom of God from the turn of the century, and his *Rediscovering the Teaching of Jesus* (London: SCM Press, 1967), seeks to determine what is authentic in the gospel tradition. An older work, T. W. Manson, *The Teaching of Jesus* (Cambridge: At the University Press, 1963), contains valuable insights.

CHAPTER FIFTEEN: *The Sermon*

An important book for scholars is M. Dibelius, *The Sermon on the Mount,* tr. C. H. Kraeling (New York: Charles Scribner's Sons, 1940). The author asserts that the Sermon's demands cannot be fully carried out in this age. They are signs of the eternal kingdom and its total claim. They spur us on toward the divine likeness. H. Windisch, *The Meaning of the Sermon on the Mount,* tr. S. M. Gilmour (Philadelphia: The Westminster Press, 1951), another book for specialists, argues for the "fulfillability" of the teachings of the Sermon. A third difficult but rewarding treatment is A. N. Wilder, *Eschatology and Ethics in the Teaching of Jesus,* rev. ed. (New York: Harper & Row, Publishers, Inc., 1950). Wilder holds that the eschatological expectation was the most significant factor in the presentation of Jesus' ethical teachings. The teachings were an emergency ethic, not of the interim (Schweitzer) but of Jesus' mission. H. K. McArthur, *Understanding the Sermon on the Mount* (New York: Harper & Row, Publishers, Inc., 1960) steers a middle course on the eschatological nature of the Sermon and furnishes a fine summary of the different ways in which Christians have regarded the Sermon during the history of the Church. A. M. Hunter, *A Pattern for Life* (Philadelphia: The Westminster Press, 1953) describes in relatively popular language the making, manner, matter, and meaning of the Sermon. C. M. Connick, *Build on the Rock, You and the Sermon on the Mount* (Westwood, N.J.: Fleming H. Revell Company, 1960) is a swiftly-moving account of the Sermon for thoughtful laymen. It grew out of the experiences of a group of prominent business and professional men who practiced the Sermon in their daily lives. A good summary of the nature and relevance of the Sermon is A. N. Wilder, "The Sermon on the Mount," in *The Interpreter's Bible,* Vol. VII, 155–64. F. W. Beare, *The Earliest Records of Jesus* (New York: Abingdon Press, 1962), pp. 52–69, is helpful. Books by Marxsen, Bornkamm, Barth, and Held, Conzelmann, Tödt, Cullmann, Fuller, and Jeremias (mentioned above in connection with chapter thirteen) and by Perrin and Manson (mentioned in connection with chapter fourteen) should be consulted.

CHAPTER SIXTEEN: *The Miracles*

J. M. Thompson, *Miracles in the New Testament* (London: Edward Arnold & Co., 1912) eliminates from the New Testament the miraculous element but retains belief in the supernatural. Rational explanations of the alleged miracles are presented. J. Wendland, *Miracles and Christianity* (London: Hodder & Stoughton, Ltd., 1911) claims that miracle has its own proper law. E. R. Micklem, *Miracles and the New Psychology* (London: Oxford University Press, 1922) stresses natural explanations of such miracles as the raising of the dead. Other works from a variety of viewpoints are: F. R. Tennant, *Miracle and Its Philosophical Presuppositions* (Cambridge: Cambridge University Press, 1925); C. J. Wright, *Miracle in History and in Modern Thought* (New York: Henry Holt & Company, Inc., 1930); C. F. Rogers, *The Case for Miracle* (London: S. P. C. K., 1936); A. Richardson, *The Miracle Stories of the Gospels* (London: Student Christian Movement Press, 1941); C. S. Lewis, *Miracles* (New York: Macmillan Company, 1947); R. M. Grant, *Miracle and Natural Law in Graeco-Roman and Early Christian Thought* (Amsterdam: N. Holland Publishing Co., 1952). Shorter treatments are given by J. Klausner, *Jesus of Nazareth* (New York: Macmillan Company, 1925), pp. 267–72, and F. W. Beare, *The Earliest Records of Jesus* (New York: Abingdon Press, 1962), pp. 69–77. The treatment of individual miracles is ably covered in the commentaries and other source books previously mentioned. S. V. McCasland, *By the Finger of God* (New York: Macmillan Company, 1951) gives a good account of the contributions of modern psychotherapy to the understanding of Jesus' healings. H. J. Held, "Matthew as Interpreter of the Miracle Stories," in Bornkamm, Barth, and Held, *Tradition and Interpretation in Matthew*, pp. 165–299, demonstrates how Matthew used the miracle material to express his theology.

CHAPTER SEVENTEEN: *The Messianic Question*

The literature on this subject is voluminous, and the conclusions reached are varied. We shall list some of the more important works. R. Bultmann, *Theology of the New Testament*, Vol. I, tr. K. Grobel (New York: Charles Scribner's Sons, 1951) is an impressive work which is critically evaluated by R. H. Fuller, *The Mission and Achievement of Jesus* (Naperville, Ill.: A. R. Allenson, 1954). R. Otto, *The Kingdom of God and the Son of Man*, rev. ed. (Boston: Beacon Press, 1943) is a classic work which has influenced all subsequent studies. T. W. Manson, *The Servant-Messiah* (Cambridge: Cambridge University Press, 1956) is a popular presentation of that author's once rather widely held position. W. Manson, *Jesus the Messiah* (Philadelphia: The Westminster Press, 1946) is written with special reference to form criticism. G. Bornkamm, *Jesus of Nazareth*, tr. I. and F. McLuskey with J. M. Robinson (New York: Harper & Row, Publishers, Inc., 1960), pp. 169–78 and Appendix III, reflects Bultmann's thought. O. Cullmann, *The Christology of the New Testament*, tr. S. C. Guthrie and C. A. M. Hall (Philadelphia: The Westminster Press, 1959) gives an extensive treatment of the titles of Jesus. The two latest books on the subject, however, are the best: R. H. Fuller, *The Foundations of New Testament Christology* (New York: Charles Scribner's Sons, 1965) and H. E. Tödt, *The Son of Man in the Synoptic Tradition*, tr. D. M. Barton (London: SCM Press, 1965).

CHAPTER EIGHTEEN: *The Journey to Jerusalem*
Consult the commentaries (*The Interpreter's Bible*, Vols. VII and VIII, *The Moffatt New Testament Commentary*, and *Harper's New Testament Commentaries*) for helpful information on Jesus' journey to Jerusalem. Major, Manson, and Wright, *The Mission and Message of Jesus*, is also valuable. Brief accounts are found in V. Taylor, *The Life and Ministry of Jesus* (New York: Abingdon Press, 1955), pp. 161–68 and in J. Klausner, *Jesus of Nazareth* (New York: Macmillan Company, 1925), pp. 304–10. A reconstruction of Jesus' ministry from the Transfiguration to the Triumphal Entry is available in M. Goguel. *The Life of Jesus* (London: George Allen & Unwin, Ltd., 1933), pp. 400–428. E. W. Saunders, *Jesus in the Gospels* (Englewood Cliffs, N.J.: Prentice-Hall, Inc., 1967), pp. 233–258, and F. W. Beare, *The Earliest Records of Jesus* (New York: Abingdon Press, 1962), pp. 190–203, are also useful. See also relevant passages in the books by Tödt and Bornkamm, Barth, and Held cited above.

CHAPTER NINETEEN: *The Jerusalem Ministry*
The commentaries mentioned above are indispensable for understanding Jesus' Jerusalem ministry, as is the work by Major, Manson, and Wright. The Temple Cleansing and the disputes in the Temple Court are graphically discussed in J. Klausner, *Jesus of Nazareth* (New York: Macmillan Company, 1925), pp. 311–23. Instructive accounts are also given in V. Taylor, *The Life and Ministry of Jesus* (New York: Abingdon Press, 1955), pp. 169–89 and in F. W. Beare, *The Earliest Records of Jesus* (New York: Abingdon Press, 1962), pp. 206–217. See also the books by Marxsen, Tödt, and Bornkamm, Barth, and Held mentioned above.

CHAPTER TWENTY: *The Conspiracy*
In addition to the commentaries and the work by Major, Manson, and Wright, the following books contain useful material: M. Goguel, *The Life of Jesus* (London: George Allen & Unwin, Ltd., 1933), pp. 429–62, 483–501; J. Klausner, *Jesus of Nazareth* (New York: Macmillan Company, 1925), pp. 324–38; E. W. Saunders, *Jesus in the Gospels* (Englewood Cliffs, N.J.: Prentice-Hall, Inc. 1967), pp. 259–271; F. W. Beare, *The Earliest Records of Jesus* (New York: Abingdon Press, 1962), pp. 219–232; V. Taylor, *The Life and Ministry of Jesus* (New York: Abingdon Press, 1955), pp. 190–201; Joachim Jeremias, *The Eucharistic Words of Jesus*, rev. ed. (Oxford: Basil Blackwell, 1966). See also relevant passages in the books by Marxsen, Tödt, Bornkamm, Barth, and Held mentioned above.

CHAPTER TWENTY-ONE: *The Condemnation and Crucifixion*

Fruitful sources for this chapter are M. Goguel, *The Life of Jesus* (London: George Allen & Unwin, Ltd., 1933), pp. 463–82, 502–51; J. Klausner, *Jesus of Nazareth* (New York: Macmillan Company, 1925), pp. 339–55; D. M. Beck, *Through the Gospels to Jesus* (New York: Harper & Row, Publishers, Inc., 1954), pp. 311–23; V. Taylor, *The Life and Ministry of Jesus* (New York: Abingdon Press, 1955), pp. 202–24; E. W. Saunders, *Jesus in the Gospels* (Englewood Cliffs, N.J.: Prentice-Hall, Inc., 1967), pp. 272–291; F. W. Beare, *The Earliest Records of Jesus* (New York: Abingdon Press, 1962), pp. 232–240. An excellent summary of the factors which led to Jesus' death is presented in Martin Dibelius, *Jesus*, tr. C. B. Hedrick and F. C. Grant (Philadelphia: The Westminster Press, 1946), chapter nine. W. Manson, *Jesus the Messiah* (Philadelphia: The Westminster Press, 1946), chapter seven, relates Jesus' death to his total ministry. The commentaries and Major, Manson, and Wright's work are most enlightening. The trial of Jesus is ably discussed in B. H. Branscomb, *The Gospel of Mark* (New York: Harper & Row, Publishers, Inc., n.d.), pp. 271–91; I. Abrahams, *Studies in Pharisaism and the Gospels*, Vol. II (Cambridge: Cambridge University Press, 1924), pp. 129–37; M. Radin, *The Trial of Jesus of Nazareth* (Chicago: University of Chicago Press, 1931); S. Zeitlin, *Who Crucified Jesus?* 2nd ed. (New York: Harper & Row, Publishers, Inc., 1947), pp. 144–79; F. J. Powell, *The Trial of Jesus Christ* (Grand Rapids: W. B. Eerdmans Publishing Co., 1949); Paul Winter, *On the Trial of Jesus* (Berlin: Walter de Gruyter & Co., 1961). The commentaries and the work by Major, Manson, and Wright are also informative for both the trial and the crucifixion.

CHAPTER TWENTY-TWO: *The Resurrection*

The resurrection of Jesus has been discussed from many different viewpoints: K. Lake, *The Historical Evidence for the Resurrection of Jesus Christ* (New York: Putnam & Company, 1907), pp. 57–202; C. R. Bowen, *The Resurrection in the New Testament* (New York: Putnam & Company, 1911), pp. 150–373; J. M. Shaw, *The Resurrection of Christ* (Edinburgh: T. & T. Clark, 1920), pp. 44–94, 123–207; S. V. McCasland, *The Resurrection of Jesus* (New York: Thomas Nelson & Sons, 1932), pp. 15–74, 169–98; A. M. Ramsey, *The Resurrection of Christ* (Philadelphia: The Westminster Press, 1946), pp. 7–81, 115–23. Excellent treatments are given in the commentaries. More general accounts are found in H. D. A. Major, in *The Mission and Message of Jesus* (New York: E. P. Dutton & Co., Inc., 1938), pp. 211–18; E. W. Saunders, *Jesus in the Gospels* (Englewood Cliffs, N.J.: Prentice-Hall, Inc., 1967), pp. 292–312; F. W. Beare, *The Earliest Records of Jesus* (New York: Abingdon Press, 1962), pp. 240–247. A well-balanced account of the relevance of psychical research to the Easter faith is contained in M. C. Perry, *The Easter Enigma* (London: Faber & Faber, Ltd., 1959). Richard R. Niebuhr, *Resurrection and Historical Reason* (New York:

Charles Scribner's Sons, 1957), is instructive. Wolfhart Pannenberg, *Jesus—God and Man* (Philadelphia: The Westminster Press, 1968), pp. 53–114, argues for the historicity of Jesus' resurrection.

CHAPTER TWENTY-THREE: *The Living Lord*

For a discussion of the history, literature, and thought of the New Testament see C. Milo Connick, *The New Testament: An Introduction to Its History, Literature, and Thought* (Encino and Belmont, Calif.: Dickenson Publishing Co., 1972). C. T. Craig, *The Beginning of Christianity* (New York and Nashville: Abingdon Press, 1943), is also helpful. F. V. Filson, *One Lord, One Faith* (Philadelphia: The Westminster Press, 1943), and John Knox, *Christ the Lord* (Chicago and New York: Willett, Clark & Company, 1945), are useful treatments of Christ as Lord. The definitive work concerning Christ and culture is H. R. Niebuhr, *Christ and Culture* (New York: Harper & Row, Publishers, Inc., 1951). Emile Cailliet, *The Christian Approach to Culture* (New York: Harper & Row, Publishers, Inc., 1953), is also suggestive. The person of Christ is ably dealt with by Walter Horton, *Our Eternal Contemporary* (New York: Harper & Row, Publishers, Inc., 1942), and W. A. Smart, *The Contemporary Christ* (New York and Nashville: Abingdon Press, 1942).

Index of Biblical References

Index of Subjects